English Skills
with Readings

English Skills with Readings

NINTH EDITION

MLA UPDATED EDITION

John Langan
Atlantic Cape Community College

Zoé L. Albright
Metropolitan Community College—Longview

ENGLISH SKILLS WITH READINGS, NINTH EDITION, MLA UPDATED EDITION

Published by McGraw-Hill Education, 2 Penn Plaza, New York, NY 10121. Copyright © 2015 by McGraw-Hill Education. All rights reserved. Printed in the United States of America. Previous editions © 2012, 2008, and 2006. No part of this publication may be reproduced or distributed in any form or by any means, or stored in a database or retrieval system, without the prior written consent of McGraw-Hill Education, including, but not limited to, in any network or other electronic storage or transmission, or broadcast for distance learning.

Some ancillaries, including electronic and print components, may not be available to customers outside the United States.

This book is printed on acid-free paper.

1 2 3 4 5 6 7 8 9 LCR 21 20 19 18 17

ISBN 978-1-259-98874-5
MHID 1-259-98874-0

ISBN 978-1-259-99619-1 (Annotated Instructor's Edition)
MHID 1-259-99619-0

Senior Vice President, Products & Markets:
   Kurt L. Strand
Vice President, General Manager, Products &
   Markets: *Michael Ryan*
Vice President, Content Production & Technology
   Services: *Kimberly Meriwether David*
Managing Director: *David S. Patterson*
Director: *Paul Banks*
Executive Brand Manager: *Kelly Villella-Canton*
Executive Director of Development: *Lisa Pinto*
Senior Marketing Manager: *Jaclyn Elkins*
Digital Development Editor: *Scott Harris*
Digital Product Analyst: *Courtney Costello*
Editorial Coordinator: *Dana Wan*

Director, Content Production: *Terri Schiesl*
Content Project Manager: *Jolynn Kilburg*
Designer: *Debra Kubiak*
Buyer: *Susan K. Culbertson*
Cover Image: ©*Tetra Images/Getty Images*
   © *Aping Vision/STS/Getty Image*
Content Licensing Specialist (Text): *Shirley Lanners*
Content Licensing Specialist (Photo):
   Shawntel Schmitt
Media Project Manager: *Jennifer Bartell*
Compositor: *MPS Limited*
Typeface: *11/13 Times LT Std*
Printer: *LSC Communications*

Library of Congress Cataloging-in-Publication Data

Langan, John, 1942-
   English skills with readings/John Langan, Atlantic Cape Community College, Zoé L. Albright,
Metropolitan Community College-Longview.—Ninth edition.
     pages cm.
  ISBN-13: 978-1-259-98874-5 (Student Edition: acid-free paper)
  ISBN-10: 1-259-98874-0 (Student Edition: acid-free paper)
  ISBN-13: (invalid) 978-1-259-99619-1 (Instructor's Edition: acid-free paper)
  ISBN-10: (invalid) 1-259-99619-0 (Instructor's Edition: acid-free paper)
  1. English language—Rhetoric. 2. English language—Grammar. 3. College readers. I. Albright, Zoé L. II. Title.
  PE1408.L3182 2014
  808'.0427—dc23

                          2013043700

The Internet addresses listed in the text were accurate at the time of publication. The inclusion of a website does not indicate an endorsement by the authors or McGraw-Hill Education, and McGraw-Hill Education does not guarantee the accuracy of the information presented at these sites.

www.mhhe.com

John Langan has taught reading and writing at Atlantic Cape Community College near Atlantic City, New Jersey, for more than twenty-five years. The author of a popular series of college textbooks on both writing and reading, John enjoys the challenge of developing materials that teach skills in an especially clear and lively way. Before teaching, he earned advanced degrees in writing at Rutgers University and in reading at Rowan University. He also spent a year writing fiction that, he says, "is now at the back of a drawer waiting to be discovered and acclaimed posthumously." While in school, he supported himself by working as a truck driver, a machinist, a battery assembler, a hospital attendant, and an apple packer. John now lives with his wife, Judith Nadell, near Philadelphia. In addition to his wife and Philly sports teams, his passions include reading and turning on nonreaders to the pleasure and power of books. Through Townsend Press, his educational publishing company, he has developed the nonprofit "Townsend Library"—a collection of more than one hundred new and classic stories that appeal to readers of any age.

John Langan

Zoé L. Albright has been involved in diverse aspects of education for eighteen years. For the last thirteen years, she has been a faculty member at Metropolitan Community College—Longview, teaching developmental writing, composition, and literature. She has created and implemented traditional and online curricula for high school and college English and composition courses and for a variety of literature courses. She continues to research new educational theory and practices. In addition to this extensive teaching experience, Zoé has most recently served as a contributing author to the Langan writing series, including the *Exploring Writing 3/e* books and *College Writing Skills with Readings 9/e*. She received her M.A. from Goldsmiths, University of London; B.S. and B.A. from the University of Idaho; and A.A. from Cottey College. Travel is one of Zoé's main passions. Whenever she travels, she incorporates what she has experienced and learned into her writing and teaching. When she is not working or traveling, she enjoys reading or pursuing her newfound interest, tennis. Zoé currently resides outside Kansas City, Missouri, with her husband and young son.

Zoé L. Albright

v

BRIEF CONTENTS

CONTENTS

CREATE-ONLY CHAPTERS

Mc Graw Hill create Using the Library
   Making Full Use of the Library's Resources

McGraw Hill **create** Combined Mastery Tests

READINGS Listed by Rhetorical Mode

Note: Some selections are listed more than once because they illustrate more than one rhetorical method of development.

EXEMPLIFICATION

PROCESS

COMPARISON AND/OR CONTRAST

DEFINITION

DIVISION-CLASSIFICATION

DESCRIPTION

CAUSE AND/OR EFFECT

NARRATION

ARGUMENT

Preface

Be inspired to make a great book, the perfect book for your course with McGraw-Hill Learning Solutions.

English Skills 11th Edition Now Available through McGraw-Hill Create™ Only

If you previously ordered *English Skills* (without readings), you can easily continue to do so by asking your McGraw-Hill representative to add all the content to a Create project and generate an ISBN, or you can take this opportunity to get creative!

In addition to reorganizing and eliminating chapters in *English Skills,* you have many other options to build the perfect book:

- Add your own materials (such as sample student paragraphs or essays) or add chapters from other McGraw-Hill textbooks.

- Add in one or two readings from Part 5 of the version with readings or a reading from the anthologies of any other McGraw-Hill Langan texts.

- Customize the readings using other McGraw Hill collections in Create, such as *The Ideal Reader* or *Cornerstones.*

McGraw-Hill Create™Only Content and ExpressBooks

The chapter "Using the Library" will be offered only through Create™ as an option to customize into your print or electronic text. Additionally, the "Combined Mastery Tests" will now be loaded individually in Create so you can add some or all of them to your text.

If you wish to consider alternate TOCs or quickly view the possibilities for customizing your book, visit www.mcgrawhillcreate.com and enter "English Skills with Readings" under the Find Content tab. Once you select the current edition of the book, click on the orange "Related Materials" button to see options. You will find an ExpressBook for the text with Part 5 readings organized by rhetorical modes, one with readings organized after each rhetorical mode chapter, and one with alternate/additional readings. You may select an ExpressBook and further customize it as you wish.

We understand that you have a unique perspective. Use McGraw-Hill Create™ Express-Books to build the text you've only imagined!

Copyright ©2015 The McGraw-Hill Companies, Inc. All rights reserved.

xix

Inspire the writing process with McGraw-Hill Digital Solutions.

McGraw-Hill provides the foundation with a suite of tools and reporting that help you and your program adapt to students' needs. Imagine the ability to identify and make real-time curriculum changes that do not require you to change your typical writing assignments or rubrics. Inspire your program, yourself, and your students with the power of better data with Connect© Writing!

Adaptive Assessment, Learning, and Practice

With Connect© Writing, your students gain access to McGraw-Hill's adaptive learning tool, Learn-Smart Achieve™, which works to identify what students know and do not know about the writing process and grammar as they answer questions that are tied to key course learning objectives. Its continually-adaptive technology and exclusive time-management features enable you and your students to monitor progress and stay on track towards mastering assigned topics.

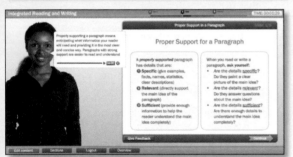

Within each topic, the system starts with a "Tune In" phase that offers a baseline assessment designed to determine how to *focus* a student's time with five learning resources tied to five objectives that are difficult for a given student. During the LearnSmart Achieve "Focus" phase, students are presented with an individualized learning experience focusing them on concepts where they need most help. The program then guides students through the "Practice" phase, continuing to assess for and remediate on those same five objectives as students work towards mastery. With an engine that incorporates metacognitive learning theory and forgetting curve theory, students indicate their confidence with each question and see a "Recharge" button that prompts them to review the concepts they are most likely to forget right before they are about to forget them.

LearnSmart Achieve reports in Connect Writing allow instructors to dig deeper and pinpoint the areas that students are struggling with the most.

Additionally, by allowing students to improve their skills at their own pace with comprehensive assignment of multiple topics, LearnSmart Achieve supports a variety of redesign models (co-requisites, boot camps, NCBOs, ABE, ALP, modularized, labs) or more-focused classroom instruction time.

Connect eBook Reader, Question Bank, and Assessments

Connect Writing includes a thematically-organized eReader of over 120 engaging source texts for reading and writing.

The Question Bank provides questions for each eBook reading designed for holistic assessment of writing skills. Questions have been tagged for topics; learning objectives; mode, purpose, and genre of the reading; academic disciplines; themes; Bloom's taxonomy; and more. Extensive filters allow instructors to select most readings and questions using these tags.

Additionally, the bank will include four pre-set, customizable, leveled assessments for use as "moment-in-time" diagnostics. These assessments will test students on the same topics and learning objectives in LearnSmart Achieve. They may be used as Level 1 and Level 2 pre- and post-tests or they may be customized into mid-term and final examinations as well as placement and exit exams using the same filters described above.

Writing Assignments with Outcomes-Based Assessment

Connect Writing provides powerful tools to facilitate performance-based, formative assessment and data collection without changing your writing assignments or rubrics. The outcomes-based tool generates clear, simple reports with visuals that enhance your ability to pinpoint strengths and weaknesses across class sections, a single class, or a series of one student's assignments. The reporting capabilities are suitable for program evaluation or accrediting bodies—allowing a variety of stakeholders a view of student progress toward program goals. Customizable grading may be adapted to your needs. These tools ensure that the set-up, management, and reporting around outcomes for your writing assignments is efficient, professional, and useful to instructors and administrators.

Writing Assignments with Peer Review

Connect Writing offers writing assignments with superior peer reviewing capabilities that enable instructors to easily assign and manage groups, deadlines, and workflow for peer review exercises. This functionality gives you and your students an engaging space and efficient process for collaborating online to improve drafts during the crucial revision step in the writing process. This experience, managed through an easy-to-use online system where students and instructors can offer and review feedback, prepares students for the group writing projects they will encounter in college and the workplace.

Along with the inspiration for reinventing your course for the 21st Century, McGraw-Hill provides the foundation with services to support your effective course integration of our technologies.

Digital Success Academy

The Digital Success Academy offers a wealth of online training resources and course creation tips for instructors. Broken down into easy-to-navigate sections, the Digital Success Academy offers Connect® 100- and 200- level video clips, Power-Point documents, and Clickthrough Guides that explain how to navigate the Connect platform and how to use course-specific features. **http://create. mcgraw-hill.com/wordpress-mu/success-academy/**

Digital Success Team

This dedicated McGraw-Hill group of individuals offer instructors one-on-one online consultations to show them the functionality of the Connect platform and to recommend the best ways to incorporate Connect within a syllabus. To request a Digital Success Team member contact you, please email your McGraw-Hill sales representative. **http://catalogs.mhhe.com/mhhe/findRep.do**

Digital Learning Consultants

Digital Learning Consultants are local specialists who work closely with your McGraw-Hill sales representative. They provide face-to-face faculty support and training. You may request a Digital Learning Consultation through your McGraw-Hill sales representative.

Digital Faculty Consultants

These experienced instructors who have used Connect in their classroom are available to offer training, suggestions, and advice about how best to integrate Connect in the classroom. To request a Digital Faculty Consultant speak with you, please email your McGraw-Hill sales representative.

National Training Webinars

McGraw-Hill offers an ongoing series of webinars for instructors to learn about the Connect platform and its course-specific tools and features. We hope you will refer to our online schedule of national training webinars and sign up to learn more about Connect!

Customer Experience Group (CXG)

This team troubleshoots technical issues and problems. To contact our customer support team, please call us at 800-331-5094 or visit us online at **http://mpss.mhhe.com/contact.php**

Hours of operation are Sunday 6 p.m.–11 p.m., Monday-Thursday 8 a.m.–11 p.m., and Friday 8 a.m.–6 p.m. Please note that all times are Central.

The Connect Community

McGraw-Hill's Connect Community is a network of passionate educators dedicated to advancing student learning via the effective use of educational technologies. Please join and participate at **http://theconnectcommunity.com**

Personal, Academic, and Workplace Writing

English Skills with Readings 9/e/English Skills 11/e expose students to examples of writing that reflect the three key realms of their lives—personal, academic, and workplace. They will find models, activities, and examples for any writing situation. This variety provides great flexibility in the kinds of assignments you prefer to give. Icons identifying personal, academic, and workplace writing are integrated throughout the chapters.

Mastering the Four Bases: Unity, Support, Coherence, Sentence Skills

English Skills with Readings 9/e emphasizes writing skills and process. By referring to a set of four skills for effective writing, it encourages new writers to see writing as a skill that can be learned and a process that must be explored. The four skills, or bases, for effective writing are as follows:

- **Unity:** Discover a clearly stated point, or topic sentence, and make sure that all other information in the paragraph or essay supports that point.

- **Support:** Support the points with specific evidence, and plenty of it.

- **Coherence:** Organize and connect supporting evidence so that paragraphs and essays transition smoothly from one bit of supporting information to the next.

- **Sentence skills:** Revise and edit so that sentences are error-free for clearer and more effective communication.

The four bases are essential to effective writing, whether it be a narrative paragraph, a cover letter for a job application, or an essay assignment.

UNITY	SUPPORT
Discover a clearly stated point, or topic sentence, and make sure that all other information in the paragraph or essay supports that point.	Support the points with specific evidence, and plenty of it.

COHERENCE	SENTENCE SKILLS
Organize and connect supporting evidence so that paragraphs and essays transition smoothly from one bit of supporting information to the next.	Revise and edit so that sentences are error-free for clearer and more effective communication.

CHAPTER-BY-CHAPTER CHANGES

In addition to maintaining the four bases framework and continuing to build in many familiar personal writing examples, *English Skills with Readings 9/e/English Skills 11/e* include the following chapter-by-chapter changes:

Part 1: Fundamentals of Effective Writing

- Coverage of four bases woven more integrally into treatment of the writing process

- Coverage of audience and purpose consolidated and repositioned to integrate better with the fundamentals of writing

- *Chapter 7: Writing in the Digital Age*—New chapter addresses key topics related to the use of technology within the writing process; best practices for students accessing the Internet, including research procedures and guidelines for evaluating digital sources; and pragmatic tips and recommendations for effective use of electronic aids

Part 2: Paragraph Development

- Clearer and more consistent heading structure added throughout Part 2

- New sample paragraphs that reflect academic and workplace writing

- Updated personal writing examples

- New Activities and Writing Assignments that reflect academic and workplace writing

- Revised writing samples to eliminate use of second-person

Part 3: Essay Development

- Coverage of essays with more than three supporting paragraphs

- Revised introductory text with explanation of how multiple modes function together in one essay

- Revised treatment of the use of questions in essay structuring

- Multiple new writing samples, Activities, and Writing Assignments that reflect academic and workplace writing

- New material on preparing for essay exams

- Inclusion of multiple across-chapter cross-references to related topics

Part 4: Handbook of Sentence Skills

- Chapters covering verbs revised to reflect better logical flow

- Grammar activities and exercises rewritten to incorporate academic and workplace-related themes

- Review Tests reworked to incorporate academic and workplace-related themes

- Revised material frequently focused on one issue so that it reads as a unified passage rather than a set of disconnected statements

- Inclusion of multiple across-chapter cross-references to related topics

- Practice section streamlined to focus on Editing Tests; Combined Mastery Tests now loaded in Create so that instructors have the option to build one or more into a customized text; both sets of tests thoroughly revised

Part 5: Readings for Writers

- Readings updated to include four new selections by diverse and well-respected authors on high-interest subjects:

   "Different Is Just Different" by Suzanne Staples Fisher

   "What Students Need to Know about Today's Job Crisis" by Don Bertram from *A Tale of Two Cities* by Charles Dickens

   "Duel at High Noon: A Replay of Cormier's Works" by Kathy Neal Headley

- Each new reading accompanied by new full set of questions and assignments

- All assignments reflect either personal, academic, or workplace-related themes

Appendixes

- Section revised to include both Sentence-Skills Diagnostic and Achievement Tests

- Full coverage of English as a Second Language re-positioned to this section

Throughout: New Emphasis on Visual Literacy

- Thought-provoking captions and prompts challenge students to analyze photographs and images to deepen critical thinking skills

Research Paper Coverage (Create):

- Updated formatting for sample student paper to better represent academic expectations

- Revised exposition to reflect updated MLA standards

Book-Specific Supplements for Instructors

The **Annotated Instructor's Edition** consists of the student text, including answers to all activities and tests, as well as a complete Instructor's Guide.

The **Online Learning Center (www.mhhe.com/langan)** offers a number of instructional materials specific to *English Skills with Readings 9/e/English Skills 11/e* including:

- An Instructor's Manual comprising Suggested Approaches and Techniques, Answer Keys for all Parts of the text, Supplementary Tests and Activities, and Portfolio Resources

- Connect Writing Chapter Correlation Grid

- PowerPoint® slides that may be tailored to course needs

- Additional tests covering the contents of each chapter

Create the Perfect Course Materials with Create™

With McGraw-Hill Create, you can easily arrange your book to align with the syllabus, eliminate chapters you do not assign, combine material from other content sources, and quickly upload content you have written, such as your course syllabus or teaching notes, to enhance the value of course materials for your students. You control the net price of the book as you build it and have the opportunity to choose format: color, black and white, and eBook. When you build a CREATE book, you'll receive a complimentary print review copy in 3 to 5 business days or a complimentary electronic review copy (eComp) via e-mail in about one hour.

Go to www.mcgrawhillcreate.com and register today!

Connect Learning Management System Integration

Connect Writing integrates with your local Learning Management System (Blackboard, Desire2Learn, and others).

MH Campus® is a new one-stop teaching and learning experience available to users of any learning management system. This complimentary integration allows faculty and students to enjoy single sign-on (SSO) access to all McGraw-Hill Higher Education materials and synchronized grade-books with our award-winning

McGraw-Hill *Connect* platform. For more information on MH Campus please visit our website at **www.mhcampus.com** or contact your local McGraw-Hill representative to find out more about installations on your campus.

Tegrity

Tegrity Campus is a service that makes class time available all the time by automatically capturing every lecture in a searchable format for students to review when they study and complete assignments. With a simple one-click start and stop process, users capture all computer screens and corresponding audio. Students replay any part of any class with easy-to-use browser-based viewing on a PC or Mac. Educators know that the more students can see, hear, and experience class resources, the better they learn. With Tegrity Campus, students quickly recall key moments by using Tegrity Campus's unique search feature. This search helps students efficiently find what they need, when they need it, across an entire semester of class recordings. Help turn all your students' study time into learning moments immediately supported by your lecture.

CourseSmart

This text is available at **www.CourseSmart.com** as an eTextbook. At CourseSmart your students can take advantage of significant savings off the cost of a print textbook, reduce their impact on the environment, and gain access to powerful tools for learning. CourseSmart eTextbooks can be viewed online or downloaded to a computer. CourseSmart offers free Apps to access the textbooks on SmartPhones and iPads. The eTextbooks allow students to do full text searches, add highlighting and notes, and share notes with classmates. CourseSmart has the largest selection of eTextbooks available anywhere. Visit **www.CourseSmart.com** to learn more and to try a sample chapter.

ACKNOWLEDGMENTS

The quality of *English Skills with Readings 9/e/ English Skills 11/e* is a testament to the suggestions and insights from instructors around the country. Many thanks to all of those who helped improve this project.

Kristina Beckman-Brito, *Pima Community College*

Cameron Bentley, *Augusta Technical College*

Darren DeFrain, *Wichita State University*

Lowrie Fawley, *Keiser University*

Holly French Hart, *Bossier Parish Community College*

Sally Hudson, *Keiser University*

Tammy McPherson, *Hinds Community College*

Judy Netherland, *Virginia Highlands Community College*

Anne Marie Prendergast, *Bergen Community College*

Jennifer Riske, *Northeast Lakeview College*

Louisa Rogers, *Keiser University*

Erin Severs, *Mohawk Valley Community College*

Patricia Sink, *Cumberland County College*

Emmie Stokes, *Augusta Technical College*

Susan Taylor, *North Florida Community College*

Karen Wright, *Glendale Community College*

We are also grateful for the talented support of our developmental team, Merryl Maleska Wilbur, Development Editor; Kelly Villella-Canton, Executive Brand Manager; Lisa Pinto, Executive Director of Development; Dana Wan, Developmental English Coordinator; and Wes Hall, text permissions editor. Without their dedication, guidance, and hard work, this edition would not have come to fruition. Working with this group of editors has truly been a wonderful and educational experience.

We also wish to express gratitude to our skilled production and design team, including Jolynn Kilburg, Content Project Manager; Debra Kubiak, Designer, Creative Services; Preston Thomas, interior and cover designer; and Emily and David Tietz, photo researchers; as well as Ruma Khurana at MPS Limited.

John Langan

Zoé L. Albright

Fundamentals of Effective Writing

College offers many different challenges for students. Knowing your individual strengths and weaknesses can help you be a successful student. Take a few minutes to think about your strengths and weaknesses as a student and jot them down. How can you use this information to be a better student?

An Introduction to Writing

This chapter will

- introduce you to the basic principles, or four bases, of effective writing

- ask you to write a simple paragraph

- explain the significance of audience and purpose for all writing

- present writing as both a skill and a process of discovery

- suggest that you keep a journal

- suggest a sequence for using this book

WHAT WOULD YOU WRITE ABOUT A JOB?

Though some of us may manage to find the job of our dreams easily, many of us have had to endure one or two jobs that were more like a nightmare. In this chapter you will read a student's paragraph about his worst job. Think about the best or worst job you have ever had. Later in the chapter you will be asked to write a paragraph of your own on this topic.

This book grows out of experiences I had when learning how to write. My early memories of writing in school are not pleasant. In middle school, I remember getting back paper after paper on which the only comment was "Handwriting very poor." In high school, the night before a book report was due, I would work anxiously at a card table in my bedroom. I was nervous and sweaty because I felt out of my element, like a person who knows only how to open a can of soup being asked to cook a five-course meal. The act of writing was hard enough, and my feeling that I wasn't any good at it made me hate the process all the more.

Luckily, in college I had an instructor who changed my negative attitude about writing. During my first semester in composition, I realized that my instructor repeatedly asked two questions about any paper I wrote: "What is your point?" and "What is your support for that point?" I learned that sound writing consists basically of making a point and then providing evidence to support or develop that point. As I understood, practiced, and mastered these and other principles, I began to write effective papers. By the end of the semester, much of my uneasiness and bad feelings about writing had disappeared. I knew that competent writing is a skill that I or anyone can learn with practice. It is a nuts-and-bolts process consisting of a number of principles and techniques that can be studied and mastered. Further, I learned that while there is no alternative to the work required for competent writing, there is satisfaction to be gained through such work. I no longer feared or hated writing, for I knew I could work at it and be good at it.

English Skills with Readings explains in a clear and direct way the four basic principles you must learn to write effectively:

1. Start with a clearly stated point.

2. Provide logical, detailed support for your point.

3. Organize and connect your supporting material.

4. Revise and edit so that your sentences are effective and error-free.

Part 1 of this book explains each of these four bases of effective writing in detail and provides many practice materials to help you achieve them.

Understanding Point and Support

An Important Difference between Writing and Talking

In everyday conversation, you make all kinds of points, or assertions. You say, for example, "I hate my job"; "Sue's a really generous person"; or "That exam was unfair." The points that you make concern such personal matters as well as, at times, larger issues: "A lot of doctors are arrogant"; "The death penalty should exist for certain crimes"; "Tobacco and marijuana are equally dangerous."

The people you are talking with do not always challenge you to give reasons for your statements. They may know why you feel as you do, or they may already agree with you, or they simply may not want to put you on the spot; so they do not always ask "Why?" But the people who *read* what you write may not know you, agree with you, or feel in any way obliged to you. If you want to communicate effectively with readers, you must provide solid evidence for any point you make. An important difference, then, between writing and talking is this: *In writing, any idea that you advance must be supported with specific reasons or details.*

Think of your readers as reasonable people. They will not take your views on faith, but they *are* willing to consider what you say as long as you support it. Therefore, remember to support with specific evidence any statement that you make.

Point and Support in a Paragraph

Suppose you and a friend are talking about jobs you have had. You might say about a particular job, "That was the worst one I ever had. A lot of hard work and not much money." For your friend, that might be enough to make your point, and you would not really have to explain your statement. But in writing, your point would have to be backed up with specific reasons and details.

Below is a paragraph, written by a student named Gene Hert, about his worst job. A *paragraph* is a short paper of 150 to 200 words. It usually consists of an opening point called a *topic sentence* followed by a series of sentences supporting that point.

Personal

My Job in an Apple Plant

Working in an apple plant was the worst job I ever had. First of all, the work was physically hard. For ten hours a night, I took cartons that rolled down a metal track and stacked them onto wooden skids in a tractor trailer. Each carton contained twenty-five pounds of bottled apple juice, and they came down the track almost nonstop. The second bad feature of the job was the pay. I was getting the minimum wage at that time, $4.50 an hour, plus fifty cents extra for working the night shift. I had to work over sixty hours a week to get decent take-home pay. Finally, I hated the working conditions. We were limited to two ten-minute breaks and an unpaid half hour for lunch. Most of my time was spent outside on the loading dock in near-zero-degree temperatures. I was very lonely on the job because I had no interests in common with the other truck loaders. I felt this isolation especially when the production line shut down for the night, and I spent two hours by myself cleaning the apple vats. The vats were an ugly place to be on a cold morning, and the job was a bitter one to have.

Notice what the details in this paragraph do. They provide you, the reader, with a basis for understanding *why* the writer makes the point that is made. Through this specific evidence, the writer has explained and successfully communicated the idea that this job was his worst one.

The evidence that supports the point in a paragraph often consists of a series of reasons followed by examples and details that support the reasons. That is true of the paragraph above: Three reasons are provided, with examples and details that back up those reasons. Supporting evidence in a paper can also consist of anecdotes, personal experiences, facts, studies, statistics, and the opinions of experts.

ACTIVITY 1

The paragraph on the apple plant, like almost any piece of effective writing, has two essential parts: (1) a point is advanced, and (2) that point is then supported. Taking a minute to outline the paragraph will help you understand these basic parts clearly. Add the words needed to complete the outline.

Point: Working in an apple plant is the worst job I ever had.

Reason 1: _____

    a. Loaded cartons onto skids for ten hours a night

    b. _____

Reason 2: _____

    a. _____

    b. Had to work sixty hours for decent take-home pay

Reason 3: _____

    a. Two ten-minute breaks and an unpaid lunch

    b. _____

    c. Loneliness on job

       (1) No interests in common with other workers

       (2) By myself for two hours cleaning the apple vats

ACTIVITY 2

See if you can complete the statements below.

1. An important difference between writing and talking is that in writing we absolutely must _____ any statement we make.

2. A _____ is made up of a point and a collection of specifics that support the point.

ACTIVITY 3

An excellent way to get a feel for the paragraph is to write one. Your instructor may ask you to do that now. The only guidelines you need to follow are the ones described here. There is an advantage to writing a paragraph right away, at a point where you have had almost no instruction. This first paragraph will give a quick sense of your needs as a writer and will provide a baseline—a standard of comparison that you and your instructor can use to measure your writing progress during the semester.

Here, then, is your topic: Write a paragraph on the best or worst job you have ever had. Provide three reasons why your job was the best or the worst, and give plenty of details to develop each of your three reasons.

Notice that the sample paragraph, "My Job in an Apple Plant," has the same format your paragraph should have. You should do what this author has done:

- State a point in the first sentence.
- Give three reasons to support the point.
- Introduce each reason clearly with signal words (such as *First of all,* *Second,* and *Finally*).
- Provide details that develop each of the three reasons.

Benefits of Paragraph Writing

Paragraph writing offers three benefits. First, mastering the structure of paragraphs will make you a better writer. For other courses, you'll often write pieces that are variations on the paragraph—for example, exam answers, summaries, response papers, and brief reports. In addition, paragraphs serve as the basic building blocks of essays, the most common form of college writing. The basic structure of the traditional paragraph, with its emphasis on a clear point and well-organized logical support, will help you write effective essays and almost every kind of paper that you will have to do.

Second, writing paragraphs strengthens your skills as a reader and listener. You'll become more aware of the ideas of other writers and speakers and the evidence they provide—or fail to provide—to support those ideas.

Most important, paragraph writing will make you a stronger thinker. Writing a solidly reasoned paragraph requires mental discipline. Creating a paragraph with an overall topic sentence supported by well-reasoned, convincing evidence is more challenging than writing a free-form or expressive paper. Such a paragraph requires you to sort out, think through, and organize ideas carefully. Traditional paragraph writing, in short, will train your mind to think clearly, and that ability will prove to be of value in every phase of your life.

Writing as a Way to Communicate with Others: Considering Audience and Purpose

When you talk, chances are you do not treat everyone the same. For example, you are unlikely to speak to your boss in the same way that you chat with a young child. Instead, you adjust what you say to suit the people who are listening to you—your *audience*. Similarly you probably change your speech each day to suit whatever *purpose* you have in mind when you are speaking. For instance, if you wanted to tell someone how to get to your new apartment, you would speak differently than if you were describing your favorite movie.

To communicate effectively, people must constantly adjust their speech to suit their audience and purpose. The same idea is true for writing. When you write for others, it is crucial to know both your purpose for writing and the audience who will be reading your work. The ability to adjust your writing to suit your purpose and audience will serve you well not only in the classroom, but in the workplace and beyond.

Purpose

The three most common purposes of writing are *to inform, to persuade*, and *to entertain*. Each is described briefly below.

- To **inform**—to give information about a subject. Authors writing to inform want to provide facts that will explain or teach something to readers. For example, an informative paragraph about sandwiches might begin, "Eating food between two slices of bread—a sandwich—is a practice that has its origins in eighteenth-century England."

- To **persuade**—to convince the reader to agree with the author's point of view on a subject. Authors writing to persuade may give facts, but their main goal is to argue or prove a point to readers. A persuasive paragraph about sandwiches might begin, "There are good reasons why every sandwich should be made with whole grain bread."

- To **entertain**—to amuse and delight; to appeal to the reader's senses and imagination. Authors write to entertain in various ways, through fiction and nonfiction. An entertaining paragraph about sandwiches might begin, "What I wanted was a midnight snack, but what I got was better—the biggest, most magical sandwich in the entire world."

Considering Purpose within Different Contexts

Of course, the *purpose* of completing any college writing assignment is to fulfill a course requirement and get a grade. But all writing—whether done for a class, a job, or any other reason—is aimed at accomplishing something far more specific.

In most cases, you will be given an assignment that explains or at least hints at that purpose. You will be able to spot clues about purpose by looking for key words in the assignment such as *define*, *contrast*, *argue*, *illustrate*, or *explain causes and/ or effects*.

For example, an assignment for a history paper might ask you to *explain* the causes of World War I. An essay question on a biology midterm might call for the *definition* of photosynthesis. A political science assignment might ask you to *contrast* the parliamentary system of government used in several European nations with the federal system used in the United States. If you are enrolled in a technical writing course, you might be asked to *describe* a machine or *analyze* a natural or mechanical *process*. Each of these tasks asks you to accomplish a specific aim.

Having a clear idea of your purpose is just as important for writing you do outside of college (what many call "real-world writing"). For example, say your employer asks you to write a report that recommends the purchase of a particular model of photocopier from a choice of three. You first might have to *contrast* each on the basis of cost, ease of use, features, and reliability. Then you might have to *argue* that even though copier A is more expensive than copiers B and C, it is preferable because it will work best with your company's computers. Note that unlike a college writing assignment, the job you have been given by your employer does not specify the approaches (*contrasting* and *arguing*) you will have to take to complete the project. You will have to figure that out for yourself by considering the writing's purpose before you begin.

As you start gathering information for your paragraph or essay, keep your purpose in mind. You might want to read your assignment several times, looking for key words such as those mentioned above, and then summarize your purpose in a short sentence of your own on a piece of scrap paper. Keep this sentence in front of you throughout the prewriting stage.

Much of the writing assigned in this book will involve some form of argumentation or persuasion. You will advance a point or thesis and then support it in a variety of ways. To some extent, also, you will write papers to inform—to provide readers with information about a particular subject. And since, in practice, writing often combines purposes, you might also find yourself providing vivid or humorous details in order to entertain your readers.

Audience

The *audience* for a piece of writing is its reader or readers, and like purpose, audience should be considered early in the writing process. In college, your primary audience will be your instructor. Your instructor, though, is really representative of the larger audience you should see yourself as writing for—an audience of educated adults who expect you to present your ideas in a clear, direct, organized way.

Some instructors will also require you to share your work with other students, either in small groups or with the class as a whole. In some cases, your writing will be judged on how well it informs or persuades your classmates. Therefore, you must keep them in mind as you write. Other academic situations in which you will want to keep your audience in mind include writing a letter to a college newspaper to express an opinion, applying for transfer to another college, or applying for a scholarship.

After you graduate, you will have ample opportunity to write to a wide range of audiences. This is when you will have to pay even more attention to evaluating your audience. For example, careers in science and the technologies require employees to write to other experts, who may know a great deal about the subject. On the other hand, scientists and technologists are often required to write to laypersons, whose knowledge of a subject might vary from adequate to nonexistent. The same is true of those who pursue careers in business, law enforcement, the legal and medical professions, the military, education, or government work.

Let's say you get a job in a town's public works department as a civil engineer and the town decides to change a two-lane road to a four-lane road. You may be asked to write a letter to residents who live along that road explaining why the job is necessary, what will be done, how long it will take, and why they may experience delays in getting home during construction. Explaining such a project to another civil engineer might not be difficult, since he or she will know about the technicalities of traffic studies, road grading, and paving. Your explanation will be fairly straightforward and will use technical terminology that this reader is sure to understand. In addition, you won't have to convince your engineering colleague that the inconvenience to residents will be worthwhile; it will be obvious to him or her that the improvements will make the road much safer. However, if you were writing to the residents—people who may not have any knowledge about road construction and repair—you would avoid using technical terminology, which they might not understand. In addition, you might have to make a real effort to convince these readers that the inconvenience they will experience during construction is worth the outcome—a much safer road.

Evaluating the Nature of Your Audience

Here are a few questions you should ask yourself when evaluating any audience. The answers to these questions will help you determine your approach to any writing project.

1. *How much does the audience already know about the subject?* If you assume that your readers know very little, you might bore them with too much basic information. But, if you assume that they know more than they do, you might confuse them by using unfamiliar technical terminology or neglecting to provide enough informative detail.

2. *Why might the reader need or want to read this material?* In college, your English professor will use your papers to evaluate your writing skills and

determine how you can strengthen them. He or she will probably also use them to establish your course grade. If, however, you are writing to a group of residents whose road is going to be closed for improvements, you will have to meet different expectations. They will want to know why the improvements are being made, how long the work will take, and what benefits they will reap from it. As taxpayers, they may also want to know how much the repaving will cost.

3. *Is your purpose simply to inform the audience? Or is it to convince readers of something as well?* If your purpose is to convince or persuade, you may want to use some of the techniques for writing arguments in Chapter 16. For example, if you are writing a letter to the editor of your local newspaper in support of the new school budget, you may have to persuade voters to approve the budget even though it is sure to raise their property taxes.

4. *What type of language should be used?* Are you writing to peers, other college students? Or are you communicating with professors, business and community leaders, or government officials? With peers, you might want to use language that is relaxed, friendly, and informal, language that will win their confidence. If you're writing to a professor, a government official, or an employer, you will have to be more formal. (You can read more about effective word choice in Chapter 40.)

TIP

In addition to focusing on audience and purpose in your writing, you should always consider your knowledge of your subject. Whenever possible, write on a subject that interests you. If you do, you will find it easier to put more time into your work. Even more important, try to write on a subject that you already know something about. If you do not have direct experience with the subject, you should at least have indirect experience— knowledge gained through thinking, prewriting, reading, or talking about the subject. If you are asked to write on a topic about which you have no experience or knowledge, you should do whatever research is required to gain the information you need. You will find many references to doing research in this book, as well as a full chapter on the topic on the CREATE site. Without direct or indirect experience, or the information you gain through research, you may not be able to provide the specific evidence needed to develop whatever point you are trying to make. Your writing will be starved for specifics.

A Note on Tone

It will be helpful for you to write some papers for a more specific audience. By doing so, you will develop an ability to choose words and adopt a tone of voice that is just right for a given purpose and a given group of people. Tone reveals the attitude that a writer has toward a subject. It is expressed through the words and details the writer selects. Just as a speaker's voice can project a range of feelings, a writer's voice can project one or more tones, or feelings: anger, sympathy, hopefulness, sadness, respect, dislike, and so on.

To appreciate differences in tone, look at the six statements below, which express different attitudes about a shabby apartment. Six different tones are used. Label each statement with the tone you think is present.

ACTIVITY 4

a. bitter	c. matter-of-fact	e. tolerant and accepting
b. sentimental	d. humorous	f. optimistic and hopeful

_____ 1. This place may be shabby, but since both of my children were born while we lived here, it has a special place in my heart.

_____ 2. The apartment is not fancy, but it meets my needs.

_____ 3. If only there were some decent jobs out there, I wouldn't be reduced to living in this miserable dump.

_____ 4. This place does need some repairs, but I'm sure the landlord will be making improvements sometime soon.

_____ 5. When we move away, we're planning to release three hundred cockroaches and two mice, so we can leave the place exactly as we found it.

_____ 6. It's a small two-bedroom apartment that needs to be repainted and have the kitchen plumbing repaired.

EXPLANATION

The tone of item 1 is sentimental. "It has a special place in my heart" expresses tender emotions. In item 2, the words "meets my needs" show that the writer is tolerant, accepting the situation while recognizing that it could be better. We could describe the tone of item 3 as bitter. The writer resents a situation that forces him or her to live in a "miserable dump." Item 4 is optimistic and hopeful, since the writer is expecting the apartment to be improved soon. The tone of item 5 is humorous. Its writer claims to be planning a comic revenge on the landlord. The tone of item 6 is matter-of-fact and objective, simply describing what needs to be done.

The "Purpose and Audience" Assignments

In all the Part 2 chapters and occasionally elsewhere in this book you will find a dedicated assignment that asks you to write with a very specific purpose in mind and for a very specific audience. You will be asked, for example, to imagine yourself as an aide at a day care center preparing instructions for children, as a high school graduate explaining to the school's principal why the school deserves a high or low rating, as an apartment tenant complaining to a landlord about neighbors, as a reporter for your college newspaper describing a potential vacation spot, and as an employee describing a new job opening at your workplace. Through these and other assignments, you will learn to adjust your style and tone of voice to a given writing situation.

Writing as a Skill

A sure way not to learn how to write competently is to believe that writing is a "natural gift" rather than a learned skill. People who think this way feel that everyone else finds writing easy and that they're "just not good at it." The result of this attitude is that people try to avoid writing and, when they do write, to do less than their best. Their attitude becomes a self-fulfilling prophecy: Their writing fails chiefly because they have brainwashed themselves into thinking that they don't have the "natural talent" needed to write.

But writing is a skill, and like most other skills, such as typing, driving, or cooking, it can be learned. If you have the determination to learn, this book will give you the practice you need to develop good writing skills.

Of course, it's frightening to sit down before a blank sheet of paper or computer screen and know that, an hour later, you may not have written a lot worth keeping. Transforming thoughts from one's head into words on a sheet of paper can be a challenge, and at times it can be frustrating. But writing is not an automatic process—we will not get something for nothing, and we shouldn't expect to. For almost everyone, competent writing comes only from plain hard work—determination and sweat. It is a head-on battle. The good news is that you can do it if you are ready to work hard.

ACTIVITY 5

To get a sense of just how you regard writing, read the following statements. Put a check (✓) beside those statements with which you agree. This activity is not a test, so try to be as honest as possible.

_____ 1. A good writer should be able to sit down and write a paper straight through without stopping.

_____ 2. Writing is a skill that anyone can learn with practice.

_____ 3. I'll never be good at writing because I make too many mistakes in spelling, grammar, and punctuation.

_____ 4. Because I dislike writing, I always start a paper at the last possible minute.

_____ 5. I've always done poorly in English, and I don't expect that to change.

Now read the following comments about the five statements. The comments will help you see if your attitude is hurting or helping your efforts to become a better writer.

COMMENTS

- Statement 1: *"A good writer should be able to sit down and write a paper straight through without stopping."*

    Statement 1 is not true. Writing is, in fact, a process. It is done not in one easy step but in a series of steps, and seldom at one sitting. If you cannot do a paper all at once, that simply means you are like most of the other people on the planet. It is harmful to carry around the false idea that writing should be easy.

- Statement 2: *"Writing is a skill that anyone can learn with practice."*

    Statement 2 is absolutely true. Writing is a skill, like driving or word processing, that you can master with hard work. If you want to learn to write, you can. It is as simple as that. If you believe this, you are ready to learn how to become a competent writer.

    Some people hold the false belief that writing is a natural gift that some have and others do not. Because of this belief, they never make a truly honest effort to learn to write—so they never learn.

- Statement 3: *"I'll never be good at writing because I make too many mistakes in spelling, grammar, and punctuation."*

    The first concern in good writing should be content—what you have to say. Your ideas and feelings are what matter most. You should not worry about spelling, grammar, or punctuation while working on content.

    Unfortunately, some people are so self-conscious about making mistakes that they do not focus on what they want to say. They need to realize that a paper is best done in stages, and that applying the rules can and should wait until a later stage in the writing process. Through review and practice, you will eventually learn how to follow the rules with confidence.

- Statement 4: *"Because I dislike writing, I always start a paper at the last possible minute."*

    This habit is all too common. You feel you are going to do poorly, and then you behave in a way that ensures you *will* do poorly! Your attitude is so negative that you defeat yourself—not even allowing enough time to really try.

    Again, what you need to realize is that writing is a process. Because it is done in steps, you don't have to get it right all at once. If you allow yourself enough time, you'll find a way to make a paper come together.

- Statement 5: *"I've always done poorly in English, and I don't expect that to change."*

Even if you did poorly in English in high school, it is in your power to make English one of your best subjects in college. If you believe writing can be learned, work hard at it! You *will* become a better writer!

Your attitude is crucial. If you continue to believe you will never be a good writer, chances are good that you will not improve. If you start believing that you *can improve*, chances are excellent that you *will improve*.

Writing as a Process of Discovery

In addition to believing that writing is a natural gift, many people believe, mistakenly, that writing should flow in a simple, straight line from the writer's head onto the page. But writing is seldom an easy, one-step journey in which a finished paper comes out in a first draft. The truth is that *writing is a process of discovery* that involves a series of steps, and those steps are usually a zigzag journey that often result in starting over at some point in the process. Look at the following illustrations of the writing process:

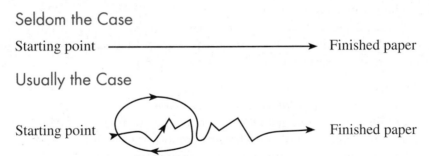

Very often, writers do not discover exactly what they want to write about until they explore their thoughts in writing. For example, Gene Hert had been asked to write about a best or worst job. Only after he did some freewriting on good and bad jobs did he realize that the most interesting details centered on his job at an apple plant. He discovered his subject in the course of writing.

Another student, Rhonda, talking afterward about a paper she wrote, explained that at first her topic was how she relaxed with her children. But as she accumulated details, she realized after a page of writing that the words *relax* and *children* simply did not go together. Her details were really examples of how she *enjoyed* her children, not how she *relaxed* with them. She sensed that the real focus of her writing should be what she did by herself to relax, and then she thought suddenly that the best time of her week was Thursday after school. "A light clicked on in my head," she explained. "I knew I had my paper." Then it was a matter of detailing exactly what she did to relax on Thursday evenings. Her paper, "How I Relax," is on page 90.

The point is that writing is often a process of continuing discovery. As you write, you may suddenly switch direction or double back. You may be working on a topic sentence and realize suddenly that it could be your concluding thought. Or you may be developing a supporting idea and then decide that it should be the main point of your paper. Chapter 2 treats the writing process directly. What is important to remember here is that writers frequently do not know their exact destination as they begin to write. Very often they discover the direction and shape of a paper during the process of writing.

Keeping a Journal

Because writing is a skill, it makes sense that the more you practice writing, the better you will write. One excellent way to get practice in writing, even before you begin composing formal paragraphs, is to keep a daily or almost daily journal. Writing a journal will help you develop the habit of thinking on paper and will show you how ideas can be discovered in the process of writing. A journal can make writing a familiar part of your life and can serve as a continuing source of ideas for papers.

At some point during the day—perhaps during a study period after your last class of the day, or right before dinner, or right before going to bed—spend fifteen minutes or so writing in your journal. Keep in mind that you do not have to plan what to write about, or be in the mood to write, or worry about making mistakes as you write; just write down whatever words come out. You should write at least one page in each session.

You may want to use a notebook that you can easily carry with you for on-the-spot writing. Or you may decide to write on loose-leaf paper that can be transferred later to a journal folder on your desk. Many students choose to keep electronic journals on their computers or online through livejournal.com or a similar Web site. No matter how you proceed, be sure to date all entries.

Your instructor may ask you to make journal entries a specific number of times a week, for a specific number of weeks. He or she may have you turn in your journal every so often for review and feedback. If you are keeping the journal on your own, try to make entries three to five times a week every week of the semester. Your journal can serve as a sourcebook of ideas for possible papers. More important, keeping a journal will help you develop the habit of thinking on paper, and it can help you make writing a familiar part of your life.

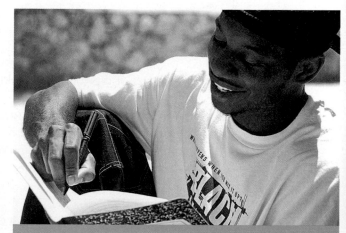

INSPIRATION TO WRITE COMES IN MANY WAYS AND at many different times. Do you think that using a handwritten versus an electronic journal might affect the notes and observations one makes? Which do you prefer and why?

ACTIVITY 6

Following is an excerpt from one student's journal. (Sentence-skills mistakes have been corrected to improve readability.) As you read, look for a general point and for supporting material that could be the basis for an interesting paper.

October 6

Today a woman came into our department at the store and wanted to know if we had any scrap lumber ten feet long. Ten feet! "Lady," I said, "anything we have that's ten feet long sure as heck isn't scrap." When the boss heard me say that, he almost canned me. My boss is a company man, down to his toe tips. He wants to make a big impression on his bosses, and he'll run us around like mad all night to make himself look good. He's the most ambitious man I've ever met. If I don't transfer out of Hardware soon, I'm going to go crazy on this job. I'm not ready to quit, though. The time is not right. I want to be here for a year and have another job lined up and have other things right before I quit. It's good the boss wasn't around tonight when another customer wanted me to carry a bookcase he had bought out to his car. He didn't ask me to help him—he expected *me to help him. I hate that kind of "You're my servant" attitude, and I told him that carrying stuff out to cars wasn't my job. Ordinarily I go out of my way to give people a hand, but not guys like him. . . .*

- If the writer of this journal is looking for an idea for a paper, he can probably find several in this single entry. For example, he might write a narrative supporting the point that "In my sales job I have to deal with some irritating customers." See if you can find another idea in this entry that might be the basis for an interesting paragraph. Write your point in the space below.

  _____

- Take fifteen minutes to prepare a journal entry right now on this day in your life. On a separate sheet of paper, just start writing about anything that you have said, heard, thought, or felt, and let your thoughts take you where they may.

Using This Text

Here is a suggested sequence for using this book if you are working on your own.

1. After completing this introduction, read the next five chapters in Part 1 and work through as many of the activities as you need to master the ideas in these chapters. At that point, you will have covered all the basic theory needed to write effective papers.

2. Turn to Appendix B and take the diagnostic test. The test will help you determine what sentence skills you need to review. Study those skills one or two at a time while you continue to work on other parts of the book. These skills will help you write effective, error-free sentences.

3. What you do next depends on course requirements, individual needs, or both. You will want to practice at least several different kinds of paragraph development in Part 2. If your time is limited, be sure to include "Exemplification" (pages 184–198), "Process" (pages 199–213), "Comparison and/or Contrast" (pages 229–249), and "Argument" (pages 305–322).

4. After you develop skill in writing effective paragraphs, go on to practice writing one or more of the several-paragraph essays described in Part 3.

5. In numerous sections throughout the book, you will find helpful information for projects that involve research.

Remember that, for your convenience, the book includes the following:

- On the inside back cover, there is a checklist of the four basic principles, or four bases, of effective writing.
- On page 542, there is a list of commonly used correction symbols.

Get into the habit of referring to these guides regularly; they'll help you produce clearly thought-out, well-written papers.

English Skills with Readings will help you learn, practice, and apply the thinking and writing skills you need to communicate effectively. But the starting point must be your determination to do the work needed to become a strong writer. The ability to express yourself clearly and logically can open doors of opportunity for you, both in school and in your career. If you decide—*and only you can decide*—that you want such language power, this book will help you reach that goal.

2

The Four Bases and the Writing Process

This chapter will

- explain and illustrate the sequence of steps in writing an effective paragraph

  - prewriting

  - revising

  - editing

- show you how to conduct a peer review and personal review

HOW DO YOU BEGIN WRITING? Getting started is often the hardest part of writing. You may have looked and felt like the student pictured here many times when working on a writing assignment. What specific methods could this student use to help get ideas flowing? As you will learn in this chapter, using various prewriting techniques can help make the writing process a lot easier.

Chapter 1 introduced you to the paragraph form and some fundamentals of writing, including the four basic principles, or four bases, of effective writing. This chapter explains and illustrates the sequence of steps—based on those principles—that you'll need to write an effective paragraph. In particular, the chapter gives special emphasis to prewriting and revising—strategies that can help with every paragraph that you write.

For many people, writing is a process that involves the following steps:

1. Discovering a point—often through prewriting.
2. Developing solid support for the point—often through more prewriting.
3. Organizing the supporting material and writing it out in a first draft.
4. Revising and then editing carefully to ensure an effective, error-free paper.

Learning this sequence will help give you confidence when the time comes to write. You'll know that you can use prewriting as a way to think on paper (or at the keyboard) and to discover gradually what ideas you want to develop, and then when you are ready, to use those ideas to write a first draft. You'll realize that you can use revising to rework a paragraph until it is strong and effective. And you'll be able to edit a paragraph so that your sentences are clear and error-free.

Throughout the process, you'll understand that there are four clear-cut goals to aim for—unity, support, organization, and error-free sentences:

Four Steps ⟶	Four Bases
1. If you make one point and stick to that point,	your writing will have *unity*.
2. If you back up the point with specific evidence,	your writing will have *support*.
3. If you organize and connect the specific evidence,	your writing will have *coherence*.
4. If you write clear, error-free sentences,	your writing will demonstrate effective *sentence skills*.

Prewriting

If you are like many people, you may have trouble getting started writing. A mental block may develop when you sit down before a blank sheet of paper or a blank screen. You may not be able to think of an interesting topic or a point to make about your topic. Or you may have trouble coming up with specific details to support your point. And even after starting a paragraph, you may hit snags—moments when you wonder "What else can I say?" or "Where do I go next?"

The following pages describe five techniques that will help you think about and develop a topic and get words on paper: (1) freewriting, (2) questioning, (3) making a list, (4) clustering, and (5) summarizing. These prewriting techniques help you think about and create material, and they are a central part of the writing process.

Technique 1: Freewriting

When you do not know what to write about a subject or when you are blocked in writing, freewriting sometimes helps. In *freewriting,* you write on your topic for ten minutes. You do not worry about spelling or punctuating correctly, about erasing mistakes, about organizing material, or about finding exact words. You just write without stopping. If you get stuck for words, you write "I am looking for something to say" or repeat words until you think of something. There is no need to feel inhibited, since mistakes *do not count* and you do not have to hand in your paper.

Freewriting will limber up your writing muscles and make you familiar with the act of writing. It is a way to break through mental blocks about writing. Since you do not have to worry about mistakes, you can focus on discovering what you want to say about a subject. Your initial ideas and impressions will often become clearer after you have gotten them down on paper, and they may lead to other impressions and ideas. Through continued practice in freewriting, you will develop the habit of thinking as you write. And you will learn a technique that is a helpful way to get started on almost any paragraph.

Freewriting: A Student Model

Gene Hert's paragraph "My Job in an Apple Plant" on page 4 was written in response to an assignment to write a paragraph on the best or worst job he ever had. Gene began by doing some general freewriting and thinking about his jobs. Here is his freewriting:

I have had good and bad jobs, that's for sure. It was great earning money for the first time. I shoveled snow for my neighbor, a friend of mine and I did the work and had snowball fights along the way. I remember my neighbor reaching into his pocket and pulling out several dollars and handing us the money, it was like magic. Then there was the lawnmowing, which was also a good job. I mowed my aunts lawn while she was away at work. Then I'd go sit by myself in her cool living room and have a coke she left in the refrigarator for me. And look through all her magazines. Then there was the apple plant job I had after high school. That was a worst job that left me totaly wiped out at the end of my shift. Lifting cartons and cartons of apple juice for bosses that treated us

continued

> *like slaves. The cartons coming and coming all night long. I started early in the evening and finished the next morning. I still remember how tired I was. Driving back home the first time. That was a lonely job and a hard job and I don't eat apples anymore.*

At this point, Gene read over his notes, and as he later commented, "I realized that I had several potential topics. I said to myself, 'What point can I make that I can cover in a paragraph? What do I have the most information about?' I decided to narrow my topic down to my awful job at the apple plant. I figured I would have lots of interesting details for that topic." Gene then did a more focused freewriting to accumulate details for a paragraph on his bad job:

> *The job I remember most is the worst job I ever had. I worked in an apple plant, I put in very long hours and would be totaly beat after ten hours of work. All the time lifting cartons of apple juice which would come racing down a metal track. The guy with me was a bit lazy at times, and I would be one man doing a two-man job. The cartons would go into a tracter trailer, we would have to throw down wooden skids to put the cartons on, then wed have to move the metal track as we filled up the truck. There is no other job I have had that even compares to this job, it was a lot worse than it seems. The bosses treated us like slaves and the company paid us like slaves. I would work all night from 7 P.M. and drive home in the morning at 5 A.M. and be bone tired. I remember my arms and sholders were so tired after the first night. I had trouble turning the steering wheel of my father's car.*

Notice that there are problems with spelling, grammar, and punctuation in Gene's freewriting. Gene was not worried about such matters, nor should he have been. At this stage, he just wanted to do some thinking on paper and get some material down on the page. He knew that this was a good first step, a good way of getting started, and that he would then be able to go on to shape that material.

You should take the same approach when freewriting: Explore your topic without worrying at all about being "correct." Figuring out what you want to say and getting raw material down on the page should have all of your attention at this early stage of the writing process.

ACTIVITY 1

To get a sense of the freewriting process, take a sheet of paper and freewrite about different jobs you have had and what you liked or did not like about them. See how much material you can accumulate in ten minutes. Remember not to worry about "mistakes"; you are just thinking on paper.

Read over the material that you generated and decide which job you have the most information about. Then do more focused freewriting on that particular job.

Technique 2: Questioning

In *questioning,* you generate ideas and details by asking as many questions as you can think of about your subject. Such questions include *Why? When? Where? Who? How? In what ways?*

Here are questions that Gene Hert asked while further developing his paragraph.

Questioning: A Student Model

Questions	Answers
What did I hate about the job?	Very hard work.
	Poor pay. Mean bosses.
How was the work hard?	Nonstop cartons of apple juice.
	Cartons became very heavy.
Why was pay poor?	$4.50 an hour (minimum wage at the time). Only fifty cents more for working the second shift. Only good money was in overtime—where you got time-and-a-half. No double time.
How were the bosses mean?	Yelled at some workers.
	Showed no appreciation.
	Created bad working conditions.
In what ways were working conditions bad?	Unheated truck in zero-degree weather.
	Floor of tractor trailer was cold steel.
	Breaks were limited—only two of them.
	Lonely job.

Asking questions can be an effective way of getting yourself to think about a topic from different angles. The questions can help you generate details about a topic and get ideas on how to organize those details. Notice how asking questions gives Gene a better sense of the different reasons why he hated the job.

To get a feel for the questioning process, use a sheet of paper to ask yourself a series of questions about your best and worst jobs. What did you like about the jobs? What did you dislike? What were the working conditions like? See how many details you can accumulate in ten minutes. Remember not to be concerned about "mistakes" because you are just thinking on paper.

ACTIVITY 2

Technique 3: Making a List

In *making a list,* also known as *brainstorming,* you create a list of ideas and details that relate to your subject. Pile these items up, one after another, without trying to sort out major details from minor ones, or trying to put the details in any special order, or even trying to spell words correctly. Your goal is to accumulate raw material by making up a list of everything about your subject that occurs to you.

After freewriting and questioning, Gene made up the following list of details.

Making a List: A Student Model

Apple factory job—worst one I ever had

Bosses were mean

Working conditions were poor

Went to work at 5 P.M., got back at 7 A.M.

Lifted cartons of apple juice for ten hours

Cartons were heavy

Only two ten-minute breaks a night

Pay was only $4.50 an hour

Just fifty cents extra for night shift

Cost of gas money to and from work

No pay for lunch break

Had to work 60 hours for good take-home pay

Loaded onto wooden skids in a truck

Bosses yelled at some workers

Temperature zero outside

Floors of trucks ice-cold metal

Nonstop pace

Had to clean apple vats after work

Slept, ate, and worked—no social life

No real friends at work

One detail led to another as Gene expanded his list. Slowly but surely, more details emerged, some of which he could use in developing his paragraph. By the time he had finished his list, he was ready to plan an outline of his paragraph and then to write his first draft.

ACTIVITY 3

To get a sense of making a list, use a sheet of paper to list a series of details about one of the best or worst jobs you ever had. Don't worry about deciding whether the details are major or minor; instead, just get down as many details as you can think of in five or ten minutes.

Technique 4: Clustering

Clustering, also known as *diagramming* or *mapping,* is another strategy that can be used to generate material for a paragraph. This method is helpful for people who like to think in a visual way. In clustering, you use lines, boxes, arrows, and circles to show relationships among the ideas and details that occur to you.

Begin by stating your subject in a few words in the center of a blank sheet of paper. Then, as ideas and details occur to you, put them in boxes or circles around the subject and draw lines to connect them to each other and to the subject. Put minor ideas or details in smaller boxes or circles, and use connecting lines to show how they relate as well.

Keep in mind that there is no right or wrong way of clustering. It is a way to think on paper about how various ideas and details relate to one another. Below is an example of what Gene might have done to develop his ideas:

Clustering: A Student Model

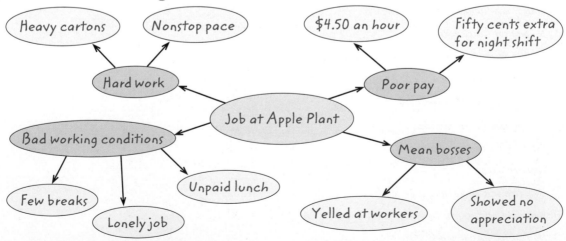

> **TIP** In addition to helping generate material, clustering often suggests ways to organize ideas and details.

Use clustering or another type of diagramming to organize the details about a best or worst job that you created for the previous activity (page 23).

ACTIVITY 4

Technique 5: Summarizing

Often, you can gather ideas and details about your topic in the work of other writers. When you *summarize* someone else's work, you condense that person's ideas and put them into your own words. Always shorter than the original, a summary is an effective way to combine new information with what you already know.

Always make sure to use your own words throughout the summary. Also, give the source of your information credit by identifying the author. For example, you might write, "Dr. Henry Davison claims that eating a lot of fiber is important to good digestion." Activities involving both summarizing and identifying sources can be found in numerous different sections throughout this book.

Writing a Topic Sentence and Preparing a Scratch Outline

After reading over the information you have gathered through one of the prewriting techniques just discussed, write a working topic sentence. A topic sentence expresses the *point* you want to make about the *subject* of your paragraph. This point, discussed further in Chapter 3, should be clearly stated and narrow, and it should be drawn from the ideas you have recorded in your prewriting.

In Chapter 1, you read Gene Hert's paragraph entitled "My Job in an Apple Plant," which responds to an assignment that asked students to discuss their best or worst jobs. Look back to Gene's freewriting (pages 20–21); you'll notice that he rewrote his first attempt, narrowing his focus to only one job in the second version. His working topic sentence emerged when he wrote his second version: "The job I remember most was the worst job I ever had." As with any other aspect of writing, however, a working topic sentence can and often should be revised for clarity and exactness. Gene revised his topic sentence in the final version of his paragraph (page 4): "Working in an apple plant was the worst job I ever had."

Once you have composed a topic sentence, you should prepare a scratch outline, which can be the *single most helpful technique* for writing a good paragraph. Though a scratch outline usually comes after you have written a working topic sentence, it may even emerge as you complete your freewriting, questioning, or other type of prewriting activity.

Making a scratch outline is part of prewriting because it is a good way to see if you need to gather more information for your paragraph. If you cannot come up with a solid outline, then you know you need to do more prewriting to clarify your main point and provide more support.

In a scratch outline, you think carefully about the point you are making, the supporting items for that point, and the order in which you will arrange those items. The scratch outline is a plan or blueprint to help you achieve a unified, supported, and well-organized paragraph.

Scratch Outline: A Student Model

In Gene's case, as he was working on his list of details, he suddenly realized what the plan of his paragraph could be. He could organize many of his details into one of three supporting groups: (1) the job itself, (2) the pay, and (3) the working conditions. He then went back to the list, crossed out items that he now saw did not fit, and numbered the items according to the group where they fit. The illustration below shows what Gene did with the list he had created.

Apple factory job—worst one I ever had

~~Bosses were mean~~

3 Working conditions were poor

~~Went to work at 5 P.M., got back at 7 A.M.~~

1 Lifted cartons of apple juice for ten hours

1 Cartons were heavy

3 Only two ten-minute breaks a night

2 Pay was only $4.50 an hour

2 Just fifty cents extra for night shift

~~Cost of gas money to and from work~~

3 No pay for lunch break

2 Had to work 60 hours for good take-home pay

1 Loaded onto wooden skids in a truck

~~Bosses yelled at some workers~~

3 Temperature zero outside

~~Floors of trucks ice-cold metal~~

1 Nonstop pace

continued

3 Had to clean apple vats after work

~~*Slept, ate, and worked—no social life*~~

3 No real friends at work

Under the list, Gene was now able to prepare his scratch outline:

The apple plant was my worst job.

1. Hard work

2. Poor pay

3. Poor working conditions

After all his prewriting, Gene was pleased. He knew that he had a promising paragraph—one with a clear point and solid support. He saw that he could organize the material into a paragraph with a topic sentence, supporting points, and vivid details. He was now ready to write the first draft of his paragraph, using his outline as a guide.

 TIP Chances are that if you do enough prewriting and thinking on paper, you will eventually discover the point and support of your paragraph.

Create a scratch outline that could serve as a guide if you were to write a paragraph on your best or worst job experience.

ACTIVITY 5

Writing a First Draft

To write your first draft, begin by reading the prewriting you completed for the assignment. Then review your working topic sentence and your scratch outline. Make sure that each item in your outline supports and develops the main point in your working topic sentence. If it doesn't, cross it out. For example, let's say Gene's scratch outline had these items: (1) hard work, (2) poor pay, (3) poor working conditions, and (4) friendly coworkers. Gene would want to eliminate item 4 because it does not support his working topic sentence—"The apple plant was my worst job."

Once you have reviewed your outline, you're ready to write your first draft. Start by writing down or typing your working topic sentence. Then put down the first item from your scratch outline in sentence form. Now write, one sentence at a time, all the specific details for that item that you gathered during prewriting. For example, look at Gene's first draft shown below. After explaining that the work was hard, Gene included the following supporting detail: "For ten hours a night, I stacked cartons that rolled down a metal track. . . ." This information is from the list Gene made during prewriting (see page 23).

When you are finished with the first outline item, go on to the next one. Following your scratch outline like a blueprint, continue to put down information gathered in your prewriting under the remaining items in your outline. Don't worry yet about grammar, punctuation, or spelling. You don't want to take time to correct sentences that you might decide to remove later.

New details and ideas may pop into your mind as you write. That's only natural. Just add the new information to your draft. Remember that writing is a process: You discover more and more about what you want to say as you work. Developing new information helps make your paragraph more convincing. More important, it shows that you are thinking critically as you work.

Writing a First Draft: A Student Model

Here is Gene's first draft, done in longhand.

~~The apple plant job was my worst.~~ Working in an apple plant was the worst job I ever had. The work was physicaly hard. For ~~a long time~~ ten to twelve hours a night, I stacked cartons that rolled down a metal track in a tracter trailer. Each carton had cans or bottles of apple juice, and they were heavy. At the same time, I had to keep a mental count of all the cartons I had loaded. The pay for the job was a bad feature. I was getting the minamum wage at that time plus fifty cents extra for night shift. I had to work a lot to get a decent take-home pay. Working conditions were poor at the apple plant, we were limited to ~~short breaks~~ two ten-minute breaks. The truck-loading dock where I was most of the time was a cold and lonely place. Then by myself cleaning up. DETAILS!

TIP After Gene finished the first draft, he was able to put it aside until the next day. You will benefit as well if you can allow some time between finishing a draft and starting to revise.

Fill in the missing words in the following explanation of Gene's first draft.

1. Gene presents his _____ in the first sentence and then crosses it out and revises it right away to make it read smoothly and clearly.

2. Notice that he continues to accumulate specific supporting details as he writes the draft. For example, he crosses out and replaces "a long time" with the more specific _____; he crosses out and replaces "short breaks" with the more specific _____.

3. There are various misspellings—for example, _____. Gene doesn't worry about spelling at this point. He just wants to get down as much of the substance of his paragraph as possible.

4. There are various punctuation errors, especially the run-on and the fragment near the (*beginning, middle, end*) _____ of the paragraph.

5. Near the close of his paragraph, Gene can't think of added details to insert, so he simply prints "_____" as a reminder to himself for the next draft.

Revising

Revising is as much a stage in the writing process as prewriting, outlining, and doing the first draft. *Revising* means that you rewrite a paragraph, building upon what has already been done, in order to make it stronger. One writer said about revision, "It's like cleaning house—getting rid of all the junk and putting things in the right order." It is not just "straightening up"; instead, you must be ready to roll up your sleeves and do whatever is needed to create an effective paragraph. Too many students think that a first draft *is* the paragraph. They start to become writers when they realize that revising a rough draft three or four times is often at the heart of the writing process.

Here are some quick tips that can help make revision easier. First, set your first draft aside for a while. You can then come back to it with a fresher, more objective point of view. Second, work from typed or printed text, preferably double-spaced so you'll have room to handwrite changes later. You'll be able to see the paragraph more impartially if it is typed than if you were just looking at your own familiar handwriting. Next, read your draft aloud. Hearing how your writing sounds will help you pick up problems with meaning as well as with style. Finally, as you do all these things, write additional thoughts and changes above the lines or in the margins of your paragraph. Your written comments can serve as a guide when you work on the next draft.

There are two stages to the revision process:

- Revising content
- Revising sentences

Revising Content

To revise the content of your paragraph, ask the questions listed in the box below.

---

1. Is my paragraph **unified**?
   - Do I have a main idea that is clearly stated at the beginning of my paragraph?
   - Do all my supporting points truly support and back up my main idea?
2. Is my paragraph **supported**?
   - Are there separate supporting points for the main idea?
   - Do I have specific evidence for each supporting point?
   - Is there plenty of specific evidence for the supporting points?
3. Is my paragraph **organized**?
   - Do I have a clear method of organizing my paper?
   - Do I use transitions and other connecting words?

The next two chapters (Chapters 3 and 4) give you practice in achieving *unity, support,* and *organization* in your writing.

Revising Sentences

To revise individual sentences in your paragraph, ask the following questions:

---

1. Do I use *parallelism* to balance my words and ideas?
2. Do I have a *consistent point of view?*
3. Do I use *specific* words?
4. Do I use *active* verbs?
5. Do I use words effectively by *avoiding slang, clichés, pretentious language,* and *wordiness?*
6. Do I *vary my sentences* in length and structure?

Chapter 5 will give you practice in revising sentences.

Revising: A Student Model

For his second draft, Gene used the word-processing program on his computer. He then printed out a double-spaced version of his paragraph, leaving himself plenty of room for handwritten revisions. Here is Gene's second draft plus the handwritten changes and additions that became his third draft.

First of all

Working in an apple plant was the worst job I ever had. The work

was physicaly hard. For ten to twelve hours a night, I stacked cartons

that rolled down a metal track in a tracter trailer. Each carton contained

25 pounds of bottled   *down the track*

~~bottles of~~ apple juice, and they came nonstop. ~~At the same time, I had~~

~~to keep a mental count of all the cartons I had loaded~~. The second bad

feature ~~that made the job a worst one was the pay~~. I was getting the

just

minamum wage at that time, $4.50 an hour. Plus fifty cents extra

the   *over sixty hours a week*   *Finally*

for night shift. I had to work ~~a lot of hours~~ to get decent take-home pay. I

hated the working conditions. We were limited to two ten-minute breaks

an unpaid half hour for lunch

and ~~the half hour for lunch was not paid~~. Most of my time was spent

loading   *near-zero-degree*

outside on the dock in ~~cold~~ temperatures. And I was very lonely on the

because   *I*

job, I had nothing in common with the other workers. ~~you~~ felt this isolation

and

especially when the production line shut down for the night I had to clean

an ugly

the apple vats. The vats were ~~a bad~~ place to be on a cold morning and

bitter

the job was a ~~bad~~ one to have.

Gene made his changes in longhand as he worked on the second draft. As you will see when you complete the activity below, his revision serves to make the paragraph more unified, supported, and organized.

Fill in the missing words.

ACTIVITY 7

1. To clarify the organization, Gene adds at the beginning of the first supporting point the transitional phrase "_____," and he sets off the third supporting point with the word "_____."

2. In the interest of (*unity, support, organization*) _____, he crosses out the sentence "_____." He realizes that

this sentence is not a relevant detail to support the idea that the work was physically hard.

3. To add more (*unity, support, organization*) _____, he changes "a lot of hours" to "_____"; he changes "on the dock" to "_____"; he changes "cold temperatures" to "_____."

4. In the interest of eliminating wordiness, he removes the words "_____" from the sixth sentence.

5. To achieve parallelism, Gene changes "the half hour for lunch was not paid" to "_____."

6. For greater sentence variety, Gene combines two short sentences, beginning the second part of the sentence with the subordinating word "_____."

7. To create a consistent point of view, Gene changes "You felt this isolation" to "_____."

8. Finally, Gene replaces the somewhat vague "bad" in "The vats were a bad place to be on a cold morning, and the job was a bad one to have" with two more precise words: "_____" and "_____."

Editing

The last major stage in the writing process is editing—checking a paragraph for mistakes in grammar, punctuation, usage, and spelling. Editing as well as proof-reading (checking a paragraph for typos and other careless errors) is explained in detail on pages 128-130.

Editing: A Student Model

After typing into his word-processing file all the revisions in his paragraph, Gene printed out another clean draft of the paragraph. He now turned his attention to editing changes, as shown on the next page.

My Job in an Apple Plant

Working in an apple plant was the worst job I ever had. First of all, the

work was ~~physicaly~~ *physically* hard. For ten to twelve hours a night, I took cartons

that rolled down a metal track and stacked them onto wooden skids in

a ~~tracter~~ *tractor* trailer. Each carton contained ~~25~~ *twenty-five* pounds of bottled apple juice,

and they came down the track almost nonstop. The second bad feature

of the job was the pay. I was getting the ~~minamum~~ *minimum* wage at that time,

$4.50 an hour, Plus just fifty cents extra for working the night shift. I had

to work over sixty hours a week to get a decent take-home pay. Finally,

I hated the working conditions. We were limited to two ten-minute breaks

and an unpaid half hour for lunch. Most of my time was spent outside on

the loading dock in near-zero-degree temperatures. And I was very lonely

on the job because I had no interests in common with the other workers.

I felt this isolation especially when the production line shut down for the

night, and I ~~had to clean~~ *spent two hours by myself cleaning* the apple vats. The vats were an ugly place to

be on a cold morning, and the job was a bitter one to have.

Once again, Gene made his changes in longhand right on the printout of his paragraph. To note these changes, complete the activity below.

Fill in the missing words.

ACTIVITY 8

1. As part of his editing, Gene checked and corrected the _____

   of three words, *physically, tractor,* and *minimum.*

2. He added _____ to set off an introductory phrase ("First of

   all") and an introductory word ("Finally") and also to connect the two com-

   plete thoughts in the final sentence.

3. He corrected a fragment ("_____") by using a comma to

   attach it to the preceding sentence.

4. He realized that a number like "25" should be _____ as

   "twenty-five."

5. And since revision can occur at any stage of the writing process, including editing, Gene makes one of his details more vivid by adding the descriptive words "_____."

All that remained for Gene to do was to enter his corrections, print out the final draft of the paragraph, and proofread it for any typos or other careless errors. He was then ready to hand it in to his instructor.

Using Peer Review

It is a good idea to have another student or peer respond to your writing before you hand it in to the instructor. On the day a rough draft is due, or on a day when you are writing paragraphs or essays in class, your instructor may ask you to pair up with another student or group of students. Each student's essay will be read and responded to by those in the group.

Ideally, read the other paragraph or essay aloud while your partner listens. If that is not practical, read it in a whisper while he or she looks on. As you read, both you

WORKING WITH ANOTHER STUDENT CAN BE BENEFICIAL FOR BOTH OF YOU.
What kinds of skills might you gain from being a peer reviewer? In what specific ways could you benefit as an author?

and your partner should look and listen for spots where the composition does not read smoothly and clearly. Check or circle the trouble spots where your reading snags.

Your partner should then re-read your work, marking possible trouble spots while doing so. Then each of you should do the following three things.

1. Identification

On a separate sheet of paper, write at the top the title and author of the composition you have read. Under it put your name as the reader of the paragraph or essay.

2. Scratch Outline

"X-ray" the paper for its inner logic by making up a scratch outline. The scratch outline need be no more than twenty words or so, but it should show clearly the logical foundation on which the paragraph or essay is built. It should identify and summarize the overall point of the paper and the three areas of support for the point.

Your outline should be organized like this:

Point: _____

Support:

1. _____

2. _____

3. _____

For example here is a scratch outline of the paper on page 215 about the benefits of exercise:

Point: *Effects of exercise can change one's life.*

Support:

1. *Burns calories for weight loss*

2. *Helps heart and circulatory system*

3. *Helps improve emotional health*

3. Comments

Under the outline, write the heading "Comments." As many people are sensitive to criticism, it is very important to be specific and constructive with your comments.

Try to avoid vague comments like "it's good"; instead offer helpful suggestions like "your topic sentence is very broad and should be narrowed down." Here are some of the general areas you should comment on while peer reviewing:

- Is there a topic sentence or thesis statement that makes a point? If not, try to suggest ways the author could improve it.

- Are there spots in the paragraph or essay where you see problems with *unity, support,* or *organization*? (You'll find it helpful to refer to the checklist on the inside back cover of this book.) If so, offer comments. For example, for an essay you might say, "More details are needed in the first supporting paragraph," or "Some details in the last supporting paragraph don't really back up your point."

- Make a note of at least two things the author did really well, such as good use of transitions or an especially realistic or vivid specific detail.

- Write down at least two things the author could do to improve the paper, such as adding detail or support in specific areas or using more vibrant and active language.

- Finally, go back to the spots where your reading of the composition snagged: Are words or ideas missing? Is there a lack of parallel structure? Is the meaning of a sentence confusing? Try to figure out what the problems are and suggest ways of fixing them.

- Although *sentence skills* are important, try not to simply edit a student's paper as you are reviewing; extra attention to grammar and punctuation should be given during the editing stage and not the revising stage.

After you have completed your evaluation of the paragraph or essay, give it to your partner and talk about the comments. As the author, you need to understand the reviewer's comments, so you should ask for clarification on anything that you don't understand. Remember not to get defensive, but see this as one part of the process of writing and a chance to improve your skills as a writer.

Doing a Personal Review

1. While you're writing and revising a paragraph or essay, you should be constantly evaluating it in terms of *unity, support,* and *organization*. Use as a guide the detailed checklist on the inside back cover of this book.

2. After you've finished the next-to-final draft of a composition, check it for the *sentence skills* listed on the inside back cover. It may also help to read your work out loud. If a given sentence does not sound right—that is, if it does not read clearly and smoothly—chances are something is wrong. In that case, revise or edit as necessary until your composition is complete.

Review Activities

You now have a good overview of the writing process, from prewriting to first draft to revising to editing. The remaining chapters in Part 1 will deepen your sense of the four goals of effective writing: unity, support, organization or coherence, and sentence skills.

To reinforce much of the information about the writing process that you have learned in this chapter, you can now work through the following activities:

1. Taking a writing inventory
2. Prewriting
3. Outlining
4. Revising

1 Taking a Writing Inventory

To evaluate your approach to the writing process, answer the questions below. This activity is not a test, so try to be as honest as possible. Becoming aware of your writing habits can help you make helpful changes in your writing.

ACTIVITY 9

---

1. When you start work on a paper, do you typically do any prewriting?

   _____ Yes   _____ Sometimes   _____ No

2. Which of the following techniques do you use?

   _____ Freewriting   _____ Clustering

   _____ Questioning   _____ Topic sentence and scratch outline

   _____ List making   _____ Other (please describe)

   _____ Summarizing

3. Which prewriting technique or techniques work best for you or do you think will work best for you?

4. Many students have said they find it helpful to handwrite a first draft and then type that draft on a computer. They then print the draft out and revise it by hand. Describe your own way of drafting and revising a paper.

---

continued

5. After you write the first draft of a paper, do you have time to set it aside for a while so that you can come back to it with a fresh eye?

6. How many drafts do you typically write when doing a paper?

7. When you revise, are you aware that you should be working toward a paper that is unified, solidly supported, and clearly organized? Has this chapter given you a better sense that unity, support, and organization are goals to aim for?

8. Do you revise a paper for the effectiveness of its sentences as well as for its content?

9. What (if any) information has this chapter given you about prewriting that you will try to apply in your writing?

10. What (if any) information has this chapter given you about revising that you will try to apply in your writing?

2 Prewriting and Scratch Outline

ACTIVITY 10

Following are examples of how the different techniques could be used to develop the topic "Inconsiderate Drivers." Identify each technique by writing F (for freewriting),

Q (for questioning), L (for listing), C (for clustering), or SO (for scratch outline) in the answer space.

_____ High beams on
Weave in and out at high speeds
Treat street like a trash can
Open car door onto street without looking
Stop on street looking for an address
Don't use turn signals
High speeds in low-speed zones
Don't take turns merging
Use horn when they don't need to
Don't give walkers the right of way
More attention to cell phone than the road

_____
What is one example of an inconsiderate driver?	A person who turns suddenly without signaling.
Where does this happen?	At city intersections or on smaller country roads.
Why is this dangerous?	You have to be alert and slow down yourself to avoid rear-ending the car in front.
What is another example of inconsideration on the road?	Drivers who come toward you at night with their high beams on.

_____ Some people are inconsiderate drivers.
1. In city:
    a. Stop in middle of street
    b. Turn without signaling
2. On highway:
    a. Leave high beams on
    b. Stay in passing lane
    c. Cheat during a merge
3. Both in city and on highway:
    a. Throw trash out of window
    b. Pay more attention to cell phone than to road

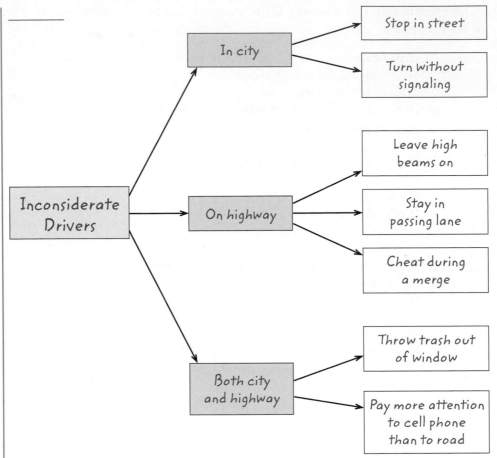

I was driving home last night after class and had three people try to blind me by coming at me with their high beams on. I had to zap them all with my high beams. Rude drivers make me crazy. The worst are the ones that use the road as a trash can. People who throw butts and cups and hamburger wrappings and other stuff out the car windows should be tossed into a trash dumpster. If word got around that this was the punishment maybe they would wise up. Other drivers do dumb things as well. I hate the person who will just stop in the middle of the street and try to figure out directions or look for a house address. Why don't they pull over to the side of the street? That hardly seems like too much to ask. Instead, they stop all traffic while doing their own thing. Then there are the people who keep what they want to do a secret. They're not going to tell you they plan to make a right- or left-hand turn. You've got to figure it out yourself when they suddenly slow down in front of you. Then there are all the people on their cell phones yakking away and not paying attention to their driving.

3 Outlining

As already mentioned (see page 25), outlining is central to writing a good paragraph. An outline lets you see, and work on, the bare bones of a paragraph, without the distraction of cluttered words and sentences. It develops your ability to think clearly and logically. Outlining provides a quick check on whether your paragraph will be *unified*. It also suggests right at the start whether your paragraph will be adequately *supported*. And it shows you how to plan a paragraph that is *well organized*.

The following series of exercises will help you develop the outlining skills so important to planning and writing a solid paragraph.

One key to effective outlining is the ability to distinguish between general ideas and specific details that fit under those ideas. Read each group of specific ideas below. Then circle the letter of the general idea that tells what the specific ideas have in common. Note that the general idea should not be too broad or too narrow. Begin by trying the example item, and then read the explanation that follows.

ACTIVITY 11

EXAMPLE

Specific ideas: runny nose, coughing, sneezing, sore throat

The general idea is:

a.) cold symptoms.

b. symptoms.

c. throat problems.

EXPLANATION

It is true that the specific ideas are all symptoms, but they have in common something even more specific—they are all symptoms of the common cold. Therefore, answer *b* is too broad; the correct answer is *a*. Answer *c* is too narrow because it doesn't cover all the specific ideas; it covers only the final item in the list ("sore throat").

1. *Specific ideas:* good student reviews, good rapport with colleagues, excellent class evaluation

    The general idea is:

    a. teaching at a community college.

    b. reasons teaching is an important profession.

    c. reasons a teacher might be rehired.

2. *Specific ideas:* baking cookies, wrapping presents, decorating a tree

    The general idea is:

    a. Christmas.

    b. activities to prepare for Christmas.

    c. activities to prepare for any holiday.

3. *Specific ideas:* putting sticky tape on someone's chair, putting a "kick me" sign on someone's back, putting hot pepper in someone's cereal

   The general idea is:

   a. practical jokes.

   b. jokes.

   c. practical jokes played on teachers.

4. *Specific ideas:* long lines at the cafeteria, lack of available parking spaces, lack of available computers and printers

   The general idea is:

   a. problems.

   b. problems on campus.

   c. problems at the dining hall.

5. *Specific ideas:* broken sidewalks, non-functioning streetlamps, crumbling bridges, uncollected trash

   The general idea is:

   a. a city in disrepair.

   b. disrepair.

   c. a street in disrepair.

ACTIVITY 12   In the following items, the specific ideas are given but the general ideas are unstated. Fill in each blank with a general heading that accurately describes the list provided.

EXAMPLE

   General idea: Household Chores

   Specific ideas: washing dishes

   preparing meals

   taking out trash

   dusting

1. *General idea:* _____

   Specific ideas: empathetic

   loyal

   kind

   supportive

2. *General idea:* _____

   Specific ideas: losing weight

   exercising more

   eating more fruits and vegetables

   eating fewer fast-food meals

3. *General idea:* _____

   Specific ideas: different colored glitter
   multi-themed craft paper
   hot glue gun
   ribbons, buttons, and bows

4. *General idea:* _____

   Specific ideas: tees

   clubs

   bag

   spiked shoes

5. *General idea:* _____

   Specific ideas: staying at Disneyworld
   spending a week on a cruise
   visiting a national park
   touring castles in England

Major and minor ideas are mixed together in the two paragraphs outlined below. Put the ideas in logical order by filling in the outlines.

ACTIVITY 13

1. *Topic sentence:* Implementing year-round school would benefit society.

   Students attend school more days than within traditional calendars
   No need to spend first quarter learning again what was forgotten over the summer
   No need for families to find childcare for the summer break
   Helps students maintain and reinforce learning
   Less review time equals more time to study new subjects
   Helps families with scheduling and budgeting
   Eliminates the expense of privately funded activities during summer
   Allows teachers to teach subjects in more depth
   More school days allow for greater exposure to new concepts and information.

   a. _____
     (1) _____
     (2) _____
   b. _____
     (1) _____
     (2) _____
   _____

c. _____

   (1) _____

   (2) _____

2. *Topic sentence:* Blogging can be a great career choice for someone with an entrepreneurial spirit.

Regular posting schedule will keep readers interested.
Sticking to one theme, like fitness, will garner regular audience.
Successful bloggers identify a popular topic and/or timely niche.
Finding thrifty ways to dress fashionably is now a popular trend.
Bloggers should participate in social bookmarking like Digg and Reddit.
Bloggers need to be visible and promote themselves.
Bloggers need to be consistent.
People like to read about health-related topics.

a. _____

   (1) _____

   (2) _____

b. _____

   (1) _____

   (2) _____

c. _____

   (1) _____

   (2) _____

ACTIVITY 14

Again, major and minor ideas are mixed together. In addition, in each outline one of the three major ideas is missing and must be added. Put the ideas in logical order by filling in the outlines that follow (summarizing as needed) and adding a third major idea.

1. *Topic sentence:* Extending the school day would have several advantages.

Help children academically
Parents know children are safe at the school
More time to spend on basics
Less pressure to cover subjects quickly
More time for extras like art, music, and sports
Help working parents
More convenient to pick up children at 4 or 5 P.M.
Teachers' salaries would be raised

a. _____

   (1) _____

   (2) _____

b. _____

   (1) _____

   (2) _____

c. _____

   (1) _____

   (2) _____

2. *Topic sentence:* By following certain hints about food, exercise, and smoking, you can increase your chances of dying young.

   Don't ever walk if you can ride instead.

   Choose foods such as bacon and lunch meats that are laced with nitrites and other preservatives.

   Be very selective about what you eat.

   If you begin to cough or feel short of breath, keep smoking.

   If a friend invites you to play an outdoor sport, open a beer instead and head for your La-Z-Boy recliner.

   Resist the urge to exercise.

   Choose foods from one of four essential groups: fat, starch, sugar, and grease.

   Smoke on a regular basis.

a. _____

   (1) _____

   (2) _____

b. _____

   (1) _____

   (2) _____

c. _____

   (1) _____

   (2) _____

Read the following two paragraphs. Then outline each one in the space provided. Write out the topic sentence in each case and summarize in a few words the primary and secondary supporting material that fits under the topic sentence.

ACTIVITY 15

1.

Academic

Properly Planning a Family Vacation

Carefully planning a family vacation *as* a family can be the difference between a wonderful vacation and a terrible one. The very first thing a family should do in deciding what type of vacation to take is to determine the budget. Figuring how much can be spent, letting everyone in the family know the budget, and staying within that budget will help alleviate the stress of worrying or arguing about money during the trip. For example, a family of six may find that its budget will necessitate travel by car rather than by plane. Once the budget has been determined, the family should focus on where to vacation. A vacation to New York would involve several different factors than planning a vacation to Canada. For instance, to enter Canada each family member will need a passport; that process can take as long as three months. The next step is to decide on possible activities. For example, if a cruise is planned and the budget permits, family members may want to examine the excursions that are offered and choose one or two. However, if the vacation is to be a road trip through Yellowstone Park, family members may want to incorporate several daily hikes to break up the monotony of driving. To help keep family peace, each family member should be allotted one activity specifically geared toward him or her. Younger children may want a day at the beach to play in the sand, but teens might prefer a visit to a specialized museum, show, or concert. The final step in planning is creating a daily itinerary. By mapping out the specific days for each activity, everyone will have a clear idea of what to expect. Including the entire family in the planning process allows each family member input and ownership of the vacation.

Topic Sentence: _____

_____

a. _____

    (1) _____

    (2) _____

    _____

b. _____

    (1) _____

    _____

    (2) _____

    _____

c. _____

(1) _____

_____

(2) _____

_____

(3) _____

_____

(4) _____

_____

d. _____

(1) _____

_____

2.

Slow Down to Slim Down

It might sound strange, but one reason people gain weight is lack of time. Most of us live such busy lives that exercising and following a sensible diet—the two most important ways to stay slim—are difficult. Walking, running, or working out at least three times a week demands sacrifice. To fit it into our schedules, we need to wake up extra early or make time after long hours at school or work, when all we want to do is lie on the couch. Moreover, physical exercise may not be part of our daily routine. To save twenty precious minutes, we drive to the post office or drugstore rather than walk, or we take the elevator to the fifth floor rather than the stairs, just to squeeze out another ten minutes. However, our need for more time also affects our diet. Too often we skip breakfast, which causes us to overeat later in the day, or we head for the drive-through and pick up some cholesterol-loaded monstrosity containing nearly 1,000 calories. Then, at lunch, we grab a burger and french fries, which we devour—in five minutes or less—while at work, while we're studying, or even while we're driving our cars. And instead of spending time cooking sensible, healthful dinners at home, we opt for fat-soaked, calorie-filled fried chicken takeout so we can get to our second jobs on time, start a ton of homework, or run off to fulfill a family obligation. In short then, we need to make time—as hard as that is—to do what's right for our bodies and ourselves. Weight gain is a major health threat because it can lead to a number of serious illnesses such as arthritis, diabetes, and heart disease. It can also affect our self-esteem and even cause depression. The lesson is clear: We need to slow down to slim down.

Topic sentence: _____

a. _____

     (1) _____

     (2) _____

b. _____

     (1) _____

     (2) _____

     (3) _____

     _____

c. _____

     (1) _____

     (2) _____

ACTIVITY 16

4 Revising

Listed in the box below are five stages in the process of composing a paragraph titled "Dangerous Places."

> 1. Prewriting (list)
> 2. Prewriting (freewriting and questioning) and scratch outline
> 3. First draft
> 4. Revising (second draft)
> 5. Revising (final draft)

The five stages appear in scrambled order below and on the next page. Write the number 1 in the blank space in front of the first stage of development and number the remaining stages in sequence.

Personal

_____

> There are some places where I never feel safe. For example, public restrooms. The ~~dirt and graffiti~~ dirt on the floors and the graffiti scrawled on the walls ~~make the room seem dangerous~~ create a sense of danger. I'm also afraid in parking lots. ~~Late at night, I don't like walking in the lot After class, I don't like the parking lot.~~ When I leave my night class or the shopping mall late the walk to the car is scary. ~~Most parking lots have large lights which make me feel at least a little better.~~ I feel least safe in our laundry room. . . . It is a depressing place . . . Bars on the windows, . . . pipes making noises, . . . cement steps the only way out. . . .

continued

_____

<u>Dangerous Places</u>
Highways
Cars—especially parking lots
Feel frightened in our laundry room
Big crowds—concerts, movies
Closed-in places
Bus and train stations
Airplane
Elevators and escalators

_____

Dangerous Places

There are some places where I never feel completely safe. For example, I seldom feel safe in public restrooms. I worry that I'll suddenly be alone there and that someone will come in to mug me. The ugly graffiti often scrawled on the walls, along with the grime and dirt in the room and crumpled tissues and paper towels on the floor, add to my sense of unease and danger. I also feel unsafe in large, dark, parking lots. When I leave my night class a little late, or I am one of the few leaving the mall at 10 P.M., I dread the walk to my car. I am afraid that someone may be lurking behind another car, ready to mug me. And I fear that my car will not start, leaving me stuck in the dark parking lot. The place where I feel least safe is the basement laundry room in our apartment building. No matter what time I do my laundry, I seem to be the only person there. The windows are barred, and the only exit is a steep flight of cement steps. While I'm folding the clothes, I feel trapped. If anyone unfriendly came down those steps, I would have nowhere to go. The pipes in the room make sudden gurgles, clanks, and hisses, adding to my unsettledness. Places like public restrooms, dark parking lots, and the basement laundry room give me the shivers.

_____

There are some places where I never feel completely safe. For example, I never feel safe in public restrooms. If I'm alone there, I worry that someone will come in to rob and mug me. The dirt on the floors and the graffiti scrawled on the walls create a sense of danger. I feel unsafe in large, dark parking lots. When I leave my night class a little late or I leave the mall at 10 P.M., the walk to the car is scary. I'm afraid that someone may be behind a car. Also that my car won't start. Another place I don't feel safe is the basement laundry room in our apartment building. No matter when I do the laundry, I'm the only person there. The windows are barred

continued

and there are steep steps. I feel trapped when I fold the clothes. The pipes in the room make frightening noises such as hisses and clanks. Our laundry room and other places give me the shivers.

_____   Some places seem dangerous and unsafe to me. For example, last night I stayed till 10:15 after night class and walked out to parking lot alone. Very scary. Also, other places I go to every day, such as places in my apartment building. Also frightened by big crowds and public restrooms.

Why was the parking lot scary?	What places in my building scare me?
Dark	Laundry room (especially)
Only a few cars	Elevators
No one else in lot	Lobby at night sometimes
Could be someone behind a car	Outside walkway at night
Cold	
2 Parking lots	
3 Laundry room	
1 Public restrooms	

ACTIVITY 17 The author of "Dangerous Places" in Activity 16 made a number of revising and editing changes between the second draft and the final draft. Compare the two drafts and, in the spaces provided below, identify five of the changes.

1. _____

2. _____

3. _____

4. _____

5. _____

The First and Second Steps in Writing

This chapter will show you how to

- begin a paragraph by making a point of some kind

- provide specific evidence to support that point

- write a simple paragraph

WHY ARE YOU IN COLLEGE? There are many different reasons for going to college. Perhaps you are studying architecture like the student pictured here. This chapter contains two student paragraphs detailing each of the writer's reasons for being in college. Think about your own reasons for attending college. You may want to make a list of these reasons. At the end of this chapter, you will be asked to write your own paragraph on why you are in college.

Chapter 2 emphasized how prewriting and revising can help you become an effective writer. This chapter focuses on the first two steps in writing an effective paragraph:

1. Begin with a point.

2. Support the point with specific evidence.

Chapters 4 and 5 then look at the third and fourth steps in writing:

3. Organize and connect the specific evidence (pages 89–110).

4. Write clear, error-free sentences (pages 111–140).

Step 1: Begin with a Point

Your first step in writing is to decide what point you want to make and to write that point in a single sentence. The point is commonly known as a *topic sentence*. As a guide to yourself and to the reader, put that point in the first sentence of your paragraph. Everything else in the paragraph should then develop and support in specific ways the single point given in the first sentence. (For information about using a working topic sentence to develop a scratch outline, see pages 25–27 in Chapter 2.)

ACTIVITY 1

Read the two student paragraphs below about families today. Which paragraph clearly supports a single point? Which paragraph rambles on in many directions, introducing a number of ideas but developing none of them?

PARAGRAPH A

> ### Changes in the Family
>
> Changes in our society in recent years have weakened family life. First of all, today's mothers spend much less time with their children. A generation or two ago, most households got by on Dad's paycheck and Mom stayed home. Now many mothers work, and their children attend an after-school program, stay with a neighbor, or go home to an empty house. Another change is that families no longer eat together. In the past, Mom would be home to fix a full dinner—salad, pot roast, potatoes, and vegetables, with homemade cake or pie to top it off. Dinner today is more likely to be takeout food or frozen dinners eaten at home, or fast food eaten out, with different members of the family eating at different times. Finally, television has taken the place of family conversation and

continued

togetherness. Back when there were traditional meals, family members would have a chance to eat together, talk with each other, and share events of the day in a leisurely manner. But now families are more likely to be looking at the TV set than talking to one another. Most homes even have several TV sets, which people watch in separate rooms. Clearly, modern life is a challenge to family life.

PARAGRAPH B

The Family

Family togetherness is very important. However, today's mothers spend much less time at home than their mothers did, for several reasons. Most fathers are also home much less than they used to be. In previous times, families had to work together running a farm. Now children are left at other places or are home alone much of the time. Some families do find ways to spend more time together despite the demands of work. Another problem is that with parents gone so much of the day, nobody is at home to prepare wholesome meals for the family to eat together. The meals Grandma used to make would include pot roast and fried chicken, mashed potatoes, salad, vegetables, and delicious homemade desserts. Today's takeout foods and frozen meals can provide good nutrition. Some menu choices offer nothing but high-fat and high-sodium choices. People can supplement prepared foods by eating sufficient vegetables and fruit. Finally, television is also a big obstacle to togetherness. It sometimes seems that people are constantly watching TV and never talking to each other. Even when parents have friends over, it is often to watch something on TV. TV must be used wisely to achieve family togetherness.

Complete the following statement: Paragraph _____ is effective because it makes a clear, single point in the first sentence and goes on in the remaining sentences to support that single point.

Paragraph A starts with a point—that changes in our society in recent years have weakened family life—and then supports that idea with examples about mothers' working, families' eating habits, and television.

Paragraph B, on the other hand, does not make and support a single point. At first we think the point of the paragraph may be that "family togetherness is very important." But there is no supporting evidence showing how important family togetherness is. Instead, the line of thought in paragraph B swerves about like a car without a steering wheel. In the second sentence, we read that "today's mothers spend much less time at home than their mothers did, for several reasons." Now we think for a moment that this may be the main point and that the author will list and explain some of those reasons. But the paragraph then goes on to comment on fathers, families in previous times, and families who find ways to spend time together. Any one of those ideas could be the focus of the paragraph, but none is. By now we are not really surprised at what happens in the rest of the paragraph. We are told about the absence of anyone "to prepare wholesome meals for the family," about what "the meals Grandma used to make" would be like, and about nutrition. The author then goes on to make a couple of points about how much people watch TV. The paragraph ends with yet another idea that does not support any previous point and that itself could be the point of a paragraph: "TV must be used wisely to achieve family togetherness." No single idea in this paragraph is developed, and the result for the reader is confusion.

In summary, while paragraph A is unified, paragraph B shows a complete lack of unity.

Step 2: Support the Point with Specific Evidence

The first essential step in writing effectively is to start with a clearly stated point. The second basic step is to support that point with specific evidence. Consider the supported point that you just read:

Point

Changes in our society in recent years have weakened family life.

Support

1. Mothers
   a. Most stayed home a generation ago
   b. Most work now, leaving children at an after-school program, or with a neighbor, or in an empty house
2. Eating habits
   a. Formerly full homemade meals, eaten together
   b. Now prepared foods at home or fast food out, eaten separately
3. Television
   a. Watching TV instead of conversing
   b. Watching in separate rooms instead of being together

The supporting evidence is needed so that we can *see and understand for ourselves* that the writer's point is sound. The author of "Changes in the Family" has supplied specific supporting examples of how changes in our society have weakened family life. The paragraph has provided the evidence that is needed for us to understand and agree with the writer's point.

Now consider the following paragraph.

The Children of Huang Shi: A Must See

By incorporating beautiful cinematography, extensive music scores, and highly talented actors, *The Children of Huang Shi* is an emotional masterpiece. The setting of the film is China during the Japanese occupation, and several filming techniques are used to immerse the viewer in the natural beauty of China. The wide angled shots of the orphans marching across the Liu Pan Shan Mountains into Mongolia demonstrate the vastness and ruggedness of China's wilderness. The film's low-key lighting hints at the fear and devastation that the Chinese were facing during this period. Additionally, the musical scores enhance the emotion evoked by this film. David Hirschfelder, known for writing the *Crouching Tiger, Hidden Dragon* score, has created music that boldly mimics the vast wilderness, and yet becomes delicate and intimate during key moments. Finally, the incredible cast enriches the audience's experience. Jonathan Rhys-Meyers realistically portrays George Hogg, the man who put his life on the line to save the fifty-six orphans. Chow Yun-Fat is very believable as Chen Hansheng, a communist resistance fighter. Michelle Yeoh is amazing as Mrs. Wang, a businesswoman who has figured out how to survive during the war. All in all, *The Children of Huang Shi* is a film that will inspire audiences for decades to come.

The author's point is that the film, *The Children of Huang Shi*, should be watched. Summarize in the spaces below the three reasons she gives to support her decision:

Reason 1: _____

Reason 2: _____

Reason 3: _____

Notice what the supporting details in this paragraph do. They provide you, the reader, with a basis for understanding why the writer believes this film should be seen. Through specific evidence, the writer has explained and communicated her point successfully. The evidence that supports the point in a paragraph often consists of a series of reasons introduced by signal words (the author here uses *Additionally* and *Finally*) and followed by examples and details that support the reasons. That is true of the sample paragraph above: Three reasons are provided, followed by examples and details that back up those reasons.

The Point as an "Umbrella" Idea

You may find it helpful to think of the point as an "umbrella" idea. Under the writer's point fits all of the other material of the paragraph. That other material is made up of specific supporting details— evidence such as examples, reasons, or facts. The diagram to the right shows the relationship for the paragraph "Good-Bye, Tony."

ACTIVITY 2

Both of the paragraphs that follow resulted from the assignment to "Write a paragraph that details your reasons for being in college." Both writers make the point that they have various reasons for attending college. Which paragraph then goes on to provide plenty of specific evidence to back up its point? Which paragraph is vague and repetitive and lacks the concrete details needed to show us exactly why the author decided to attend college?

> **HINT** Imagine that you've been asked to make a short film based on each paragraph. Which one suggests specific pictures, locations, words, and scenes you could shoot? That is the one that uses concrete details.

PARAGRAPH A

Reasons for Going to College

I decided to attend college for various reasons. One reason is self-respect. For a long time now, I have had little self-respect. I spent a lot of time doing nothing, just hanging around or getting into trouble, and eventually I began to feel bad about it. Going to college is a way to start feeling better about myself. By accomplishing things, I will improve my self-image. Another reason for going to college is that things happened in my life that made me think about a change. For one thing, I lost the part-time job I had. When I lost the job, I realized I would have to do something in life, so I thought about school. I was in a rut and needed to get out of it but did not know how. But when something happens that is out of your control, then you have to make some kind of decision. The most important reason for college, though, is to fulfill my dream. I know I need an education, and I want to take the courses I need to reach the position that I think I can handle. Only by qualifying yourself can you get what you want. Going to college will help me fulfill this goal. These are the main reasons why I am attending college.

PARAGRAPH B

Why I'm in School

There are several reasons I'm in school. First of all, my father's attitude made me want to succeed in school. One night last year, after I had come in at 3 A.M., my father said, "Mickey, you're a bum. When I look at my son, all I see is a good-for-nothing bum." I was angry, but I knew my father was right in a way. I had spent the last two years working at odd jobs at a pizza parlor and luncheonette, trying all kinds of drugs with my friends. That night, though, I decided I would prove my father wrong. I would go to college and be a success. Another reason I'm in college is my girlfriend's encouragement. Marie has already been in school for a year, and she is doing well in her computer courses. Marie helped me fill out my application and register for courses. She even lent me sixty-five dollars for textbooks. On her day off, she lets me use her car so I don't have to take the college bus. The main reason I am in college is to fulfill a personal goal: for the first time in my life, I want to finish something. For example, I quit high school in the eleventh grade. Then I enrolled in a government job-training program, but I dropped out after six months. I tried to get a high school equivalency diploma, but I started missing classes and eventually gave up. Now I am in a special program where I will earn my high school degree by completing a series of five courses. I am determined to accomplish this goal and to then go on and work for a degree in hotel management.

Complete the following statement: Paragraph _____ provides clear, vividly detailed reasons why the writer decided to attend college.

Paragraph B is the one that solidly backs up its point. The writer gives us specific reasons he is in school. On the basis of such evidence, we can clearly understand his opening point. The writer of paragraph A offers only vague, general reasons for being in school. We do not get specific examples of how the writer was "getting into trouble," what events occurred that forced the decision, or even what kind of job he or she wants to qualify for. We sense that the feeling expressed is sincere, but without particular examples we cannot really see why the writer decided to attend college.

Reinforcing Point and Support

You have learned the two most important steps in writing effectively: making a point and supporting that point. Take a few minutes now to do the following activity. It will strengthen your ability to recognize a *point* and the *support* for that point.

ACTIVITY 3

In the following groups, one statement is the general point and the other statements are specific support for the point. Identify each point with a P and each statement of support with an S.

EXAMPLE

___S___   My college is only three miles from my house.

___S___   It's on a bus line that passes a block from my house.

___S___   When the weather is good, I can walk to school in about forty-five minutes.

___P___   For me, the college I attend is easy to get to.

EXPLANATION

The point—that the writer's college is easy for the writer to get to—is strongly supported by the three specific details stated.

---

1. _____   This has been a wonderful week.

   _____   I won a hundred dollars in the state lottery.

   _____   I received an A on my chemistry exam.

   _____   My boss just gave me a raise.

2. _____   Some people skip breakfast.

   _____   Some people have poor eating habits.

   _____   Some people always order supersize portions.

   _____   Some people eat almost no fruits or vegetables.

3. _____   My blood pressure has dropped.

   _____   This new exercise program must be working.

   _____   I have lost ten pounds in three weeks.

   _____   I don't tire as easily as I used to.

4. _____   Cats are clean and do not require much attention.

   _____   Cats like living indoors and are safe to have around children.

_____ Cats are inexpensive to feed and easy to keep healthy.

_____ There are definite advantages to having a cat as a pet.

5. _____ She is eating less red meat, fewer fatty foods, and more vegetables.

_____ Jane is taking better care of herself.

_____ She exercises at least four times a week.

_____ Jane made sure to get a flu shot this year.

6. _____ My work hours are flexible.

_____ I love my job at the day care center.

_____ The children are easy to work with.

_____ The center is bright and cheerful.

7. _____ The bread the waiter brought us is stale.

_____ We've been waiting for our main course for more than an hour.

_____ It is time to speak to the restaurant manager.

_____ The people next to us are awfully loud.

8. _____ Carla asks people questions about themselves.

_____ Carla is a pleasure to be around.

_____ Carla has a great smile.

_____ Carla really listens to people when they talk.

9. _____ The library subscribes to more than five hundred magazines and newspapers.

_____ Students have online access to thirty-five academic databases to which the college subscribes.

_____ Several expert librarians are always present to help students locate resources.

_____ Our college library has excellent resources.

_____ The library's DVD collection has recently been expanded.

_____ There are more than 150,000 books in our library.

10. _____ My older brother is a computer nerd.

_____ My sister wants to go to dental school.

_____ My younger brother wants to become a history teacher.

_____ The children in my family have different academic and career goals.

_____ I have a flair for foreign languages and want to become a diplomat.

11. _____ Though a mosquito is small, it has power.

    _____ A mosquito can find you in the dark.

    _____ A mosquito can keep you awake all night.

    _____ A mosquito can make you scratch yourself until you bleed.

12. _____ Because sending e-mail is so simple, family and friends may use e-mail messages to stay in close touch.

    _____ When people are upset, they may send off an angry e-mail before they consider the consequences.

    _____ The jokes, petitions, and other e-mails that friends so easily forward can become a real nuisance.

    _____ The ease of using e-mail can be both a blessing and a curse.

13. _____ When some people answer the phone, their first words are "Who's this?"

    _____ Some people never bother to identify themselves when calling someone.

    _____ Some people have terrible telephone manners.

    _____ Some people hang up without even saying good-bye.

14. _____ One mother created what she called the homework zone—the kitchen table after dinner—where she and her young children did their assignments.

    _____ Some adult students have taken classes at a nearby community college during their lunch hour.

    _____ Adult students often find creative ways to balance school, employment, and family responsibilities.

    _____ By listening to recorded lectures in the car, working students turn travel time into learning time.

15. _____ Moviegoers can take several simple steps to save money at the movie theater.

    _____ Bringing homemade popcorn to the movies is cheaper than buying expensive theater popcorn.

    _____ Buying candy at a grocery store, not a theater, cuts candy costs in half.

    _____ Going to movies early in the day reduces ticket prices by as much as three dollars each.

The Importance of *Specific* Details

The point that opens a paragraph is a general statement. The evidence that supports a point is made up of specific details, reasons, examples, and facts.

Specific details have two key functions. First of all, details *excite the reader's interest.* They make writing a pleasure to read, for we all enjoy learning particulars about other people—what they do and think and feel. Second, details *support and explain a writer's point;* they give the evidence needed for us to see and understand a general idea. For example, the writer of "*The Children of Huang Shi*: A Must See" provides details that make vividly clear why a person should see the film. She specifies the filming techniques used to immerse the viewer (wide angled shots and low-key lighting). She explains how the music enhances the emotions the audience experiences (bold, delicate, and intimate). She tells why the cast enriches the audience's enjoyment of the movie (realistically portrays; believable as communist resistance fighter; amazing as a businesswoman).

The writer of "Why I'm in School" provides equally vivid details. He gives clear reasons for being in school (his father's attitude, his girlfriend's encouragement, and his wish to fulfill a personal goal) and backs up each reason with specific details. His details give us many sharp pictures. For instance, we hear the exact words his father spoke: "Mickey, you're a bum." He tells us exactly how he was spending his time ("working at odd jobs at a pizza parlor and luncheonette, trying all kinds of drugs with my friends"). He describes how his girlfriend helped him (filling out the college application, lending money and her car). Finally, instead of stating generally that "you have to make some kind of decision," as the writer of "Reasons for Going to College" does, he specifies that he has a strong desire to finish college because he dropped out of many schools and programs in the past: high school, a job-training program, and a high school equivalency course.

In both "*The Children of Huang Shi*: A Must See" and "Why I'm in School," then, the vivid, exact details capture our interest and enable us to share in the writer's experience. In the first case, we gain a specific and deep grasp of the writer's opinions; in the second, we see people's actions and hear their words. The details provide pictures that make each of us feel "I am there." The particulars also allow us to understand each writer's point clearly. We are shown exactly why the first writer feels the movie is worth seeing and exactly why the second writer is attending college.

Each of the five points below is followed by two attempts at support (*a* and *b*). Write S (for *specific*) in the space next to the one that succeeds in providing specific support for the point. Write X in the space next to the one that lacks supporting details.

ACTIVITY 4

1. My cat is extremely bright.

   _____ a. He knows how to solve problems. He also recognizes people he knows.

_____ b. When he gets lost in the basement, he simply grasps the door latch, pulls down on it, and opens the door. He also distinguishes between family members and strangers. When a classmate of mine came by last week, my cat jumped on my lap and rubbed himself against my face, but he refused to go near our guest.

2. The thrift store was terribly filthy.

_____ a. The first thing I noticed was the awful smell as soon as I entered the door. It reminded me of unwashed socks in a locker room. The floor had a shiny, greasy film on it that looked like an oil slick on water. None of the clothes had been washed.

_____ b. It had an awful smell. The floor was sticky and gross. The clothes were dirty. It was hard to miss that smell, which was just really awful to experience.

3. Professor DeMarco is an excellent math teacher.

_____ a. He keeps extra office hours for students who are having trouble understanding the homework or the material presented in class. He questions students individually in class to make sure that everyone understands what is being discussed. If not, he explains the subject again in a different way to make it clearer.

_____ b. He cares about students, makes his classes interesting, and has taught me a great deal. I think these must be the reasons he is well liked and considered such a good teacher.

4. My brother-in-law is a workaholic.

_____ a. He works twelve hours a day at the accounting firm he started. Then he comes home, gulps down some dinner, opens his briefcase, turns on his computer, and puts in another three hours.

_____ b. He's at it all the time. He spends a lot of time at the office even though he's the boss. Then he comes home and does more work. Sometimes he's working late into the night.

5. Blue Stem is my favorite restaurant.

_____ a. The food is very good. The décor and atmosphere are really cool, making this a really popular place in town. In fact, it's one of the most popular places in town. Also, the staff is friendly.

_____ b. The food is well prepared and creative. The atmosphere is upbeat and funky. The décor is very comfortable, yet trendy. The wait staff is attentive and helpful.

EXPLANATION

The specific support for point 1 is answer *b,* which vividly describes the cat's behavior to prove that he is bright. For point 2, answer *a* gives specific examples to describe why and exactly how the store was filthy. For point 3, answer *a* goes beyond general statements and opinions about the professor. For point 4, answer *a* goes beyond telling us that the brother-in-law is a workaholic; it also gives examples of his day and evening work habits. For point 5, answer *b* provides more specific adjectives to support why the restaurant is good.

In each case the specific evidence enables us *to see for ourselves* that the writer's point is valid.

ACTIVITY 5

Follow the directions for Activity 4.

1. Students use their phones in a variety of ways.

    _____ a. Students call and text their friends, use various apps for different activities, take pictures of friends and family, and listen to music.

    _____ b. Students call and text their friends, use apps like Facebook and Twitter, take and share pictures with Instagram, and listen to music through iTunes and Pandora.

2. Soccer is a better sport than football.

    _____ a. Soccer fans are known for their passionate support of their teams. Soccer matches last ninety minutes compared to football games that can go on and on. Soccer matches involve a lot of game time, but football games have a lot of downtime.

    _____ b. Although players in both types of sports incur concussions, soccer players suffer fewer concussions than do football players. Soccer matches last ninety minutes compared to football games that typically run three hours. Soccer is played by both men and women, but football is a predominantly male sport.

3. Rico knew very little about cooking when he got his first apartment.

    _____ a. He had to live on whatever he had in the freezer for a while. He was not any good in the kitchen and had to learn very slowly. More often than not, he would learn how to cook something only by making mistakes first.

_____   b. He lived on macaroni and cheese TV dinners for three weeks. His idea of cooking an egg was to put a whole egg in the microwave, where it exploded. Then he tried to make a grilled cheese sandwich by putting slices of cheese and bread in a toaster.

4. Small children can have as much fun with ordinary household items as with costly toys.

_____   a. A large sheet thrown over a dining room table makes a great hideout. Banging pot covers together creates a tremendous crash that kids love. Also, children really enjoy turning large cardboard boxes into trains, cars, and airplanes and "driving" them around the house.

_____   b. Kids can make musical instruments out of practically anything. The result is a lot of noise and fun. They can easily create their own play areas as well by using a little imagination. There is simply no need to have to spend a lot of money on playthings.

5. Speaking before a group is a problem for many people.

_____   a. They become uncomfortable even at the thought of speaking in public. They will go to almost any length to avoid speaking to a group. If they are forced to do it, they can feel so anxious that they actually develop physical symptoms.

_____   b. Stage fright, stammering, and blushing are frequent reactions. Some people will pretend to be ill to avoid speaking publicly. When asked to rank their worst fears, people often list public speaking as even worse than death.

The Importance of *Adequate* Details

One of the most common and most serious problems in students' writing is inadequate development. You must provide *enough* specific details to support fully the point you are making. You could not, for example, submit a paragraph about your brother-in-law being rude and provide only a single short example. You would have to add several other examples or provide an extended example of your brother-in-law's rudeness. Without such additional support, your paragraph would be underdeveloped.

At times, students try to disguise an undersupported point by using repetition and wordy generalities. You saw this, for example, in paragraph A ("Reasons for Going to College") on page 56. Be prepared to do the plain hard work needed to ensure that each of your paragraphs has full, solid support.

The following paragraphs were written on the same topic, and each has a clear opening point. Which one is adequately developed? Which one has few particulars and uses mostly vague, general, wordy sentences to conceal the fact that it is starved for specific details?

ACTIVITY 6

PARAGRAPH A

Florida

Florida, the Sunshine State, is known as a place where many senior citizens spend their retirement because of the fabulous weather. However, this state offers something for people of all ages. Recreational opportunities are abundant. First, Florida is a peninsula—that is, two-thirds of it is surrounded by water—so there are plenty of places to go swimming, boating, fishing, wind surfing, and water skiing. In the interior, Florida offers many gorgeous lakes for similar activities or simply for observing animals such as alligators, snakes, panthers, tortoises, herons, ibis, egrets, cranes, and flamingos in their native habitats. Florida is also an entertainment mecca. Besides the most famous attractions—Disney World, Universal Studios, and Busch Gardens—there are theme parks such as SeaWorld, Legoland, and Discovery Cove. In addition, every major city has theaters, museums, and concert halls of all kinds. One of the most fascinating is the Salvador Dalí Museum in St. Petersburg, which features the works of the famous Spanish artist. Floridians are also proud of their great professional athletic teams, such as the Miami Dolphins, the Tampa Bay Buccaneers, the Florida Marlins, the Tampa Bay Rays, and the Miami Heat. Daytona Beach, right off Route 95 on Florida's eastern coast, is home to what some people call the World Series of stock car racing. Finally, Florida has many fine colleges and universities, from local community colleges, such as Miami-Dade Community College, to Florida State University and the University of Florida. Perhaps all of this is why this state has had the greatest rate of population growth in the country.

PARAGRAPH B

Florida

Lots of older people retire to Florida because of the weather. After all, it's not called the Sunshine State for nothing. However, that is not the only reason that more and more people are moving to Florida from other parts of the country. There's simply a lot to do there, which makes the state very

continued

attractive to potential newcomers. First, there's water sports. One can swim or just relax at one of Florida's many beaches. Then there are many lakes where the state's exotic wildlife can be seen in their natural habitats. Also, Florida is an entertainment mecca. Theme parks attract millions of visitors from all over the world the year round. Seniors, adults, and children really love these places. They are certainly family friendly. In addition, every major city has theaters, museums, and concert halls of all kinds. Floridians also love their professional sports teams, and almost every professional sport is represented, including stock car racing. Finally, there are many excellent colleges and universities in the state. Perhaps all of this is why this state has had the greatest rate of population growth in the country.

Complete the following statement: Paragraph _____ provides an adequate number of specific details to support its point.

Paragraph A offers detailed examples of Florida's many attractions. Paragraph B, on the other hand, is underdeveloped. Paragraph B speaks only of "water sports" such as swimming, but paragraph A mentions boating, fishing, surfing, and water skiing, as well. Paragraph B talks in a general way about Florida as an entertainment mecca, but paragraph A mentions specific attractions such as Disney World and Universal Studios. When discussing Florida's sports, paragraph B claims that the state has many professional teams, but paragraph A names several teams, such as the Dolphins and the Marlins. In short, paragraph A has the detail that paragraph B lacks.

To check your understanding of the chapter so far, see if you can answer the following questions.

1. It has been observed: "To write well, the first thing that you must do is decide what nail you want to drive home." What is meant by *nail*?

   _____

2. How do you drive home the nail in the paragraph?

   _____

   _____

3. What are the two reasons for using specific details in your writing?

   a. _____

   b. _____

Practice in Making and Supporting a Point

You now know the two most important steps in competent writing: (1) making a point and (2) supporting that point with specific evidence. The purpose of this section is to expand and strengthen your understanding of these two basic steps.

You will first work through a series of activities on *making* a point:

1. Identifying Common Errors in Topic Sentences
2. Understanding the Two Parts of a Topic Sentence
3. Selecting a Topic Sentence
4. Writing a Topic Sentence: I
5. Writing a Topic Sentence: II

You will then sharpen your understanding of specific details by working through a series of activities on *supporting* a point:

6. Recognizing Specific Details: I
7. Recognizing Specific Details: II
8. Providing Supporting Evidence
9. Identifying Adequate Supporting Evidence
10. Adding Details to Complete a Paragraph
11. Writing a Simple Paragraph

1 Identifying Common Errors in Topic Sentences

When writing a point, or topic sentence, people sometimes make mistakes that undermine their chances of producing an effective paper. One mistake is to substitute an announcement of the topic for a true topic sentence. Other mistakes include writing statements that are too broad or too narrow. Following are examples of all three errors, along with contrasting examples of effective topic sentences.

Announcement

My car is the concern of this paragraph.

The statement above is a simple announcement of a subject, rather than a topic sentence expressing an idea about the subject.

Statement That Is Too Broad

Many people have problems with their cars.

The statement is too broad to be supported adequately with specific details in a single paragraph.

Statement That Is Too Narrow

My car is a Ford Focus.

The preceding statement is too narrow to be expanded into a paragraph. Such a narrow statement is sometimes called a *dead-end statement* because there is no place to go with it. It is a simple fact that does not need or call for any support.

Effective Topic Sentence

I hate my car.

The statement above expresses an opinion that could be supported in a paragraph. The writer could offer a series of specific supporting reasons, examples, and details to make it clear why he or she hates the car.

Here are additional examples:

Announcements

The subject of this paper will be my apartment.

I want to talk about increases in the divorce rate.

Statements That Are Too Broad

The places where people live have definite effects on their lives.

Many people have trouble getting along with others.

Statements That Are Too Narrow

I have no hot water in my apartment at night.

Almost one of every two marriages ends in divorce.

Effective Topic Sentences

My apartment is a terrible place to live.

The divorce rate is increasing for several reasons.

ACTIVITY 7

For each pair of sentences below, write *A* beside the sentence that only *announces* a topic. Write *OK* beside the sentence that *advances an idea* about the topic.

1. _____ a. This paper is about what not to do on a first date.

   _____ b. There are three things to avoid so the first date isn't the last date.

2. _____ a. I am going to write about my job as a Starbucks barista.

   _____ b. Working at Starbucks as a barista was the best job I had during college.

3. _____ a. Keeping to a strict budget is this paragraph's focus.

   _____ b. College students can save money by giving up cigarettes, beer, and pizza.

4. _____ a. In several ways, the tennis club in my town is a great bargain.

   _____ b. This paragraph will deal with the local tennis club.

5. _____ a. My paper will discuss the topic of fishing.

_____ b. The following steps will help anyone become a great fisher.

For each pair of sentences below, write *TN* beside the statement that is *too narrow* to be developed into a paragraph. Write *OK* beside the statement in each pair that could be developed into a paragraph.

ACTIVITY 8

1. _____ a. I do push-ups and sit-ups each morning.

_____ b. Exercising every morning has had positive effects on my health.

2. _____ a. José works nine hours a day and then goes to school three hours a night.

_____ b. José is an ambitious man.

3. _____ a. I started college after being away from school for seven years.

_____ b. Several of my fears about returning to school have proved to be groundless.

4. _____ a. I watched a show on the Discovery Channel.

_____ b. The Discovery Channel show on chimpanzees that I watched provided information on language acquisition that I can use when writing my psychology paper.

5. _____ a. My brother was depressed yesterday for several reasons.

_____ b. Yesterday my brother had to pay fifty-two dollars for a motor tune-up.

For each pair of sentences below, write *TB* beside the statement that is *too broad* to be supported adequately in a short paper. Write *OK* beside the statement that makes a limited point.

ACTIVITY 9

1. _____ a. Angela is very intelligent.

_____ b. Angela has the qualifications to be a great lawyer.

2. _____ a. Computers are very helpful.

_____ b. Writing a paper on a computer can save a student time, money, and headaches.

3. _____ a. I chose to take Advanced Placement English for three reasons.

_____ b. I have always loved studying.

4. _____ a. Weddings are a waste of money.

_____ b. Engaged couples are often so excited about the wedding that they overspend.

5. _____ a. Golf is a great sport that has taught me much.

_____ b. I have learned to be both physically fit and morally honest through the sport of golf.

2 Understanding the Two Parts of a Topic Sentence

As stated earlier, the point that opens a paragraph is often called a *topic sentence.* When you look closely at a point, or topic sentence, you can see that it is made up of two parts:

1. The *limited topic*
2. The writer's *attitude* toward, or idea about, the limited topic

The writer's attitude, point of view, or idea is usually expressed in one or more *key words.* All the details in a paragraph should support the idea expressed in the key words. In each of the topic sentences below, a single line appears under the topic and a double line under the idea about the topic (expressed in a key word or key words):

My dog is extremely stubborn.

Texting while driving is against the law in many states.

The kitchen is the most widely used room in my house.

Voting should be required by law in the United States.

My pickup truck is the most reliable vehicle I have ever owned.

In the first sentence, the topic is *dog,* and the key words that express the writer's idea about his topic are that his dog is *extremely stubborn.* In the second sentence, the topic is *texting while driving,* and the key words that determine the focus of the paragraph are *against the law.* Notice each topic and key word or key words in the other three sentences as well.

ACTIVITY 10

For each point below, draw a single line under the topic and a double line under the idea about the topic.

1. The house provided every comfort a young person would want.
2. Spaniards eat dinner very late.
3. Nurses at our local hospital are well trained.
4. The capital of Hungary, which is Budapest, was once two separate cities.

5. Finding information for research papers has become easier because of the Internet.

6. The zoo contains many exotic animals.

7. Post-partum depression has several warning signs.

8. Ladybugs are very beneficial for gardeners.

9. The city's new bridge has several drawbacks.

10. The Senate voted to increase funding to the nation's schools.

11. The age that teenagers can get their drivers' licenses should be raised to eighteen.

12. The school cafeteria should provide higher quality food.

13. Advertisers should follow stricter regulations.

14. My boss is a very unkind person.

15. Developers should be required to plant two new trees for every one they remove.

16. My horse is very temperamental.

17. The violence in many movies is too graphic.

18. Neglected children often turn out to have problems later in life.

19. Television advertisements for prescription medications should not be allowed to air.

20. Elementary-school teachers are often very selfless.

3 Selecting a Topic Sentence

Remember that a paragraph is made up of a topic sentence and a group of related sentences developing the topic sentence. It is also helpful to remember that the topic sentence is a *general* statement. The other sentences provide specific support for the general statement.

Each group of sentences below could be written as a short paragraph. Circle the letter of the topic sentence in each case. To find the topic sentence, ask yourself, "Which is a general statement supported by the specific details in the other three statements?"

Begin by trying the example item below. First circle the letter of the sentence you think expresses the main idea. Then read the explanation.

ACTIVITY 11

EXAMPLE

a. If you stop carrying matches or a lighter, you can cut down on impulse smoking.

b. If you sit in no-smoking areas, you will smoke less.

(c.) You can behave in ways that will help you smoke less.

d. By keeping a record of when and where you smoke, you can identify the most tempting situations and then avoid them.

EXPLANATION

Sentence *a* explains one way to smoke less. Sentences *b* and *d* also provide specific ways to smoke less. In sentence *c*, however, no one specific way is explained. The words *ways that will help you smoke less* refer only generally to such methods. Therefore, sentence *c* is the topic sentence; it expresses the author's main idea. The other sentences support that idea by providing examples.

1. a. The kitchen and the baths had been remodeled.
   b. The house was well maintained.
   c. The roof, furnace, and air conditioner were new.
   d. The yard had just been landscaped.

2. a. This car costs less than comparable models.
   b. My car is economical.
   c. It gets forty-one miles per gallon.
   d. After 75,000 miles, I have replaced only the tires and brakes.

3. a. The last time I ate at the diner, I got food poisoning and was sick for two days.
   b. The city inspector found roaches and mice in the diner's kitchen.
   c. Our town diner is a health hazard and ought to be closed down.
   d. The toilets in the diner often back up, and the sinks have only a trickle of water.

4. a. The History Channel and the Discovery Channel are informative.
   b. Viewers of shows like *This Old House* can learn a lot about home maintenance.
   c. Television can be a tool for education.
   d. Several cable networks offer shows discussing important health issues.

5. a. In early colleges, students were mostly white males.
   b. Colleges of two centuries ago were quite different from today's schools.
   c. All students in early colleges had to take the same courses.
   d. The entire student body at early schools would be only a few dozen people.

4 Writing a Topic Sentence: I

The following activity will give you practice in writing an accurate point, or topic sentence—one that is neither too broad nor too narrow for the supporting material in a paragraph. Sometimes you will construct your topic sentence after you have decided which details you want to discuss. An added value of this activity is that it shows you how to write a topic sentence that will exactly match the details you have developed.

ACTIVITY 12

1. *Topic sentence:* _____

   _____

   a. Thomas Jefferson read Latin, Greek, French, Italian, and other foreign languages.
   b. His library contained more than 6,400 books.
   c. He designed his magnificent mansion at Monticello after teaching himself architecture.
   d. He was an excellent writer, an accomplished musician, and a political genius.

2. *Topic sentence:* _____

   _____

   a. Only about thirty people came to the dance, instead of the expected two hundred.
   b. The band arrived late and spent an hour setting up.
   c. There were at least three males at the dance to every female.
   d. An hour after the dance started, it ended because of a power failure.

3. *Topic sentence:* _____

   _____

   a. We had to wait half an hour even though we had reserved a table.
   b. Our appetizer and main course arrived at the same time.
   c. The busboy ignored our requests for more water.
   d. The wrong desserts were served to us.

4. *Topic sentence:* _____

   _____

   a. People who settled the American frontier had to clear dense forests.
   b. They had to fight off deadly diseases that threatened them and their animals.
   c. The weather, which was unpredictable, sometimes destroyed their crops.
   d. Because knowledge of farming methods was limited, they sometimes failed to grow enough food to sustain themselves.

5. *Topic sentence:* _____

_____

    a. The crowd scenes were crudely spliced from another film.

    b. Mountains and other background scenery were just painted cardboard cutouts.

    c. The "sync" was off, so that you heard voices even when the actors' lips were not moving.

    d. The so-called monster was just a spider that had been filmed through a magnifying lens.

5 Writing a Topic Sentence: II

Often you will start with a general topic or a general idea of what you want to write about. You may, for example, want to write a paragraph about some aspect of school life. To come up with a point about school life, begin by limiting your topic. One way to do this is to make a list of all the limited topics you can think of that fit under the general topic.

ACTIVITY 13

Following are five general topics and a series of limited topics that fit under them. Make a point out of *one* of the limited topics in each group.

HINT To create a topic sentence, ask yourself, "What point do I want to make about _____ (*my limited topic*)?"

EXAMPLE

Recreation

- Movies
- Dancing
- TV shows
- Reading
- Sports parks

Your point: *Sports parks today have some truly exciting games.*

1. Your school

- Instructor
- Cafeteria
- Specific course

- Particular room or building
- Particular policy (attendance, grading, etc.)
- Classmate

Your point: _____

_____

2. Job
   - Pay
   - Boss
   - Working conditions
   - Duties
   - Coworkers
   - Customers or clients

   Your point: _____

   _____

3. Money
   - Budgets
   - Credit cards
   - Dealing with a bank
   - School expenses
   - Ways to get it
   - Ways to save it

   Your point: _____

   _____

4. Living dangerously
   - Sky diving
   - Drag racing
   - Unprotected sex
   - Drinking and driving
   - Snowbarding and skiing accidents

   Your point: _____

   _____

5. Sports
    - A team's chances
    - At your school
    - Women's team
    - Recreational versus spectator
    - Favorite team
    - Outstanding athlete

    Your point: _____

    _____

6   Recognizing Specific Details: I

Specific details are examples, reasons, particulars, and facts. Such details are needed to support and explain a topic sentence effectively. They provide the evidence needed for readers to understand, as well as to feel and experience, a writer's point.

Here is a topic sentence followed by two sets of supporting sentences. Which set provides sharp, specific details?

Topic Sentence

Some poor people must struggle to make meals for themselves.

Set A

They gather up whatever free food they can find in fast-food restaurants and take it home to use however they can. Instead of planning well-balanced meals, they base their diet on anything they can buy that is cheap and filling.

Set B

Some make tomato soup by adding hot water to the free packets of ketchup they get at McDonald's. Others buy cans of cheap dog food and fry it like hamburger.

Set B provides specific details: Instead of a general statement about "free food they find in fast-food restaurants and take . . . home to use however they can," we get a vivid detail we can see and picture clearly: "make tomato soup [from] free packets of ketchup." Instead of a general statement about how the poor will "base their diet on anything they can buy that is cheap and filling," we get exact and vivid details: "Others buy cans of cheap dog food and fry it like hamburger."

Specific details are often like the information we might find in a movie script. They provide us with such clear pictures that we could make a film of them if we wanted to. You would know just how to film the information given in set B. You would show a poor person breaking open a packet of ketchup from McDonald's and mixing it with water to make a kind of tomato soup. You would show someone opening a can of dog food and frying its contents like hamburger.

In contrast, the writer of set A fails to provide the specific information needed. If you were asked to make a film based on set A, you would have to figure out for yourself what particulars you were going to show.

When you are working to provide specific supporting information in a paper, it might help to ask yourself, "Could someone easily film this information?" If the answer is "yes," you probably have good details.

Each topic sentence below is followed by two sets of supporting details (*a* and *b*). Write *S* (for *specific*) in the space next to the set that provides specific support for the point. Write *G* (for *general*) next to the set that offers only vague, general support.

ACTIVITY 14

1. *Topic sentence*: Attila the Hun was a fierce and bloody ruler.

   _____ a. After he became king of the Huns (A.D. 434), a people who lived in an area of eastern Europe that approximates the site of modern Hungary, Attila murdered his brother and coruler, Bleda. Then he wreaked havoc on eastern and central Europe, conquering many peoples who lived in that area, which now includes Poland, the Czech Republic, Austria, Slovakia, and Romania. In 450, he invaded Gaul (now France), which was a Roman province, and later Italy, where he killed thousands of people, wiped out several villages and small cities, and burned farmland.

   _____ b. Attila became king of the Huns in the fifth century. The Huns lived in central Europe. Shortly after taking the throne, he killed his brother. Then he attacked his neighbors, conquering many of the people around him. He also invaded France and Italy, where he killed thousands of others and caused much destruction.

2. *Topic sentence:* Roberta is very aggressive.

   _____ a. Her aggressiveness is apparent in both her personal and her professional life. She is never shy about extending social invitations. And while some people are turned off by her aggressive attitude, others are impressed by it and enjoy doing business with her.

   _____ b. When she meets a man she likes, she is quick to say, "Let's go out sometime. What's your phone number?" In her job as a furniture salesperson, she will follow potential customers out onto the sidewalk as she tries to persuade them to buy.

3. *Topic sentence:* Our new kitten causes us lots of trouble.

_____ a. He has shredded the curtains in my bedroom with his claws. He nearly drowned when he crawled into the washing machine. And my hands look like raw hamburger from his playful bites and scratches.

_____ b. He seems to destroy everything he touches. He's always getting into places where he doesn't belong. Sometimes he plays too roughly, and that can be painful.

4. *Topic sentence:* My landlord is softhearted.

_____ a. Even though he wrote them himself, he sometimes ignores the official apartment rules in order to make his tenants happy.

_____ b. Although the lease states "No pets," he brought my daughter a puppy after she told him how much she missed having one.

5. *Topic sentence:* The library is a distracting place to try to study.

_____ a. It's hard to concentrate when a noisy eight-person poker game is going on on the floor beside you. It's also distracting to overhear remarks like, "Hey, Baby, what's your mother's address? I want to send her a thank-you card for having such a beautiful daughter."

_____ b. Many students meet in the library to do group activities and socialize with one another. Others go there to flirt. It's easy to get more interested in all that activity than in paying attention to your studies.

7 Recognizing Specific Details: II

ACTIVITY 15

At several points in the following paragraphs, you are given a choice of two sets of supporting details. Write *S* (for *specific*) in the space next to the set that provides specific support for the point. Write *G* (for *general*) next to the set that offers only vague, general support.

PARAGRAPH 1

My daughter's boyfriend is a good-for-nothing young man. After knowing him for just three months, everyone in our family is opposed to the relationship. For one thing, Russell is lazy.

_____ a. He is always finding an excuse to avoid putting in an honest day's work. He never pitches in and helps with chores around our house, even when he's asked directly to do so. And his attitude about his job isn't any better. To hear him tell it, he deserves special treatment in the workplace. He thinks he's gone out of his way if he just shows up on time.

_____ b. After starting a new job last week, he announced this Monday that he wasn't going to work because it was his *birthday*—as if he were somebody special. And when my husband asked Russell to help put storm windows on the house next Saturday, Russell answered that he uses his weekends to catch up on sleep.

Another quality of Russell's which no one likes is that he is cheap.

_____ c. When my daughter's birthday came around, Russell said he would take her out to Baldoni's, a fancy Italian restaurant. Then he changed his mind. Instead of spending a lot of money on a meal, he said, he wanted to buy her a really nice pair of earrings. So my daughter cooked dinner for him at her apartment. But there was no present, not even a little one. He claims he's waiting for a jewelry sale at Macy's. I don't think my daughter will ever see that "really nice" gift.

_____ d. He makes big promises about all the nice things he's going to do for my daughter, but he never comes through. His words are cheap, and so is he. He's all talk and no action. My daughter isn't greedy, but it hurts her when Russell says he's going to take her someplace nice or give her something special and then nothing happens.

Worst of all, Russell is mean.

_____ e. Russell seems to get special pleasure from hurting people when he feels they have a weak point. I have heard him make remarks that to him were funny but were really very insensitive. You've got to wonder about someone who needs to be ugly to other people just for the sake of being powerful. Sometimes I want to let him know how I feel.

_____ f. When my husband was out of work, Russell said to him, "Well, you've got it made now, living off your wife." After my husband glared at him, he said, "Why're you getting sore? I'm just kidding." Sometimes he snaps at my daughter, saying things like "Don't make me wait—there are plenty of other babes who would like to take your place." At such times I want to toss him out to the curb.

Everyone in the family is waiting anxiously for the day when my daughter will see Russell the way the rest of us see him.

PARAGRAPH 2

Many adult children move back in with their parents for some period of time. Although living with Mom and Dad again has some advantages, there are certain problems that are likely to arise. One common problem is that children may expect their parents to do all the household chores.

_____ a. They never think that they should take on their share of work around the house. Not only do they not help with their parents' chores; they don't even take responsibility for the extra work that their presence creates. Like babies, they go through the house making a mess that the parents are supposed to clean up. It's as if they think their parents are their servants.

_____ b. They expect meals to appear on the table as if by magic. After they've eaten, they go off to work or play, never thinking about who's going to do the dishes. They drop their dirty laundry beside the washing machine, assuming that Mom or Dad will attend to it and return clean, folded clothes to their bedroom door. And speaking of their bedrooms: Every day they await the arrival of Mom's Maid Service to make the bed, pick up the floor, and dust the furniture.

Another frequent problem is that parents forget their adult children are no longer adolescents.

_____ c. Parents like this want to know everything about their adult children's lives. They don't think their kids, even though they are adults, should have any privacy. Whenever they see their children doing anything, they want to know all the details. It's as though their children are still teenagers who are expected to report all their activities. Naturally, adult children get irritated when they are treated as if they were little kids.

_____ d. They may insist upon knowing far more about their children's comings and goings than the children want to share. For example, if such parents see their adult son heading out the door, they demand, "Where are you going? Who will you be with? What will you be doing? What time will you be back?" In addition, they may not let their adult child have any privacy. If their daughter and a date are sitting in the living room, for instance, they may join them there and start peppering the young man with questions about his family and his job, as if they were interviewing him for the position of son-in-law.

Finally, there may be financial problems when an adult child returns to live at home.

_____ e. Having an extra adult in the household creates extra expenses. But many adult children don't offer to help deal with those extra costs. Adult children often eat at home, causing the grocery bill to climb. They may stay in a formerly unused room, which now needs to be heated and lit. They produce extra laundry to be washed. They run up the family's cell-phone bills. For all these reasons, adult children should expect to pay a reasonable fee to their parents for room and board.

_____ f. It's expensive to have another adult living in the household. Adult children would be paying a lot of bills on their own if they weren't staying with their parents. It's only fair that they share the expenses at their parents' house. They should consider all the ways that their living at home is increasing their parents' expenses. Then they should insist on covering their share of the costs.

8 Providing Supporting Evidence

Provide three details that logically support each of the following points, or topic sentences. Your details can be drawn from your own experience, or they can be invented. In each case, the details should show in a specific way what the point expresses in only a general way. You may state your details briefly in phrases, or as complete sentences.

ACTIVITY 16

EXAMPLE

The student had several ways of passing time during the dull lecture.

Shielded his eyes with his hand and dozed awhile.

Read the sports magazine he had brought to class.

Made an elaborate drawing on a page of his notebook.

1. I could tell I was coming down with the flu.

   _____

   _____

   _____

2. There are several ways to save gas.

   _____

   _____

   _____

3. I had car problems recently.

   _____

   _____

   _____

4. When money gets tight, there are several ways to economize.

_____

_____

_____

5. Some people have dangerous driving habits.

_____

_____

_____

9 Identifying Adequate Supporting Evidence

ACTIVITY 17

Three of the following paragraphs provide sufficient details to support their topic sentences convincingly. Write *AD*, for *adequate development*, beside those paragraphs. There are also two paragraphs that, for the most part, use vague, general, or wordy sentences as a substitute for concrete details. Write *U*, for *underdeveloped*, beside those paragraphs.

_____   1.   **My Husband's Stubbornness**

My husband's worst problem is his stubbornness. He simply will not let any kind of weakness show. If he isn't feeling well, he refuses to admit it. He will keep on doing whatever he is doing and will wait until the symptoms get almost unbearable before he will even hint that anything is the matter with him. Then things are so far along that he has to spend more time recovering than he would if he had a different attitude. He also hates to be wrong. If he is wrong, he will be the last to admit it. This happened once when we went shopping, and he spent an endless amount of time going from one place to the next. He insisted that one of them had a fantastic sale on things he wanted. We never found a sale, but the fact that this situation happened will not change his attitude. Finally, he never listens to anyone else's suggestions on a car trip. He always knows he's on the right road, and the results have led to a lot of time wasted getting back in the right direction. Every time one of these incidents happens, that only means that it is going to happen again in the future.

_____   2.   **The Aztecs**

Before the Spaniards came to Mexico, the native inhabitants had developed advanced civilizations. For example, when the Europeans arrived, the Aztecs controlled much of the southwestern portion of

continued

present-day Mexico. They had built cities that were as large as, or larger than, many European cities of the sixteenth century. In fact, their capital, Tenochtitlán, had 200,000 to 300,000 inhabitants, more than any European capital. The Aztecs built immense temples and government buildings, and they developed a vibrant economy. In the central market of Tenochtitlán, 60,000 people conducted business each day. They also developed a writing system based on pictographs (small pictures), wrote poetry, recorded their history, and composed music. Their government and armies were highly organized. They created a system to collect taxes, they practiced a sophisticated system of religion, and they even took a census.

3.   **Social Saving**

The power of the group is often stronger than the power of the individual. This is demonstrated in the blossoming of online group coupon sites like LivingSocial, Groupon, and Dealster. By exercising group buying power, users are able to save money on food, clothing, and entertainment. Most sites offer discounts of at least 50 percent for consumers. Many sites like BuyWithMe and Gilt City can be personalized to help users find deals in specific cities. These are good sites not just for people who live in the area, but also for savvy travelers. For example, in preparation for a visit to San Francisco, travelers can subscribe to Gilt City and purchase coupons to be used during the vacation. The coupons could be applied toward a six-course dinner or the opportunity to watch the America's Cup finals aboard a WWII Liberty Ship. BuyWithMe is not just a social group coupon, but a portion of each of the proceeds goes to local charities—often chosen by the customer from a provided list. Such charities might include local schools, the Leukemia and Lymphoma Society, or museums. Group buying power was, is, and will continue to be a powerful economical force.

4.   **Qualities in a Friend**

There are several qualities I look for in a friend. A friend should give support and security. A friend should also be fun to be around. Friends can have faults, like anyone else, and sometimes it is hard to overlook them. But a friend can't be dropped because he or she has faults. A friend should stick around, even in bad times. There is a saying that "a friend in need is a friend indeed." I believe this means that there are good friends and fair-weather friends. The

continued

second type is not a true friend. He or she is the kind of person who runs when there's trouble. Friends don't always last a lifetime. Someone who is believed to be a best friend may lose contact if he or she moves to a different area or goes around with a different group of people. A friend should be generous and understanding. Friends do not have to be exactly like each other. Sometimes friends are opposites, but they still like each other and get along. Since I am a very quiet person, I can't say that I have many friends. But these are the qualities I believe a friend should have.

5.   **Learning Outside the Classroom**

Colleges should require that all students take a service learning course. Service learning not only combines classroom study and community service, but it introduces students to hands-on training and helps create a sense of well-being in students. Students in biology classes often partake in waterway clean-up projects. These students gain a sense of contributing to their community and helping improve the environment, while at the same time they are able to study plants and wildlife and learn just how humans positively and negatively affect specific ecosystems. Students in education classes can volunteer at local schools, offering services like free tutoring, aiding teachers, and campus clean-up programs. Not only will this volunteer work have a positive impact on the schools' communities, but it will introduce future teachers to ways of bettering the very environments they will be working in. Students in English composition classes can participate in local adult literacy programs, helping tutor adults in reading and writing. As these students gain a sense of purpose and help increase community literacy, they will also be improving their own reading and writing skills. Service learning improves both classroom learning and lifelong learning and should be a requirement for every college graduate.

10 Adding Details to Complete a Paragraph

ACTIVITY 18

Each of the following paragraphs needs specific details to back up its supporting points. In the spaces provided, add a sentence or two of realistic details for each supporting point. The more specific you are, the more convincing your details are likely to be.

1.   **A Pushover Instructor**

We knew after the first few classes that the instructor was a pushover. First of all, he didn't seem able to control the class.

_____

_____

_____

In addition, he made some course requirements easier when a few students complained.

_____

_____

_____

Finally, he gave the easiest quiz we had ever taken.

_____

_____

_____

2.

Helping a Parent in College

   There are several ways a family can help a parent who is attending college. First, family members can take over some of the household chores that the parent usually does.

_____

_____

_____

Also, family members can make sure that the student has some quiet study time.

_____

_____

_____

Last, families can take an interest in the student's problems and accomplishments.

_____

_____

_____

11 Writing a Simple Paragraph

You know now that an effective paragraph does two essential things: (1) It makes a point. (2) It provides specific details to support that point. You have considered a number of paragraphs that are effective because they follow these two basic steps or ineffective because they fail to follow them.

You are ready, then, to write a simple paragraph of your own. Choose one of the three assignments below, and follow carefully the guidelines provided.

WRITING ASSIGNMENT 1

Turn back to the activity on pages 81–82, and select the point for which you have the best supporting details. Develop that point into a paragraph by following these steps.

a. If necessary, rewrite the point so that the first sentence is more specific or suits your purpose more exactly. For example, you might write the second point as follows: "Saving gas will help you economize and protect the environment."

b. Provide several sentences of information to develop each of your three supporting details fully. Make sure that all the information in your paragraph truly supports your point.

c. Use the words *First of all, Second,* and *Finally* to introduce your three supporting details.

d. Conclude your paragraph with a sentence that refers to your opening point. This last sentence "rounds off" the paragraph and lets the reader know that your discussion is complete. For example, the paragraph "Changes in the Family" on page 52 begins with "Changes in our society in recent years have weakened family life." It closes with a statement that refers to, and echoes, the opening point: "Clearly, modern life is a challenge to family life."

e. Supply a title based on your point. For instance, point 4 on page 82 might have the title "Ways to Economize."

Use the following list to check your paragraph for each of the above items:

YES	NO	
____	____	Do you begin with a point?
____	____	Do you provide relevant, specific details that support the point?
____	____	Do you use the words *First of all, Second,* and *Finally* to introduce your three supporting details?
____	____	Do you have a closing sentence?
____	____	Do you have a title based on your point?
____	____	Are your sentences clear and free of obvious errors?

WRITING ASSIGNMENT 2

In this chapter you have read two paragraphs (pages 56–57) on reasons for being in college. For this assignment, write a paragraph describing your own reasons for being in college. You might want to look first at the following list of common reasons students give for going to school. Write a check mark next to each reason that applies to you. If you have reasons for being in college that are not listed here, add them to the list. Then select your three most important reasons for being in school, and generate specific supporting details for each reason.

Before starting, reread paragraph B on page 57. *You must provide comparable specific details of your own.* Make your paragraph truly personal; do not fall back on vague generalities like those in paragraph A on page 56. As you work on your paragraph, use the checklist for Writing Assignment 1 as a guide.

APPLY IN MY CASE | **Reasons Students Go to College**

———— To have some fun before getting a job

———— To prepare for a specific career

———— To please their families

———— To educate and enrich themselves

———— To be with friends who are going to college

———— To take advantage of an opportunity they didn't have before

———— To find a husband or wife

———— To see if college has anything to offer them

———— To do more with their lives than they've done so far

———— To take advantage of Veterans Administration benefits or other special funding

———— To earn the status that they feel comes with a college degree

———— To get a new start in life

———— Other: _____

WRITING ASSIGNMENT 3

Interview someone in the class. Take notes as you ask the person a series of questions.

How to Proceed

a. Begin by asking a series of factual questions about the person. You might ask such questions as

• Where is the person from? Where does he or she live now?

- Does the person have brothers or sisters? Does the person live with other people, or alone?
- What kinds of jobs (if any) has the person had? Where does he or she work now?
- What are the person's school or career plans? What courses is he or she taking?
- What are the person's favorite leisure activities?

Work at getting specific details rather than general ones. You do not want your introduction to include lines such as "Regina graduated from high school and worked for a year." You want to state specific places and dates: "Regina graduated from DeWitt Clinton High School in the Bronx in 2011. Within a week of graduation, she had gotten a job as a secretary for a branch of the Allstate Insurance Company located in Queens." Or if you are writing about a person's favorite activities, you do not want to simply say, "Regina enjoys watching TV in her few spare hours." Instead, go on and add details such as "Her favorite shows are *The Bachelor*, *The Colbert Report*, and *Glee*."

b. Then ask a series of questions about the person's attitudes and thoughts on various matters. You might ask the person's feeling about his or her

- Writing ability
- Parents
- Boss (if any)
- Courses
- Past schooling
- Strengths and talents
- Areas for self-improvement

You might also ask what things make the person angry or sad or happy, and why.

c. After collecting all this information, use it in three paragraphs. Begin your introduction to the person with a line like "This is a short introduction to _____. Some interesting biographical information about him (her) is _____." You might then begin your second paragraph with the line "_____ has a _____ attitude toward his/her past schooling and writing ability." Your third paragraph could then start out by saying "_____ is proud of his/her (insert strength/talent), but is hoping to improve his/her _____ in the future."

The Third Step in Writing

This chapter will show you how to

- organize specific evidence in a paper by using a clear method of organization

- connect the specific evidence by using transitions and other connecting words

HOW DO YOU STUDY FOR A TEST? Look at this photograph, and write a paragraph in which you tell a new college student how to study for an important exam. Once you have read through Chapter 4, read your paragraph again. Did you use *time order, emphatic order,* or a combination of both to organize your paragraph?

You know from Chapter 3 that the first two steps in writing an effective paragraph are making a point and supporting the point with specific evidence. This chapter deals with the third step. You'll learn the chief ways to organize and connect the supporting information in a paper.

Step 3: Organize and Connect the Specific Evidence

At the same time that you are generating the specific details needed to support a point, you should be thinking about ways to organize and connect those details. All the details in your paper must *cohere,* or stick together; when they do, your reader will be able to move smoothly from one bit of supporting information to the next. This chapter discusses the following ways to organize and connect supporting details: (1) common methods of organization, (2) transition words, and (3) other connecting words.

Common Methods of Organization: Time Order and Emphatic Order

Time order and emphatic order are common methods used to organize the supporting material in a paper. (You will learn more specialized methods of development in Part 2 of the book.)

Time order simply means that details are listed as they occur in time. *First* this is done; *next* this; *then* this; *after* that, this; and so on. Here is a paragraph that organizes its details through time order.

How I Relax

The way I relax when I get home from school on Thursday night is, first of all, to put my three children to bed. Next, I run hot water in the tub and put in lots of scented bubble bath. As the bubbles rise, I undress and get into the tub. The water is relaxing to my tired muscles, and the bubbles are tingly on my skin. I lie back and put my feet on the water spigots, with everything but my head under the water. I like to stick my big toe up the spigot and spray water over the tub. After about ten minutes of soaking, I wash myself with scented soap, get out and dry myself off, and put on my nightgown. Then I go downstairs and make myself a ham, lettuce, and tomato sandwich on rye bread and pour myself a tall glass of iced tea with plenty of sugar and ice cubes. I carry these into the living room and turn on the television. To get comfortable, I sit on the couch with a pillow behind me and my legs under me. I enjoy watching *The Daily Show* or a late movie. The time is very peaceful after a long, hard day of housecleaning, cooking, washing, and attending night class.

Fill in the missing words: "How I relax" uses the following words to help show time order: _____, _____, _____, _____, and _____.

Emphatic order is sometimes described as "save-the-best-'til-last" order. It means that the most interesting or important detail is placed in the last part of a paper. (In cases where all details seem equal in importance, the writer should impose a personal order that seems logical or appropriate to the details.) The last position in a paper is the most emphatic position because the reader is most likely to remember the last thing read. *Finally, last of all,* and *most important* are typical words and phrases showing emphasis. The following paragraph organizes its details through emphatic order.

Academic

The *National Enquirer*

There are several reasons why the *National Enquirer* is so popular. First of all, the paper is advertised on television. In the ads, attractive-looking people say, with a smile, "I want to know!" as they scan the pages of the *Enquirer.* The ads reassure people that it's all right to want to read stories such as "Heartbreak for Jennifer Lopez" or "Prince's Fiancée in New Royal Topless Scandal." In addition, the paper is easily available. In supermarkets, convenience stores, and drugstores, the *Enquirer* is always displayed in racks close to the cash register. As customers wait in line, they can't help being attracted to the paper's glaring headlines. Then, on impulse, customers will add the paper to their other purchases. Most of all, people read the *Enquirer* because they love gossip. We find other people's lives fascinating, especially if those people are rich and famous. We want to see and read about their homes, their clothes, and their friends, lovers, and families. We also take a kind of mean delight in their unflattering photos and problems and mistakes, perhaps because we envy them. Even though we may be ashamed of our interest, it's hard to resist buying a paper that promises "The Forbidden Love of Paris Hilton" or "Film Star Who Now Looks Like a Cadaver" or even "Hollywood Star Wars: Who Hates Whom and Why." The *Enquirer* knows how to get us interested and make us buy.

Fill in the missing words: The paragraph lists a total of _____ different reasons people read the *National Enquirer.* The writer of the paragraph feels that the most important reason is _____. He or she signals this reason by using the emphasis words _____.

Some paragraphs use a *combination of time order and emphatic order.* For example, "Why I'm in School" on page 57 includes time order: It moves from the night the writer's father confronted him to his current enrollment in a special program of five courses. In addition, the writer uses emphatic order, ending with the most important reason (signaled by the words "The main reason") for returning to school.

Transition Words

Look at the following items. Then check (✓) the one that is easier to read and understand.

_____ Our landlord repainted our apartment. He replaced the dishwasher.

_____ Our landlord repainted our apartment. Also, he replaced the dishwasher.

You probably found the second item easier to understand. The word *also* makes it clear that the writer is adding a second way the landlord has been of help. *Transitions,* or *transition words,* are signal words that help readers follow the direction of the writer's thoughts. They show the relationship between ideas, connecting thoughts. They are "bridge" words, carrying the reader across from one idea to the next.

Paperback books cost less than hardbacks.  , they are easier to carry.

Two major types of transitions are of particular help when you write: words that show *addition* and words that show *time.*

Words That Show Addition

Check (✓) the item that is easier to read and understand.

1. _____ a. A drinking problem can destroy a person's life. It can tear a family apart.

   _____ b. A drinking problem can destroy a person's life. In addition, it can tear a family apart.

2. _____ a. One way to lose friends is always to talk and never to listen. A way to end friendships is to borrow money and never pay it back.

   _____ b. One way to lose friends is always to talk and never to listen. Another way to end friendships is to borrow money and never pay it back.

In the pair of sentences about a drinking problem, the words *In addition* help make the relationship between the two sentences clear. The author is describing two effects of a drinking problem: it can destroy a life and a family. *In addition, another,* and words like these are known as *addition words.* In the pair of sentences about losing friends, you probably found the second item easier to understand. The word *Another* makes it clear that the writer is describing a second way to lose friends.

Addition words signal added ideas. They help writers organize information and present it clearly to readers. Some common words that show addition are listed in the following box.

Addition Words

one	to begin with	in addition
first	another	next
first of all	second	last (of all)
for one thing	also	finally

Words That Show Time

Check (✓) the item that is easier to read and understand.

1. _____ a. I had blood work done. I went to the doctor.

   _____ b. I had blood work done. Then I went to the doctor.

The word *Then* in the second item makes clear the relationship between the sentences. After having blood work done, the writer goes to the doctor. *Then* and words like it are *time words,* which carry the reader from one idea to the next.

I had blood work done. ———————— I went to the doctor.

Here are some more pairs of sentences. Check (✓) the item in each pair that contains a time word and so is easier to read and understand.

2. _____ a. Every week my uncle studies the food ads to see which stores have the best specials. He clips all the coupons.

   _____ b. Every week my uncle studies the food ads to see which stores have the best specials. Next, he clips all the coupons.

3. _____ a. Carmen took a very long shower. There was no hot water left for anyone else in the house.

   _____ b. Carmen took a very long shower. After that, there was no hot water left for anyone else in the house.

In the pair of sentences about the uncle, the word *Next* helps make the relationship between the two sentences clear. The uncle studies ads, and then he clips coupons. In the second pair of sentences, the word *after* makes the relationship clear. After Carmen's long shower, there was no hot water left for anyone else.

Time words tell us *when* something happened in relation to when something else happened. They help writers organize and make clear the order of events, stages, and steps in a process. Below are some common words that show time.

Time Words

before	next	later
first	as	after
second	when	finally
third	while	then

ACTIVITY 1

1. Fill in each blank with the appropriate addition transition from the list that follows. Use each transition once.

   another   finally   one

   > There are some widely popular but inappropriate methods that people have to combat stress. _____ common strategy is to consume massive quantities of junk food, which is easily done thanks to all the ever-present convenience stores and fast-food restaurants. _____ way to deal with stress is to doze or sleep for hours and hours, even during the day.
   >
   > _____, watching hours of nonstop TV can put people in a stupor that helps them forget the problems of everyday life.

2. Fill in each blank with the appropriate time transition from the list that follows. Use each transition once.

   then   next   before   first   after

   > I do not like to write. In fact, I dislike writing so much that I have developed a series of steps for postponing the agony of doing writing assignments. _____ I tell myself that to proceed without the proper

continued

equipment would be unwise. So I go out to buy a new pen, and this

kills at least an hour. _____, I begin to stare at the blank page.

_____ long, however, I realize that writing may also require thought, so I begin to think deeply about my subject. Soon I feel drowsy. This naturally leads to the conclusion that I need a nap because I can't throw

myself into my writing until I am at my very best. _____ a refreshing nap, I again face the blank page. It is usually at this stage that I actually

write a sentence or two—disappointing ones. I _____ wisely decide that I need inspiration, perhaps from an interesting magazine or my new XBox game. If I feel a bit guilty, I comfort myself with the knowledge that, as any artist knows, these things cannot be rushed.

3. Underline the three *addition* signals in the following paragraph.

Academic

States should consider getting rid of state lotteries for several reasons. First of all, the way lotteries are advertised is problematic. The commercials promote the lotteries as an easy way to get rich and find happiness. In fact, the odds against getting rich are astronomical, and it is common to see a news story featuring someone who won millions in the lottery and who is claiming bankruptcy within five years. Another reason is that lotteries take advantage of the people who can least afford them. Reports like "Why the Poor Play the Lottery" by Jens Beckert and Mark Lutter have shown that people with lower incomes are more likely to play the lottery than people with higher incomes. As these authors point out, "low-income individuals spend a larger share of their incomes on lottery tickets than those with higher incomes." This is the harshest reality of the lotteries: the state is encouraging people of limited means not to save their money but to throw it away on a state-supported pipe dream. Last, and most importantly, state lotteries don't raise the kind of revenue they promise. According to Dr. Patrick Briney's report, "Eight Reasons to Oppose a State Lottery," presented to the Arkansas Republican Assembly in 2000, "Thirty-seven states sponsoring lotteries . . . generated $123 in per capita sales [which] amounts to approximately less than one-half of one penny for each dollar of personal income." This amount of money is small compared to what sales, property, and gas taxes could generate. If states want to increase revenue, they need to find better ways than lotteries.

4.   Underline the three *time* signals in the following paragraph.

> Of the three meals eaten each day, dinner offers the best opportunity for families to sit down together and connect with one another. First, the morning meal that begins the day is typically very hectic. Many times children are rushing out the door to catch the school bus while parents are scrambling to make it to work on time. Breakfast often includes Pop-Tarts eaten on school buses, lattes purchased from local coffee shops, or doughnuts found in employee workrooms. Next, midday meals are rarely eaten as a family. Children eat their lunches at school, often on different schedules from their siblings. Parents may eat their lunches at their desks while working or in a restaurant with colleagues. Even parents who work at home aren't able to meet up with family members because schedules often conflict. Finally, the evening meal often offers the only time when the family is able to connect. Parents have returned from work and children have returned from school. Even though there may be the occasional evening activity that might prevent a dinner together, families should be able to find at least three or four nights a week in which to reconnect.

Other Kinds of Transitions

In the following box are other common transitional words, grouped according to the kind of signal they give readers. In the paragraphs you write, you will most often use addition words (like *first, also, another,* and *finally*), but all of the following signals are helpful to know as well.

Other Common Transitional Words

Space signals: next to, across, on the opposite side, to the left, to the right, in front, in back, above, below, behind, nearby

Change-of-direction signals: but, however, yet, in contrast, otherwise, still, on the contrary, on the other hand

Illustration signals: for example, for instance, specifically, as an illustration, once, such as

Conclusion signals: therefore, consequently, thus, then, as a result, in summary, to conclude, last of all, finally

1. Underline the four space signals in the following paragraph:

> The Lincoln Memorial is located in Washington, D.C. Its cornerstone was laid in 1915. Around the Memorial's exterior are thirty-six columns representing the thirty-six states of the nation at the time of President Abraham Lincoln's death in 1865. In front of the building is a large and imposing staircase leading to three large rooms. In the middle room is a statue of the President sitting in a large chair. To the left and right of this room are the north and south chambers, on the walls of which are inscribed quotations from Lincoln's Gettysburg Address and Second Inaugural Address.

2. Underline the four *change-of-direction signals* in the following paragraph.

> In some ways, train travel is superior to air travel. People always marvel at the speed with which airplanes can zip from one end of the country to another. Trains, on the other hand, definitely take longer. But sometimes longer can be better. Traveling across the country by train allows people to experience the trip more completely. They get to see the cities and towns, mountains and prairies that too often pass by unnoticed when they fly. Another advantage of train travel is comfort. Traveling by plane means wedging adult-sized bodies into narrow seats, bumping knees on the back of the seat, and having to pay five dollars for a tiny bag of pretzels. In contrast, the seats on most trains are spacious and comfortable, permitting even the longest-legged traveler to stretch out and watch the scenery just outside the window. And when train travelers grow hungry, they can get up and stroll to the dining car, where they can order anything from a simple snack to a gourmet meal. There's no question that train travel is definitely slow and old-fashioned compared with air travel. However, in many ways it is much more civilized.

3. Underline the three *illustration signals* in the following selection.

> Status symbols are all around us. The cars we drive, for instance, say something about who we are and how successful we have been. The auto makers depend on this perception of automobiles, designing their commercials to show older, well-established people driving luxury sedans and young, fun-loving people driving to the beach in sports cars. Clothing, too, has always been a status symbol. Specifically, schoolchildren are often rated by their classmates according to the brand names of their clothing. Another example of a status symbol is the cell phone. This

continued

device, not so long ago considered a novelty, is now used by almost everyone. Being without a cell phone in the twenty-first century is like being without a regular phone in the 1990s.

4. Underline the *conclusion signal* in the following paragraph.

A hundred years ago, miners used to bring caged canaries down into the mines with them to act as warning signals. If the bird died, the miners knew that the oxygen was running out. The smaller animal would be affected much more quickly than the miners. In the same way, animals are acting as warning signals to us today. Baby birds die before they can hatch because pesticides in the environment cause the adults to lay eggs with paper-thin shells. Fish die when lakes are contaminated with acid rain or poisonous mercury. The dangers in our environment will eventually affect all life on earth, including humans. Therefore, we must pay attention to these early warning signals. If we don't, we will be as foolish as a miner who ignored a dead canary—and we will die.

Other Connecting Words

In addition to transitions, there are three other kinds of connecting words that help tie together the specific evidence in a paper: *repeated words, pronouns,* and *synonyms.*

Repeated Words

Many of us have been taught by English instructors—correctly so—not to repeat ourselves in writing. However, repeating key words can help tie ideas together. In the paragraph that follows, the word *business* is repeated to remind readers of the key idea on which the discussion is centered. Underline the word the six times it appears.

Everyone remembers Thomas Alva Edison (1847–1931) as a great inventor; after all, he was issued more than one thousand patents by the United States government, more than any other person to date. However, he also had a head for business. When he was ten years old, he started a fresh produce business, growing vegetables on his family farm and selling them locally. Later, he began selling sandwiches, newspapers, and other goods to train commuters, a business that grew to such an extent that he had to hire other boys to help him. In 1870, Edison established a business in New Jersey manufacturing stock tickers and telegraph equipment. By 1872, sponsored by the Western Union Company, he opened a laboratory

continued

in Menlo Park, New Jersey. This new business yielded such extraordinary inventions as the phonograph, a new telephone transmitting device, and of course the incandescent lightbulb. By the time the United States entered World War I (1917), Edison had become a very wealthy man, having patented, manufactured, and marketed inventions affecting every sector of American business, from the film industry to cement manufacturing.

Pronouns

Pronouns (*he, she, it, you, they, this, that,* and others) are another way to connect ideas as you develop a paper. Using pronouns to take the place of other words or ideas can help you avoid needless repetition. (Be sure, though, to use pronouns with care in order to avoid the unclear or inconsistent pronoun references described in Chapters 25 and 26 of this book.) Underline the eight pronouns in the passage that follows, noting at the same time the words that the pronouns refer to.

A professor of nutrition at a major university recently advised his students that they could do better on their examinations by eating lots of sweets. He told them that the sugar in cakes and candy would stimulate their brains to work more efficiently, and that if the sugar was eaten for only a month or two, it would not do them any harm.

Synonyms

Using *synonyms*—words that are alike in meaning—can also help move the reader from one thought to the next. In addition, the use of synonyms increases variety and interest by avoiding needless repetition of the same words. Underline the three words used as synonyms for *false ideas* in the following passage.

There are many false ideas about suicide. One wrong idea is that a person who talks about suicide never follows through. The truth is that about three out of every four people who commit suicide speak of it to one or more other persons ahead of time. Another misconception is that a person who commits suicide is poor or downtrodden. Actually, poverty appears to be a deterrent to suicide rather than a predisposing factor. A third myth about suicide is that people considering suicide will eventually take their lives one way or another, whether or not the most obvious means of suicide is removed from their reach. In fact, to those attempting suicide as a kind of cry for help, removing a convenient means of taking one's life, such as a gun, shows that someone cares and is paying attention.

ACTIVITY 3

Read the selection below, and then answer the questions about it that follow.

Health Inspection Report: Main Street Grill

The following is a summary of the May 2013 report that recommends the Main Street Grill be closed immediately:

[1]The entry of the restaurant is in dire need of repair. [2]Several windows have large cracks, and none have screens. [3]The front steps are missing a handrail, and one stair tread has a large hole in its middle. [4]The front door does not close properly, allowing flies freedom to enter the establishment. [5]Immediately inside the entryway, sections of broken flooring have been temporarily covered with loose boards. [6]Many of them show signs of wood rot and decay. [7]The interior of the restaurant does not appear to have been cleaned in several years and is extremely dirty. [8]Layers of dust and grease were visible on the lighting fixtures and appliances. [9]The floor, where it wasn't broken, was a dingy gray that was slippery and dangerous. [10]The kitchen contains several non-working pieces of equipment. [11]Fifteen extension cords were being used to connect appliances to one outlet. [12]Foods were not being stored at the proper temperatures. [13]Tests showed meats at 105 degrees Fahrenheit and milk at 52 degrees Fahrenheit. [14]Proper restaurant and employee health standards were not being upheld during the inspection. [15]Workers were not wearing hairnets, nor did any of them wash their hands while the inspection was happening. [16]This is the third time that Main Street Grill has failed a health inspection; no improvements have been made since the last visit. [17]The restaurant must be closed immediately.

QUESTIONS

1. How many times is the word *restaurant* used? _____

2. Write here the pronoun that is used to refer to *stair tread* (sentence 3): _____; *boards* (sentence 6): _____; *floor* (sentence 9): _____

3. Write here the word that is used as a synonym for *dirty* (sentence 9):

   _____

   the words that are used as a synonym for *appliances* (sentence 10):

   _____

   the word that is used as a synonym for *employees* (sentence 15):

   _____

Complete the following statements.

1. *Time order* means _____

_____

2. *Emphatic order* means _____

_____

3. _____ are signal words that help readers follow the
direction of a writer's thought.

4. In addition to transitions, three other kinds of connecting words
that help link sentences and ideas are repeated words, _____,
and _____.

Practice in Organizing and Connecting Specific Evidence

You now know the third step in effective writing: organizing and connecting the
specific evidence used to support the main point of a paper. This closing section
will expand and strengthen your understanding of the third step in writing.

You will work through the following series of activities:

- Organizing through Time Order
- Organizing through Emphatic Order
- Organizing through a Combination of Time Order and Emphatic Order
- Identifying Transitions
- Identifying Transitions and Other Connecting Words

Organizing through Time Order

Use time order to organize the scrambled list of sentences below. Write the number
1 beside the point that all the other sentences support. Then number each supporting sentence as it occurs in time.

ACTIVITY 4

Academic

_____   Once a working thesis has been created, the student should continue researching by taking notes, with a more focused attention to the information that supports the working thesis.

_____   Writing a research paper should be done as a process.

_____ Once a subject is chosen, the student should then narrow it to a limited research topic that the instructor approves.

_____ A proven method of note-taking, for example an online source like Noodle Tools or a low-tech approach like index cards, should be employed.

_____ The student should next edit the final, revised version of the paper. During this stage, the student should double-check that the bibliographic entries on his or her "Works Cited" list correspond to the cited material in the essay.

_____ Once the majority of the research has been gathered and noted, the student should then start outlining his or her paper. The instructor may require a long, formal outline, but a scratch outline will do at this stage.

_____ First, a student should choose a broad subject that is interesting, unless the instructor assigns a subject.

_____ The next step the student should take is preliminary research to make sure that the topic can be researched easily via the college library and/or reputable electronic sources.

_____ After the rough draft has been completed, the student should plan to revise his or her draft as many times as needed. The student should not panic if he or she realizes that more information is needed, thus leading to more research. This is not unusual.

_____ After the preliminary research is completed, the next step is homing in on exactly what the student wants to prove or say about the topic and using this idea to create a working thesis.

_____ Finally, the student should proofread the edited copy as carefully as possible.

_____ The outline should then serve as a guide for the student to begin drafting his or her paper, citing and identifying research sources as they are incorporated into the paper.

Organizing through Emphatic Order

ACTIVITY 5 Use emphatic order (order of importance) to arrange the following scrambled list of sentences. Write the number 1 beside the point that all the other sentences support. Then number each supporting sentence, starting with what seems to be the least important detail and ending with the most important detail.

_____ The people here are all around my age and seem to be genuinely friendly and interested in me.

_____ The place where I live has several important advantages.

_____ The schools in this neighborhood have a good reputation, so I feel that my daughter is getting a good education.

_____ The best thing of all about this area, though, is the school system.

_____ Therefore, I don't have to put up with public transportation or worry about how much it's going to cost to park each day.

_____ The school also has an extended after-school program, so I know my daughter is in good hands until I come home from work.

_____ First of all, I like the people who live in the other apartments near mine.

_____ Another positive aspect of this area is that it's close to where I work.

_____ That's more than I can say for the last place I lived, where people stayed behind locked doors.

_____ The office where I'm a receptionist is only a six-block walk from my house.

_____ In addition, I save a lot of wear and tear on my car.

Organizing through a Combination of Time Order and Emphatic Order

Use a combination of time and emphatic order to arrange the scrambled list of sentences below. Write the number 1 beside the point that all the other sentences support. Then number each supporting sentence. Paying close attention to transitional words and phrases will help you organize and connect the supporting sentences.

ACTIVITY 6

Personal

_____ I did not see the spider but visited my friend in the hospital, where he suffered through a week of nausea and dizziness because of the poison.

_____ We were listening to the radio when we discovered that nature was calling.

_____ As I got back into the car, I sensed, rather than felt or saw, a presence on my left hand.

_____ After these two experiences, I suspect that my fear of spiders will be with me until I die.

_____ The first experience was the time when my best friend received a bite from a black widow spider.

_____ I looked down at my hand, but I could not see anything because it was so dark.

_____ I had two experiences when I was sixteen that are the cause of my *arachnophobia,* a terrible and uncontrollable fear of spiders.

_____ We stopped the car at the side of the road, walked into the woods a few feet, and watered the leaves.

_____ My friend then entered the car, putting on the dashboard light, and I almost passed out with horror.

_____ I saw the bandage on his hand and the puffy swelling when the bandage was removed.

_____ Then it flew off my hand and into the dark bushes nearby.

_____ I sat in the car for an hour afterward, shaking and sweating and constantly rubbing the fingers of my hand to reassure myself that the spider was no longer there.

_____ But my more dramatic experience with spiders happened one evening when another friend and I were driving around in his car.

_____ Almost completely covering my fingers was a monstrous brown spider, with white stripes running down each of a seemingly endless number of long, furry legs.

_____ Most of all, I saw the ugly red scab on his hand and the yellow pus that continued oozing from under the scab for several weeks.

_____ I imagined my entire hand soon disappearing as the behemoth relentlessly devoured it.

_____ At the same time, I cried out "Arghh!" and flicked my hand violently back and forth to shake off the spider.

_____ For a long, horrible second it clung stickily, as if intertwined for good among the fingers of my hand.

Identifying Transitions

ACTIVITY 7

Fill in each blank with the appropriate addition transition from the following list. Use each transition once.

| also | second | for one thing | last of all |

Academic

Why School May Frighten a Young Child

School may be frightening to young children for a number of reasons. _____, the regimented environment may be a new and disturbing experience. At home, children may have been able to do what they wanted when they wanted to do it. In school, however, they

continued

are given set times for talking, working, playing, eating, and even using

the restroom. A _____ source of anxiety may be the public method of discipline that some teachers use. Whereas at home children are scolded in private, in school they may be held up to embarrassment and ridicule in front of their peers. "Bonnie," the teacher may say, "why are you the only one in class who didn't do your homework?" Or, "David, why are you the only one who can't work quietly at your seat?" Children

may _____ be frightened by the loss of personal attention. Their little discomforts or mishaps, such as tripping on the stairs, may bring instant sympathy from a parent; in school, there is often no one to notice, or the teacher is frequently too busy to care and just says, "Go do

your work. You'll be all right." _____, a child may be scared by the competitive environment of the school. At home, one hopes, such competition for attention is minimal. But in school, children may vie for the teacher's approving glance or tone, or for stars on a paper, or for favored seats in the front row. For these and other reasons, it is not surprising that children may have difficulty adjusting to school.

Fill in each blank with the appropriate time transition from the list that follows. Use each transition once.

ACTIVITY 8

then   first   after   as   later

A Victory for Big Brother

In one of the most terrifying scenes in all of literature, George Orwell in his classic novel *1984* describes how a government known as Big Brother destroys a couple's love. The couple, Winston and Julia, fall in love

and meet secretly, knowing the government would not approve. _____ informers turn them in, a government agent named O'Brien takes steps

to end their love. _____ he straps Winston down and explains that

he has discovered Winston's worst fear. _____ he sets a cage with two giant, starving sewer rats on the table next to Winston. He says that when he presses a lever, the door of the cage will slide up, and the rats

will shoot out like bullets and bore straight into Winston's face. _____ Winston's eyes dart back and forth, revealing his terror, O'Brien places

continued

his hand on the lever. Winston knows that the only way out is for Julia to take his place. Suddenly, he hears his own voice screaming, "Do it to Julia! Not me! Julia!" Orwell does not describe Julia's interrogation, but

when Julia and Winston see each other _____, they realize that each has betrayed the other. Their love is gone. Big Brother has won.

ACTIVITY 9

Fill in each blank with the transition word or phrase from the list that follows. Use each transition once.

in summary   in addition   however   specifically

The Aspen Venue

WB&E Engineering has designed an events center for the city of Greenville in order to provide a complex to better serve the needs of the community. The new center will work well for a group as small as twenty-five or as large as three hundred. To blend in with the city's historic roots,

it will be built in Georgian style, _____ using hand-hewed brick from the Greenville Brick Company. The interior design will incorporate soaring twenty-foot ceilings, hardwood oak floors, crystal chandeliers, and stained-glass pieces from local artisans. The bathrooms have been specially fashioned to reflect key periods in Greenville's history. The two kitchens have been designed with the highest quality fixtures and appliances. Each floor holds two large halls that can be combined to create one larger hall.

_____, all of the halls open up to heated balconies that offer expansive views of Greenville. The quality of construction will ensure that multiple functions can be hosted without crossover noise. The total events space in the building is six thousand square feet split among the three levels.

No extra parking will be provided with this venue; _____, city

parking will adequately accommodate the needed spaces. _____, this facility will service the city by offering a functional and flexible space that will be both beautiful and practical.

ACTIVITY 10

Fill in each blank with the appropriate addition or change-of-direction transitions from the list that follows. Use each transition once.

fourth   but   yet   another
for one thing   second   however   last

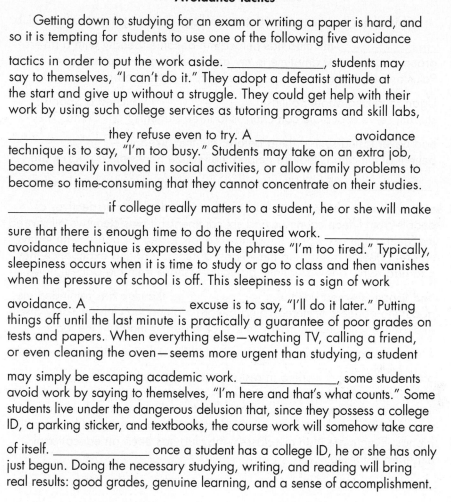

Avoidance Tactics

Getting down to studying for an exam or writing a paper is hard, and so it is tempting for students to use one of the following five avoidance

tactics in order to put the work aside. _____, students may say to themselves, "I can't do it." They adopt a defeatist attitude at the start and give up without a struggle. They could get help with their work by using such college services as tutoring programs and skill labs,

_____ they refuse even to try. A _____ avoidance technique is to say, "I'm too busy." Students may take on an extra job, become heavily involved in social activities, or allow family problems to become so time-consuming that they cannot concentrate on their studies.

_____ if college really matters to a student, he or she will make

sure that there is enough time to do the required work. _____ avoidance technique is expressed by the phrase "I'm too tired." Typically, sleepiness occurs when it is time to study or go to class and then vanishes when the pressure of school is off. This sleepiness is a sign of work

avoidance. A _____ excuse is to say, "I'll do it later." Putting things off until the last minute is practically a guarantee of poor grades on tests and papers. When everything else—watching TV, calling a friend, or even cleaning the oven—seems more urgent than studying, a student

may simply be escaping academic work. _____, some students avoid work by saying to themselves, "I'm here and that's what counts." Some students live under the dangerous delusion that, since they possess a college ID, a parking sticker, and textbooks, the course work will somehow take care

of itself. _____ once a student has a college ID, he or she has only just begun. Doing the necessary studying, writing, and reading will bring real results: good grades, genuine learning, and a sense of accomplishment.

Fill in each blank with the appropriate transition from the following list. Use each transition once.

Copyright ©2015 The McGraw-Hill Companies, Inc. All rights reserved.

ACTIVITY 11

Addition transitions: first of all, second, finally

Time transition: when

Illustration transition: once

Change-of-direction transition: however

Conclusion transition: as a result

Joining a Multicultural Club

One of the best things I've done in college is joining a multicultural club.

_____, the club has helped me become friendly with a diverse group of people. At any time in my apartment, I can have someone from Pakistan or Sweden chatting about music, or someone from Russia or

Uganda talking about politics. _____, I watched a Spanish student serve *chocolate con churros* to three students from China. They

had never tasted such a thing before, but they liked it. A _____ benefit of the club is that it's helped me realize how similar people are.

_____ the whole club first assembled, we wound up having

a conversation about dating and sex that included the perspectives of people from fifteen countries and six continents! It was clear we all shared the feeling that sex was fascinating. The talk lasted for hours, with many different people describing the wildest or funniest dating experience they had had. Only a few students, particularly those from the United States

and Japan, seemed bashful. _____, the club has reminded me about the dangers of stereotyping. Before I joined the club, my only direct experience with people from China was ordering meals in the local

Chinese restaurant. _____, I believed that most Chinese people

ate lots of rice and worked in restaurants. In the club, _____ I met Chinese people who were soccer players, English majors, and math tutors. I've also seen Jewish and Muslim students—people who I thought would never get along—drop their preconceived notions and become friends. Even more than my classes, the club has been an educational experience for me.

Identifying Transitions and Other Connecting Words

ACTIVITY 12

This activity will give you practice in identifying transitions and other connecting words that are used to help tie ideas together.

Section A—Transitions

Locate the transitional word in each sentence, and write it in the space provided.

1. I decided to pick up a drop-add form from the registrar's office. However, I changed my mind when I saw the long line of students waiting there.

_____

2. In England, drivers use the left-hand side of the road. Consequently, in a car the steering wheel is on the right side.

_____

3. Crawling babies will often investigate new objects by putting them in their mouths. Therefore, parents should be alert for any pins, tacks, or other dangerous items on floors and carpets.

_____

4. One technique that advertisers use is to have a celebrity endorse a product. The consumer then associates that product with the star qualities of the celebrity.

_____

Section B—Repeated Words

In the space provided, write the repeated words.

5. The tall ships moved majestically into the harbor. Along the docks were thousands of people who had come to witness the harbor spectacle.

_____

6. Many researchers believe that people have weight set-points their bodies try to maintain. This may explain why many dieters return to their original weight.

_____

7. At the end of the concert, thousands of fans held up lighters in the darkened stadium. The sea of lighters signaled that the fans wanted an encore.

_____

8. Establishing credit is important for everyone. A good credit history is often necessary when you are applying for a loan or credit card.

_____

Section C—Synonyms

In the space provided, write the synonym for the underlined word.

9. Entering the five-thousand-year-old tomb, the archaeologists found that it had been ransacked by thieves hundreds of years before. However, several of the fine earthen jars had been left intact by the robbers.

_____

10. Women's clothes, in general, use less material than men's clothes. Yet women's garments usually cost more than men's.

    _____

11. The temperance movement in this country sought to ban alcohol. Drinking liquor, movement leaders said, led to violence, poverty, prostitution, and insanity.

    _____

12. For me, apathy quickly sets in when the weather becomes hot and sticky. This listlessness disappears when the humidity decreases.

    _____

Section D—Pronouns

In the space provided, write the word referred to by the underlined pronoun.

13. At the beginning of the twentieth century, bananas were still an oddity in the United States. Some people even attempted to eat them with the skin on.

    _____

14. Canning vegetables is easy and economical. It can also be very dangerous.

    _____

15. Members of the United States Congress always seem to be campaigning. After all, they have to stand for reelection every two years.

    _____

The Fourth Step in Writing

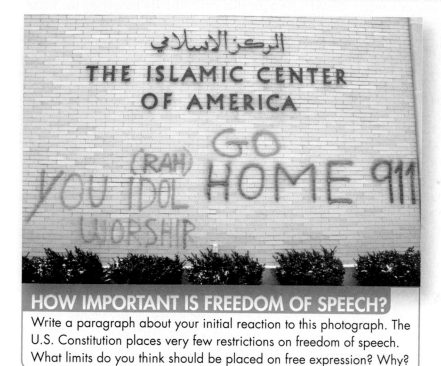

HOW IMPORTANT IS FREEDOM OF SPEECH?

Write a paragraph about your initial reaction to this photograph. The U.S. Constitution places very few restrictions on freedom of speech. What limits do you think should be placed on free expression? Why?

Step 4: Write Clear, Error-Free Sentences

So far, this book has emphasized the first three steps in writing an effective paragraph: making a point (Chapter 3), supporting the point (Chapter 3), and organizing and connecting the evidence (Chapter 4). This chapter focuses on the fourth step: writing clear, error-free sentences. You'll learn how to revise a paragraph so that your sentences flow smoothly and clearly. Then you'll review how to edit a paragraph for mistakes in grammar, punctuation, and spelling.

Revising Sentences

The following strategies will help you to revise your sentences effectively.

- Use parallelism.
- Use a consistent point of view.

- Use specific words.
- Use concise wording.
- Vary your sentences.

Use Parallelism

Words in a pair or a series should have a parallel structure. By balancing the items in a pair or a series so that they have the same kind of structure, you will make a sentence clearer and easier to read. Notice how the parallel sentences that follow read more smoothly than the nonparallel ones.

Nonparallel (Not Balanced)	Parallel (Balanced)
I resolved to lose weight, to study more, and *watching* less TV.	I resolved to lose weight, to study more, and to watch less TV. (A balanced series of *to* verbs: *to lose, to study, to watch*)
A consumer group rates my car as noisy, expensive, and *not having much safety*.	A consumer group rates my car as noisy, expensive, and unsafe. (A balanced series of descriptive words: *noisy, expensive, unsafe*)
Lola likes wearing soft sweaters, eating exotic foods, and *to bathe* in scented bath oil.	Lola likes wearing soft sweaters, eating exotic foods, and bathing in scented bath oil. (A balanced series of *-ing* words: *wearing, eating, bathing*)
Single life offers more freedom of choice; *more security is offered by marriage*.	Single life offers more freedom of choice; marriage offers more security. (Balanced verbs and word order: *single life offers . . . ; marriage offers . . .*)

TIP You need not worry about balanced sentences when writing first drafts. But when you rewrite, try to put matching words and ideas into matching structures. Such parallelism will improve your writing style.

ACTIVITY 1   Cross out and revise the unbalanced part of each of the following sentences.

EXAMPLE

When Gail doesn't have class, she uses her time to clean house, ~~getting~~ her laundry done, and to buy groceries.

1. Lola plans to become a model, a lawyer, or to go into nursing.

2. Filling out an income tax form is worse than wrestling a bear or to walk on hot coals.

3. The study-skills course taught me how to take more effective notes, to read a textbook chapter, and preparing for exams.

4. Home Depot has huge sections devoted to plumbing equipment, electrical supplies, and tools needed for carpentry.

5. When visiting Chicago, make sure to visit its wonderful art museum, eat some deep-dish pizza, and taking a stroll along the Lake Michigan shoreline.

6. Filled with talent and ambitious, Eduardo worked hard at his sales job.

7. Viewing the Grand Canyon for the first time, we felt exeitement, peaceful, and awed at the same time.

8. Cindy's cat likes sleeping in the dryer, lying in the bathtub, and to chase squirrels.

9. The weather was hot, there were crowds in the city, and the buses were on strike.

10. People in the lobby munched popcorn, sipped sodas, and were shuffling their feet impatiently.

Use a Consistent Point of View

Consistency with Verbs

Do not shift verb tenses unnecessarily. If you begin writing a paper in the present tense, don't shift suddenly to the past. If you begin in the past, don't shift without reason to the present. Notice the inconsistent verb tenses in the following example:

Incorrect   The shoplifter *walked* quickly toward the front of the store. When a clerk *shouts* at him, he *started* to run.

The verbs must be consistently in the present tense:

Correct   The shoplifter *walks* quickly toward the front of the store. When a clerk *shouts* at him, he *starts* to run.

Or the verbs must be consistently in the past tense:

Correct   The shoplifter *walked* quickly toward the front of the store. When a clerk *shouted* at him, he *started* to run.

ACTIVITY 2

In each passage, one verb must be changed so that it agrees in tense with the other verbs. Cross out the incorrect verb, and write the correct form above each crossed-out verb.

EXAMPLE

    carried
Kareem wanted to be someplace else when the dentist ~~carries~~ in a long needle.

1. I listened to music and surfed the Internet before I decide to do some homework.

2. The hitchhiker stopped me as I walks from the turnpike rest station and said, "Are you on your way to San Jose?"

3. During both World War I and World War II, Switzerland was neutral. Therefore, some refugees from Nazi Germany escape to that country.

4. Molly's grandfather was a college English professor. Only after he retires did he learn to read Italian.

5. In the movie, artillery shells exploded on the hide of the reptile monster. The creature just grinned, tosses off the shells, and kept eating people.

6. Several months a year, monarch butterflies come to live in a spot along the California coast. Thousands and thousands of them hang from the trees and fluttered through the air in large groups.

7. After waking up each morning, Harry stays in bed for a while. First he stretches and yawned loudly, and then he plans his day.

8. The salespeople at Biggs's Department Store are very helpful. When people asked for a product the store doesn't carry or is out of, the salesperson recommends another store.

9. The American Revolution began in 1775, when the British fire upon Americans at Lexington and Concord, Massachusetts. However, trouble had been brewing since Britain imposed new taxes on the colonies in 1766.

10. Smashed cars, ambulances, and police cars blocked traffic on one side of the highway. On the other side, traffic slows down as drivers looked to see what had happened.

Consistency with Pronouns

Pronouns should not shift point of view unnecessarily. When writing a paper, be consistent in your use of first-, second-, or third-person pronouns.

Type of Pronoun	Singular	Plural
First-person pronouns	I (my, mine, me)	we (our, us)
Second-person pronouns	you (your)	you (your)
Third-person pronouns	he (his, him)	they (their, them)
	she (her)	
	it (its)	

TIP

Any person, place, or thing, as well as any indefinite pronoun like *one*, *anyone*, *someone*, and so on, is a third-person word.

If you start writing in the third person *she*, don't jump suddenly to the second person *you*. Or if you are writing in the first person *I*, don't shift unexpectedly to *one*. Look at the examples that follow.

Inconsistent

I enjoy movies like *The Return of the Vampire* that frighten *you*. (A very common mistake people make is to let *you* slip into their writing after they start with another pronoun.)

As soon as a tourist enters Arlington National Cemetery, where many of America's military heroes are buried, *you* begin to realize how costly the price of liberty is.

(Again, *you* is a shift in point of view.)

Consistent

I enjoy movies like *The Return of the Vampire* that frighten me.

As soon as a tourist enters Arlington National Cemetery, where many of America's military heroes are buried, *he or she* begins to realize how costly the price of liberty is.

(See also the coverage of *his or her* references on pages 417–418.)

Cross out inconsistent pronouns in the following sentences, and write the correct form of the pronoun above each crossed-out word. You may have to change the form of the verb as well.

ACTIVITY 3

EXAMPLE

My dreams are always the kind that haunt ~~you~~ *me* the next day.

1. Whenever we take our children on a trip, you have to remember to bring snacks, tissues, and toys.

2. In our society, we often need a diploma before you can be hired for a job.

3. This summer, I worked for the city sanitation department, a job in which you learn a lot about people's consumption habits.

4. If a student organizes time carefully, you can accomplish a great deal of work.

5. Although I know you should watch your cholesterol intake, I can never resist an ear of corn dripping with melted butter.

6. Good conversationalists have the ability to make the person they were talking to feel as if they are the only other person in the room.

7. We never go to the Salad Bowl anymore, because you wait so long to be seated and the waiters usually make mistakes with the order.

8. I read over my notes before class because one can never tell when there will be a quiz.

9. Our time was limited, so we decided not to go to the Gettysburg National Military Park because you would need to spend an entire day for a worthwhile visit.

10. In my job as store manager, I'm supposed to be nice to the customer even if they are being totally unreasonable.

Use Specific Words

To be an effective writer, you must use specific words rather than general words. Specific words create pictures in the reader's mind. They help capture interest and make your meaning clear. Compare the following general and specific sentences:

General	Specific
The boy came down the street.	Theo ran down Woodlawn Avenue.
A bird appeared on the grass.	A blue jay swooped down onto the frost-covered lawn.
She stopped the car.	Jackie slammed on the brakes of her Hummer.

The specific sentences create clear pictures in our minds. The details *show* us exactly what has happened.

Here are four ways to make your sentences specific.

1. Use exact names.

She loves her *car*.

Renée loves her *Honda*.

2. Use lively verbs.

The garbage truck *went* down Front Street.

The garbage truck *rumbled* down Front Street.

3. Use descriptive words (modifiers) before nouns.

A girl peeked out the window.

A *chubby six-year-old* girl peeked out the *dirty kitchen* window.

4. Use words that relate to the five senses: sight, sound, taste, smell, and touch.

That woman is a karate expert.

That *tiny, silver-haired* woman is a karate expert. (*sight*)

When the dryer stopped, a signal sounded.

When the dryer stopped, a *loud buzzer* sounded. (*sound*)

Lola offered me an orange slice.

Lola offered me a *sweet, juicy* orange slice. (*taste*)

The real estate agent opened the door of the closet.

The real estate agent opened the door of the *cedar-scented* closet. (*smell*)

I pulled the blanket around me to fight off the wind.

I pulled the *fluffy* blanket around me to fight off the *chilling* wind. (*touch*)

This activity will give you practice in replacing vague, indefinite words with sharp, specific words. Add three or more specific words to replace the general word or words underlined in each sentence. Make changes in the wording of a sentence as necessary.

ACTIVITY 4

EXAMPLE

My bathroom cabinet contains <u>many drugs</u>.

My bathroom cabinet contains aspirin, antibiotics, tranquilizers, and codeine

cough medicine.

1. My Netflix queue <u>is long and has many items</u>.

_____

_____

2. At Worlds of Fun, I went on <u>a lot of rides</u>.

_____

_____

3. Saturday is my day to run errands.

_____

_____

4. The room was a mess.

_____

_____

5. Recently we visited several museums.

_____

_____

ACTIVITY 5

Again, you will practice changing vague, indefinite writing into lively, image-filled writing that helps capture the reader's interest and makes your meaning clear. With the help of the methods described on pages 52–60 and 74–85, add specific details to the sentences that follow. Note the examples.

EXAMPLE

The person got out of the car.

The elderly man painfully lifted himself out of the white Buick

station wagon.

The fans enjoyed the victory.

Many of the fifty thousand fans stood, waved banners, and cheered wildly when Barnes

scored the winning touchdown.

1. The college offers a variety of intramural sports.

_____

_____

2. The animal ran away.

_____

_____

3. An accident occurred.

_____

_____

4. The instructor came into the room.

_____

_____

5. Luis is interested in electronic gadgets.

_____

_____

_____

_____

Use Concise Wording

Wordiness—using more words than necessary to express a meaning—is often a sign of lazy or careless writing. Your readers may resent the extra time and energy they must spend when you have not done the work needed to make your writing direct and concise.

Here are examples of wordy sentences:

> Anne is of the opinion that the death penalty should be allowed.

> The country of Colombia has as its capital the city known as Bogotá.

Omitting needless words improves the sentences:

> Anne supports the death penalty.

> The capital of Colombia is Bogotá.

The following box lists some wordy expressions that could be reduced to single words.

Kate Taylor/www.CartoonStock.com

Wordy Form	Short Form
a large number of	many
a period of a week	a week
arrive at an agreement	agree
at an earlier point in time	before
at the present time	now

continued

Wordy Form	Short Form
big in size	big
owing to the fact that	because
during the time that	while
five in number	five
for the reason that	because
good benefit	benefit
in every instance	always
in my own opinion	I think
in the event that	if
in the near future	soon
in this day and age	today
is able to	can
large in size	large
plan ahead for the future	plan
postponed until later	postponed
red in color	red
return back	return

ACTIVITY 6

Rewrite the following sentences, omitting needless words.

1. The headquarters of the U.S. Central Intelligence Agency, which collects information important to maintaining the security and safety of the entire nation, is located in Langley, Virginia, a suburb just outside of the nation's capital, which is Washington, D.C.

    _____

    _____

2. The agency that is known as the U.S. Central Intelligence Agency grew out of what was called the Office of Strategic Services, an organization founded in the year 1942 to gather strategic information important and useful in fighting the Second World War.

    _____

    _____

3. The president of the United States of America during 1947, Harry S. Truman, was the president who signed the act known as the National Security Act,

which specifically called out and created the U.S. Central Intelligence Agency by name.

_____

_____

4. The act that gave the U.S. Central Intelligence Agency its name and purpose also created a position known as the Director of Central Intelligence who acted as the main person who advised the president of the United States on matters that involved or related to security affecting the nation.

_____

_____

5. In the year 2004, the 108th Congress, which includes both the Senate and the House of Representatives, passed an act called the Intelligence Reform and Terrorism Prevention Act of 2004 that amended the National Security Act to create a Director of National Intelligence who took over the presidential advisor position formerly held by the Director of Central Intelligence.

_____

_____

_____

Vary Your Sentences

One aspect of effective writing is to vary your sentences. If every sentence follows the same pattern, writing may become monotonous. This chapter explains four ways you can create variety and interest in your writing style. The first two ways involve coordination and subordination—important techniques for achieving different kinds of emphasis.

The following are four methods you can use to make your sentences more varied and more sophisticated:

- Add a second complete thought (coordination).
- Add a dependent thought (subordination).
- Begin with a special opening word or phrase.
- Place adjectives or verbs in a series.

Revise by Adding a Second Complete Thought (Coordination)

When you add a second complete thought to a simple sentence, the result is a *compound* (or double) sentence. The two complete statements in a compound sentence are usually connected by a comma plus a joining, or *coordinating,* word (*and, but, for, or, nor, so, yet*).

Use a compound sentence when you want to give equal weight to two closely related ideas. The technique of showing that ideas have equal importance is called *coordination*. Following are some compound sentences. Each contains two ideas that the writer regards as equal in importance.

The Roman Colosseum was the site where gladiatorial contests once took place, but it is now a major tourist attraction.

I repeatedly failed the math quizzes, so I decided to drop the course.

Darrell turned all the lights off, and then he locked the office door.

ACTIVITY 7   Combine the following pairs of simple sentences into compound sentences. Use a comma and a logical joining word (*and, but, for, so, yet*) to connect each pair.

 HINT   If you are not sure what *and, but, for,* and *so* mean, see pages 384–385.

EXAMPLE

- The cars crept along slowly.
- Visibility was poor in the heavy fog.

   The cars crept along slowly, for visibility was poor in the heavy fog.

   _____

1. • The Vikings sailed as far west as North America.
   • They built cities as far east as Russia.

   _____

   _____

2. • George Washington did not have an extensive military education.
   • When he became general of the Continental Army, he got some on-the-job training.

   _____

   _____

3. • The Wailing Wall in Jerusalem is an important religious site for Jews.
   • It is visited by people of all faiths.

   _____

   _____

4. • Mold grew on my leather boots.
    • The closet was warm and humid.

    _____

    _____

5. • My father has a high cholesterol count.
    • He continues to eat red meat almost every day.

    _____

    _____

Revise by Adding a Dependent Thought (Subordination)

When you add a dependent thought to a simple sentence, the result is a complex sentence.* A dependent thought begins with a word or phrase such as one of the following.

Dependent Words

after	if, even if	when, whenever
although, though	in order that	where, wherever
as	since	whether
because	that, so that	which, whichever
before	unless	while
even though	until	who, whoever
how	what, whatever	whose

A *complex* sentence is used to emphasize one idea over another. Look at the following complex sentence:

Although I lowered the thermostat, my heating bill remained high.

The idea that the writer wants to emphasize here—*my heating bill remained high*—is expressed as a complete thought. The less important idea—*Although I lowered my thermostat*—is subordinated to this complete thought. The technique of giving one idea less emphasis than another is called *subordination*.

---

*The two parts of a complex sentence are sometimes called an *independent clause* and a *dependent clause*. A *clause* is simply a word group that contains a subject and a verb. An independent clause expresses a complete thought and can stand alone. A dependent clause does not express a complete thought in itself and "depends on" the independent clause to complete its meaning. Dependent clauses always begin with a dependent, or subordinating, word.

Following are other examples of complex sentences. In each case, the part starting with the dependent word is the less emphasized part of the sentence.

Even though I was tired, I stayed up to watch the horror movie.

Before I take a bath, I check for spiders in the tub.

When Vera feels nervous, she pulls on her earlobe.

ACTIVITY 8

Use logical subordinating words to combine the following pairs of simple sentences into sentences that contain a dependent thought. Place a comma after a dependent statement when it starts the sentence.

EXAMPLE

Drew Carey is the host of *The Price is Right*.

He wrote and acted in *The Drew Carey Show*.

Before Drew Carey became the host of The Price is Right, he wrote and acted in

The Drew Carey Show.

1. Ronald Reagan started his career as a radio announcer.
    He ended it by holding the highest office in the land.

    _____

    _____

2. Hugh Jackman became famous as Wolverine of the *X-Men* movies.
    He once made a living as Coco the Clown, performing at children's parties.

    _____

    _____

3. Michael Bloomberg is the 108th mayor of New York City and a very wealthy man.
    He was once a parking lot attendant.

    _____

    _____

4. Barack Obama was an Illinois senator.
    He became the 44th president in 2009.

    _____

    _____

5. Alan Rickman starred as Severus Snape in the *Harry Potter* films.

    A new generation of fans was introduced to this well-respected actor.

    _____

    _____

Revise by Beginning with a Special Opening Word or Phrase

Among the special openers that can be used to start sentences are (1) *-ed* words, (2) *-ing* words, (3) *-ly* words, (4) *to* word groups, and (5) prepositional phrases. Here are examples of all five kinds of openers:

-ed word

Tired from a long day of work, Sharon fell asleep on the sofa.

-ing word

Using a thick towel, Mel dried his hair quickly.

-ly word

Reluctantly, I agreed to rewrite the paper.

to word group

To get to the church on time, you must leave now.

prepositional phrase

With Fred's help, Martha planted the evergreen shrubs.

Combine each pair of simple sentences into one sentence by using the opener shown at the left and omitting repeated words. Use a comma to set off the opener from the rest of the sentence.

ACTIVITY 9

EXAMPLE

-ing word
- The toaster refused to pop up.
- It buzzed like an angry hornet.

  Buzzing like an angry hornet, the toaster refused to pop up.

  _____

1. • In 1980, the U.S. Olympic hockey team was determined to take the gold medal.
   • It beat the Soviet team, which was rated the world's finest.

   _____

   _____

-ed word

-*ing* word | 2. • The star player glided down the court.
  • He dribbled the basketball like a pro.

_____

_____

-*ly* word | 3. • No pedestrians were hurt when a large chunk of ice fell from the roof of the building.
  • That was lucky.

_____

_____

to word group | 4. • The little boy likes to annoy his parents.
  • He pretends not to hear them.

_____

_____

prepositional phrase | 5. • People must wear rubber-soled shoes.
  • They must do this in the gym.

_____

_____

Revise by Placing Adjectives or Verbs in a Series

Various parts of a sentence may be placed in a series. Among these parts are adjectives (descriptive words) and verbs. Here are examples of both in a series.

Adjectives

The *black, smeary* newsprint rubbed off on my *new butcher-block* table.

Verbs

The quarterback *fumbled* the ball, *recovered* it, and *sighed* with relief.

ACTIVITY 10

In each group, combine the simple sentences into one sentence by using adjectives or verbs in a series and by omitting repeated words. In most cases, use a comma between the adjectives or verbs in a series.

EXAMPLE

• Before Christmas, I made fruitcakes.
• I decorated the house.
• I wrapped dozens of toys.

Before Christmas, I made fruitcakes, decorated the house, and wrapped

dozens of toys.

1. • The latte was steaming.
   • The latte was hot.
   • The latte was foamy.
   • The latte burned the roof of my mouth.

2. • The first Starbucks coffee shop opened in 1971.
   • The coffee shop was located in Seattle.
   • The coffee shop sold roasted beans.
   • The coffee shop did not brew or serve coffee.

3. • George Washington Carver was born into slavery.
   • He became an inventor.
   • He became an agricultural chemist.
   • He became an expert on successful farming practices.

4. • Alexander Hamilton was a soldier.
   • He fought in the American Revolutionary War.
   • He was a Founding Father.
   • He was the first Secretary of the Treasury of the United States.

5. • Al Capone was a gangster.
   • He lived in Chicago.
   • He made money by running gambling rackets.
   • He made money by running bootlegging rackets.
   • He played an infamous role in the St. Valentine's Day Massacre.

Editing Sentences

After revising sentences in a paragraph so that they flow smoothly and clearly, you need to edit the paragraph for mistakes in grammar, punctuation, mechanics, usage, and spelling. Even if a paragraph is otherwise well written, it will make an unfavorable impression on readers if it contains such mistakes. To edit a paragraph, check it against the agreed-upon rules or conventions of written English—simply called *sentence skills* in this book. Here are the most common of these conventions:

> ✓ Write complete sentences rather than fragments.
> ✓ Do not write run-ons.
> ✓ Use verb forms correctly.
> ✓ Make sure that subject, verbs, and pronouns agree.
> ✓ Eliminate faulty modifiers.
> ✓ Use pronoun forms correctly.
> ✓ Use capital letters where needed.
> ✓ Use the following marks of punctuation correctly: apostrophe, quotation marks, comma, semicolon, colon, hyphen, dash, parentheses.
> ✓ Use correct manuscript form.
> ✓ Eliminate slang, clichés, and pretentious words.
> ✓ Check for possible spelling errors.
> ✓ Eliminate careless errors.

These sentence skills are treated in detail in Part 4 of this book, and they can be referred to easily as needed. Both the list of sentence skills on the inside back cover and the correction symbols on page 542 include page references so that you can turn quickly to any skill you want to check.

Tips for Editing

Here are four tips that can help you edit the next-to-final draft of a paragraph for sentence-skills mistakes:

1. Have at hand two essential tools: a good dictionary (see page 490) and a grammar handbook (you can use the one in this book on pages 357–542).

2. Use a sheet of paper to cover your paragraph so that you will expose only one sentence at a time. Look for errors in grammar, spelling, and typing. It may help to read each sentence out loud. If a sentence does not read clearly and smoothly, chances are something is wrong.

3. Pay special attention to the kinds of errors you tend to make. For example, if you tend to write run-ons or fragments, be on the lookout for those errors.

4. Try to work on a printed draft, where you'll be able to see your writing more objectively than you can on a handwritten page or computer screen; use a pen with colored ink so that your corrections will stand out.

A Note on Proofreading

Proofreading means checking the final, edited draft of your paragraph closely for typos and other careless errors. An effective strategy is to read your paper backward, from the last sentence to the first. This helps keep you from getting caught up in the flow of the paper and missing small mistakes. Here are six useful proofing symbols.

Proofing Symbol	Meaning	Example
^	insert missing letter or word	belíeve
ℒ	omit	in the ~~the~~ meantime
∽	reverse order of words or letters	once a upon time
#	add space	alltogether
⌒	close up space	foot ball
cap lc /	add a capital (or a lowercase) letter	My persian Cat

If you have to make a lot of corrections, type in the corrections and reprint the page.

In the spaces below this paragraph, write the numbers of the ten word groups that contain fragments or run-ons. Then, in the spaces between the lines, edit by making the necessary corrections. One is done for you as an example.

ACTIVITY 11

Academic

¹Two groups of researchers have concluded that "getting cold" has little to do with "catching a cold." ²When the experiment was done for the first time, ³Researchers exposed more than four hundred people to the cold

continued

virus, 4Then divided those people into three groups. 5One group, wearing winter coats, sat around in ten-degree temperature. the second group was placed in sixty-degree temperature, 6With the third group staying in a room, 7Where it was eighty degrees. 8The number of people who actually caught colds was the same, 9In each group. 10Other researchers repeated this experiment ten years later. 11This time they kept some subjects cozy and warm they submerged others in a tank filled with water, 12Whose temperature had been lowered to seventy-five degrees. 13They made others sit around in their underwear in forty-degree temperature. 14The results were the same, the subjects got sick at the same rate. 15Proving that people who get cold do not always get colds.

1. ___2___   2. _____   3. _____   4. _____   5. _____

6. _____   7. _____   8. _____   9. _____   10. _____

 A series of editing tests appears on pages 528–541. You will probably find it most helpful to take these tests after reviewing the sentence-skills handbook in Part 4.

Practice in Revising Sentences

You now know the fourth step in effective writing: revising and editing sentences. You also know that practice in *editing* sentences is best undertaken after you have worked through the sentence skills in Part 4. The focus in this closing section, then, will be on *revising* your work—using a variety of methods to ensure that your sentences flow smoothly and are clear and interesting. You will work through review tests that cover the following topics:

- Using parallelism
- Using a consistent point of view
- Using specific words
- Using concise wording
- Varying your sentences

Using Parallelism

Cross out the unbalanced part of each sentence. In the space provided, revise the unbalanced part so that it matches the other item or items in the sentence. One is done for you as an example.

EXAMPLE

The professor warned his students that he would give surprise tests, ~~the assignment of term papers~~, and allow no makeup exams.

assign term papers

1. As the elderly woman climbed the long staircase, she breathed hard and was grabbing the railing tightly.

2. Making a big dinner is a lot more fun than to clean up after it.

3. Many people want a career that pays high wages, provides a complete benefits package, and offering opportunities for promotion.

4. Many of today's action movies have attractive actors, fantastic special effects, and dialogue that is ridiculous.

5. The neighborhood group asked the town council to repair the potholes and that a traffic signal be installed.

6. Pesky mosquitoes, humidity that is high, and sweltering heat make summer unpleasant in Louisiana.

7. Penicillin, the first wonder drug, has many uses: to treat syphilis, to fight bacterial infections in wounds, and even curing eye and ear infections.

8. The state of Georgia offers a varied landscape with the Blue Ridge Mountains in the north and the Okefenokee Swamp is found in the south.

9. The old historic house had a broken garage door, shutters that were peeling, and a crumbling chimney.

_____

10. In the early nineteenth century, Newburyport, Massachusetts, was a ship-building center, a trade and commerce port, and a city where there were many fine ship captains' homes.

_____

Using a Consistent Point of View

REVIEW TEST 2

In the following passage, change verbs as needed so that they are consistently in the past tense. Cross out each incorrect verb and write the correct form above it, as shown in the example. You will need to make nine corrections.

Late one rainy night, Mei Ling woke to the sound of steady dripping.
When she got out of bed to investigate, a drop of cold water ~~splashes~~ _splashed_
onto her arm. She looks up just in time to see another drop form on the
ceiling, hang suspended for a moment, and fall to the carpet. Stumbling
to the kitchen, Mei Ling reaches deep into one of the cabinets and lifts
out a large roasting pan. As she did so, pot lids and baking tins clattered
out and crash onto the counter. Mei Ling ignored them, stumbled back
to the bedroom, and places the pan on the floor under the drip. But a
minute after sliding her icy feet under the covers, Mei Ling realized she
is in trouble. The sound of each drop hitting the metal pan echoed like a
gunshot in the quiet room. Mei Ling feels like crying, but she finally thought
of a solution. She got out of bed and returns a minute later with a thick
bath towel. She lined the pan with the towel and crawls back into bed.

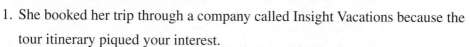

REVIEW TEST 3

Cross out the inconsistent pronouns in the following sentences and revise by writing the correct form of the pronoun above each crossed-out word.

EXAMPLE

    Melissa saved her money so ~~you~~ *she* could take a dream vacation.

1. She booked her trip through a company called Insight Vacations because the tour itinerary piqued your interest.

2. While traveling through England, Melissa asked her tour guide if you would be able to see the Tower of London from her hotel room.

3. The RHS Chelsea Flower Show was the first activity you participated in after everyone got settled into the hotel.

4. When it was time to head to Paris, the tour guide reminded Melissa that you would need to be at the train station at 7:00 a.m.

5. The guide told the tour group members they should visit the Louvre Museum in Paris because she could get an education in art just by looking at the paintings.

6. Melissa's favorite part of the Louvre was the "From Palace to Museum" visitor trail that took you more than three hours to complete.

7. After experiencing Paris, Melissa was looking forward to the next part of our trip, which was a train ride to Rome.

8. Melissa begged the tour guide to immediately take them and the other group members to the Vatican.

9. As she stood looking at the Vatican, Melissa exclaimed, "This is the most beautiful building you have ever seen!"

10. Melissa spent her final day in Rome eating gelato by the Trevi Fountain and planning the next vacation you could dream about.

Using Specific Words

REVIEW TEST 4

Revise the following sentences, replacing vague, indefinite words with sharp, specific ones.

1. The refrigerator was well stocked with *food*.

    _____

    _____

    _____

2. Lin brought *lots of reading materials* to keep her busy in the hospital waiting room.

_____

_____

3. To do well in school, a student needs *certain qualities.*

_____

_____

4. The table at the wedding reception was full of *a variety of appetizers.*

_____

_____

5. As I grew older and less stupid, I realized that money cannot buy *certain things.*

_____

_____

REVIEW TEST 5

With the help of the methods described on pages 116–117 and summarized below, add specific details to the sentences that follow.

1. Use exact names.
2. Use lively verbs.
3. Use descriptive words (modifiers) before nouns.
4. Use words that relate to the senses—sight, hearing, taste, smell, touch.

1. The movie was good.

_____

_____

2. My exam was hard.

_____

_____

_____

3. His professor is strange.

_____

_____

4. The building is unique.

   _____

   _____

5. The city was crowded.

   _____

   _____

Using Concise Wording

Rewrite the following sentences, omitting needless words.

1. There was this one girl in my class who rarely, if ever, did her homework.

   _____

   _____

2. Judging by the looks of things, it seems to me that it will probably rain very soon.

   _____

   _____

3. Seeing as how the refrigerator is empty of food, I will go to the supermarket in the very near future.

   _____

   _____

4. In this day and age it is almost a certainty that someone you know will be an innocent victim of criminal activity.

   _____

   _____

5. In my personal opinion it is correct to say that the spring season is the most beautiful period of time in the year.

   _____

   _____

Rewrite the following sentences, omitting needless words.

1. Workers who are employed on a part-time basis are attractive to a business because they do not have to be paid as much as full-time workers for a business.

   _____

   _____

2. During the time that I was sick and out of school, I missed a total of three math tests.

   _____

   _____

3. The game, which was scheduled for later today, has been canceled by the officials because of the rainy weather.

   _____

   _____

4. At this point in time, I am quite undecided and unsure about just which classes I will take during this coming semester.

   _____

   _____

5. An inconsiderate person located in the apartment next to mine keeps her radio on too loud a good deal of the time, with the result being that it is disturbing to everyone in the neighboring apartments.

   _____

   _____

Varying Your Sentences

Using coordination, subordination, or both, combine each of the following groups of simple sentences into one longer sentence. Omit repeated words. Various combinations are possible, so for each group, try to find the combination that flows most smoothly and clearly.

1. • My grandmother is eighty-six.
   • She drives to Florida alone every year.

- She believes in being self-reliant.

_____

_____

2. • Dr. Martin Luther King, Jr. was a Baptist minister.
   • He led the Southern Christian Leadership Conference.
   • He helped create this organization in 1957.

_____

_____

3. • The United States Constitution was adopted in 1787.
   • The Declaration of Independence was written in 1776.
   • Both documents were approved at meetings in Philadelphia.

_____

_____

4. • A volcano erupts.
   • It sends tons of ash into the air.
   • This creates flaming orange sunsets.

_____

_____

5. • A telephone rings late at night.
   • We answer it fearfully.
   • It could bring tragic news.

_____

_____

REVIEW TEST 9

Using coordination, subordination, or both, combine each of the following groups of simple sentences into two longer sentences. Omit repeated words. Various combinations are possible, so for each group, try to find the combination that flows most smoothly and clearly.

1. • Wendy pretended not to overhear her coworkers.
   • She couldn't stop listening.
   • She felt deeply embarrassed.

• They were criticizing her work.

_____

_____

_____

2. • Tony got home from the shopping mall.
   • He discovered that his rented tuxedo did not fit.
   • The jacket sleeves covered his hands.
   • The pants cuffs hung over his shoes.

_____

_____

_____

3. • The boys waited for the bus.
   • The wind shook the flimsy shelter.
   • They shivered with cold.
   • They were wearing thin jackets.

_____

_____

_____

4. • The First Amendment to the United States Constitution guarantees
     freedom of religion.
   • It also guarantees freedom of assembly.
   • Other rights it guarantees are freedom of speech and freedom of the press.

_____

_____

_____

5. • Gary was leaving the store.
   • The shoplifting alarm went off.
   • He had not stolen anything.
   • The clerk had forgotten to remove the magnetic tag.
   • The tag was on a shirt Gary had bought.

_____

_____

_____

REVIEW TEST 10

PART A

Combine the simple sentences into one sentence by using the opener shown in the margin and omitting repeated words. Use a comma to set off the opener from the rest of the sentence.

1. • We were exhausted from four hours of hiking.

   • We decided to stop for the day.

   _____

   _____   *-ed* word

2. • Gus was staring out the window.

   • He didn't hear the instructor call on him.

   _____

   _____   *-ing* word

3. • The surgeon closed the incision of the patient on whom she had just operated.

   • She was careful when she did this.

   _____

   _____   *-ly* word

4. • Steve traveled to Cairo, Egypt.

   • He wanted to see the Great Pyramid.

   _____

   _____   *to* word group

5. • Joanne goes online to e-mail her friends.

   • She does this during her lunch breaks.

   _____

   _____   prepositional phrase

PART B

Combine the simple sentences in each group into one sentence by using adjectives or verbs in a series and by omitting repeated words. In most cases, use a comma between the adjectives or verbs in a series.

6. • The photographer waved a teddy bear at the baby.

   • He made a funny face.

- He quacked like a duck.

_____

_____

7. • The bucket held a bunch of daisies.
   • The bucket was shiny.
   • The bucket was aluminum.
   • The daisies were fresh.
   • The daisies were white.

_____

_____

8. • Amy poured herself a cup of coffee.
   • She pulled her hair back into a ponytail.
   • She opened her textbook.
   • She sat down at her desk.
   • She fell asleep.

_____

_____

9. • The box in the dresser drawer was stuffed with letters.
   • The box was cardboard.
   • The dresser drawer was locked.
   • The letters were faded.
   • The letters were about love.

_____

_____

10. • The speaker was eloquent.
    • The speaker was learned.
    • He moved to the podium.
    • The podium was on the stage of the auditorium.
    • The auditorium was crowded.

_____

_____

Four Bases for Revising Writing

This chapter will show you how to evaluate a paragraph for

- unity
- support
- coherence
- sentence skills

HOW DO YOU KNOW WHEN TO ACCEPT ADVICE?

Very often, our own interests and goals are different from those our friends and family want for us. Write a paragraph about a time you "did your own thing" instead of following the advice of someone close to you. Why did you make the decision you did? How did the other person react? Looking back, do you still feel you made the right decision?

This chapter discusses the four bases—unity, support, coherence, and sentence skills—and shows how these four bases can be used to evaluate and revise a paragraph. The box on the next page, originally presented in Chapter 2, is helpful in illustrating how you can use the four bases to evaluate your writing and make decisions about revising.

Four Steps $\longrightarrow$	Four Bases
1. If you make one point and stick to that point,	your writing will have *unity*.
2. If you back up the point with specific evidence,	your writing will have *support*.
3. If you organize and connect the specific evidence,	your writing will have *coherence*.
4. If you write clear, error-free sentences,	your writing will demonstrate effective *sentence skills*.

Base 1: Unity

Understanding Unity

The following two paragraphs were written by students on the topic "Why Students Drop Out of College." Read them and decide which one makes its point more clearly and effectively, and why.

PARAGRAPH A

Why Students Drop Out

Students drop out of college for many reasons. First of all, some students are bored in school. These students may enter college expecting nonstop fun or a series of fascinating courses. When they find out that college is often routine, they quickly lose interest. They do not want to take dull required courses or spend their nights studying, so they drop out. Students also drop out of college because the work is harder than they thought it would be. These students may have made decent grades in high school simply by showing up for class. In college, however, they may have to prepare for two-hour exams, write fifteen-page term papers, or make detailed presentations to a class. The hard work comes as a shock, and students give up. Perhaps the most common reason students drop out is that they are having personal or emotional problems. Younger students, especially, may be attending college at an age when they are

continued

also feeling confused, lonely, or depressed. These students may have problems with roommates, family, boyfriends, or girlfriends. They become too unhappy to deal with both hard academic work and emotional troubles. For many types of students, dropping out seems to be the only solution they can imagine.

PARAGRAPH B

Student Dropouts

There are three main reasons students drop out of college. Some students, for one thing, are not really sure they want to be in school and lack the desire to do the work. When exams come up, or when a course requires a difficult project or term paper, these students will not do the required studying or research. Eventually, they may drop out because their grades are so poor they are about to flunk out anyway. Such students sometimes come back to school later with a completely different attitude about school. Other students drop out for financial reasons. The pressures of paying tuition, buying textbooks, and possibly having to support themselves can be overwhelming. These students can often be helped by the school because financial aid is available, and some schools offer work-study programs. Finally, students drop out because they have personal problems. They cannot concentrate on their courses because they are unhappy at home, they are lonely, or they are having trouble with boyfriends or girlfriends. Instructors should suggest that such troubled students see counselors or join support groups. If instructors would take a more personal interest in their students, more students would make it through troubled times.

Fill in the blanks: Paragraph _____ makes its point more clearly and effectively

because _____

_____

_____

ACTIVITY 1

Paragraph A is more effective because it is *unified.* All the details in paragraph A are *on target;* they support and develop the single point expressed in the first sentence—that students drop out of college for many reasons.

On the other hand, paragraph B contains some details irrelevant to the opening point—that there are three main reasons students drop out. These details should be omitted in the interest of paragraph unity. Go back to paragraph B and cross out the sections that are off target—the sections that do not support the opening idea.

You should have crossed out the following sections: "Such students sometimes . . . attitude about school"; "These students can often . . . work-study programs"; and "Instructors should suggest . . . through troubled times."

The difference between these two paragraphs leads us to the first base, or standard, of effective writing: *unity*. To achieve unity is to have all the details in your paragraph related to the single point expressed in the topic sentence, the first sentence. Each time you think of something to put in, ask yourself whether it relates to your main point. If it does not, leave it out. For example, if you were writing about a certain job as the worst job you ever had and then spent a couple of sentences talking about the interesting people you met there on that job, you would be missing the first and most essential base of good writing.

Checking for Unity

To check a paragraph for unity, ask yourself these questions:

1. Is there a clear opening statement of the point of the paragraph?
2. Is all the material on target in support of the opening point?

Base 2: Support

Understanding Support

The following student paragraphs were written on the topic "An Important Book." Both are unified, but one communicates more clearly and effectively. Which one, and why?

PARAGRAPH A

Controversial Adventures

The Adventures of Huckleberry Finn by Mark Twain has been causing controversy since it was written. When first printed in 1885, Twain's book was considered as nothing more than garbage with absolutely no moral

continued

or literary value. In fact, the Concord Public Library refused to shelve the book after the library committee met and agreed that "it contain[ed] but little humor . . . of a very coarse type . . . being more suited to the slums than to intelligent, respectable people." Later, many claimed that the book glamorized juvenile delinquency. Huckleberry Finn is a runaway who engages in many questionable activities while harboring a fugitive. Since the 1960s, however, it is the language in *Huckleberry Finn* that has caused the most offense. In fact, in 2011, *Publisher's Weekly* released a story about a new edition that eliminated the offending language in order to create a "more politically correct" version. Regardless of the controversy, *The Adventures of Huckleberry Finn* will continue to be read by future generations.

PARAGRAPH B

Controversial Adventures

The Adventures of Huckleberry Finn by Mark Twain has been causing controversy since it was first written. In fact, since its publication, Twain's book has never been without controversy and detractors. When first printed in 1885, the book was considered as nothing more than garbage with absolutely no moral or literary value. In the 1900s, many claimed that the book glamorized juvenile delinquency and this caused a great deal of concern. Since the 1960s, however, most people have been offended by the use of language in Huckleberry Finn. Regardless of the controversy, *The Adventures of Huckleberry Finn* will continue to be read by future generations.

Fill in the blanks: Paragraph _____ makes its point more clearly and effectively

because _____

_____

_____

ACTIVITY 2

Paragraph A is more effective, for it offers specific examples that explain the controversial history that the novel has experienced.

Paragraph B, on the other hand, gives no specific evidence. The writer makes several statements about possible reasons that the novel has been controversial, but doesn't support those statements with evidence. Why was it considered garbage? How did it glamorize juvenile delinquency? Why is the language offensive? We are interested about the novel's history, but without the specific details, we cannot understand it.

Consideration of these two paragraphs leads us to the second base of effective writing: *support*. After realizing the importance of specific supporting details, one student writer revised a paragraph she had done on a restaurant job as the worst job she ever had. In the revised paragraph, instead of talking about "unsanitary conditions in the kitchen," she referred to such specifics as "green mold on the bacon" and "ants in the potato salad." All your paragraphs should include many vivid details!

Checking for Support

To check a paragraph for support, ask yourself these questions:

1. Is there *specific* evidence to support the opening point?
2. Is there *enough* specific evidence?

Base 3: Coherence

Understanding Coherence

The following two paragraphs were written on the topic "The Best or Worst Job You Ever Had." Both are unified and both are supported. However, one communicates more clearly and effectively. Which one, and why?

PARAGRAPH A

Pantry Helper

My worst job was as a pantry helper in one of San Diego's well-known restaurants. I had an assistant from three to six in the afternoon who did little but stand around and eat the whole time she was there. She would listen for the sound of the back door opening, which was a sure sign the boss was coming in. The boss would testily say to me, "You've got a lot of things to do here, Alice. Try to get a move on." I would come in at two o'clock to relieve the woman on the morning shift. If her day was busy, that meant I would have to prepare salads,

continued

slice meat and cheese, and so on. Orders for sandwiches and cold platters would come in and have to be prepared. The worst thing about the job was that the heat in the kitchen, combined with my nerves, would give me an upset stomach by seven o'clock almost every night. I might be going to the storeroom to get some supplies, and one of the waitresses would tell me she wanted a bacon, lettuce, and tomato sandwich on white toast. I would put the toast in and head for the supply room, and a waitress would holler out that her customer was in a hurry. Green flies would come in through the torn screen in the kitchen window and sting me. I was getting paid only $7.05 an hour. At five o'clock, when the dinner rush began, I would be dead tired. Roaches scurried in all directions whenever I moved a box or picked up a head of lettuce to cut.

PARAGRAPH B

My Worst Job

The worst job I ever had was as a waiter at the Westside Inn. First of all, many of the people I waited on were rude. When a baked potato was hard inside or a salad was flat or their steak wasn't just the way they wanted it, they blamed me, rather than the kitchen. Or they would ask me to light their cigarettes, or chase flies from their tables, or even take their children to the bathroom. Also, I had to contend not only with the customers but with the kitchen staff as well. The cooks and busboys were often undependable and surly. If I didn't treat them just right, I would wind up having to apologize to customers because their meals came late or their water glasses weren't filled. Another reason I didn't like the job was that I was always moving. Because of the constant line at the door, as soon as one group left, another would take its place. I usually had only a twenty-minute lunch break and a ten-minute break in almost nine hours of work. I think I could have put up with the job if I had been able to pause and rest more often. The last and most important reason I hated the job was my boss. She played favorites, giving some of the waiters and waitresses the best-tipping repeat customers and preferences on holidays. She would hover around during my break to make sure I didn't take a second more than the allotted time. And even when I helped out by working through a break, she never had an appreciative word but would just tell me not to be late for work the next day.

ACTIVITY 3

Fill in the blanks: Paragraph _____ makes its point more clearly and effectively because _____

_____

_____

Paragraph B is more effective because the material is organized clearly and logically. Using emphatic order, the writer gives us a list of four reasons why the job was so bad: rude customers, an unreliable kitchen staff, constant motion, and—most of all—an unfair boss. Further, the writer includes transitional words that act as signposts, making movement from one idea to the next easy to follow. The major transitions are *First of all, Also, Another reason,* and *The last and most important reason.*

While paragraph A is unified and supported, the writer does not have any clear and consistent way of organizing the material. Partly, emphatic order is used, but this is not made clear by transitions or by saving the most important reason for last. Partly, time order is used, but it moves inconsistently from two to seven to five o'clock.

These two paragraphs lead us to the third base of effective writing: *coherence.* The supporting ideas and sentences in a composition must be organized so that they cohere, or "stick together." As has already been mentioned, key techniques for tying material together are a clear method of organization (such as time order or emphatic order), transitions, and other connecting words.

Checking for Coherence

To check a paragraph for coherence, ask yourself these questions:

1. Does the paragraph have a clear method of organization?
2. Are transitions and other connecting words used to tie the material together?

Base 4: Sentence Skills

Understanding Sentence Skills

Two versions of a paragraph follow. Both are unified, supported, and organized, but one version communicates more clearly and effectively. Which one, and why?

PARAGRAPH A

Social Not-Working

¹The workplace environment is being affected by social networking sites such as Facebook, Twitter, and Pinterest. ²First, most people don't consider it a negative habit to check Twitter during the work day, but it is actually stealing. ³People who constantly check Twitter when they should be working are stealing time from the company. ⁴If, for example, Sam gets paid ten dollars an hour and he spends one hour a week looking at Twitter, he is being paid for one hour that he is not working. ⁵In other words, he is stealing ten dollars a week from the company. ⁶Over the course of a year, that could add up to more than five hundred dollars. ⁷Second, people who use company computers to check Pinterest during the workday are misusing company equipment. ⁸Although it might seem harmless, this use of company equipment is no different from driving a company car or using company furniture for personal reasons; maintenance, service, and upgrades cost and must be budgeted. ⁹Taking a company car on a personal trip or borrowing company furniture to decorate a house are forbidden; most companies don't allow personal use of company computers either. ¹⁰In addition, many company computers contain private and sensitive material that could be compromised if an employee is on a social networking site. ¹¹Finally, people who check Facebook during work hours can lose focus on their work, causing delays and poor performance. ¹²Something exciting or disturbing that is posted could have an impact on the employee, and his or her ability to work could be affected. ¹³Although people like to stay connected with each other during the day, company employees need to limit their use of social networking sites to private equipment during lunch hours, breaks, or non-working hours.

PARAGRAPH B

"Social Not-Working"

¹The workplace environment is being affected by social networking sites such as Facebook, Twitter, and Pinterest. ²First, most people doesn't consider it a negative habit to check Twitter during the workday, but it is actually stealing. ³People who constantly check Twitter when they should be working are stealing time from the company. ⁴If, for example, Sam gets paid ten dollars an hour and he spends one hour a week looking

continued

at Twitter he is being paid for one hour that he is not working. ⁵In other words, stealing ten dollars a week from the company. ⁶Over the course of a year, that could add up to more than five hundred dollars. ⁷Second, people who be using company computers to check Pinterest during the workday are misusing company equipment. ⁸Although it might seem harmless, this use of company equipment is no different from to drive a company car or using company furniture for personal reasons; maintenance, service, and upgrades cost and must be budgeted. ⁹Taking a company car on a personal trip or borrowing company furniture to decorate a house are forbidden; most companies dont allow personal use of company computers either. ¹⁰In addition, many company computers contain private and sensitive material that could be compromised if an employee is on a social networking site. ¹¹Finally, people who check Facebook during work hours can zone out, causing delays and poor performance. ¹²Something exciting or disturbing that is posted could have an impact on the employee, his or her ability to work could be affected. ¹³Although people like to stay connected with each other during the day, company employees need to limit their use of social networking sites to private equipment during lunch hours, breaks, or non-working hours.

ACTIVITY 4

Fill in the blanks: Paragraph _____ makes its point more clearly and effectively because _____

_____

_____

Paragraph A is more effective because it incorporates *sentence skills,* the fourth base of competent writing.

ACTIVITY 5

See if you can identify the ten sentence-skills mistakes in paragraph B. Do this, first of all, by going back and underlining the ten spots in paragraph B that differ in wording or punctuation from paragraph A. Then identify the ten sentence-skills mistakes by circling what you feel is the correct answer in each of the following ten statements.

HINT   Comparing paragraph B with the correct version may help you guess correct answers even if you are not familiar with the names of certain skills.

1. The title should not be set off with
   a. capital letters.
   b. quotation marks.
2. In word group 2, there is a
   a. mistake in parallelism.
   b. dangling modifier.
   c. mistake in subject-verb agreement.
   d. sentence fragment.
3. In word group 4, there is a
   a. missing comma.
   b. sentence fragment.
   c. mistake in subject-verb agreement.
   d. mistake involving an irregular verb.
4. In word group 5, there is a
   a. missing comma.
   b. missing apostrophe.
   c. sentence fragment.
   d. dangling modifier.
5. In word group 7, there is a
   a. nonstandard English verb.
   b. run-on.
   c. comma mistake.
   d. missing capital letter.
6. In word group 8, there is a
   a. misplaced modifier.
   b. dangling modifier.
   c. mistake in parallelism.
   d. run-on.
7. In word group 9, there is a
   a. missing apostrophe.
   b. missing quotation mark.
   c. mistake involving an irregular verb.
   d. missing capital latter.
8. In word group 11, there is a
   a. mistake involving an irregular verb.
   b. sentence fragment.
   c. mistake in subject-verb agreement.
   d. slang phrase.
9. In word group 12, there is a
   a. sentence fragment.
   b. run-on.
   c. missing apostrophe.
   d. dangling modifier.
10. In word group 13, there is a
    a. mistake in parallelism.
    b. mistake involving an irregular verb.
    c. sentence fragment.
    d. missing capital letter.

You should have chosen the following answers:

1. b   2. c   3. a   4. c   5. a
6. c   7. a   8. d   9. b   10. d

Part 4 of this book explains these and other sentence skills. You should review all the skills carefully. Doing so will ensure that you know the most important rules of grammar, punctuation, and usage—rules needed to write clear, error-free sentences.

Checking for Sentence Skills

Sentence skills and the other bases of effective writing are summarized in the following chart and on the inside back cover of the book.

A Summary of the Four Bases of Effective Writing

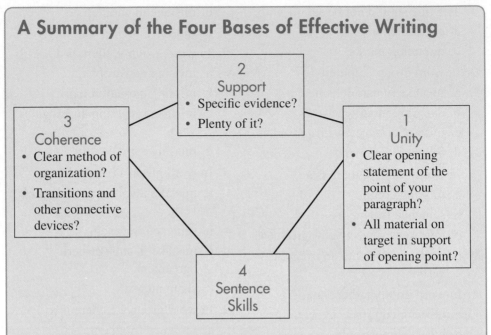

**2
Support**
- Specific evidence?
- Plenty of it?

**3
Coherence**
- Clear method of organization?
- Transitions and other connective devices?

**1
Unity**
- Clear opening statement of the point of your paragraph?
- All material on target in support of opening point?

**4
Sentence Skills**

- Fragments eliminated? (page 367)
- Run-ons eliminated? (381)
- Correct verb forms? (402)
- Subject and verb agreement? (410)
- Faulty modifiers eliminated? (433)
- Faulty pronouns eliminated? (416; 422)
- Capital letters used correctly? (447)
- Punctuation marks where needed?
  a. Apostrophes (460)
  b. Quotation marks (468)
  c. Commas (476)
  d. Semicolons; colons (485)
  e. Hyphens; dashes (485)
  f. Parentheses (485)
- Correct paper format? (442)
- Needless words eliminated? (119; 521)
- Effective word choices? (521)
- Possible spelling errors checked? (499)
- Careless errors eliminated through proofreading? (129)
- Sentences varied? (121)

Practice in Using the Four Bases

You are now familiar with four bases, or standards, of effective writing: unity, support, coherence, and sentence skills. In this closing section, you will expand and strengthen your understanding of the four bases as you work through the following activities:

1. Evaluating Scratch Outlines for Unity
2. Evaluating Paragraphs for Unity
3. Evaluating Paragraphs for Support
4. Evaluating Paragraphs for Coherence
5. Revising Paragraphs for Coherence
6. Evaluating Paragraphs for All Four Bases: Unity, Support, Coherence, and Sentence Skills

1 Evaluating Scratch Outlines for Unity

The best time to check a paragraph for unity is at the outline stage. A scratch outline, as explained on page 25, is one of the best techniques for getting started with a paragraph.

Look at the following scratch outline that one student prepared and then corrected for unity.

I had a depressing weekend.

1.   Hay fever bothered me

2.   Had to pay seventy-seven-dollar car bill

3.   ~~Felt bad~~

4.   Boyfriend and I had a fight

5.   ~~Did poorly in my math test today as a result~~

6.   My mother yelled at me unfairly

Four reasons support the opening statement that the writer was depressed over the weekend. The writer crossed out "Felt bad" because it was not a reason for her depression. (Saying that she felt bad is only another way of saying that she was depressed.) She also crossed out the item about the math test because the point she is supporting is that she was depressed over the weekend.

In each outline, cross out the items that do not support the opening point. These items must be omitted in order to achieve paragraph unity.

ACTIVITY 6

1. In 1699, the Pennsylvania Religious Society of Friends argued against the evil of slavery.

   a. Pennsylvania is named after William Penn.

b. They argued that taking someone's freedom is the same as taking his or her life.

c. The wealth that comes from slavery is the product of violence.

d. The Civil War ended slavery in the United States.

e. The Society of Friends denied the claim that the Bible allowed slavery.

2. The twentieth century achieved much toward the control of infectious diseases.

a. Penicillin and other antibacterial medicines were discovered.

b. Sanitary sewer systems were built in many cities.

c. School lunch programs offered low-cost meals to students.

d. Many communities developed water purification systems.

e. More was learned about psychological diseases.

3. There are several ways to get better mileage in your car.

a. Check air pressure in tires regularly.

b. Drive at no more than fifty-five miles per hour.

c. Orange and yellow cars are the most visible.

d. Avoid jackrabbit starts at stop signs and traffic lights.

e. Always have duplicate ignition and trunk keys.

4. My swimming instructor helped me overcome my terror of the water.

a. He talked with me about my fears.

b. I was never good at sports.

c. He showed me how to hold my head under water and not panic.

d. I held on to a floating board until I was confident enough to give it up.

e. My instructor was on the swimming team at his college.

5. Fred Wilkes is the best candidate for state governor.

a. He has fifteen years' experience in the state senate.

b. His son is a professional football player.

c. He has helped stop air and water pollution in the state.

d. His opponent has been divorced.

e. He has brought new industries and jobs to the state.

2 Evaluating Paragraphs for Unity

ACTIVITY 7

Each of the following five paragraphs contains sentences that are off target—sentences that do not support the opening point—and so the paragraphs are not unified. In the interest of paragraph unity, such sentences must be omitted.

Cross out the irrelevant sentences and write the numbers of those sentences in the spaces provided. The number of spaces will tell you the number of irrelevant sentences in each paragraph.

1.

A Kindergarten Failure

[1]In kindergarten I experienced the fear of failure that haunts many schoolchildren. [2]My moment of panic occurred on my last day in kindergarten at Charles Foos Public School in Riverside, California. [3]My family lived in California for three years before we moved to Omaha, Nebraska, where my father was a personnel manager for Mutual of Omaha. [4]Our teacher began reading a list of names of all those students who were to line up at the door in order to visit the first-grade classroom. [5]Our teacher was a pleasant-faced woman who had resumed her career after raising her own children. [6]She called off every name but mine, and I was left sitting alone in the class while everyone else left, the teacher included. [7]I sat there in absolute horror. [8]I imagined that I was the first kid in human history who had flunked things like crayons, sandbox, and sliding board. [9]Without getting the teacher's permission, I got up and walked to the bathroom and threw up into a sink. [10]Only when I ran home in tears to my mother did I get an explanation of what had happened. [11]Since I was to go to a parochial school in the fall, I had not been taken with the other children to meet the first-grade teacher at the public school. [12]My moment of terror and shame had been only a misunderstanding.

The numbers of the irrelevant sentences: _____ _____

2.

How to Prevent Cheating

[1]Instructors should take steps to prevent students from cheating on exams. [2]To begin with, instructors should stop reusing old tests. [3]A test that has been used even once is soon known on the student grapevine. [4]Students will check with their friends to find out, for example, what was on Dr. Thompson's biology final last term. [5]They may even manage to find a copy of the test itself, "accidentally" not turned in by a former student of Dr. Thompson's. [6]Instructors should also take some commonsense precautions at test time. [7]They should make students separate themselves—by at least one seat—during an exam, and they should watch the class closely. [8]The best place for the instructor to sit is in the rear of the room, so that a student is never sure if the instructor is looking at him or her. [9]Last of all, instructors must make it clear to students that there will be stiff penalties for cheating. [10]One of the problems with our school systems is a lack of discipline. [11]Instructors never used to give in to students' demands or put up with bad behavior, as they do today. [12]Anyone caught cheating should immediately receive a zero for the exam. [13]A person even suspected of cheating should be forced to take an alternative exam in the instructor's office. [14]Because cheating is unfair to honest students, it should not be tolerated.

The numbers of the irrelevant sentences: _____ _____

3.

Other Uses for Cars

¹Many people who own a car manage to turn the vehicle into a trash can, a clothes closet, or a storage room. ²People who use their cars as trash cans are easily recognized. ³Empty snack bags, hamburger wrappers, pizza cartons, soda cans, and doughnut boxes litter the floor. ⁴On the seats are old scratched CDs, blackened fruit skins, crumpled receipts, crushed cigarette packs, and used tissues. ⁵At least the trash stays in the car, instead of adding to the litter on our highways. ⁶Other people use a car as a clothes closet. ⁷The car contains several pairs of shoes, pants, or shorts, along with a suit or dress that's been hanging on the car's clothes hanger for over a year. ⁸Sweaty, smelly gym clothes will also find a place in the car, a fact passengers quickly discover. ⁹The world would be better off if people showed more consideration of others. ¹⁰Finally, some people use a car as a spare garage or basement. ¹¹In the backseats or trunks of these cars are bags of fertilizer, beach chairs, old textbooks, chainsaws, or window screens that have been there for months. ¹²The trunk may also contain an extra spare tire, a dented hubcap, a gallon container of window washer fluid, and old stereo equipment. ¹³If apartments offered more storage space, probably fewer people would resort to using their cars for such storage purposes. ¹⁴All in all, people get a lot more use out of their cars than simply the miles they travel on the road.

The numbers of the irrelevant sentences: _____   _____   _____

4.

Why Adults Visit Amusement Parks

¹Adults visit amusement parks for several reasons. ²For one thing, an amusement park is a place where it is acceptable to "pig out" on junk food. ³At the park, everyone is drinking soda and eating popcorn, ice cream, or hot dogs. ⁴No one seems to be on a diet, and so buying all the junk food one can eat is a guilt-free experience. ⁵Parks should provide stands where healthier food, such as salads or cold chicken, would be sold. ⁶Another reason people visit amusement parks is to prove themselves. ⁷They want to visit the park that has the newest, scariest ride in order to say that they went on the Parachute Drop, the seven-story Elevator, the Water Chute, or the Death Slide. ⁸Going on a scary ride is a way to feel courageous and adventurous without taking much of a risk. ⁹Some rides, however, can be dangerous. ¹⁰Rides that are not properly inspected or maintained have killed people all over the country. ¹¹A final reason people visit amusement parks is to escape from everyday pressures. ¹²When people are poised at the top of a gigantic roller coaster, they are not thinking of bills, work, or personal problems. ¹³A scary ride empties the mind of all worries—except making it to the bottom alive. ¹⁴Adults at an amusement park may claim they have come for their children, but they are there for themselves as well.

The numbers of the irrelevant sentences: _____ _____ _____

5.

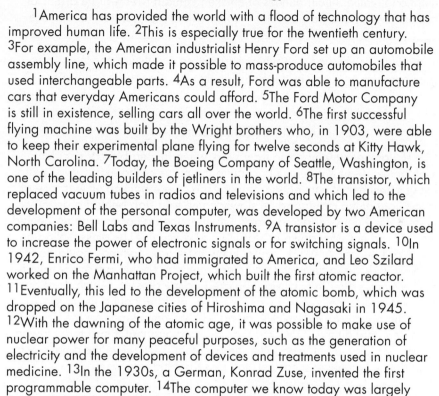

American Technology

[1]America has provided the world with a flood of technology that has improved human life. [2]This is especially true for the twentieth century. [3]For example, the American industrialist Henry Ford set up an automobile assembly line, which made it possible to mass-produce automobiles that used interchangeable parts. [4]As a result, Ford was able to manufacture cars that everyday Americans could afford. [5]The Ford Motor Company is still in existence, selling cars all over the world. [6]The first successful flying machine was built by the Wright brothers who, in 1903, were able to keep their experimental plane flying for twelve seconds at Kitty Hawk, North Carolina. [7]Today, the Boeing Company of Seattle, Washington, is one of the leading builders of jetliners in the world. [8]The transistor, which replaced vacuum tubes in radios and televisions and which led to the development of the personal computer, was developed by two American companies: Bell Labs and Texas Instruments. [9]A transistor is a device used to increase the power of electronic signals or for switching signals. [10]In 1942, Enrico Fermi, who had immigrated to America, and Leo Szilard worked on the Manhattan Project, which built the first atomic reactor. [11]Eventually, this led to the development of the atomic bomb, which was dropped on the Japanese cities of Hiroshima and Nagasaki in 1945. [12]With the dawning of the atomic age, it was possible to make use of nuclear power for many peaceful purposes, such as the generation of electricity and the development of devices and treatments used in nuclear medicine. [13]In the 1930s, a German, Konrad Zuse, invented the first programmable computer. [14]The computer we know today was largely the product of the work of scientists at several American companies and universities, including IBM, Remington Rand, and Harvard University.

The numbers of the irrelevant sentences: _____ _____ _____ _____ _____

3 Evaluating Paragraphs for Support

ACTIVITY 8

The five paragraphs that follow lack sufficient supporting details. In each paragraph, identify the spot or spots where more specific details are needed.

1.

Chicken: Our Best Friend

[1]Chicken is the best-selling meat today for a number of good reasons. [2]First of all, its reasonable cost puts it within everyone's reach. [3]Chicken is popular, too, because it can be prepared in so many different ways.

continued

> 4It can, for example, be cooked by itself, in spaghetti sauce, or with noodles and gravy. 5It can be baked, boiled, broiled, or fried. 6Chicken is also convenient. 7Last and most important, chicken has a high nutritional value. 8Four ounces of chicken contain twenty-eight grams of protein, which is almost half the recommended daily dietary allowance.

Fill in the blanks: The first spot where supporting details are needed occurs after sentence number _____. The second spot occurs after sentence number _____.

2.

> ### A Car Accident
>
> 1I was on my way home from work when my terrible car accident took place. 2As I drove my car around the curve of the expressway exit, I saw a number of cars ahead of me. 3They were backed up because of a red light at the main road. 4I slowly came to a stop behind a dozen or more cars. 5In my rearview mirror, I then noticed a car coming up behind me that did not slow down or stop. 6I had a horrible, helpless feeling as I realized the car would hit me. 7I knew there was nothing I could do to signal the driver in time, nor was there any way I could get away from the car. 8Minutes after the collision, I picked up my glasses, which were on the seat beside me. 9My lip was bleeding, and I got out a tissue to wipe it. 10The police arrived quickly, along with an ambulance for the driver of the car that hit me. 11My car was so damaged that it had to be towed away. 12Today, eight years after the accident, I still relive the details of the experience whenever a car gets too close behind me.

Fill in the blank: The point where details are needed occurs after sentence number _____.

3.

> ### Tips on Bringing Up Children
>
> 1In some ways, children should be treated as mature people. 2For one thing, adults should not use baby talk with children. 3Using real words with children helps them develop language skills more quickly. 4Baby talk makes children feel patronized, frustrated, and confused, for they want to understand and communicate with adults by learning their speech. 5So animals should be called cows and dogs, not "moo-moos" and "bow-wows." 6Second, parents should be consistent when disciplining children. 7For example, if a parent tells a child, "You cannot have dessert unless you put away your toys," it is important that the parent follow through on the warning. 8By being consistent, parents will teach children responsibility

continued

and give them a stable center around which to grow. ⁹Finally, and most important, children should be allowed and encouraged to make simple decisions. ¹⁰Parents will thus be helping their children prepare for the complex decisions that they will have to deal with in later life.

Fill in the blank: The spot where supporting details are needed occurs after sentence number _____.

4.

Being on TV

¹People act a little strangely when a television camera comes their way. ²Some people behave as if a crazy puppeteer were pulling their strings. ³Their arms jerk wildly about, and they begin jumping up and down for no apparent reason. ⁴Often they accompany their body movements with loud screams, squeals, and yelps. ⁵Another group of people engage in an activity known as the cover-up. ⁶They will be calmly watching a sports game or other televised event when they realize the camera is focused on them. ⁷The camera operator can't resist zooming in for a close-up of these people. ⁸Then there are those who practice their funny faces on the unsuspecting public. ⁹They take advantage of the television time to show off their talents, hoping to get that big break that will carry them to stardom. ¹⁰Finally, there are those who pretend they are above reacting for the camera. ¹¹They wipe an expression from their faces and appear to be interested in something else. ¹²Yet if the camera stays on them long enough, they will slyly check to see if they are still being watched. ¹³Everybody's behavior seems to be slightly strange in front of a TV camera.

Fill in the blanks: The first spot where supporting details are needed occurs after sentence number _____. The second spot occurs after sentence number _____.

5.

Culture Conflict

¹I am in a constant tug-of-war with my parents over conflicts between their Vietnamese culture and American culture. ²To begin with, my parents do not like me to have American friends. ³They think that I should spend all my time with other Vietnamese people and speak English only when necessary. ⁴I get into an argument whenever I want to go to a fast-food restaurant or a movie at night with my American friends. ⁵The conflict with my parents is even worse when it comes to plans for a career. ⁶My parents want me to get a degree in science and then go on to medical school. ⁷On the other hand, I think I want to become a teacher. ⁸So far I have

continued

been taking both science and education courses, but soon I will have to concentrate on one or the other. 9The other night my father made his attitude about what I should do very clear. 10The most difficult aspect of our cultural differences is the way our family is structured. 11My father is the center of our family, and he expects that I will always listen to him. 12Although I am twenty-one years old, I still have a nightly curfew at an hour which I consider insulting. 13Also, I am expected to help my mother perform certain household chores that I've really come to hate. 14My father expects me to live at home until I am married to a Vietnamese man. 15When that happens, he assumes I will obey my husband just as I obey him. 16I do not want to be a bad daughter, but I want to live like my American female friends.

Fill in the blanks: The first spot where supporting details are needed occurs after sentence number _____. The second spot occurs after sentence number _____. The third spot occurs after sentence number _____.

4 Evaluating Paragraphs for Coherence

ACTIVITY 9

Answer the questions about coherence that follow each of the two paragraphs below.

Work

1.

Grant Proposal

1The Longview Preschool, a non-profit preschool in Longview, Washington, is seeking a grant of $129,334 to improve our services. 2Our school currently services 279 at-risk students from the lowest socio-economic group in the area, and we have 36 full-time teachers. 3Our objective is that by the end of the year, at least two-thirds of our 55 pre-K students will demonstrate kindergarten preparedness. 4This would be an increase of 22 percent from our previous year. 5Most important, to better implement curriculum and prepare our students, we plan to increase our hours for pre-K students to five days a week, and four-year-old students to four days a week. 6Our tuition is currently $255 per month for three days a week. 7However, as 95 percent of our students already receive government assistance, increasing costs to the families is not feasible. 8The remaining portion of our grant request will cover the costs of increased teacher pay, student tuition, and facility overhead. 9The total amount required to cover these costs would be $126,225, an increase of $1530 per pre-K student and $765 per four-year-old student per year. 10Our second goal is to improve the curriculum used within the classroom. 11We plan to move from our current curriculum to the award-winning The Creative Curriculum. 12Preschool students who have been taught by teachers using this program have consistently demonstrated a higher level of kindergarten preparedness;

continued

after researching numerous programs, we believe this program is the best fit for our school. ¹³This award-winning curriculum will cost $2,149. ¹⁴As part of meeting this objective, we will be increasing the number of staff who hold Child Development Associate (CDA) licenses. ¹⁵The cost of preparation and licensing will be $960. ¹⁶Currently, 14 of our 36 staff hold CDA licenses through the Council for Professional Recognition. ¹⁷Our intention is to increase that number to 30. ¹⁸The funding from the grant will cover class and materials costs, as well as license fees. ¹⁹Better prepared teachers, stronger curriculum, and increased instructional time will ensure that Longview Preschool meets the needs of the community.

a. The paragraph should use emphatic order. Write 1 before the goal that seems slightly less important than the other two goals, 2 before the second most important goal, and 3 before the most important goal.

_____ Lengthened school week

_____ Teacher licensing and preparation

_____ New curriculum

b. Before which of the three goals should the transitional words *One important goal* be added? _____

c. Before which of the three goals could the transition words *In addition* be added? _____

d. Which words show emphasis in sentence 5? _____

e. What is a synonym for the word *feasible* in sentence 7? _____

2.

Apartment Hunting

¹Apartment hunting is a several-step process that all potential renters should follow. ²They should visit and carefully inspect the most promising apartments. ³They should check each place for signs of unwanted guests such as roaches or mice. ⁴Making sure that light switches and appliances work and that there are enough electrical outlets are also important steps. ⁵Turning faucets on and off and flushing the toilet will help potential renters to be sure that the plumbing works smoothly. ⁶Talking to the landlord for a bit can help develop a feeling for the kind of person he or she is. ⁷If a problem develops after renters have moved in, they will want to know that a decent and capable person is there to handle the matter. ⁸People should find out what's available that matches their interests. ⁹The town newspaper and local real estate offices can provide lists of apartments for rent. ¹⁰Family and friends may be able to give leads. ¹¹And local schools

continued

may have a housing office that keeps a list of approved apartments for rent.
12Potential renters should decide what they need in an apartment. 13If they
can afford no more than four hundred dollars a month, they need to find
a place that will cost no more than that. 14If location near work or school
is important, these factors should be considered. 15For those who plan to
cook, a place with a workable kitchen is important. 16By taking these steps,
anyone should be ready to select the apartment that is best for him or her.

a. The paragraph should use time order. Write 1 before the step that should
   come first, 2 before the intermediate step, and 3 before the final step.

   _____ Visit and carefully inspect the most promising apartments.

   _____ Decide what one needs.

   _____ Find out what is available that matches interests.

b. Before which of the three steps could the transitional words *The first step
   is* to be added? _____

c. Before which step could the transitional words *After a person has
   decided what he or she is looking for, the next step is to* be added?

   _____

d. Before which step could the transitional words *The final step* be added?

   _____

e. To whom does the pronoun *he or she* in sentence 6 refer? _____

f. What is a synonym for *landlord* in sentence 7? _____

g. What is a synonym for *apartment* in sentence 13? _____

5 Revising Paragraphs for Coherence

The two paragraphs in this section begin with a clear point, but in each case the
supporting material that follows the point is not coherent. Read each paragraph and
the comments that follow it on how to organize and connect the supporting material. Then do the activity for the paragraph.

PARAGRAPH 1

Personal   A Difficult Period

Since I arrived in the Bay Area in midsummer, I have had the most
difficult period of my life. I had to look for an apartment. I found only
one place that I could afford, but the landlord said I could not move in until
it was painted. When I first arrived in San Francisco, my thoughts were to

continued

stay with my father and stepmother. I had to set out looking for a job so that I could afford my own place, for I soon realized that my stepmother was not at all happy having me live with them. A three-week search led to a job shampooing rugs for a housecleaning company. I painted the apartment myself, and at least that problem was ended. I was in a hurry to get settled because I was starting school at the University of San Francisco in September. A transportation problem developed because my stepmother insisted that I return my father's bike, which I was using at first to get to school. I had to rely on a bus that often arrived late, with the result that I missed some classes and was late for others. I had already had a problem with registration in early September. My counselor had made a mistake with my classes, and I had to register all over again. This meant that I was one week late for class. Now I'm riding to school with a classmate and no longer have to depend on the bus. My life is starting to order itself, but I must admit that at first I thought it was hopeless to stay here.

EXPLANATION

The writer of this paragraph has provided a good deal of specific evidence to support the opening point. The evidence, however, needs to be organized. Before starting the paragraph, the writer should have decided to arrange the details by using time order. He or she could then have listed in a scratch outline the exact sequence of events that made for such a difficult period.

ACTIVITY 10

Here is a list of the various events described by the writer of paragraph 1. Number the events in the correct time sequence by writing 1 in front of the first event that occurred, 2 in front of the second event, and so on.

Since I arrived in the Bay Area in midsummer, I have had the most difficult period of my life.

_____ I had to search for an apartment I could afford.

_____ I had to find a job so that I could afford my own place.

_____ My stepmother objected to my living with her and my father.

_____ I had to paint the apartment before I could move in.

_____ I had to find an alternative to unreliable bus transportation.

_____ I had to register again for my college courses because of a counselor's mistake.

Your instructor may now have you rewrite the paragraph on separate paper. If so, be sure to use time signals such as *first, next, then, during, when, after,* and *now* to help guide your reader from one event to the next.

PARAGRAPH 2

Lionel Hampton in Idaho

Music students should plan to visit the University of Idaho and include the Lionel Hampton Jazz Festival in their visit. The festival, usually held in February, brings together famous jazz musicians with students of all ages, from elementary school to college. Music students can participate in master class workshops, learning from some of the greatest jazz artists. Once Lionel Hampton pledged his support, the festival grew. In addition to the headliners, the Lionel Hampton Jazz Festival offers numerous workshops and opportunities for participants to learn. It has featured famous jazz artists like Dizzy Gillespie, Bobby McFerrin, and Doc Severinsen. Participants can attend smaller, more intimate concerts that often include question and answer sessions. They receive trophies and awards for their performances. Elementary and middle school students benefit from the festival as the artists spend time visiting the surrounding schools and introducing students to the beauty of jazz. Two of the most exciting events for students are the Young Artists Concerts and Hamp's Club. Both of these events highlight students and groups who have been selected for recognition. Students perform in front of large audiences. There are jazz festivals around the United States; the Lionel Hampton Jazz Festival is one that should not be missed. This four-day event began as a local celebration, but gained national recognition when Ella Fitzgerald headlined.

EXPLANATION

The writer of this paragraph provides a number of specifics that support the opening point. However, the supporting material has not been organized clearly. Before writing this paragraph, the author should have (1) decided to arrange the supporting evidence by using emphatic order and (2) listed in a scratch outline the reasons students should visit the jazz festival. The writer could also have determined which reason to use in the emphatic final position of the paper.

ACTIVITY 11

Create a clear outline for paragraph 2 by filling in the scheme below. The outline is partially completed.

Music students should plan to visit the University of Idaho and include the Lionel Hampton Jazz Festival in their visit.

Reason   1. _Brings together famous jazz musicians with students of all ages_____

Details   a. _____

               _____

               b. _____

               _____

c. _____

_____

2. *Offers numerous workshops and opportunities for participants to learn* _____   Reason

   a. _____   Details

   b. *Master class workshops* _____

   c. _____

3. _____   Reason

   a. *Events such as Hamp's Club recognize students and groups* _____   Details

   b. _____

   c. _____

Your instructor may have you rewrite the paragraph on separate paper. If so, be sure to introduce each of the three reasons with transitions such as *First, Another reason,* and *Finally.* You may also want to use repeated words, pronouns, and synonyms to help tie your sentences together.

6 Evaluating Paragraphs for All Four Bases: Unity, Support, Coherence, and Sentence Skills

In this activity, you will evaluate paragraphs in terms of all four bases: unity, support, coherence, and sentence skills. Evaluative comments follow each paragraph below. Circle the letter of the statement that best applies in each case.

ACTIVITY 12

1.

Texting

    Cell phone texting is ruining people's understanding of proper English skills. First, texting is causing a generation of people to acquire weak writing skills. Secondly, people are forgetting how to use proper grammar and sentence structure. Instead of writing in complete sentences, people write short phrases that are often sentence fragments. Finally, texting is creating a generation of people who cannot spell properly. If we aren't careful, soon people won't be able to write, spell, or properly communicate with each other.

---

a. The paragraph is not unified.

b. The paragraph is not adequately supported.

c. The paragraph is not well organized.

d. The paragraph does not show a command of sentence skills.

e. The paragraph is well written in terms of the four bases.

2.

Bullying

In recent years, the frequency of bullying in schools has increased. The National Education Association estimates that 160,000 children stay home from school regularly. Because they fear being bullied. In fact, fifteen percent of absenteeism is caused by the fear of being bullied, and at least one out of every six children is a victim of bullying. Believed to have low esteem, psychologists once thought that bullies were children who had been bullied themselves, either at school or at home. And that they intimidated others to bolster their egos. However, new research shows that many bullies have high self-esteem, they engage in such behavior because they take pleasure in threatening and even harming others. Bullying can be stopped. The *Stop Bullying* Web site advises victims of bullying to report it to teachers or counselors. Also to join groups in which others will lend support against bullies. Finally, to confront the bully if it's safe to do so.

a. The paragraph is not unified.
b. The paragraph is not adequately supported.
c. The paragraph is not well organized.
d. The paragraph does not show a command of sentence skills.
e. The paragraph is well written in terms of the four bases.

3.

Asking Girls Out

There are several reasons I have trouble asking girls to go out with me. I have asked some girls out and have been turned down. This is one reason that I can't talk to them. At one time I was very shy and quiet, and people sometimes didn't even know I was present. I can talk to girls now as friends, but as soon as I want to ask them out, I usually start to become quiet, and a little bit of shyness comes out. When I finally get the nerve up, the girl will turn me down, and I swear that I will never ask another one out again. I feel sure I will get a refusal, and I have no confidence in myself. Also, my friends mock me, though they aren't any better than I am. It is very discouraging when my friends get on me. Sometimes I just stand there and wait to hear what line the girl will use. The one they use a lot is "We like you as a friend, Ted, and it's better that way." All my past experiences with girls have been just as bad. One girl used me to make her old boyfriend jealous. Then when she succeeded, she started going out with him again. I had a bad experience when I took a girl to the prom. I spent a lot of money on her. Two days later, she told me that she was getting serious with another guy. I feel that when I meet a girl I have to be sure I can trust her. I don't want her to turn on me.

a. The paragraph is not unified.
b. The paragraph is not adequately supported.
c. The paragraph is not well organized.
d. The paragraph does not show a command of sentence skills.
e. The paragraph is well written in terms of the four bases.

4.

A Change in My Writing

A technique of my present English instructor has corrected a writing problem that I've always had. In past English courses, I had major problems with commas in the wrong places, bad spelling, capitalizing the wrong words, sentence fragments, and run-on sentences. I never had any big problems with unity, support, or coherence, but the sentence skills were another matter. They were like little bugs that always appeared to infest my writing. My present instructor asked me to rewrite papers, just concentrating on sentence skills. I thought that the instructor was crazy because I didn't feel that rewriting would do any good. I soon became certain that my instructor was out of his mind, for he made me rewrite my first paper four times. It was very frustrating, for I became tired of doing the same paper over and over. I wanted to belt my instructor against the wall when I'd show him each new draft and he'd find skills mistakes and say, "Rewrite." Finally, my papers began to improve and the sentence skills began to fall into place. I was able to see them and correct them before turning in a paper, whereas I couldn't before. Why or how this happened I don't know, but I think that rewriting helped a lot. It took me most of the semester, but I stuck it out and the work paid off.

a. The paragraph is not unified.
b. The paragraph is not adequately supported.
c. The paragraph is not well organized.
d. The paragraph does not show a command of sentence skills.
e. The paragraph is well written in terms of the four bases.

5.

Luck and Me

I am a very lucky man, though the rest of my family has not always been lucky. Sometimes when I get depressed, which is too frequently, it's hard to see just how lucky I am. I'm lucky that I'm living in a country that is free. I'm allowed to worship the way I want to, and that is very important to me. Without a belief in God a person cannot live with any real certainty in life. My relationship with my wife is a source of good fortune for me. She gives me security, and that's something I need a lot. Even with these positive realities in my life, I still seem to find time for insecurity, worry, and, worst of all, depression. At times in my life I have had bouts of terrible luck. But overall, I'm a very lucky guy. I plan to further develop the positive aspects of my life and try to eliminate the negative ones.

a. The paragraph is not unified.
b. The paragraph is not adequately supported.
c. The paragraph is not well organized.
d. The paragraph does not show a command of sentence skills.
e. The paragraph is well written in terms of the four bases.

Writing in the Digital Age

This chapter will

- offer tips for writing on-screen

- provide information on using digital and electronic resources at each stage of the writing process

- explain and illustrate how to use the Internet to find books and articles on a topic

- show you how to evaluate Internet sources

- present a preview of Part 2

HOW HAS TECHNOLOGY HELPED YOU? Laptops, smart phones, and tablets have all made it much easier to have technology on the go. Write a paragraph in which you describe one of your favorite places to study and write. What type of place is it? What is it about that space that inspires you? Do you prefer to be there alone or with others?

In the last decade, computers, tablets, and online resources have become increasingly more important to the writing process. Almost all instructors require that papers be typed and printed (rather than handwritten), and most students use word-processing programs like Google Docs or Microsoft Word to compose, revise, and edit essays. Online resources provide a wide array of opportunities for brainstorming, learning more about topics, and sharing ideas with peers. Even if you don't currently own a computer or if you do but it needs maintenance, your school has one or more computer labs with machines specifically for student use. These labs are sometimes staffed, and if they aren't, most computers have very user-friendly interfaces and Help programs.

Tips for Writing On-Screen

- If you are using your school's computer center, allow enough time. You may have to wait for a computer or printer to be free, or your school may have sign-up sheets in the lab or online. In addition, you may need several sessions at the computer and printer to complete your paper.

- When using word-processing programs like Microsoft Word or Google Docs *save your work frequently as you write your draft*. In addition to saving on the computer, back files up on an external disk, a flash drive, or a server. Most computers will auto-save your work, but any file that is not saved may be lost if the program quits, the computer crashes, or the power is turned off.

- Always keep your work in multiple places—the hard drive you are working on; a backup device such as a flash drive or external hard drive; and a server such as Dropbox or iCloud. You can also e-mail a copy to yourself.

- Print out your work at least at the end of every session. Then not only will you have your most recent draft to work on away from the computer, you'll also have a copy in case something should happen to your files.

- Before making major changes in a paper, create a copy of your file. For example, if your file is titled "Worst Job," create a file called "Worst Job 2" or "Worst Job 2-9-15" (using the date as a reference). Then make all your changes in that file. If the changes don't work out, you can always go back to the original file.

Using Digital and Electronic Resources at Each Stage of the Writing Process

Word-processing programs like Microsoft Word or Google Docs make it easy for you to experiment with ideas and wording throughout your paper. They also allow you to create and save many versions.

Following are ways to use computers at each stage of the writing process. Note that the sections that follow correspond to the stages of the writing process described in Chapter 2, pages 18–50. Note, too, that although Gene Hert, the student author of "My Job in an Apple Plant," preferred to handwrite his early stages, the computer offers a valuable alternative.

Prewriting

If you're a fast typist, many kinds of prewriting will work well on the computer. With freewriting in particular, you can get ideas onto the screen almost as quickly as they occur to you. A passing thought that could be productive is not likely to get lost. You may even find it helpful, when freewriting, to dim the screen of your monitor so that you can't see what you're typing. If you temporarily cannot see the screen, you won't have to worry about grammar or spelling or typing errors (all of which do not matter in prewriting); instead, you can concentrate on getting down as many ideas and details as possible about your subject.

After you complete your prewriting, it's often very helpful to print out a hard copy of what you've done. With a clean printout in front of you, you'll be able to see everything at once and revise and expand your work with handwritten comments in the margins of the paper. Alternately, you can continue to work on-screen and track your changes there.

Working on a computer also makes it easy for you to experiment with the wording of the point (also called a working topic sentence or working thesis) of your paper. You can try a number of versions in a short time. After you have decided on the version that works best, you can easily delete the other versions, simply move them to a temporary "leftover" section at the end of the paper, or move them to a new file.

Preparing a Scratch Outline

If you used listing as a prewriting technique, you may easily be able to turn your list into an outline. Use the cut and paste functions to shuffle the ideas around until you find the best order of supporting points and details for your paper. You can easily delete any ideas that do not fit and add new ideas as needed.

You can also create scratch outlines using Web-based programs like Work-Flowy (also available as an app for most smartphones) and ThinkLinkr. Both tools can be used, as well, to jumpstart brainstorming and take notes, and they allow you to share and work together on outlines with others. This can be useful when getting peer feedback or working on a group writing project.

TIP

At any point in the prewriting, outlining, or drafting process, you might experience writer's block or need some inspiration. One way to get ideas flowing is to do some Google searches based on key words in your topic. For instance, you could do a search for "worst jobs" and find some funny lists or sad stories on the topic. Maybe an anecdote by someone else will help you remember a specific detail from your own experience. It's a little too easy to get caught up in Web searching for hours, so restrict your search to ten or twenty minutes. Set an alarm so you won't go over your time limit.

If you are trying to find a new topic or can't think of one, try reviewing recent e-mails, text messages, posts on Twitter or Facebook, or even your school library Web site. What have you been talking about with friends, family, or classmates? What topics have been hotly discussed on your campus? Try writing about something that interests you.

Writing the First Draft

Like many writers, you may want to write your first draft by hand and then type it into the computer for revision. The process of simply typing out a handwritten draft for the first time may provide opportunities for making some changes and improvements. Once you have a draft on the screen, you will find it much easier to revise than a handwritten one.

If you feel comfortable composing directly on the screen, you can benefit from a number of special features. For example, if you have written an anecdote in your freewriting that you plan to use in your paper, simply copy the story from your free-writing file and insert it where it fits into your paper. You can refine it then or later. Or if you discover while typing that a sentence is out of place, cut it out from where it is and paste it wherever you wish. And if while writing you realize that an earlier sentence can be expanded, just go back to that point and type in the added material.

As you write a first draft, it can be tempting to break things up by texting, visiting Twitter, answering e-mails, or streaming a film. Avoid the temptation by turning off your phone and hiding these other options. One way to do this is by drafting with a program like Typewriter, TextRoom, JDarkRoom, or FocusCopy. If you use a Mac, WriteRoom is a good option. Each of these programs turns your screen into a blank sheet of paper or chalkboard, and there are options to shield you from alerts about new messages or updates of any kind. You are also free from

DO YOU THINK COMPUTERS AND TABLETS HAVE MADE IT EASIER OR MORE complicated to do research? Do you like the accessibility of electronic resources or do you spend too much time on social networking sites? When you choose research materials, do you prefer electronic or print? Jot down several specific methods you typically employ for research. Highlight one that you feel you could improve and explain why.

the distractions of choices; without menus and, for instance, font options, you can focus on the writing itself. If you'd prefer to use an online text editor instead of one you have to download, try DarkCopy. When you're ready to start formatting your paper, you can copy and paste it into the word-processing program you normally use; TextRoom allows you to export text directly to Google Docs.

Revising

It is during revision that the virtues of word-processing programs really shine. All substituting, adding, deleting, and rearranging can be done easily within an existing file. All changes instantly take their proper places within the paper, not scribbled above the line or squeezed into the margin. Also, you can choose to track your changes within a draft, instead of saving multiple versions, and leave comments and questions for yourself in the margins with a Comments (or similarly named) feature. You can concentrate on each change you want to make, because you never have to type from scratch or work on a messy draft. You can carefully go through your paper to check that all your supporting evidence is relevant and to add new support as needed here and there. Anything you decide to eliminate can be deleted quickly and neatly. Anything you add can be inserted precisely where you choose. You can undo edits easily, too. If you change your mind, all you have to do is delete or cut and paste. Then you can sweep through the paper focusing on other changes: improving word choice, increasing sentence variety, eliminating wordiness, and so on.

If you are like some students, you will find it convenient to print out a hard copy of your file at various points throughout the revision. Make sure your paper is double spaced to make it easier to revise in longhand. The double spacing will give you room to add, cross out, and indicate changes that you can quickly make when you revise the document.

Editing and Proofreading

Editing and proofreading also benefit richly from word processing. Instead of crossing or whiting out mistakes, or rewriting an entire paper to correct numerous errors, you can make all necessary changes within the most recent draft. If you find editing or proofreading on the screen hard on your eyes, print out a copy. Mark any corrections on that copy, and then transfer them to the final draft.

If the word-processing software you're using includes spelling and grammar checks, by all means use them. The spell-check function tells you when a word is not in the computer's dictionary. Keep in mind, however, that the spell-check cannot tell you how to spell a name correctly or when you have mistakenly used, for example, *their* instead of *there*. To a spell-check, *Thank ewe four the complement* is as correct as *Thank you for the compliment*. Also use the grammar-checker with caution. Any errors it doesn't uncover are still your responsibility, and it sometimes points out mistakes where there are none.

A freshly printed paper, with its clean appearance and attractive formatting, looks so good that you may think it is in better shape than it really is. Do not be fooled by your paper's appearance. Take sufficient time to review your grammar, punctuation, and spelling carefully.

Even after you hand in your paper, save the digital file. Your teacher may ask you to do some revising, and then the file will save you from having to type the paper from scratch.

Occasionally, you may be asked to submit a paper in electronic form, either through e-mail or on a school server or FTP site or cloud. In these cases, always double check that the file has gone through. Get confirmation from your instructor, not just from the system or destination itself. Submit a paper electronically only if your instructor specifically asks this of you.

TIP

In future assignments, you may be asked to incorporate images or links into a paper. Think of these as garnishes on a dinner plate or lemon slices in glasses of water—they are there to add a bit of color and flavor, but not to overwhelm the main dish. Incorporate visuals or links into a paper only with your instructor's approval and guidance.

Know and follow rules, both legal and ethical, about when and how to use others' images and how to credit them. You probably know the saying "A picture speaks a thousand words." Remember this when selecting an image; aim to find one that illustrates or supports your paper's main idea.

Links should be used when they provide useful information that enhances the content of your paper. As with images, avoid links that might distract readers from the central point of your paper.

Using the Internet

The Internet can aid and enhance your writing in numerous ways. It can be especially valuable in aiding you in doing research for a paper or essay but it can also help you check dates, names, and background information for any kind of writing. Here we will look at how you can use the Internet to find books and articles on a particular topic. We will also discuss the important issue of learning how to evaluate Internet sources, as these sources vary greatly in their quality and reliability.

HAVE YOU USED AN ELECTRONIC SOURCE TO ORDER books? What is your favorite method of acquiring e-books? In a few lines, describe the difference between browsing in a brick and mortar bookstore or library and browsing online for a book.

Find Books on Your Topic

To find current books, go to your college's catalog, which you may be able to access from home, and look for books published recently. Another approach is to go online and search the Web site of a commercial bookseller such as Amazon.com (www.amazon.com) or Barnes and Noble Books (www.barnesandnoble.com). You can search for books on these sites for free, and you are under no obligation to buy a book.

Use the "Browse" Tab

On the Web site of a commercial bookseller, click on "Books" and then "Browse." You'll get a list of general categories to search. Suppose you are reporting on the development of the modern telescope. When you click "Browse subjects" on Amazon.com, you get a list of categories that includes "Science & Math." Clicking on that category displays a list of subcategories, one of which is "Astronomy & Space Science." Clicking on this subcategory brings up more subcategories, including "Telescopes." Finally, clicking on "Telescopes" gives you a list of recent books on the topic. You can click on each title for information about each book. All this browsing can be done very easily and will help you research your topic quickly.

Use the "Search" Box

If you are preparing a paper on some aspect of photography, type the word "photography" in the search box. You'll then get a list of books on that subject. Just looking at the list may help you narrow your subject and decide on a specific topic to develop. For instance, one student typed "photography" in the search box on Barnes and Noble's site and got a list of 13,000 books on the subject. Considering only part of that list helped her realize that she wanted to write on some aspect of photography during the U.S. Civil War. She typed "Civil War photography" and got a list of 200 titles. After looking at information about twenty of those books, she was able to decide on a limited topic for her paper.

A Note on the Library of Congress

The commercial bookstore sites are especially quick and easy to use. But to find additional books on your topic, you can also visit the Library of Congress Web site (www.loc.gov). The Library of Congress, in Washington, D.C., has copies of all books published in the United States. Its online catalog contains about twelve million entries. You can browse this catalog by subject or search by keywords. The search form permits you to check only those books that interest you. Click on the "Full Record" option to view publication information about a book, as well as its call numbers. You can then try to obtain the book from your college library or through an interlibrary loan.

Other Points to Note

Remember that at any time you can use your printer to quickly print information presented on the screen. (For example, the student planning a paper on photography in the Civil War could print a list of the twenty books, along with sheets of information about individual books.) You could then go to your library knowing exactly what books you want to borrow. If your own local or school library is accessible online, you can visit in advance to find out whether it has the books you want. Also, if you have time and money, you may want to purchase them from a local bookshop or an online bookstore, such as Amazon. Used books are often available at greatly reduced cost, and they often ship out in only a few days.

Find Articles on Your Topic

There are many online sources that will help you find articles on your subject. Following are descriptions of some of them.

Online Databases

Most college and public libraries provide online computer-search services known as *online databases* or *library subscription services*. Using any of these services, you can type in keywords and quickly search many periodicals for articles on your subject. Some databases, such as General Science Index, cover a specific discipline, but others, such as Academic Search Elite, are more general.

Often, articles you find will appear as "full text." This means that you can print the entire article from your computer. In other cases, only an *abstract* (summary) of the article will be available. However, abstracts are valuable too, because they allow you to determine whether the article is relevant to your research and whether you should continue searching for the full text.

Finally, database articles appear in *HTML* or *PDF* format or in both. Articles in HTML (*hypertext markup language*) have been reformatted for publication on the Internet. Those in PDF (*portable document format*) are exact reproductions of a print document.

Your library may use a service that provides access to many online databases. EBSCOhost, Infotrac, and ProQuest are such services. Here are a few online databases that have proven useful for new student researchers.

Academic Search Premier covers a variety of disciplines and includes full-text articles and abstracts of articles from more than 4,400 periodicals.

CGP (Catalog of U.S. Government Publications) contains documents published by the U.S. government.

Cumulative Index to Nursing and Allied Health Literature (CINAHL) provides access to articles found in more than 1,800 professional journals in the health professions.

ERIC (Education Resources Information Center) makes available articles from professional journals, reports, and speeches having to do with education.

General Science Index lists articles on biology, chemistry, physics, and the other physical sciences.

JSTOR (Journal Storage) provides full-text articles found in back issues of journals in the humanities, social sciences, and natural sciences.

New York Times **Index** lists articles published in this newspaper since 1913.

PsychInfo is published by the American Psychological Association. It includes abstracts of books, articles, and doctoral dissertations in psychology. It also provides access to full-text articles through PsycARTICLES.

Wilson Humanities Index covers more than 500 English-language periodicals in disciplines such as archaeology, the classics, art, history, theater, music, literature, philosophy, and religion.

Google and the Google logo are registered trademarks of Google Inc., used with permission.

HERE ARE TWO TIPS TO HELP YOU SIFT THROUGH MULTITUDES OF search results: Instead of starting with the top-listed page, use the list of results to find the right keywords to narrow and refine your research. Then use those keywords in a more academic search engine like Google Scholar. Or, you might start by employing a search engine that focuses on specific types of Web sites, such as academic or medical.

Online Magazine, Newspaper, and Journal Articles

Although your college library may subscribe to online databases, another online research service, one that you can subscribe to individually on a home computer, is *Question.* You may be able to get a free one-day trial subscription or pay for a monthly subscription at limited cost. This service provides millions of newspaper articles as well as thousands of book chapters and television and radio transcripts.

Search Engines

An Internet search engine will help you quickly go through a vast amount of information on the Web to find articles about almost any topic. Google, the most commonly used search engine, can be accessed by typing "www.google.com." A screen will then appear with a box in which you can type one or more keywords. For example, if you are thinking of doing a paper on yoga, you simply enter the keyword, "yoga." Within a second or so you will get a list of millions of articles and sites on the Web about the subject of yoga.

You should then try to narrow your topic by adding other keywords. For instance, if you typed "health benefits of yoga," you would get a considerably reduced list of articles and sites. If you narrowed your potential topic further by typing "effects of yoga on reducing stress," you would get a far more focused list. Google does a superior job of returning hits that are genuinely relevant to your search, so just scanning only the early part of a list may be enough to provide you with the information you need.

Very often your challenge with searches will be getting too much information rather than too little. Try making your keywords more specific, or use different combinations of keywords. You might also try using Google Scholar or another search engine, such as Bing. In addition, consult the search engine's built-in "Advanced Search" feature for tips on successful searching.

Finally, save the addresses of relevant Web sites that you may want to visit again. The browser that you are using (for example, Internet Explorer or Safari) will probably have a "Bookmark" or "Favorite Places" option. With the click of a mouse, you can bookmark a site. You will then be able to return to it simply by clicking on its name in a list, rather than having to remember and type its address.

ACTIVITY 1

1. Using your library's list of databases, find a database that would give you information about the following subjects and write the title of that database.

   a. career preparation: _____

   b. Sigmund Freud: _____

   c. space travel: _____
   d. a new state law: _____

2. Using one of the online databases to which your college subscribes, find an article on organic gardening.

   a. Name of the database you used _____

   b. Article title _____

   c. Author (if given) _____

   d. Name of magazine, journal, or newspaper _____

   e. Pages (if given) _____

   f. Date _____

Evaluating Internet Sources

Keep in mind that the quality and reliability of information you find on the Internet may vary widely. Anyone with a bit of computer know-how can create a Web site and post information there. That person may be a Nobel Prize winner, a leading authority in a specialized field, a high school student, or a crackpot. Be careful, then, to look closely at your source in the following ways.

Guidelines for Evaluating Online Sources

1. **Internet address:** In a Web address, the three letters after the "dot" identify the domain. The most common domains are .com, .edu, .gov, .net, and .org. You can't always determine a Web site's reliability by the domain type. Almost anyone can get a Web address ending in *.com* or *.org.* So you must examine every Web site carefully. Consider these three points: author, internal evidence, and date.

2. **Author:** What credentials does the author have? What academic degrees does he or she hold? Does the author work for a college, university, well-respected think tank, or research group? Has he or she published other material on the topic?

3. **Internal evidence:** Does the author seem to proceed objectively—presenting all sides of the issue fairly before stating his or her own views?

   Does the sponsor of the Web site seem to be an objective source? For example, it would be fair to assume that a Web article from the American Medical Association discussing irradiated food treats the subject objectively. Can you say the same for an article appearing on the Web site of an irradiated-food distributor?

   Does the author provide adequate support for his or her views? Or does he or she make unsupported generalizations—claims that are simply not backed up with studies or the opinions of other experts?

   Was the article first published in a print version? Is the publisher of this print version reliable? If the article was not first published in print, could it have been, or is it so outlandish that no publisher would take the financial risk of backing it?

4. **Date:** Is the information up to date? Check at the top or bottom of the document for copyright, publication, or revision dates. Knowing such data will help you decide whether the material is current enough for your purposes. For example, would a ten-year-old article on computer viruses yield useful information for a paper that discusses ways to protect today's computers? Probably not.

PART A   Go to www.google.com and search for the word "democracy." Then complete the items below.

1. How many items did your search yield?

    _____

2. In the early listings, you will probably find each of the following domains: edu, gov, org, and com. Pick one site with each domain and write its full address.

    a. Address of one .com site you found:

    _____

    b. Address of one .gov site:

    _____

    c. Address of one .org site:

    _____

    d. Address of one .edu site:

    _____

PART B   Circle *one* of the sites you identified above and use it to complete the following evaluation.

3. Name of site's author or authoring institution:

    _____

4. Is site's information current (within two years)?

    _____

5. Does the site serve obvious business purposes (with advertising or attempts to sell products)?

    _____

6. Does the site have an obvious connection to a governmental, commercial, business, or religious organization? If so, which one?

    _____

7. Does the site's information seem fair and objective?

    _____

8. Based on the information above, would you say the site appears reliable?

    _____

ACTIVITY 3

Select one of the following areas or (with your instructor's permission) an area of your own choice:

Acid rain	Mind-body medicine
Airport security	New remedies for allergies
All-electric cars	New treatments for insomnia
Alzheimer's disease	Noise control
Animal rights movement	Nursing home costs
Animals nearing extinction	Online gambling
Assisted suicide	Organ donation
Autism	Origins of Kwanzaa
Best job prospects today	Pollution of drinking water
Bill of Rights	Prenatal care
Cell phones and driving	Prison reform
Censorship on the Internet	Privacy and technology
Charter schools	Problems of retirement
Child abuse	Recent consumer frauds
Climate change	Ritalin and children
Cremation	Self-help groups
Declaration of Independence	Sexual harassment
Drug treatment programs	Steroids and professional athletes
Everyday addictions	Stress reduction in the workplace
Fertility drugs	Surrogate mothers
Food poisoning (salmonella)	The Aztecs
Forecasting earthquakes	The Maya
Health insurance reform	The next ice age
Heroes for today	Toxic waste disposal
Holistic healing	Vegetarianism/Veganism
HPV immunizations	Violence in videogames
Magna Carta	Witchcraft today
Medical marijuana	

First, look up your topic in a search engine like Google (or Google Scholar if your instructor specifies that your sources need to be academic) and read through the results. In order to narrow your search, note the most prevalent main subject headings and tag words. Employing your library's catalog and database, use the tag words to locate books and articles about your chosen topic. Locate several sources you think might be beneficial.

1. Topic
2. Three books that either cover the topic directly or at least touch on the topic in some way. Include

   Author

   Title

   Place of publication

   Publisher

   Date of publication
3. Three articles on the topic published in 2007 or later. Include

   Title of article

   Author (if given)

   Title of magazine

   Date

   Pages (if given)
4. Finally, write a paragraph describing exactly how you went about researching your topic. In addition, include a photocopy or printout of one of the three articles.

A Look Ahead to Part 2

Patterns of Paragraph Development

Traditionally, writing has been divided into the following patterns of development.

- Exposition
    - Exemplification
    - Process
    - Cause and/or effect
    - Comparison and/or contrast
    - Definition
    - Classification
- Description
- Narration
- Argumentation

   In *exposition,* the writer provides information about and explains a particular subject. Patterns of development within exposition include *exemplification*, or giving examples; detailing a *process* of doing or making something; analyzing *causes and effects; comparing* and *contrasting; defining* a term or concept; and *dividing* something into parts or *classifying* it into categories.

In addition to the six exposition patterns of development, three other patterns are common: *description, narration,* and *argumentation.* A *description* is a verbal picture of a person, place, or thing. In *narration,* a writer tells the story of something that happened. Finally, in *argumentation,* a writer attempts to support a controversial point or defend a position on which there is a difference of opinion.

The pages ahead present individual chapters on each pattern. You will have a chance, then, to learn nine different patterns or methods for organizing material in your papers. Each pattern has its own internal logic and provides its own special strategies for imposing order on your ideas.

As you practice each pattern, you should remember the following Tip.

> **TIP**
>
> While each paragraph that you write will involve one predominant pattern, very often one or more additional patterns may be involved as well. For instance, the paragraph, "*The Children of Huang Shi*: A Must See," presents a series of examples to support the argument that people should watch this film. But the author also uses description to support each of his/her points (low-key lighting, vastness and ruggedness of China's wilderness, delicate and intimate music).
>
> No matter which pattern or patterns you use, each paragraph will probably involve some form of argumentation. You will advance a point and then go on to support your point. To convince the reader that your point is valid, you may use exemplification, narration, description, or some other pattern of organization. Among the paragraphs you will read in Part 2, one writer supports the point that a favorite outdoor spot is like "heaven" by providing a number of descriptive details. Another labels a certain experience in his life as heartbreaking and then uses a narrative to demonstrate the truth of his statement. A third writer advances the opinion that good horror movies can be easily distinguished from bad horror movies and then supplies comparative information about both to support her claim. Much of your writing, in short, will have the purpose of persuading your reader that the idea you have advanced is valid.

The Progression in Each Chapter

After each type of paragraph development is explained, student papers illustrating that type are presented. These are followed by questions about the paragraphs. The questions relate to unity, support, and coherence—three of the four bases of effective writing. You are then asked to write your own paragraph. In most cases, the first assignment is fairly structured and provides a good deal of guidance for the writing process. The other assignments offer a wide choice of writing topics. At least one assignment will require some simple research. The final assignment always requires writing with a specific purpose and for a specific audience.

Paragraph Development

This photograph is clearly making a statement. Write a paragraph about what you think that statement is and why you came to that conclusion. You may want to use personal experience to strengthen the support in your paragraph.

Exemplification

This chapter will explain and illustrate how to

- develop an exemplification paragraph

- write an exemplification paragraph

- revise an exemplification paragraph

In addition, you will read and evaluate

- three student paragraphs

ARE WE A HEALTH-CONSCIOUS NATION? Look at this photograph and write a paragraph in which you answer that question. Use examples found in the media, in the photograph, or in your own daily observations to support your point. Consider how and why some examples are stronger than others in helping to support a position.

In our daily conversations, we often provide *examples*—that is, details, particulars, specific instances—to explain statements that we make. Consider the several statements and supporting examples in the box below.

Statement	Examples
Wal-Mart was crowded today.	There were at least four carts waiting at each of the checkout counters, and it took me forty-five minutes to get through a line.
The corduroy shirt I bought is poorly made.	When I washed it, the colors began to fade, one button cracked and another fell off, a shoulder seam opened, and the sleeves shrank almost two inches.
Success in college requires students to practice commonsense habits.	Regular attendance is necessary for mastering the complex ideas taught in college. Keeping up with the assigned reading prepares students for class and increases their grasp of the material. Careful note taking is essential to studying for and passing examinations.

In each case, the examples help us *see for ourselves* the truth of the statement that has been made. In paragraphs, too, explanatory examples help the audience fully understand a point. Lively, specific examples also add interest to a paragraph.

In this chapter, you will be asked to provide a series of examples to support a topic sentence. Providing examples to support a point is one of the simplest and most common methods of paragraph development. To prepare for this assignment, read the following paragraphs, which all use examples to develop their points, and answer the questions.

Evaluating Student Paragraphs

Confessions of an Internet Addict

¹My addiction to the Internet is causing several problems in my life. ²The first issue is my expanding waistline. ³I used to enjoy exercising and playing tennis four days a week, but now my need to catch up on Twitter and read the latest sports blogs has stopped me from exercising. ⁴In the last six months, I have followed every major sports story, but I have also gained thirty pounds. ⁵The second issue is my online shopping. ⁶I no longer have to leave the house to buy groceries, clothes, or cleaning supplies. ⁷With the quick touch of a button, I can have my items ordered, and within days, delivered. ⁸The worst issue, however, is my dying social life. ⁹Whenever a friend texts to meet up, I usually ignore the text or respond that I am busy. ¹⁰Fewer and fewer friends are texting anymore, so even if I wanted to go out, I don't have anyone to meet. ¹¹Although the Internet benefits most people, it has had a negative impact on my life.

Office Politics

¹Office politics is a destructive game played by several types of people. ²For instance, two supervisors may get into a conflict over how to do a certain job. ³Instead of working out an agreement like adults, they carry on a power struggle that turns the poor employees under them into human Ping-Pong balls being swatted between two angry players. ⁴Another common example of office politics is the ambitious worker who takes credit for other people's ideas. ⁵He or she will chat in a "friendly" fashion with inexperienced employees, getting their ideas about how to run the office more smoothly. ⁶Next thing you know, Mr. or Ms. Idea-Stealer is having a closed-door session with the boss and getting promotion points for his or her "wonderful creativity." ⁷Yet another illustration of office politics is the spy. ⁸This employee acts very buddy-buddy with other workers, often dropping little comments about things he or she doesn't like in the workplace. ⁹The spy encourages people to talk about their problems at work, that they don't like their boss, the pay, and the working conditions. ¹⁰Then the spy goes straight back and repeats all he or she has heard to the boss, and the employees get blamed for their "poor attitude." ¹¹A final example of office politics is people who gossip. ¹²Too often, office politics can turn a perfectly fine work situation into a stressful one.

A Visit to Utah's National Parks

¹Some of the most interesting national parks in the United States are found in Utah. ²For example, Zion National Park contains a canyon that is almost one-half mile deep. ³It also features massive cliffs of deep red and brown that overlook rivers and green, wooded trails. ⁴Visitors to Bryce Canyon National Park are treated to interesting rock formations shaped by wind erosion. ⁵Included are several large solid rock horseshoes, which are topped with delicate stone columns in fantastic shapes. ⁶South Dakota's Badlands National Park is another place one can see landforms created by erosion. ⁷In most cases, it's the wind that has cut the stone, but in others water from rivers—long dried up—has done the sculpting. ⁸Utah's Arches National Park is well named because of its stone arches. ⁹Tourists are often seen photographing the park's beautiful red-rock formations, whose shading varies with changes in sunlight as the day goes on. ¹⁰Petroglyphs, or engravings in the surface of rocks, can be found in Canyonlands National Park in the southeastern part of Utah. ¹¹Many of these carvings are more than one thousand years old. ¹²Finally, Capitol Reef National Park is interesting because of its large white rock that looks a lot like the United States Capitol in Washington, D.C.

ABOUT UNITY

1. Which two sentences in "A Visit to Utah's National Parks" are irrelevant to the point that "interesting national parks . . . are found in Utah"?

   _____   _____

ABOUT SUPPORT

2. In "Confessions of an Internet Addict," how many examples does the writer provide of his/her addiction?

   _____ two _____ three _____ four _____ six

3. After which sentence in "Office Politics" are specific details needed?

   _____

ABOUT COHERENCE

4. What are the four transition words or phrases that are used to introduce each new example in "Office Politics"?

   _____   _____ _____ _____

QUESTIONS

5. Identify at least three transitional words or phrases used to introduce examples in "A Visit to Utah's National Parks."

    _____   _____   _____

6. Which paragraph clearly uses emphatic order to organize its details, saving for last what the writer regards as the most important example?

    _____

Developing an Exemplification Paragraph

Development through Prewriting

Backing up your statements with clear, specific illustrations is the key to a successful exemplification paragraph. When Charlene, the writer of "Office Politics," was assigned an examples paragraph, she at first did not know what to write about.

Then her instructor made a suggestion. "Imagine yourself having lunch with some friends," the instructor said. "You're telling them *how* you feel about something and *why*. Maybe you're saying, 'I am so mad at my boyfriend!' or 'My new apartment is really great.' You wouldn't stop there—you'd continue by saying what your boyfriend does that is annoying, or in what way your apartment is nice. In other words, you'd be making a general point and backing it up with examples. That's what you need to do in this paragraph."

That night, Charlene was on the telephone with her brother. She was complaining about the office where she worked. "Suddenly I realized what I was doing," Charlene said. "I was making a statement—I hate the politics in my office—and giving examples of those politics. I knew what I could write about!"

Charlene began preparing to write her paragraph by freewriting. She gave herself ten minutes to write down everything she could think of on the subject of politics in her office. This is what she wrote:

> *Of all the places I've ever worked this one is the worst that way. Can't trust anybody there—everybody's playing some sort of game. Worst one of all is Bradley and the way he pretends to be friendly with people. Gets them to complain about Ms. Bennett and Mr. Hankins and then runs back to them and reports everything. He should realize that people are catching on to his game and figuring out what a jerk he is. Melissa steals people's ideas and then takes credit for them. Anything*

continued

to get brownie points. She's always out for herself first, you can tell. Then there's all the gossip that goes on. You think you're in a soap opera or something, and it's kind of fun in a way but it also is very distracting people always talking about each other and worrying about what they say about you. And people talk about our bosses a lot. Nobody knows why Ms. Bennett and Mr. Hankins hate each other so much but they each want the workers on their side. You do something one boss's way, but then the other boss appears and is angry that you're not doing it another way. You don't know what to do at times to keep people happy.

Charlene read over her freewriting and then spent some time asking questions about her paragraph. "Exactly what do I want my point to be?" she asked. "And exactly how am I going to support that point?" With that in mind, she worked on several scratch outlines and wound up with the following:

Office politics are ruining the office.

1. *Bradley reports people's complaints.*

2. *Melissa steals ideas.*

3. *People gossip.*

4. *Ms. Bennett and Mr. Hankins make workers choose sides.*

Working from this outline, she then wrote the following first draft:

My office is being ruined by office politics. It seems like everybody is trying to play some sort of game to get ahead and don't care what it does to anybody else. One example is Bradley. Although he pretends to be friendly with people he isn't sincere. What he is trying to do is get them to complain about their bosses. Once they do, he goes back to the bosses and tells them what's been said and gets the worker in trouble. I've seen the same kind of thing happen at two other offices

continued

where I've worked. Melissa is another example of someone who plays office politics games. She steals other people's ideas and takes the credit for them. I had a good idea once on how to reduce office memos. I told her we ought to use e-mail to send office memos instead of typing them on paper. She went to Ms. Bennett and pretended the idea was hers. I guess I was partly to blame for not acting on the idea myself. And Ms. Bennett and Mr. Hankins hate each other and try to get us to take sides in their conflict. Then there is all the gossip that goes on. People do a lot of backbiting, and you have to be very careful about your behavior or people will start talking about you. All in all, office politics is really a problem where I work.

Development through Revising

After completing her first draft, Charlene put it aside until the next day. When she reread it, this was her response:

"I think the paragraph would be stronger if I made it about office politics in general instead of just politics in my office. The things I was writing about happen in many offices, not just in mine. And our instructor wants us to try some third-person writing. Also, I need to make better use of transitions to help the reader follow as I move from one example to another."

With these thoughts in mind, Charlene began revising her paragraph, and after several drafts she produced the paragraph that appears on page 186.

Writing an Exemplification Paragraph

WRITING ASSIGNMENT 1

The assignment here is to complete an unfinished paragraph (in the box), which has as its topic sentence, "People use MP3 players for more than just listening to music." Provide the supporting details needed to develop the examples. The first example is done for you.

Uses for MP3 Players

People use MP3 players for more than just listening to music. Many people wear earpieces connected to iPods or other MP3 players just so they can drown out annoying noises. *In a large city, being exposed to the roar of buses and trains for more than a few minutes can be nerve-wracking. Then there are the cars and taxis that blow their horns at each other and at pedestrians as they bully their way through traffic.*

Being plugged into an electronic device can also come in handy on a crowded bus, train, or other type of public transportation.

_____

_____

_____

Listening to background music on an MP3 player can help one concentrate on important tasks even when in busy places where others are coming and going and talking among themselves.

_____

_____

_____

---

continued

Finally, listening to these devices helps drown out unwanted noise at home.

_____

_____

_____

PREWRITING

a. On a separate piece of paper, jot down a couple of answers for each of the following questions.

- How can being plugged into an MP3 player help people avoid noise pollution on a bus, train, or other type of public transportation? What kinds of noise distractions have you experienced when using public transportation?

- What tasks do you find easier to concentrate on when listening to music that comes through an earpiece? Why does the music make it easier to concentrate on these tasks even when you are in a place that is crowded and noisy? Name specific places that you often find crowded and noisy.

- What kinds of unwanted noises annoy or disturb you at home? Does such noise break your concentration when you are trying to do something important? What are some of these tasks or projects?

Your instructor may ask you to work with one or two other students in generating the details needed to develop the three examples in the paragraph. The groups may then be asked to read their details aloud, with the class deciding which details are the most effective for each example.

Here and in general in your writing, try to generate *more* supporting material than you need. You are then in a position to choose the most convincing details for your paragraph.

b. Read over the details you have generated and decide which sound most effective. Jot down additional details as they occur to you.

c. Take your best details, reshape them as needed, and use them to complete the paragraph explaining why people plug into electronic devices.

REVISING

Read over the paragraph you have written. Ask yourself these questions.

FOUR BASES Checklist: Exemplification

ABOUT *UNITY*

✔ Do all of the examples I provide support the central idea that people use MP3 players for several reasons?

ABOUT *SUPPORT*

✔ Are there enough examples to make my point about MP3 players and convince others to agree with me?

✔ Do I appeal to my readers' senses with vivid, specific examples?

ABOUT *COHERENCE*

✔ Have I presented the examples in my paragraph in the most effective order?

ABOUT *SENTENCE SKILLS*

✔ Have I used specific rather than general words?

✔ Are my sentences varied in length and structure?

✔ Have I checked for spelling and other sentence skills, as listed on the inside back cover of the book?

Continue revising your work until you can answer "yes" to each of these questions.

WRITING ASSIGNMENT 2

Personal

Write an exemplification paragraph about techniques you use to make it through a day of school or work. These may include

Caffeine	Food
A system of rewards	Fantasizing
Humor	Speaking with friends
Praying or meditating	Just keeping busy

You might organize the paragraph by using time order. Show how you turn to your supports at various times during the day in order to cope with fatigue or boredom. For example, in the morning you might use coffee (with its dose of caffeine) to get started. Later in the day, you might go on to use other caffeine-related supports, such as drinking a Red Bull.

PREWRITING

a. Select the technique you will write about.

b. Make a list of examples that will support your point. A list for someone who uses caffeine might look like this:

Make pot of coffee
Purchase large Diet Vanilla Coke
Drink Red Bull
Eat chocolate bar
Buy coffee at Starbucks
Eat ice cream
Take two Excedrin
Munch on Perky Jerky

c. Read over your list and see how you might organize your items to reflect time order. The list above, for example, could be sequenced from morning to night.

   1. Consume high amounts of caffeine in the morning.
      a. Make a pot of coffee as soon as wake up
      b. Take two Excedrin before leaving house
      c. Purchase Starbucks double-shot latte at 10:00 a.m.
   2. Eat foods with caffeine in the afternoon
      a. Munch on Perky Jerky throughout the afternoon
      b. Eat chocolate bar and drink Red Bull for afternoon snack
   3. Continue consuming caffeine in the evening
      a. Purchase large Diet Vanilla Coke on way home
      b. Eat bowl of Bang! Caffeinated Ice Cream after dinner

d. Write the topic sentence of your paragraph. You should include the specific technique you are writing about. For example, you might write, "Without constant doses of caffeine, I cannot make it through the day."

   Remember to focus on only one specific technique, not a vague, general way of coping.

e. Now you have a topic sentence and an outline and are ready to write the first draft of your paragraph. Remember, as you flesh out the examples, that your goal is not just to *tell* us about the technique but to *show* us how it helps you get through the day.

REVISING

It's hard to criticize your own work honestly, especially right after you've finished writing. If at all possible, put your paragraph away for a day or so and then return to it. Better yet, wait a day and then read it aloud to a friend whose judgment you trust.

Read the paragraph with these questions in mind.

FOUR BASES Checklist: Exemplification

ABOUT *UNITY*

✔ Does my topic sentence clearly state what I am writing about and how this technique helps me through the day?

✔ Do the examples I provide truly demonstrate how and why I use this technique?

✔ Is there any irrelevant material that should be eliminated or rewritten?

ABOUT *SUPPORT*

✔ Have I provided enough specific details to solidly support my point?

ABOUT *COHERENCE*

✔ Have I organized my essay into a time-ordered paragraph?

✔ Have I used transition words to help readers follow my train of thought?

ABOUT *SENTENCE SKILLS*

✔ Have I used a consistent point of view throughout my essay?

✔ Have I used specific rather than general words?

✔ Have I used concise wording?

✔ Are my sentences varied?

✔ Have I proofread my essay for spelling and other sentence skills, as listed on the inside back cover of the book?

As you revise your essay through one or more additional drafts, continue to refer to this checklist until you can answer "yes" to each question.

WRITING ASSIGNMENT 3

Write a paragraph that uses examples to develop one of the following statements or a related statement of your own.

1. The daily life of a college student is filled with conflicts.

2. The Internet cannot always be a trusted source of information.

3. Abundant evidence exists that the United States has become a health-conscious nation.

4. Students attend college for various reasons.

5. One of my instructors, _____, has some good (*or* unusual) teaching techniques.

6. Travel is a great way to broaden an individual's way of thinking.

7. Wasted electricity is all around us.

8. Colleges have resources to help students succeed.

9. Apple and Microsoft should offer their products for free.

10. Dating in the workplace can be difficult.

11. It is easy to find opportunities to exercise in a normal, daily routine without going to a gym or jogging.

12. Some students at _____ do not care about learning (*or* are overly concerned about grades).

Be sure to choose examples that truly support your topic sentence. They should be relevant facts, statistics, personal experiences, or incidents you have heard or read about. Organize your paragraph by listing several examples that support your point. Save the most vivid, most convincing, or most important example for last.

WRITING ASSIGNMENT 4

As the cartoon on page 197 suggests, the diet of many Americans is not healthy. We eat too much junk food and far too much cholesterol. Write a paragraph with a topic sentence like one of those below:

The diet of the average American is unhealthy.

The diet of many American families is unhealthy.

Many schoolchildren in America do not have a healthy diet.

PREWRITING

a. To gather information you may need to do some research. In addition to the Internet, you'll find useful material if you go to the library and search

Dan Rosandich/www.CartoonStock.com

through article indexes for recent news magazines. (If you need help, ask your instructor or a reference librarian.) Or interview friends and acquaintances who might have a specific experience or a strong opinion about this topic.

b. To generate ideas for your essay, try the following exercise. Pretend that a visitor from Mars who has never heard of an unhealthy diet has asked you to explain it, as well as why you have the attitude you do toward it. Using the technique of freewriting—not worrying about sentence structure, organization, spelling, repetition, and so on—write an answer for the Martian. Throw in every reason you can think of to support your opinion.

c. As you look over the writing you've done for the Martian, note the strongest points. From them, select your three main supporting points. Are there other thoughts in your writing that can be used as supporting details for those points?

DRAFTING

a. Write your three supporting points. As you include your researched material, make sure you credit your sources. For instance, if you gathered information from a local nutrition council, you might want to include this sentence, "According to the El Paso Nutrition Council, '63 percent of families eat fast-food at least once a day'."

b. In your concluding statement, summarize the problem and restate why it is a problem.

WRITING ASSIGNMENT 5

Writing for a Specific Purpose and Audience

In this exemplification paragraph, you will write with a specific purpose and for a specific audience. Imagine that you are writing a television review for a college newspaper read by students just like you and your classmates. Your purpose will be to *recommend* the television programs you think are most worth watching.

Notice that the topic for this assignment is very broad. How can you discuss the many television shows you think are worth watching in a single paragraph? You decide to do some prewriting to narrow your topic.

Here's where paying attention to the specific needs or interests of your intended audience—students like you—can help. Through prewriting, you realize that reality shows, game shows, and crime dramas are among this group's favorite types of television programs. You decide to limit your paragraph to shows from one of these categories.

The next step is to express the point you want to make in a topic sentence. For example, you might start with "The most entertaining (reality shows, game shows, crime dramas) this season are _____, _____, and _____."

You see that you will have to do some more prewriting—in this case, research—to develop specific details for your paragraph. Begin by watching various episodes of the type of show you have chosen. Take detailed notes on what qualities make a specific show particularly entertaining. Is it suspenseful, clever, humorous, realistic? Write down examples that illustrate each of these qualities. Now, pick three shows you would recommend to readers.

When you write your outline, list the titles of the shows as your major headings. Then under each heading list two or three specific details that make that show particularly entertaining. For example, you might describe how a character's outrageous actions in a particular episode made you laugh.

After you have written the first draft of your paragraph, read it to make sure that your topic sentence is limited and clear, that you have included enough detail, and that your paragraph is both unified and coherent. Then revise and edit.

Process

This chapter will explain and illustrate how to

- develop a process paragraph
- write a process paragraph
- revise a process paragraph

In addition, you will read and evaluate

- three student process paragraphs

HOW DO YOU NAVIGATE ONLINE? Write a paragraph that informs a particular reader how to "surf the Web." For instance, you might tell film buffs how to find out about their favorite directors, or budding astronomers where to find the most up-to-date information online, or students where to find help in one or more of their courses. Be sure to imagine a specific audience with specific interests and take readers through the process of browsing the Internet step by step.

Every day we perform many activities that are *processes*—that is, series of steps carried out in a definite order. Many of these processes are familiar and automatic: for example, tying shoelaces, changing sheets, using a vending machine, and starting a car. We are thus seldom aware of the sequence of steps making up each activity. In other cases, such as when we are asked for directions to a particular place, or when we try to read and follow the directions for a new game, we may be painfully conscious of the whole series of steps involved in the process.

In this chapter, you will be asked to write a process paragraph—one that explains clearly how to do or make something. To prepare for this assignment, you should first read the student process papers below and then respond to the questions that follow.

TIP

In process writing, you are often giving instructions to the reader, so the pronoun *you* can appropriately be used. One of the following model paragraphs uses *you*—as indeed does much of this book, which gives instruction on how to write effectively. As a general rule, though, do not use *you* in your writing. Two of the following models demonstrate effective ways to write process paragraphs without using *you*.

Evaluating Student Paragraphs

Sneaking into the House at Night

[1]The first step I take is bringing my key along with me. [2]Obviously, I don't want to have to knock on the door at 1:30 in the morning and rouse my parents out of bed. [3]Second, I make it a point to stay out past midnight. [4]If I come in before then, my father is still up, and I'll have to face his disapproving look. [5]All I need in my life is for him to make me feel guilty. [6]Trying to make it as a college student is as much as I'm ready to handle. [7]Next, I am careful to be very quiet upon entering the house. [8]This involves lifting the front door up slightly as I open it, so that it does not creak. [9]It also means treating the floor and steps to the second floor

continued

like a minefield, stepping carefully over the spots that squeak. ¹⁰When I'm upstairs, I stop briefly in the bathroom without turning on the light. ¹¹Finally, I tiptoe to my room, put my clothes in a pile on a chair, and slip quietly into bed. ¹²With my careful method of sneaking into the house at night, I have avoided some major hassles with my parents.

Protecting the Skin

¹Being exposed to the sun or ultraviolet light regularly or for long periods can harm a person's skin. ²It can even cause skin cancer. ³There are several things that can be done to prevent this. ⁴First, a person should stay away from tanning booths. ⁵They are simply not safe. ⁶They use ultraviolet rays, which over time can cause severe damage. ⁷Second, and for the same reason, a person shouldn't use sun lamps or sit in the sun with a shiny reflector under the chin. ⁸Many young people use artificial tanning devices or sit under sun reflectors to clear up their complexions. ⁹However, there are many safer methods to solve acne problems. ¹⁰Next, even if a person doesn't have fair skin, it's important to avoid exposure to the sun especially during the hours of 11 A.M. to 3 P.M., when its rays are strongest. ¹¹Finally and most important, a person should wear a hat and cover both arms and legs when out in the sun for any length of time. ¹²In addition, he or she should use a sunscreen that has a sun protection factor (SPF) of 30. ¹³However, it should be remembered that many sun protectors wash off during swimming, so they must be reapplied. ¹⁴Also, it's worth noting that even the best sunscreen can't protect the human body from prolonged exposure.

Dealing with Verbal Abuse

¹If you are living with someone who abuses you verbally with criticism, complaints, and insults, you should take steps to change your situation. ²First, realize that you are not to blame for his or her abusive behavior. ³This may be difficult for you to believe. ⁴Years of verbal abuse have probably convinced you that you're responsible for everything that's wrong with your relationship. ⁵But that is a lie. ⁶If your partner is verbally

continued

abusive, it is that person's responsibility to learn why he or she chooses to deal with problems by saying nasty things. 7Perhaps he observed his father treating his mother that same way. 8Maybe she never learned any more positive ways to deal with negative emotions, like anger, fear, or disappointment. 9Steps two and three need to be done one right after the other. 10Step two is for you to announce that you will no longer tolerate being verbally abused. 11State that you are a person who deserves respect and civil behavior, and that you will accept no less. 12Next, offer to go with him or her to talk to a counselor who will help both of you learn new ways to communicate. 13While your partner learns to express his or her feelings without attacking you, you can learn to stand up for yourself and express your feelings clearly. 14If he or she refuses to take responsibility for changing abusive behavior, then you must consider step four: to leave that person. 15You were not put here on earth to have your self-concept demolished by serving as someone else's verbal punching bag.

QUESTIONS

ABOUT UNITY

1. Which paragraph lacks an opening topic sentence?

   _____

2. Which two sentences in "Sneaking into the House at Night" should be eliminated in the interest of paragraph unity? (*Write the sentence numbers here.*)

   _____   _____

ABOUT SUPPORT

3. After which sentence in "Protecting the Skin" are supportive details or examples needed?

   _____

4. Summarize the four steps in the process of dealing with verbal abuse.

   a. _____
   b. _____
   c. _____
   d. _____

ABOUT COHERENCE

5. Which of these paragraphs use or uses time order?

   _____

Which use or uses emphatic order?

_____

6. Which transition words introduce the first, second, and third steps in "Sneaking into the House at Night"?

_____   _____   _____

Developing a Process Paragraph

Development through Prewriting

To be successful, a process essay must explain clearly each step of an activity. The key to preparing to write such an essay is thinking through the activity as though you're doing it for the first time. Selma is the author of "Dealing with Verbal Abuse." As she considered possible topics for her paper, she soon focused on a situation in her own life: living with an abusive man. Selma had not known how to change her situation. But with the help of a counselor, she realized there were steps she could take—a process she could follow. She carried out that process and finally left her abusive partner. Remembering this, Selma decided to write about how to deal with abuse.

She began by making a list of the steps she followed in coping with her own abusive relationship. This is what she wrote:

> Tell him you won't accept any more abuse.
>
> Open your own checking account.
>
> Apply for credit cards in your own name.
>
> Offer to go with him to counseling.
>
> Realize you're not to blame.
>
> Learn to stand up for yourself.
>
> Go into counseling yourself if he won't do it.
>
> Call the police if he ever becomes violent.
>
> Leave him if he refuses to change.

Next, she numbered the steps in the order in which she had performed them. She crossed out some items she realized weren't really part of the process of dealing with verbal abuse.

2   Tell him you won't accept any more abuse.

~~Open your own checking account.~~

~~Apply for credit cards in your own name.~~

3   Offer to go with him to counseling.

1   Realize you're not to blame.

5   Learn to stand up for yourself.

4   Go into counseling yourself if he won't do it.

~~Call the police if he ever becomes violent.~~

6   Leave him if he refuses to change.

Then Selma grouped her items into four steps. Those steps were (1) realize you're not to blame; (2) tell the abuser you won't accept more abuse; (3) get into counseling, preferably with him; and (4) if necessary, leave him.

Selma was ready to write her first draft. Here it is.

Some people think that "abuse" has to mean getting punched and kicked, but that's not so. Verbal abuse can be as painful inside as physical abuse is on the outside. It can make you feel worthless and sad. I know because I lived with a verbally abusive man for years. Finally I found the courage to deal with the situation. Here is what I did. With the help of friends, I finally figured out that I wasn't to blame. I thought it was my fault because that's what he always told me—that if I wasn't so stupid, he wouldn't criticize and insult me. When I told him I wanted him to stop insulting and criticizing me, he just laughed at me and told me I was a crybaby. One of my friends suggested a counselor, and I asked Harry to go talk to him with me. We went together once but Harry wouldn't go back. He said he didn't need anyone to tell him how to treat his woman. I wasn't that surprised because Harry grew up with a father who treated his mother like dirt and his mom just accepts it to this day. Even after Harry refused to go see the counselor, though, I kept going. The counselor

continued

helped me see that I couldn't make Harry change, but I was still free to make my own choices. If I didn't want to live my life being Harry's verbal punching bag, and if he didn't want to change, then I would have to. I told Harry that I wasn't going to live that way anymore. I told him if he wanted to work together on better ways to communicate, I'd work with him. But otherwise, I would leave. He gave me his usual talk about "Oh, you know I don't really mean half the stuff I say when I'm mad." I said that wasn't a good enough excuse, and that I did mean what I was saying. He got mad all over again and called me every name in the book. I stuck around for a little while after that but then realized "This is it. I can stay here and take this or I can do what I know is right for me." So I left. It was a really hard decision but it was the right one. Harry may be angry at me forever but I know now that his anger and his verbal abuse are his problem, not mine.

Development through Revising

After Selma had written her first draft, she showed it to a classmate for her comments. Here is what the classmate wrote in response:

In order for this to be a good process essay, I think you need to do a couple of things.

First, although the essay is based on what you went through, I think it's too much about your own experience. I'd suggest you take yourself out of it and just write about how any person could deal with any verbally abusive situation. Otherwise this paper is about you and Harry, not the process.

Second, you need a clear topic sentence that tells the reader what process you're going to explain.

Third, I'd use transitions like "first" and "next" to make the steps in the process clearer. I think the steps are all there, but they get lost in all the details about you and Harry.

When Selma reread her first draft, she agreed with her classmate's suggestions. She then wrote the version of "Dealing with Verbal Abuse" that appears on pages 201–202.

Writing a Process Paragraph

Choose one of the topics below to write about in a process paragraph.

How to feed a family on a budget

How to break up with a boyfriend or girlfriend

How to keep your computer up-to-date and virus-free

How to change a car or bike tire

How to get rid of house or garden pests, such as mice, roaches, or wasps

How to play a simple game like checkers, tic-tac-toe, or an easy card game

How to shorten a skirt or pants

How to meet new people, for either dating or friendship

How to plant a garden

How to deal with a nosy person

How to fix a leaky faucet, a clogged drain, or the like

How to make tomato sauce

How to study for an important exam

How to conduct a yard or garage sale

How to wash dishes efficiently, clean a bathroom, or do laundry

PREWRITING

a. Begin by freewriting on your topic for ten minutes. Do not worry about spelling, grammar, organization, or other matters of form. Just write whatever comes into your head regarding the topic. Keep writing for more than ten minutes if ideas keep coming to you. This freewriting will give you a base of raw material to draw from during the next phase of your work on the paragraph. After freewriting, you should have a sense of whether there is enough material available for you to write a process paragraph about the topic. If so, continue as explained below. If there is not enough material, choose another topic and freewrite about *it* for ten minutes.

b. Write a clear, direct topic sentence stating the process you are going to describe. For instance, if you are going to describe a way to study for major exams, your topic sentence might be "My study-skills instructor has suggested a good way to study for major exams." Or you can state in your topic sentence the process and the number of steps involved: "My technique for changing a bike tire involves four main steps."

c. List all the steps you can think of that may be included in the process. Don't worry, at this point, about how each step fits or whether two steps overlap. Here, for example, is the list prepared by the author of "Sneaking into the House at Night":

> Quiet on stairs
> Come in after Dad's asleep
> House is freezing at night
> Bring key
> Know which steps to avoid
> Lift up front door
> Late dances on Saturday night
> Don't turn on bathroom light
> Avoid squeaky spots on floor
> Get into bed quietly

d. Number your items in the order in which they occur; strike out items that do not fit in the list; add others that come to mind. The author of "Sneaking into the House at Night" did this step as follows:

> ~~Quiet on stairs~~
> 2 Come in after Dad's asleep
> ~~House is freezing at night~~
> 1 Bring key
> 5 Know which steps to avoid
> 3 Lift up front door
> ~~Late dances on Saturday night~~
> 6 Don't turn on bathroom light
> 4 Avoid squeaky spots on floor
> 8 Get into bed quietly
> 7 Undress quietly

e. Use your list as a guide to write the first draft of your paragraph. As you write, try to think of additional details that will support your opening sentence. Do not expect to finish your composition in one draft. After you complete your first rough draft, in fact, you should be ready to write a series of drafts as you work toward the goals of unity, support, and coherence.

REVISING

After you have written the first draft of your paragraph, set it aside for a while if you can. Then read it out loud, either to yourself or (better yet) to a friend or classmate who will be honest with you about how it sounds. You (or you and your friend) should keep these points in mind.

FOUR BASES Checklist: Process

ABOUT *UNITY*

✔ An effective process composition describes a series of events in a way that is clear and easy to follow. Are the steps in your paragraph described in a clear, logical way?

ABOUT *SUPPORT*

✔ Does your paragraph explain every necessary step so that a reader could perform the task described?

ABOUT *COHERENCE*

✔ Have you used transitions such as *first, next, also, then, after, now, during,* and *finally* to make the paper move smoothly from one step to another?

ABOUT *SENTENCE SKILLS*

✔ Is the point of view consistent? For example, if you begin by writing "This is how I got rid of mice" (first person), do not switch to "You must buy the right traps" (second person). Write this paragraph either from the first-person point of view (using *I* and *we*) or from the second-person point of view (*you*)—do not jump back and forth from one to the other.

✔ Have you corrected any sentence-skills mistakes that you noticed while reading the paragraph out loud? Have you checked the composition for sentence skills, including spelling, as listed on the inside back cover of this book?

Continue revising your work until you and your reader can answer "yes" to each of these questions.

Write a paragraph about one of the following processes. For this assignment, you will be working with more general topics than those in Writing Assignment 1. In fact, many of the topics are so broad that entire books have been written about them. A big part of your task, then, will be to narrow the topic down enough so that it can be covered in one paragraph. Then you'll have to invent your own steps for the process. In addition, you'll need to make decisions about how many steps to include and the order in which to present them.

How to break a bad habit such as smoking, overeating, or excess drinking

How to improve a course you have taken

How to help someone you know to feel happy

How to be less concerned about yourself and more concerned about others

How to improve the place where you work

How to show appreciation to others

How to get someone to forgive you

How to be more "green"

How to make your life less hectic

How to be a good parent

How to fail at something (the paragraph written on this topic is intended to be funny)

How to flirt

PREWRITING

a. Choose a topic that appeals to you. Then ask yourself, "How can I make this broad, general topic narrow enough to be covered in a paragraph?" A logical way to proceed would be to think of a particular time you have gone through this process. For instance, if the general topic is "How to decorate economically," you might think about a time you decorated your own apartment.

b. Write a topic sentence about the process you are going to describe. Your topic sentence should clearly reflect the narrowed-down topic you have chosen. If you chose the topic described in step *a*, for example, your topic sentence could be "I made my first apartment look nice without spending a fortune."

c. Make a list of as many different items as you can think of that concern your topic. Don't worry about repeating yourself, about putting the items in order, about whether details are major or minor, or about spelling. Simply make a list of everything about your topic that occurs to you.

Here, for instance, is a list of items generated by the student writing about decorating her apartment on a budget:

> Bought pretty towels and used them as wall hangings
>
> Trimmed overgrown shrubs in front yard
>
> Used old mayonnaise jars for vases to hold flowers picked in the yard
>
> Found an old oriental rug at a yard sale
>
> Painted mismatched kitchen chairs in bright colors
>
> Kept dishes washed and put away
>
> Bought a slipcover for a battered couch
>
> Used pink lightbulbs
>
> Hung pretty colored sheets over the windows

d. Next, decide what order you will present your items in and number them. (As in the example of "decorating an apartment," there may not be an order that the steps *must* be done in. If that is the case, you'll need to make a decision about a sequence that makes sense, or that you followed yourself.) As you number your items, strike out items that do not fit in the list and add others that you think of, like this:

> 6   Bought pretty towels and used them as wall hangings
>
>   ~~Trimmed overgrown shrubs in front yard~~
>
> 7   Used old mayonnaise jars for vases to hold flowers picked in the yard
>
> 4   Found an old oriental rug at a yard sale
>
> 2   Painted mismatched kitchen chairs in bright colors
>
>   ~~Kept dishes washed and put away~~
>
> 1   Bought a slipcover for a battered couch
>
> 8   Used pink lightbulbs
>
> 5   Hung pretty colored sheets over the windows
>
> 3   Built bookshelves out of cinder blocks and boards

e. Referring to your list of steps, write the first draft of your paper. Add additional steps as they occur to you.

REVISING

If you can, put your first draft away for a day or so and then return to it. Read it out loud to yourself or, better yet, to a friend who will give you honest feedback.

Here are questions to ask yourself as you read over your first draft and the drafts to follow.

FOUR BASES Checklist: Process

ABOUT *UNITY*

✔ Have I included a clear topic sentence that tells what process I will be describing?

✔ Is the rest of my paragraph on target in support of my topic sentence?

ABOUT *SUPPORT*

✔ Have I included all the essential information so that anyone reading my paper could follow the same process?

ABOUT *COHERENCE*

✔ Have I made the sequence of steps easy to follow by using transitions like *first, second, then, next, during,* and *finally*?

ABOUT *SENTENCE SKILLS*

✔ Have I used a consistent point of view throughout my paragraph?

✔ Have I used specific rather than general words?

✔ Have I used concise wording?

✔ Are my sentences varied?

✔ Have I checked for spelling and other sentence skills, as listed on the inside back cover of the book?

Continue revising your work until you can answer "yes" to each of these questions.

WRITING ASSIGNMENT 3

Write in detail about a person who provided help at an important time in your life. State in the first sentence who the person is, the person's relationship to you (friend, father, cousin, etc.), and the situation the person helped you with. For example, "My grandmother's support helped me greatly during the difficult time when my parents were getting divorced" or "My grandmother guided me through all the preparations necessary for my wedding." Then provide specific examples (the person's words and actions) to show the process in which he or she helped you get through the situation or prepare for the event.

To support the topic sentence in the first example, you could say that your grandmother called you every day, met with you once a week, or attended all of your basketball games or drama performances to help you cope with the stress at home. You might add that in particularly trying moments your grandmother took you for long walks in the park, along the lake, or in other peaceful places, to encourage you and cheer you up with words of comfort and wisdom.

To support the topic sentence in the second example, you might enumerate the specific steps in planning the wedding: going bridal shopping, meeting with the minister, and making the major decisions leading up to your wedding. You will want to include ways in which your grandmother's guidance helped you during each step. For example, you might show how her pragmatic approach helped you save money in times when your emotions overtook logic and include specific instances of this help.

WRITING ASSIGNMENT 4

Write a paragraph for a younger brother, sister, or other relative on the steps involved in preparing for a successful interview. You can find information on the Internet, so do some research on the topic first. Read at least three different Web sites for information. Your reading will help you think about how to proceed. Remember, however, that any information you take from another source, such as a Web site, must be properly credited whether you write it word-for-word (quotation) or in your own words (paraphrase).

After gathering information, note which steps seem to be repeated most often or are stressed in the various sites you researched. Condense this information into four or five basic steps. Try to rewrite the steps in your own words (paraphrase), but be sure to acknowledge where the information originated. For example, you might write a statement such as, "According to numerous sources, including the *Wall Street Journal,* an important first step in the process is appearing well-manicured—dressing professionally, having clean and neatly trimmed hair, and keeping breath mints handy."

Writing for a Specific Purpose and Audience

In this process paragraph, you will write with a specific purpose and for a specific audience. You have two options.

OPTION 1

Imagine that you have a part-time job helping out in a day care center. The director, who is pleased with your work and wants to give you more responsibility, has put you in charge of a group activity (for example, an exercise session, an alphabet lesson, or a valentine-making project). But before you actually begin the activity, the director wants to see a summary of how you would go about it. What advance preparation would be needed, and what exactly would you be doing throughout the time of the project? Write a paragraph explaining the steps you would follow in conducting the activity.

OPTION 2

Imagine you have been asked to write a letter or e-mail message to members of your college's next incoming class. Explain one thing that these future college students can do to improve their chances of succeeding. For example, explain how to take notes, how to study for an exam, or how to make use of the college's tutoring services.

10

Cause and/or Effect

This chapter will explain and illustrate how to

- develop a cause and/or effect paragraph
- write a cause and/or effect paragraph
- revise a cause and/or effect paragraph

In addition, you will read and evaluate

- three student cause and/or effect paragraphs

HOW DOES TERRORISM AFFECT DAILY LIFE?

Write a paragraph in which you explain the effects of a significant terrorist attack, like the one pictured here from the 2013 Boston Marathon, on the city in which the attack occurred and on the nation. Think about how such an event might affect daily life. What changes might it cause in the public's acceptance of increased security vis-à-vis the right to privacy? How might it affect you personally?

What caused Will to drop out of school? Why are reality TV shows so popular? Why does our football team do so poorly each year? How has retirement affected Mom? What effects does divorce have on children? Every day we ask such questions and look for answers. We realize that situations have causes and also effects—good or bad. By examining causes and effects, we seek to understand and explain things.

In this chapter, you will be asked to do some detective work by examining the causes or the effects of something. First read the three student paragraphs that follow and answer the questions about them. All three paragraphs support their opening points by explaining a series of causes and/or effects.

Evaluating Student Paragraphs

The Benefits of Exercise

¹The effects of regular exercise can change a person's life. ²First, walking or running three miles a day can burn about 250 calories. ³That adds up to a weight loss of about half a pound a week even without dieting! ⁴Over a year, about twenty-six pounds can be shed. ⁵Second, exercise helps the heart and circulatory system, thereby increasing the flow of oxygen and, in the long run, lessening the chances of contracting heart disease. ⁶Perhaps most significantly, however, exercise releases endorphins, compounds produced by glands in the body, which help fight depression and improve one's emotional health!

Treatment of American Indians

¹Two major policies, the Indian Removal Act of 1830 and the Dawes Severalty Act of 1887, had profound and lasting effects on American Indians. ²In 1830, President Andrew Jackson signed the act that authorized the United States government to transfer eastern American Indians like the Cherokee into unclaimed western territories. ³After several years of court battles, what followed was one of the most heartbreaking events in early American history—The Trail of Tears. ⁴Thousands of Cherokee men, women, and children were forced to march over a thousand miles to Oklahoma. ⁵Estimates say that at least four thousand died on the journey. ⁶It is terrible that people had to suffer like this and it should not have been

continued

allowed to happen. 7Then, in 1887, the Dawes Act gave the United States government the right to divide reservation lands among individual American Indians and their families. 8In other words, it offered plots of land to those who were willing to sign a registry, anglicize their name, and renounce allegiance to their tribe. 9Reservations were broken up, tribes fought among themselves, and the unity that was central to tribes' survival disappeared. 10Today, there are about three hundred reservations in the United States, but there are over five hundred recognized tribes. 11Most reservations are located in the western portion of the United States in areas that often lack natural resources, and many have high rates of poverty and unemployment.

Why I Stopped Smoking

1For one thing, I realized that my cigarette smoke bothered others, irritating people's eyes and causing them to cough and sneeze. 2They also had to put up with my stinking smoker's breath. 3Also, cigarettes are a messy habit. 4Our house was littered with ashtrays piled high with butts, matchsticks, and ashes, and the children were always knocking them over. 5Cigarettes are expensive, and I estimated that the carton a week that I was smoking cost me about $2,000 a year. 6Another reason I stopped was that the message about cigarettes being harmful to health finally got through to me. 7I'd known they could hurt the smoker—in fact, a heavy smoker I know from work is in Eagleville Hospital now with lung cancer. 8But when I realized what secondhand smoke could do to my wife and children, causing them bronchial problems and even increasing their risk of cancer, it really bothered me. 9Cigarettes were also inconvenient. 10Whenever I smoked, I would have to drink something to wet my dry throat, and that meant I had to keep going to the bathroom all the time. 11I sometimes seemed to spend whole weekends doing nothing but smoking, drinking, and going to the bathroom. 12Most of all, I resolved to stop smoking because I felt exploited. 13I hated the thought of wealthy, greedy corporations making money off my sweat and blood. 14The rich may keep getting richer, but—at least as regards cigarettes—with no thanks to me.

QUESTIONS

ABOUT UNITY

1. Which sentence in "Treatment of American Indians" does not support the opening idea and should be omitted?

   _____

2. Which of the above paragraphs lacks a topic sentence?

   _____

ABOUT SUPPORT

3. How many separate causes are given in "Why I Stopped Smoking"?

_____ four   _____ six   _____ seven   _____ eight

4. How many effects of regular exercise are discussed in "The Benefits of Exercise"?

_____ one   _____ two   _____ three   _____ four

ABOUT COHERENCE

5. Which sentences in "Treatment of American Indians" contain transition words or phrases? (Write the sentence numbers here.)

_____   _____   _____   _____   _____

6. In "The Benefits of Exercise," what words signal the effect the author thinks is most important?

_____

Developing a Cause and/or Effect Paragraph

Development through Prewriting

In order to write a good cause and/or effect paragraph, you must clearly define an effect (*what* happened) and the contributing causes (*why* it happened). In addition, you will need to provide details that support the causes and effects you're writing about.

Jerome is the student author of "Why I Stopped Smoking." As soon as the topic occurred to him, he knew he had his *effect* (he had stopped smoking). His next task was to come up with a list of *causes* (reasons he had stopped). He decided to make a list of all the reasons for his quitting smoking that he could think of. This is what he came up with:

Annoyed others

Messy

Bad for health

Expensive

Taking his list, Jerome then jotted down details that supported each of those reasons:

Annoyed others

Bad breath

Irritates eyes

Makes other people cough

People hate the smell

Messy

Ashtrays, ashes, butts everywhere

Messes up my car interior

Bad for health

Marco in hospital with lung cancer

Secondhand smoke dangerous to family

My morning cough

Expensive

Carton a week costs more than $2,000 a year

Tobacco companies getting rich off me

Jerome then had an effect and four causes with details to support them. On the basis of this list, he wrote a first draft.

My smoking annoyed other people, making them cough and burning their eyes. I bothered them with my smoker's breath. Nonsmokers usually hate the smell of cigarettes and I got embarrassed when nonsmokers visited my house. I saw them wrinkle their noses in disgust at the smell. It is a messy habit. My house was full of loaded ashtrays that the kids were always knocking over. My car was messy too. A guy from work, Marco, who has smoked for years, is in the hospital now with lung

continued

cancer. It doesn't look as though he's going to make it. Secondhand smoke is bad for people too and I worried it would hurt my wife and kids. Also I realized I was coughing once in a while. The price of cigarettes keeps going up and I was spending too much on smokes. When I see things in the paper about tobacco companies and their huge profits it made me mad.

Development through Revising

The next day, Jerome traded first drafts with his classmate Roger. This is what Roger had to say about Jerome's work.

The biggest criticism I have is that you haven't used many transitions to tie your sentences together. Without them, the paragraph sounds like a list, not a unified piece of writing.

Is one of your reasons more important than the others? If so, it would be good if you indicated that.

You could add a little more detail in several places. For instance, how could secondhand smoke hurt your family? And how much were you spending on cigarettes?

As Jerome read his own paper, he realized he wanted to add one more reason to his paragraph: the inconvenience to himself. "Maybe it sounds silly to write about always getting drinks and going to the bathroom, but that's one of the ways that smoking takes over your life that you never think about when you start," he said. Using Roger's comments and his own new idea, he produced the paragraph that appears on page 216.

Writing a Cause and/or Effect Paragraph

WRITING ASSIGNMENT 1

Choose one of the three topic sentences and brief outlines below. Each is made up of three supporting points (causes or effects). Your task is to turn the topic sentence and outline into a cause or effect paragraph.

OPTION 1

Topic sentence: There are several reasons why some high school graduates are unable to read.

(1) Failure of parents (*cause*)
(2) Failure of schools (*cause*)
(3) Failure of students themselves (*cause*)

OPTION 2

Topic sentence: Living with roommates (or family) makes attending college difficult.

HAVE YOU EVER SHARED A ROOM WITH SOMEONE? BRAINSTORM A LIST OF THE benefits and the drawbacks. What advice would you give someone who was living with a roommate for the first time?

(1) Late-night hours (*cause*)

(2) More temptations (*cause*)

(3) More distractions (*cause*)

OPTION 3

Topic sentence: Attending college has changed my personality in positive ways.

(1) More confident (*effect*)

(2) More knowledgeable (*effect*)

(3) More adventurous (*effect*)

PREWRITING

a. After you've chosen the option that appeals to you most, jot down all the details you can think of that might go under each of the supporting points. Use a separate piece of paper for your lists. Don't worry yet about whether you can use all the items—your goal is to generate more material than you need. Here, for example, are some of the details generated by the author of "The Benefits of Exercise" to back up her supporting points:

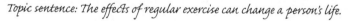

Topic sentence: The effects of regular exercise can change a person's life.

1. *Helps lose weight*

    a. *Running/walking three miles can burn about 250 calories*

    b. *This adds up to half a pound a week*

    c. *Can lose about twenty-six pounds a year*

    d. *Swimming or lifting weights for an hour equally effective*

2. *Helps circulatory system, lungs*

    a. *Lowers heart rate*

    b. *Increases oxygen flow*

    c. *Lessens chances of developing heart disease*

    d. *Increases lung capacity*

3. *Helps improve emotional health*

    a. *Makes for better sleep*

    b. *Relieves tension*

    c. *Releases endorphins, which help fight depression*

    d. *Improves emotional outlook*

b. Now go through the details you have generated and decide which are most effective. Strike out the ones you decide are not worth using. Do other details occur to you? If so, jot them down as well.

c. Now you are ready to write your paragraph. Begin the paragraph with the topic sentence you chose. Make sure to develop each of the supporting points from the outline into a complete sentence, and then back it up with the best of the details you have generated.

REVISING

Review your paragraph with these questions in mind.

FOUR BASES Checklist: Cause and/or Effect

ABOUT *UNITY*

✔ Have I begun the paragraph with the topic sentence provided?

✔ Are any sentences in my paragraph not directly relevant to this topic sentence?

ABOUT *SUPPORT*

✔ Is each supporting point stated in a complete sentence?

✔ Have I provided effective details to back up each supporting point?

ABOUT *COHERENCE*

✔ Have I used transitions such as *in addition, another thing,* and *also* to make relationships between the sentences clear?

ABOUT *SENTENCE SKILLS*

✔ Have I avoided wordiness?

✔ Have I proofread the paragraph for sentence-skills errors, including spelling, as listed on the inside back cover of the book?

Revise your paragraph until you are sure the answer to each question is "yes."

WRITING ASSIGNMENT 2

Most of us find it easy to criticize other people, but we may find it harder to give compliments. In this assignment, you will be asked to write a one-paragraph letter praising someone. The letter may be to a person you know (for instance, a parent, relative, or friend); to a public figure (an actor, politician, religious leader, sports star, and so on); or to a company or an organization (for example, a newspaper, a government agency, a store where you shop, or the manufacturer of a product you own).

PREWRITING

a. The fact that you are writing this letter indicates that its recipient has had an *effect* on you: You like, admire, or appreciate the person or organization. Your job will be to put into words the *causes,* or reasons, for this good feeling. Begin by making a list of reasons for your admiration. Here, for example, are a few reasons a person might praise an automobile manufacturer:

> My car is dependable.
>
> The price was reasonable.
>
> I received prompt action on a complaint.
>
> The car is well-designed.
>
> The car dealer was honest and friendly.
>
> The car has needed little maintenance.

Reasons for admiring a parent might include these:

> You are patient with me.
>
> You are fair.
>
> You have a great sense of humor.
>
> You encourage me in several ways.
>
> I know you have made sacrifices for me.

Develop your own list of reasons for admiring the person or organization you've chosen.

b. Now that you have a list of reasons, you need details to back up each reason. Jot down as many supporting details as you can for each reason. Here is what the writer of a letter to the car manufacturer might do:

My car is dependable.

Started during last winter's coldest days when neighbors' cars wouldn't start

Has never stranded me anywhere

The price was reasonable.

Costs less than other cars in its class

Came standard with more options than other cars of the same price

I received prompt action on a complaint.

When I complained about rattle in door, manufacturer arranged for a part to be replaced at no charge

The car is well-designed.

Controls are easy to reach

Dashboard gauges are easy to read

The car dealer was honest and friendly.

No pressure, no fake "special deal only today"

The car has needed little maintenance.

Haven't done anything but regular tune-ups and oil changes

---

c. Next, select from your list the three or four reasons that you can best support with effective details. These will make up the body of your letter.

d. For your topic sentence, make the positive statement you wish to support. For example, the writer of the letter to the car manufacturer might begin like this: "I am a very satisfied owner of a 2010 Accord."

e. Now combine your topic sentence, reasons, and supporting details, and write a draft of your letter.

REVISING

If possible, put your letter aside for a day. Then read it aloud to a friend. As you and he or she listen to your words, you should both keep these questions in mind.

FOUR BASES Checklist: Cause and/or Effect

ABOUT *UNITY*

✔ Is the topic sentence a positive statement that is supported by the details?

✔ Is the rest of my letter on target in support of my topic sentence?

ABOUT *SUPPORT*

✔ Does the letter clearly state several different reasons for liking and admiring the person or organization?

✔ Is each of those reasons supported with specific evidence?

ABOUT *COHERENCE*

✔ Are the sentences linked with transitional words and phrases?

ABOUT *SENTENCE SKILLS*

✔ Have I avoided wordiness?

✔ Are my sentences varied?

✔ Have I checked for spelling and other sentence skills, as listed on the inside back cover of the book?

Continue revising your work until you and your reader can answer "yes" to each of these questions.

WRITING ASSIGNMENT 3

Personal

Write a paragraph about a particular addiction. You might write about someone you know who is addicted to smoking, drinking, shopping, playing video games, or surfing the Internet. In your paragraph, discuss several possible reasons for this addiction, or several effects on the person's life.

Here are some sample topic sentences for such a paragraph:

> My cousin is addicted to overeating, and her addiction is harming her in a number of ways.

> There were at least three reasons why I became addicted to cigarettes.

> Although shopping can be a pleasant activity, addictive shopping can be destructive for several reasons.

STUDY THE POSTER PICTURED HERE.
What does it seem to suggest? How do the woman's expression and clenched fists help you better understand the meaning of the poster?

WRITING ASSIGNMENT 4

Personal

Are you as good a writer as you want to be? Write a paragraph analyzing the reasons you have become a good writer or explaining why you are not as good as you'd like to be. Begin by considering some factors that may have influenced your writing ability.

Your family background: Did you see people writing at home? Did your parents respect and value the ability to write?

Your school experience: Did you have good writing teachers? Did you have a history of failure or success with writing? Was writing fun, or was it a chore? Did your school emphasize writing?

Social influences: How did your school friends do at writing? What were your friends' attitudes toward writing? What feelings about writing did you pick up from TV or the movies?

You might want to organize your paragraph by describing the three greatest influences on your skill (or your lack of skill) as a writer. Show how each of these has contributed to the present state of your writing.

Here are some sample topic sentences for such a paragraph:

> There are three main reasons I have been unsuccessful in my writing.

> I am a strong writer because of my mother, my teachers, and my grandmother.

> Since my friends all enjoyed writing, I began to learn to like it.

WRITING ASSIGNMENT 5

Explore the reasons behind an event making news in your town or on your campus. For example, you might want to focus on the causes of

A change in parking regulations or fees

An increase in tuition or student fees

The hiring of a new professor or dean

A local tax increase

The election of a local official

The construction or closing of a public school

A change in school district boundaries

Research the reasons for the event by talking to school or local officials, reading current newspapers, reading government or school district Web sites, watching local newscasts, or consulting an Internet news source.

Decide on the major cause or causes of the event and their specific effects. Then write a paragraph explaining in detail the causes and/or effects. To avoid any possible plagiarism, you will want to properly credit your sources. Below is a sample topic sentence for this assignment.

> The fifth accident in two months caused by drag racing in the college's main parking lot has created serious concern among students, faculty, and staff, who are demanding that campus police patrol that area more frequently.

Notice that the sentence contains general words such as *concern, demanding,* and *frequently,* which can summarize specific supporting details. Support for *frequently,* for example, might include details about how often campus police currently patrol the area and how often the campus community would like them to do so.

WRITING ASSIGNMENT 6

Writing for a Specific Purpose and Audience

In this paragraph, you will write with a specific purpose and for a specific audience. Choose one of the following options.

OPTION 1

Assume that your boss has asked you to prepare a report about an issue that is affecting your career field. In your report, you should explain what has caused this issue. For instance, nurses might be affected by a rise in workload because of a lack of qualified nurses, budget cuts, or an increase in patients. Or the health of city workers could be compromised because of the need to work in old buildings with poor air duct systems, mold problems, or poor heating.

OPTION 2

Alternatively, think about the effects that this issue might have on your career field. Write a report to your boss indicating what the impact of this issue will be on you. For instance, nurses who have larger workloads may be suffering exhaustion that could lead to mistakes made on the job. Or employees who are highly allergic to mold could wind up missing multiple days of work, thus burdening other employees who would need to cover their shifts.

Comparison and/or Contrast

This chapter will explain and illustrate how to

- develop a comparison and/or contrast paragraph
- write a comparison and/or contrast paragraph
- revise a comparison and/or contrast paragraph

In addition, you will study and evaluate

- three student comparison and/or contrast paragraphs and three additional paragraphs
- two common methods of development in a comparison and/or contrast paragraph

HOW DO EXPERIENCES COMPARE OR CONTRAST?

Look at this photograph and write a paragraph in which you compare or contrast the experience of attending a sporting event in person versus that of viewing one on television. Be sure to note how spectators in the photo are acting. Use one or more examples from this photo to support your point.

Comparison and contrast are two everyday thought processes. When we *compare* two things, we show how they are similar; when we *contrast* two things, we show how they are different. We might compare or contrast two brand-name products (for example, Nike versus New Balance running shoes), two television shows, two instructors, two jobs, two friends, or two courses of action we could take in a given situation. The purpose of comparing or contrasting is to understand each of the two things more clearly and, at times, to make judgments about them.

In this chapter, you will learn about two common methods of developing a comparison and/or contrast paragraph. First, read the two paragraphs that follow and focus on the particular way each develops its points.

Evaluating Student Paragraphs

Landenburg: Then and Now

¹Landenburg has changed for the better over the last ten years. ²Twenty years ago, the town experienced an economic downturn. ³The electrical supply factory, which employed more than five hundred people, had just closed down. ⁴The hundred-year-old high school needed repair: Its roof leaked, the masonry was cracked, the heating system was undependable, and its outside walls were covered with graffiti. ⁵The science labs contained only outdated or broken equipment. ⁶Students were using books that were very old, and pages were missing in some of them. ⁷Barker Avenue, the town's main shopping area, contained several boarded-up storefronts, and most of the other stores advertised going-out-of-business sales. ⁸There were always plenty of parking spaces because fewer and fewer customers shopped there. ⁹It was as if an economic disease had attacked the heart of Landenburg. ¹⁰About ten years ago, however, things changed. ¹¹The local economy got better. ¹²A manufacturer of automobile brake pads relocated in Landenburg, building a huge factory just outside of town. ¹³Then a restaurant supply factory moved in, and last year the state university broke ground for an extension campus two miles away. ¹⁴As a result, many new jobs have been created, and with increased tax revenues, the town was able to replace the old high school with one that has modern laboratories and offers students brand-new books. ¹⁵The new jobs have also boosted consumer confidence. ¹⁶The downtown shopping area has several new stores and restaurants. ¹⁷A ten-screen movie complex just opened, and not one of the town's commercial buildings is for rent. ¹⁸And because of the increased activity, downtown parking spaces are sometimes impossible to find. ¹⁹The entire town seems to have gotten a lot healthier.

Day versus Evening Students

¹As a part-time college student who has taken both day and evening courses, I have observed notable differences between day and evening students. ² First of all, day and evening students differ greatly in age, styles, and interests. ³The students in my daytime classes are all about the same age, with similar clothing styles and similar interests. ⁴Most are in their late teens to early twenties, and whether male or female, they

continued

pretty much dress alike. [5]Their uniform consists of jeans, a T-shirt, running shoes, a baseball cap, and maybe a gold earring or two. [6]They use the same popular slang, talk about the same movies and TV shows, and know the same musical artists. [7]But students in my evening courses are much more diverse. [8]Some are in their late teens, but most range from young married people in their twenties and thirties to people my grandparents' age. [9]Generally, their clothing is more formal than the day students'. [10]They are dressed for the workplace, not for a typical college classroom. [11]Many of the women wear skirts or dresses; the men often wear dress shirts or sweaters. [12]And they are more comfortable talking about mortgages or work schedules or child care than about what was on TV last night. [13]Day and evening students also have very different responsibilities. [14]For day students, college and a part-time job are generally the only major responsibilities. [15]They have plenty of time to study and get assignments done. [16]However, evening students lead much more complicated lives than most day students. [17]They may come to campus after putting in a nine-to-five day at work. [18]Most have children to raise or grandchildren to baby-sit for. [19]When they miss a class or hand in an assignment late, it's usually because of a real problem, such as a sick child or an important deadline at work. [20]Finally, day and evening students definitely have different attitudes toward school. [21]Day students often seem more interested in the view out the window or the cute classmate in the next row than in what the instructor is saying. [22]They doze, draw cartoons, whisper, and write notes instead of paying attention. [23]In contrast, evening students sit up straight, listen hard, and ask the instructor lots of questions. [24]They obviously are there to learn, and they don't want their time wasted. [25]In short, day students and night students are as different as . . . day and night.

THE STUDENT WRITER OF "DAY versus Evening Students" uses the different appearances of day and evening students to support his or her argument. Looking at the woman pictured here, would you say she is a day or an evening student, or not a student at all? What generalizations do we often make about people based on their appearance? Are these generalizations fair? Write a paragraph in which you explore this topic.

Complete this comment: The difference in the methods of contrast in the two paragraphs is that

_____

_____

_____

Compare your answer with the following explanation of the two methods of development used in comparison and/or contrast paragraphs.

Two Common Methods of Development

There are two common methods, or formats, of development in a comparison and/or contrast paper. One format presents the details *one side at a time*. The other presents the details *point by point*. Each format is explained below.

One Side at a Time

Look at the outline of "Landenburg: Then and Now":

Topic sentence: Landenburg has changed for the better over the last ten years.

A. *Landenburg 20 years ago (first half of paragraph)*

   1. *Economic downturn*

   2. *Electrical supply factory closes*

   3. *More than 500 jobs lost*

   4. *High school in disrepair, poorly equipped*

   5. *Many downtown shops closed or closing*

B. *Landenburg today (second half of paragraph)*

   1. *Things change; local economy better*

   2. *New companies move in; state university building extension campus*

   3. *New jobs created*

   4. *New high school built—modern labs, new books*

   5. *Revival of downtown shopping district*

When you use the one-side-at-a-time method, follow the same order of points of contrast or comparison for each side, as in the outline above. For example, both the first half of the paper and the second half begin with the same idea: the state of the economy. Then both sides go on to companies, jobs, the high school, and so on.

Point by Point

Now look at the outline of "Day versus Evening Students":

> _Topic sentence:_ _There are notable differences between day and night students._
>
> A. _Age and related interests and tastes in clothing_
>   1. _Youthful nature of day students_
>   2. _Older nature of evening students_
> B. _Amount of responsibilities_
>   1. _Lighter responsibilities of day students_
>   2. _Heavier responsibilities of evening students_
> C. _Attitude toward school_
>   1. _Casual attitude of day students_
>   2. _Serious attitude of evening students_

The outline shows how the two kinds of students are contrasted point by point. First, the writer contrasts the ages, clothing styles, and interests of daytime students and evening students. Next, the writer contrasts the limited responsibilities of the daytime students with the heavier responsibilities of the evening students. Finally, the writer contrasts the casual attitude toward school of the daytime students and the serious attitude of the evening students.

When you begin a comparison and/or contrast paper, you should decide right away which format you are going to use: one side at a time or point by point. An outline is an essential step in helping you decide which format will be more workable for your topic. Keep in mind, however, that an outline is just a guide, not a permanent commitment. If you later feel that you've chosen the wrong format, you can reshape your outline to the other format.

Complete the statements and the partial outline that follow.

1. **The United States Congress: Two Branches**

   The United States Congress, the federal government's law-making branch, is made up of two different bodies: the Senate and the House of Representatives. The Senate consists of one hundred members, two

continued

from each state. Until 1913, senators were elected by state legislatures, but the Seventeenth Amendment to the Constitution, approved in that year, now requires the direct election of senators by each state's citizens. Senators serve six-year terms, and about one-third of the members are eligible for reelection every two years. The presiding officer of the Senate is the vice president of the United States. The House of Representatives has 435 members representing congressional districts across the United States. The boundaries of a congressional district are determined, theoretically at least, by the number of people residing in the district. Therefore, while New Jersey has twelve congressional districts, Wyoming, with a much smaller population, has only one. Members of the House serve for two-year terms, at the end of which all members must be reelected if they wish to continue. The presiding officer of this body is the Speaker of the House, who is elected by members of the majority party. Whenever the two branches pass different versions of a bill, a committee consisting of both representatives and senators meets to resolve the differences.

Topic sentence: The United States Congress, the federal government's law-making branch, is made up of two different bodies: the Senate and the House of Representatives.

   a. The Senate
      (1) Consists of 100 members
      (2) Before 1913 was elected by state legislature; today is elected by citizens
      (3) Senators serve six-year terms, one-third up for reelection every two years
      (4) VP is presiding officer

   b. House of Representatives
      (1) Consists of 435 members; each congressional district contains (theoretically) about same number of people
      (2) Members directly elected by citizens of district
      (3) Members serve two-year terms, then must be reelected to continue
      (4) Speaker of the House is presiding officer—elected by members of House's majority party.

   c. Joint committee of House and Senate resolves differences in bills

Complete the following statement: Paragraph 1 uses the _____ method of development.

2.

Good and Bad Horror Movies

A good horror movie is easily distinguishable from a bad one. A good horror movie, first of all, has both male and female victims. Both sexes suffer terrible fates at the hands of monsters and maniacs. Therefore, everyone in the audience has a chance to identify with the victim. Bad horror movies, on the other hand, tend to concentrate on women, especially half-dressed ones. These movies are obviously prejudiced against half the human race. Second, a good horror movie inspires compassion for its characters. For example, the audience will feel sympathy for the victims in the horror classics about the Wolfman, played by Lon Chaney Jr., and also for the Wolfman himself, who is shown to be a sad victim of fate. In contrast, a bad horror movie encourages feelings of aggression and violence in viewers. For instance, in the *Halloween* films, the murders are seen from the murderer's point of view. The effect is that the audience stalks the victims along with the killer and feels the same thrill he does. Finally, every good horror movie has a sense of humor. In *Alien*, as a crew member is coughing and choking just before the horrible thing bursts out of his chest, a colleague chides him, "The food ain't *that* bad, man." Humor provides relief from the horror and makes the characters more human. A bad horror movie, though, is humorless and boring. One murder is piled on top of another, and the characters are just cardboard figures. Bad horror movies may provide cheap thrills, but the good ones touch our emotions and live forever.

Topic sentence: A good horror movie is easily distinguished from a bad one.

   a. Kinds of victims

      (1) ______________________

      (2) ______________________

   b. Effect on audience

      (1) ______________________

      (2) ______________________

   c. Tone

      (1) ______________________

      (2) ______________________

Complete the following statement: Paragraph 2 uses the _________ method of development.

Evaluating Additional Paragraphs

Read these additional paragraphs of comparison and/or contrast, and then answer the questions that follow.

My Broken Dream

¹When I became a police officer in my town, the job was not as I had dreamed it would be. ²I began to dream about being a police officer at about age ten. ³I could picture myself wearing a handsome blue uniform with an impressive-looking badge on my chest. ⁴I could also picture myself driving a powerful patrol car through town and seeing everyone stare at me with envy. ⁵But most of all, I dreamed of wearing a gun and using all the equipment that "TV cops" use. ⁶I knew everyone would be proud of me. ⁷I could almost hear the guys on the block saying, "Boy, Steve made it big. ⁸Did you hear he's a cop?" ⁹I dreamed of leading an exciting life, solving big crimes, and meeting lots of people. ¹⁰I knew that if I became a cop, everyone in town would look up to me. ¹¹However, when I actually did become a police officer, I soon found out that the reality was different. ¹²My first disappointment came when I was sworn in and handed a well-used, baggy uniform. ¹³My disappointment continued when I was given a badge that looked like something pulled out of a cereal box. ¹⁴I was assigned a beat-up old junker and told that it would be my patrol car. ¹⁵It had a striking resemblance to a car that had lost in a demolition derby at a stock-car raceway. ¹⁶Disappointment seemed to continue. ¹⁷I soon found out that I was not the envy of all my friends. ¹⁸When I drove through town, they acted as if they had not seen me, despite the gun and nightstick at my side. ¹⁹I was told I was crazy doing this kind of job by people I thought would look up to me. ²⁰My job was not as exciting as I had dreamed it would be, either. ²¹Instead of solving robberies and murders every day, I found that I spent a great deal of time comforting a local resident because a neighborhood dog had watered his favorite bush.

Two Views on Toys

¹Children and adults have very different preferences. ²First, there is the matter of taste. ³Adults pride themselves on taste, while children ignore the matter of taste in favor of things that are fun. ⁴Adults, especially grandparents, pick out tasteful toys that go unused, while children love the cheap playthings advertised on television. ⁵Second, of course, there is the matter of money. ⁶The new games on the market today are a case

continued

in point. 7Have you ever tried to lure a child away from some expensive game in order to get him or her to play with an old-fashioned game or toy? 8Finally, there is a difference between an adult's and a child's idea of what is educational. 9Adults, filled with memories of their own childhood, tend to be fond of the written word. 10Today's children, on the other hand, concentrate on anything electronic. 11These things mean much more to them than to adults. 12Next holiday season, examine the toys that adults choose for children. 13Then look at the toys the children prefer. 14You will see the difference.

Ice Hockey and Soccer

1Like ice hockey, soccer is a game whose aim is scoring goals against the opposing team. 2Both are team sports in which the most important position is that of goaltender or goalie. 3This is the player who defends the team's goal or net. 4Unlike ice hockey, which is played on an indoor ice rink or a frozen pond or lake, soccer is played outside on a grassy field. 5In an ice hockey match, only six players from each team can be on the ice at one time. 6Ice hockey players wear a lot of protective equipment such as helmets, shin guards, and padded gloves. In a soccer match, each team fields eleven players. 7Both sports require a great deal of energy. 8Ice hockey players seem to be constantly in motion, and soccer players race up and down the field almost nonstop. 9However, they wear little protective gear. 10Their uniforms consist of soccer shoes, socks, shorts, and jerseys.

ABOUT UNITY

QUESTIONS

1. Which paragraph lacks a topic sentence?

_____

2. Which paragraph has a topic sentence that is too broad?

_____

ABOUT SUPPORT

3. Which paragraph contains almost no specific details?

_____

4. Which paragraph provides the most complete support?

_____

5. What method of development (one side at a time or point by point) is used in "My Broken Dream"?

_____

In "Two Views on Toys"?

_____

6. Which paragraph offers specific details but lacks a clear, consistent method of development?

_____

Developing a Comparison and/or Contrast Paragraph

Development through Prewriting

Molly, the author of "Landenburg: Then and Now," had little trouble thinking of a topic for her comparison or contrast paper.

"My instructor said, 'You might compare or contrast two individuals, two places, two situations, or the same place at different times'. I immediately thought about the town in which I was born—the difference that ten years has made is amazing."

Because she is a person who likes to think visually, Molly started preparing for her paragraph by clustering. She found this a helpful way to "see" the differences between her hometown as it is now and as it was.

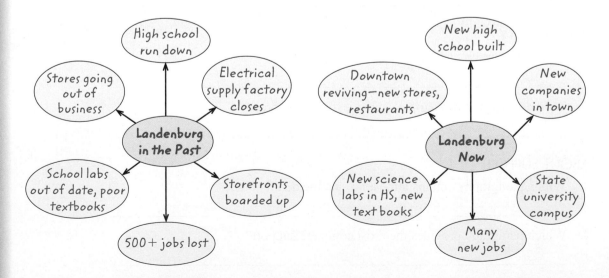

Taking a detail first from the "Landenburg in the past" part of the diagram, then one from the "Landenburg now" part, then another from the "Landenburg in the past" section, and so on, Molly began to write her paragraph using the point-by-point method:

Landenburg has changed for the better over the last 10 years. Twenty years ago, the town experienced an economic downturn. The electrical supply factory closed down about 10 years ago. However, things changed when a maker of automobile brake pads built a factory just outside of town. When the electrical supply factory closed, more than 500 people lost their jobs. The new company brought back many of those jobs. In addition, there's another new factory that manufactures restaurant equipment, and it employs about 150 additional people. Last year, the state university broke ground for a new extension campus. When the economy was bad, there was little money to spend on education, and the old high school was in disrepair. The science labs were outdated, and the textbooks were old and falling apart.

Molly stopped here because she wasn't satisfied with the way the paragraph was developing. "I wanted the reader to picture the way Landenburg had been years ago without interrupting that picture with a description of what it's like today. So I decided to try the one-side-at-a time approach, instead." Here is Molly's next draft:

Landenburg: Then and Now

Landenburg has changed for the better over the last ten years. Twenty years ago, the town experienced an economic downturn. The electrical supply factory had just closed down. The old high school needed repair. I remember my grandmother telling me that she had graduated from Landenburg High School and that she had met my grandfather there in an algebra class. The high school's outside walls were covered with graffiti. Students used books that were very old. Barker Avenue, the town's main shopping area, looked like a ghost town. It was as if an economic disease had attacked Landenburg. About ten years ago, however, things changed. A manufacturer of automobile brake pads decided to relocate in Landenburg, and it built a huge factory just outside of town. I

continued

worked there one summer and made enough to pay for half of my college tuition that year. It was hard, dirty work, and there was no air conditioning. So on really hot days, I was miserable. As a result of this new factory, however, many new jobs have replaced those lost when the electrical supply factory closed, and with increased tax revenues, the town was able to replace the old high school. The entire town seems to have gotten a lot healthier. The new jobs have also boosted consumer confidence. The downtown shopping area is busier than ever. A ten-screen movie complex just opened. A restaurant supply factory decided to move in, and last year the state university broke ground for an extension campus two miles away. These events have also helped build confidence.

Development through Revising

Molly's instructor reviewed her first draft. Here are his comments:

All of this is very interesting, but some of your details are out of order—for example, you mention the opening of the restaurant-equipment plant and the work on the state university's extension campus after discussing the creation of new jobs and the boost in consumer confidence. Shouldn't the order be reversed? After all, the new plant and the new college campus are among the reasons that the local economy is getting better.

More descriptive details are needed! For instance, you say that the downtown area once "looked like a ghost town." Exactly what does a ghost town look like? Describe what you saw there. Also, what do you mean by "the old high school needed repair"? How old was it, and what kind of repairs did it need?

You include some unnecessary information; for example, the details about your grandmother and grandfather meeting in a high school algebra class and those that have to do with your work at the brake-pad factory. Everything in your paragraph should support your topic sentence.

Following her instructor's suggestions (and remembering a few more details she wanted to include), Molly wrote the version of her paragraph that appears on page 230.

Writing a Comparison and/or Contrast Paragraph

Personal

Write a comparison and/or contrast paragraph on one of the topics listed below. Alternately, select one of the photos below and write a comparison and/or contrast paragraph about the items or persons depicted.

Two cars	Two places you would like to live
Two cartoon strips	Two singers or groups
Two coworkers	Two teachers
Two drivers	Two teams
Two homes	Two types of diets
Two courses you've taken	Two jobs you have held
Two members of a family	Two ways of using technology for communication
Two periods in your life	
Two pets	Two vacations you've taken

PREWRITING

a. Choose your topic, the two subjects you will write about.

b. Decide whether your paragraph will *compare* the two subjects (discuss their similarities), *contrast* them (discuss their differences), or use a combination (discuss both similarities and differences). For example, you might write about how a musical group you enjoy differs from a musical group you dislike. You might discuss both important differences and basic similarities between two employers you have had or describe the similarities between two homes you've lived in. Or you might contrast a job you've had in a car factory with a job you've had as a receptionist.

c. Write a direct topic sentence for your paragraph. Here's an example: "My job in a car-parts factory was very different from my job as a receptionist."

d. Come up with at least three strong points to support your topic sentence. If you are contrasting two jobs, for example, your points might be that they differed greatly (1) in their physical setting, (2) in the skills they required, and (3) in the people they brought you into contact with.

e. Use your topic sentence and supporting points to create a scratch outline for your paragraph. For the paragraph about jobs, the outline would look like this:

Topic sentence: My job in a car-parts factory was very different from my job as a receptionist.

1. The jobs differed in physical setting.

2. The jobs differed in the skills they required.

3. The jobs differed in the people they brought me into contact with.

---

f. Under each of your supporting points, jot down as many details as occur to you. Don't worry yet about whether the details all fit perfectly or whether you will be able to use them all. Your goal is to generate a wealth of material to draw on. An example:

Topic sentence: My job in a car-parts factory was very different from my job as a receptionist.

1. The jobs differed in physical setting.

Factory loud and dirty

Office clean and quiet

Factory full of machines, hunks of metal, tools

---

continued

Office full of desks, files, computers

Factory smelled of motor oil

Office smelled of new carpet

Windows in factory too high and grimy to look out of

Office had clean windows onto street

2. *The jobs differed in the skills and behavior they required.*

   Factory required physical strength

   Office required mental activity

   Didn't need to be polite in factory

   Had to be polite in office

   Didn't need to think much for self in factory

   Constantly had to make decisions in office

3. *The jobs differed in the people they brought me into contact with.*

   In factory, worked with same crew every day

   In office, saw constant stream of new customers

   Most coworkers in factory had high-school education or less

   Many coworkers and clients in office well educated

   Coworkers in factory spoke variety of languages

   Rarely heard anything but English in office

g. Decide which format you will use to develop your paragraph: one side at a time or point by point. Either is acceptable; it is up to you to decide which you prefer. The important thing is to be consistent: whichever format you choose, be sure to use it throughout the entire paragraph.

h. Write the first draft of your paragraph.

REVISING

Put your writing away for a day or so. You will return to it with a fresh perspective and a better ability to critique what you have done.

Reread your work with these questions in mind.

FOUR BASES Checklist: Comparison and/or Contrast

ABOUT *UNITY*

✔ Does my topic sentence make it clear what two things I am comparing or contrasting?

✔ Do all sentences in the paragraph stay on-topic?

ABOUT *SUPPORT*

✔ Have I compared or contrasted the subjects in at least three important ways?

✔ Have I provided specific details that effectively back up my supporting points?

ABOUT *COHERENCE*

✔ If I have chosen the point-by-point format, have I consistently discussed a point about one subject, then immediately discussed the same point about the other subject before moving on to the next point?

✔ If I have chosen the one-side-at-a-time format, have I discussed every point about one of my subjects, then discussed the same points *in the same order* about the second subject?

✔ Have I used appropriate transitions, such as *first, in addition, also,* and *another way,* to help readers follow my train of thought?

ABOUT *SENTENCE SKILLS*

✔ Have I carefully proofread my paragraph, using the list on the inside back cover of the book, and corrected all sentence-skills mistakes, including spelling?

Continue revising your work until you can answer "yes" to each of these questions.

WRITING ASSIGNMENT 2

Write a paragraph in which you compare or contrast your life in the real world with your life in an imagined "perfect world." Your paragraph may be humorous or serious.

PREWRITING

a. As your "real life" and "ideal life" are too broad for a paragraph, choose three specific areas to focus on. You might select any of the areas below, or think of a specific area yourself.

work	friends
money	possessions
romance	housing
physical location	talents
personal appearance	

b. Write the name of one of your three areas (for example, "work") across the top of a page. Divide the page into two columns. Label one column "real world" and the other "perfect world." Under "real world," write down as many details as you can think of describing your real-life work situation. Under "perfect world," write down details describing what your perfect work life would be like. Repeat the process on separate pages for your other two major areas.

c. Write a topic sentence for your paragraph. Here's an example: "In my perfect world, my life would be quite different in the areas of work, money, and housing."

d. Decide which approach you will take: one side at a time or point by point.

e. Write a scratch outline that reflects the format you have selected. The outline for a point-by-point format would look like this:

Topic sentence: In my perfect world, my life would be quite different in the areas of work, money, and housing.

1. *Work*

   a. *Real-life work*

   b. *Perfect-world work*

continued

2. *Money*

    a. Real-life money

    b. Perfect-world money

3. *Housing*

    a. Real-life housing

    b. Perfect-world housing

The outline for a one-side-at-a-time format would look like this:

Topic sentence: In my perfect world, my life would be quite different in the areas of work, money, and housing.

1. *Real life*

    a. Work

    b. Money

    c. Housing

2. *Perfect world*

    a. Work

    b. Money

    c. Housing

f. Drawing from the three pages of details you generated in step *b*, complete your outline by jotting down your strongest supporting details for each point.

g. Write the first draft of your paragraph.

REVISING

Reread your paragraph, and then show it to a friend who will give you honest feedback. You should both review it with these questions in mind.

FOUR BASES Checklist: Comparison and/or Contrast

ABOUT *UNITY*

✔ Does the topic sentence make it clear what three areas of life are being compared or contrasted?

✔ Is the rest of my paragraph on target in support of my topic sentence?

ABOUT *SUPPORT*

✔ Does the paragraph provide specific details that describe both the "real-life" situation and the "perfect-world" situation?

ABOUT *COHERENCE*

✔ Does the paragraph follow a consistent format: point by point or one side at a time?

ABOUT *SENTENCE SKILLS*

✔ Have I used a consistent point of view throughout my paragraph?

✔ Have I used specific rather than general words?

✔ Have I avoided wordiness?

✔ Are my sentences varied?

✔ Have I checked for spelling and other sentence skills, as listed on the inside back cover of the book?

Continue revising your work until you and your reader can answer "yes" to each of these questions.

WRITING ASSIGNMENT 3

Write a contrast paragraph on one of the topics below.

- Shopping at a brick-and-mortar store versus online shopping
- A favorite holiday and a holiday you don't like
- A positive way of handling a problem versus a negative way of handling a problem

- A parent who works outside of the home versus a parent who works in the home
- News in a newspaper versus news on television or the Internet
- The hero and the villain in a movie, TV show, or novel
- The neighborhood you live in and the neighborhood you want to live in
- A supportive boss and a non-supportive boss
- A job you loved and a job you hated
- Your parents' beliefs and values versus your beliefs and values

Follow the directions for prewriting and rewriting given in Writing Assignment 2.

WRITING ASSIGNMENT 4

Academic

Write a paragraph in which you compare and/or contrast two famous portraits at the National Portrait Gallery.

a. Go to www.npg.si.edu
b. In the search box, type in a famous person like Albert Einstein.
c. Take notes on the similarities and differences of the two portraits you choose. For instance, a search for Albert Einstein will bring up numerous paintings, photos, and drawings, each of which will share commonalities while at the same time exhibit differences.
d. Create a topic sentence like the sample ones below:

The extremely realistic etching by Julius C. Turner provides a very different image from the oil painting by Josef Scharl.

The photos by Philippe Halsman and Fred Stein share similar qualities.

After you have done your research, follow the directions for prewriting and rewriting given in Writing Assignment 2.

WRITING ASSIGNMENT 5

Academic

Writing for a Specific Purpose and Audience

In this comparison and contrast paragraph, you will write with a specific purpose and for a specific audience. Imagine that you are living in an apartment building in which new tenants are making life unpleasant for you and the others who live on your floor. Write a letter of complaint to your landlord comparing *and* contrasting life before and after the tenants arrived.

Your purpose is to get your landlord to do something about the problem or problems created by the new tenants. To achieve this purpose, use as many specific and convincing details as you can. For example, don't just write that your neighbors have lots of parties. Instead, say that guests come and go until 2 or 3 A.M. or that the music is so loud it shakes the walls and keeps you up all night.

Your audience—the landlord—has an interest in keeping *all* tenants happy. So be sure to stress how all of the residents on your floor have been complaining about the newcomers.

You might want to focus on one or more of the following:

Noise	Parking situation
Trash	Damage to the building
Safety hazards	Police have been called during parties

Definition

This chapter will explain and illustrate how to

- develop a definition paragraph
- write a definition paragraph
- revise a definition paragraph

In addition, you will read and evaluate

- three student definition paragraphs

HOW DO YOU DEFINE A QUALITY? What are some words that come to mind as you look at this photograph? Write a paragraph in which you define one of these terms. For example, you may look at the photograph and think "challenge," "frustration," "obstacle," or "courage."

In talking with other people, we sometimes offer informal definitions to explain just what we mean by a particular term. Suppose, for example, we say to a friend, "Karen can be so clingy." We might then expand on our idea of "clingy" by saying, "You know, a clingy person needs to be with someone every single minute. If Karen's best friend makes plans that don't include her, she becomes hurt. And when she dates someone, she calls him several times a day and gets upset if he even goes to the grocery store without her. She hangs on to people too tightly." In a written definition, we make clear in a more complete and formal way our own personal understanding of a term. Such a definition typically starts with one meaning of a term. The meaning is then illustrated with a series of examples or a story.

The simplest way to state the meaning of a word is to follow the lead of scientists, who first classify an animal or plant by general category or class (*genus*) and then by the specific characteristics of the animal or plant (*species*). Thus you could say that a dog is a mammal (general category) that has four legs, a tail, and an ability to bark (specific characteristics). In one of the paragraphs that follow, the writer begins by defining *hypnotherapy* as a "medical treatment" (general category). The definition then explains that this treatment is used "while the patient is hypnotized" (specific characteristic).

After discussing the meaning of a term, provide as many examples and details as you can to clarify your point. In the paragraph entitled "The Liberal Arts," which follows, the writer gives several examples of the types of subjects included in the liberal arts. In "Hypnotherapy" the writer supplies a few examples of the uses of this medical practice.

To continue developing your definition, you might consider defining by contrast. That means telling your reader what the term does *not* mean or distinguishing it from other terms with which it is sometimes confused. For example, the writer of "Hypnotherapy" contrasts that term with *mesmerism*. The author of "The Liberal Arts" contrasts the liberal arts course of study with vocational, professional, and technical courses of study.

In this chapter, you will be asked to write a paragraph that begins with a one-sentence definition; that sentence will be the topic sentence. To prepare for this assignment, first read the three student papers that follow. They are all examples of definition paragraphs. Then answer the accompanying questions.

Evaluating Student Paragraphs

Hypnotherapy

¹Hypnotherapy is a medical treatment that is used while the patient is hypnotized. ²The word hypnosis comes from the Greek word *hypnos*, which means "sleep." ³Under hypnosis, the patient is very susceptible to suggestions from the doctor, who uses these suggestions to aid in the treatment. ⁴The British surgeon James Braid used this method during minor operations to lessen the patient's discomfort. ⁵Today, it is used to treat insomnia, depression, and emotional problems. ⁶Hypnotherapy has been used to ease a pregnant woman's anxiety, even during childbirth. ⁷Mesmerism, founded by Franz Anton Mesmer, is often confused with hypnotism and therefore with hypnotherapy. ⁸Mesmer studied medicine at the University of Vienna, but he was also an astrologer. ⁹However, mesmerism has been discredited as a therapy by the medical profession. ¹⁰Unlike hypnotherapy, the theory behind mesmerism is that every individual has magnetic fluid flowing through his or her body. ¹¹This fluid is supposed to be susceptible to blockages, thus causing physical or emotional ailments. ¹²Mesmer's claim that he could use a force called "animal magnetism" to probe a subject's unconscious through this fluid was proven false by Braid and those who followed him. ¹³Although many people misunderstand hypnotherapy because of false theories like mesmerism, hypnotherapy is an accepted and widely used treatment.

Disillusionment

¹Disillusionment is the feeling we have when one of our most cherished beliefs is stolen from us. ²I learned about disillusionment firsthand the day Mr. Keller, our eighth-grade teacher, handed out the grades for our class biology projects. ³I had worked hard to assemble what I thought was the best insect collection any school had ever seen. ⁴For weeks, I had set up homemade traps around our house, in the woods, and in vacant lots. ⁵At night, I would stretch a white sheet between two trees, shine a lantern on it, and collect the night-flying insects that gathered there. ⁶With my own money, I had bought killing jars, insect pins, gummed labels, and display boxes. ⁷I carefully arranged related insects together, with labels listing each scientific name and the place and date of capture. ⁸Slowly and painfully, I wrote and typed the report that accompanied my project at the school science fair. ⁹In contrast, my friend Eddie did almost nothing for his project.

continued

¹⁰He had his father, a psychologist, build an impressive maze complete with live rats and a sign that read, "You are the trainer." ¹¹A person could lift a little plastic door, send a rat running through the maze, and then hit a button to release a pellet of rat food as a reward. ¹²This exhibit turned out to be the most popular one at the fair. ¹³I felt sure that our teacher would know that Eddie could not have built it, and I was certain that my hard work would be recognized and rewarded. ¹⁴Then the grades were finally handed out, and I was crushed. ¹⁵Eddie had gotten an A plus, but my grade was a B. ¹⁶I suddenly realized that honesty and hard work don't always pay off in the end. ¹⁷The idea that life is not fair, that sometimes it pays to cheat, hit me with such force that I felt sick. ¹⁸I will never forget that moment.

The Liberal Arts

¹Most colleges offer at least some liberal arts classes. ²The vast majority, in fact, offer liberal arts courses of study. ³These are unlike professional, vocational, or technical courses of study, which focus on specific skills or on areas that prepare students for certain specific occupations. ⁴Instead, the liberal arts tend to be wider in scope and to provide all students—not just those majoring in a liberal arts subject—with the general knowledge they will need to be well-rounded members of the community. ⁵The liberal arts, which are often grouped with the natural sciences, include communication, literature, history, language, the social sciences, philosophy, and mathematics. ⁶In addition to teaching an accepted body of knowledge, liberal arts classes also teach students the kinds of skills they will need to continue learning on their own after they graduate. ⁷For example, many courses in literature, history, and philosophy require critical reading, research, and writing. ⁸The term *liberal* comes from the Latin word *liber*, meaning "free," for when the liberal arts were taught in antiquity they were intended for free men. ⁹Training in specific skills, on the other hand, was reserved for slaves. ¹⁰The liberal arts are also called the humanities, because they aim at helping people become more civilized, that is, more human.

ABOUT UNITY

QUESTIONS

1. Which paragraph places its topic sentence within the paragraph rather than, more appropriately, at the beginning?

_____

2. Which sentence in "Hypnotherapy" should be omitted in the interest of paragraph unity? (*Write the sentence number here.*) _____

ABOUT SUPPORT

3. Which paragraph develops its definition through examples?

    _____

4. Which paragraph develops its definition through a single extended example?

    _____

ABOUT COHERENCE

5. Which paragraph uses emphatic order, saving the best detail for last?

    _____

6. Which paragraph uses time order to organize its details?

    _____

Developing a Definition Paragraph

Development through Prewriting

When Harry, the author of "Disillusionment," started working on his assignment, he did not know what he wanted to write about. He looked around the house for inspiration. His two-year-old twins racing around the room made him think about defining "energy." The fat cat asleep on a sunny windowsill suggested that he might write about "laziness" or "relaxation." Still not sure of a topic, he looked over his notes from that day's class. His instructor had jotted a list of terms on the blackboard, saying, "Maybe you could focus on what one of these words has meant in your own life." Harry looked over the words he had copied down: *honesty, willpower, faith, betrayal, disillusionment.* "When I got to the word 'disillusionment,' the eighth-grade science fair flashed into my mind," Harry said. "That was a bitter experience that definitely taught me what disillusionment was all about."

Because the science fair had occurred many years before, Harry had to work to remember it well. He decided to try the technique of questioning himself to come up with the details of what had happened. Here are the questions Harry asked himself and the answers he wrote:

When did I learn about disillusionment?

When I was in eighth grade

Where did it happen?

At the school science fair

continued

<u>Who was involved?</u>

Me, Eddie Loomis and his father, and Mr. Keller

<u>What happened?</u>

I had worked very hard on my insect collection. Eddie had done almost nothing but he had a rat maze that his father had built. I got a B on my project while Eddie got an A+.

<u>Why was the experience so disillusioning?</u>

I thought my hard work would be rewarded. I was sure Mr. Keller would recognize that I had put far more effort into my project than Eddie had. When Eddie won, I learned that cheating can pay off and that honest work isn't always rewarded.

<u>How did I react?</u>

I felt sick to my stomach. I wanted to confront Mr. Keller and Eddie and make them see how unfair the grades were. But I knew I'd just look like a poor loser, so I didn't do anything.

<u>On the basis of this experience, how would I define disillusionment?</u>

It's finding out that something you really believed in isn't true.

Drawing from the ideas generated by his self-questioning, Harry wrote the following draft of his paragraph:

Disillusionment is finding out that one of your most important beliefs isn't true. I learned about disillusionment at my eighth-grade science fair. I had worked very hard on my project, an insect collection. I was sure it would get an A. I had worked so hard on it, even spending nights outside making sure it was very good. My friend Eddie also did a project, but he barely worked on his at all. Instead, he had his

continued

father build a maze for a rat to run through. The trainer lifted a little plastic door to let the rat into the maze, and if it completed the maze, the trainer could release a pellet of food for it to eat. It was a nice project, but the point is that Eddie hadn't made it. He just made things like the banner that hung over it. Mr. Keller was our science teacher. He gave Eddie an A+ and me just a B. So that really taught me about disillusionment.

Development through Revising

The next day, Harry's instructor divided the class into groups of three. The groups reviewed each member's paragraph. Harry was grouped with Curtis and Jocelyn. After reading through Harry's paper several times, the group had the following discussion:

"My first reaction is that I want to know more about your project," said Jocelyn. "You give details about Eddie's, but not many about your own. What was so good about it? You need to show us, not just tell us. Also, you said that you worked very hard, but you didn't show us how hard."

"Yeah," said Harry. "I remember my project clearly, but I guess the reader has to know what it was like and how much effort went into it."

Curtis said, "I like your topic sentence, but when I finished the paragraph I wasn't sure what 'important belief' you'd learned wasn't true. What would you say that belief was?"

Harry thought a minute. "I'd believed that honest hard work would always be rewarded. I found out that it doesn't always happen that way, and that cheating can actually win."

Curtis nodded. "I think you need to include that in your paper."

Jocelyn added, "I'd like to read how you felt or reacted after you saw your grade, too. If you don't explain that, the paragraph ends sort of abruptly."

Harry agreed with his classmates' suggestions. After he had gone through several revisions, he produced the version that appears on pages 252–253.

Writing a Definition Paragraph

WRITING ASSIGNMENT 1

Write a paragraph that defines the term *TV addict*. Base your paragraph on the topic sentence and three supporting points provided below.

Topic sentence: Television addicts are people who will watch all the programs they can, for as long as they can, without doing anything else.

(1) TV addicts, first of all, will watch anything on the tube, no matter how bad it is. . . .

(2) In addition, addicts watch more hours of TV than normal people do. . . .

(3) Finally, addicts feel that TV is more important than other people or any other activities that might be going on. . . .

JOT DOWN SOME IDEAS ABOUT HOW TO AVOID the time trap of mindless TV surfing.

PREWRITING

a. Generate as many examples as you can for each of the three qualities of a TV addict. You can do this by asking yourself the following questions:

- What are some truly awful shows that I (or TV addicts I know) watch just because the television is turned on?

- What are some examples of the large amounts of time that I (or TV addicts I know) watch television?

- What are some examples of ways that I (or TV addicts I know) neglect people or give up activities in order to watch TV?

Write down every answer you can think of for each question. At this point, don't worry about writing full sentences or even about grammar or spelling. Just get your thoughts down on paper.

b. Look over the list of examples you have generated. Select the strongest examples you have thought of. You should have at least two or three for each quality. If not, ask yourself the questions in step *a* again.

c. Write out the examples you will use, this time expressing them in full, grammatically correct sentences.

d. Start with the topic sentence and three points provided in the assignment. Fill in the examples you've generated to support each point and write a first draft of your paragraph.

REVISING

Put your first draft away for a day or so. When you come back to it, reread it critically, asking yourself these questions.

FOUR BASES Checklist: Definition

ABOUT *UNITY*

✔ Have I used the topic sentence and the three supporting points that were provided?

✔ Does every sentence in my paragraph help define the term *TV addict*?

ABOUT *SUPPORT*

✔ Have I backed up each supporting point with at least two examples?

✔ Does each of my examples truly illustrate the point that it backs up?

ABOUT *COHERENCE*

✔ Have I used appropriate transitional language (*another, in addition, for example*) to tie my thoughts together?

✔ Are all the transitional words correctly used?

ABOUT *SENTENCE SKILLS*

✔ Have I carefully proofread my paragraph, using the list on the inside back cover of the book, and corrected all sentence-skills mistakes, including spelling?

✔ Have I used a consistent point of view throughout my paragraph?

Keep revising your paragraph until you can answer "yes" to each question.

Write a paragraph that defines one of the following terms. Each term refers to a certain kind of person.

Academic

Artist	Darwin Award winner	Idealist	Philanthropist
Beauty	Fair-weather friend	Intellect	Procrastinator
Brainiac	Feminist	Introvert	Pushover
Charmer	Flirt	Know-it-all	Romantic
Chocoholic	Friend-padder	Leader	Self-promoter
Compliment-seeker	Geek	Manipulator	Showoff
Con-artist	Genius	Optimist	Slacker
Control freak	Good neighbor	Pack rat	Snob
Coward	Good sport	Pessimist	Workaholic

PREWRITING

a. Write a topic sentence for your definition paragraph. This is a two-part process:

- *First,* place the term in a class, or category. For example, if you are writing about a certain kind of person, the general category is *person.* If you are describing a type of friend, the general category is *friend.*

- *Second,* describe what you consider the special feature or features that set your term apart from other members of its class. For instance, say what *kind* of person you are writing about or what *type* of friend.

In the following topic sentence, try to identify three things: the term being defined, the class it belongs to, and the special feature that sets the term apart from other members of the class.

A chocoholic is a person who craves chocolate.

The term being defined is *chocoholic.* The category it belongs to is *person.* The words that set *chocoholic* apart from any other person are *craves chocolate.*

Below is another example of a topic sentence for this assignment. It is a definition of *whiner.* The class, or category, is underlined: A whiner is a type of person. The words that set the term *whiner* apart from other members of the class are double-underlined.

A whiner is a person who feels wronged by life.

In the following sample topic sentences, underline the class and double-underline the special features.

A shopaholic is a person who needs new clothes to be happy.

The class clown is a student who gets attention through silly behavior.

A worrywart is a person who sees danger everywhere.

b. Develop your definition by using one of the following methods:

Examples. Give several examples that support your topic sentence.

Extended example. Use one longer example to support your topic sentence. *Contrast.* Support your topic sentence by contrasting what your term *is* with what it is *not*. For instance, you may want to define a *fair-weather friend* by contrasting his or her actions with those of a true friend.

c. Once you have created a topic sentence and decided how to develop your paragraph, make a scratch outline. If you are using a contrast method of development, remember to present the details one side at a time or point by point (see pages 232–233).

d. Write a first draft of your paragraph.

REVISING

As you revise your paragraph, keep these questions in mind.

FOUR BASES Checklist: Definition

ABOUT *UNITY*

✔ Does my topic sentence (1) place my term in a class and (2) name some special features that set it apart from its class?

✔ Is the rest of my paragraph on target in support of my topic sentence?

ABOUT *SUPPORT*

✔ Have I made a clear choice to develop my topic sentence through several examples, or one extended example, or contrast?

ABOUT *COHERENCE*

✔ If I have chosen to illustrate my topic through contrast, have I consistently followed either a point-by-point or a one-side-at-a-time format?

✔ Have I used appropriate transitions (*another, in addition, in contrast, for example*) to tie my thoughts together?

ABOUT *SENTENCE SKILLS*

✔ Have I used a consistent point of view throughout my paragraph?

✔ Have I used specific rather than general words?

✔ Have I avoided wordiness?

✔ Are my sentences varied?

✔ Have I checked for spelling and other sentence skills, as listed on the inside back cover of the book?

Continue revising your work until you can answer "yes" to each of these questions.

WRITING ASSIGNMENT 3

Think of a word that people would use to describe you. In a paragraph, define that word by using personal examples and details. You may want to brainstorm some words you think define you, or you may want to talk to family members to come up with ideas. The paragraph below demonstrates a student's response to this assignment.

Floor-Cleaning Freak

My family considers me a floor-cleaning freak. I use my DustBuster to snap up crumbs seconds after they fall. When a rubber heel mark appears on my vinyl floor, I run for the steel wool. As I work in my kitchen preparing meals, I constantly scan the tiles, looking for spots where some liquid has been spilled or for a crumb that has somehow miraculously escaped my vision. After I scrub and wax my floors, I stand to one side of the room and try to catch the light in such a way as to reveal spots that have gone unwaxed. As I travel from one room to the other, my experienced eye is faithfully searching for lint that may have invaded my domain since my last passing. If I discover an offender, I discreetly tuck it into my pocket. The amount of lint I have gathered in the course of the day is the ultimate test of how diligently I am performing my task. I give my vacuum cleaner quite a workout, and I spend an excessive amount on replacement bags. My expenses for floor-cleaners and wax are alarmingly high, but somehow this does not stop me. Where my floors are concerned, money is not a consideration!

WRITING ASSIGNMENT 4

Earlier in this chapter you read a paragraph defining *hypnotherapy*. Write an extended definition paragraph in which you explain another scientific or medical term.
Here are a few terms you might choose from:

Electromagnetism	Post-partum depression
Hypertension	Social anxiety disorder
Inertia	Dissociative fugue
Isotope	Munchausen syndrome
Magnetic resonance imaging	Synesthesia
Photosynthesis	Kinesthesia

It will probably be helpful to do some background research. You might use the Internet to access an online medical site such as the Mayo Clinic or a scientific site like Science.gov. To avoid plagiarism, credit the sources you use and put quotation marks around any definitions or statements you use from those sources. For instance, if you are defining "schizophrenia" and you use the wording of the Mayo

Clinic definition, you would want to write it in the following manner: "According to the Mayo Clinic, 'Schizophrenia is a group of severe brain disorders in which people interpret reality abnormally.'" To extend your definition, you will want to use one of the methods described on page 251 and in Writing Assignment 2.

WRITING ASSIGNMENT 5

Personal

Examine this photograph. What words come to mind immediately? Perhaps "jubilant" or "victorious"? Brainstorm one word that you feel best describes the emotion depicted here and write a paragraph that defines that word. Alternately, you might imagine the exact opposite of the scene shown here—at the very moment that this photo is being shot, how is the other team feeling? Choose one word for that feeling and write a paragraph describing it.

WRITING ASSIGNMENT 6

Work

Writing for a Specific Purpose and Audience

In this definition paragraph, you will write with a specific purpose and for a specific audience. Imagine that you work in an office building in which an environmental problem has developed. You and your coworkers have been experiencing symptoms of illness, such as flu-like feelings and headaches. What used to be an exciting and invigorating place to work has become plagued by lassitude. Your supervisor seems to be oblivious to the root of the problem and you feel it would be beneficial to provide factual information for him. You research the phenomenon of "sick building syndrome." In a well-written, factual memo, describe and define the problem for your boss. Your extended definition should include specific details that demonstrate how people are feeling as well as technical and documented characteristics of the syndrome. Instead of writing "people are tired," you might write "People are experiencing respiratory problems. Poor ventilation or indoor pollutants, which are elements of sick building syndrome, may be the cause." Your purpose is not to offer solutions, but simply to define the problem and the syndrome in a business-like manner.

Division-Classification

This chapter will explain and illustrate how to

- develop a division-classification paragraph
- write a division-classification paragraph
- revise a division-classification paragraph

In addition, you will read and evaluate

- three student division-classification paragraphs

HOW MANY KINDS OF ART ARE HERE? Art comes in many forms. Write a paragraph in which you discuss two different art media and/or two different styles within those media. Include details about what makes each unique.

If you were doing the laundry, you might begin by separating the clothing into piles. You might put all the whites in one pile and all the colors in another. Or you might classify the laundry not according to color but according to fabric—putting all cottons in one pile, polyesters in another, and so on. *Classifying* is the process of taking many things and separating them into categories. We generally classify to better manage or understand many things. Librarians classify books into groups (fiction, travel, health, etc.) to make them easier to find. A scientist sheds light on the world by classifying all living things into two main groups: animals and plants.

Dividing, in contrast, is taking one thing and breaking it down into parts. We often divide, or analyze, to better understand, teach, or evaluate something. For instance, a tinkerer might take apart a clock to see how it works; a science text might divide a tree into its parts to explain their functions. A music reviewer may analyze the elements of a band's performance—for example, the skill of the various players, rapport with the audience, selections, and so on.

In short, if you are classifying, you are sorting *numbers of things* into categories. If you are dividing, you are breaking *one thing* into parts. It all depends on your purpose—you might classify flowers into various types or divide a single flower into its parts.

In this chapter, you will be asked to write a paragraph in which you classify a group of things into categories according to a single principle. To prepare for this assignment, first read the paragraphs below, and then work through the questions and the activity that follow.

Evaluating Student Paragraphs

Five Stages of Grief

[1]Elizabeth Kübler-Ross introduced the world to the five stages of grief in her book *On Death and Dying.* [2]The first stage is called denial. [3]In this stage, those who are terminally ill ignore their sickness. [4]They claim to be fine and refuse to acknowledge reality. [5]However, this stage is usually short-lived as the second stage, anger, takes over. [6]During this stage, the individual will typically claim that it's not fair he or she is sick. [7]Family members are often the target of the anger as the individual lashes out at the

continued

world. 8The third stage, bargaining, however, reflects a completely different attitude. 9When the bargaining doesn't work, the fourth stage, depression, sets in. 10During this time, the individual decides that since he or she is going to die, nothing matters. 11Some people become reclusive during this period. 12The final stage, acceptance, is the time that the individual realizes nothing can be done and he or she should prepare for the outcome. 13Many times, once the individual who is dying enters this stage, he or she will start giving away possessions and reconnecting with family and friends. 14Some people go through the stages quickly, while others move through them slowly; some cycle back through stages before moving on. 15Although there is no one "right" way to experience grief, the stages Kübler-Ross defined have helved us greatly in our overall understanding of the process.

The Diversity of Africa

1We often think of Africa as a place covered with jungles and inhabited by people who practice the same culture. 2The northern part of Africa is mainly desert, except for the very edge, which borders the Mediterranean Sea. 3The Sahara, the world's largest desert, is located in this part of the continent. 4So are countries such as Morocco, Algeria, Libya, Mauritania, and Egypt. In these countries the vast majority of the population speaks Arabic and practices Islam. 5In the middle of the continent, one finds the Sudan, Africa's largest country, which offers a wide variety of landscapes: desert, grassland, and mountain. 6Other countries found in the middle part of Africa are Ethiopia, the Congo, Nigeria, Ghana, Uganda, and Kenya. 7The best-known countries in the southern part of the continent are Angola, Zimbabwe, Zambia, and South Africa. 8The landscape in the first three of these southern countries consists mostly of grasslands with some mountains. 9The languages of these countries include English as well as native tongues. 10Many southern African countries have Christian majorities. 11In Mauritius, however, there are more Hindus than Christians or Muslims. 12Finally, the nation of South Africa seems to mirror the rest of the continent in its diversity. 13Here there are mountains, grasslands, and seashore. 14Eleven official languages are spoken in this country: Afrikaans, English, isiNdebele, isiXhosa, isiZulu, Sepedi, Sesotho, Setswana, siSwati, Tshivenda, and Xitsonga. 15What's more, several very different faiths are represented in South Africa, including Hinduism, Judaism, Islam, many sects of Christianity, and a wide variety of native religions.

Three Kinds of Dogs

[1]A city walker will notice that most dogs fall into one of three categories. [2]First there are the big dogs, which are generally harmless and often downright friendly. [3]They walk along peacefully with their masters, their tongues hanging out and big goofy grins on their faces. [4]Apparently they know they're too big to have anything to worry about, so why not be nice? [5]Second are the spunky medium-sized dogs. [6]When they see a stranger approaching, they go on alert. [7]They prick up their ears, they raise their hackles, and they may growl a little deep in their throats. [8]"I could tear you up," they seem to be saying, "but I won't if you behave yourself." [9]Unless the walker leaps for their master's throat, these dogs usually won't do anything more than threaten. [10]The third category is made up of the shivering neurotic little yappers whose shrill barks could shatter glass and whose needle-like little teeth are eager to sink into a friendly outstretched hand. [11]Walkers always wonder about these dogs—don't they know that people who really wanted to could squash them under their feet like bugs? [12]Apparently not, because of all the dogs a walker meets, these provide the most irritation. [13]Such dogs are only one of the potential hazards that the city walker encounters.

QUESTIONS

ABOUT UNITY

1. Which paragraph lacks a topic sentence?

   _____

2. Which sentence in "Three Kinds of Dogs" should be eliminated in the interest of paragraph unity? (*Write the sentence number here.*) _____

ABOUT SUPPORT

3. Of the three parts of Africa discussed in "The Diversity of Africa," which one needs more specific detail?

   _____

4. After which sentence in "Five Stages of Grief" are supporting details needed? (*Write the sentence number here.*) _____

ABOUT COHERENCE

5. Which sentences in "Three Kinds of Dogs" contain addition transition words or phrases? (*Write the sentence numbers here.*) _____ _____ _____

6. What type of order does "Five Stages of Grief" use to organize its details?

   _____

This activity will sharpen your sense of the classifying process. In each of the ten groups, cross out the one item that has not been classified on the same basis as the other three. Also, indicate in the space provided the single principle of classification used for the remaining three items. Note the examples.

ACTIVITY 1

EXAMPLES

Water
a. Cold
b. ~~Lake~~
c. Hot
d. Lukewarm
Unifying principle:
Temperature

Household pests
a. ~~Mice~~
b. Ants
c. Roaches
d. Flies
Unifying principle:
Insects

1. Eyes
   a. Blue
   b. Nearsighted
   c. Brown
   d. Hazel
   Unifying principle:

2. Mattresses
   a. Double
   b. Twin
   c. Queen
   d. Firm
   Unifying principle:

3. Zoo animals
   a. Flamingo
   b. Peacock
   c. Polar bear
   d. Ostrich
   Unifying principle:

4. Vacation
   a. Summer
   b. Holiday
   c. Seashore
   d. Weekend
   Unifying principle:

5. Books
   a. Novels
   b. Biographies
   c. Boring
   d. Short stories
   Unifying principle:

6. Wallets
   a. Leather
   b. Plastic
   c. Stolen
   d. Fabric
   Unifying principle:

7. Newspaper
   a. Wrapping garbage
   b. Editorials
   c. Making paper planes
   d. Covering floor while painting
   Unifying principle:

   _____

8. Students
   a. First-year
   b. Transfer
   c. Junior
   d. Sophomore
   Unifying principle:

   _____

9. Exercise
   a. Running
   b. Swimming
   c. Gymnastics
   d. Fatigue
   Unifying principle:

   _____

10. Leftovers
    a. Cold chicken
    b. Feed to dog
    c. Reheat
    d. Use in a stew
    Unifying principle:

    _____

Developing a Division-Classification Paragraph

Development through Prewriting

Marcus walked home from campus to his apartment, thinking about the assignment to write a division-classification paragraph. As he strolled along his familiar route, his observations made him think of several possibilities. "First I thought of writing about the businesses in my neighborhood, dividing them into the ones run by Hispanics, Asians, and African Americans," he said. "When I stopped in at my favorite coffee shop, I thought about dividing the people who hang out there. There is a group of old men who meet to drink coffee and play cards, and there are students like me, but there didn't seem to be a third category and I wasn't sure two was enough. As I continued walking home, though, I saw Mr. Enriquez and his big golden retriever, and a woman with two nervous little dogs that acted as if they wanted to eat me, and the newsstand guy with his mutt that's always guarding the place, and I thought 'Dogs! I can classify types of dogs.'"

But how would he classify them? Thinking further, Marcus realized that he thought of dogs as having certain personalities depending on their size. "I know there are exceptions, of course, but since this was going to be a lighthearted, even comical paragraph, I thought it would be OK if I exaggerated a bit." He wrote down his three categories:

Big dogs

Medium-sized dogs

Small dogs

Under each division, then, he wrote down as many characteristics as he could think of:

Big dogs	Medium-sized dogs	Small dogs
calm	spunky	nervous
friendly	energetic	trembling
good-natured	ready to fight	noisy
dumb	protective	yappy
lazy	friendly if they know you	snappy
		annoying

Marcus then wrote a topic sentence: "Dogs seem to fall into three categories." Using that topic sentence and a scratch outline he produced from his prewriting, he wrote the following paragraph:

Most dogs seem to fall into one of three categories. First there are the big dumb friendly dogs. They give the impression of being sweet but not real bright. One example of this kind of dog is Lucy. She's a golden retriever belonging to a man in my neighborhood. Lucy goes everywhere with Mr. Enriquez. She doesn't even need a leash but just follows him. Dogs like Lucy never bother anybody. She just lies at Mr. Enriquez's feet when he stops to talk to anyone. The guy who runs the corner newsstand I pass every day has a spunky medium-sized dog. Once the dog knows you he's friendly and even playful. But he's always on the lookout for a stranger who might mean trouble. For a dog who's not very big he can make himself look pretty fierce if

continued

he wants to. Then there are my least favorite kind of dogs. Little nervous yappy ones.
My aunt used to have a Chihuahua like that. It knew me for nine years and still
went crazy shaking and yipping at me every time we met. She loved that dog but I
can't imagine why. If I had a dog it would definitely come from category 1 or 2.

Development through Revising

Marcus traded his first draft with a fellow student, Rachel, and asked her to give him feedback. Here are the comments Rachel wrote on his paper:

This is a change in point of view—you haven't been using "you" before.

Is this the beginning of a second category? That's not clear.

Not a complete sentence.

Most dogs seem to fall into three categories.
First there are the big dumb friendly dogs. They
give the impression of being sweet but not real
bright. One example of this kind of dog is Lucy,
a golden retriever belonging to a man in my
neighborhood. Lucy goes everywhere with Mr.
Enriquez. She doesn't even need a leash but just
follows him everywhere. Lucy never bothers
you. She just lies at Mr. Enriquez's feet when he
stops to talk to anyone. The guy who runs the
corner newsstand I pass every day has a spunky
medium-sized dog. Once the dog knows you
he's friendly and even playful. But he's always
on the lookout for a stranger who might mean
trouble. For a dog who's not very big he can
make himself look pretty fierce if he wants to
scare you. Then there are my least favorite kind
of dogs. Little nervous yappy ones. My aunt used

continued

to have a Chihuahua like that. It knew me for nine years and still went crazy shaking and yipping at me every time we met. She loved that dog but I can't imagine why. If I had a dog it would definitely come from category 1 or 2.

Another change in point of view—you've gone from writing in the third person to "you" to "me."

Marcus—I think you need to make your three categories clearer. Your first one is OK— "big dogs," which you say are friendly—but categories 2 and 3 aren't stated as clearly.

It's distracting to have your point of view change from third person to "you" to "me."

Since you're trying to divide and classify all dogs, I'm not sure it's a good idea to talk only about three individual dogs. This way it sounds as if you're just describing those three dogs instead of putting them into three groups.

When Marcus considered Rachel's comments and reread his paragraph, he agreed with what she had written. "I realized it was too much about three particular dogs and not enough about the categories of dogs," he said. "I decided to revise it and focus on the three classes of dogs."

Marcus then wrote the version that appears on page 266.

Writing a Division-Classification Paragraph

WRITING ASSIGNMENT 1

Following are four options to develop into a classification paragraph. Each one presents a topic to classify into three categories. Choose one option to develop into a paragraph.

OPTION 1

College Campuses

(1) The pristine suburban campus

(2) The noisy urban campus

(3) The isolated rural campus

OPTION 2

College Professors

(1) The one who speaks in a monotone

(2) The one who wants to be every student's friend

(3) The one who is passionate about teaching

OPTION 3

College Students

(1) Those who work hard to achieve a goal

(2) Those who don't know why they're in college

(3) Those who just want to get by

OPTION 4

College Roommates

(1) The life of the party

(2) The depressed homesick whiner

(3) The overly serious studier

WHICH OF THE SIX categories listed under "College Students" and "College Roommates" do you think this student falls into? (You might find that one, two, or more categories fit.) Write a paragraph explaining what you observe in the photo that leads you to this/these classification(s).

PREWRITING

a. Begin by freewriting on your topic. For five or ten minutes, simply write down everything that comes into your head when you think about "students," "professors," or whichever topic you chose. Don't worry about grammar, spelling, or organization—just write.

b. Now that you've "loosened up your brain" a little, try asking yourself questions about the topic and writing down your answers. If you are writing about students, for instance, you might ask questions like these:

- How do the three kinds of students prepare for their classes?

- How many classes will each student take?

- What do the different kinds of students do during the semester?

- How long does each type of student spend studying, partying, working?

Write down whatever answers occur to you for these and other questions. Again, do not worry at this stage about writing correctly. Instead, concentrate on getting down all the information you can think of that supports your three points.

c. Reread the material you have accumulated. If some of the details you have written make you think of even better ones, add them. Select the details that best support your three points. Number them in the order you will present them.

d. Restate your topic as a grammatically complete topic sentence. For example, if you're writing about professors, your topic sentence might be "College professors can be classified into three categories." Turn each of your three supporting points into a full sentence as well.

e. Using your topic sentence and three supporting sentences and adding the details you have generated, write the first draft of your paragraph.

REVISING

Put away your work for a day or so. Then reread it with a critical eye, asking yourself or a peer reviewer these questions.

FOUR BASES Checklist: Division-Classification

ABOUT *UNITY*

✔ Does my paragraph include a complete topic sentence and three supporting points?

✔ While classifying the various types of my chosen topic, have I also kept that subject unified?

ABOUT *SUPPORT*

✔ Have I backed up each supporting point with strong, specific details?

✔ Have I given examples of each type of college student, roommate, campus, or professor?

ABOUT *COHERENCE*

✔ Does the paragraph successfully classify types of college students, roommates, campuses, or professors?

ABOUT *SENTENCE SKILLS*

✔ Have I carefully proofread my paragraph, using the list on the inside back cover of the book, and corrected all sentence-skills mistakes, including spelling?

✔ Have I used specific rather than general words?

Continue revising your work until you can answer "yes" to each of these questions.

WRITING ASSIGNMENT 2

We don't often think about our own hometown from the perspective of a tourist. However, it is always a good idea to have suggestions available of things to do for people who are visiting. In preparation for visitors, you are to look at what activities are available to do in your city and classify them in a logical way, so you can provide travelling advice to any group that might visit.

PREWRITING

a. Classify the activities you are considering writing about into three categories. Remember: *You must use a single principle of division when you create your three categories.* For example, you might classify the activities as family friendly, teens only, and adults only, or you might categorize the activities as inexpensive, reasonably priced, and splurges. However, you wouldn't want to categorize your activities as family friendly, outdoor, and inexpensive as these are all different principles of division.

b. Once you have a satisfactory three-part division, spend at least five minutes freewriting about each of your three points. Don't be concerned yet with grammar, spelling, or organization. Just write whatever comes into your mind about each of the three points.

c. Expand your topic into a fully stated topic sentence.

d. At this stage, you have all three elements of your paragraph: the topic sentence, the three main points, and the details needed to support each point. Now weave them all together in one paragraph.

REVISING

Do not attempt to revise your paragraph right away. Put it away for a while, if possible until the next day. When you reread it, try to be as critical of it as you would be if someone else had written it. As you go over the work, ask yourself the questions in the Four Bases chart on the next page.

Continue revising until you are sure the answer to each question is "yes."

FOUR BASES Checklist: Division-Classification

ABOUT *UNITY*

✔ Have I divided my topic into three distinct parts?

✔ Is each of those parts based on the same principle of division?

ABOUT *SUPPORT*

✔ Have I provided effective details to back up each of my three points?

✔ Have I given each of the three parts approximately equal weight, devoting the same amount of time to each part?

ABOUT *COHERENCE*

✔ Have I used appropriate transitions and other connective devices to weave my paragraph together?

ABOUT *SENTENCE SKILLS*

✔ Have I used a consistent point of view throughout my paragraph?

✔ Have I used specific rather than general words?

✔ Have I avoided wordiness and used concise wording?

✔ Are my sentences varied?

✔ Have I checked for spelling and other sentence skills, as listed on the inside back cover of the book?

WRITING ASSIGNMENT 3

People often assume different roles and different attitudes according to the immediate situation, or context, in which they find themselves. Examples of different types of roles might be student, parent, sister, friend, boss, and employee. Identify several roles that you adopt on a regular basis and write a paragraph that explores how you act and feel in each role. Another approach to this assignment would be to write how different people react to you in your different roles. For instance, think about how your professor might greet you if you bumped into him or her in the supermarket or how your boss might treat you if you happened to meet on the playground as you both watched your children.

WRITING ASSIGNMENT 4

When we go to a restaurant, we probably hope that the service will be helpful, the atmosphere will be pleasant, and the food will be tasty. But as the following cartoon suggests, restaurants that are good in all three respects may be hard to find. Write a review of a restaurant, analyzing its (1) service, (2) atmosphere, and (3) food. Visit a restaurant for this assignment, or draw on an experience you have had recently. Freewrite or make a list of observations about such elements as

Quantity of food you receive	Attitude of the servers
Taste of the food	Efficiency of the servers
Temperature of the food	Decor (take into consideration whether
Freshness of the ingredients	it's a chain restaurant)
How the food is presented	Level of cleanliness
(garnishes, dishes, and so on)	Noise level and music, if any

Feel free to write about details other than those listed above. Just be sure each detail fits into one of your three categories: food, service, or atmosphere.

For your topic sentence, rate the restaurant by giving it from one to five stars, on the basis of your overall impression. Include the restaurant's name and location in your topic sentence. Here are some examples:

Guido's, an Italian restaurant downtown, deserves three stars.

The McDonald's on Route 70 merits a four-star rating.

The Circle Diner in Westfield barely earns a one-star rating.

Think about what makes this cartoon amusing. Select and describe one aspect about the text and one about the image that explain the cartoon's humor.

"The little sad faces next to some items mean they don't taste very good."

Leo Cullum/The New Yorker Collection/www.cartoonbank.com

WRITING ASSIGNMENT 5

Writing for a Specific Purpose and Audience

In this division-classification paragraph, you will write with a specific purpose and for a specific audience. Suppose you are working at a car wash, a beauty salon, a restaurant, an automobile service center, or some other establishment that offers three different versions of a service: economy, full-service, and high-end. For each service, explain what is covered, what is done, and what is charged. Another option is to describe three versions of a product sold where you work. For example, let's say you're employed by a fast-food hamburger restaurant. You might describe three different versions of the same meal by discussing what they cost, what they include, and what size each part of the meals comes in.

Description

This chapter will explain and illustrate how to

- develop a descriptive paragraph
- write a descriptive paragraph
- revise a descriptive paragraph

In addition, you will read and evaluate

- three student descriptive paragraphs

HOW DO DETAILS CREATE THE WHOLE?
Just as an artist uses paint to create a picture for viewers, writers use words to paint a picture in their readers' minds. In both kinds of creations, the use of details is critical. Study the top image and the called-out detail in this painting. Select either the detail or the whole image and write a paragraph describing it to someone who has never seen the painting. As you write, consider how the detail relates to the whole.

When you describe something or someone, you give your readers a picture in words. To make this "word picture" as vivid and real as possible, you must observe and record specific details that appeal to your readers' senses (sight, hearing, taste, smell, and touch). More than any other type of writing, a descriptive paragraph needs sharp, colorful details.

Here is a description in which only the sense of sight is used:

A rug covers the living-room floor.

In contrast, here is a description rich in sense impressions:

A thick, reddish-brown shag rug is laid wall to wall across the living-room floor. The long, curled fibers of the shag seem to whisper as you walk through them in your bare feet, and when you squeeze your toes into the deep covering, the soft fibers push back at you with a spongy resilience.

Sense impressions include sight (*thick, reddish-brown shag rug; laid wall to wall; walk through them in your bare feet; squeeze your toes into the deep covering; push back*), hearing (*whisper*), and touch (*bare feet, soft fibers, spongy resilience*). The sharp, vivid images provided by the sensory details give us a clear picture of the rug and enable us to share the writer's experience.

In addition to sensory detail, you can include details about how a person behaves, how a thing operates, or what happens in a place. In other words, you can relate actions to help convey your *dominant impression* of your subject. This is called *narration,* a writing technique discussed in Chapter 15. For example, in "Paradise Pond," a paragraph that follows, the writer includes certain actions such as the golfers warning him about certain "critters" that live in the pond. He also tells us about his fishing bobber plunging into the water as a bass tugs at the end of his line. In "My Teenage Son's Room," the writer mentions the gerbil that scratches "against the cage wall." In addition we get a picture of the writer's son, Greg, tossing balls of papers into a "'basket'—the trash can."

In this chapter, you will be asked to describe a person, place, or thing for your readers by using words rich in sensory details. To prepare for the assignment, first read the three paragraphs that follow and then answer the accompanying questions.

Evaluating Student Paragraphs

My Teenage Son's Room

¹I push open the door with difficulty. ²The doorknob is loose and has to be jiggled just right before the catch releases from the doorjamb. ³Furthermore, as I push at the door, it runs into a basketball shoe lying on the floor. ⁴I manage to squeeze in through the narrow opening. ⁵I am immediately aware of a pungent odor in the room, most of which is coming from the closet, to my right. ⁶That's the location of a white wicker clothes hamper, heaped with grass-stained jeans, sweat-stained T-shirts, and old-fish-scented socks. ⁷But the half-eaten burrito, lying dried and unappetizing on the bedside table across the room, contributes a bit of aroma, as does the glass of curdled sour milk sitting on the sunny windowsill. ⁸To my left, the small wire cage on Greg's desk is also fragrant, but pleasantly. ⁹From its nest of sweet-smelling cedar chips, the gerbil peers out at me with its bright eyes, its tiny claws scratching against the cage wall. ¹⁰The floor around the wastebasket that is next to the desk is surrounded by what appears to be a sprinkling of snowballs. ¹¹They're actually old wadded-up school papers, and I can picture Greg sitting on his bed, crushing them into balls and aiming them at the "basket"—the trash can. ¹²I glance at the bed across from the desk and chuckle because pillows stuffed under the tangled nest of blankets make it look as if someone is still sleeping there, though I know Greg is in history class right now. ¹³I step carefully through the room, trying to walk through the obstacle course of science-fiction paperbacks, a wristwatch, sports magazines, and a dust-covered computer on which my son stacks empty soda cans. ¹⁴I leave everything as I find it, but tape a note to Greg's door saying, "Isn't it about time to clean up?"

Paradise Pond

¹It wasn't a pond at all, just a large water hole on a golf course. ²But it was my little piece of heaven. ³Long shards of sweet grass rose on every shore, completely encircling the water except for a small clearing where I could fish. ⁴Sometimes a musty, half-sweet odor rose from the brown muck that collected around the green and yellow grass, but usually the air was clear, cool, and refreshing. ⁵I was after blue gills and bass, which had somehow found their way into the pond and which I could sometimes see swimming in the sandy shallows. ⁶On the other side of the pond, the golfers, playing hole 10, scowled at me, and they called out warnings about "critters" that lived there. ⁷The only other sound was the crack of a steel seven iron that struck a

continued

ball and sent it flying toward the flag, which waved in the cool, silent breeze. ⁸I only chuckled, my eyes fixed on the bobber that I was certain would soon plunge deep into the water as a large-mouth bass tugged on the line.

Karla

¹Karla, my brother's new girlfriend, is a catlike creature. ²Framing her face is a layer of sleek black hair that always looks just-combed. ³Her face, with its wide forehead, sharp cheekbones, and narrow, pointed chin, resembles a triangle. ⁴Karla's skin is a soft, velvety brown. ⁵Her large brown eyes slant upward at the corners, and she emphasizes their angle with a sweep of maroon eye shadow. ⁶Karla's habit of looking sidelong out of the tail of her eye makes her appear cautious, as if she were expecting something to sneak up on her. ⁷Her nose is small and flat. ⁸The sharply outlined depression under it leads the observer's eye to a pair of red-tinted lips. ⁹With their slight upward tilt at the corners, Karla's lips make her seem self-satisfied and secretly pleased. ¹⁰One reason Karla may be happy is that she recently was asked to be in a local beauty contest. ¹¹Her long neck and slim body are perfectly in proportion with her face. ¹²Karla manages to look elegant and sleek no matter how she is standing or sitting, for her body seems to be made up of graceful angles. ¹³Her slender hands are tipped with long, polished nails. ¹⁴Her narrow feet are long, too, but they appear delicate even in flat-soled running shoes. ¹⁵Somehow, Karla would look perfect in a cat's jeweled collar.

ABOUT UNITY

1. Which paragraph lacks a topic sentence?

_____

2. Which sentence in the paragraph about Karla should be omitted in the interest of paragraph unity? (*Write the sentence number here.*) _____

ABOUT SUPPORT

3. Label as *sight, touch, hearing,* or *smell* all the sensory details in the following sentences taken from the three paragraphs. The first sentence is done for you as an example.

   a. Sometimes a musty, half-sweet odor rose from the brown muck

      that collected around the green and yellow grass, but usually the

      air was clear, cool, and refreshing.

b. I only chuckled, my eyes fixed on the bobber that I was certain would soon plunge deep into the water as a large-mouth bass tugged on the line.

c. Her slender hands are tipped with long, polished nails.

d. That's the location of a white wicker clothes hamper, heaped with grass-stained jeans, sweat-stained T-shirts, and old-fish-scented socks.

4. After which sentence in "Paradise Pond" are specific details needed?

_____

ABOUT COHERENCE

5. Spatial signals (*above, next to, to the right,* and so on) are often used to help organize details in a descriptive paragraph. List four space signals that appear in "My Teenage Son's Room":

_____   _____   _____   _____   _____   _____

6. The writer of "Karla" organizes the details by observing Karla in an orderly way. Which of Karla's features is described first? _____ Which is described last? _____ Check the method of spatial organization that best describes the paragraph:

_____ Interior to exterior

_____ Near to far

_____ Top to bottom

Developing a Descriptive Paragraph

Development through Prewriting

When Victor was assigned a descriptive paragraph, he thought at first of describing his own office at work. He began by making a list of details he noticed while looking around the office.

> *adjustable black chair*   *computer*
>
> *beige desk*   *pictures of Marie and kids on desk*
>
> *piles of papers*   *desk calendar*

But Victor quickly became bored. Here is how he describes what happened next:

"As I wrote down what I saw in my office, I was thinking, 'What a drag.' I gave up and worked on something else. Later that evening I told my wife that I was going to write a boring paragraph about my boring office. She started laughing at me. I said, 'What's so funny?' and she said, 'You're so certain that a writing assignment has to be boring that you deliberately chose a subject that bores you. How about writing about something you care about?' At first I was annoyed, but then I realized she was right. When I hear 'assignment' I automatically think 'pain in the neck' and just want to get it over with."

Victor's attitude is not uncommon. Many students who are not experienced writers don't take the time to find a topic that interests them. They grab the one closest at hand and force themselves to write about it just for the sake of completing the assignment. Like Victor, they ensure that they (and probably their instructors as well) will be bored with the task.

That evening, Victor remembered the days when, as a boy, he used to fish "the pond," really a water hole on a local public golf course in Florida. "As I remembered the 'pond,' I recalled a lot of descriptive details—sounds, smells, sights," said Victor. "I realized not only that it would be more fun to describe a place like that than my bland, boring office, but also that I would actually find it an interesting challenge to make my reader see the pond through my words."

Victor now began to make a list of details about the pond:

Brown muck surrounding the pond

Tall sweet grass

Golfers on the 10th hole

Steel clubs cracking against hard golf balls

A clear spot in the weeds—a place to fish

Blue gills, large-mouth bass

Musty smell, sweet

"Watch out for snakes, kid"

Bobber plunges into the water—a strike

Great feeling at the end of the line, bass tugs away

As he looked over his list of details, the word that came to mind was "paradise." Victor remembered this place fondly, as a beautiful and peaceful haven. He decided his topic sentence would be "It was my little piece of heaven." He then wrote this first draft:

It was my little piece of heaven, beautiful and peaceful. Grass completely surrounded the pond except for one small clearing where I could fish. All I cared about was catching fish, and I kept my eye on that bobber, waiting for it to disappear into the water. The golfers warn me to watch for snakes. I didn't care about the golfers' warnings. The only other sound is a club hitting the ball. An odor rose from the muck that collects around the grass, but it's not bad. Usually the air is refreshing. Watch out for the "critters."

Development through Revising

The next day, Victor's instructor asked to see the students' first drafts. This is what she wrote in response to Victor's:

This is a very good beginning. You have provided some strong details that appeal to the reader's sense of smell, hearing, and sight.

In your next draft, organize your paragraph better. Try spatial order. For example, you might describe the grass that surrounds the pond, then mention the fact that you found an open spot to fish from, and then tell us about the golfers' warnings. You can then end logically by explaining how you reacted to their warnings.

I encourage you to become even more specific in your details. For instance, what kind of fish were you after? As you work on each sentence, ask yourself if you can add more descriptive details to paint a more vivid picture in words.

In response to his instructor's suggestions, Victor rewrote the paragraph, beginning with the sweet grass on the shore. Then he mentioned the fish in the water. Next he focused on the golfers on the other side of the pond. He ended the paragraph with a sentence that brought the reader back to his fishing on the shoreline. He then added some more vivid details throughout and produced the paragraph that appears on pages 280–281.

Writing a Descriptive Paragraph

Having the ideal study environment is different for each of us. Write a paragraph that describes the ideal study environment for you. What type of atmosphere helps you focus? What should your reader understand about your study zone? Why is this environment so effective for you?

Personal

PREWRITING

a. After you decide where you best study, prepare a list of all the details you can think of that support the topic. For example, a student who planned to describe studying in her dorm room made this list:

> audio system
> computer
> small window
> small pink lamp
> photos of family
> photos of friends
> bookcase
> whiteboard with to-do lists

b. You may want to use other prewriting techniques, such as freewriting or questioning, to develop more details for your topic. As you continue prewriting, keep the following in mind:

- Everything in the paragraph should support your point. For example, if you are writing about a dorm room, every detail should serve to show why that room facilitates studying. Other details—for example, dirty clothes and strange wall color—should be omitted.

- Description depends on the use of specific rather than general descriptive words. Examples are given on the next page.

SELECT ONE DETAIL FROM THIS photo and write a brief paragraph describing exactly what and how that item contributes to the mess in this scene.

General	Specific
Mess on the floor	The obstacle course of science-fiction paperbacks, a wristwatch, sports magazines, and a dust-covered computer on which my son stacks empty soda cans
Ugly turtle tub	Large plastic tub of dirty, stagnant water with a motionless turtle
Bad smell	Unpleasant mixture of strong chemical deodorizers, urine-soaked newspapers, and musty sawdust
Nice skin	Soft, velvety brown skin

Remember that you want your readers to experience the room vividly. Your words should be as detailed as a clear photograph, giving readers a real feel for the room. Appeal to as many senses as possible. Most of your description will involve the sense of sight, but you may be able to include details about touch, hearing, and smell as well.

- Spatial order is a good way to organize a descriptive paragraph. Move as a visitor's eye might move around the room, from right to left or from larger items to smaller ones. Here are a few transition words that show spatial relationships:

to the left	above	across from
to the right	below	nearby
next to	on the opposite side	

Such transitions will help prevent you—and your reader—from getting lost as the description proceeds.

c. Before you write, make a scratch outline based on your list. Here is one possible outline of the paragraph about studying in the dorm room. Note that the details are organized according to spatial order—starting with the window at the outside edge of the room and moving in toward the center.

Topic sentence: The best place for me to study is in my dorm room.

1. Window
2. Walls
3. Whiteboard
4. Bookcase
5. Desk
6. Lamp

---

d. Then proceed to write a first draft of your paragraph.

REVISING

Read your descriptive paragraph slowly out loud to a friend. Ask the friend to close his or her eyes and try to picture the room as you read. Read it aloud a second time. Ask your friend to answer these questions.

FOUR BASES Checklist: Description

ABOUT *UNITY*

✔ Does every detail in the paragraph support the topic sentence?

ABOUT *SUPPORT*

✔ Are the details specific and vivid rather than general?

✔ Has the writer included details that appeal to as many senses as possible?

ABOUT *COHERENCE*

✔ Does the paragraph follow a logical spatial order?

✔ Has the writer used transitions (such as *on top of, beside, to the left of*) to help the reader follow that order?

ABOUT *SENTENCE SKILLS*

✔ Has the writer carefully proofread his or her paragraph, using the list on the inside back cover of the book, and corrected all sentence-skills mistakes, including spelling?

Continue revising your work until you and your reader can answer "yes" to each of these questions.

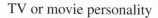

WRITING ASSIGNMENT 2

Write a paragraph describing a specific person. Select a dominant impression of the person, and use only details that will convey that impression. You might want to write about someone who falls into one of these categories:

TV or movie personality	Coworker
Brother or sister	Clergyman or clergywoman

Employer	Police officer
Child	Store owner or manager
Older person	Bartender
Close friend	Joker
Enemy or rival	Doctor or nurse

PREWRITING

a. Reread the paragraph about Karla that appears earlier in this chapter. Note the dominant impression that the writer wanted to convey: that Karla is a catlike person. Having decided to focus on that impression, the writer included only details that contributed to her point. Similarly, you should focus on one dominant aspect of your subject's appearance, personality, or behavior.

   Once you have chosen the person you will write about and the impression you plan to portray, put that information into a topic sentence. Here are some examples of topic sentences that mention a particular person and the dominant impression of that person:

   Kate gives the impression of being permanently nervous.

   The candidate for the Senate looked like a movie star.

   The child was an angelic little figure.

   The dental receptionist was extremely reassuring.

   The TV newscaster seems as synthetic as a piece of Styrofoam.

   Our neighbor is a fussy person.

   The rock singer seemed to be plugged into some special kind of energy source.

   The police office inspired confidence.

   My friend Jeffrey is a slow, deliberate person.

   The owner of that grocery store seems burdened with troubles.

b. Make a list of the person's qualities that support your topic sentence. Write quickly; don't worry if you find yourself writing down something that doesn't quite fit. You can always edit the list later. For now, just write down all the details that occur to you that support the dominant impression you want to convey. Include details that involve as many senses as possible (sight, sound, hearing, touch, smell). For instance, here's a list one writer jotted down to support the sentence "The child was an angelic little figure":

soft brown ringlets of hair

pink cheeks

wide shining eyes

shrieking laugh

joyful smile

starched white dress

white flowers in hair

c. Edit your list, striking out details that don't support your topic sentence and adding others that do. The author of the paragraph on an angelic figure crossed out one detail from the original list and added a new one:

soft brown ringlets of hair

pink cheeks

wide shining eyes

~~shrieking laugh~~

joyful smile

starched white dress

white flowers in hair

~~sweet singing voice~~

d. Decide on a spatial order of organization. In the example above, the writer ultimately decided to describe the child from head to toe.

e. Make a scratch outline for your paragraph, based on the organization you have chosen.

f. Then proceed to write a first draft of your paragraph.

REVISING

Put your paragraph away for a day or so if at all possible. Then ask yourself and a peer editor these questions.

FOUR BASES Checklist: Description

ABOUT *UNITY*

✔ Does my topic sentence make a general point about the person?

ABOUT *SUPPORT*

✔ Do descriptions of the appearance, tone of voice, and expressions of the people involved paint a clear picture of the person?

ABOUT *COHERENCE*

✔ Have I used transitional words, such as *first, later,* and *then*?

ABOUT *SENTENCE SKILLS*

✔ Have I used a consistent point of view throughout my paragraph?

✔ Have I used specific rather than general words?

✔ Have I avoided wordiness?

✔ Are my sentences varied?

✔ Have I checked for spelling and other sentence skills, as listed on the inside back cover of the book?

Continue revising your work until you can answer "yes" to each of these questions.

WRITING ASSIGNMENT 3

Write a paragraph describing the cartoon shown here so that a person who has never seen it will be able to visualize it and fully understand it.

In order to write such a complete description, you must notice and report *every detail* in the cartoon. The details include such things as the way the room is arranged; the objects present in the room; what the characters are doing with those objects; the expressions on the characters' faces; and any motions that are occurring. Remember as you are describing the cartoon to give special attention to the same elements that the cartoonist gives special attention to. Your goal should be this: Someone who reads your description of the cartoon will understand it as fully as someone who saw the cartoon itself.

Dan Reynolds @ www.CartoonStock.com

WRITING ASSIGNMENT 4

Imagine you have been asked to be part of an experiment. This experiment requires you to sit on one side of a curtain and describe yourself in enough detail that a sketch artist on the other side of the curtain can create a perfect picture of you. Select colorful detailed descriptions that support a dominant impression of you. Once you decide on the impression you wish to convey, compose a topic sentence, such as one of those below, that summarizes the details you will use.

My face is interesting because my individual features contrast with one another dramatically.

My facial features convey my Hawaiian heritage.

My large piercing eyes dominate my otherwise plain features.

After you have written your paragraph, you may want to give it to a friend or classmate to see if he or she thinks your description is accurate.

WRITING ASSIGNMENT 5

Writing for a Specific Purpose and Audience

In this description paragraph, you will write with a specific purpose and for a specific audience. Imagine that you work for a marketing firm and have to create an advertising campaign. Choose an object that you need to promote and then write a paragraph describing that object, how it is used, and why it would make a good purchase. Include as many sensory details as possible—details that will emotionally connect the buyer to the product. Once you decide on the impression you want to convey, compose a topic sentence like the one below that summarizes the details:

> No household should be without the amazing, all-purpose, environmentally friendly, lawn care system known as "The Goat."

Remember to provide colorful detailed descriptions to help your readers picture the image you are writing about. Note the contrast in the two items below:

> *Lacks rich descriptive details:* Our lawn looked really nice after it had been cut.

> *Includes rich descriptive details:* After we used "The Goat" for the first time, our lawn was trimmed to a neat uniform one-inch height and was a shining, beautiful dark green from all the natural fertilizer.

This chapter will explain and illustrate how to

- develop a narrative paragraph
- write a narrative paragraph
- revise a narrative paragraph

In addition, you will read and evaluate

- three student narrative paragraphs

HOW REALISTIC ARE YOUR MEMORIES? Adults sentimentally think of childhood as a time of happy, carefree innocence, as depicted in this photograph. Yet during childhood most of us witnessed events that began to make us aware that life was not always happy or fair. What such events do you remember? Select one and write a paragraph about it. What impression did it make on you?

At times we make a statement clear by relating in detail something that has happened. In the story we tell, we present the details in the order in which they happened. A person might say, for example, "I was embarrassed yesterday," and then go on to illustrate the statement with the following narrative:

> I was hurrying across campus to get to a class. It had rained heavily all morning, so I was hopscotching my way around puddles in the pathway. I called to two friends ahead to wait for me, and right before I caught up to them, I came to a large puddle that covered the entire path. I had to make a quick choice of either stepping into the puddle or trying to jump over it. I jumped, wanting to seem cool, since my friends were watching, but didn't clear the puddle. Water splashed everywhere, drenching my shoe, sock, and pants cuff, and spraying the pants of my friends as well. "Well done, Dave!" they said. My embarrassment was all the greater because I had tried to look so casual.

The speaker's details have made his moment of embarrassment vivid and real for us, and we can see and understand just why he felt as he did.

In addition to vivid details that convey action, you might want to include both characters and *dialogue* (what people say) in your narrative. For example, in "Heartbreak" we meet Bonnie, the writer's former girlfriend. When he asks her about her new love interest ("Who is Blake?"), Bonnie asks him, "What do you want to hear about—my classes or Blake?"

In this chapter, you will be asked to tell a story that illustrates or explains some point. The paragraphs below all present narrative experiences that support a point. Read them and then answer the questions that follow.

Evaluating Student Paragraphs

Heartbreak

¹Bonnie and I had gotten engaged in August, just before she left for college at Penn State. ²A week before Thanksgiving, I drove up to see her as a surprise. ³When I knocked on the door of her dorm room, she was indeed surprised, but not in a pleasant way. ⁴She introduced me to her roommate, who looked uncomfortable and quickly left. ⁵I asked Bonnie

continued

how classes were going, and at the same time I tugged on the sleeve of my heavy sweater in order to pull it off. 6As I was slipping it over my head, I noticed a large photo on the wall—of Bonnie and a tall guy laughing together. 7It was decorated with paper flowers and a yellow ribbon, and on the ribbon was written "Bonnie and Blake." 8"What's going on?" I said. 9I stood there stunned and then felt anger that grew rapidly. 10"Who is Blake?" I asked. 11Bonnie laughed nervously and said, "What do you want to hear about—my classes or Blake?" 12I don't really remember what she then told me, except that Blake was a sophomore math major. 13I felt a terrible pain in the pit of my stomach, and I wanted to rest my head on someone's shoulder and cry. 14I wanted to tear down the sign and run out, but I did nothing. 15Clumsily I pulled on my sweater again. 16My knees felt weak, and I barely had control of my body. 17I opened the room door, and suddenly more than anything I wanted to slam the door shut so hard that the dorm walls would collapse. 18Instead, I managed to close the door quietly. 19I walked away understanding what was meant by a broken heart.

James Smith's Remarkable Career

1Until his recent retirement, James Smith was a partner and highly successful attorney at Lowell and Lowell. 2For more than thirty-five years, his practice focused exclusively on environmental law and international treaties and regulations. 3Before coming to Lowell and Lowell, Mr. Smith received his bachelor's degree in human physiology from Gonzaga University. 4In 1989, Mr. Smith graduated from Cornell University Law School, earning a J.D./LL.M in International and Comparative Law. 5In his many years at Lowell and Lowell, Mr. Smith became known for litigation for stricter standards for watershed pollution control. 6He regularly represented clients in environmental cases where individual plaintiffs sought statutory and/or punitive damages on behalf of themselves and a class. 7Over the years, Mr. Smith successfully litigated numerous high profile class actions against pharmaceutical companies, gas and oil companies, and the commercial fishing industry. 8He worked on public safety initiatives along the Mississippi and Gulf Coast areas and made frequent trips to meet with people in those regions. 9In 2012, he successfully won a class action suit against British Petroleum for the Deepwater Horizon oil spill. 10In 2014, he testified in the congressional hearing for new EPA standards; his testimony was key to the passing of the standards. 11At his retirement party last month, several clients spoke warmly and appreciatively about his tireless work on their behalf, and the firm presented Mr. Smith with a special plaque commemorating his many achievements.

The End of Smallpox

¹The deadly infectious disease known as smallpox killed millions over the centuries. ²Today, however, the disease has been completely eliminated. ³Smallpox began in Africa, some scientists believe, and then moved to Asia thousands of years ago. ⁴The first signs that smallpox could be eradicated came about one thousand years ago in Asia. ⁵About the year 1040, it was discovered that pulverizing the scabs of smallpox victims and blowing the dust into the nose of a healthy person would make that person immune. ⁶Then, at the end of the eighteenth century, a British doctor, Edward Jenner, found that farmworkers who got cowpox, a disease that attacks cows and oxen, became immune to smallpox. ⁷Cowpox also affects rodents such as mice and voles. ⁸Soon thereafter, Jenner developed a vaccine by using the pus in a farmworker's cowpox boil to make a serum that he injected into a healthy young boy. ⁹Several weeks later, the boy was exposed to smallpox, but he never developed the disease. ¹⁰In the late 1960s, an attempt to eradicate smallpox was launched by the World Health Organization, and since 1980, no additional cases of smallpox have been confirmed.

QUESTIONS

ABOUT UNITY

1.   Which paragraph lacks a topic sentence?

_____

Write a topic sentence for the paragraph.

_____

_____

2.   Which sentence in "The End of Smallpox" should be omitted in the interest

of paragraph unity? (*Write the sentence number here.*) _____

ABOUT SUPPORT

3.   What is for you the best (most real and vivid) detail or image in the
paragraph "Heartbreak"?

_____

_____

What is the best detail or image in "James Smith's Remarkable Career"?

_____

_____

What is the best detail or image in "The End of Smallpox"?

_____

_____

4.   Which paragraph includes the actual words spoken by the participants?

_____

_____

ABOUT COHERENCE

5.   Do the three paragraphs use time order or emphatic order to organize details?

_____

6.   What are the seven transition words or phrases used in "The End of Smallpox"?

_____

_____

Developing a Narrative Paragraph

Development through Prewriting

Gary's instructor was helping her students think of topics for their narrative paragraphs. "A narrative is simply a story that illustrates a point," she said. "That point is often about an emotion you felt. Looking at a list of emotions may help you think of a topic. Ask yourself what incident in your life has made you feel any of these emotions."

The instructor then jotted these feelings on the board:

Anger	Thankfulness
Embarrassment	Loneliness
Jealousy	Sadness
Amusement	Terror
Confusion	Relief

As Gary looked over the list, he thought of several experiences in his life. "The word 'angry' made me think about a time when I was a kid. My brother took my skateboard without permission and left it in the park, where it got stolen. 'Amused' made me think of when I watched my roommate, who claimed he spoke Spanish, try to bargain with a street vendor in Mexico. He got so flustered that he ended up paying even more than the vendor had originally asked for. When I got to 'sad', though, I thought about when I visited Bonnie and found out she was dating someone else. 'Sad' wasn't a strong enough word, though—I was heartbroken. So I decided to write about heartbreak."

Gary's first step was to do some freewriting. Without worrying about spelling or grammar, he simply wrote down everything that came into his mind concerning his visit to Bonnie. Here is what he came up with:

I hadn't expected to see Bonnie until Christmas. We'd got engaged just before she went off to college. The drive to Penn State took ten hours each way and that seemed like to much driving for just a weekend visit. But I realized I had a long weekend over Thanksgiving I decided to surprise her. I think down deep I knew something was wrong. She had sounded sort of cool on the phone and she hadn't been writing as often. I guess I wanted to convince myself that everything was OK. We'd been dating since we were 16 and I couldn't imagine not being with her. When I knocked at her dorm door I remember how she was smiling when she opened the door. Her expression changed to one of surprise. Not happy surprise. I hugged her and she sort of hugged me back but like you'd hug your brother. Another girl was in the room. Bonnie said, "This is Pam," and Pam shot out of the room like I had a disease. Everything seemed wrong and confused. I started taking off my sweater and then I saw it. On a bulletin board was this photo of Bonnie with Blake, the guy she had been messing around with. They broke up about a year later, but by then I never wanted to see Bonnie again. I couldn't believe Bonnie would start seeing somebody else when we were planning to get married. It had even been her idea to get engaged. Before she left for college. Later on I realized that wasn't the first dishonest thing she'd done. I got out of there as quick as I could.

Development through Revising

Gary knew that the first, freewritten version of his paragraph needed work. Here are the comments he made after he reread it the following day.

"Although my point is supposed to be that my visit to Bonnie was heartbreaking, I didn't really get that across. I need to say more about how the experience felt.

"I've included some information that doesn't really support my point. For instance, what happened to Bonnie and Blake later isn't important here. Also, I think

continued

I spend too much time explaining the circumstances of the visit. I need to get more quickly to the point where I arrived at Bonnie's dorm.

    "I think I should include more dialogue, too. That would make the reader feel more like a witness to what really happened."

With this self-critique in mind, Gary revised his paragraph until he had produced the version that appears on pages 294–295.

Writing a Narrative Paragraph

WRITING ASSIGNMENT 1

Write a paragraph that narrates one of the scenarios listed below.

- A time when one of your ideas or beliefs was challenged or destroyed
- How a story/movie or character in a story/movie had a great effect on you
- A time when you witnessed an act of heroism
- An experience you had in another country
- Your best or worst job interview
- A time when you failed or succeeded at something

The experience you write about should be limited in time, like the experiences in "Heartbreak," which occurred within a relatively short period.

PREWRITING

a. Begin by freewriting. Think of an experience or event that caused you to feel a certain emotion strongly. Then spend ten minutes writing freely about the experience. Do not worry at this point about such matters as spelling or grammar or putting things in the right order. Instead, just try to get down all the details you can think of that seem related to the experience.

b. This preliminary writing will help you decide whether your topic is promising enough to develop further. If it is not, choose another scenario and repeat step *a*. If it does seem promising, do three things:

- First, write your topic sentence, underlining the emotion you will focus on. For example, "My first job interview for a teaching position was one of the most embarrassing days of my life."
- Second, make a list of all the details involved in the experience.
- Then number these details according to the order in which they occurred.

c. Referring to your list of details, write a rough draft of your paragraph. Use time signals such as *first, then, after, next, while, during,* and *finally* to help connect details as you move from the beginning to the middle to the end of your narrative. Be sure to include not only what happened but also how you felt about what was going on.

REVISING

Put your first draft away for a day or so. When you return to it, read it over, asking yourself these questions.

FOUR BASES Checklist: Narration

ABOUT *UNITY*

✔ Does my paragraph have a clearly stated topic sentence, including a dominant impression?

✔ Are there any off-topic sentences I should eliminate for the sake of paragraph unity?

ABOUT *SUPPORT*

✔ Have I provided rich, specific details that will appeal to my reader?

ABOUT *COHERENCE*

✔ Have I used time order to narrate the experience from beginning to end?

✔ Have I used time signals to help readers follow my train of thought?

ABOUT *SENTENCE SKILLS*

✔ Have I carefully proofread my paragraph for spelling and other sentence skills, as listed on the inside back cover of the book?

✔ Have I used a consistent point of view throughout my paragraph?

✔ Have I used specific rather than general words?

✔ Have I used verb tenses consistently and correctly? (This is especially important when relaying a story.)

Continue revising your work until you can answer "yes" to each of these questions.

WRITING ASSIGNMENT 2

When applying for scholarships, students often submit copies of their transcripts, a resume that demonstrates their community service and school involvement, and a letter stating their qualifications. For this assignment, write a story about yourself that demonstrates why you should be awarded the scholarship.

PREWRITING

a. If you are unsure of the types of scholarship available to students, speak with someone in your school's financial aid office or search online at a site like CollegeBoard.com.

b. Decide what points you will make about why you deserve the scholarship. What things have you done that make you worthy? How can you best demonstrate your qualifications?

c. Write your topic sentence. The topic sentence should state why you deserve and qualify for the scholarship. Here are some possibilities:

> Although my grades may not be as high as some students, the experiences I have had working to help support my family since I was fourteen tell what has been most significant in my life.

> The changes I have gone through as I have volunteered at the animal shelter have prepared me to be a great veterinarian and an ideal candidate for the Bonner County Biology Scholarship.

d. Use the questioning technique to remind yourself of details that will make your narrative come alive. Ask yourself questions like these and write down your answers:

- What are the scholarship requirements?

- How do I qualify for the scholarship?

- What incidents or experiences in my past support my application?

- Why should I get the scholarship over other applicants?

e. Drawing details from the notes you have written, write the first draft of your paragraph. Remember to use time signals such as *then, after that, during, meanwhile,* and *finally* to connect one sentence to another.

REVISING

After you have put your paragraph away for a day, read it to a friend who will give you honest feedback. You and your friend should consider the questions in the Four Bases checklist on the next page.

FOUR BASES Checklist: Narration

ABOUT *UNITY*

✔ Does my topic sentence make a general point about why I should receive the scholarship?

ABOUT *SUPPORT*

✔ Have I provided rich, specific details that will appeal to my reader?

ABOUT *COHERENCE*

✔ Is the sequence of events made clear by transitional words such as *first, later,* and *then*?

ABOUT *SENTENCE SKILLS*

✔ Have I carefully proofread my paragraph for spelling and other sentence skills, as listed on the inside back cover of the book?

✔ Have I used a consistent point of view throughout my paragraph?

✔ Have I avoided wordiness?

✔ Are my sentences varied?

Continue revising your work until you and your reader can answer "yes" to each of these questions.

WRITING ASSIGNMENT 3

Write a one-paragraph e-mail to your boss describing how something at the company could be done better. In your paragraph, identify the problem—supporting it with a story that demonstrates the problem. Your story should include details about a specific incident that occurred, which revealed or uncovered the nature and depth of the problem. Then suggest a possible solution. You must explain why your solution will work, so you will want to check Chapter 16, "Argument," to help you create a persuasive tone for both your story and solution. Keep in mind that writing to a boss requires formal language and detailed support. A memo also requires proper formatting that includes the sender, addressee, date, and subject matter. Refer to the following sample memo, which illustrates a topic sentence and proper formatting.

To: Tom Jones

Subject: Paper Usage at Acme Widgets, Inc.

Attachment: 2012 HR Paper Report

Dear Mr. Jones:

I would like to relay an experience I've had recently that demonstrates what I feel is a serious problem concerning current paper usage at Acme Widgets, Inc., as well as offer a solution about how our company could save $1000 per month by making some very small changes.

Sincerely,
Jane Smith
Manager, Human Resources
Acme Widgets, Incorporated
600 South Smith Road
New York, NY 62210
(555) 555-5555
jane.smith@gmail.com

WRITING ASSIGNMENT 4

Personal

Write a paragraph that shows the truth or falsity of a popular belief such as one from the list below. Base your story on a personal experience, but feel free to fictionalize as well.

- Haste makes waste.
- Don't count your chickens before they hatch.
- A bird in the hand is worth two in the bush.
- It isn't what you know; it's who you know.
- You really never know people until you see them in an emergency.
- If you don't help yourself, no one else will.
- An ounce of prevention is worth a pound of cure.
- You get what you pay for.
- A fool and his money are soon parted.
- Nice guys finish last.

Begin with a topic sentence that expresses your agreement or disagreement with the saying or belief—for example:

> "Never give advice to a friend" is not always good advice, as I learned after helping a friend reunite with her boyfriend.

Remember that the purpose of your story is to support your topic sentence. Omit details that don't support it. Also feel free to make up details that will.

WRITING ASSIGNMENT 5

Writing for a Specific Purpose and Audience

Your employer is updating the company's Web site. One of the new features of the Web site is a biographical anecdote for every employee. It is your job to write the paragraph that will accompany your photo. Your anecdote should relate a signifi-cant experience in your work life that illustrates such factors as, for example, your work-related competencies, how your educational background has helped you on the job, how long you have been with the company, or any major projects you have completed. Keep in mind that this personal story is intended to help potential clients get to know employees, so it should have a serious tone. A sample topic sentence has also been provided for you:

> On my first day teaching at State University—fourteen years ago—something happened that immediately helped me understand why this was the right place for me to be working.

Argument

This chapter will explain and illustrate how to

- develop an argument paragraph

- write an argument paragraph

- revise an argument paragraph

In addition, you will read and evaluate

- three student argument paragraphs

IS PRIVACY A RIGHT OR PRIVILEGE? Do agencies like the National Security Agency and state and local police have the right to invade our private lives? Do you think a person's right to privacy is more important than national security? Write a paragraph in which you argue for or against a person's full right to privacy.

Most of us know someone who enjoys a good argument. Such a person usually challenges any sweeping statement we might make. "Why do you say that?" he or she will ask. "Give your reasons." Our questioner then listens carefully as we cite our reasons, waiting to see if we really do have solid evidence to support our point of view. In an argument such as the one going on in the cartoon, the two parties each present their supporting evidence. The goal is to determine who has the more solid evidence to support his or her point of view. A questioner may make us feel a bit nervous, but we may also appreciate the way he or she makes us think through our opinions.

The ability to advance sound, compelling arguments is an important skill in everyday life. We can use argument to get an extension on a term paper, obtain a favor from a friend, or convince an employer that we are the right person for a job. Understanding persuasion based on clear, logical reasoning can also help us see through the sometimes faulty arguments advanced by advertisers, editors, politicians, and others who try to bring us over to their side.

In this chapter, you will be asked to argue a position and defend it with a series of solid reasons. In a general way, you are doing the same thing with all the paragraph assignments in the book: making a point and then supporting it. The difference here is that, in a more direct and formal manner, you will advance a point about which you feel strongly and seek to persuade others to agree with you.

Strategies for Argument

Because argument assumes controversy, you have to work especially hard to convince readers of your position. Here are four strategies you can use to help win over readers whose viewpoint may differ from yours.

Provide Logical Support

The best way to prove a point or to persuade someone to do something is simply to provide enough evidence or support for your position. Thus, if you are trying to persuade the president of your college to hire more librarians, you might explain that you had to wait for more than an hour to get the help you needed when recently researching a paper topic.

But you wouldn't stop there. You might get a hundred other students to attest to the same problem by signing a petition. You might also find out the student-librarian ratios at other colleges and compare them with the ratio at your school. Finally, you might conduct a survey to estimate the number of students who use the library each semester or the number of research papers that are assigned at your school each term. All of this would provide hard evidence to help you make your case. Of course, you would want to present your position logically and fairly. In this case, it seems only logical and fair that if students are being requested to do library research, enough librarians should be on hand to assist them.

Another good example is demonstrated in "Recommendation for Continued Employment," one of the sample paragraphs below. In this paragraph, several distinct and specific factors are provided as evidence to support the writer's position.

In what ways does this cartoon represent a "good" argument? At the same time, what makes it humorous?

Anticipate Opposing Arguments

Another way to strengthen your argument is to anticipate and address opposing arguments. Let's say the college's budget is stretched to the limit. If so, the college president might respond to your argument simply by stating that the lack of funds prevents the hiring of more librarians. If you believe this to be true, the first thing to do is to admit that it is. The next is to offer a solution to the problem, perhaps by suggesting that money from a less important aspect of college operations be shifted to the library's budget. Of course, if you don't believe that the opposing argument is true, you will have to disprove it convincingly before you move on.

Establish Your Credibility

Yet another important requirement for arguing persuasively is to establish your credibility. In other words, you will need to convince your readers that you know what you are talking about and that your opinion is sound. For example, in "Living Alone," a student paragraph that follows, the writer establishes his credibility by telling us that he "lived alone for ten years before [he] got married."

Appeal to Your Audience

Finally, remember that tone and audience are even more important to argument than to other types of writing. While you may want to appeal to your readers' self-interest and emotions, try to remain as clear, levelheaded, and courteous as you can. Because you are attempting to persuade readers to accept your viewpoint, it is important not to anger them by referring to them or their opinions in rude or belittling terms. Stay away from sweeping statements like "Everybody knows that…." or "People with any intelligence agree that…." Also, keep the focus on the issue you are discussing, not on the people involved in the debate. Don't write, "*My opponents* claim that surveillance cameras are acceptable in all public spaces." Instead, write, "*Supporters of widespread use of surveillance cameras* say that cameras should be allowed in all public spaces." Terms like *my opponents* imply that the argument is between you and anyone who disagrees with you. By contrast, saying *supporters of widespread use of surveillance cameras* suggests that those who don't agree with you are nevertheless reasonable people who are willing to consider differing opinions.

Evaluating Student Paragraphs

Let's Ban Proms

¹While many students regard proms as peak events in high school life, I believe that high school proms should be banned. ²One reason is that even before the prom takes place, it causes problems. ³Teenagers are separated into "the ones who were asked" and "the ones who weren't." ⁴Being one of those who weren't asked can be heartbreaking to a sensitive young person. ⁵Another pre-prom problem is money. ⁶The price of the various items needed can add up quickly to a lot of money. ⁷The prom itself can be unpleasant and frustrating, too. ⁸At the beginning of the evening, the girls enviously compare dresses while the boys sweat nervously inside their rented suits. ⁹During the dance, the couples who have gotten together only to go to the prom have split up into miserable singles. ¹⁰When the prom draws to a close, the popular teenagers drive off happily to other parties while the less popular ones head home, as usual. ¹¹Perhaps the main reason proms should be banned, however, is the drinking and driving that go on after the prom is over. ¹²Teenagers pile into their cars on their way to "after-proms" and pull out the bottles and cans stashed under the seat. ¹³By the time the big night is finally over, at 4 or 5 A.M., students are trying to weave home without encountering the police or a roadside tree. ¹⁴Some of them do not make it, and prom night turns into tragedy. ¹⁵For all these reasons, proms have no place in our schools.

Recommendation for Continued Employment

¹After evaluating Ms. Davis, the committee recommends that she be offered a contract to continue teaching in the English Department for the 2014–2015 school year. ²It is evident that Ms. Davis is highly knowledgeable about the subject matter. ³In the two years she has been teaching, she has taught English Composition I and II, Women's Literature, Humanities Past and Present, American Indian Literature, and Masterpieces of American Literature. ⁴Her degrees in composition and rhetoric and anthropology are an asset to our department. ⁵Because her background is varied, she is able to teach a diversity of courses with a strong body of knowledge that has proven to be valuable to our students. ⁶Second, her rapport with students is also to be commended. ⁷As her evaluations demonstrate, Ms. Davis often spends several hours a week tutoring students who are struggling and working with students who want to go further. ⁸She has even offered extra study sessions outside of normal classroom time in preparation for examinations. ⁹Very few professors offer extra study sessions. ¹⁰Additionally, her commitment to the college community has been outstanding. ¹¹She has participated in the First Learning Year Team, the Senate Curriculum Committee, the Global Education and Assessment Team, and the Small Technology Committee. ¹²Many colleagues have submitted letters of support applauding her collegiality and passion for education. ¹³Finally, in keeping with our mission of "serving communities," Ms. Davis has been a volunteer at Literacy Now, a non-profit adult literacy group. ¹⁴She volunteers six hours a week as a literacy tutor, and during the summer is a literacy trainer. ¹⁵Ms. Davis is an asset to the English Department and should be offered continued employment.

Living Alone

¹Living alone is quite an experience. ²I know because I lived alone for ten years before I got married. ³People who live alone, for one thing, have to learn to do all kinds of tasks by themselves. ⁴They must learn— even if they have had no experience—to put up curtains and shades, set up an Internet router, temporarily dam an overflowing toilet, cook a meal, and sort the laundry. ⁵When there is no father, husband, mother, or wife to depend on, a person can't fall back on the excuse, "I don't know how to do that." ⁶Those who live alone also need the strength to deal with people. ⁷Alone, singles must face noisy neighbors, unresponsive landlords, dishonest repair people, and aggressive bill collectors. ⁸Because there

continued

are no buffers between themselves and the outside world, people living alone have to handle every visitor—friendly or unfriendly—alone. 9Finally, singles need a large dose of courage to cope with occasional panic and unavoidable loneliness. 10That weird thump in the night is even more terrifying when there is no one in the next bed or the next room. 11Frightening weather or unexpected bad news is doubly bad when the worry can't be shared. 12Even when life is going well, little moments of sudden loneliness can send shivers through the heart. 13Struggling through such bad times taps into reserves of courage that people may not have known they possessed. 14Facing everyday tasks, confronting all types of people, and handling panic and loneliness can shape singles into brave, resourceful, and more independent people.

QUESTIONS

ABOUT UNITY

1. The topic sentence in "Living Alone" is too broad. Circle the topic sentence below that states accurately what the paragraph is about.

   a. Living alone can make one a better person.

   b. Living alone can create feelings of loneliness.

   c. Living alone should be avoided.

2. Which sentence in "Recommendation for Continued Employment" should be eliminated in the interest of paragraph unity? (*Write the sentence number here.*) _____

3. How many reasons are given to support the topic sentence in each paragraph?

   a. In "Let's Ban Proms"   _____ one _____ two _____ three _____ four

   b. In "Recommendation for Continued Employment"

   _____ one _____ two _____ three _____ four

   c. In "Living Alone"   _____ one _____ two _____ three _____ four

4. After which sentence in "Let's Ban Proms" are more specific details needed? ____

ABOUT COHERENCE

5. Which paragraph uses a combination of time and emphatic order to organize its details? _____

6. What are the three main transition words or phrases in "Living Alone"?

   _____   _____   _____

Complete the outline below of "Recommendation for Continued Employment" by summarizing in a few words the supporting material that fits under the topic sentence. Write in the main points of support for the topic sentence. In the spaces after the letters, write in the examples used to support the four main points. Three items have been provided for you.

ACTIVITY 1

Topic sentence: After evaluating Ms. Davis, the committee recommends that she be offered a contract to continue teaching in the English Department for the 2014–2015 school year.

1. Evident that Ms. Davis is highly knowledgeable about the subject matter _____

    a. _____

    _____

    b. _____

    _____

    c. _____

    _____

2. _____

    _____

    a. _____

    _____

    b. Offered extra study sessions outside of normal classroom time _____

3. _____

    _____

    a. _____

    _____

    b. _____

    _____

4. _____

    _____

    a. Volunteers as literacy tutor six hours a week _____

    b. _____

    _____

ACTIVITY 2 As discussed in this chapter, learning to create an argument in writing is an important skill. However, arguments can often be made through images as well.

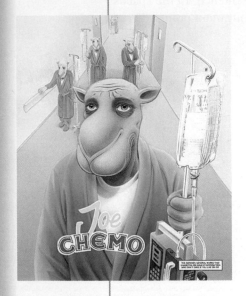

As you look at this poster, analyze the argument being made. What message does the image convey? Is the argument effective? Why or why not?

_____

_____

_____

_____

_____

_____

Study this poster. Summarize its message in one sentence. How do its elements work to create a particular impression? Is its argument different from the poster above? Which poster is more effective in your opinion? Why?

_____

_____

_____

_____

_____

_____

Developing an Argument Paragraph

Development through Prewriting

Yolanda is the student author of "Let's Ban Proms." She decided on her topic after visiting her parents' home one weekend and observing her younger brother's concern about his upcoming prom.

"I really felt bad for Martin as I saw what he was going through," Yolanda said. "He's usually a happy kid who enjoys school. But this weekend he wasn't talking about his track meets or term papers or any of the things he's usually chatting about. Instead he was all tied up in knots about his prom. The girl he'd really wanted to go with had already been asked, and so friends had fixed him up with a girl he barely knew who didn't have a date either. Neither of them was excited about being together, but they felt that they just 'had' to go. And now he's worried about how to afford renting a tux, and how will he get a cool car to go in, and all that stuff. It's shaping up to be a really stressful, expensive evening. When I was in high school, I saw a lot of bad things associated with the prom, too. I hate to see young kids feeling pressured to attend an event that is fun for only a few."

Yolanda began prewriting by making a list of all the negative aspects of proms. This is what she came up with:

Drinking after prom

Car accidents (most important!)

Competition for dates

Preparation for prom cuts into school hours

Rejection of not being asked

Waste of school money

Going with someone you don't like

Separates popular from unpopular

Expensive

Bad-tempered chaperones

Next, Yolanda numbered the details in the order she was going to present them. She also struck out details she decided not to use:

6   Drinking after prom

7   Car accidents (most important!)

3   Competition for dates

~~Preparation for prom cuts into school hours~~

1   Rejection of not being asked

~~Waste of school money~~

4   Going with someone you don't like

5   Separates popular from unpopular

2   Expensive

~~Bad-tempered chaperones~~

Drawing from these notes, Yolanda wrote the following first draft of her paragraph:

In my opinion, high school proms should be banned. First, they cause unhappiness by separating students into "the ones who were asked" and "the ones who weren't." Proms are also expensive, as anyone who has attended one knows. The competition for dates can damage previously strong friendships. Many couples get together only in order to have a date for the prom and do not enjoy each other's company. After the prom, too, the kids are separated into "more popular" and "less popular" groups, with the popular ones going to after-prom parties. The biggest reason to ban proms, though, is the prom-night drinking that commonly occurs. Teenagers hide liquor in their cars and then try to drive home drunk. Some of them do not make it. For all these reasons, proms should be banned.

Development through Revising

Yolanda's instructor reviewed her first draft and made these comments:

> The order of your paragraph could be made stronger. Although you make good use of emphatic order (by ending with "the biggest reason to ban proms"), it's less clear that the paragraph is also organized according to time—in other words, you move from before the prom starts to during the prom to after it. Better use of transitional language will make the organization more clear.
>
> Also, you could make the paragraph more alive by including concrete details and illustrations. Your main points would be stronger with such support.

With these comments in mind, Yolanda revised her paragraph until she produced the version that appears on page 308.

Writing an Argument Paragraph

WRITING ASSIGNMENT 1

Choose one of the topics below and follow the directions. The purpose is to take a strong stand. You must support your claim with at least three reasons.

- Write a letter to the editor arguing against or supporting the banning of a specific book like *To Kill a Mockingbird, Slaughterhouse Five, The Adventures of Huckleberry Finn,* or a book of your choosing.

- Write a letter to the editor arguing that cigarette and alcohol advertising on television and in magazines should (*or* should not) be banned.

- Your college has just announced that the grading scale is going to be changed from a 10-point scale (80-90, 90-100) to a 7-point scale (87-93, 94-100). Write a paragraph in which you support or oppose this decision.

- Your local school district is going to require all students to wear school uniforms. Write a paragraph (either as a student attending or as a parent) in which you support or oppose this decision.

- As you are applying for a new job, your potential employer requests to see your social networking profiles. Write a letter expressing why you don't think this is a valid way to check a potential employee's background.

- As you are starting your new job, you are informed that you get eight days of holiday and vacation time a year. Write a paragraph explaining why you believe you should get more holidays and longer vacations.

- Since the current age for a person to get his or her own credit card is eighteen, many credit card companies canvas college campuses and encourage college students to sign up for multiple cards. Write a paragraph arguing that the minimum age for a credit card should be raised from eighteen to twenty-one years.

PREWRITING

a. Make up brief outlines for any three of the statements above. Make sure you have three separate and distinct reasons for each statement. Below is an example of a brief outline for a paragraph making another point.

Large cities should outlaw passenger cars.

1. *Cut down on smog and pollution*

2. *Cut down on noise*

3. *Make more room for pedestrians*

b. Decide, perhaps through discussion with your instructor or classmates, which of your outlines is the most promising for development into a paragraph. Make sure your supporting points are logical by asking yourself in each case, "Does this item truly support my topic sentence?"

c. Do some prewriting. Prepare a list of all the details you can think of that might support your point. Don't limit yourself; include more details than you can actually use. Here, for example, are details generated by the writer of "Living Alone":

Deal with power failures	*Noisy neighbors*
Nasty landlords	*Develop courage*
Scary noises at night	*Do all the cooking*
Spiders	*Home repairs*
Bill collectors	*Obscene phone calls*
Frightening storms	*Loneliness*

d. Decide which details you will use to develop your paragraph. Number the details in the order in which you will present them. Because presenting the strongest reason last (emphatic order) is the most effective way to organize an argument paragraph, be sure to save your most powerful reason for last. Here is how the author of "Living Alone" made decisions about details:

1	Deal with power failures
4	Nasty landlords
7	Scary noises at night
	~~Spiders~~
6	Bill collectors
8	Frightening storms
5	Noisy neighbors
10	Develop courage
2	Do all the cooking
3	Home repairs
	~~Obscene phone calls~~
9	Loneliness

e. Write the first draft of your paragraph. As you write, develop each reason with specific details. For example, in "Living Alone," notice how the writer makes the experience of living alone come alive with phrases like "That weird thump in the night" or "little moments of sudden loneliness can send shivers through the heart."

REVISING

Put your paragraph away for a day or so. Then look over the checklist that follows.

FOUR BASES Checklist: Argument

ABOUT *UNITY*

✔ Imagine that your audience is a jury who will ultimately render a verdict on your argument. Have you presented a convincing case? If you were on the jury, would you both understand and be favorably impressed by this argument?

✔ Does every one of your supporting points help prove the argument stated in your topic sentence?

ABOUT *SUPPORT*

✔ Have you backed up your points of support with specific details?

✔ Have you appealed to your readers' senses with these details?

ABOUT *COHERENCE*

✔ Have you used emphatic order in your paragraph, saving the most important, strongest detail for last?

ABOUT *SENTENCE SKILLS*

✔ Have you used strong verbs (rather than *is* and *to be*) throughout?

✔ Have you used active verbs in your writing?

✔ Have you checked your paper for sentence-skills mistakes, including spelling? Use the checklist on the inside back cover of this book.

Continue revising your work until you can answer "yes" to each of these questions.

WRITING ASSIGNMENT 2

Write a paragraph in which you take a stand on one of the controversial points below. Support the point with three reasons.

- Students should not be required to attend high school.
- Prisoners who have served their time and who have been released should be allowed to vote.
- The government should set up centers where sick or elderly people can live at a minimal cost to them or their family.

- College writing classes should be on a pass/fail system.
- Students should be required to take an age-appropriate economics class every year from first grade through twelfth grade.
- Public schools should mandate school uniforms.
- Prostitution should be legalized.
- People older than ninety-five should be prohibited from driving.
- No state should allow legal use of medical marijuana.

PREWRITING

a. As a useful exercise to help you begin developing your argument, your instructor might give class members a chance to "stand up" for what they believe in. One side of the front of the room should be designated *strong agreement* and the other side *strong disagreement,* with an imaginary line representing varying degrees of agreement or disagreement in between. The instructor will read one value statement at a time from the list above, and students will move to the appropriate spot, depending on their degree of agreement or disagreement. Some time will be allowed for students, first, to discuss with those near them the reasons they are standing where they are; and, second, to state to those at the other end of the scale the reasons for their position.

b. Begin your paragraph by writing a sentence that expresses your attitude toward one of the value statements above—for example, "I feel that prostitution should be legalized."

c. Outline the reason or reasons you hold the opinion that you do. Your support may be based on your own experience, the experience of someone you know, or logic. For example, an outline of a paragraph based on one student's logic looked like this:

I feel that prostitution should be legalized for the following reasons:

1. *Prostitutes would then have to pay their fair share of income tax.*

2. *Government health centers would administer regular checkups. This would help prevent the spread of AIDS and venereal disease.*

3. *Prostitutes would be able to work openly and independently and would not be controlled by pimps and gangsters.*

4. *Most of all, prostitutes would be less looked down on—an attitude that is psychologically damaging to those who may already have emotional problems.*

d. Write a first draft of your paragraph, providing specific details to back up each point in your outline.

REVISING

Put your paragraph away for at least a day. Ask a friend whose judgment you trust to read and critique it. Your friend should consider each of these questions.

FOUR BASES Checklist: Argument

ABOUT *UNITY*

✔ Does the topic sentence clearly state the writer's opinion on a controversial subject?

ABOUT *SUPPORT*

✔ Does the paragraph include at least three separate and distinct reasons that support the author's argument?

✔ Is each of the three reasons backed up by specific, relevant evidence?

ABOUT *COHERENCE*

✔ Has the author saved the most powerful reason for last?

ABOUT *SENTENCE SKILLS*

✔ Has the author used a consistent point of view throughout the paragraph?

✔ Has the author used specific rather than general words?

✔ Has the author avoided wordiness?

✔ Has the author checked for spelling and other sentence skills, as listed on the inside back cover of the book?

Continue revising your work until you and your reader can answer "yes" to each of these questions.

WRITING ASSIGNMENT 3

Where do you think it is best to bring up children—in the country, the suburbs, or the city? Write a paragraph in which you argue that one of those three environments is best for families with young children. Your argument should cover two types of reasons: (1) the advantages of living in the environment you've chosen and (2) the disadvantages of living in the other places. Use the following, or something much like it, for your topic sentence:

> For families with young children, (*the country, a suburb,* or *the city*) _____ is the best place to live.

For each reason you advance, include at least one persuasive example. For instance, if you argue that the cultural life in the city is one important reason to live there, you should explain in detail how going to a science museum is interesting and helpful to children. After deciding on your points of support, arrange them in a brief outline, saving your strongest point for last. In your paragraph, introduce each of your reasons with an addition transition, such as *first of all, another, also,* and *finally*.

WRITING ASSIGNMENT 4

Currently, when high school students in America graduate, they have the option of continuing their education or working, in contrast to countries like Switzerland and Israel that require either military or civilian service for a minimum period of time. Some countries, like Austria, allow conscientious objectors to participate in a civilian corps instead of military service. In this assignment, you are to argue that all high school graduates must participate in AmeriCorps for a minimum of twelve months. Your argument will require you to visit the AmeriCorps Web site (http://www.americorps.gov) to learn about the three different programs and their projects and benefits. Use the following, or something similar, for your topic sentence:

> Upon graduating from high school, all American students should be required to participate in AmeriCorps for a minimum period of twelve months, after which they can enter college, enter the workforce, or re-enter AmeriCorps.

For each reason you advance, include at least one persuasive example. Support can be presented as narrative stories from your life, as contrasting examples, and/or as steps in a process. If you use facts to support your argument, and these facts come from the AmeriCorps Web site, you will need to credit your source in order to avoid plagiarism. After deciding on your points of support, arrange them in a brief outline, saving your strongest point for last. In your paragraph, introduce each of your reasons with an additional transition, such as *first of all, another, also,* and *finally*.

WRITING ASSIGNMENT 5

Writing for a Specific Purpose and Audience

In this argument paragraph, you will write with a specific purpose and for a specific audience. Imagine you have just returned from a trip to England. While you were there, you discovered that students are awarded for being in school by receiving discounted tickets on trains, in the theaters, and to museums. You have decided to write a letter to your local city council, urging them to encourage local businesses to start offering discounts to students. Be sure to address how this will benefit both students and business owners.

For instance, you might suggest that the local art museum offer a five-dollar admission price to students, which could increase student interest, possibly leading to future volunteer docents. If your city has a professional sports team, you could suggest that the team allow students to purchase same day tickets for ten dollars, increasing the future fan base, as well as ensuring larger crowds at games. Or you might suggest that local restaurants offer students a 15 percent discount on their bills within specific hours, thus encouraging business during typically slower times.

Because many businesses may not want to increase the number of students visiting their establishments, you will need to construct a strong objective argument that will demonstrate specifics ways in which the businesses could actually profit. In addition to the kinds of ideas included above, you might point out that student use of social media could lead to increased patronage—students will be more likely to publicly promote those businesses who recognize them as appreciated customers. In sum, a good argument will emphasize that offering these discounts is a win-win situation for both parties involved.

Essay Development

Write two to three paragraphs about what you plan to do after graduating from college.

Writing the Essay

This chapter will explain and illustrate

- the differences between a paragraph and an essay
- the structure of an essay

This chapter will also show how to

- plan an essay
- begin an essay
- tie an essay's supporting paragraphs together
- conclude an essay
- prepare for and take an essay exam

In addition, you will read and consider

- one model essay
- three student essays

HOW DO YOU COMMUNICATE BEST? Technology continues to change the way people communicate in their personal, college, and work lives. Write two or more paragraphs about a technology you use frequently that has changed the way you communicate with others.

What Is an Essay?

Differences Between an Essay and a Paragraph

An essay is simply a paper of several paragraphs, rather than one paragraph, that supports a single point. In an essay, subjects can and should be treated more fully than they would in a single-paragraph paper. Unlike paragraphs that are usually developed using one mode of writing, like description, essays are usually developed using several modes of writing to support the single point.

The main idea or point developed in an essay is called the *thesis statement* or *thesis sentence* (rather than, as in a paragraph, the *topic sentence*). The thesis statement appears in the introductory paragraph, and it is then developed in the supporting paragraphs that follow. A concluding paragraph closes the essay.

The nine different patterns of paragraph writing you learned in Part 2—*exemplification, narration, description, process, cause and/or effect, comparison and/or contrast, definition, division-classification*, and *argument*—can also be used to write essays. Because essays are much longer works than paragraphs, it is common that multiple patterns are incorporated to fully support the thesis statement. For example, a history student may need to employ exemplification, cause and/or effect, and argument in a class paper. Or a scientist preparing a report may need to utilize description, definition, and argument to defend his or her hypothesis. A real estate agent may employ description and narration to write about a house for sale. Everyday writing involves determining which patterns to use and how best to organize them to effectively support your purpose.

The Structure of an Essay

The diagram on page 327 shows the basic structure of an essay with three supporting paragraphs. You can refer to this as a guide while writing your own essays.

Most college essays will require more than three paragraphs of support; however, the process of developing an essay remains the same regardless of the number of supporting paragraphs.

A Model Essay

Gene, the writer of the paragraph on working in an apple plant (page 4), later decided to develop his subject more fully. Here is the essay that resulted.

My Job in an Apple Plant

[1]In the course of working my way through school, I have taken many jobs I would rather forget. [2]I have spent nine hours a day lifting heavy automobile and truck batteries off the end of an assembly belt. [3]I have

Introductory
paragraph

continued

risked the loss of eyes and fingers working a punch press in a textile factory. 4I have served as a ward aide in a mental hospital, helping care for brain-damaged men who would break into violent fits at unexpected moments. 5But none of these jobs was as dreadful as my job in an apple plant. 6The work was physically hard; the pay was poor; and, most of all, the working conditions were dismal.

First supporting paragraph

7First, the job made enormous demands on my strength and energy. 8For ten hours a night, I took cartons that rolled down a metal track and stacked them onto wooden skids in a tractor trailer. 9Each carton contained twelve heavy bottles of apple juice. 10A carton shot down the track about every fifteen seconds. 11I once figured out that I was lifting an average of twelve tons of apple juice every night. 12When a truck was almost filled, I or my partner had to drag fourteen bulky wooden skids into the empty trailer nearby and then set up added sections of the heavy metal track so that we could start routing cartons to the back of the empty van. 13While one of us did that, the other performed the stacking work of two men.

Second supporting paragraph

14I would not have minded the difficulty of the work so much if the pay had not been so poor. 15I was paid the minimum wage at that time, $4.50 an hour, plus just fifty cents extra for working the night shift. 16Because of the low salary, I felt compelled to get as much overtime pay as possible. 17Everything over eight hours a night was time-and-a-half, so I typically worked twelve hours a night. 18On Friday I would sometimes work straight through until Saturday at noon—eighteen hours. 19I averaged over sixty hours a week but did not take home much more than $220.

Third supporting paragraph

20But even more than the low pay, what upset me about my apple plant job was the working conditions. 21Our humorless supervisor cared only about his production record for each night and tried to keep the assembly line moving at breakneck pace. 22During work I was limited to two ten-minute breaks and an unpaid half hour for lunch. 23Most of my time was spent outside on the truck loading dock in near-zero-degree temperatures. 24The steel floors of the trucks were like ice; the quickly penetrating cold made my feet feel like stone. 25I had no shared interests with the man I loaded cartons with, and so I had to work without companionship on the job. 26And after the production line shut down and most people left, I had to spend two hours alone scrubbing clean the apple vats, which were coated with a sticky residue.

Concluding paragraph

27I stayed on the job for five months, all the while hating the difficulty of the work, the poor money, and the conditions under which I worked. 28By the time I quit, I was determined never to do such degrading work again.

Introductory Paragraph

> Introduction
> Thesis statement
> Plan of development:
> Points 1, 2, 3

The *introduction* attracts the reader's interest.

The *thesis statement* (or *thesis sentence*) states the main idea advanced in the essay.

The *plan of development* is a list of points that support the thesis. The points are presented in the order in which they will be developed in the essay.

First Supporting Paragraph

> Topic sentence (point 1)
> Specific evidence

The *topic sentence* advances the first supporting point for the thesis, and the *specific evidence* in the rest of the paragraph develops that first point.

Second Supporting Paragraph

> Topic sentence (point 2)
> Specific evidence

The *topic sentence* advances the second supporting point for the thesis, and the *specific evidence* in the rest of the paragraph develops that second point.

Third Supporting Paragraph

> Topic sentence (point 3)
> Specific evidence

The *topic sentence* advances the third supporting point for the thesis, and the *specific evidence* in the rest of the paragraph develops that third point.

Concluding Paragraph

> Summary, conclusion,
> or both

A *summary* is a brief restatement of the thesis and its main points. A *conclusion* is a final thought or two stemming from the subject of the essay.

Important Points about the Essay

Introductory Paragraph

An introductory paragraph has certain purposes or functions and can be constructed using various methods.

Purposes of the Introduction

An introductory paragraph should do three things:

1. Attract the reader's *interest*. Using one of the suggested methods of introduction described below can help draw the reader into your essay.

2. Present a *thesis sentence*—a clear, direct statement of the central idea that you will develop in your essay. The thesis statement, like a topic sentence, should have a key word or key words reflecting your attitude about the subject. For example, in the essay on the apple plant job, the key word is *dreadful*.

3. Indicate a *plan of development*—a preview of the major points that will support your thesis statement, listed in the order in which they will be presented. In some cases, the thesis statement and plan of development may appear in the same sentence. In some cases, also, the plan of development may be omitted.

ACTIVITY 1

1. In "My Job in an Apple Plant," which sentences are used to attract the reader's interest?

   _____ sentences 1 to 3 _____ 1 to 4 _____ 1 to 5

2. The thesis in "My Job in an Apple Plant" is presented in

   _____ sentence 4 _____ sentence 5 _____ sentence 6

3. Is the thesis followed by a plan of development?

   _____ Yes _____ No

4. Which words in the plan of development announce the three major supporting points in the essay? Write them below.

   a. _____

   b. _____

   c. _____

Common Methods of Introduction

Here are some common methods of introduction. Use any one method, or a combination of methods, to introduce your subject in an interesting way.

1. **Broad statement.** Begin with a broad, general statement of your topic and narrow it down to your thesis statement. Broad, general statements ease the reader into your thesis statement by providing a background for it. In "My Job in an Apple Plant," Gene writes generally on the topic of his worst jobs and then narrows down to a specific worst job.

2. **Contrast.** Start with an idea or situation that is the opposite of the one you will develop. This approach works because your readers will be surprised, and then intrigued, by the contrast between the opening idea and the thesis that follows it. Here is an example of a "contrast" introduction by a student writer:

> When I was a girl, I never argued with my parents about differences between their attitudes and mine. My father would deliver his judgment on an issue, and that was usually the end of the matter. Discussion seldom changed his mind, and disagreement was not tolerated. But the situation is different with today's parents and children. My husband and I have to contend with radical differences between what our children think about a given situation and what we think about it. We have had disagreements with all three of our daughters, Stephanie, Diana, and Giselle.

Personal

3. **Relevance.** Explain the importance of your topic. If you can convince your readers that the subject applies to them in some way, or is something they should know more about, they will want to continue reading. The introductory paragraph of "Sports-Crazy America" (page 334) provides an example of a "relevance" introduction.

4. **Incident or story.** Use an incident or brief story. Stories are naturally interesting. They appeal to a reader's curiosity. In your introduction, an anecdote will grab the reader's attention right away. The story should be brief and should be related to your central idea. The incident in the story can be something that happened to you, something that you may have heard about, or something that you have read about in a newspaper or magazine. Here is an example of a paragraph that begins with a story:

> The husky man pushes open the door of the bedroom and grins as he pulls out a .38 revolver. An elderly man wearing thin pajamas looks at him and whimpers. In a feeble effort at escape, the old man slides out of his bed and moves to the door of the room. The husky man, still

continued

grinning, blocks his way. With the face of a small, frightened animal, the old man looks up and whispers, "Oh, God, please don't hurt me." The grinning man then fires four times. The television movie cuts now to a soap commercial, but the little boy who has been watching the set has begun to cry. Such scenes of direct violence on television must surely be harmful to children for a number of psychological reasons.

5. **Quotation.** A quotation can be something you have read in a book or an article. It can also be something that you have heard: a popular saying or proverb ("Never give advice to a friend"); a current or recent advertising slogan ("Just do it"); a favorite expression used by your friends or family ("My father always says . . ."). Using a quotation in your introductory paragraph lets you add someone else's voice to your own. Here is an example of a paragraph that begins with a quotation:

"Evil," wrote the philosopher Martin Buber, "is lack of direction." In my school days as a fatherless boy, with a mother too confused by her own life to really care for me, I strayed down a number of dangerous paths. Before my eighteenth birthday, I had been a car thief, a burglar, and a drug dealer.

6. **Startling statement or statistic.** Some essays start with statements or statistics (numbers) that may shock readers and get them so interested that they want to read more. Read the following paragraph, which uses both statistics and a startling statement:

The Spanish influenza (flu) was a pandemic that, between 1918 and 1920, reached every corner of the earth, including the Arctic and the most remote Pacific islands. Unlike most other flus, this one attacked healthy young men and women primarily, not the very old or the very young. Scientists estimate that the disease killed between 50 million and 100 million people worldwide. Even more significantly, the Spanish influenza was caused by a strain of the H1N1 virus that threatens the world today.

Supporting Paragraphs

Many essays have three supporting points, detailed at length within three separate paragraphs. However, more developed essays require four or more body paragraphs to support the thesis. This is very common in essays with thesis statements that omit a plan of development. Each of the supporting paragraphs should begin with a *topic sentence* that states the point to be detailed in that paragraph. Just as a thesis provides a focus for the entire essay, the topic sentence provides a focus for a supporting paragraph.

ACTIVITY 2

1. What is the topic sentence for the first supporting paragraph of "My Job in an Apple Plant"? (*Write the sentence number here.*) _____

2. What is the topic sentence for the second supporting paragraph? _____

3. What is the topic sentence for the third supporting paragraph? _____

Transitional Sentences

In paragraphs, transitions and other connective devices (pages 92–101) are used to help link sentences. Similarly, in an essay *transitional sentences* are used to help tie the supporting paragraphs together. Such transitional sentences usually occur near the end of one paragraph or the beginning of the next.

In "My Job in an Apple Plant," the first transitional sentence is this:

> I would not have minded the difficulty of the work so much if the pay had not been so poor.

In this sentence, the key word *difficulty* reminds us of the point of the first supporting paragraph, while *pay* tells us the point to be developed in the second supporting paragraph.

Here is the other transitional sentence in "My Job in an Apple Plant":

ACTIVITY 3

> But even more than the low pay, what upset me about my apple plant job was the working conditions.

Complete the following statement: In the sentence above, the key words _____ echo the point of the second supporting paragraph, and the key words _____ announce the topic of the third supporting paragraph.

Concluding Paragraph

The concluding paragraph often summarizes the essay by briefly restating the thesis and, at times, the main supporting points. Also, the conclusion brings the paper to a natural and graceful end, sometimes leaving the reader with a final thought on the subject.

ACTIVITY 4

1. Which sentence in the concluding paragraph of "My Job in an Apple Plant" restates the thesis and supporting points of the essay? _____

2. Which sentence contains the concluding thought of the essay? _____

Evaluating Student Essays

Read the three student essays below and then answer the questions that follow.

Summer Read-a-thons

¹I remember when I was growing up that I spent many sunny afternoons in my backyard. ²I was fortunate to have a carefree happy mother who enjoyed reading and helped books come alive. ³We would spread out a blanket on the long green grass and have read-a-thons together. ⁴Reading became a doorway into a new and exciting world that I have often chosen to enter. ⁵I fell in love with reading in my yard, where my kind mother helped me find my imagination, learn about the world, and learn more about myself.

⁶At first my mother would bribe me with candy and popcorn, enticing me onto the reading blanket, but soon I would gladly assemble near her ready for the adventures to begin. ⁷She would ask me what book I wanted to hear for the day. ⁸Did I want to listen to a story of a little mouse that lived in a hotel and snuck around at night, flying through the hallways on his *real* toy-sized motorcycle? ⁹Or perhaps I would prefer finding myself in the middle of the Salem witch trials running for my life with Kit Tyler from *The Witch of Blackbird Pond?*

¹⁰My mom would help me think about new ideas through books. ¹¹We would read a story together and then discuss deep topics about what symbolism we found. ¹²One of my favorite discussions we had sparked from the book *Mrs. Frisby and the Rats of NIMH.* ¹³It's about Mrs. Frisby, a mother field mouse and her determination to protect her children, especially her young, ill son. ¹⁴She needs additional help from some neighbors who happen to be rats. ¹⁵The other animals have

continued

previously been afraid of the rats on this farm because they have strange ways and do strange things. [16]Mrs. Frisby learns not to judge only by appearance. [17]One young rat is especially notable as he gives his life for his fellow rats because it is the right thing to do. [18]He became a hero of mine. [19]As a young child I learned about service and sacrifice from this simple, yet beautifully told story of rats and mice. [20]I learned not to be as judgmental, and my imagination grew abundantly.

[21]As I grew older, I developed a love for novels, biographies, and historical fiction. [22]I especially enjoyed reading about World War II. [23]In the book *The Hiding Place*, by Corrie ten Boom, I felt as if I knew Corrie and her sister Betsie, and was alongside them as they helped hide Jews from the Gestapo. [24]They had tremendous courage and became symbols of bravery and tenacity. [25]I learned much from these young girls as I read about the Nazis taking all of their possessions and locking them into a concentration camp, and about how they suffered and endured so many indignities. [26]If I am ever feeling sorry for myself or that the world is out to get me, I think about Corrie ten Boom and her story, and I am humbled and grateful for my simple life.

[27]Like the previous books, Catherine Clinton's book also inspired me. [28]In *Harriet Tubman: The Road to Freedom*, a book about the Underground Railroad during the Civil War era, Harriet helps to free three hundred slaves and guides them north to safety. [29]I was in awe of the miracles that happened in her quest. [30]No one was captured; again and again she found families to hide fleeing slaves. [31]I found myself wishing I could meet her and talk with her about how she became so daring, so willing to sacrifice her own life for others. [32]An enjoyment of history developed from these books, and I couldn't get enough of them. [33]I wanted to immerse myself in them and learn about other leaders throughout history, what made them strong, what made them act! [34]Harriet Tubman's story inspired me to do more, to be less selfish, and to be more understanding of different cultures and different beliefs. [35]I learned that it is good to have a strong opinion, but I should listen to others, and be compassionate in my judgments.

[36]Now that I am older, I am thankful my mother loved to read, and that she had the insight to hold those summer read-a-thons to help me develop a deep love of reading that has stayed with me throughout my life. [37]I still think back to those summer days beside her in my yard, and the contentment I felt, hearing her laughter and gaining strength from her soft-spoken words. [38]I remember the encouragement she gave me, telling me that I could do anything I put my mind to, and that I was smart and capable. [39]I am grateful my mother brought reading to life, and I discovered a part of me that I hadn't realized was there to find.

Sports-Crazy America

1Almost all Americans are involved with sports in some way. 2They may play basketball or volleyball or go swimming or skiing. 3They may watch football or basketball games on the high school, college, or professional level. 4Sports may seem like an innocent pleasure, but it is important to look under the surface. 5In reality, sports have reached a point where they play too large a part in daily life. 6They take up too much media time, play too large a role in the raising of children, and give too much power and prestige to athletes.

7The overemphasis on sports can be seen most obviously in the vast media coverage of athletic events. 8It seems as if every bowl game play-off, tournament, trial, bout, race, meet, or match is shown on one television channel or another. 9On Saturday and Sunday, a check of *TV Guide* will show countless sports programs on network television alone, and countless more on cable stations. 10In addition, sports make up about 30 percent of local news at six and eleven o'clock, and network world news shows often devote several minutes to major American sports events. 11Radio offers a full roster of games and a wide assortment of sports talk shows. 12Furthermore, many daily newspapers such as *USA Today* are devoting more and more space to sports coverage, often in an attempt to improve circulation. 13The newspaper with the biggest sports section is the one people will buy.

14The way we raise and educate our children also illustrates our sports mania. 15As early as age six or seven, kids are placed in little leagues, often to play under screaming coaches and pressuring parents. 16Later, in high school, students who are singled out by the school and by the community are not those who are best academically but those who are best athletically. 17And college sometimes seems to be more about sports than about learning. 18The United States may be the only country in the world where people often think of their colleges as teams first and schools second. 19The names Ohio State, Notre Dame, and Southern Cal mean "sports" to the public.

Maria Sharapova
and her Aquaracer Diamonds.

WHAT ARE YOU MADE OF?

TAGHeuer
SWISS AVANT-GARDE SINCE 1860

Available at TAG Heuer-Westfield, London and selected fine jewellers nationwide. For further information please call 0800 037 9658, or visit www.tagheuer.com

WHY DOES AN ATHLETE'S ENDORSEMENT help sell a product? Would you be willing to pay extra for a product, knowing that it cost more because of endorsement fees? Make a list of your responses and ideas.

continued

20Our sports craziness is especially evident in the prestige given to athletes in the United States. 21For one thing, we reward them with enormous salaries. 22In 2006, for example, baseball players averaged over $2.8 million a year; the average annual salary in the United States was $44,389. 23Besides their huge salaries, athletes receive the awe, the admiration, and sometimes the votes of the public. 24Kids look up to someone like LeBron James or Tom Brady as a true hero; adults wear the jerseys and jackets of their favorite teams. 25Former players become senators and congressmen. 26And a famous athlete like Serena Williams needs to make only one commercial for advertisers to see the sales of a product boom.

27Americans are truly mad about sports. 28Perhaps we like to see the competitiveness we experience in our daily lives acted out on playing fields. 29Perhaps we need heroes who can achieve clear-cut victories in a short time, of only an hour or two. 30Whatever the reason, the sports scene in this country is more popular than ever.

An Interpretation of *Lord of the Flies*

1Modern history has shown us the evil that exists in human beings. 2Assassinations are common, governments use torture to discourage dissent, and six million Jews were exterminated during World War II. 3In *Lord of the Flies*, William Golding describes a group of schoolboys shipwrecked on an island with no authority figures to control their behavior. 4One of the boys soon yields to dark forces within himself, and his corruption symbolizes the evil in all of us. 5First, Jack Merridew kills a living creature; then, he rebels against the group leader; and finally, he seizes power and sets up his own murderous society.

6The first stage in Jack's downfall is his killing of a living creature. 7In Chapter 1, Jack aims at a pig but is unable to kill. 8His upraised arm pauses "because of the enormity of the knife descending and cutting into living flesh, because of the unbearable blood," and the pig escapes. 9Three chapters later, however, Jack leads some boys on a successful hunt. 10He returns triumphantly with a freshly killed pig and reports excitedly to the others, "I cut the pig's throat." 11Yet Jack twitches as he says this, and he wipes his bloody hands on his shorts as if eager to remove the stains. 12There is still some civilization left in him.

13After the initial act of killing the pig, Jack's refusal to cooperate with Ralph shows us that this civilized part is rapidly disappearing. 14With no adults around, Ralph has made some rules. 15One is that a signal fire must be kept burning. 16But Jack tempts the boys watching the fire

continued

to go hunting, and the fire goes out. ¹⁷Another rule is that at a meeting, only the person holding a special seashell has the right to speak. ¹⁸In Chapter 5, another boy is speaking when Jack rudely tells him to shut up. ¹⁹Ralph accuses Jack of breaking the rules. ²⁰Jack shouts: "Bollocks to the rules! We're strong—we hunt! If there's a beast, we'll hunt it down! We'll close in and beat and beat and beat—!" ²¹He gives a "wild whoop" and leaps off the platform, throwing the meeting into chaos. ²²Jack is now much more savage than civilized.

²³The most obvious proof of Jack's corruption comes in Chapter 8, when he establishes his own murderous society. ²⁴Insisting that Ralph is not a "proper chief" because he does not hunt, Jack asks for a new election. ²⁵After he again loses, Jack announces, "I'm going off by myself . . . . Anyone who wants to hunt when I do can come too." ²⁶Eventually, nearly all the boys join Jack's "tribe." ²⁷Following his example, they paint their faces like savages, sacrifice to "the beast," brutally murder two of their schoolmates, and nearly succeed in killing Ralph as well. ²⁸Jack has now become completely savage— and so have the others.

²⁹Through Jack Merridew, then, Golding shows how easily moral laws can be forgotten. ³⁰Freed from grown-ups and their rules, Jack learns to kill living things, defy authority, and lead a tribe of murdering savages. ³¹Jack's example is a frightening reminder of humanity's potential for evil. ³²The "beast" the boys try to hunt and kill is actually within every human being.

QUESTIONS

1. In which essay does the thesis statement appear in the last sentence of the introductory paragraph? _____

2. In the essay on *Lord of the Flies,* which sentence of the introductory paragraph contains the plan of development? _____

3. Which method of introduction is used in "Summer Read-a-thons"?
   a. Broad statement   c. Incident or story
   b. Relevance/importance of topic   d. Quotation

4. Write a brief outline of the points developed in "Summer Read-a-thons":

   a. _____

   b. _____

   c. _____

   d. _____

5. Which *two* essays use a transitional sentence between the first and second supporting paragraphs?

   _____

6. *Complete the following statement:* Emphatic order is shown in the last supporting paragraph of "Sports-Crazy America" with the words _____ _____ and in the last supporting paragraph of "An Interpretation of *Lord of the Flies*" with the words _____.

7. Which essay uses time order as well as emphatic order to organize its three supporting paragraphs? _____

8. List four major transitions used in the supporting paragraphs of "An Interpretation of *Lord of the Flies*."

   a. _____   c. _____

   b. _____   d. _____

9. Which essay includes a sentence in the concluding paragraph that summarizes three main supporting points? _____

10. Which essay includes two final thoughts in its concluding paragraph?

    _____

11. What three modes of writing does the author employ in "Summer Read-a-thons"?
    a. exemplification, narration, definition
    b. exemplification, narration, description
    c. narration, comparison and/or contrast, description
    d. argument, comparison and/or contrast, description

12. The primary mode of writing used in "An Interpretation of *Lord of the Flies*" is argument. What is a secondary mode?

    _____

    _____

Planning the Essay

Determining Audience and Purpose

When you are writing an essay, planning is crucial for success. Start by thinking about your purpose (what you want your essay to accomplish) and intended audience (the person or persons who will read the essay).

In Chapter 1, you learned that, often, an assignment clearly states or at least hints at what the essay is supposed to accomplish—its intended purpose. Key words such as *define, contrast, argue, illustrate,* or *explain causes and effects,* can reveal the assignment's purpose. The box on pages 347–348 explains such terms, and Chapters 8–16 discuss how to develop specific types of paragraphs for these purposes. So before you begin collecting information for your essay through prewriting, spend a few minutes thinking about the purpose your paper is intended to fulfill.

Now determine who your reader is. Sometimes this will simply be your instructor. At other times you may be writing for a wider and more diverse audience, such as the other students in your class, the student body of your college, or the employees of a company you work for.

To clearly define your audience, ask yourself these questions:

1. Why does this person want to read my essay? What does he or she want to gain or learn from it?

2. Does the reader need to make a decision based upon what I have written? Is the reader leaning one way or the other? Does the reader hold an opinion that is opposite to the one I am defending?

3. Is the reader simply seeking new information, or does he or she need to answer a specific question or to solve a specific problem?

4. Is the reader looking for a recommendation on a course of action. (For example, a movie reviewer makes recommendations aimed at people choosing a movie to see.)

5. How much does my reader know about my subject? Is he new to the subject, or does she know a lot about it already? Will I have to define basic terms, or can I use these terms without explaining what they mean? (For example, you might define the word *tweeting* to a senior citizen who does not own a computer. But would you have to explain this term to one of your peers?)

6. Am I writing to readers who have strong political, religious, or other beliefs? If you are stating an opposite opinion, you might have to be extra careful to word your ideas so as not to offend the audience.

Once you have answered these questions in your head, on a piece of paper, or on a computer, you will have a much clearer idea of your audience's background, needs, and purpose for reading. More important, you will be able to tailor your essay so that it contains ideas, information, and techniques that will appeal to your intended audience and, thus, improve your chances of writing an effective essay.

Outlining the Essay

Another important step in planning the essay is outlining. You can make a plan of your essay by outlining in two ways.

1. Prepare a scratch outline. This should consist of a short statement of the thesis followed by the main supporting points for the thesis. Here is Gene's scratch outline for his essay on the apple plant:

Working at an apple plant was my worst job.

1. Hard work

2. Poor pay

3. Bad working conditions

Do not underestimate the value of this initial outline—or the work involved in achieving it. Be prepared to do a good deal of plain hard thinking at this first and most important stage of your essay.

2. Prepare a more detailed outline. The outline form on page 340 will serve as a guide. Your instructor may ask you to submit a copy of this form either before you actually write an essay or along with your finished essay.

Practice in Writing the Essay

In this section, you will expand and strengthen your understanding of the essay as you work through the following activities.

Understanding the Two Parts of a Thesis Statement

In this chapter, you have learned that effective essays center on a thesis, or main point, that a writer wishes to express. This central idea is usually presented as a *thesis statement* in an essay's introductory paragraph.

Just like the topic sentence of a paragraph, a good thesis statement does two things. First, it tells readers an essay's *topic*. Second, it presents the *writer's attitude, opinion, idea,* or *point* about that topic. For example, look at the following thesis statement:

Celebrities are often poor role models.

In this thesis statement, the topic is *celebrities;* the writer's main point is celebrities are *often poor role models.*

Introduction

Body

Concluding
Paragraph

Form for Planning an Essay

Opening remarks:

Thesis statement _____

_____

Plan of development (if used)

Supporting Paragraph 1

Topic sentence _____

_____

Specific supporting details _____

_____

Supporting Paragraph 2

Topic sentence _____

_____

Specific supporting details _____

_____

Supporting Paragraph 3 (4, 5, . . .)

Topic sentence _____

_____

Specific supporting details _____

_____

Summary, Conclusion or both

Thesis restated _____

_____

Closing remarks _____

_____

For each thesis statement below, single-underline the topic and double-underline the main point that the writer wishes to express about the topic.

1. Several teachers have played important roles in my life.

2. A period of loneliness in life can actually have certain benefits.

3. Owning an old car has its own special rewards.

4. Learning to write takes work, patience, and a sense of humor.

5. Advertisers use several clever sales techniques to promote their message.

6. The police in large cities often have to do more than fight crime.

7. Working part time and going to college full time requires self-sacrifice, energy, and an ability to manage one's time.

8. My study habits in college benefited greatly from a course on note taking, textbook study, and test-taking skills.

9. The best teachers encourage their students, provide them with extra help, and present the material in a clear and interesting manner.

10. Parents should take certain steps to encourage their children to enjoy reading.

Supporting the Thesis with Specific Evidence

The first essential step in writing a successful essay is to form a clearly stated thesis. The second basic step is to support the thesis with specific reasons or details—just as you would support the topic sentence of a paragraph.

To ensure that your essay will have adequate support, you may find an informal outline very helpful. Write down a brief version of your thesis idea, and then work out and jot down the three or more points that will support your thesis.

Here is the scratch outline that was prepared for one essay:

The college cafeteria is poorly managed.

The checkout lines are always long.

The floor and tables are often dirty.

Food choices are often limited.

A scratch outline like the one above looks simple, but developing it often requires a good deal of careful thinking. The time spent on developing a logical outline is invaluable, though. Once you have planned the steps that logically support your thesis, you will be in an excellent position to go on to write an effective essay.

ACTIVITY 6

Following are five informal outlines in which two points (*a* and *b*) are already provided. Complete each outline by adding a third logical supporting point (*c*).

1. Poor grades in school can have various causes.
    a. Family problems
    b. Study problems

    c. _____

2. My landlord adds to the stress in my life.
    a. Keeps raising the rent
    b. Expects me to help maintain the apartment

    c. _____

3. My mother (*or some other adult*) has three qualities I admire.
    a. Sense of humor
    b. Patience

    c. _____

4. The first day in college was nerve-racking.
    a. Meeting new people
    b. Dealing with the bookstore

    c. _____

5. Staying healthy while carrying a full course load in college takes planning.
    a. Set aside at least seven hours a day for sleep
    b. Choose foods that are nutritious; avoid those loaded with sugar and fat

    c. _____

Identifying Introductions

The box lists six common methods for introducing an essay; each is discussed in this chapter.

1. Broad statement	4. Incident or story
2. Contrast	5. Quotation
3. Relevance	6. Startling statement or statistic

ACTIVITY 7

After reviewing the six methods of introduction on pages 328–330, refer to the box above and read the following seven introductory paragraphs. Then, in the space provided, write the number of the kind of introduction used in each paragraph. Each kind of introduction is used once.

PARAGRAPH A

_____

In a perfect school, students would treat each other with affection and respect. Differences would be tolerated, and even welcomed. Kids would become more popular by being kind and supportive. Students would go out of their way to make sure one another felt happy and comfortable. But most schools are not perfect. Instead of being places of respect and tolerance, they are places where the hateful act of bullying is widespread.

PARAGRAPH B

_____

Students have to deal with all kinds of problems in schools. There are the problems created by difficult classes, by too much homework, or by personality conflicts with teachers. There are problems with scheduling the classes they need and still getting some of the ones they want. There are problems with bad cafeteria food, grouchy principals, or overcrowded classrooms. But one of the most difficult problems of all has to do with a terrible situation that exists in most schools: bullying.

PARAGRAPH C

_____

Eric, a new boy at school, was shy and physically small. He quickly became a victim of bullies. Kids would wait after school, pull out his shirt, and punch and shove him around. He was called such names as "Mouse Boy" and "Jerk Boy." When he sat down during lunch hour, others would leave his table. In gym games he was never thrown the ball, as if he didn't exist. Then one day he came to school with a gun. When the police were called, he told them he just couldn't take it anymore. Bullying had hurt him badly, just as it hurts many other students. Every member of a school community should be aware of bullying and the three hateful forms that it takes: physical, verbal, and social bullying.

PARAGRAPH D

_____

A British prime minister once said, "Courage is fire, and bullying is smoke." If that is true, there is a lot of "smoke" present in most schools today. Bullying in schools is a huge problem that hurts both its victims and the people who practice it. Physical, verbal, and social bullying are all harmful in their own ways.

PARAGRAPH E

_____

A pair of students bring guns and homemade bombs to school, killing a number of their fellow students and teachers before taking their own lives. A young man hangs himself on Sunday evening rather than attend school the following morning. A junior high school girl is admitted to the emergency room after cutting her wrists. What do all these horrible reports have to do with each other? All were reportedly caused by a terrible practice that is common in schools: bullying.

PARAGRAPH F

_____

It is estimated that 23 percent of all students in American middle schools have experienced bullying. More than 20 percent have admitted to engaging in bullying themselves. Moreover, 8 percent complain of being bullied at least once each week. At times, victims of bullying become depressed, suffer from chronic health problems, and even contemplate suicide.

Revising an Essay for All Four Bases: Unity, Support, Coherence, and Sentence Skills

You know from your work on paragraphs that there are four "bases" a paper must cover to be effective. In the following activity, you will evaluate and revise an essay in terms of all four bases: *unity, support, coherence,* and *sentence skills.*

ACTIVITY 8

Comments follow each supporting paragraph and the concluding paragraph. Circle the letter of the *one* statement that applies in each case.

A Hateful Activity: Bullying

PARAGRAPH 1: INTRODUCTION

Eric, a new boy at school, was shy and physically small. He quickly became a victim of bullies. Kids would wait after school, pull out his shirt, and punch and shove him around. He was called such names as "Mouse Boy" and "Jerk Boy." When he sat down during lunch hour, others would leave his table. In gym games he was never thrown the ball, as if he didn't exist. Then one day he came to school with a gun. When the police were called, he told them he just couldn't take it anymore. Bullying had hurt him badly, just as it hurts many other students. Every member of a school community should be aware of bullying and the three hateful forms that it takes: physical, verbal, and social bullying.

PARAGRAPH 2: FIRST SUPPORTING PARAGRAPH

Bigger or meaner kids try to hurt kids who are smaller or unsure of themselves. They'll push kids into their lockers, knock books out of their hands, or shoulder them out of the cafeteria line. In gym class, a bully often likes to kick kids' legs out from under them while they are running. In the classroom, bullies might kick the back of the chair or step on the foot of the kids they want to intimidate. Bullies will corner a kid in a bathroom. There the victim will be slapped around, will have his or her clothes half pulled off, and might even be shoved into a trash can. Bullies will wait for kids after school and bump or wrestle them around, often while others are looking on. The goal is to frighten kids as much as possible and try to make them cry. Physical bullying is more common among boys, but it is not unknown for girls to be physical bullies as well. The victims are left bruised and hurting, but often in even more pain emotionally than bodily.

a. Paragraph 2 contains an irrelevant sentence.
b. Paragraph 2 lacks transition words.
c. Paragraph 2 lacks supporting details at one key spot.
d. Paragraph 2 contains a fragment and a run-on.

PARAGRAPH 3: SECOND SUPPORTING PARAGRAPH

Perhaps even worse than physical attack is verbal bullying, which uses words, rather than hands or fists, as weapons. We may be told that "sticks and stones may break my bones, but words can never harm me," but few of us are immune to the pain of a verbal attack. Like physical bullies, verbal bullies tend to single out certain targets. From that moment on, the victim is subject to a hail of insults and put-downs. These are usually delivered in public, so the victim's humiliation will be greatest: "Oh, no; here comes the nerd!" "Why don't you lose some weight, blubber boy?" "You smell as bad as you look!" "Weirdo." "Fairy." "Creep." "Dork." "Slut." "Loser." Verbal bullying is an equal-opportunity activity, with girls as likely to be verbal bullies as boys. If parents don't want their children to be bullies like this, they shouldn't be abusive themselves. Meanwhile, the victim retreats farther and farther into his or her shell, hoping to escape further notice.

a. Paragraph 3 contains an irrelevant sentence.
b. Paragraph 3 lacks transition words.
c. Paragraph 3 lacks supporting details at one key spot.
d. Paragraph 3 contains a fragment and a run-on.

PARAGRAPH 4: THIRD SUPPORTING PARAGRAPH

As bad as verbal bullying is, many would agree that the most painful type of bullying of all is social bullying. Many students have a strong need for the comfort of being part of a group. For social bullies, the pleasure of belonging to a group is increased by the sight of someone who is refused entry into that group. So, like wolves targeting the weakest sheep in a herd, the bullies lead the

continued

> pack in isolating people who they decide are different. Bullies do everything they can to make those people feel sad and lonely. In class and out of it, the bullies make it clear that the victims are ignored and unwanted. As the victims sink farther into isolation and depression, the social bullies—who seem to be female more often than male—feel all the more puffed up by their own popularity.

a.   Paragraph 4 contains an irrelevant sentence.
b.   Paragraph 4 lacks transition words.
c.   Paragraph 4 lacks supporting details at one key spot.
d.   Paragraph 4 contains a fragment and a run-on.

PARAGRAPH 5: CONCLUDING PARAGRAPH

> Whether bullying is physical, verbal, or social, it can leave deep and lasting scars. If parents, teachers, and other adults were more aware of the types of bullying, they might help by stepping in. Before the situation becomes too extreme. If students were more aware of the terrible pain that bullying causes, they might think twice about being bullies themselves, their awareness could make the world a kinder place.

a.   Paragraph 5 contains an irrelevant sentence.
b.   Paragraph 5 lacks transition words.
c.   Paragraph 5 lacks supporting details at one key spot.
d.   Paragraph 5 contains a fragment and a run-on.

Preparing for Essay Exams

In many classes, instructors administer examinations with questions to be answered in short but fully developed essays. Here are a few suggestions for taking such exams and completing such essays.

1.   Keep to a schedule. Reserve enough time to complete the essay, depending on how much the essay contributes to the overall test grade. For example, if the essay question is worth 50 points of the test's 100 points, plan to spend at least half the test period writing the essay.

2.   Make sure you understand the test question well. Read through it a few times if you have to. Then follow the directions carefully.

3.   Look for key words to determine exactly what the question is asking you to do. This is perhaps the most important part of the process. If the question asks you to *analyze* the long-term effects of the Civil War, you will need to do more than just say that the South lost and some of its major cities were greatly damaged. If you are asked to *compare* and *contrast* the economies of the South and North before the Civil War, you will have to do more than simply explain how they were different (contrast). If you are asked to explain what *causes* a tsunami, don't describe the devastation when the 2004 tsunami struck southern Asia.

Here is a list of key terms you might encounter on essay exams.

Term	Meaning	Example
Analyze	Divide into component parts or aspects, and then explain how each part relates to the whole.	*Analyze* the imagery in William Shakespeare's Sonnet 116.
Compare	Draw similarities between items.	*Compare* the composition of the ancient Roman senate to that of the modern United States senate.
Contrast	Explain differences between items.	How are the jobs of a local police officer and an FBI agent *different*?
Criticize	Give the positive and negative points of a subject as well as evidence for those positions.	*Criticize* the American government's handling of the IRS scandal of 2013.
Define	Give the formal meaning of a term.	*Define* "the American Dream" as it is used in *Death of a Salesman*.
Describe	Create a verbal picture. However, sometimes *describe* means "discuss" or even "narrate" in an essay exam.	*Describe* the symptoms seen in people who suffered from bubonic plague. *Describe* (discuss) the economic effects of recent income tax rate reductions.
Diagram	Make a drawing and label it.	*Diagram* the nervous system.
Discuss	Explain, analyze, and/or evaluate.	*Discuss* the advantages of regular aerobic exercise.
Enumerate	List items.	*Enumerate* the rights guaranteed in the Bill of Rights.
Evaluate	Weigh, assess, or appraise.	*Evaluate* the effectiveness of using electronic calculators to teach college algebra.
Explain	Depending on the rest of the question, list causes or effects or tell how something is done.	*Explain* the *effects* of America's entry into World War II on its economy. *Explain* the *process* that immigrants must go through to become citizens.

continued

Term	Meaning	Example
Illustrate	Provide examples.	*Illustrate* the following statement: "The computer is an invaluable academic tool."
Interpret	Analyze and explain the meaning or significance of something.	*Interpret* the significance of the religious imagery used in two of Hawthorne's short stories.
Justify	Give reasons for something.	*Justify* the Twenty-second Amendment.
List	Give a series of points and number them 1, 2, 3, and so on.	*List* and *explain* the major steps in the writing process.
Outline	Give the main points and important secondary points. Put main points at the margin and indent secondary points under the main points. Relationships may also be described with logical symbols, as follows: 1. _____ a. _____ b. _____ 2. _____	*Outline* the timeline of the Civil War.
Prove	Provide a logical argument supported by facts.	*Prove* the claim that the Greek gods displayed human qualities.
Relate	Show connections among things.	*Relate* America's belief of "manifest destiny" to the Mexican-American War.
State	Give the main points.	*State* the reasons that led to the automobile industry crisis and bailout of 2008–2010.
Summarize	Give a condensed account of the main points.	*Summarize* the role of FEMA in natural disasters.
Trace	Track the progress of something.	*Trace* the major events that ended apartheid in South Africa.

4. Jot down a rough outline of what you want to say in your essay.

5. Leave enough time to edit and proofread your essay for glaring errors before you submit your test paper to the instructor.

Essay Assignments

HINTS

Keep the points below in mind when writing an essay on any of the topics that follow.

1. Your first step is planning your essay. Determine your audience and your purpose. Prepare both a scratch outline and a more detailed outline.

2. While writing your essay, use the checklist below to make sure that your essay touches all four bases of effective writing.

3. Each essay will require support that incorporates different modes of writing. Relevant chapters are listed in each assignment. You will want to review those chapters as necessary.

4. Don't forget to give your essay a title.

FOUR BASES Checklist: Essays

BASE 1: *UNITY*

✔ Clearly stated thesis in the introductory paragraph of your essay

✔ All the supporting paragraphs on target in backing up your thesis

BASE 2: *SUPPORT*

✔ Three or more separate supporting points for your thesis

✔ *Specific* evidence for each of the supporting points

✔ *Plenty* of specific evidence for each supporting point

BASE 3: *COHERENCE*

✔ Clear method of organization

✔ Transitions and other connecting words

✔ Effective introduction and conclusion

BASE 4: *SENTENCE SKILLS*

✔ Clear, error-free sentences (use the checklist on the inside back cover of this book)

WRITING ASSIGNMENT 1

Defining Community

Write an essay that defines and illustrates what the word *community* means to you. To fully address this assignment, consider the following questions:

- When you think about the word *community,* what initially comes to mind?
- Where do you think your ideas about community originate?
- What roles do communities play in modern life?
- What does it mean to be a member of a community?
- What communities do you belong to?
- What does it mean to be part of these communities?
- Are there any communities you would like to belong to?
- What it is about these communities that interest you?

After you have answered the questions, think about which ideas you are most drawn to. From these ideas, create a strong thesis statement that you can fully support in your essay.

Depending on the type of support you choose to incorporate, you may need to review Chapter 12, "Definition"; Chapter 8, "Exemplification"; and Chapter 11, "Comparison and/or Contrast."

WRITING ASSIGNMENT 2

Recalling a Mistake

Write an essay about the biggest mistake you made within the past year. Describe the mistake and show how its effects have convinced you that it was the wrong thing to do. For instance, if you write about "taking a full-time job while going to school" as your biggest mistake, show the problems it caused. (You might discuss such matters as low grades, constant exhaustion, and poor performance at work.)

To get started, make a list of all the things you did last year that, with hindsight, now seem to be mistakes. Then select the action that has had the most serious consequences for you and that you can discuss in detail. Make a brief outline to guide you as you write, as in the example below.

Thesis: Buying a used car to commute to school was the worst mistake of last year.

1. *Unreliable—late for class or missed class*

2. *Expenses for insurance, repairs*

3. *Led to an accident*

Good support will include narration (Chapter 15), effects (Chapter 10), and argument (Chapter 16).

WRITING ASSIGNMENT 3

Analyzing Lives

Write an essay the claims that students' lives are much more difficult than professors' lives (or vice-versa). As preparation, you will need to speak with both professors and students and ask questions like:

Daily life: What does a typical day look like for you? What are your responsibilities? Do you have time each day just for yourself?

Academic life: How much time do you spend preparing for class? How much time do you spend in class? How much time do you spend grading (professors only)?

Social life: How much time do you spend participating in social activities?

Personal life: Do you work outside of your academic life? Do you have added responsibilities you haven't addressed?

Once you have gathered information, you will want to write an essay that asserts one group has a tougher life than the other. One way to organize your essay would be creating a paragraph for each of the categories; another way to organize it would be to write all the information that supports the thesis about one group and then follow with information about the other group. You will want to review Chapter 11, "Comparison and/or Contrast," and Chapter 16, "Argument," to help create a persuasive and effective essay.

WRITING ASSIGNMENT 4

Reflecting on Your Writing

Are you as good a writer as you want to be? Write an essay analyzing the reasons you have become a good writer or explaining why you are not as good as you'd like to be. Begin by considering some factors that may have influenced your writing ability.

Your family background: Did you see people writing at home? Did your parents respect and value the ability to write?

Your school experience: Did you have good writing teachers? Did you have a history of failure or success with writing? Was writing fun, or was it a chore? Did your school emphasize writing?

Social influences: How did your school friends do at writing? What were your friends' attitudes toward writing? What feelings about writing did you pick up from TV or the movies?

You might want to organize your essay by describing the three greatest influences on your skill (or your lack of skill) as a writer. Show how each of these has contributed to the present state of your writing. You will want to review Chapter 10, "Cause and/or Effect," and Chapter 16, "Argument," to help create a persuasive and effective essay.

WRITING ASSIGNMENT 5

Abolishing Unjust, Unnecessary Rules

Write an essay in which you discuss one or more rules, requirements, laws, policies or regulations that you think should be abolished because they are unjust or are unnecessary or for any other reason you believe is appropriate. Among the examples you might wish to discuss are the following:

- A code enforced by a club, sorority, or house of worship to which you belong
- A policy your employer wants you to follow
- A graduation requirement at your high school or college
- A law enforced by your state or community
- A rule or practice your family observes

If you want, pick unrelated rules or policies enforced by different organizations or people. In your thesis statement, however, explain why you oppose these laws or rules. For example, let's say that your employer wants you to wear conservative clothes to work even though you work in the stockroom; that your college wants you to complete a course covering computer programs that you've already mastered; and that the volunteer fire company you belong to requires your attendance at a Halloween dance. Your thesis might read as follows: "Certain rules and regulations, like those enforced by my employer, my college, and my fire company, are simply unnecessary." Note that such a thesis includes a plan of development. In other words, you will discuss your employer first, your college second, and your fire company last.

Another way you might want to focus your paper is to write an extended explanation of one rule. A thesis statement for this type of paper might read: "My family's requirement that everyone eat dinner together every Friday night is unfair and needs to be reconsidered for several reasons." Note that this thesis does not include a plan of development, but an effective essay would use emphatic order to create the most persuasive tone.

Regardless of which direction you choose for your essay, you will want to review Chapter 16, "Argument"; Chapter 8, "Exemplification"; Chapter 10, "Cause and/or Effect"; and, possibly, Chapter 13, "Division-Classification" to help you write a persuasive and effective essay.

WRITING ASSIGNMENT 6

Describing Your Characteristics

It has been said that the older we get, the more we see our parents in ourselves. Indeed, our temperament and many of our habits (good and bad) and beliefs can often be traced to one of our parents.

Write a paragraph in which you describe three characteristics you have "inherited" from a parent. You might want to think about your topic by asking yourself a series of questions: "How am I like my mother (or father)?"; "When and where am I like her (or him)?"; "Why am I like her (or him)?"

One student who wrote such a paper used the following thesis statement: "Although I hate to admit it, I know that in several ways I'm just like my mom." She then went on to describe how she works too hard, worries too much, and judges other people too harshly. Another student wrote, "I resemble my father in my love of TV sports, my habit of putting things off, and my reluctance to show my feelings."

Be sure to include examples and support for each of the characteristics you mention. For ideas about the types of support you will want to include, review Chapter 15, "Narration"; Chapter 14, "Description"; and Chapter 11, "Comparison and/or Contrast."

TELEVISION SHOWS, LIKE *GAME OF THRONES*, OFTEN become part of our culture, influencing language, social engagements, and even workplace conversations. Do you think this is a problem or just a way to relax? Write a thesis statement that expresses your view.

WRITING ASSIGNMENT 7

Reviewing a TV Show or Movie

Write an essay about a television show or movie you have seen very recently. The thesis of your essay will be that the show (or movie) has both good and bad features. (If you are writing about a TV series, be sure that you evaluate only one episode.)

Your essay should include a brief summary of the show or movie. Don't get bogged down in small details, but provide enough information so that a reader who hasn't seen the show or movie can understand your essay. You will also need to include evidence that supports the good and bad features of the show or movie. Such features might be:

- Fanciful or realistic plot
- Well-constructed or confusing plot
- Good and average/bad scenery and/or special effects
- Good and average/bad aspects of the acting
- Believable characters and/or those that are flat, cardboard-like
- Strong, clever ending or predictable ending

Remember to create a topic sentence for each paragraph and to include only information that supports your topic sentence. You will want to review Chapter 13, "Division-Classification"; Chapter 14, "Description"; and Chapter 16, "Argument"; to create a strong, convincing essay.

WRITING ASSIGNMENT 8

Describing Demands in Life

College demands a lot. You must attend classes, take notes, read textbooks, study for quizzes, write papers—the list goes on. In addition to school, you probably have other demands or expectations in your life. What are those demands? Write an essay that focuses on three demands or expectations that compete for your time. To help you get started, here is a list common to college students:

Job	Other family members
Housing	Financial debt
Children	Living expenses
Transportation	Hobbies, sports, activities
Spouse or significant other	Partying/socializing
Health conditions	Daily tasks (laundry, errands)

In your thesis statement, let your readers know what your three demands/expectations are and how they affect your life. Each of these demands should be developed in a separate paragraph. Each paragraph should have its own detailed examples. To create a strong essay, you will want to review Chapter 16, "Argument"; Chapter 13, "Division-Classification"; Chapter 10, "Cause and/or Effect"; and Chapter 8, "Exemplification."

WRITING ASSIGNMENT 9

Profiling Heroes

Many people would agree that three men who died in recent years were a credit to the human race. Neil Armstrong, the first person to walk on the moon, helped inspire generations of young children to study math, science, and engineering and

to quite literally reach for the stars. Charles Schultz was the creator of the world-famous comic strip *Peanuts,* whose characters dealt with anxieties we could all understand. Christopher Reeve played Superman in the movies but became one in real life by fighting a spinal-cord injury. Write an essay in which each of your supporting paragraphs explains in detail why each of these people can be regarded as a hero for humanity. You will need an introduction and thesis statement that encompasses all three men. Your conclusion will need to close the entire essay and restate your thesis. Chapter 16, "Argument"; Chapter 14, "Description"; and Chapter 10, "Cause and/or Effect," will help you create a convincing and effective essay.

WRITING ASSIGNMENT 10

Writing for a Specific Purpose and Audience

In this piece, you will write with a specific purpose and for a specific audience. Imagine that you are an outside consultant called in as a neutral observer to examine the high school you attended, which is now up for an accreditation review. After your visit, you must send the school board a well-written letter in which you describe the most striking features (good, bad, or both) of the school and evidence for each of these features.

In order to write the letter, you may want to think about the following features of your high school:

- Attitude of the teachers, student body, or administration
- Condition of the buildings and classrooms
- Curriculum
- How classes are conducted
- Extracurricular activities
- Crowded or uncrowded conditions

- Typical class size
- Availability of sports facilities and fields
- Number of Advanced Placement courses offered

Be sure to include an introduction, a clear thesis statement, clear topic sentences for each supporting paragraph, and a conclusion.

You will want to review Chapter 16, "Argument"; Chapter 14, "Description"; and Chapter 13, "Division-Classification"; to help you write a persuasive letter with a formal tone.

Handbook of Sentence Skills

Identify the misspelling in each sign. How does the error in the first sign completely change the sign's meaning? What are the effects of the misspelling in the second sign? How can you correct each?

Grammar

REPAIRS IN PROGRESS

STAIRWELL CLOSE
TO ALL TRAFFIC

To ensure your safety, these stairs
are undergoing extensive repairs

We apologize for the inconvenience.

To access Columbus please use the
stairwell at the east end (back toward
the lake) of the Sheraton Hotel.

WHY IS GRAMMAR IMPORTANT? Which one incorrect word completely alters the meaning that the sign is trying to convey? Which additional errors in punctuation do you see? How would you change this sign's wording to make it grammatically correct?

Subjects and Verbs

The basic building blocks of English sentences are subjects and verbs. Understanding them is an important first step toward mastering a number of sentence skills.

Every sentence has a subject and a verb. Who or what the sentence speaks about is called the subject; what the sentence says about the subject is called the verb.

The children laughed.

Several branches fell.

Most students passed the test.

That man is a hero.

A Simple Way to Find a Subject

To find a subject, ask *who* or *what* the sentence is about. As shown below, your answer is the subject.

Who is the first sentence about? Children

What is the second sentence about? Several branches

Who is the third sentence about? Most students

Who is the fourth sentence about? That man

A Simple Way to Find a Verb

To find a verb, ask what the sentence *says about* the subject. As shown below, your answer is the verb.

What does the first sentence *say about* the children? They laughed.

What does the second sentence *say about* the branches? They fell.

What does the third sentence *say about* the students? They passed.

What does the fourth sentence *say about* that man? He is (a hero).

A second way to find the verb is to put *I, you, we, he, she, it,* or *they* (whichever form is appropriate) in front of the word you think is a verb. If the result makes sense, you have a verb. For example, you could put *they* in front of *laughed* in the first sentence above, with the result, *they laughed,* making sense. Therefore you know that *laughed* is a verb. You could use *they* or *he,* for instance, to test the other verbs as well.

Finally, it helps to remember that most verbs show action. In the sentences already considered, the three action verbs are *laughed, fell,* and *passed.* Certain other verbs, known as *linking verbs,* do not show action. They do, however, give information about the subject. In "That man is a hero," the linking verb *is* tells us that the man is a hero. Other common linking verbs include *am, are, was, were, feel, appear, look, become,* and *seem.*

ACTIVITY 1   In each of the following sentences, draw one line under the subject and two lines under the verb.

1. Blood flows from the heart to the lungs via the pulmonary arteries.

2. The curious child stared silently at the shopping mall Santa.

3. The city-states of ancient Greece were ruled by various kinds of governments.

4. Cotton shirts feel softer than polyester ones.

5. The fog rolled into the cemetery.

6. Yoko invited her friends to dinner.

7. A green fly stung her on the ankle.

8. Every year, the Nile River flooded the land it bordered, depositing fertile soil on its banks.

9. The elderly man sat for a few minutes on the park bench.

10. With their fingers, the children drew pictures on the steamed window.

More about Subjects and Verbs

1. A pronoun (a word such as *he, she, it, we, you,* or *they* used in place of a noun) can serve as the subject of a sentence. For example:

    He seems like a lonely person.
    They both like to gamble.

    Without a surrounding context (so that we know who *He* or *They* refers to), such sentences may not seem clear, but they *are* complete.

2. A sentence may have more than one verb, more than one subject, or several subjects and verbs:

My heart skipped and pounded.

The money and credit cards were stolen from the wallet.

Dave and Ellen prepared the report together and presented it to the class.

3. The subject of a sentence never appears within a prepositional phrase. A *prepositional phrase* is simply a group of words that begins with a preposition. Following is a list of common prepositions.

Prepositions

about	before	by	inside	over
above	behind	during	into	through
across	below	except	of	to
among	beneath	for	off	toward
around	beside	from	on	under
at	between	in	onto	with

Cross out prepositional phrases when you are looking for the subject of a sentence.

Under my pillow I found a quarter left by the tooth fairy.

One of the yellow lights at the school crossing began flashing.

The comics pages of the newspaper have disappeared.

In spite of my efforts, Bob dropped out of school.

During a rainstorm, I sat in my car reading magazines.

4. Many verbs consist of more than one word. Here, for example, are some of the many forms of the verb *smile*.

Forms of *smile*

smile	smiled	should smile
smiles	were smiling	will be smiling
does smile	have smiled	can smile
is smiling	had smiled	could be smiling
are smiling	had been smiling	must have smiled

5. Words like *not, just, never, only,* and *always* are not part of the verb, although they may appear within the verb.

> Larry did not finish the paper before class.
> The road was just completed last week.

6. No verb preceded by *to* is ever the verb of a sentence.

> My car suddenly began to sputter on the freeway.
> I swerved to avoid a squirrel on the road.

7. No *-ing* word by itself is ever the verb of a sentence. (It may be part of the verb, but it must have a helping verb in front of it.)

> They leaving early for the game. (not a sentence, because the verb is not complete)
> They are leaving early for the game. (a sentence)

ACTIVITY 2

Draw a single line under the subjects and a double line under the verbs in the following sentences. Be sure to include all parts of the verb.

1. A large meteor heading for Earth raced across the galaxy.

2. Parts of my car were manufactured in Canada.

3. Vampires and werewolves are repelled by garlic.

4. Three people in the long bank line looked impatiently at their watches.

5. The pelting rain had pasted wet leaves all over the car.

6. She has decided to find a new apartment.

7. The trees in the mall were glittering with tiny white lights.

8. The puppies slipped and tumbled on the vinyl kitchen floor.

9. Spain and Portugal occupy the Iberian Peninsula and share a border.

10. We have not met our new neighbors in the apartment building.

REVIEW TEST

Draw a single line under the subjects and a double line under the verbs. Note that many sentences have multiple subjects and multiple verbs. Cross out prepositional phrases as necessary to find the subjects.

1. John Muir is known as the "Father of the National Park Service."

2. Muir was born in Scotland, but his family moved to the United States in 1849.

3. As a freshman at the University of Wisconsin, he studied chemistry, but he was soon introduced to botany.

4. In 1867, Muir embarked on a 1,000-mile journey from Indianapolis to Florida; he studied the flora and fauna, met people, and learned about America.

5. After his long walk, Muir sailed to San Francisco and immediately traveled to Yosemite.

6. His experience in Yosemite and Ralph Waldo Emerson's essays on nature inspired Muir, and he published articles about his experiences.

7. After Yosemite, Muir traveled to Utah, Alaska, and Mt. Rainier.

8. Muir convinced President Roosevelt that Yosemite, Mt. Rainier, and the Grand Canyon must be protected.

9. In 1890, 1,500 acres of Yosemite were established as preserved land.

10. This paved the way for the creation of more than 50 protected parks now within the United States National Parks System.

Sentence Sense

As a speaker of English, you already possess the most important of all sentence skills. You have *sentence sense*—an instinctive feel for where a sentence begins, where it ends, and how it can be developed. You learned sentence sense automatically and naturally, as part of learning the English language, and you have practiced it through all the years that you have been speaking English. It is as much a part of you as your ability to speak and understand English is a part of you.

How Does Sentence Sense Relate to You as a Writer?

Sentence sense can help you recognize and avoid fragments and run-ons, two of the most common and most serious sentence-skills mistakes in written English. Sentence sense will also help you to place commas, spot awkward and unclear phrasing, and add variety to your sentences.

You may ask, "If I already have this 'sentence sense,' why do I still make mistakes in punctuating sentences?" One answer could be that your past school experiences in writing were unrewarding or unpleasant. English courses may have been a series of dry writing topics and heavy doses of "correct" grammar and usage, or they may have given no attention at all to sentence skills. For any of these reasons, or perhaps for other reasons, the instinctive sentence skills you practice while *speaking* may turn off when you start *writing*. The very act of picking up a pen or sitting down to type may shut down your natural system of language abilities and skills.

Turning On Your Sentence Sense

Chances are that you don't *read a paper aloud* after you write it, and that you don't do the next best thing: read it "aloud" in your head. But reading aloud is essential to turn on the natural language system within you. By reading aloud, you will be able to hear the points where your sentences begin and end. In addition, you will be able to pick up any trouble spots where your thoughts are not communicated clearly and well.

The activities that follow will help you turn on and rediscover the enormous language power within you. You will be able to see how your built-in sentence sense can guide your writing just as it guides your speaking.

Each item that follows lacks basic punctuation. There is no period to mark the end of one sentence and no capital letter to mark the start of the next. Read each item aloud (or in your head) so that you "hear" where each sentence begins and ends. Your voice will tend to drop and pause at the point of each sentence break. Draw a light slash mark (/) at every point where you hear a break. Then go back and read the item a second time. If you are now sure of each place where a split occurs, insert a period and change the first small letter after it to a capital. Minor pauses are often marked in English by commas; these are already inserted. Part of item 1 is done for you as an example.

ACTIVITY 1

1. Americans devalue literacy. The closing of bookstores like Borders demonstrates this lack of value. However, if reading books were banned, the value of literacy would increase. During Prohibition, the government banned alcohol people didn't stop drinking. Instead, they went to great lengths to obtain a drink they didn't care if they broke the law to get one. Americans often desire what has been taken away. The American government should ban the reading of all books. By banning books, Americans will see the importance of reading and literacy.

2. Lola hates huge tractor trailers that sometimes tailgate her Honda Civic the enormous smoke-belching machines seem ready to swallow her small car she shakes her fist at the drivers, and she screams out many angry words recently she had a very satisfying dream she broke into an army supply depot and stole a bazooka she then became the first person in history to murder a truck.

3. The right to freedom of religion, press, and expression is guaranteed in an amendment to the United States Constitution it is fundamental to our country it lets Americans express themselves and their beliefs. This amendment sets America apart from so many other countries. Countries like Nigeria and North Korea don't allow their citizens to freely practice whatever religion they want similarly, these countries do not welcome free speech or free press to lose these freedoms would mean that a key part of America would be lost.

Any threat to the First Amendment should be fought with a vigor and passion that reflects our forefathers.

4. Cities across the nation are dealing with neighborhood blight. People are unable or unwilling to care for their houses and yards neighborhoods become run-down and unsafe. Crime goes up. Cities don't have the money or resources to fix these problems often, volunteer organizations go into these neighborhoods to help paint, mow, and do general clean-up however, what cities are overlooking is an untapped, inexpensive labor force. People who have been convicted of lesser crimes and sentenced to extended periods in city and county jails should be required to do community service as part of their sentence. Everyone wins with a program like this inmates gain a sense of pride cities save money neighborhoods are improved.

5. the Federalists, a faction that arose during the administration of President George Washington (1789–97), favored a strong central government it was led by Alexander Hamilton, Washington's secretary of the Treasury. Hamilton and his followers also believed in supporting the rights of landowners and business people they were opposed by the Democratic-Republican Party the Federalists were against the War of 1812 with Great Britain however, President James Madison, a member of the opposing party, was re-elected therefore, the war continued by 1824, the Federalists had lost much of their power, and soon the party went out of existence.

Summary: Using Sentence Sense

You probably did well in locating the end stops in these selections—proving to yourself that you *do* have sentence sense. This instinctive sense will help you deal with fragments and run-ons, perhaps the two most common sentence-skills mistakes.

Remember the importance of *reading your paper aloud.* By reading aloud, you turn on the natural language skills that come from all your experience of speaking English. The same sentence sense that helps you communicate effectively in speaking will help you communicate effectively in writing.

Fragments

This chapter will explain how to avoid the most common types of fragments. A fragment is a word group that lacks a subject or a verb and/or one that does not express a complete thought.

What Are Fragments?

Every sentence must have a subject and a verb and must express a complete thought. As explained above, a word group that lacks a subject or a verb and does not express a complete thought is a *fragment*. The most common types of fragments are

1. Dependent-word fragments
2. *-ing* and *to* fragments
3. Added-detail fragments
4. Missing-subject fragments

Once you understand what specific kinds of fragments you write, you should be able to eliminate them from your writing. The following pages explain all four types of fragments.

Dependent-Word Fragments

Some word groups that begin with a dependent word are fragments. Here is a list of common dependent words.

Dependent Words

after	if, even if	when, whenever
although, though	in order that	where, wherever
as	since	whether
because	that, so that	which, whichever
before	unless	while
even though	until	who, whoever
how	what, whatever	whose

Whenever you start a sentence with one of these words, you must be careful that a fragment does not result.

The word group beginning with the dependent word *After* in the example below is a fragment.

After I learned the price of new cars. I decided to keep my old pickup.

A *dependent statement*—one starting with a dependent word such as *After*—cannot stand alone. It depends on another statement to complete the thought. "After I learned the price of new cars" is a dependent statement. It leaves us hanging. We expect to find out—in the same sentence—*what happened after* the writer learned the price of new cars. When a writer does not follow through and complete a thought, a fragment results.

To correct the fragment, simply follow through and complete the thought:

After I learned the price of new cars, I decided to keep my old pickup.

Remember, then, that *dependent statements by themselves are fragments.* They must be attached to a statement that makes sense standing alone.

Here are two other examples of dependent-word fragments:

My daughter refused to stop eating sugar. Unless I stopped also.

He made an early appointment. Which he did not intend to keep.

"Unless I stopped also" is a fragment; it does not make sense standing by itself. We want to know—in the same statement—*what would not happen unless* the writer stopped also. The writer must complete the thought. Likewise, "Which he did not intend to keep" is not in itself a complete thought. We want to know in the same statement what *which* refers to.

Additional information about dependent words and phrases can be found on pages 123–125. In that discussion, dependent words are also referred to as subordinating words.

Correcting a Dependent-Word Fragment

In most cases you can correct a dependent-word fragment by attaching it to the sentence that comes after it or to the sentence that comes before it:

After I learned the price of new cars, I decided to keep my old pickup.
(*The fragment has been attached to the sentence that comes after it.*)

My daughter refused to stop eating sugar unless I stopped also.
(*The fragment has been attached to the sentence that comes before it.*)

He made an early appointment, which he did not intend to keep.
(*The fragment has been attached to the sentence that comes before it.*)

Another way of connecting a dependent-word fragment is simply to eliminate the dependent word by rewriting the sentence:

I learned the price of new cars and decided to keep my old pickup.

She wanted me to stop also.

He did not intend to keep it.

Do not use this method of correction too frequently, however, for it may cut down on interest and variety in your writing style.

TIPS

1. Use a comma if a dependent-word group comes at the beginning of a sentence (see also page 368):

    After I learned the price of new cars, I decided to keep my old pickup.

    However, do not generally use a comma if the dependent-word group comes at the end of a sentence:

    My daughter refused to stop eating sugar unless I stopped also.

    He made an early appointment, which he did not intend to keep.

2. Sometimes the dependent words *who, that, which,* or *where* appear not at the very start, but near the start, of a word group. A fragment often results:

    The town council decided to put more lights on South Street.
    A place where several people have been mugged.

    "A place where several people have been mugged" is not in itself a complete thought. We want to know in the same statement *where the place was* that several people were mugged. The fragment can be corrected by attaching it to the sentence that comes before it:

    The town council decided to put more lights on South Street, a place where several people have been mugged.

Turn each of the following dependent-word groups into a sentence by adding a complete thought. Put a comma after the dependent-word group if a dependent word starts the sentence.

ACTIVITY 1

EXAMPLES

Although I arrived in class late

Although I arrived in class late, I still did well on the test.

_____

The little boy who plays with our daughter

The little boy who plays with our daughter just came down with German measles.

_____

1. After we stopped for gas

    _____

    _____

2. If I want to live a healthier life

    _____

    _____

3. The car that we bought

    _____

    _____

4. When I made the Dean's List

    _____

    _____

5. Before my father got married

    _____

    _____

ACTIVITY 2

Working with a partner, underline the dependent-word fragment or fragments in each item. Then correct each fragment by attaching it to the sentence that comes before or the sentence that comes after it—whichever is more logical. Put a comma after the dependent-word group if it starts the sentence. Note: One item includes two different fragments.

1. Although the Devil's Tomato and Blue Nightshade are related to the tomato and potato. They are both highly toxic plants. They should not be eaten in a salad or baked.

    _____

    _____

    _____

2. The Adam and Eve orchid grows in Connecticut. It is hard to spot. Because its leaves have withered by the time it blooms.

    _____

    _____

    _____

3. Most people think about the fish-eating sea anemone. When the word "anemone" is mentioned. However, there are nineteen species of non-fish-eating anemone wildflowers found throughout the United States.

_____

_____

_____

4. Although it might seem strange to give someone a bouquet of Cat's Ear. This tiny yellow flower is actually an aster. It makes a beautiful bouquet. Because of its sunny color and daisy-like appearance.

_____

_____

_____

5. Since the Indian Pipe lacks chlorophyll and grows near fungi. Many people often mistake it for a mushroom instead of a flower. Its white color has given it the name Ghost Flower.

_____

_____

_____

6. Many homeowners spend time and energy trying to eliminate the dandelions in their yards. Even though harvesting the plants might be a better use of their time. The petals of the flowers add color and flavor to salads, the leaves can be eaten, and dandelion wine is a popular drink in many Midwestern states.

_____

_____

_____

_____

-ing and to Fragments

When an -ing word appears at or near the start of a word group, a fragment may result. Such fragments often lack a subject and part of the verb. Underline the word groups in the examples below that contain -ing words. Each is a fragment.

EXAMPLE 1

I spent almost two hours on the phone yesterday. Trying to find a garage to repair my car. Eventually I had to have it towed to a garage in another town.

EXAMPLE 2

Maggie was at first happy with the used SUV she bought from a neighbor. Not realizing until a week later that the vehicle averaged just nine miles per gallon of gas.

EXAMPLE 3

He looked forward to the study period at school. It being the only time he could sit unbothered and dream about his future. He imagined himself as a lawyer with lots of money and women to spend it on.

People sometimes write -*ing* fragments because they think the subject in one sentence will work for the next word group as well. Thus, in the first example, the writer thinks that the subject *I* in the opening sentence will also serve as the subject for "Trying to find a garage to repair my car." But the subject must actually be *in* the sentence.

Correcting -*ing* Fragments

1.   Attach the -*ing* fragment to the sentence that comes before it or the sentence that comes after it, whichever makes sense. Example 1 could read: "I spent almost two hours on the phone yesterday, trying to find a garage to repair my car."

2.   Add a subject and change the -*ing* verb part to the correct form of the verb. Example 2 could read: "She did not realize until a week later that the vehicle averaged just nine miles per gallon of gas."

3.   Change *being* to the correct form of the verb *be* (*am, are, is, was, were*). Example 3 could read: "It was the only time he could sit unbothered and dream about his future."

Correcting *to* Fragments

When *to* appears at or near the start of a word group, a fragment sometimes results:

> I plan on working overtime. To get this job finished. Otherwise, my boss may get angry at me.

The second word group is a fragment and can be corrected by adding it to the preceding sentence:

> I plan on working overtime to get this job finished.

Underline the *-ing* fragment in each of the items that follow. Then make it a sentence by rewriting it, using the method described in parentheses.

EXAMPLE

A thunderstorm was brewing. A sudden breeze shot through the windows. Driving the stuffiness out of the room. (Add the fragment to the preceding sentence.)

A sudden breeze shot through the windows, driving the stuffiness out of the room.

_____

(In the example, a comma is used to set off "driving the stuffiness out of the room," which is extra material placed at the end of the sentence.)

1. Establishing a research laboratory in Menlo Park, New Jersey (1876). Edison set the standard for modern industrial research. (Add the fragment to the sentence that comes after it.)

_____

_____

2. He works 10 hours a day. Then going to class for 2½ hours. It is no wonder he writes fragments. (Connect the fragment by adding the subject *he* and changing *going* to the proper form of the verb, *goes*.)

_____

_____

3. Charlotte loved the classic movie *Gone with the Wind,* but Clyde hated it. His chief objection being that it lasted four hours. (Correct the fragment by changing *being* to the proper verb form, *was*.)

_____

_____

ACTIVITY 3

Underline the *-ing* or *to* fragment or fragments in each item. Then rewrite each item, using one of the methods of correction described on page 372.

1. A mysterious package arrived on my porch yesterday. Bearing no return address. I half expected to find a bomb inside.

_____

_____

ACTIVITY 4

2. Jack bundled up and went outside on the bitterly cold day. To saw wood for his fireplace. He returned half frozen with only two logs.

    _____

    _____

3. Tariq read an entire novel on his seventeen-hour flight. Traveling to South Africa. He also wrote three letters.

    _____

    _____

4. Being an excellent math student. Nadia had no difficulty impressing her algebra professor.

    _____

    _____

5. Typing furiously. Luis attempted to finish his paper before class. However, he didn't leave time for proofreading. The result being a paper riddled with errors.

    _____

    _____

Added-Detail Fragments

Added-detail fragments lack a subject and a verb. They often begin with one of the following words.

also	except	including
especially	for example	such as

See if you can locate and underline the one added-detail fragment in each of the examples that follow:

EXAMPLE 1

I love to cook and eat Italian food. Especially spaghetti and lasagna. I make everything from scratch.

EXAMPLE 2

The class often starts late. For example, yesterday at a quarter after nine instead of at nine sharp. Today the class started at five after nine.

EXAMPLE 3

He failed a number of courses before he earned his degree. Among them, English I, Economics, and General Biology.

People often write added-detail fragments for much the same reason they write *-ing* fragments. They think the subject and verb in one sentence will serve for the next word group as well. But the subject and verb must be in *each* word group.

Correcting Added-Detail Fragments

1. Attach the fragment to the complete thought that precedes it. Example 1 could read: "I love to cook and eat Italian food, especially spaghetti and lasagna."

2. Add a subject and a verb to the fragment to make it a complete sentence. Example 2 could read: "The class often starts late. For example, yesterday it began at a quarter after nine instead of at nine sharp."

3. Change words as necessary to make the fragment part of the preceding sentence. Example 3 could read: "Among the courses he failed before he earned his degree were English I, Economics, and General Biology."

Underline the fragment in each of the items below. Then make it a sentence by rewriting it, using the method described in parentheses.

ACTIVITY 5

Personal

EXAMPLE

The brightly painted furniture movement has changed my mind about colors. <u>Like bright teal and yellow.</u> I am thinking about redecorating my dining room. (Add the fragment to the preceding sentence.)

The brightly painted furniture movement has changed my mind about colors like

bright teal and yellow.

1. Last week, I read a good article on how to repaint furniture to embrace bold colors. For example, the different types of paint strippers to buy. It also discussed different types of paint. (Correct the fragment by adding the subject and verb *explained*.)

_____

_____

2. I was very fascinated by the Annie Sloan chalk paint. It doesn't require much preparation. Such as stripping and sanding. According to the article, Annie Sloan paint is almost foolproof. (Add the fragment to the preceding sentence.)

_____

_____

3. I decided to give the paint a try and painted my dining room table Old White and my chairs English Yellow. With stenciled borders on the chairbacks in bright teal. (Correct the fragment by adding the subject and verb *embellished*.)

_____

_____

ACTIVITY 6

Underline the added-detail fragment in each item. Then rewrite that part of the item needed to correct the fragment. Use one of the three methods of correction described above.

1. It's always hard for me to get up for work. Especially on Monday after a holiday weekend. However, I always wake up early on free days.

_____

_____

2. Tony has enormous endurance. For example, the ability to run five miles in the morning and then play basketball all afternoon.

_____

_____

3. Montgomery is the capital of Alabama. As well as being a major furniture-manufacturing center.

_____

_____

4. I love visiting Arizona. Especially Sedona. However, I always bring a lot of sun protection.

_____

_____

5. One of my greatest joys in life is eating desserts. Such as cherry cheesecake and vanilla cream puffs. Almond fudge cake makes me want to dance.

_____

_____

Missing-Subject Fragments

In each example below, underline the word group in which the subject is missing.

EXAMPLE 1

The truck skidded on the rain-slick highway. But missed a telephone pole on the side of the road.

EXAMPLE 2

Michelle tried each of the appetizers on the table. And then found that, when the dinner arrived, her appetite was gone.

People write missing-subject fragments because they think the subject in one sentence will apply to the next word group as well. But the subject, as well as the verb, must be in *each* word group to make it a sentence.

Correcting Missing-Subject Fragments

1. Attach the fragment to the preceding sentence. Example 1 could read: "The truck skidded on the rain-slick highway but missed a telephone pole on the side of the road."

2. Add a subject (which can often be a pronoun standing for the subject in the preceding sentence). Example 2 could read: "She then found that, when the dinner arrived, her appetite was gone."

Work with a partner to underline the missing-subject fragment in each item. Together, rewrite that part of the item needed to correct the fragment. Use one of the two methods of correction described above.

ACTIVITY 7

1. I tried on an old suit hanging in our basement closet. And discovered, to my surprise, that it was too tight to button.

   _____

   _____

2. When Mary had a sore throat, friends told her to gargle with salt water. Or suck on an ice cube. The worst advice she got was to avoid swallowing.

   _____

   _____

3. Montana is bordered by North Dakota and South Dakota to the east. Also by Wyoming to the south. To the north of the state lies Canada.

   _____

   _____

TIPS

Check for Fragments

1. Read your paper aloud from the *last* sentence to the *first*. You will be better able to see and hear whether each word group you read is a complete thought.

2. If you think a word group is a fragment, ask yourself: Does this contain a subject and a verb and express a complete thought?

3. More specifically, be on the lookout for the most common fragments:

   • Dependent-word fragments (starting with words such as *after*, *because*, *since*, *when*, and *before*)

   • *-ing* and *to* fragments (*-ing* or *to* at or near the start of a word group)

   • Added-detail fragments (starting with words such as *for example*, *such as*, *also*, and *especially*)

   • Missing-subject fragments (a verb is present but not the subject)

REVIEW TEST 1

Underline the two fragments in each item. Then rewrite the item in the space provided, making the changes needed to correct the fragments.

EXAMPLE

The people at the sandwich shop save money. <u>By watering down the coffee.</u> <u>Also, using the cheapest grade of hamburger.</u> Few people go there anymore.

The people at the sandwich shop save money by watering down the coffee. Also, they use the cheapest grade of hamburger. . . .

1. Gathering speed with enormous force. The plane was suddenly in the air. Then it began to climb sharply. And several minutes later leveled off.

   _____

   _____

   _____

2. After visiting Montevideo, the capital of Uruguay. We flew to Buenos Aires, Argentina. And then to Santiago, Chile.

   _____

   _____

   _____

3. Running untouched into the end zone. The halfback raised his arms in triumph. Then he slammed the football to the ground. And did a little victory dance.

_____

_____

_____

4. The Greek scientist Archimedes (287–212 B.C.) invented many interesting devices. Such as huge mirrors that, reflecting the sun's rays, set the invading Roman ships on fire. However, his efforts at repelling the enemy were unsuccessful.

_____

_____

_____

5. While we waited in a line to see the Claude Monet paintings at the museum. A famous actor entered the building. And caused an enormous commotion.

_____

_____

_____

REVIEW TEST 2

Read the paragraph below and correct each fragment. You should find a total of seven fragments.

EXAMPLE

When students enter college, ͭ̑hey meet many new people.

Academic

    Although college students will meet different types of people. The two most prominent types will likely be happy people and pessimistic people. Happy people are the ones others want to be around. Because they treat everyone with kindness instead of harboring grudges. Happy people look at complications as positive challenges and embrace the excitement of working through difficulties. They don't make excuses or worry about small things. Able to truly listen to others. They form good friendships. Pessimists can be tiring to be around. Since their attitude is so bad.

continued

These people typically look at problems in a negative light. They often frown, grumble, or complain to everyone they meet. Although they aren't necessarily unkind. They don't welcome challenges, and they bemoan the hurdles instead. Worrying about themselves. Pessimistic people don't always make great friends. They are often so busy focusing on the bad things that they become lonely and miserable. After a few semesters in college. Most students will be able to quickly identify those who are happy and those who are not.

REVIEW TEST 3

1. _____
2. _____
3. _____
4. _____
5. _____
6. _____
7. _____
8. _____
9. _____
10. _____
11. _____
12. _____
13. _____
14. _____
15. _____
16. _____
17. _____
18. _____
19. _____
20. _____

Each word group in the student paragraph following is numbered. In the space provided, write C if a word group is a *complete sentence;* write F if it is a *fragment.* You will find seven fragments in the paragraph.

Personal

A Disastrous First Date

¹My first date with Donna was a disaster. ²I decided to take her to a small Italian restaurant. ³That my friends told me had reasonable prices. ⁴I looked over the menu and realized I could not pronounce the names of the dishes. ⁵Such as "veal piccata" and "fettucini alfredo." ⁶Then I noticed a burning smell. ⁷The candle on the table was starting to blacken. ⁸And scorch the back of my menu. ⁹Trying to be casual, I quickly poured half my glass of water onto the menu. ¹⁰When the waiter returned to our table. ¹¹He asked me if I wanted to order some wine. ¹²I ordered a bottle of Blue Nun. ¹³The only wine that I had heard of and could pronounce. ¹⁴The waiter brought the wine, poured a small amount into my glass, and waited. ¹⁵I said, "You don't have to stand there. We can pour the wine ourselves." ¹⁶After the waiter put down the wine bottle and left. ¹⁷Donna told me I was supposed to taste the wine. ¹⁸Feeling like a complete fool. ¹⁹I managed to get through the dinner. ²⁰However, for weeks afterward, I felt like jumping out of a tenth-story window.

On a separate piece of paper, correct the fragments you have found. Attach each fragment to the sentence that comes before or after it, or make whatever other change is needed to turn the fragment into a sentence.

Run-Ons

A run-on occurs when two sentences are run together with no adequate sign given to mark the break between them. This chapter will explore two types of run-ons and explain how to avoid them.

What Are Run-Ons?

As mentioned, a *run-on* occurs when two sentences are run together with no adequate sign given to mark the break between them.* Some run-ons have no punctuation at all to mark the break between the thoughts. Such run-ons are known as *fused sentences:* They are fused, or joined together, as if they were only one thought.

FUSED SENTENCES

My grades are very good this semester my social life rates only a C.

Our father was a madman in his youth he would do anything on a dare.

In other run-ons, known as *comma splices,* a comma is used to connect, or "splice" together, the two complete thoughts. However, a comma alone is *not enough* to connect two complete thoughts. Some connection stronger than a comma alone is needed.

COMMA SPLICES

My grades are very good this semester, my social life rates only a C.

Our father was a madman in his youth, he would do anything on a dare.

Comma splices are the most common kind of run-on. Students sense that some kind of connection is needed between two thoughts and so put a comma at the dividing point. But the comma alone is not sufficient: A stronger, clearer mark is needed

---

*Notes:

1. Some instructors regard all run-ons as fused sentences. But for many other instructors, and for our purposes in this book, the term *run-on* applies equally to fused sentences and comma splices. The bottom line is that you do not want either fused sentences or comma splices in your writing.

2. Some instructors refer to each complete thought in a run-on as an *independent clause.* A *clause* is simply a group of words having a subject and a verb. A clause may be *independent* (expressing a complete thought and able to stand alone) or *dependent* (not expressing a complete thought and not able to stand alone). A run-on is two independent clauses run together with no adequate sign given to mark the break between them.

3. Pages 121–125 in Chapter 5, "The Fourth Step in Writing," demonstrate how to take simple sentences and make them compound or complex sentences without creating run-ons.

between the two thoughts. Additional information about comma use, as well as additional practice, is provided in Chapter 34.

TIP

People often write run-ons when the second complete thought begins with one of the following words.

I	we	there	now
you	they	this	then
he, she, it		that	next

Remember to be on the alert for run-ons whenever you use one of those words in writing a paper.

Correcting Run-Ons

Here are four common methods of correcting a run-on:

1. Use a period and a capital letter to break the two complete thoughts into separate sentences.

   My grades are very good this semester. My social life rates only a C.
   Our father was a madman in his youth. He would do anything on a dare.

2. Use a comma plus a joining word (*and, but, for, or, nor, so, yet*) to connect the two complete thoughts.

   My grades are very good this semester, but my social life rates only a C.
   Our father was a madman in his youth, for he would do anything on a dare.

3. Use a semicolon to connect the two complete thoughts.

   My grades are very good this semester; my social life rates only a C.
   Our father was a madman in his youth; he would do anything on a dare.

4. Use subordination.

   Although my grades are very good this semester, my social life rates only a C.
   Because my father was a madman in his youth, he would do anything on a dare.

The following pages will give you practice in all four methods of correcting a run-on. The use of subordination is explained on page 389.

Method 1: Period and a Capital Letter

One way of correcting a run-on is to use a period and a capital letter at the break between the two complete thoughts. Use this method especially if the thoughts are not closely related or if another method would make the sentence too long.

Locate the split in each of the following run-ons. Each is a *fused sentence*—that is, each consists of two sentences that are fused, or joined together, with no punctuation between them. Reading each fused sentence aloud will help you "hear" where a major break or split in the thought occurs. At such a point, your voice will probably drop and pause.

Correct the run-on by putting a period at the end of the first thought and a capital letter at the start of the next thought.

ACTIVITY 1

Academic

EXAMPLE

Each year, music lovers around the United States look forward to the Grammy Awards. The award is given by the National Academy of Recording Arts and Sciences.

1. The first Grammy Awards ceremony was held on May 4, 1959 the artists were recognized for their contributions to the music industry during 1958.

2. There are several categories some of these categories are "Album of the Year" and "Song of the Year."

3. Henry Mancini was the winner of the first "Album of the Year" his album was titled *The Music from Peter Gunn.*

4. Two albums by Frank Sinatra competed against Mancini's unfortunately, neither *Come Fly With Me* nor *Only The Lonely* gained enough votes to win.

5. The first winner of "Song of the Year" was Domenico Modugno his song "Nel Blu Dipinto Blu (Volare)" can still be heard in many Italian restaurants across America.

6. In 2013, the "Album of the Year" award was given to Mumford & Sons they are an English folk rock band whose music has become popular with multiple generations.

7. That same year, the "Song of the Year" was given to "We Are Young" the song beat out "The A Team," "Adorn," and "Call Me Maybe."

8. Some of the newer Grammy categories are "Best Classical Compendium," "Best Latin Jazz Album," and "Best Urban Contemporary Album" these three categories brought the number of possible awards to eighty-one.

9. Most of the awards are presented prior to the show only about ten or eleven of the awards are given during the live show.

10. The Grammy Awards ceremony is always a star-filled night with incredible music performances millions of people tune in every year to see who the newest winners will be.

ACTIVITY 2

Working in pairs, locate the split in each of the following run-ons. Some of the run-ons are fused sentences, and some are *comma splices*—run-ons spliced, or joined together, with only a comma. Correct each run-on by putting a period at the end of the first thought and a capital letter at the start of the next thought.

1. A bird got into the house through the chimney we had to catch it before our cat did.

2. Some so-called health foods are not so healthy many are made with oils that raise cholesterol levels.

3. We sat only ten feet from the magician we still couldn't see where all the birds came from.

4. Jerome needs only five hours of sleep each night his wife needs at least seven.

5. Our image of dentistry will soon change dentists will use lasers instead of drills.

6. Gail got to school early to study for a math test when she got there, she found school had closed because of a water-main break.

7. There were several unusual hairstyles at the party one woman had bright green braids.

8. Todd saves all his magazines once a month, he takes them to a nearby nursing home.

9. The mountain ranges of Europe include the Pyrenees and the Alps the Himalayas are in Asia.

10. In the nineteenth century, showboats had stages on which actors and musicians performed they sailed up and down major rivers such as the Mississippi.

Method 2: Comma and a Joining Word

A second way of correcting a run-on is to use a comma plus a joining word to connect the two complete thoughts. Joining words (also called *conjunctions*) include *and, but, for, or, nor, so,* and *yet.* Here is what the four most common joining words mean:

> *and* in addition to, along with
>
> > His feet hurt from the long hike, and his stomach was growling.

(*And* means "in addition": His feet hurt from the long hike; *in addition,* his stomach was growling.)

but however, except, on the other hand, just the opposite

   I remembered to get the cocoa, but I forgot the marshmallows.

(*But* means "however": I remembered to get the cocoa; *however,* I forgot the marshmallows.)

for because, the reason that, the cause of something

   She was afraid of not doing well in the course, for she had always had bad luck with English before.

(*For* means "because" or "the reason that": She was afraid of not doing well in the course; *the reason* was that she had always had bad luck with English before.)

> **HINT** If you are not comfortable using *for,* use *because* instead in the activities that follow. If you do use *because,* omit the comma before it.

so as a result, therefore

   The windshield wiper was broken, so she was in trouble when the rain started.

(*So* means "as a result": The windshield wiper was broken; *as a result,* she was in trouble when the rain started.)

Insert the joining word (*and, but, for, so*) that logically connects the two thoughts in each sentence.

ACTIVITY 3

1. The Vikings were the first Europeans to land in the Americas, _____ Columbus is usually given credit for the discovery.

2. The Law of the Sea treaty agreed to in 1982 prohibits ocean pollution, _____ it also limits a nation's territorial waters to twelve miles.

3. Clyde asked his wife if she had any bandages, _____ he had just sliced his finger with a paring knife.

4. A group of teens talked and giggled loudly during the movie, _____ the ushers asked them to leave.

5. The restaurant was beautiful, _____ the food was overpriced.

ACTIVITY 4

Add a complete, closely related thought to go with each of the following statements. Use a comma plus the joining word at the left when you write the second thought.

EXAMPLE

for

Lola spent the day walking barefoot, *for the heel of one of her shoes had come off.*

but

1. She wanted to go to the party _____

and

2. Tony washed his car in the morning _____

so

3. The day was dark and rainy _____

for

4. We missed the bus this morning _____

but

5. I wish I could spend more time with my family _____

Method 3: Semicolon

A third method of correcting a run-on is to use a semicolon to mark the break between two thoughts. A *semicolon* (;) is made up of a period above a comma and is sometimes called a *strong comma*. The semicolon signals more of a pause than a comma alone but not quite the full pause of a period.

Semicolon Alone

Here are some earlier sentences that were connected with a comma plus a joining word. Notice that a semicolon alone, unlike a comma alone, can be used to connect the two complete thoughts in each sentence:

The Law of the Sea treaty agreed to in 1982 prohibits ocean pollution; it also limits a nation's territorial waters to twelve miles.

She was afraid of not doing well in the course; she had always had bad luck with English before.

The restaurant was beautiful; the food was overpriced.

The semicolon can add to sentence variety. For some people, however, the semicolon is a confusing mark of punctuation. Keep in mind that if you are not comfortable using it, you can and should use one of the first two methods of correcting a run-on.

Insert a semicolon where the break occurs between the two complete thoughts in each of the following run-ons.

ACTIVITY 5

EXAMPLE

I missed the bus by seconds;there would not be another for half an hour.

1. Some people have trouble with standardized tests the very idea of taking one makes them panic.

2. Pat retired at age forty she had won six million dollars in the state lottery.

3. The current was too strong Byron decided not to risk crossing the river.

4. Tony never goes to a certain gas station anymore he found out that the service manager overcharged him for a valve job.

5. The washer shook and banged with its unbalanced load then it began to walk across the floor.

Semicolon with a Transitional Word

A semicolon is sometimes used with a transitional word and a comma to join two complete thoughts.

We were short of money; therefore, we decided not to eat out that weekend.

The roots of a geranium have to be crowded into a small pot; otherwise, the plants may not flower.

I had a paper to write; however, my brain had stopped working for the night.

Following is a list of common transitional words (also known as *adverbial conjunctions*). Brief meanings are given for the words.

Transitional Word	Meaning
however	but
nevertheless	but
on the other hand	but
instead	as a substitute
meanwhile	in the intervening time
otherwise	under other conditions
indeed	in fact
in addition	and
also	and
moreover	and
futhermore	and
as a result	in consequence
thus	as a result
consequently	as a result
therefore	as a result

ACTIVITY 6

Choose a logical transitional word from the list in the box and write it in the space provided. Put a semicolon *before* the connector and a comma *after* it.

EXAMPLE

Exams are over _____*; however,*_____ I still feel tense and nervous.

1. I did not understand her point _____ I asked her to repeat it.

2. John wasn't willing to pay two hundred dollars for a fancy dinner _____ he had no problem investing this amount in stocks.

3. Post offices are closed for today's holiday _____ no mail will be delivered.

4. Mac and Alana didn't have a fancy wedding _____ they used their money for a nice honeymoon.

5. We're sure he didn't get the invitation _____ he would have come to the party.

Punctuate each sentence by using a semicolon and a comma.

EXAMPLE

My brother's asthma was worsening;as a result, he quit the soccer team.

1. We observed a blue heron standing by the side of the lake in addition we saw an ibis that had built a nest nearby.

2. Arnie tried to straighten his tie however he almost strangled himself.

3. Our instructor was absent therefore the test was postponed.

4. I had no time to shop for a gift instead I gave my friend a gift certificate to her favorite store.

5. Lola loves the velvety texture of cherry Jell-O moreover she loves to squish it between her teeth.

Method 4: Subordination

A fourth method of joining related thoughts is to use subordination. *Subordination* is a way of showing that one thought in a sentence is not as important as another thought.

Here are three earlier sentences that have been recast so that one idea is subordinated to (made less important than) the other idea:

When the window shade snapped up like a gunshot, her cat leaped four feet off the floor.

Because my father was a madman in his youth, he would do anything on a dare.

Although my grades are very good this year, my social life rates only a C.

Notice that when we subordinate, we use dependent words such as *when, because,* and *although.* Here is a brief list of common dependent words.

Common Dependent Words

after	before	unless
although	even though	until
as	if	when
because	since	while

ACTIVITY 8

Choose a logical dependent word from the box on page 389 and write it in the space provided. Then team up with a partner and compare your answers.

EXAMPLE

_____*Because*_____ I had so much to do, I never even turned on the TV last night.

1. _____ the roads became snow covered, we decided to stay home.

2. _____ "All Natural" was printed in large letters on the yogurt carton, the fine print listing the ingredients told a different story.

3. _____ Phil had eaten a second helping of lasagna, he had no room left for dessert.

4. _____ the vampire movie was over, my children were afraid to go to bed.

5. _____ you have a driver's license and two major credit cards, that store will not accept your check.

A Review: How to Check for Run-Ons

1. To see if a sentence is a run-on, read it aloud and listen for a break marking two complete thoughts. Your voice will probably drop and pause at the break.

2. To check an entire paper, read each sentence aloud from the *last* one to the *first*. Doing so will help you hear and see each complete thought.

3. Be on the lookout for words that can lead to run-on sentences:

I	he, she, it	they	this	next
you	we	there	that	then

4. Correct run-on sentences by using one of the following methods:
   - Period and capital letter
   - Comma and joining word (*and, but, for, or, nor, so, yet*)
   - Semicolon
   - Subordination

Some of the run-ons that follow are fused sentences, having no punctuation between the two complete thoughts; others are comma splices, having only a comma between the two complete thoughts. Correct the run-ons by using one of the following methods:

- Period and capital letter
- Comma and one of the following joining words: *for, and, nor, but, or, yet, so*
- Semicolon
- One of the following dependent words: *after, although, as, because, before, even though, since, until, when*

Do not use the same method of correction for every sentence.

EXAMPLE

Three people did the job, *but* I could have done it alone.

1. There are a number of suits and jackets on sale they all have very noticeable flaws.

2. Many computer systems come with printers, I had to pay extra for mine.

3. Marilyn took Professor Stewart's Introduction to Literature class, she had a greater appreciation for poetry.

4. The power went off for an hour during the night all the clocks in the house must be reset.

5. Gas-saving hybrid vehicles are now available, they make up only a fraction of the new-car market.

6. The course on the history of UFOs sounded interesting, it turned out to be very dull.

7. Everything on the menu of Angie's Pancake House sounded delicious they wanted to order the entire menu.

8. Denise has a photographic memory after reading a page of text, she can recite it word for word.

9. Marc used to be a fast-food junkie now he eats only fruits, vegetables, and nuts.

10. The college has been able to operate within its budget it won't need to raise tuition.

REVIEW TEST 2

There are two run-ons in each passage. Correct them by using the following methods:

- Period and capital letter
- Comma and one of these joining words: *and, but,* or *so*
- One of these dependent words: *although, because,* or *when*

1. The medical researcher was honored by her colleagues who could have dreamed that a cure for such a deadly disease could ever be found? Her research had taken years she was persistent. She never gave up.

   _____

   _____

   _____

2. Small feet were admired in ancient China, some female infants had their feet tightly bound. The feet then grew into a tiny, deformed shape. The women could barely walk their feet were crippled for life.

   _____

   _____

   _____

3. Kanye insisted on dressing himself for nursery school. It was a cold winter day, he put on shorts and a tank top. He also put on cowboy boots over his bare feet. He liked his image in the mirror his mother made him change.

   _____

   _____

   _____

4. A stimulating scent such as peppermint can help people concentrate better. The idea has practical applications, studies have shown that students do better on tests when peppermint is in the air. Maybe scented air could improve students' performance, it might help office workers be more alert, too.

   _____

   _____

   _____

REVIEW TEST 3

Locate and correct the five run-ons in the passage that follows. Do not use the same method of correction for every sentence.

Work

Employers are always looking for great employees who are conscientious, focused, and analytical. First, conscientious employees take pride in their work and want to do their best they make sure they contribute the best work possible and meet deadlines. If they run into a problem, they first try to solve it on their own if they cannot solve the problem, they seek the help necessary to complete the task. Second, focused employees don't waste time. They arrive punctually and use the time at work to do work they don't talk frivolously to their friends or family on the phone. They don't surf the Internet for amusing YouTube videos, they don't stand around idly chatting with coworkers. Finally, analytical employees see a problem and work to solve the issue they are striving to make things better. If they see a better way that something could be done, they try to implement it. Employees who have these three qualities will always be in demand.

22 Regular and Irregular Verbs

> Every verb has four principal parts: present, past, past participle, and present participle. These parts can be used to build all the verb *tenses* (the times shown by a verb).

A Brief Review of Regular Verbs

The past and past participle of a regular verb are formed by adding -*d* or -*ed* to the present. The *past participle* is the form of the verb used with the helping verbs *have, has,* or *had* (or some form of *be* with passive verbs). The *present participle* is formed by adding -*ing* to the present. Here are the principal forms of some regular verbs. Most verbs in English are regular.

Present	Past	Past Participle	Present Participle
crash	crashed	crashed	crashing
shiver	shivered	shivered	shivering
kiss	kissed	kissed	kissing
apologize	apologized	apologized	apologizing
tease	teased	teased	teasing

Irregular Verbs

Irregular verbs have irregular forms in the past tense and past participle. For example, the past tense of the irregular verb *know* is *knew,* and the past participle is *known.*

Almost everyone has some degree of trouble with irregular verbs. When you are unsure about the form of a verb, you can check the following list of irregular verbs. (The present participle is not shown on this list because it is formed simply by adding -*ing* to the base form of the verb.) Or you can check a dictionary, which gives the principal parts of irregular verbs.

A List of Irregular Verbs

Present	Past	Past Participle
arise	arose	arisen
awake	awoke *or* awaked	awoken *or* awaked
be (am, are, is)	was (were)	been
become	became	become
begin	began	begun
bend	bent	bent
bite	bit	bitten
blow	blew	blown
break	broke	broken
bring	brought	brought
build	built	built
burst	burst	burst
buy	bought	bought
catch	caught	caught
choose	chose	chosen
come	came	come
cost	cost	cost
cut	cut	cut
do (does)	did	done
draw	drew	drawn
drink	drank	drunk
drive	drove	driven
eat	ate	eaten
fall	fell	fallen
feed	fed	fed
feel	felt	felt
fight	fought	fought
find	found	found
fly	flew	flown
forget	forgot	forgotten

continued

Present	Past	Past Participle
freeze	froze	frozen
get	got	got *or* gotten
give	gave	given
go (goes)	went	gone
grow	grew	grown
have (has)	had	had
hear	heard	heard
hide	hid	hidden
hold	held	held
hurt	hurt	hurt
keep	kept	kept
know	knew	known
lay	laid	laid
lead	led	led
leave	left	left
lend	lent	lent
let	let	let
lie	lay	lain
lose	lost	lost
make	made	made
meet	met	met
pay	paid	paid
ride	rode	ridden
ring	rang	rung
rise	rose	risen
run	ran	run
say	said	said
see	saw	seen
sell	sold	sold
send	sent	sent
shake	shook	shaken

continued

Present	Past	Past Participle
shrink	shrank	shrunk
shut	shut	shut
sing	sang	sung
sit	sat	sat
sleep	slept	slept
speak	spoke	spoken
spend	spent	spent
stand	stood	stood
steal	stole	stolen
stick	stuck	stuck
sting	stung	stung
swear	swore	sworn
swim	swam	swum
take	took	taken
teach	taught	taught
tear	tore	torn
tell	told	told
think	thought	thought
throw	threw	thrown
wake	woke *or* waked	woken *or* waked
wear	wore	worn
win	won	won
write	wrote	written

Cross out the incorrect verb form in each of the following sentences. Then write the correct form of the verb in the space provided.

ACTIVITY 1

EXAMPLE

_____*caught*_____ I ~~catched~~ sixteen largemouth bass on my fishing trip.

_____ 1. The real estate agent selled my house in only two weeks.

_____ 2. In yoga this morning, I falled asleep during savasana.

_____ 3. She sweared that she hadn't borrowed my sweater, but I had a picture of her wearing it.

_____ 4. During the ceremony, we taked turns reading poems to the audience.

_____ 5. The professor had wrote the assignment on the board, but I had forgotten to write it in my calendar.

_____ 6. As the sun rised over the mountains, John knew it was going to be a hot day.

_____ 7. Taika had drove four hours before she thought to check her gas tank.

_____ 8. Tommy gived his favorite toy to the Oklahoma tornado relief charity.

_____ 9. By the time my son had awoke from his nap, I had finished

_____   cleaning the kitchen.

_____ 10. That dog in our neighborhood has bited three people!

ACTIVITY 2

For each of the italicized verbs, fill in the three missing forms in the following order:

(a) Present tense, which takes an -s ending when the subject is *he, she, it,* or any *one person* or *thing* (see pages 403–404)

(b) Past tense

(c) Past participle—the form that goes with the helping verb *have, has,* or *had*

After completing the activity, compare answers with a partner.

EXAMPLE

My uncle likes to *give* away certain things. He (a) _____*gives*_____ old,

threadbare clothes to the Salvation Army. Last year he (b) _____*gave*_____

me a worthless television set with a burned-out picture tube. He has

(c) _____*given*_____ away stuff that a junk dealer would reject.

1. It's fun to *freeze* Hershey bars. A Hershey bar (a) _____ in half an

   hour. Once I (b) _____ a bottle of Pepsi. I put it in the freezer to

   chill and then forgot about it. Later I opened the freezer and discovered that it

   had (c) _____ and exploded.

2. Natalie *speaks* French. She *(a)* _____ German, too. Her grand-mother *(b)* _____ both languages and taught them to her. Since she was a baby, Natalie has *(c)* _____ them both as well as she speaks English.

3. My cousin has always liked to *write*. He usually *(a)* _____ short stories. However, he just *(b)* _____ a book of poetry, which he is getting published. He has even *(c)* _____ a play.

4. I *go* to parties a lot. Often Camille *(a)* _____ with me. She *(b)* _____ with me just last week. I have *(c)* _____ to parties every Friday for the past month.

5. My brother likes to *throw* things. Sometimes he *(a)* _____ socks into his bureau drawer. In high school he *(b)* _____ footballs while quarterbacking the team. And he has *(c)* _____ Frisbees in our backyard for as long as I can remember.

6. I would like to *see* a UFO. I spend hours looking at the night sky, hoping to *(a)* _____ one. A neighbor of ours claims he *(b)* _____ one last month. But he says he has *(c)* _____ the Abominable Snowman, too.

7. I often *lie* down for a few minutes after a hard day's work. Sometimes my cat *(a)* _____ down near me. Yesterday was Saturday, so I *(b)* _____ in bed all morning. I probably would have *(c)* _____ in bed all afternoon, but I wanted to get some planting done in my vegetable garden.

8. To *teach* in college has been Claire's life-long dream. Currently, she *(a)* _____ English at the YWCA to newly arrived immigrants. Last year, she *(b)* _____ at a private high school, and before that she had *(c)* _____ at the local community college part time.

9. The government plans to *give* citizens more tax credits in order to encourage energy savings. It already *(a)* _____ a $3,000 credit to those who buy hybrid vehicles. Last year, it *(b)* _____ my uncle a tax credit for installing solar panels on his house, and it had *(c)* _____ him money the year before to help pay for the

cost of replacement windows.

10. Martha likes to *eat*. She *(a)* _____ as continuously as some
people smoke. Once she *(b)* _____ a large pack of cookies in half
an hour. Even if she has *(c)* _____ a heavy meal, she often starts
munching snacks right afterward.

REVIEW TEST 1

Underline the correct verb in the parentheses.

1. As I began my speech, my hands (shaked, shook) so badly I nearly dropped
my notes.

2. Oscar came into the gym and (began, begun) to practice on the parallel bars.

3. The food she donated (feed, fed) three families during the holidays.

4. Even though my father (teached, taught) me how to play baseball, I never enjoyed any part of the game.

5. When I (lent, lend) him the money yesterday, I knew he would pay me back.

6. The bank had (growed, grown) from a small savings and loan to a large re-
gional mortgage company.

7. Lola (brang, brought) a sweatshirt with her, for she knew the mountains got
cold at night.

8. The red maple that had (stood, standed) in the yard for one hundred years
was blown over by a strong wind.

9. The audience (burst, bursted) into laughter when the comedian told his favorite joke.

10. Anthony (sweared, swore) that he had locked the front door.

11. Someone (leaved, left) his or her books in the classroom.

12. Fran's muscle was (tore, torn) when she slipped on the wet pavement.

13. If I hadn't (threw, thrown) away the receipt, I could have gotten my money
back.

14. I would have (become, became) very angry if you had not intervened.

15. As the flowerpot (fell, falled) from the windowsill, the little boy yelled,
"Bombs away!"

REVIEW TEST 2

Cross out the incorrect verb form in each of the following sentences. Then write the correct verb form in the space provided.

_____ 1. She had wore her best dress for the party, but it still wasn't fancy enough.

_____ 2. He has builded four houses and remodeled three office buildings.

_____ 3. As Jane standed in the aisle at the grocery store and stared at the different types of bread, she couldn't choose which one to purchase.

_____ 4. The little boy falled off the monkey bars and broke his arm.

_____ 5. Even though my son is eight years old, he has never swam.

_____ 6. The children had growed much taller over the course of the summer, so their mother took them shopping for new clothes.

_____ 7. If I had knowed how much I would like Indian food, I would have started eating it much earlier in my life.

_____ 8. The minister has spoke to his community about helping the homeless.

_____ 9. Peter was afraid of horses, so it was quite a triumph when he finally rided one.

_____ 10. After the earthquake shaked the building, the people were relieved that no one was hurt.

_____ 11. He was asked to bring chips and salsa to the party, but he brang a vegetable platter instead.

_____ 12. Steven has flew to Budapest three times this year.

_____ 13. The young child was very tired so he lied down to take a nap.

_____ 14. Last night, before he went to bed, Tom feeded his pets.

_____ 15. On two occasions, Henry has saw his girlfriend skateboarding with her friends.

Standard English Verbs

Many people have grown up in communities where nonstandard verb forms are used in everyday life. Such forms include *I thinks, he talk, it done, we has, you was,* and *she don't.* Community dialects have richness and power but are a drawback in college and the world at large, where standard English verb forms must be used. Standard English helps ensure clear communication among English-speaking people everywhere, and it is especially important in the world of work.

This chapter compares community dialect and standard English forms of one regular verb and three common irregular verbs.

Regular Verbs: Dialect and Standard Forms

The chart below compares community dialect (nonstandard) and standard English forms of the regular verb *smile*.

Smile			
Community Dialect (Do not use in your writing)		**Standard English** (Use for clear communication)	
Present tense			
I smiles	we smiles	I smile	we smile
you smiles	you smiles	you smile	you smile
he, she, it smile	they smiles	he, she, it smiles	they smile
Past tense			
I smile	we smile	I smiled	we smiled
you smile	you smile	you smiled	you smiled
he, she, it smile	they smile	he, she, it smiled	they smiled

One of the most common nonstandard forms results from dropping the endings of regular verbs. For example, people might say "David never *smile* anymore" instead of "David never *smiles* anymore." Or they will say "Before he lost his job, David *smile* a lot" instead of "Before he lost his job, David *smiled* a lot." To avoid such nonstandard usage, memorize the forms shown above for the regular verb *smile*. Then use the activities that follow to help you develop a habit of including verb endings when you write.

Present-Tense Endings

The verb ending -*s* or -*es* is needed with a regular verb in the present tense when the subject is *he, she, it,* or any *one person* or *thing*. Consider the following examples of present-tense endings.

He	He yell*s*.
She	She throw*s* things.
It	It really anger*s* me.
One person	Their son storm*s* out of the house.
One person	Their frightened daughter crouch*es* behind the bed.
One thing	At night the house shake*s*.

All but one of the ten sentences that follow need *s* or *es* verb endings. Cross out the nonstandard verb forms, and write the standard forms in the spaces provided. Mark the one sentence that needs no change with a *C* for *correct*.

ACTIVITY 1

EXAMPLE

_____*wants*_____ Dana always ~~want~~ the teacher's attention.

_____ 1. Recently, I bought a computer that operate very fast.

_____ 2. Don't eat a fish that smell funny.

_____ 3. Claire plan to enter the contest.

_____ 4. Whole-wheat bread taste better to me than rye bread.

_____ 5. Bob work as a security guard at the mall.

_____ 6. The city seem to glow in the early morning sun.

_____ 7. Wanda makes me angry sometimes.

_____ 8. Troy run faster than anybody else on the track team.

_____ 9. She live in a rough section of town.

_____ 10. Martha like mystery novels better than romances.

ACTIVITY 2

Work with a partner to rewrite the short passage below, adding present-tense *-s* or *-es* verb endings wherever needed. Underline each ending as you add it. You should find a total of twelve endings to change.

> There are three main stages of a tick's life: larva, nymph, and adult. The larva is generally the size of a grain of salt. The larva itself hatch from an egg and then immediately look for a host. The search for a host can last as long as a year! As soon as it find a host, it attach itself and begin feeding on the host's blood. After a few days, it fall off, molt, and enter the nymph stage. This stage can take anywhere from one to three weeks. The nymph now has to find a new host. Once again, this search can take months. After it find a host, it repeat the feeding cycle, drop off, molts, and enters the adult stage. As an adult, it seeks a host, seeks a mate, and then die within two years.

_____

_____

_____

_____

_____

_____

_____

_____

Past-Tense Endings

The verb ending *-d* or *-ed* is needed with a regular verb in the past tense.

A midwife deliver*ed* my baby.

The visitor puzzl*ed* over the campus map.

The children watch*ed* cartoons all morning.

ACTIVITY 3

All but one of the ten sentences that follow need *-d* or *-ed* verb endings. Cross out the nonstandard verb forms, and write the standard forms in the spaces provided. Mark the one sentence that needs no change with a *C*.

EXAMPLE

_____*failed*_____ Yesterday I ~~fail~~ a chemistry quiz.

_____ 1. Lily want to go to the concert on Saturday.

_____ 2. The Vietnamese student struggle with the new language.

_____ 3. In the past, the requirement for a bachelor of arts degree include two years' study of a foreign language.

_____ 4. The tired mother turned on the TV for him.

_____ 5. Many newcomers to the community attend the recent town hall meeting.

_____ 6. The weather forecaster promise blue skies, but rain began early this morning.

_____ 7. Sam attempt to put out the candle flame with his finger.

_____ 8. However, he end up burning himself.

_____ 9. On the bus, Yolanda listen to music on her iPod.

_____ 10. As the photographer was about to take a picture of the smiling baby, a sudden noise frighten the child and made her cry.

Rewrite the following short passage, adding past-tense *-d* or *-ed* verb endings wherever needed. Underline each ending as you add it. You should find a total of twelve endings to change.

ACTIVITY 4

Personal

> I smoke for two years and during that time suffer no real side effects. Then my body attack me. I start to have trouble falling asleep, and I awaken early every morning. My stomach digest food very slowly, so that at lunchtime I seem to be still full with breakfast. My lips and mouth turn dry, and I swallow water constantly. Also, mucus fill my lungs and I cough a lot. I decide to stop smoking when my wife insist I take out more life insurance for our family.

_____

_____

_____

_____

_____

_____

_____

Three Common Irregular Verbs: Dialect and Standard Forms

The following charts compare community dialect and standard English forms of the common irregular verbs *be, have,* and *do.* (For more on irregular verbs, see pages 394–401.)

Be

Community Dialect (Do not use in your writing)		Standard English (Use for clear communication)	
Present tense			
I be (*or* is)	we be	I am	we are
you be	you be	you are	you are
he, she, it be	they be	he, she, it is	they are
Past tense			
I were	we was	I was	we were
you was	you was	you were	you were
he, she, it were	they was	he, she, it was	they were

Have

Community Dialect (Do not use in your writing)		Standard English (Use for clear communication)	
Present tense			
I has	we has	I have	we have
you has	you has	you have	you have
he, she, it have	they has	he, she, it has	they have
Past tense			
I has	we has	I had	we had
you has	you has	you had	you had
he, she, it have	they has	he, she, it had	they had

Do

Community Dialect (Do not use in your writing)		Standard English (Use for clear communication)	
Present tense			
I does	we does	I do	we do
you does	you does	you do	you do
he, she, it do	they does	he, she, it does	they do
Past tense			
I done	we done	I did	we did
you done	you done	you did	you did
he, she, it done	they done	he, she, it did	they did

TIP Many people have trouble with the negative form of *do*. They will say, for example, "He don't agree" instead of "He doesn't agree," or they will say "The door don't work" instead of "The door doesn't work." Be careful to avoid the common mistake of using *don't* instead of *doesn't*.

Underline the standard form of *be, have,* or *do*.

ACTIVITY 5

1. Crystal (have, has) such a nice singing voice that she often sings solos at our choir concerts.
2. The women at the factory (is, are) demanding to be paid the same wages as men.
3. The island of Corsica (has, have) belonged to France since the eighteenth century.
4. Rod and Arlene (was, were) ready to leave for the movies when the baby began to wail.
5. Our art class (done, did) the mural on the wall of the cafeteria.
6. If I (have, has) the time later, I will help you set up your new laser printer.
7. Jesse (be, is) the best basketball player at our school.
8. The Finnish government (has, have) installed stop signals in road pavements because pedestrians who are texting sometimes get hurt when they cross the street.
9. Vanessa wears the same perfume that Anya (do, does), but their clothing styles are very different.
10. The science instructor said that the state of California (be, is) likely to have a major earthquake any day.

ACTIVITY 6

Fill in each blank with the standard form of *be, have,* or *do.*

San Diego's Balboa Park _____ some beautiful features. One of
the most famous parts of the park _____ the San Diego Zoo. The zoo
_____ more than four thousand rare, exotic, and endangered animals.
Just a short walk from the zoo _____ the Natural History Museum. The
museum _____ numerous hands-on exhibits and _____ located on
El Prado, the central road in Balboa Park. The architecture surrounding El
Prado _____ Spanish; visitors to the area feel as if they _____ no
longer in modern California. At the far western edge of El Prado _____
the Old Globe Theater. The theater company _____ performances
ranging from Shakespeare to Monty Python. The park _____ also
home to multiple gardens including the Japanese Friendship Garden,
the Desert Garden, and the Zoro Garden. A trip to Balboa _____
not seem complete without a visit to The Prado Restaurant, voted one of
"America's Best Restaurants" by *Gourmet* magazine.

REVIEW TEST 1

Underline the standard verb form.

1. Jason (be, is) the luckiest guy I know; he has won the lottery four times.
2. Johanna (love, loves) to walk in the rain.
3. She (has, have) more than two thousand songs in her iTunes library.
4. We (was, were) supposed to go skiing last weekend, but the snow melted.
5. Jabril and Trevin (do, does) their homework in the college library.
6. John's dog (eats, eat) his food out of a large, crystal bowl.
7. Don (likes, like) to smile at everyone on campus.
8. We (had, has) a test in psychology last week.
9. Every morning, my cat hungrily (stare, stares) at the birds in our feeders.
10. No one (wants, want) to buy the house that is for sale in my neighborhood.
11. Gardeners often (has, have) dirty fingers even if they use gloves.
12. Since 1976, Manila (have been, has been) the capital of the independent
    Republic of the Philippines.

13. Both of the ships (was, were) built in Brooklyn, New York.

14. I (watched, watch) *American Idol* until Simon Cowell left the show.

15. My teacher (encourages, encourage) me to be a better person and do my best in everything.

REVIEW TEST 2

Cross out the two nonstandard verb forms in each sentence below. Then write the standard English verbs in the spaces provided.

EXAMPLE

_____ *is* _____   When our teacher ~~be~~ angry, his eyelid ~~begin~~ to twitch.

_____ *begins* _____

_____   1. My mother work for the local newspaper; she take classified ads over the phone.

_____

_____   2. Caesar conquer Gaul in 58 B.C.; he then invade Britain.

_____

_____   3. Peter and his sister owns a fast-food restaurant that offer gourmet takeout.

_____

_____   4. Henry love to go camping until two thieves in the campground remove his cooler, stove, and sleeping bag from his tent.

_____

_____   5. Last week the supermarket have a special on orange juice, just when I needs some.

_____

_____   6. Although my little girls knows they shouldn't tease the cat, they often dresses up the animal in doll clothes.

_____

_____   7. Whenever my brothers watches *Monday Night Football,* they screams at the TV as if they are actually at the game.

_____

_____   8. The large red fire engines gleams in the afternoon sun as they rushes through traffic on the busy boulevard.

_____

_____   9. I show the receipt to the manager to prove that the clerk had accidentally overcharge me.

_____

_____   10. As far as our son be concerned, oatmeal taste like soggy cardboard.

_____

Subject-Verb Agreement

A verb must agree with its subject in number. A *singular subject* (one person or one thing) takes a singular verb. A *plural subject* (more than one person or thing) takes a plural verb. Mistakes in subject-verb agreement are sometimes made in the situations listed below (each situation is explained on the following pages):

1. When words come between the subject and the verb
2. When a verb comes before the subject
3. With compound subjects
4. With indefinite pronouns

Words between Subject and Verb

Words that come between the subject and the verb do not change subject-verb agreement. In the sentence

The <u>tomatoes</u> in this salad <u>are</u> brown and mushy.

the subject (<u>tomatoes</u>) is plural, and so the verb (<u>are</u>) is plural. The words *in this salad* that come between the subject and the verb do not affect subject-verb agreement.

To help find the subject of certain sentences, you should cross out prepositional phrases (see page 361):

<u>Nell</u>, ~~with her three dogs close behind~~, <u>runs</u> around the park every day.

The <u>seams</u> ~~in my new coat~~ <u>have split</u> after only two wearings.

ACTIVITY 1

Underline the correct verb form in the parentheses.

1. The decisions of the judge (seem, seems) questionable.

2. The flakes in this cereal (taste, tastes) like sawdust.

3. The list of books for my American literature course (are, is) posted on the class Web site.

4. Many people in Europe (speak, speaks) several languages.

5. An ability to read a compass and a map (are, is) essential to surviving in the wild.

6. That silk flower by the candles (look, looks) real.

7. Opinions about the latest renovations to the Student Center (was, were) discussed at the meeting.

8. The rust spots on the back of Emily's car (need, needs) to be cleaned with a special polish.

9. The collection of medicine bottles in my parents' bathroom (overflow, overflows) the cabinet shelves.

10. A schedule of all the intramural tennis matches (appear, appears) on the coach's office door.

Verb before Subject

A verb agrees with its subject even when the verb comes *before* the subject. Words that may precede the subject include *there, here,* and, in questions, *who, which, what,* and *where.*

> On Glen's doorstep were two police officers.
> There are many pizza places in our town.
> Here is your receipt.
> Where are they going to sleep?

If you are unsure about the subject, look at the verb and ask *who* or *what.* With the first example above, you might ask, "*Who* were on the doorstep?" The answer, *police officers,* is the subject.

Working with a partner, write the correct form of the verb in each space provided.

ACTIVITY 2

is, are   1. What _____ the capital of Idaho?

was, were   2. Among the guests _____ a private detective.

do, does   3. Where _____ students like to congregate on campus?

is, are   4. There _____ many interesting things to see in Mexico.

rest, rests   5. In that grave _____ the bones of my great-grandfather.

was, were   6. There _____ so many important problems to be solved that we got to work immediately.

is, are	7. Why _____ the lights turned off?
stand, stands	8. Across the street _____ the post office.
is, are	9. Here _____ the tickets for tonight's game.
has, have	10. When _____ the people of this city ever not been able to trust the police?

Compound Subjects

Subjects joined by *and* generally take a plural verb.

Maple syrup and sweet butter taste delicious on pancakes.

Fear and ignorance have a lot to do with hatred.

When subjects are joined by *either . . . or, neither . . . nor, not only . . . but also,* the verb agrees with the subject closer to the verb.

Neither TV shows nor the Internet is as enjoyable to me as spending time with my friends.

The nearer subject, *Internet,* is singular, and so the verb is singular.

ACTIVITY 3   Write the correct form of the verb in the space provided.

stays, stay	1. Our cats and dog _____ at a neighbor's house when we go on vacation.
Is, Are	2. _____ the birthday cake and ice cream ready to be served?
holds, hold	3. Staples and Scotch tape _____ all our old photo albums together.
was, were	4. Tom and Pam _____ able to pay for their new car in cash.
support, supports	5. Neither the mayor nor the members of the city council _____ the new state mandate.
are, is	6. Tokyo and Beijing _____ capitals of Asian countries.
was, were	7. Owning a car and having money in my pocket _____ the chief ambitions of my adolescence.
visits, visit	8. My aunt and uncle from Ireland _____ us every other summer.
was, were	9. Before they saw a marriage therapist, Peter and Jenny _____ planning to get divorced.
favor, favors	10. Not only the dean but also the faculty members _____ adopting changes to the curriculum.

Indefinite Pronouns

The following words, known as *indefinite pronouns,* always take singular verbs.

(*-one* words)	(*-body* words)	(*-thing* words)	
one, no one	nobody	nothing	each
anyone	anybody	anything	either
everyone	everybody	everything	neither
someone	somebody	something	

 TIP   *Both* always takes a plural verb.

Write the correct form of the verb in the space provided.

ACTIVITY 4

is, are   1. Everybody at my new school _____ friendly.

has, have   2. Neither of them _____ made it to the wrestling finals.

knows, know   3. Nobody in my family _____ how to swim.

believe, believes   4. Each of three candidates _____ he or she won the debate.

tell, tells   5. Something _____ me that she will succeed.

pitches, pitch   6. If each of us _____ in, we can finish this job in an hour.

was, were   7. Everyone we invited _____ asked to bring a story to share.

provides, provide   8. Neither of the restaurants _____ facilities for the handicapped.

likes, like   9. No one in our family _____ housecleaning, but we all take a turn at it.

steals, steal   10. Someone in our neighborhood _____ vegetables from people's gardens.

REVIEW TEST 1

Underline the correct verb in parentheses.

1. Many people who are interested in the weather and weather patterns (like, likes) to study NOAA's Web site.

2. What do the letters "NOAA" (stand, stands) for?

3. The answer to that question (are, is) the "National Oceanic and Atmospheric Administration."

4. The scientists who work at NOAA (compile, compiles) weather data from all over the world.

5. Airlines like Delta (consult, consults) the data provided by NOAA to help pilots know what type of weather to expect.

6. Each spring (come, comes) sooner or later depending on the prediction of the famous groundhog, Punxsutawney Phil, on February 2, Groundhog Day.

7. American's obsession with the groundhog's prediction (fascinate, fascinates) me.

8. Of course, not everyone (believes, believe) Punxsutawney.

9. Meteorologists and their high-tech tools (is, are) much better predictors of the weather.

10. A student training to become a meteorologist (has, have) to take numerous math and science courses.

11. Terms like *diurnal*, *additive data*, and *indefinite ceiling* (is, are) part of a meteorologist's vocabulary.

12. Most meteorologists make a modest living, but some like Sam Champion on *Good Morning America* (earn, earns) more than a million dollars a year.

REVIEW TEST 2

Each of the following passages contains *two* mistakes in subject-verb agreement. Find these two mistakes and cross them out. Then write the correct form of each verb in the space provided.

1. *Rick Steves's Europe* is a very interesting and popular show on Public Broadcasting Station (PBS). Rick Steves himself host it. What are his secret? The answer is an emphasis on unique, independent travel.

   a. _____

   b. _____

2. Rick Steves's show emphasize traveling throughout the world. On each show, there are a special destination highlighted. Steves explains how to best experience that destination.

    a. _____

    b. _____

3. Just about everyone enjoy his show, "Florentine Delights and Tuscan Side Trips," in which he guides the audience through a trip to Lucca, a walled city in Tuscany. He and his crew also visits Pisa and celebrate its famous leaning tower.

    a. _____

    b. _____

4. Many of his shows features unique lodgings. For instance, in the Swiss Alps, he and his crew stays at the Gasthous Ascher. This is a hut that has been built on the side of the mountain.

    a. _____

    b. _____

5. There is more angles to Rick Steves's career than just his PBS show. Besides that show, he has a radio show on National Public Radio and a tour company. The tour company specialize in European vacations.

    a. _____

    b. _____

Pronoun Agreement and Reference

Pronouns are words that take the place of nouns (persons, places, or things). In fact, the word *pronoun* means "for a noun." Pronouns are shortcuts that keep you from unnecessarily repeating words in writing. Here are some examples of pronouns:

> Shirley has not finished the paper *she* was assigned. (*She* is a pronoun that replaces *Shirley*.)

> Tony swung so heavily on the tree branch that *it* snapped. (*It* replaces *branch*.)

> When the three little pigs saw the wolf, *they* pulled out cans of Mace. (*They* is a pronoun that takes the place of *pigs*.)

This chapter presents rules that will help you avoid two common mistakes people make with pronouns. The rules are as follows:

1. A pronoun must agree in number with the word or words it replaces.
2. A pronoun must refer clearly to the word it replaces.

Pronoun Agreement

A pronoun must agree in number with the word or words it replaces. If the word a pronoun refers to is singular, the pronoun must be singular; if that word is plural, the pronoun must be plural. (Note that the word a pronoun refers to is also known as the *antecedent*.)

Barbara agreed to lend me her Ray Charles CDs.

People walking the trail must watch their step because of snakes.

In the first example, the pronoun *her* refers to the singular word *Barbara*; in the second example, the pronoun *their* refers to the plural word *People*.

Write the appropriate pronoun (*their, they, them, it*) in the blank space in each of the following sentences.

ACTIVITY 1

EXAMPLE

I lifted the pot of hot potatoes carefully, but _____*it*_____ slipped out of my hand.

1. People should try to go into a new situation with _____ minds open, not with opinions already firmly formed.

2. Fred never misses his daily workout; he believes _____ keeps him healthy.

3. Citizens of New Orleans are proud of _____ city's heritage.

4. For some students, college is often their first experience with an unsupervised learning situation, and _____ are not always ready to accept the responsibility.

5. Our new neighbors moved in three months ago, but I have yet to meet _____

Indefinite Pronouns

The following words, known as *indefinite pronouns,* are always singular.

(*-one* words)	(*-body* words)	
one, no one	nobody	each
anyone	anybody	either
everyone	everybody	neither
someone	somebody	

If a pronoun in a sentence refers to one of those singular words, the pronoun should be singular.

Each father felt that (his) child should have won the contest.

One of the women could not find (her) purse.

Everyone must be in (his) seat before the instructor takes attendance.

In each example, the circled pronoun is singular because it refers to one of the special singular words.

The last example is correct if everyone in the class is a man. If everyone in the class is a woman, the pronoun would be *her.* If the class has both women and men, the pronoun form would be *his or her:*

Everyone must be in his or her seat before the instructor takes attendance.

Some writers follow the traditional practice of using *his* to refer to both women and men. Many now use *his or her* to avoid an implied sexual bias. To avoid using *his* or the somewhat awkward *his or her,* a sentence can often be rewritten in the plural:

Students must be in their seats before the instructor takes attendance.

ACTIVITY 2

Underline the correct pronoun. Check your answers against a partner's.

1. Some young man has blocked the parking lot exit with (his, their) sports car.

2. An elderly, stylishly dressed gentleman sporting a top hat and tails made (his, their) way into the fashionable restaurant.

3. Neither of the men arrested as terrorists would reveal (his, their) real name.

4. Anyone who joins the Women's Civic Club can add (her, their) voice to the discussions held at monthly meetings.

5. Each of the president's female advisors offered (her, their) opinion about the abortion bill.

Pronoun Reference

A sentence may be confusing and unclear if a pronoun appears to refer to more than one word, or if the pronoun does not refer to any specific word. Look at this sentence:

Joe almost dropped out of high school, for he felt *they* emphasized discipline too much.

Who emphasized discipline too much? There is no specific word that *they* refers to. Be clear:

Joe almost dropped out of high school, for he felt *the teachers* emphasized discipline too much.

Below are sentences with other kinds of faulty pronoun reference. Read the explanations of why they are faulty and look carefully at how they are corrected.

Faulty	Clear
June told Margie that *she* lacked self-confidence. (*Who* lacked self-confidence: June or Margie? Be clear.)	June told Margie, "You lack self-confidence." (Quotation marks, which can sometimes be used to correct an unclear reference, are explained on pages 468–475.)
Nancy's mother is a hairdresser, but Nancy is not interested in *it.*	Nancy's mother is a hairdresser, but Nancy is not interested in becoming one.

Faulty

(There is no specific word that *it* refers to. It would not make sense to say, "Nancy is not interested in hairdresser.")

Ron blamed the police officer for the ticket, *which* was foolish. (Does *which* mean that the ticket was foolish or that Ron's blaming the officer was foolish? Be clear.)

Clear

Foolishly, Ron blamed the police officer for the ticket.

Rewrite each of the following sentences to make the vague pronoun reference clear. Add, change, or omit words as necessary.

ACTIVITY 3

EXAMPLE

Our cat was friends with our hamster until he bit him.

Until the cat bit the hamster, the two were friends.

1. They found him not guilty, and she set him free immediately.

    _____

    _____

2. They claim that if the American colonists had lost the Revolutionary War, we would still be governed by Britain.

    _____

    _____

3. Telephone personnel provide assistance when they're not working correctly.

    _____

    _____

4. Jeanne told Maria she had been promoted.

    _____

    _____

5. I love Parmesan cheese on veal, but it does not always digest well.

    _____

    _____

REVIEW TEST 1

Cross out the pronoun error in each sentence, and write the correct word(s) on the line following the sentence. Then in the space provided, write whether the rule being followed is about pronoun agreement or about pronoun reference.

EXAMPLES

Pronoun Agreement   Many students begin college without any idea what ~~he or she~~ will study. ____they____

Pronoun Reference   The years pass quickly, and they will soon need to focus on a main interest. ____students____

_____   1. If a person wants to become a high school history teacher, they should major in secondary education. _____

_____   2. Astronomers are scientists who study the stars; they often are out very late at night. _____

_____   3. College students wanting to be cryptologists need to study math, and he or she will also need to be good at solving puzzles and creating and breaking codes. _____

_____   4. All students who want to enter law school and who expect college admissions personnel to consider their applications must take the LSAT before they will look at the application. _____

_____   5. Anybody who wants to be a firefighter will need to be in top physical condition to pass their physical examination. _____

_____   6. Not all food service workers need college degrees, but they can help with advancement. _____

_____   7. A student who wants to study the field of biomedical engineering should be prepared to spend his college years taking chemistry, biology, anatomy, and engineering classes. _____

_____   8. Zoologists work at zoos and aquariums with animals, and they often travel to natural habitats to learn more. _____

_____   9. Everyone who wants to become a doctor will have to pass their United States Medical Licensing Exam. _____

_____ 10. A student who wants to work outdoors could choose to be a fish and game warden, but they should be prepared to major in wildlife management. _____

REVIEW TEST 2

Underline the correct word in parentheses.

1. Philip is the kind of father who likes to keep in close contact with (his, their) children.

2. Hoping to be first in line when (they, the ushers) opened the doors, we arrived two hours early for the concert.

3. If a person really wants to appreciate good coffee, (he or she, they) should drink it black.

4. I have been interested in gardening ever since my grandmother kept (a garden, one) in her backyard.

5. Lois often visits the reading center in school, for she finds that (they, the tutors) give her helpful instruction.

6. Nobody in our house can express (his or her, their) opinion without starting an argument.

7. As the room got colder, everybody wished for (his or her, their) coat.

8. Each of my brothers has had (his, their) apartment broken into.

9. If someone is going to write a composition, (he or she, they) should prepare at least one rough draft.

10. My uncle gets into the movies for half price; (that discount, it) is one of the advantages of being a senior citizen.

11. I've been taking cold medicine, and now (it, the cold) is better.

12. Each one of the Boy Scouts was required to bring (his, their) sleeping bags.

13. An annual flu shot is a good idea; (it, they) will help children and older people stay healthy.

14. Indira had been following the legislators' views on immigration laws, and she could not believe how many times (they, the legislators' views) changed.

15. Both the front door and the back door of the abandoned house had fallen off (its, their) hinges.

Pronoun Types

This chapter describes some common types of pronouns: subject and object pronouns, possessive pronouns, and demonstrative pronouns.

Subject and Object Pronouns

Pronouns change their form depending on the purpose they serve in a sentence. In the box that follows is a list of subject and object pronouns.

Subject Pronouns	Object Pronouns
I	me
you	you (*no change*)
he	him
she	her
it	it (*no change*)
we	us
they	them

Subject Pronouns

Subject pronouns are subjects of verbs.

> *She* is wearing blue nail polish on her toes. (*She* is the subject of the verb *is wearing.*)
>
> *They* ran up three flights of stairs. (*They* is the subject of the verb *ran.*)
>
> *We* children should have some privacy too. (*We* is the subject of the verb *should have.*)

Rules for using subject pronouns, and several kinds of mistakes people sometimes make with subject pronouns, are explained in the pages that follow.

Rule 1

Use a subject pronoun in spots where you have a compound (more than one) subject.

Incorrect	Correct
Sally and *me* are exactly the same size.	Sally and *I* are exactly the same size.
Her and *me* share our wardrobes with each other.	*She* and *I* share our wardrobes with each other.

> **TIP**
>
> If you are not sure what pronoun to use, try each pronoun by itself in the sentence. The correct pronoun will be the one that sounds right. For example, "Her shares her wardrobe" does not sound right. "She shares her wardrobe" does.

Rule 2

Use a subject pronoun after forms of the verb *be*. Forms of *be* include *am, are, is, was, were, has been,* and *have been.*

It was *I* who called you a minute ago and then hung up.

It may be *they* entering the diner.

It was *he* who put the white tablecloth into the washing machine with a red sock.

The sentences above may sound strange and stilted to you because they are seldom used in conversation. When we speak with one another, forms such as "It was me," "It may be them," and "It is him" are widely accepted. In formal writing, however, the grammatically correct forms are still preferred.

> **TIP**
>
> To avoid having to use the subject pronoun form after *be*, you can simply reword a sentence. Here is how the preceding examples could be reworded:
>
> I was the one who called you a minute ago and then hung up.
>
> They may be the ones entering the diner.
>
> He put the white tablecloth into the washing machine with a red sock.

Rule 3

Use subject pronouns after *than* or *as*. The subject pronoun is used because a verb is understood after the pronoun.

Mark can hold his breath longer than *I* (can). (The verb *can* is understood after *I*.)

Her thirteen-year-old daughter is as tall as *she* (is). (The verb *is* is understood after *she*.)

You drive much better than *he* (drives). (The verb *drives* is understood after *he*.)

TIP   Avoid mistakes by mentally adding the "missing" verb at the end of the sentence.

Object Pronouns

Object pronouns (for example, *me, him, her, us, them*) are the objects of verbs or prepositions. (*Prepositions* are connecting words like *for, at, about, to, before, by, with,* and *of.* See also page 361.)

Lee pushed *me.* (*Me* is the object of the verb *pushed.*)

We dragged *them* all the way home. (*Them* is the object of the verb *dragged.*)

She wrote all about *us* in her diary. (*Us* is the object of the preposition *about.*)

Vera passed a note to *him* as she walked to the pencil sharpener. (*Him* is the object of the preposition *to.*)

People are sometimes uncertain about which pronoun to use when two objects follow the verb.

Incorrect	Correct
I argued with his sister and *he.*	I argued with his sister and *him.*
The cashier cheated Rick and *I.*	The cashier cheated Rick and *me.*

TIP   If you are not sure which pronoun to use, try each pronoun by itself in the sentence. The correct pronoun will be the one that sounds right. For example, "I argued with he" does not sound right; "I argued with him" does.

ACTIVITY 1   Underline the correct subject or object pronoun in each of the following sentences. Then show whether your answer is a subject or an object pronoun by circling S or O in the margin. The first one is done for you as an example.

Ⓢ O   1. Darcy and (she, her) kept dancing even after the band stopped playing.

S O   2. Both Sam and (I, me) submitted proposals for the project.

S O   3. Dawn is good at bowling, but her little sister is even better than (she, her).

S O   4. Their track team won because they practiced more than (we, us).

S O   5. (We, Us) choir members get to perform for the governor.

S O   6. The rest of (they, them) came to the wedding by train.

S O   7. (Her, She) and Albert have teamed up to study for the chemistry exam.

S O   8. Between you and (I, me), I don't believe in flying saucers.

S O   9. Tony and (he, him) look a lot alike, but they're not even related.

S O   10. Gordon asked Steve and (her, she) to join his study group.

Possessive Pronouns

Possessive pronouns show ownership or possession.

> Using a small branch, Stu wrote *his* initials in the wet cement.
>
> The furniture is *mine,* but the car is *hers.*

Here is a list of possessive pronouns:

my, mine	our, ours
your, yours	your, yours
his	their, theirs
her, hers	
its	

 TIP   A possessive pronoun *never* uses an apostrophe. (See also page 463.)

Incorrect	Correct
That earring is *her's.*	That earring is *hers.*
The orange cat is *theirs'.*	The orange cat is *theirs.*

Cross out the incorrect pronoun form in each of the sentences below. Write the correct form in the space at the left.

ACTIVITY 2

EXAMPLE

___*ours*___   The house with the maroon shutters ~~is ours'~~.

_____ 1. A porcupine has no quills on it's belly.

_____ 2. The desk chair we just bought is less comfortable than her's

_____ 3. You can easily tell which team is ours' by when we cheer.

_____ 4. It's banks swollen, the river nearly overflowed into the middle of town.

_____ 5. Grandma's silverware and dishes will be yours' when you get married.

Demonstrative Pronouns

Demonstrative pronouns point to or single out a person or thing. There are four demonstrative pronouns:

this	these
that	those

Generally speaking, *this* and *these* refer to things close at hand; *that* and *those* refer to things farther away. These four pronouns are commonly used in the role of demonstrative adjectives as well.

This milk has gone sour.

My wife insists on saving all *these* cooking magazines.

I almost tripped on *that* roller blade at the bottom of the steps.

Those plants in the corner don't get enough light.

> **TIP** Do not use *them, this here, that there, these here,* or *those there* to point out. Use only *this, that, these,* or *those.*

ACTIVITY 3

Cross out the incorrect form of the demonstrative pronoun and write the correct form in the space provided.

EXAMPLE

*Those*   ~~Those there~~ tires look worn.

_____ 1. This here child has a high fever.

_____ 2. Them birds on the lawn are crows.

_____ 3. These here mistakes in his paper need correcting.

_____ 4. That there umpire won't stand for any temper tantrums.

_____ 5. I am saving them old baby clothes for my daughter's dolls.

Read the paragraph and underline the correct word in the parentheses.

Three notable writers, Charlotte, Emily, and Anne Brontë, wrote and published in the 1800s before women authors were widely accepted. The sisters are well known in literary circles, but few know (their, them) personal history. (Theirs', Their) family moved to Haworth in 1820 when Reverend Patrick Brontë was appointed curate of Haworth. In 1821, Patrick's wife, Maria, died; (this, this here) meant that he had to care for his children (five girls and one boy). To help (he, him), Maria's sister, Elizabeth, moved in and took over the care of the children. In 1824, four of the girls were sent to the Clergy Daughters' School at Cowan Bridge. (That there, That) school was a very cruel and terrible place, and the two oldest girls died as a result of (it's, its) poor food and harsh conditions. Reverend Brontë decided that (he, him) and Elizabeth should educate the remaining four children—Charlotte, Emily, Anne, and Branwell—at home. During this time, the girls spent many hours developing (her, their) creativity. In 1842, Elizabeth died, leaving some money to the family. In 1846, the girls used part of the money to have their poems published. Because women writers weren't widely received, (they, them) titled the book *Poems by Currer, Ellis, and Acton Bell*. The book of poems sold only two copies. However, Charlotte's novel *Jane Eyre* was published in 1847 to great success. The Lowood School that Jane attends in the novel was modeled after the sisters' experience at the Clergy Daughters' School. Later that year, Emily and Anne published *Wuthering Heights* and *Agnes Grey*, respectively. All three books were originally written under (their, them) male pseudonyms. Anne published another novel the following year, *The Tenant of Wildfell Hall*. Although her true identity was soon to be known, she published that novel, too, under (hers', her) male pseudonym. Despite the women's success in the publishing world, 1848 was the beginning of a very sad time for the Brontë family. Between September 24, 1848 and May 28, 1849, Branwell, Emily, and Anne all died of tuberculosis. To cope with her sadness, Charlotte turned to her writing. In 1849, (she, her) published *Shirley*, and in 1853 *Villette*. She married Arthur Bell Nicholls in 1854, but didn't have the opportunity to enjoy (these, this) newly found happiness. She died in 1855 while expecting her first child. (These, These here) three writers of Victorian England had very short and difficult lives, but (them, they) left a unique and lasting literary legacy.

Adjectives and Adverbs

Adjectives and adverbs are descriptive words. Their purpose is to make the meaning of the words they describe more specific.

Adjectives

What Are Adjectives?

Adjectives describe nouns (the names of persons, places, or things) or pronouns.

> Ernie is a *rich* man. (The adjective *rich* describes the noun *man.*)
>
> He is also *generous.* (The adjective *generous* describes the pronoun *he.*)
>
> Our *gray* cat sleeps a lot. (The adjective *gray* describes the noun *cat.*)
>
> She is *old.* (The adjective *old* describes the pronoun *she.*)

Adjectives usually come before the word they describe (as in *rich man* and *gray cat*). But they come after forms of the verb *be* (*is, are, was, were,* and so on). They also follow verbs such as *look, appear, seem, become, sound, taste,* and *smell.*

> That speaker was *boring.* (The adjective *boring* describes the speaker.)
>
> The Petersons are *homeless.* (The adjective *homeless* describes the Petersons.)
>
> The soup looked *good.* (The adjective *good* describes the soup.)
>
> But it tasted *salty.* (The adjective *salty* describes the pronoun *it.*)

Using Adjectives to Compare

Adjectives are often used to compare things or people. Use the comparative form of the adjective if two things or people are being compared. Use the superlative form of the adjective if three or more people or things are being compared.

For nearly all one-syllable adjectives and some two-syllable adjectives, add *-er* when comparing two things and *-est* when comparing three or more things.

> My sister's handwriting is *neater* than mine, but Mother's is the *neatest.*
>
> Charles is *wealthier* than Thomas, but James is the *wealthiest* of the brothers.
>
> Note: The *y* in *wealthy* has been changed to an *i.*

For some two-syllable adjectives and all longer adjectives, add *more* when comparing two things and *most* when comparing three or more things.

In general, scorpion venom is *more poisonous* than bee venom, but the *most poisonous* venom comes from snakes.

Basketball is *more exciting* than baseball, but football is the *most exciting* sport of all.

You can usually tell when to use *more* and *most* by the sound of a word. For example, you can probably tell by its sound that "carefuller" would be too awkward to say and that *more careful* is thus correct.

There are many words for which both *-er* or *-est* and *more* or *most* are equally correct. For instance, either "a more fair rule" or "a fairer rule" is correct.

To form negative comparisons, use *less* and *least*.

When kids called me "Dum-dum," I tried to look *less* hurt than I felt.

Arthur spent *less* time on the project than anyone else, yet he won first prize.

Suzanne is the most self-centered, *least* thoughtful person I know.

Points to Remember about Comparing

Point 1

Use only one form of comparison at a time. In other words, do not use both an *-er* ending and *more* or both an *-est* ending and *most*.

Incorrect	Correct
My southern accent is always *more stronger* after I visit my family in Georgia.	My southern accent is always *stronger* after I visit my family in Georgia.
My *most luckiest* day was the day I met my wife.	My *luckiest* day was the day I met my wife.

Point 2

Learn the irregular forms of the following words.

	Comparative (for Comparing Two Things)	Superlative (for Comparing Three or More Things)
bad	worse	worst
good, well	better	best
little (in amount)	less	least
much, many	more	most

Do not use both *more* and an irregular comparative or *most* and an irregular superlative.

Incorrect	Correct
It is *more better* to stay healthy than to have to get healthy.	It is *better* to stay healthy than to have to get healthy.
Yesterday I went on the *most best* date of my life—and all we did was go on a picnic.	Yesterday I went on the *best* date of my life—and all we did was go on a picnic.

ACTIVITY 1   Add to each sentence the correct form of the word in the margin.

EXAMPLES

bad   The _____*worst*_____ meal I have ever had was at Bert's Bacteria Bonanza and Barbecue.

wonderful   The day I sold my boat was even *more wonderful* than the day I bought it.

good   1. The Grammy awards are given to the _____ recording artists of each year.

intelligent   2. Sandra is even _____ than her sister, who holds a doctorate in physics.

angry   3. Among all of the protesters, he seemed to be the _____.

light   4. A pound of feathers is no _____ than a pound of stones.

little   5. The _____ expensive way to accumulate a wardrobe is to buy used clothing whenever possible.

Adverbs

What Are Adverbs?

Adverbs describe verbs, adjectives, or other adverbs. They usually end in *-ly*.

The referee *suddenly* stopped the fight. (The adverb *suddenly* describes the verb *stopped*.)

Her yellow rosebushes are *absolutely* beautiful. (The adverb *absolutely* describes the adjective *beautiful*.)

The auctioneer spoke so *terribly* fast that I couldn't understand him. (The adverb *terribly* describes the adverb *fast*.)

A Common Mistake with Adverbs and Adjectives

People often mistakenly use an adjective instead of an adverb after a verb.

Incorrect	Correct
I jog *slow*.	I jog *slowly*.
The nervous witness spoke *quiet*.	The nervous witness spoke *quietly*.
The first night I quit smoking, I wanted a cigarette *bad*.	The first night I quit smoking, I wanted a cigarette *badly*.

Underline the adjective or adverb needed.

ACTIVITY 2

> **HINT** Remember: Adjectives describe nouns or pronouns. Adverbs describe verbs, adjectives, or other adverbs.

1. During a quiet moment in class, my stomach rumbled (loud, loudly).

2. I'm a (slow, slowly) reader, so I have to put aside more time to study than some of my friends.

3. Thinking no one was looking, my daughter (quick, quickly) peeked into the bag to see what we had bought for her.

4. The train raced (swift, swiftly) across the frozen prairie.

5. Mr. Mendoza is (slight, slightly) younger than his wife, but he looks much older than she.

Well and *Good*

Two words that are often confused are *well* and *good. Good* is an adjective; it describes nouns. *Well* is usually an adverb, and when it is, it describes verbs. But *well* (rather than *good*) is used as an adjective to refer to a person's health.

Write *well* or *good* in each of the sentences that follow. Compare your answers with a partner's.

ACTIVITY 3

1. I could tell by the broad grin on Della's face that the news was _____.

2. They say my grandfather sang so _____ that even the wind stopped to listen.

3. After she got a flu shot, Kathy did not feel _____.

4. The artist who painted the mural at our school did a _____ job.

5. People who eat _____ usually know something about nutrition.

REVIEW TEST 1

Underline the correct word or words in the parentheses.

1. Alexandrite is a very rare gemstone that is (more valuable, most valuable) than a diamond.

2. The doctor predicted that Ben would soon be (good, well) enough to go home.

3. The (little, less) time I spend worrying about a problem, the easier it is to solve.

4. Light walls make a room look (more large, larger) than dark walls do.

5. Jean is one of the (brightest, most brightest) women I have ever met.

6. The moth (continuous, continuously) thumped against the screen.

7. The Amish manage (good, well) without radios, telephones, or television.

8. When the prisoners of war were taken into the military compound, the guards were warned not to treat them (bad, badly).

9. It is (good, better) to teach people to fish than to give them fish.

10. Our new senator is (more honest, honester) than the last.

REVIEW TEST 2

The following paragraph contains ten errors in adjective and adverb use. Draw a line through each error and write the correct word in the space above.

Egypt has always been a popularly destination for travelers who want to learn about the ancient world. It is the oldest constant inhabited region in the world. Archaeologists and scholars believe people have been living in the region since 6500 BC. Some of the most good tourist attractions are the Pyramid of Djoser, the Egyptian Museum, the Temple of Karnak, and the Pyramids at Giza. The Pyramid of Djoser is considered the firstly Egyptian pyramid and is a step pyramid. The Egyptian Museum houses more than 120,000 ancient Egyptian antiquities, most notable, artifacts from the Valley of the Kings and the Tomb of Tutankhamen. The Temple of Karnak is the larger ancient religious site ever built and includes three main temples, additional more small temples, and several outer temples. The most well known tourist destination is Giza. The Great Pyramid of Khufu at Giza is the bigger pyramid in Egypt and, in fact, the biggest in the world. A visit to Egypt will be educationally for all and offers a well way for tourists to learn about ancient cultures.

Misplaced and Dangling Modifiers

Modifiers are descriptive words. Misplaced modifiers are words that, because of awkward placement, do not describe what the author intended them to describe. Dangling modifiers are descriptive words that open a sentence; like misplaced modifiers, they also do not describe what the author intended them to describe.

What Misplaced Modifiers Are and How to Correct Them

As mentioned, *misplaced modifiers* are awkwardly placed words that do not describe the words the writer intended them to describe. Misplaced modifiers often obscure the meaning of a sentence. To avoid them, place words as close as possible to what they describe.

Misplaced Words

Tony bought an old car from a crooked dealer *with a faulty transmission.*
(The *dealer* had a faulty transmission?)

I *nearly* earned two hundred dollars last week.
(You just missed earning two hundred dollars, but in fact earned nothing?)

Bill yelled at the howling dog *in his underwear.*
(The *dog* wore underwear?)

Correctly Placed Words

Tony bought an old car with a faulty transmission from a crooked dealer.
(The words describing the old car are now placed next to "car.")

I earned nearly two hundred dollars last week.
(The meaning—that you earned a little under two hundred dollars—is now clear.)

Bill, in his underwear, yelled at the howling dog.
(The words describing Bill are placed next to "Bill.")

ACTIVITY 1

Underline the misplaced word or words in each sentence. Then rewrite the sentence, placing related words together and thereby making the meaning clear.

EXAMPLES

The Birth of Venus by Sandro Botticelli features a beautiful woman standing on a seashell <u>in the halls of the Uffizi Gallery in Italy</u>.

In the halls of the Uffizi Gallery in Italy, The Birth of Venus by Sandro Botticelli features a beautiful woman standing on a seashell.

Leonardo da Vinci's *The Last Supper* <u>on the wall of Santa Maria delle Grazie church</u> is a large fresco style painting <u>in Milan, Italy</u>.

Leonardo da Vinci's The Last Supper is a large fresco style painting on the wall of Santa Maria delle Grazie church in Milan, Italy.

1. Michelangelo Merisi da Caravaggio's painting *Medusa* by Perseus the Greek hero depicts the moment she realizes her head has been severed.

   _____

   _____

2. *The Scream* by Edvard Munch, one of the most well-known paintings in history, shows an individual on a bridge screaming.

   _____

   _____

3. *The Two Fridas* by Frida Kahlo most likely portrays the painter's feelings about her divorce with one Frida displaying a whole heart and the second Frida displaying a wounded bleeding heart.

   _____

   _____

   _____

4. Matisse created after he could no longer paint gouache découpée works like *The Snail*.

   _____

   _____

5. Winslow Homer painted *The Blue Boat*, which depicts two men fishing in a small blue canoe in 1892.

   _____

   _____

6. Mary Cassatt was an American artist who illustrated the connection in her paintings between a mother and child.

_____

_____

7. Paul Klee's *Static-Dynamic Gradation,* may just look like a bunch of squares, but is actually a study of hues, colors, and contrast.

_____

_____

8. Edward Hopper's *Nighthawks* became even more famous on coffee mugs when Starbucks used the image.

_____

_____

9. Francisco Goya painted *La Cometa*, which means "kite" in the 1770s; it illustrates a group of people who are watching a kite flying.

_____

_____

10. Georgia O'Keeffe developed a style of painting that was strongly influenced by the New Mexico countryside and colors after a visit to Santa Fe in 1929.

_____

_____

What Dangling Modifiers Are and How to Correct Them

A modifier that opens a sentence must be followed immediately by the word it is meant to describe. Otherwise, the modifier is said to be *dangling,* and the sentence takes on an unintended meaning. For example, in the sentence

While smoking a pipe, my dog sat with me by the crackling fire.

the unintended meaning is that the *dog* was smoking the pipe. What the writer meant, of course, was that *he,* the writer, was smoking the pipe. The dangling modifier could be corrected by placing *I,* the word being described, directly after the opening modifier and revising as necessary:

While smoking a pipe, *I sat with* my dog by the crackling fire.

The dangling modifier could also be corrected by placing the subject within the opening word group:

> While *I was* smoking my pipe, my dog sat with me by the crackling fire.

Here are other sentences with dangling modifiers. Read the explanations of why they are dangling and look carefully at how they are corrected.

Dangling

Swimming at the lake, a rock cut Sue's foot.
(*Who* was swimming at the lake? The answer is not *rock* but *Sue*. The subject *Sue* must be added.)

While eating my sandwich, five mosquitoes bit me.
(*Who* is eating the sandwich? The answer is not *five mosquitoes,* as it unintentionally seems to be, but *I*. The subject *I* must be added.)

Getting out of bed, the tile floor was so cold that Yoko shivered all over.
(*Who* got out of bed? The answer is not *tile floor* but *Yoko*. The subject *Yoko* must be added.)

To join the team, a C average or better is necessary.
(*Who* is to join the team? The answer is not *C average* but *you*. The subject *you* must be added.)

Correct

Swimming at the lake, Sue cut her foot on a rock.
Or: When Sue was swimming at the lake, she cut her foot on a rock.

While *I* was eating my sandwich, five mosquitoes bit me.
Or: While eating my sandwich, *I* was bitten by five mosquitoes.

Getting out of bed, *Yoko* found the tile floor so cold that she shivered all over.
Or: When *Yoko* got out of bed, the tile floor was so cold that she shivered all over.

To join the team, *you* must have a C average or better.
Or: For *you* to join the team, a C average or better is necessary.

The preceding examples make clear the two ways of correcting a dangling modifier. Decide on a logical subject and do one of the following:

1. Place the subject *within* the opening word group.

> When Sue was swimming at the lake, she cut her foot on a rock.

TIP In some cases an appropriate subordinating word such as *when* must be added, and the verb may have to be changed slightly as well.

2.   Place the subject right *after* the opening word group.

> Swimming at the lake, Sue cut her foot on a rock.

Ask *Who?* as you look at the opening words in each sentence. The subject that answers the question should be nearby in the sentence. If it is not, provide the logical subject by using either method of correction described above.

EXAMPLE

> While setting up camp, a bear was spotted.
>
> *While we were setting up camp, we spotted a bear.*
>
> _____

or   *While setting up camp, we spotted a bear.*

_____

1.   Watching the horror movie, goose bumps covered my spine.

_____

_____

2.   After putting on a wool sweater, the room didn't seem as cold.

_____

_____

3.   Walking down the stairs, loud music could be heard.

_____

_____

4.   To assess the effects of a possible tuition hike, several students were interviewed.

_____

_____

5.   Joining several college clubs, Antonio's social life became more active.

_____

_____

6.   While visiting the Jungle Park Safari, a baboon scrambled onto the hood of their car.

_____

_____

7. When only a boy, that wild horse was trained.

_____

_____

8. Standing at the ocean's edge, the wind coated my glasses with a salty film.

_____

_____

9. After laughing for two hours straight, Rita's stomach started to ache.

_____

_____

10. Using binoculars, the hawk was clearly seen following its prey.

_____

_____

REVIEW TEST 1

In each pair below, one sentence is correct and one contains an error. Underline the misplaced word or words in each sentence that has an error. Write *M* for *misplaced modifier* or *C* for *correct* in front of each sentence.

_____ 1. Having been held up, the police were called by the store owner.

_____ 2. Having been held up, the store owner called the police.

_____ 3. I noticed a crack in the window walking into the delicatessen.

_____ 4. Walking into the delicatessen, I noticed a crack in the window.

_____ 5. Though he thought the job was long-term, Sam worked in Phoenix only one day.

_____ 6. Though he thought the job was long-term, Sam only worked in Phoenix one day.

_____ 7. With great delight, the children were ready to devour the luscious dessert.

_____ 8. The children were ready to devour the luscious dessert with great delight.

_____ 9. In a secondhand store, Willie found a television set that had been stolen from me last month.

_____ 10. Willie found a television set in a secondhand store that had been stolen from me last month.

In each pair below, one sentence is correct and one contains an error. Write *D* for *dangling* or *C* for *correct* in the blank next to each sentence. Remember that the opening words are a dangling modifier if they have no nearby logical subject to modify.

____ 1. Advertising on *Craigslist,* Ian's car was quickly sold.

____ 2. By advertising on *Craigslist,* Ian quickly sold his car.

____ 3. After painting the downstairs, the house needed airing to clear out the fumes.

____ 4. After we painted the downstairs, the house needed airing to clear out the fumes.

____ 5. Believing Venice to be the most romantic city in Europe, a visit there was planned for our honeymoon.

____ 6. Believing Venice to be the most romantic city in Europe, we planned a visit there for our honeymoon.

____ 7. After picking out a suit, a tie and a shirt were added to my list.

____ 8. After picking out a suit, I added a tie and a shirt to my list.

____ 9. Casting his fishing line into the lake, a largemouth bass could be felt grabbing his bait.

____ 10. Casting his fishing line into the lake, Matthew could feel a largemouth bass grabbing his bait.

Make the changes needed to correct the misplaced and dangling modifiers in the following sentences.

1. Willa Cather, author of *O Pioneers*, often wrote about women doing unusual things in her books.

_____

_____

2. A disturbing short story, Edgar Allan Poe's "The Fall of the House of Usher" contains the standard features of a Gothic story.

_____

_____

3. Kate Chopin wrote about the oppression of women in traditional society in many stories.

   _____

   _____

4. In "And of Clay Are We Created," Isabel Allende writes about how the death of a young girl affects a young man with deep feeling.

   _____

   _____

5. Often reflecting very real situations and violent deaths, Ambrose Bierce wrote many short stories.

   _____

   _____

6. Reading "The Metamorphosis" by Franz Kafka, an unexplained fear of apples and large bugs is caused.

   _____

   _____

7. F. Scott Fitzgerald is best known for his novel, which takes place in the 1920s, *The Great Gatsby*.

   _____

   _____

8. Credited as the father of the American short story, "Rip Van Winkle" was written by Washington Irving.

   _____

   _____

9. Although "The Lottery" by Shirley Jackson was written in 1948, it is influencing other stories still in the twenty-first century.

   _____

   _____

10. Overlooking the connection and courage her family offers in "Everyday Use," Alice Walker writes about a young woman, Dee, who strives to find her identity.

   _____

   _____

Mechanics

○ ○ ○   TKTS

To:	Jason.Smith@email.com
From:	Logan.OKelly@email.com
Subject:	TKTS
Date:	May 9, 2014 Signature: Logan

Jason,

omw 2 work, i bought tkts to *Betrayal* 4 next wkd. imho, it's the best new Broadway play, and since gmta, i thought u would want 2 go w/ me. wrud after wrk today? let's meet to plan.

CUL.

Logan

WHEN ARE ABBREVIATIONS APPROPRIATE?

Many people use abbreviations in their e-mail and text messages. What is your personal view about that use? Are these kinds of abbreviations ever appropriate in your college papers? Why or why not?

Paper Format

This chapter will describe the required manuscript format, or the formal characteristics, for any paper you hand in.

Guidelines for Formatting a Paper

When you hand in a paper for any of your courses, probably the first thing you will be judged on is its format. It is important, then, that you do certain things to make your papers look attractive, neat, and easy to read.

Here are guidelines to follow in preparing a paper for an instructor:

1. Use full-size theme or printer paper, 8½ by 11 inches.

2. Leave wide margins (1 inch) on all four sides of each page. In particular, do not crowd the right-hand or bottom margin. The white space makes your paper more readable; also, the instructor has room for comments.

3. If you write by hand:
   a. Use a pen with blue or black ink (*not* a pencil).
   b. Do not overlap letters. Do not make decorative loops on letters. On narrow-ruled paper, write only on every other line.
   c. Make all your letters distinct. Pay special attention to *a, e, i, o,* and *u*—five letters that people sometimes write illegibly.
   d. Keep your capital letters clearly distinct from small letters. You may even want to print all the capital letters.
   e. Make commas, periods, and other punctuation marks firm and clear. Leave a slight space after each period.

4. Center the title of your paper on the first line of page 1. Do *not* put quotation marks around the title, do not underline it, and do not put a period after it. Capitalize all the major words in a title, including the first and last words. Short connecting words within a title such as *of, for, the, in,* and *to* are not capitalized. Skip a line between the title and the first line of your text.

5. Indent the first line of each paragraph about five spaces (half an inch) from the left-hand margin.

6. When you type, use double-spacing between lines and leave an extra space after each period.

7. Whenever possible, avoid breaking (hyphenating) words at the end of lines. If you must break a word, break only between syllables (see page 487). Do not break words of one syllable.

8. Write your name, the date, and the course number where your instructor asks for them.

Also keep in mind these important points about the *title* and *first sentence* of your paper:

9. The title should simply be several words that tell what the paper is about. It should usually *not* be a complete sentence. For example, if you are writing a paper about one of the most frustrating jobs you have ever had, the title could be just "A Frustrating Job."

10. Do not rely on the title to help explain the first sentence of your paper. The first sentence must be independent of the title. For instance, if the title of your paper is "A Frustrating Job," the first sentence should *not* be "It was working as a babysitter." Rather, the first sentence might be "Working as a babysitter was the most frustrating job I ever had."

Identify the mistakes in format in the following lines from a student paper. Explain the corrections in the spaces provided. One correction is provided as an example.

ACTIVITY 1

	"Charles Darwin: his voyage on the ship beagle"
	He was a man who put forth the theories of evolution and natural selection.
	Darwin was the naturalist aboard the English ship Beagle (1831-36), which made
	a nearly five-year journey all over the globe. Its official mission was to chart the
	coastline of South America. However, on that journey, Darwin started collecting
	information that would form the basis of his scientific career.

1. *Hyphenate only between syllables.* _____

2. _____

3. _____

4. _____

5. _____

6. _____

ACTIVITY 2

A title often reflects the purpose of the paper. For an essay, the title can be based on the thesis statement. For a paragraph, the title can be based on the topic sentence. Both the thesis and/or the topic sentence express the topic and the main idea of the paper. Following are five topic sentences from student papers. Working with a partner, write a suitable and specific title for each paper, basing the title on the topic sentence. (Note the example.)

EXAMPLE

Compromise in a Relationship

Learning how to compromise is essential to a good relationship.

1. *Title:* _____
    Some houseplants are dangerous to children and pets.

2. *Title:* _____
    Some herbicides can be as dangerous to human beings as to weeds.

3. *Title:* _____
    You don't have to be a professional to take good photographs if you keep a few guidelines in mind.

4. *Title:* _____
    My husband is compulsively neat.

5. *Title:* _____
    Insulating a home well can save the owner a great deal of money on heating and cooling.

ACTIVITY 3

As has already been stated, you must *not* rely on the title to help explain your first sentence. In four of the five sentences that follow, the writer has, inappropriately, used the title to help explain the first sentence.

Rewrite these four sentences so that they stand independent of the title. Write *Correct* under the one sentence that is independent of the title.

EXAMPLE

Title: My Career Plans

First sentence: They have changed in the last six months.

Rewritten: *My career plans have changed in the last six months.*

1. *Title:* Contending with Dogs

   First sentence: This is the main problem in my work as a mail carrier.

   Rewritten: _____

   _____

   _____

2. *Title:* Study Skills

   First sentence: Good study skills are necessary if a person is to do well in college.

   Rewritten: _____

   _____

   _____

3. *Title*: Black Bears

   First Sentence: We saw several of them as we drove across the Blue Ridge Mountains.

   Rewritten: _____

   _____

   _____

4. *Title:* The Renaissance

   First Sentence: It was the period that followed the Middle Ages in Europe.

   Rewritten: _____

   _____

   _____

5. *Title:* Cell Phones

   First sentence: Many motorists have learned the hard way just how dangerous these handy tools can be.

   Rewritten: _____

   _____

   _____

REVIEW TEST

In the space provided, rewrite the following sentences from a student paper. Correct the mistakes in format.

	"beijing: china's capital then and now"
	This city is the capital of the People's Republic of China. It is the second largest city
	city in China; Shanghai is the largest. For more than seven hundred years, on and off,
	Beijing has been the seat of the Chinese government. For a time, its name was Peking.
	However, when the Communists took over the country in 1949, they gave the city back
	its ancient name. Important tourist sites in and near Beijing include the Forbidden
	City, the Summer Palace, the Beijing Zoo, and the Great Wall.

Capital Letters

This chapter will describe main uses of capital letters; secondary uses of capital letters; and unnecessary uses of capital letters.

Main Uses of Capital Letters

Capital letters are used with

1. The first word in a sentence or a direct quotation
2. Names of persons and the word *I*
3. Names of particular places
4. Names of days of the week, months, and holidays
5. Names of commercial products (brand names)
6. Names of organizations such as religious and political groups, associations, companies, unions, and clubs
7. Titles of books, magazines, newspapers, articles, stories, poems, films, podcasts, television shows, songs, papers that you write, and the like

Each use is illustrated on the pages that follow.

First Word in a Sentence or Direct Quotation

The panhandler touched me and asked, "Do you have any change?"

↑   ↑

(Capitalize the first word in the sentence.)   (Capitalize the first word in the direct quotation.)

"If you want a ride," said Tawana, "get ready now. Otherwise, I'm going alone."

(*If* and *Otherwise* are capitalized because they are the first words of sentences within a direct quotation. But *get* is not capitalized, because it is part of the first sentence within the quotation.)

Names and Titles

Names of Persons and the Word I

Last night I ran into Tony Curry and Lola Morrison.

Names of Particular Places

Charlotte graduated from Fargone High School in Orlando, Florida. She then moved with her parents to Bakersfield, California, and worked for a time there at Alexander's Gift House. Eventually she married and moved with her husband to the Naval Reserve Center in Atlantic County, New Jersey. She takes courses two nights a week at Stockton State College. On weekends she and her family often visit the nearby Wharton State Park and go canoeing on the Mullica River. She does volunteer work at Atlantic City Hospital in connection with the First Christian Church. In addition, she works during the summer as a hostess at Convention Hall and the Holiday Inn.

But   Use small letters if the specific name of a place is not given.

Charlotte sometimes remembers her unhappy days in high school and at the gift shop where she worked after graduation. She did not imagine then that she would one day be going to college and doing volunteer work for a church and a hospital in the community where she and her husband live.

Names of Days of the Week, Months, and Holidays

I was angry at myself for forgetting that Sunday was Mother's Day.

During July and August, Fred works a four-day week, and he has Mondays off.

Bill still has a scar on his ankle from a cherry bomb that exploded near him one Fourth of July and a scar on his arm where he stabbed himself with a fishhook on a Labor Day weekend.

But   Use small letters for the seasons—summer, fall, winter, spring.

Names of Commercial Products

After brushing with Colgate toothpaste in the morning, Clyde typically has a glass of Tropicana orange juice and Total cereal with milk, followed by a Marlboro cigarette.

My sister likes to play Monopoly and Cranium; I like chess and poker; my brother likes Scrabble, baseball, and table tennis.

But   Use small letters for the *type* of product (toothpaste, orange juice, cereal, cigarette, and so on).

Names of Organizations Such as Religious and Political Groups, Associations, Companies, Unions, and Clubs

Fred Grencher was a Lutheran for many years but converted to Catholicism when he married. Both he and his wife, Martha, are members of the Democratic Party. Both belong to the American Automobile Association. Martha works part-time as a refrigerator salesperson at Sears. Fred is a mail carrier and belongs to the Postal Clerks' Union.

Tony met Lola when he was a Boy Scout and she was a Campfire Girl; she asked him to light her fire.

Titles of Books, Magazines, Newspapers, Articles, Stories, Poems, Films, Television Shows, Songs, Papers That You Write, and the Like

On Sunday Lola read the first chapter of *I Know Why the Caged Bird Sings,* a book required for her writing course. She looked through her parents' copy of the *New York Times.* She then read an article titled "Thinking about a Change in Your Career" and a poem titled "Some Moments Alone" in *Cosmopolitan* magazine. At the same time, she listened to an old Beatles album, *Abbey Road.* In the evening she watched *60 Minutes* on television and an old movie, *High Noon,* starring Gary Cooper. Then from 11 P.M. to midnight she worked on a paper titled "Uses of Leisure Time in Today's Culture" for her sociology class.

Cross out the words that need capitals in the following sentences. Then write the capitalized forms of the words in the spaces provided. The number of spaces tells you how many corrections to make in each case.

ACTIVITY 1

EXAMPLE

Nathaniel ~~hawthorne~~ wrote a novel entitled the *Scarlet letter* and a short story called "Young ~~goodman brown~~."

   Hawthorne   *Letter*   *Goodman*   *Brown*

1. My son, jonah, loves to read the magazine, *popular mechanics.*

   _____   _____   _____

2. In december 2012, *popular mechanics* celebrated its 110th anniversary with a special edition, which i gave to my son for christmas.

   _____   _____   _____   _____

   _____

3. One of the headlines on the front cover was "110 predictions for the next 110 years."

   _____   _____   _____

4. One of the predictions is that self-healing concrete will be used for bridges. This concrete was invented by university of michigan engineer victor li.

_____   _____   _____   _____

5. Another prediction, made by ibm, is that people will no longer need to use passwords because such programs as face-recognition software and retinal scans will be widely available.

_____

6. Several predictions are focused on how robots are going to change our lives. Engineers at purdue university are working on robots to replace scrub nurses. Other scientists are working on robots that will deliver food carts and move patients.

_____   _____

7. My son was most excited about the prediction made by dr. fred calef of the mars science laboratory.

_____   _____   _____   _____

_____   _____

8. Dr. calef explains that scientists have been unable to confirm that dark matter exists. He states, "it's like a hidden magnet…," and goes on to say that we can see what it pulls but we can't see the source.

_____   _____

9. Dr. calef and micho kaku, a theoretical physicist, believe that scientists will discover actual evidence of the existence of dark matter, possibly in the next fifteen years.

_____   _____   _____

10. My favorite prediction is the new self-cleaning clothing designed by engineers in china; i hope that it makes my maytag washer obsolete!

_____   _____   _____

Other Uses of Capital Letters

Capital letters are also used with

1. Names that show family relationships
2. Titles of persons when used with their names
3. Specific school courses
4. Languages
5. Geographic locations

6. Historical periods and events

7. Races, nations, and nationalities

8. Opening and closing of a letter

Each use is illustrated on the pages that follow.

Names and Titles

Names That Show Family Relationships

I got Mother to babysit for me.

I went with Grandfather to the church service.

Uncle Carl and Aunt Lucy always enclose twenty dollars with birthday cards.

But Do not capitalize words like *mother, father, grandmother, aunt,* and so on, when they are preceded by a possessive word (*my, your, his, her, our, their*).

I got my mother to babysit for me.

I went with my grandfather to the church service.

My uncle and aunt always enclose twenty dollars with birthday cards.

Titles of Persons When Used with Their Names

I wrote to Senator Grabble and Congresswoman Punchie.

Professor Snorrel sent me to Chairperson Ruck, who sent me to Dean Rappers.

He drove to Dr. Helen Thompson's office after the cat bit him.

But Use small letters when titles appear by themselves, without specific names.

I wrote to my senator and my congresswoman.

The professor sent me to the chairperson, who sent me to the dean.

He drove to the doctor's office after the cat bit him.

Specific School Courses

I got an A in both Accounting and Small Business Management, but I got a C in Human Behavior.

But Use small letters for general subject areas.

I enjoyed my business courses but not my psychology or language courses.

Miscellaneous Categories

Languages

She knows German and Spanish, but she speaks mostly American slang.

Geographic Locations

I grew up in the Midwest. I worked in the East for a number of years and then moved to the West Coast.

But   Use small letters for directions.

A new high school is being built at the south end of town.

Because I have a compass in my car, I know that I won't be going east or west when I want to go north.

Historical Periods and Events

Hector did well answering an essay question about the Second World War, but he lost points on a question about the Great Depression.

Races, Nations, and Nationalities

The research study centered on African Americans and Hispanics.

They have German knives and Danish glassware in the kitchen, an Indian wood carving in the bedroom, Mexican sculptures in the study, and a Turkish rug in the living room.

Opening and Closing of a Letter

Dear Sir:

Dear Madam:

Sincerely yours,

Truly yours,

TIP   Capitalize only the first word in a closing.

ACTIVITY 2

Working with a partner, cross out the words that need capitals in the following sentences. Then write the capitalized forms of the words in the spaces provided. The number of spaces tells you how many corrections to make in each case.

1. The first european city I ever visited was london; the last was rome.

   _____   _____   _____

2. The e-mail letter began, "dear friend—You must send twenty copies of this message if you want good luck."

   _____

3. A retired army officer, captain Evert Johnson, is teaching a course called military history. He once served in the middle east.

   _____   _____   _____

4. aunt Sarah and uncle Hal, who are mormons, took us to their church services when we visited them in the midwest.

   _____   _____   _____   _____

5. While visiting san francisco, Liza stopped in at a buddhist temple and talked to a chinese lawyer there.

   _____   _____   _____   _____

Unnecessary Use of Capitals

Many errors in capitalization are caused by using capitals where they are not needed. Pages 448–452 in this chapter provide examples and explanations of words that do *not* need capitals.

Cross out the incorrectly capitalized words in the following sentences. Then write the correct forms of the words in the spaces provided. The number of spaces tells you how many corrections to make in each sentence.

ACTIVITY 3

1. My cousin is taking a course in Russian History at a College in Moscow.

   _____   _____

2. I love the television Commercials of some Insurance companies; they make Me break out laughing.

   _____   _____   _____

3. A front-page Newspaper story about the crash of a commercial Jet has made me nervous about my Overseas trip.

   _____   _____   _____

4. During a Terrible Blizzard in 1888, People froze to Death on the streets of New York.

   _____   _____   _____   _____

5. I asked the Bank Officer at Citibank, "How do I get a Card to use the automatic teller machines?"

   _____   _____   _____

REVIEW TEST 1

The following professional e-mail contains errors in capitalization. Draw a line through each error. Add or delete capitals where needed. You should make thirty-two corrections in all.

EXAMPLE:

Travel World is located in ċheyenne, the Ċapital of the State of Ẇyoming.

Work

John C. Traveler
678 Smith lane
Cheyenne, Wyoming 12345

dear Mr. traveler:

Thank you for coming into travel world to inquire about possible Vacation destinations for you and your family. After much research, we have found a family-friendly biking Tour Company, called Backroads, and an itinerary that is within the price range you provided for us. the dates for this tour are July 1 through July 6. This tour includes an extra activity because of the july fourth holiday.

Backroads offers a wonderful family biking vacation in maine. You will fly into Portland and meet your shuttle at the Portland Regency hotel. The shuttle will take you to your hotel in Camden. The first two days will be spent in Camden; the rides include views of Penobscot bay and the hills. On the Third day, you will have the opportunity to choose any of three biking routes to Belfast. That afternoon will be spent in acadia national park, located on Mount Desert Island. Day four will be spent exploring Acadia along the car-free trails. That night, in addition to a regular visit to a Maine lobster pound, you will participate in the Bar Harbor independence day festivities. Day five includes two biking routes on Isleford, an island in the Cranberry isles that is now a thriving Artists' Community. The last day includes a five-mile or twelve-mile bike ride within the region of paradise hill before the shuttle returns you to portland for your final evening before your departure.

continued

In anticipation of your possible booking, i have held this itinerary under your name. This hold is good for the next forty-eight hours. Please give us a call and we can discuss the Pricing and Payment options with you.

Thank you again for your business.

Sincerely yours,

Jacqueline McCoy

travel specialist

Travel world

123 Voyager Way

Cheyenne, Wyoming 12345

(123) 456-7890

REVIEW TEST 2

On separate paper, do the following:

1. Write seven sentences demonstrating the seven main uses of capital letters (page 447).

2. Write eight sentences demonstrating the eight additional uses of capital letters (pages 450–451).

Numbers and Abbreviations

This chapter will describe the proper use of numbers and abbreviations.

Numbers

Rule 1

Spell out numbers that can be expressed in one or two words. Otherwise, use numerals—the numbers themselves.

> During the past five years, more than twenty-five barracuda have been caught in the lake.
>
> The parking fine was ten dollars.
>
> In my grandmother's attic are eighty-four pairs of old shoes.

But

> Each year about 250 baby trout are added to the lake.
>
> My costs after contesting a parking fine in court were $135.
>
> Grandmother has 382 back copies of *Reader's Digest* in her attic.

Rule 2

Be consistent when you use a series of numbers. If some numbers in a sentence or paragraph require more than two words, then use numerals throughout the selection:

> During his election campaign, State Senator Mel Grabble went to 3 county fairs, 16 parades, 45 cookouts, and 112 club dinners, and delivered the same speech 176 times.

Rule 3

Use numerals for dates, times, addresses, percentages, and parts of a book.

> The letter was dated April 3, 1872.
>
> My appointment was at 6:15. (*But:* Spell out numbers before *o'clock*. For example: The doctor didn't see me until seven o'clock.)
>
> He lives at 212 West 19th Street.

About 20 percent of our class dropped out of school.

One cause of the Civil War is explained in Chapter 9, page 244, of our history textbook.

Cross out the mistakes in numbers and write the corrections in the spaces provided.

ACTIVITY 1

1. Pearl Harbor was attacked on December the seventh, nineteen forty-one.

    _____   _____

2. The city council decided to install 8 new traffic lights and 30 new stop signs.

    _____   _____

3. The Memorial Day parade will start at 11:00 o'clock; 30 organizations are expected to march.

    _____   _____

Abbreviations

While abbreviations are a helpful time-saver in note taking, you should avoid most abbreviations in formal writing. Listed below are some of the few abbreviations that can be used acceptably in compositions. Note that a period is used after most abbreviations.

1. Mr., Mrs., Ms., Jr., Sr., Dr. when used with proper names:

    Mr. Tibble   Dr. Stein   Ms. O'Reilly

2. Time references:

    A.M. or a.m.   P.M. or p.m.   B.C. or A.D.   B.C.E. or C.E.

3. First or middle name in a signature:

    R. Anthony Curry   Otis T. Redding   J. Alfred Prufrock

4. Organizations and common terms known primarily by their initials:

    FBI   UN   CBS   CD   DVD

Cross out the words that should not be abbreviated and correct them in the spaces provided. Then compare your answers with a partner's.

ACTIVITY 2

1. On Mon. afternoon, Feb. 10, 2010, at five min. after two o'clock, my son was born.

    _____   _____   _____

2. For six years I lived at First Ave. and Gordon St. right next to Shore Memorial Hosp., in San Fran., Calif.

    _____   _____   _____   _____   _____

3. After we completed the chem. exam, Dr. Andrews announced she had been asked to serve as Dean of Science at Aubury U. in Ariz.

    _____   _____

REVIEW TEST

The following e-mail contains errors in capitalization and the use of numbers and abbreviations. Rewrite the e-mail to correct these errors in the margins or in spaces between the lines. You should make twenty corrections in all.

From: Sherry Piper

Sent: Monday, September 29, 2014

To: Prof. Eric Dvorak

Subject: Online English 101 h.w.

Dear Prof. Dvorak:

i wanted to be sure I understood our h.w. and test review material for this week's Module and eng. exam. By tues., Oct. seventh, I am supposed to answer the 4 questions that cover chapters five and six, turn in my Research Paper, and complete the exam that covers the writing process, up-to-date doc, and annotated bibs. I believe you expect everything to be turned in by 1 o'clock that day. Is this all correct?

Thank you,

Sherry P.

Punctuation

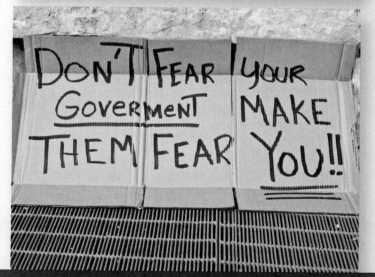

CAN YOU IDENTIFY THE MISUSED PUNCTUATION?

How could you correct the errors? Have you seen similar mistakes in signs posted on campus? on the road or in ads? in a newspaper?

Apostrophes

The two main uses of the apostrophe are

1. To show the omission of one or more letters in a contraction
2. To show ownership or possession

Each use is explained on the pages that follow.

Apostrophe in Contractions

A *contraction* is formed when two words are combined to make one word. An apostrophe is used to show where letters are omitted in forming the contraction. Here are two contractions:

have + not = haven't (*o* in *not* has been omitted)

I + will = I'll (*wi* in *will* has been omitted)

The following are some other common contractions:

I + am = I'm	it + is = it's
I + have = I've	it + has = it's
I + had = I'd	is + not = isn't
who + is = who's	could + not = couldn't
do + not = don't	I + would = I'd
did + not = didn't	they + are = they're

TIP *Will* + *not* has an unusual contraction, *won't.*

Combine the following pairs of words into contractions. One is done for you.

ACTIVITY 1

1. we + are = _we're_
2. are + not = _____
3. you + are = _____
4. they + have = _____
5. could + not = _____

6. should + not = _____
7. have + not = _____
8. who + is = _____
9. does + not = _____
10. there + is = _____

Working with a partner, write the contractions for the words in parentheses. One is done for you.

ACTIVITY 2

1. Denise (should not) _shouldn't_ complain about the cost of food if (she is) _she's_ unwilling to grow her own by planting a garden in her backyard.

2. (We have) _____ been planting our own garden for three years, and my family (will not) _____ even consider purchasing vegetables at the grocery store.

3. (We are) _____ planning to expand our garden this year; (it is) _____ our goal to make it twice the size that it was last year.

4. Last year, I (did not) _____ have enough room to grow cucumbers, squash, and pumpkins, but (I will) _____ have more than enough room this year.

5. (I would) _____ be willing to show Denise how to garden if (she is) _____ interested.

TIP Even though contractions are common in everyday speech and in written dialogue, it is usually best to avoid them in formal writing.

Apostrophe to Show Ownership or Possession

To show ownership or possession, we can use such words as *belongs to, possessed by, owned by,* or (most commonly) *of.*

the jacket that *belongs to* Tony

the grades *possessed by* James

the gas station *owned by* our cousin

the footprints *of* the animal

But often the quickest and easiest way to show possession is to use an apostrophe plus *s* (if the word is not a plural ending in -*s*). Thus we can say

> Tony's jacket
>
> James's grades
>
> our cousin's gas station
>
> the animal's footprints

Points to Remember

1. The *'s* goes with the owner or possessor (in the examples given, *Tony, James, cousin, the animal*). What follows is the person or thing possessed (in the examples given, *jacket, grades, gas station, footprints*).

2. When *'s* is handwritten in cursive script, there should always be a break between the word and the *'s*.

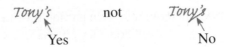

Tony's   not   *Tony's*

Yes   No

3. A singular word ending in -*s* (such as *James* in the earlier example) also shows possession by adding an apostrophe plus *s* (*James's*).

ACTIVITY 3

Rewrite the italicized part of each of the sentences below, using *'s* to show possession. Remember that the *'s* goes with the owner or possessor.

EXAMPLE

> *The toys belonging to the children* filled an entire room.
>
> _The children's toys_____

1. *The old car owned by Fred* is a classic.

   _____

2. *The concentration of my grandfather* has improved because of the new medication.

   _____

3. *The owner of the pit bull* was arrested after the dog attacked a child.

   _____

4. *The drill of the dentist* did not hurt because he had injected my gums with Novocaine.

   _____

5. *The van owned by Dennis* was recalled because of an engine defect.

   _____

6. Is this *the hat of somebody?*

_____

7. She will probably hate *the surprise ending of the movie.*

_____

8. *The cords coming from the computer* were so tangled they looked like spaghetti.

_____

9. *The energy level possessed by the little boy* is much higher than hers.

_____

10. *The leaves of the maple tree* were turning a deep red.

_____

ACTIVITY 4

Add *'s* to each of the following words to make them the possessors or owners of something. Then write sentences using the words. Your sentences can be serious or playful. One is done for you.

1. Van Gogh ____*Van Gogh's*____   ____*Van Gogh's left ear was severed from his head.*____

   _____

2. llama _____   _____

   _____

3. zombie _____   _____

   _____

4. Monopoly _____   _____

   _____

5. thief _____   _____

   _____

Apostrophe versus Possessive Pronouns

Do not use an apostrophe with possessive pronouns. They already show ownership. Possessive pronouns include *his, hers, its, yours, ours,* and *theirs.*

Incorrect	Correct
The bookstore lost its' lease.	The bookstore lost its lease.
The racing bikes were theirs'.	The racing bikes were theirs.
The change is your's.	The change is yours.
His' problems are ours', too.	His problems are ours, too.
His' skin is more sunburned than her's.	His skin is more sunburned than hers.

Apostrophe versus Simple Plurals

When you want to make a word plural, just add -s at the end of the word. Do *not* add an apostrophe. For example, the plural of the word *movie* is *movies,* not *movie's* or *movies'.* Look at this sentence:

>   Lola adores Tony's broad shoulders, rippling muscles, and warm eyes.

The words *shoulders, muscles,* and *eyes* are simple plurals, meaning *more than one shoulder, more than one muscle, more than one eye.* The plural is shown by adding only -s. On the other hand, the *'s* after *Tony* shows possession—that the shoulders, muscles, and eyes belong to Tony.

ACTIVITY 5

In the space provided under each sentence, add the one apostrophe needed and explain why the other word or words ending in -s are simple plurals.

EXAMPLE
Karens tomato plants are almost six feet tall.

Karens: *Karen's, meaning "belonging to Karen"*

plants: *plural meaning "more than one plant"*

1. The restaurants reputation brought hungry diners from miles around.

   restaurants: _____

   diners: _____

   miles: _____

2. Marios sweater was made in Ireland by monks.

   Marios: _____

   monks: _____

3. As Tinas skill at studying increased, her grades improved.

   Tinas: _____

   grades: _____

4. After I had visited the deans office, I decided to spend more time with my books.

   deans: _____

   books: _____

5. I bought two magazines and a copy of Stephen Kings latest novel at the bookstore.

   magazines: _____

   Kings: _____

6. After six weeks without rain, the nearby streams started drying up, and the lakes water level fell sharply.

weeks: _____

streams: _____

lakes: _____

7. Rebeccas hooded red cloak makes her look like a fairy-tale character, but her heavy black boots spoil the effect.

Rebeccas: _____

boots: _____

8. When the brakes failed on Eriks truck, he narrowly avoided hitting several parked cars and two trees.

brakes: _____

Eriks: _____

cars: _____

trees: _____

9. Suddenly, the clouds opened and the skys bounty drenched the dry fields.

clouds: _____

skys: _____

fields: _____

10. My parents like Floridas winters, but they prefer to spend their summers back home in Maine.

parents: _____

Floridas: _____

winters: _____

summers: _____

Apostrophe with Plural Words Ending in -*s*

Plurals that end in -*s* show possession simply by adding the apostrophe (rather than an apostrophe plus *s*):

My *parents'* station wagon is ten years old.

The *students'* many complaints were ignored by the high school principal.

All the *Boy Scouts'* tents were damaged by the hailstorm.

ACTIVITY 6

In each sentence, cross out the one plural word that needs an apostrophe. Then write the word correctly, with the apostrophe, in the space provided. An example has been provided.

EXAMPLE

The ~~surgeons~~ break room was one of the nicest rooms in the hospital.

_____*surgeons'*_____

1. My two kittens toys were scattered all over the downstairs rooms.

    _____

2. The snakes atrium was large enough for three of the creatures to live comfortably.

    _____

3. The attorneys assistants planned the holiday party.

    _____

4. My sons tree house, which they built themselves, holds eight people.

    _____

5. Three of the teachers classrooms had no air conditioning.

    _____

REVIEW TEST 1

In the paragraph below, underline the words that either need apostrophes or have misused apostrophes. Then, in the spaces between the lines, correct the mistakes. You should make eleven corrections in all.

Spiders silk is an amazing substance! Paul Hillyard says in *The Book of the Spider* (1994), "For an equal [diameter], spider silk is stronger than steel and about as strong as nylon. It is, however, much more resilient and can stretch several time's before breaking—it is twice as elastic as nylon and more difficult to break than rubber." Because of it's strength and durability, many scientists are studying spider's dragline silk, a silk that can be extended 30 to 50 percent of it's length before it breaks. The U.S. Army is interested in spider silk to use in product's like bulletproof vests, and medical scientists are interested in creating artificial ligaments

continued

and tendons from spider silk. All these study's show that spider silk has the qualities' to be useful, but creating enough has proven difficult. One researcher, however, has been genetically modifying goats to produce the spider silk protein in the goats milk. Once the milk is specially processed, threads of spider silk are created. Researchers' are also studying alfalfa plants ability to produce the silk protein. One day in the near future, spider silk may be mass produced by non-spider methods.

REVIEW TEST 2

Make the following words possessive and then use at least five of them in a not-so-serious paragraph that tells a story. In addition, use at least three contractions in the paragraph.

detective	restaurant	Angelo	student
Phoenix	sister	children	oak tree
skunk	Jimmy Fallon	boss	Lady Gaga
customer	dentist	police car	yesterday
instructor	everyone	mob	Chicago

Quotation Marks

The two main uses of quotation marks are

1. To set off the exact words of a speaker or a writer
2. To set off the titles of short works such as newspaper and magazine articles

Each use is explained on the pages that follow.

Quotation Marks to Set Off Exact Words of a Speaker or Writer

Use quotation marks when you want to show the exact words of a speaker or a writer.

- "Say something tender to me," whispered Lola to Tony.
  (Quotation marks set off the exact words that Lola spoke to Tony.)

- Mark Twain once wrote, "The more I know about human beings, the more I like my dog."
  (Quotation marks set off the exact words that Mark Twain wrote.)

- "The only dumb question," the instructor said, "is the one you don't ask."
  (Two pairs of quotation marks are used to enclose the instructor's exact words.)

- Sharon complained, "I worked so hard on this paper. I spent two days getting information in the library and online and two days writing it. Guess what grade I got on it?"
  (Note that the end quotation marks do not come until the end of Sharon's speech. Place quotation marks before the first quoted word of a speech and after the last quoted word. As long as no interruption occurs in the speech, do not use quotation marks for each new sentence.)

Complete the following statements explaining how capital letters, commas, and periods are used in quotations. Refer to the four examples as guides.

> **HINT** In the four preceding examples, notice that a comma sets off the quoted part from the rest of the sentence. Also observe that commas and periods at the end of a quotation always go *inside* quotation marks.

1. Every quotation begins with a _____ letter.

2. When a quotation is split (as in the sentence above about dumb questions), the second part does not begin with a capital letter unless it is

    a _____ sentence.

3. _____ are used to separate the quoted part of a sentence from the rest of the sentence.

4. Commas and periods that come at the end of a quotation should go _____ the quotation marks.

    The answers are *capital, new, Commas,* and *inside.*

Place quotation marks around the exact words of a speaker or writer in the sentences that follow.

ACTIVITY 1

Academic

1. Joylynn entered the Office of the Registrar and asked, Is this where I speak to someone about my degree program?

2. The clerk responded, No. You need to go down the hall to the Advising Office, and someone will help you there.

3. Thank you, replied Joylynn. I appreciate your help.

4. When she entered the Advising Office, Joylynn said, Good morning. I was told this is where I can speak with someone about my degree program.

5. Yes, replied the administrative assistant. I will need to get some information from you first. Please fill out the highlighted portions of this form, and I will let an advisor know you are here.

6. Joylynn, Mr. Saunders will see you now, announced the assistant as she directed Joylynn to an office.

7. Good morning, Joylynn. Please have a seat, stated Mr. Saunders as she entered his office.

8. Mr. Saunders, I know I am only a freshman, but I would really like to discuss my degree plan, so I can make sure I am taking the proper classes, Joylynn spoke directly to the advisor after she had sat down.

9. Mr. Saunders smiled at Joylynn and replied, I am impressed that you are planning and organizing so early.

10. After speaking with Mr. Saunders for an hour, Joylynn politely said, Thank you so much for your help.

ACTIVITY 2

After you complete each part of this activity, go over your responses with a partner. An example is provided for each part.

1. Write a sentence in which you quote a favorite expression of someone you know. Identify the relationship of the person to you.

   EXAMPLE
   My father often said, "When one door closes, another opens."

   _____

   _____

   _____

   _____

2. Write a quotation that contains the words *Tony asked Lola*. Write a second quotation that includes the words *Lola replied*.

   EXAMPLE
   "I think I've lost my sunglasses. Have you seen them?" Tony asked Lola. "Try checking on top of your head," Lola replied.

   _____

   _____

   _____

3. Copy a sentence or two that interest you from a book or magazine. Identify the title and author of the work.

   EXAMPLE
   In Night Shift, Stephen King writes, "I don't like to sleep with one leg sticking out. Because if a cool hand ever reached out from under the bed and grasped my ankle, I might scream."

   _____

   _____

   _____

Indirect Quotations

An *indirect quotation* is a rewording of someone else's comments, rather than a word-for-word direct quotation. The word *that* often signals an indirect quotation. Quotation marks are *not* used with indirect quotations.

Direct Quotation	Indirect Quotation
Fred said, "The distributor cap on my car is cracked."	Fred said that the distributor cap on his car was cracked.
(Fred's exact spoken words are given, so quotation marks are used.)	(We learn Fred's words indirectly, so no quotation marks are used.)
Sally's note to Jay read, "I'll be working late. Don't wait up for me."	Sally left a note for Jay saying she would be working late and he should not wait up for her.
(The exact words that Sally wrote in the note are given, so quotation marks are used.)	(We learn Sally's words indirectly, so no quotation marks are used.)

Rewrite the following sentences, changing words as necessary to convert the sentences into direct quotations. The first one is done for you as an example.

ACTIVITY 3

1. The instructor told everyone to take out a pen and sheet of paper.

   The instructor said, "Take out a pen and sheet of paper."

2. A student in the front row asked if this was a test.

   _____

3. The instructor replied that it was more of a pop quiz.

   _____

4. She claimed that anyone who had completed last night's homework would do well.

   _____

5. Another student responded that this would be easy for him.

Quotation Marks to Set Off Titles of Short Works

Titles of short works are usually set off by quotation marks, while titles of long works are italicized. Use quotation marks around titles of short works, such as articles that appear in books, newspapers, journals, or magazines; chapters in a book; short stories; short poems; and songs. On the other hand, italicize the titles of books, magazines, newspapers, journals, plays, movies, record albums, and television shows.

Quotation Marks	Italics (or Underlining)
the chapter "So You Want War"	in the book *American Lion*
the article "Getting a Fix on Repairs"	in the newspaper the *New York Times*
the article "The Myelin Brake"	in the magazine *Science*
the essay "Lifting the Veil"	in the book *Inventing the Truth*
the story "The Night the Bed Fell"	in the book *A Thurber Carnival*
the poem "Easter, 1916"	in the book *The Yeats Reader*
the song "Bold as Love"	in the album *Continuum*
	the television show *The Daily Show*
	the movie *Gone with the Wind*

TIP When you are typing a paper, you should always italicize longer works; however, if you are turning in handwritten work, longer works should be underlined. For example, *The Hunger Games* by Suzanne Collins would be handwritten <u>The Hunger Games</u> by Suzanne Collins.

 ACTIVITY 4 Use quotation marks or underline (or italicize) as needed.

1. Whenever Gina sees the movie The Sound of Music, the song near the end, Climb Every Mountain, makes her cry.

2. Discover magazine contains an article entitled Lost Cities of the Amazon.

3. I printed out an article titled Too Much Homework? from the online version of Time to use in my sociology report.

4. Tiffany's favorite movie is Raiders of the Lost Ark, and her favorite television show is CSI: Miami.

5. Our instructor gave us a week to buy the textbook titled Personal Finance and to read the first chapter, Work and Income.

6. Every holiday season, our family watches the movie A Christmas Carol on television.

7. Looking around to make sure no one he knew saw him, Bob bought the newest National Enquirer in order to read the story called Man Explodes on Operating Table.

8. Edgar Allan Poe's short story The Murders in the Rue Morgue and his poem The Raven are in a paperback titled Great Tales and Poems of Edgar Allan Poe.

9. After Pablo bought a copy of Time magazine, he read a story entitled Stem Cell Progress and then looked for a review of the movie Avatar.

10. The night before his exam, he discovered with horror that the chapter Becoming Mature was missing from Childhood and Adolescence, the psychology text that he had bought secondhand.

Other Uses of Quotation Marks

1. Quotation marks are used to set off special words or phrases from the rest of a sentence:

   Many people spell the words "a lot" as *one* word, "alot," instead of correctly spelling them as two words.

   I have trouble telling the difference between "their" and "there."

2. Single quotation marks are used to mark off a quotation within a quotation.

   The instructor said, "Know the chapter titled 'Status Symbols' in *Adolescent Development* if you expect to pass the test."

   Susan said, "One of my favorite Mae West lines is 'I used to be Snow White, but I drifted'."

REVIEW TEST 1

Insert quotations marks as needed and underline titles that should be italicized in the sentences that follow.

1. Cool Hand Luke was released in 1967, and since then the Captain's words have become infamous. The Captain said, What we've got here . . . is a failure to communicate.

2. In the movie, A League of Their Own, the character played by Tom Hanks demonstrates his frustration at having to manage an All-American Girls Professional Baseball League team when he yells, There's no crying in baseball!

3. The movie Smoke Signals is based on the story, This Is What It Means to Say Phoenix, Arizona, which is the fifth in a series of stories in the book, The Lone Ranger and Tonto Fistfight in Heaven, by Sherman Alexie.

4. Near the end of the 1987 film, Dirty Dancing, Johnny Castle says, Nobody puts Baby in a corner.

5. According to Odeon Cinemas in London, The Terminator contains the most memorable line of any movie. In the film, Arnold Schwarzenegger says, I'll be back.

6. Ian Fleming's book, For Your Eyes Only, contains five short stories: From a View to a Kill, For Your Eyes Only, Quantum of Solace, Risico, and The Hildebrand Rarity.

7. After being a YouTube and Facebook sensation, Walk off the Earth released its debut album, R.E.V.O., in 2013; it included the powerful song, Red Hands, but didn't include the fun parody of Madonna's Material Girl.

8. Every time we leave Kansas on our drives to Colorado, my husband says, Toto, I've got a feeling we're not in Kansas anymore. He tries to sound like Dorothy in The Wizard of Oz, but he never succeeds.

9. Harrison Ford's characters have produced many memorable quotes. In Raiders of the Lost Ark, Indiana Jones says, It's not the years, honey. It's the mileage. In Star Wars, Hans Solo says, Look, I ain't in this for your revolution, and I'm not in it for you, Princess. I expect to be well paid. I'm in it for the money.

10. The Complete Collected Poems of Maya Angelou includes the poem, Phenomenal Woman, which celebrates being a woman, and the poem, Still I Rise, which asks the question, Does my sassiness upset you?

11. Two of the bestselling albums in 2013 were Justin Timberlake's The 20/20 Experience, and Bruno Mars's Unorthodox Jukebox, while in that same year Draft Punk's song, Get Lucky, was one of the bestselling singles.

12. My friend Taryn's favorite movie is The Princess Bride. Hello. My name is Inigo Montoya. You killed my father. Prepare to die, she says over and over every time she watches the film.

13. Jack Dawson yells, I'm the king of the world! in the movie, Titanic; this made my nine-year-old son laugh so hysterically that we were kicked out of the theater.

14. Master Yoda says, Fear is the path to the dark side. Fear leads to anger. Anger leads to hate. Hate leads to suffering. I sense much fear in you. Despite this warning to Anakin in Star Wars: Episode 1—The Phantom Menace, Anakin still turns to the dark side and ultimately becomes Darth Vader.

15. In The Hobbit: An Unexpected Journey, Gandalf says, I'm looking for someone to share in an adventure ; Bilbo Baggins initially declines the offer, but his curiosity prevails and he leaves the Shire.

Look at the comic strip below and write a full description that will enable people who have not read the comic strip to visualize it clearly and appreciate its humor. Describe the setting and action in each panel, and enclose the words of the speakers in quotation marks.

BABY BLUES © 2007 Baby Blues Partnership. Dist. by King Features Syndicate

Commas

Commas often (though not always) signal a minor break or pause in a sentence. There are six main uses of the comma. This chapter will describe each.

Six Main Uses of the Comma

Commas are used mainly as follows:

1. To separate items in a series
2. To set off introductory material
3. Before and after words that interrupt the flow of thought in a sentence
4. Before two complete thoughts connected by *and, but, for, or, nor, so, yet*
5. To set off a direct quotation from the rest of a sentence
6. For certain everyday material

You may find it helpful to remember that the comma often marks a slight pause, or break, in a sentence. Read aloud the sentence examples given for each use, and listen for the minor pauses, or breaks, that are signaled by commas.

Comma between Items in a Series

Use commas to separate items in a series.

> Do you drink tea with milk, lemon, or honey?
>
> Today the dishwasher stopped working, the garbage bag split, and the refrigerator turned into a freezer.
>
> The talk shows enraged him so much he did not know whether to laugh, cry, or throw up.
>
> Reiko awoke from a restless, nightmare-filled sleep.

a. The final comma in a series is optional, but it is often used.

b. A comma is used between two descriptive words in a series only if *and* inserted between the words sounds natural. You could say:

> Reiko awoke from a restless *and* nightmare-filled sleep.

But notice in the following sentence that the descriptive words do not sound natural when *and* is inserted between them. In such cases, no comma is used.

> Wanda drove a shiny blue Corvette. (A shiny *and* blue Corvette doesn't sound right, so no comma is used.)

Place commas between items in a series.

ACTIVITY 1

1. Caleb packed his golf clubs tees shoes and water bottle in his golf bag.
2. My favorite outfit to wear around the house is baggy sweats a cotton T-shirt and flip-flops.
3. Professor Jones lectured about global warming at the University of Washington the University of Oregon and the University of Montana.
4. Michelle loved her torn worn gardening pants.
5. Thomas swam one mile ran four miles and biked sixteen miles before 6:00 A.M.

Comma after Introductory Material

Use a comma to set off introductory material.

> After punching the alarm clock with his fist, Bill turned over and went back to sleep.
>
> Looking up at the sky, I saw a man who was flying faster than a speeding bullet.
>
> Holding a baited trap, Clyde cautiously approached the gigantic mousehole.
>
> In addition, he held a broom in his hand.
>
> Also, he wore a football helmet in case a creature should leap out at his head.

a. If the introductory material is brief, the comma is sometimes omitted. In the activities here, you should use the comma.

b. A comma is also used to set off extra material at the end of a sentence. Here are two sentences where this comma rule applies:

> A sudden breeze shot through the windows, driving the stuffiness out of the room.
>
> I love to cook and eat Italian food, especially eggplant rollatini and lasagna.

ACTIVITY 2

Working with a partner, place commas after introductory material.

1. After the Civil War my ancestor opened a grocery store in Indianapolis.

2. Feeling brave and silly at the same time Tony volunteered to go onstage and help the magician.

3. While I was eating my tuna sandwich the cats circled my chair like hungry sharks.

4. Because the Antonelli children grew up near the sea they learned to swim when they were young. Even though the water is still very cold in early March the family celebrates the first day of spring with a quick dip!

5. At first putting extra hot pepper flakes on the pizza seemed like a good idea. However I felt otherwise when flames seemed about to shoot out of my mouth.

Comma around Words Interrupting the Flow of Thought

Use commas before and after words or phrases that interrupt the flow of thought in a sentence.

My brother, a sports nut, owns over five thousand baseball cards.

That reality show, at long last, has been canceled.

The children used the old Buick, rusted from disuse, as a backyard clubhouse.

Usually you can "hear" words that interrupt the flow of thought in a sentence. However, if you are not sure that certain words are interrupters, remove them from the sentence. If it still makes sense without the words, you know that the words are interrupters and the information they give is nonessential. Such nonessential information is set off with commas. In the sentence

Dody Thompson, who lives next door, won the javelin-throwing competition.

the words *who lives next door* are extra information, not needed to identify the subject of the sentence, *Dody Thompson.* Put commas around such nonessential information. On the other hand, in the sentence

The woman who lives next door won the javelin-throwing competition.

the words *who lives next door* supply essential information—information needed for us to identify the woman being spoken of. If the words were removed from the sentence, we would no longer know who won the competition. Commas are *not* used around such essential information.

Here is another example:

Wilson Hall, which the tornado destroyed, was ninety years old.

Here the words *which the tornado destroyed* are extra information, not needed to identify the subject of the sentence, *Wilson Hall.* Commas go around such nonessential information. On the other hand, in the sentence

The building that the tornado destroyed was ninety years old.

the words *that the tornado destroyed* are needed to identify the building. Commas are *not* used around such essential information.

As noted above, however, most of the time you will be able to "hear" words that interrupt the flow of thought in a sentence, and you will not have to think about whether the words are essential or nonessential.

Use commas to set off interrupting words.

ACTIVITY 3

1. During Dan's teenage years when he lived on Long Island Dan often went crabbing in the Great South Bay.
2. Dracula who had a way with women is Tony's favorite movie hero. He feels that the Wolfman on the other hand showed no class in wooing women.
3. Driving from Minneapolis to Chicago especially during a heavy snowstorm can be unnerving.
4. Mowing the grass especially when it is six inches high is my least favorite job.
5. My cousin Lucille who is wearing the black dress with the white pearls looks very stylish this evening.

Comma between Complete Thoughts

Use a comma between two complete thoughts connected by *and, but, for, or, nor, so, yet.*

The wedding was scheduled for four o'clock, but the bride changed her mind at two.

We could always tell when our instructor felt disorganized, for his shirt would not be tucked in.

Rich has to work on Monday nights, so he always remembers to record the TV football game.

a. The comma is optional when the complete thoughts are short.

Grace has a headache and Mark has a fever.

Her soda was watery but she drank it anyway.

The day was overcast so they didn't go swimming.

b.   Be careful not to use a comma in sentences having *one* subject and a *double* verb. The comma is used only in sentences made up of two complete thoughts (two subjects and two verbs). In the following sentence, there is only one subject (*Kevin*) with a double verb (*will go* and *forget*). Therefore, no comma is needed:

> Kevin will go to a party tonight and forget all about tomorrow's exam.

Likewise, the following sentence has only one subject (*Rita*) and a double verb (*was* and *will work*); therefore, no comma is needed:

> Rita was a waitress at the Red Lobster last summer and probably will work there this summer.

ACTIVITY 4   In the following sentences, place a comma before each joining word that connects two complete thoughts (two subject-verb combinations). Do *not* place a comma within the sentences that have only one subject and a double verb; label these as "correct."

1. The oranges in the refrigerator were covered with blue mold and the potatoes in the cupboard felt like sponges.
2. All the pants in the shop were on sale but not a single pair was my size.
3. Martha often window-shops in the malls for hours and comes home without buying anything.
4. Martin Fizz never brought much money to restaurants and quite often he relied on friends to pick up his tab.
5. The whole family searched the yard inch by inch but never found Mom's missing wedding ring.
6. The mayor walked up to the podium and she delivered the most inspiring speech of her career.
7. No one volunteered to read his or her paper out loud so the instructor called on Amber.
8. The aliens in the science fiction film visited our planet in peace but we greeted them with violence.
9. I felt like shouting at the gang of boys but didn't dare open my mouth.
10. Lenny will not succeed in college or he will decide to start attending classes this semester.

Comma with Direct Quotations

Use a comma to set off a direct quotation from the rest of a sentence.

> His father shouted, "Why don't you go out and get a job?"

> "Our modern world has lost a sense of the sacredness of life," the speaker said.

"No," said Celia to Jerry. "I won't write your paper for you."

"Can anyone remember," wrote Emerson, "when the times were not hard and money not scarce?"

TIP Commas and periods at the end of a quotation go inside quotation marks. See also page 469.

Use commas to set off quotations from the rest of the sentence.

ACTIVITY 5

1. Su Lin turned to her husband and said "The man may be the head of the family, but the woman is the neck that turns the head."

2. My partner on the dance floor said "Don't be so stiff. You look as if you swallowed an umbrella."

3. The question on the anatomy test read "What human organ grows faster than any other, never stops growing, and always remains the same size?"

4. The student behind me whispered "The skin."

5. "Everyone is wise" says my eighty-year-old grandmother "until he speaks."

Comma with Everyday Material

Use a comma with certain everyday material.

Persons Spoken To

Tina, go to bed if you're not feeling well.

Sara, where did you put my shoes?

Are you coming with us, Owen?

Dates

March 4, 2007, is the day Martha buried her third husband.

Addresses

Tony's grandparents live at 183 Roxborough Avenue, Cleveland, Ohio 44112.

TIP No comma is used to mark off the zip code.

Openings and Closings of Letters

Dear Santa,

Dear Ben,

Sincerely yours,

Truly yours,

> **TIP** In formal letters, a colon is used after the opening: Dear Sir: *or* Dear Madam: *or* Dear Dr. Nathan: *or* Dear Ms. Merletto:

Numbers

The dishonest dealer turned the used car's odometer from 98,170 miles to 39,170 miles.

ACTIVITY 6

Place commas where needed. Compare your answers with a partner's.

1. I expected you to set a better example for the others Mike.

2. Liz with your help I passed the test.

3. The movie stars Kitty Litter and Dredge Rivers were married on September 12 2006 and lived at 3865 Sunset Boulevard Los Angeles California for one month.

4. They received 75000 congratulatory fan letters and were given movie contracts worth $3000000 in the first week of their marriage.

5. Kitty left Dredge on October 12 2006 and ran off with their marriage counselor.

REVIEW TEST 1

Insert commas where needed. In the space provided below each sentence, summarize briefly the rule or rules that explain the use of the comma or commas.

1. "Although men have more upper-body strength" said the lecturer "women are more resistant to fatigue."

_____

2. George and Ida sat down to watch the football game with chips salsa pretzels cheese and two frosty bottles of beer.

_____

3. Tax forms though shortened and revised every year never seem to get any simpler.

_____

4. I think Roger that you had better ask someone else for your $2500 loan.

_____

5. Sandra may decide to go to college full-time or she may start by enrolling in a couple of evening courses.

_____

6. My mother who makes the best lasagna in the world was born in Naples.

_____

7. Although I knew exactly what was happening the solar eclipse caused me to feel some anxiety.

_____

8. "Don't bend over to pet the dog" I warned "or he'll bite you."

_____

9. Upon the death of Queen Elizabeth I of England in 1603 James VI of Scotland became James I of England.

_____

10. The company agreed to raise a senior bus driver's salary to $42000 by January 1 2015.

_____

11. The bookstore specializes in science fiction biography and mysteries.

_____

12. Many people who had kidney transplants years ago needed to take immune-suppressing drugs but that has become less common because of new medical technology.

_____

REVIEW TEST 2

Insert commas where needed in the business letter on the next page. You should use a total of twelve commas.

May 15 2015

The Jumping Bean
230 North Columbus Street
Lancaster Ohio 43130

Mr. Larry Smithe
420 West Hubert Avenue
Lancaster Ohio 43130

Dear Mr. Smithe:

We would like to express our gratitude for your kind and generous donation to the City Neighborhood Improvement Fund. When your check for $1200 was received our employees were overcome with emotion. Your gift helped us reach our donation goal of $10000.

As you know the money raised will be used to improve several of our more blighted neighborhoods. Some of the projects the fund will cover are simple enhancements like painting and yard work but the balance of the funds will be used for larger projects like fixing roofs porches and sidewalks.

Our employees are looking forward to participating in this citywide project and your donation has demonstrated what a generous community we live in.

We would again like to express our gratitude.

Sincerely

Jameson Roaster
Jameson Roaster, CEO
The Jumping Bean

Other Punctuation Marks

This chapter will describe other punctuation marks including the colon, the dash, the hyphen, parentheses, and the semicolon.

Colon (:)

Use the colon at the end of a complete statement to introduce a list, a long quotation, or an explanation.

List

The following were my worst jobs: truck loader in an apple plant, assembler in a battery factory, and attendant in a state mental hospital.

Long Quotation

Thoreau explains in *Walden:* "I went to the woods because I wished to live deliberately, to front only the essential facts of life, and see if I could not learn what it had to teach, and not, when I came to die, discover that I had not lived."

Explanation

There are two softball leagues in our town: the fast-pitch league and the lob-pitch league.

Place colons where needed.

ACTIVITY 1

1. In his book, *Illiterate America,* Jonathan Kozol gives startling information "Twenty-five million American adults cannot read the poison warnings on a can of pesticide, a letter from their child's teacher, or the front page of a daily paper. An additional thirty-five million read only at a level which is less than equal to the full survival needs of our society. Together, these sixty million people represent more than one-third of the entire adult population."

2. The Girl Scout troop had a profitable cookie sale 400 boxes of Thin Mints, 350 boxes of Lemonades, and 200 boxes of Shout Outs! were sold.

3. I like to exercise, but there are three things I refuse to do run long distances, swim in a lake or ocean, or participate in a group exercise class.

Semicolon (;)

The main use of the semicolon is to mark a break between two complete thoughts, as explained on page 386. Another use of the semicolon is to mark off items in a series when the items themselves contain commas. Here are some examples:

Winning prizes at the national flower show were Roberta Collins, Alabama, azaleas; Sally Hunt, Kentucky, roses; and James Weber, California, Shasta daisies.

The following books must be read for the course: *The Color Purple,* by Alice Walker; *In Our Time,* by Ernest Hemingway; and *Man's Search for Meaning,* by Victor Frankl.

ACTIVITY 2

Working with a partner, place semicolons where needed.

1. The specials at the restaurant today are eggplant Parmesan, for $16.95 black beans and rice, for $9.95 and chicken potpie, for $11.95.

2. The view of Washington's Mount Rainier was spectacular the peak was snow covered, but the lower half was covered with green forests.

3. Lola's favorite old movies are *To Catch a Thief,* starring Cary Grant and Grace Kelly *Animal Crackers,* a Marx Brothers comedy and *The Wizard of Oz,* with Judy Garland.

Dash (—)

A dash signals a pause longer than a comma but not as complete as a period. Use a dash to set off words for dramatic effect.

I didn't go out with him a second time—once was more than enough.

Some of you—I won't mention you by name—cheated on the test.

It was so windy that the VW passed him on the highway—overhead.

> **TIP**
>
> a. The dash can be formed on a keyboard by striking the hyphen twice (--). Keyboard shortcuts for both Mac and PC users can also be used to form dashes. In handwriting, the dash is as long as two letters would be.
>
> b. Be careful not to overuse dashes.

ACTIVITY 3

Place dashes where needed.

1. The neighbors threw loud parties that lasted long into the night often, in fact, until 2:00 or 3:00 A.M.

2. Three makes of luxury cars a Lexus, a Cadillac, and a Lincoln were the prizes in the church raffle.

3. The package finally arrived badly damaged.

Hyphen (-)

1. Use a hyphen with two or more words that act as a single unit describing a noun.

   > When Jeff removed his mud-covered boots, he discovered a thumb-size hole in his sock.

   > I both admire and envy her well-rounded personality.

   > When the man removed his blue-tinted shades, Lonnell saw the spaced-out look in his eyes.

2. Use a hyphen to divide a word at the end of a line of writing. When you need to divide a word at the end of a line, divide it between syllables. Use your dictionary to be sure of correct syllable divisions (see also page 493).

   > When Josh lifted the hood of his car, he realized one of the radiator hoses had broken.

 TIP
   a.   Do not divide words of one syllable.
   b.   Do not divide a word if you can avoid doing so.

Place hyphens where needed.

ACTIVITY 4

1. A lily covered pond and a jasmine scented garden greeted us as we walked into the museum's atrium.
2. When Gwen turned on the porch light, ten legged creatures scurried every where over the crumb filled floor.
3. Will had ninety two dollars in his pocket when he left for the supermarket, and he had twenty two dollars when he got back.

Parentheses ( )

Parentheses are used to set off extra or incidental information from the rest of a sentence.

> The section of that book on the medical dangers of abortion (pages 125 to 140) is outdated.

> Yesterday at Hamburger House (my favorite place to eat), the french-fry cook asked me to go out with him.

 TIP

Do not use parentheses too often in your writing.

ACTIVITY 5

Add parentheses where needed.

1. Before Theodore Roosevelt officially named the White House in 1901, the building was known by several different names the President's Palace, President's House, the Executive Mansion.

2. President Taft 1909–1913 established many things during his term in office, including a postal savings system.

3. Franklin D. Roosevelt FDR and John F. Kennedy JFK are often referred to by their initials.

REVIEW TEST

At the appropriate spot, place the punctuation mark shown in the margin.

; 1. Gdansk is a major Polish port it is located on a branch of the Vistula River.

— 2. The Vistula River with a length of 651 miles is the largest river in Poland.

- 3. Gdansk is part of a three city urban area with a population of over 450,000.

( ) 4. The city has two ports, Nowy Port "New Port" and Port Pólnocny "North Port".

: 5. Arthur Schopenhauer, a Gdansk native and famous philosopher, wrote in *Wisdom of Life and Counsels and Maxims* "It is a wise thing to be polite; consequently, it is a stupid thing to be rude. To make enemies by unnecessary and willful incivility is just as insane a proceeding as to set your house on fire. For politeness is like a counter—an avowedly false coin, with which it is foolish to be stingy."

Word Use

CAN YOU FIND THE ERROR ON THIS CANDY HEART?

Which chapter in this section do you think might cover such an error? In a sentence or two, explain how and why this error affects the meaning of this message.

Using the Dictionary

The dictionary is a valuable tool. To help you use it, this chapter explains essential information about dictionaries and the information they provide.

Owning Your Own Dictionaries

You can benefit greatly by owning two dictionaries. First, you should own a paperback dictionary that you can carry with you. Second, you should own a desk-size, hardcover dictionary that you keep in the room where you study. Either dictionary pictured below, as well as The Merriam-Webster Dictionary, would be an excellent choice. They are all available in both hardcover and paperfack format.

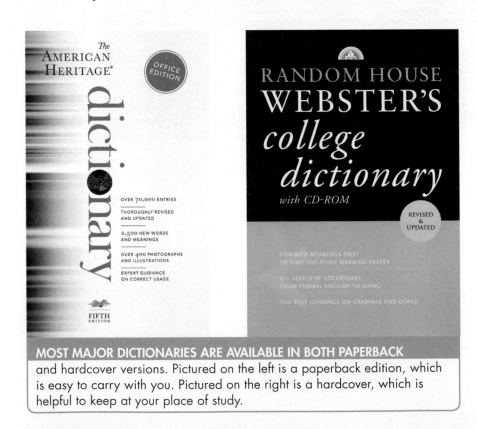

MOST MAJOR DICTIONARIES ARE AVAILABLE IN BOTH PAPERBACK and hardcover versions. Pictured on the left is a paperback edition, which is easy to carry with you. Pictured on the right is a hardcover, which is helpful to keep at your place of study.

Hardbound dictionaries contain a good deal more information than the paperback editions. For instance, a desk-size dictionary defines far more words than a paperback dictionary. And there are more definitions per word, as well. Although desk-size dictionaries cost more, they are worth the investment, because they are valuable study aids.

Dictionaries are often updated to reflect changes that occur in the language. New words come into use, and old words take on new meanings. So you should not use a dictionary that has been lying around the house for a number of years. Instead, buy yourself a new dictionary. It is easily among the best investments you will ever make.

Dictionaries on Your Computer

If you use a computer, you will likely have two additional ways to look up a word: online dictionaries and a dictionary that may come with your computer software.

Online Dictionaries

When a computer is connected to the Internet, it is easy to check words online. Here are three sites with online dictionaries:

www.merriam-webster.com

www.dictionary.com

www.oxforddictionaries.com/us

For example, if you go online to www.merriam-webster.com and type in "benefit," you may see the page shown below.

By permission from Merriam-Webster's Collegiate® Dictionary, 11th edition.© 2013 by Merriam-Webster, Inc. (www.Merriam-Webster.com)

COMPARE THIS ENTRY FROM AN ONLINE DICTIONARY TO the entry for the same word as it appears in a print dictionary (next page). What differences do you notice?

Notice the speaker icon next to the word *benefit*. If you click on this icon, the word will be pronounced for you.

Often, you will also get information on *synonyms* (words with meanings similar to those of the word you have looked up) and *antonyms* (words with meanings opposite to those of the word you have looked up).

Software Dictionaries

Many word-processing programs come with a built-in dictionary. For example, if you use Microsoft Word on a Macintosh, click "Tools" and then choose "Dictionary."

Understanding a Dictionary Entry

Look at the information provided for the word *benefit* in the following entry from *Random House Webster's College Dictionary:*

Spelling and syllabication

Pronunciation

Parts of speech

ben•e•fit (ben′ə fit), *n.* **1.** something that is advantageous or good. **2.** a payment made to help someone or given by a benefit society, insurance company, or public agency. **3.** a social event or a performance for raising money for an organization, cause, or person. **4.** *Archaic.* an act of kindness. —*v t.* **5.** to do good to: be of service to: *a health program to benefit everyone.* —*v.i.* **6.** to derive benefit; profit: *to benefit from experience.* —*idiom.* **7. benefit of the doubt,** a favorable opinion or judgment adopted despite uncertainty. [*1350–1400; late ME benefytt,* ME *b(i)enfet* < AF *benfet,* MF *bienfatt* < L *benefactum,* orig. ptp. of *benefacere;* see BENEFACTION] —Syn. See ADVANTAGE

Meanings

Random House Webster's College Dictionary, 2005. Published by Random House Reference.

Spelling

The first bit of information, in the boldface (heavy-type) entry itself, is the spelling of *benefit.* You probably already know the spelling of *benefit,* but if you didn't, you could find it by pronouncing the syllables in the word carefully and then looking it up in the dictionary.

ACTIVITY 1

Use your dictionary to correct the spelling of the following words:

compatable _____   silable _____

althogh _____   troble _____

highschool _____   untill _____

embelish _____	fancyer _____
systimatise _____	prepostrous _____
alot _____	comotion _____
attenshun _____	Vasaline _____
wierd _____	fatel _____
laffed _____	busines _____
alright _____	jenocide _____
fony _____	poluted _____
kriterion _____	attornies _____
hetirosexual _____	chalange _____

Syllabication

The second bit of information that the dictionary gives, also in the boldface entry, is the syllabication of *benefit*. Note that a dot separates each of the syllables.

Use your dictionary to mark the syllable divisions in the following words. Also indicate how many syllables are in each word.

j i t t e r	(_____ syllables)
m o t i v a t e	(_____ syllables)
o r a n g u t a n	(_____ syllables)
i n c o n t r o v e r t i b l e	(_____ syllables)

Noting syllable divisions will enable you to *hyphenate* a word: divide it at the end of one line of writing and complete it at the beginning of the next line. You can correctly hyphenate a word only at a syllable division, and you may have to check your dictionary to make sure of the syllable divisions.

Pronunciation

The third bit of information in the dictionary entry is the pronunciation of *benefit*: (ben′ə fit). You already know how to pronounce *benefit,* but if you didn't, the information within the parentheses would serve as your guide. Use your dictionary to complete the following exercises that relate to pronunciation.

Vowel Sounds

You will probably use the pronunciation key in your dictionary mainly as a guide to pronouncing vowel sounds (vowels are the letters *a, e, i, o,* and *u*). Following is a part of the pronunciation key in the *Random House Webster's College Dictionary:*

a bat   ā say   e set   ē bee   i big

The key tells you, for example, that the sound of the short *a* is like the *a* in *bat,* the sound of the long *a* is like the *a* in *say,* and the sound of the short *e* is like the *e* in *set.*

Now look at the pronunciation key in your own dictionary. The key is probably located in the front of the dictionary or at the bottom of alternate pages. What common word in the key tells you how to pronounce each of the following sounds?

ī _____   ŭ _____

ŏ _____   oŏ _____

ō _____   oō _____

(Note that a long vowel always has the sound of its own name.)

The Schwa (ə)

The symbol ə looks like an upside-down *e.* It is called a *schwa,* and it stands for the unaccented sound in such words as *ago, item, easily, gallop,* and *circus.* More approximately, it stands for the sound *uh*—like the *uh* that speakers sometimes make when they hesitate. Perhaps it would help to remember that *uh,* as well as ə, could be used to represent the schwa sound.

Here are some of the many words in which the schwa sound appears: *imitation (im-uh-tā' shuhn* or *im-ə-tā' shən); elevate (el' uh-vāt* or *el' ə-vāt); horizon (huh-rī' zuhn* or *hə-rī' zən).* Open your dictionary to any page, and you will almost surely be able to find three words that make use of the schwa in the pronunciation in parentheses after the main entry.

In the spaces below, write three words that make use of the schwa, and their pronunciations.

1. _____   (_____)
2. _____   (_____)
3. _____   (_____)

Accent Marks

Some words contain both a primary accent, shown by a heavy stroke ('), and a secondary accent, shown by a lighter stroke ('). For example, in the word *controversy (kon' trə vûr' se),* the stress, or accent, goes chiefly on the first syllable *(kon'),* and, to a lesser extent, on the third syllable *(vûr').*

Use your dictionary to add stress marks to the following words:

preclude (pri klood)

atrophy (at rə f ē)

inveigle (in vā gəl)

ubiquitous (yoo bik wi təs)

prognosticate (prog nos ti kāt)

Full Pronunciation

Use your dictionary to write the full pronunciation (the information given in parentheses) for each of the following words.

1. migration _____   11. combustible _____

2. diatribe _____   12. antipathy _____

3. inheritance _____   13. capricious _____

4. panacea _____   14. schizophrenia _____

5. esophagus _____   15. seismological _____

6. independence _____   16. internecine _____

7. chronological _____   17. amalgamate _____

8. vicarious _____   18. quixotic _____

9. quiescent _____   19. laissez-faire _____

10. parsimony _____

20. antidisestablishmentarianism (This word is probably not in a paperback dictionary, but if you can say *establish* and if you break the rest of the word into individual syllables, you should be able to pronounce it.)

_____

Now practice pronouncing each word. Use the pronunciation key in your dictionary as an aid to sounding out each syllable. Do *not* try to pronounce a word all at once; instead, work on mastering *one syllable at a time*. When you can pronounce each of the syllables in a word successfully, then say them in sequence, add the accents, and pronounce the entire word.

Parts of Speech

The next bit of information that the dictionary gives about *benefit* is *n*. This abbreviation means that the meanings of *benefit* as a noun will follow.

Use your dictionary if necessary to fill in the meanings of the following abbreviations:

    v. = _____   sing. = _____

    adj. = _____   pl. = _____

Principal Parts of Irregular Verbs

Benefit is a regular verb and forms its principal parts by adding *-ed* or *-ing* to the stem of the verb. When a verb is irregular, the dictionary lists its principal parts. For example, with *give* the present tense comes first (the entry itself, *give*).

Next comes the past tense (*gave*), and then the past participle (*given*)—the form of the verb used with such helping words as *have, had,* and *was.* Then comes the present participle (*giving*)—the *-ing* form of the verb.

Look up the principal parts of the following irregular verbs and write them in the spaces provided. The first one has been done for you.

Present	Past	Past Participle	Present Participle
tear	*tore*	*torn*	*tearing*
go	_____	_____	_____
know	_____	_____	_____
steal	_____	_____	_____

Plural Forms of Irregular Nouns

The dictionary supplies the plural forms of all irregular nouns. (Regular nouns like *benefit* form the plural by adding *-s* or *-es.*) Give the plurals of the following nouns. If two forms are shown, write down both.

analysis _____

dictionary _____

criterion _____

activity _____

thesis _____

Meanings

When a word has more than one meaning, the meanings are numbered in the dictionary, as with the word *benefit.* In many dictionaries, the most common meanings of a word are presented first. The introductory pages of your dictionary will explain the order in which meanings are presented.

ACTIVITY 3 Use the sentence context to try to explain the meaning of the underlined word in each of the following sentences. Write your definition in the space provided. Then look up and record the dictionary meaning of the word. Be sure to select the meaning that fits the word as it is used in the sentence.

1. In anthropology class, we studied the <u>indigenous</u> people of New Guinea.

   Your definition: _____

   Dictionary definition: _____

2. On the test, we had to put several historical events into <u>chronological</u> order.

   Your definition: _____

   Dictionary definition: _____

3. The FBI <u>squelched</u> the terrorists' plan to plant a bomb in the White House.

   Your definition: _____

   Dictionary definition: _____

4. One of the <u>cardinal</u> rules in our house was "Respect other people's privacy."

   Your definition: _____

   Dictionary definition: _____

5. A special <u>governor</u> prevents the school bus from traveling more than fifty-five miles an hour.

   Your definition: _____

   Dictionary definition: _____

Usage Labels

As a general rule, use only standard English words in your writing. If a word is not standard English, your dictionary will probably give it a usage label like one of the following: *informal, nonstandard, slang, vulgar, obsolete, archaic, rare.*

Look up the following words and record how your dictionary labels them. Remember that a recent hardbound desk dictionary will always be the best source of information about usage.

flunk _____

tough (meaning "unfortunate, too bad") _____

creep (meaning "an annoying person") _____

ain't _____

scam _____

Synonyms

A *synonym* is a word that is close in meaning to another word. Using synonyms helps you avoid unnecessary repetition of the same word in a paper. A paperback dictionary is not likely to give you synonyms for words, but a good desk dictionary or an online dictionary will. You might also want to own a *thesaurus,* a book that lists synonyms and *antonyms* (words approximately opposite in meaning to another word). You can also find a thesaurus online—for example, www .merriam-webster.com will give you access to a thesaurus as well as a dictionary.

Consult a desk dictionary that gives synonyms for the following words, and write the synonyms in the spaces provided.

heavy _____

escape _____

necessary _____

Improving Spelling

Poor spelling often results from bad habits developed in early school years. With work, you can correct such habits. If you can write your name without misspelling it, there is no reason why you can't do the same with almost any word in the English language. Following are six steps you can take to improve your spelling.

Step 1: Use the Dictionary

Get into the habit of using the dictionary (see pages 490–498). When you write a paper, allow yourself time to look up the spelling of all those words you are unsure about. Do not overlook the value of this step just because it is such a simple one. By using the dictionary, you can probably make yourself a 95 percent better speller.

Step 2: Keep a Personal Spelling List

Keep a list of words you misspell, and study these words regularly. To do this, create a chart with the headings "Incorrect Spelling," "Correct Spelling," and "Points to Remember." You can do this in a notebook or a computer file. This chart will become a personal spelling list that you can consult regularly.

To master the words on your list, do the following:

1. Write down any hint that will help you remember the spelling of a word. For example, you might want to note that *occasion* is spelled with two *c*'s and one *s,* or that *all right* is two words, not one word.

2. Study a word by looking at it, saying it, and spelling it. You may also want to write out the word one or more times, or "air-write" it with your finger in large, exaggerated motions.

3. When you have trouble spelling a long word, try to break the word into syllables and see whether you can spell each syllable. For example, *inadvertent* can be spelled easily if you can hear and spell in turn its four syllables: *in ad ver tent.* And *consternation* can be spelled easily if you hear and spell in

turn its four syllables: *con ster na tion*. Remember, then: Try to see, hear, and spell long words syllable by syllable.

4. Keep in mind that review and repeated self-testing are the keys to effective learning. When you are learning a series of words, go back after studying each new word and review all the preceding ones.

Step 3: Master Commonly Confused Words

Master the meanings and spellings of the commonly confused words on pages 511–520. Your instructor may assign twenty words at a time for you to study and may give you a series of quizzes until you have mastered the words.

Step 4: Use a Computer's Spell-Checker

Most word-processing programs feature a spell-checker that will identify incorrect words and suggest correct spellings. If you are unsure how to use yours, consult the program's "help" function. Spell-checkers are not foolproof; they will, for example, fail to catch misused homonyms like the words *your* and *you're*.

Step 5: Understand Basic Spelling Rules

Explained briefly here are three rules that may improve your spelling. While exceptions sometimes occur, the rules hold true most of the time.

Rule 1: Changing y to i

When a word ends in a consonant plus *y*, change *y* to *i* when you add an ending (but keep the y before *-ing*).

try + ed = tried	easy + er = easier
defy + es = defies	carry + ed = carried
ready + ness = readiness	penny + less = penniless

Rule 2: Final Silent e

Drop a final *e* before an ending that starts with a vowel (the vowels are *a, e, i, o,* and *u*).

create + ive = creative	believe + able = believable
nerve + ous = nervous	share + ing = sharing

Keep the final *e* before an ending that starts with a consonant.

extreme + ly = extremely	life + less = lifeless
hope + ful = hopeful	excite + ment = excitement

Rule 3: Doubling a Final Consonant

Double the final consonant of a word when all three of the following are true:

a. The word is one syllable or is accented on the last syllable.

b. The word ends in a single consonant preceded by a single vowel.

c. The ending you are adding starts with a vowel.

shop + er = shopper	thin + est = thinnest
equip + ed = equipped	submit + ed = submitted
swim + ing = swimming	drag + ed = dragged

Working with a partner, combine the following words and endings by applying the three rules above.

ACTIVITY 1

1. worry + ed = _____

2. write + ing = _____

3. marry + es = _____

4. run + ing = _____

5. terrify + ed = _____

6. dry + es = _____

7. forget + ing = _____

8. care + ful = _____

9. control + ed = _____

10. debate + able = _____

Step 6: Study a Basic Word List

Study the spellings of the words in the list on pages 502–507. They are five hundred of the words most often used in English. Your instructor may assign twenty-five or fifty words for you to study at a time and give you a series of quizzes until you have mastered the list.

Five Hundred Basic Words

ability	approve	breast
absent	argue	breathe
accept	around	brilliant
accident	arrange	brother
ache	attempt	building
across	attention	bulletin
address	August	bureau
advertise	automobile	business
advice	autumn	came
after	avenue	can't
again	awful	careful 75
against	awkward	careless
agree	back	cereal
all right	balance	certain
almost	bargain	chair
a lot	beautiful	change
already	because	charity
also	become 50	cheap
although	been	cheat
always	before	cheek
amateur	begin	chicken
American	being	chief
among	believe	children
amount	between	choose
angry 25	bicycle	church
animal	black	cigarette
another	blue	citizen
answer	board	city
anxious	borrow	close
appetite	bottle	clothing
apply	bottom	coffee
approach	brake	collect

continued

Five Hundred Basic Words (*continued*)

college	doubt	foreign
color	down	forty
come	dozen	forward
comfortable **100**	during	found
company	each	fourteen
condition	early	Friday
conversation	earth	friend
copy	easy	from
daily	education	gallon
danger	eight	garden
daughter	either	general
daybreak	empty	get
dear	English	good
death	enough	grammar
December	entrance	great **175**
decide	evening	grocery
deed	everything	grow
dentist	examine	guess
deposit	except	half
describe	exercise	hammer
did	exit	hand
died	expect **150**	handkerchief
different	fact	happy
dinner	factory	having
direction	family	head
discover	far	heard
disease	February	heavy
distance	few	high
doctor **125**	fifteen	himself
does	fight	hoarse
dollar	flower	holiday
don't	forehead	home

continued

Five Hundred Basic Words (*continued*)

hospital	lesson	**225**	mountain
house	letter		mouth
however	life		much
hundred	light		must
hungry	listen		nail
husband	little		near
instead	loaf		needle
intelligence **200**	loneliness		neither
interest	long		never
interfere	lose		newspaper
interrupt	made		nickel
into	making		niece
iron	many		night
itself	March		ninety
January	marry		noise
July	match		none
June	matter		not
just	may		nothing
kindergarten	measure		November **275**
kitchen	medicine		now
knock	men		number
knowledge	middle		ocean
labor	might		o'clock
laid	million		October
language	minute		offer
last	mistake **250**		often
laugh	Monday		old
learn	money		omit
led	month		once
left	more		one
leisure	morning		only
length	mother		operate

continued

Five Hundred Basic Words (*continued*)

opinion		pretty		sandwich	
opportunity		probably		Saturday	
optimist		promise		say	
original		psychology		school	
ought		public	325	scissors	
ounce		pursue		season	
overcoat		put		see	
pain		quart		sentence	
paper		quarter		September	
part		quick		service	
peace		quiet		seventeen	
pear	300	quit		several	
pencil		quite		shoes	
penny		quiz		should	
people		raise		sight	
perfect		read		since	
period		ready		sister	
person		really		sixteenth	
picture		reason		sleep	
piece		receive		smoke	
pillow		recognize		soap	
place		refer		soldier	
plain		religion		something	375
please		remember		sometimes	
pocket		repeat		soul	
policeman		resource		soup	
possible		restaurant		south	
post office		ribbon		stamp	
potato		ridiculous		state	
power		right	350	still	
prescription		said		stockings	
president		same		straight	

continued

Five Hundred Basic Words (*continued*)

street	thread	view
strong	three	villain 450
student	through	visitor
studying	Thursday	voice
such	ticket	vote
suffer	time	wage
sugar	tired	wagon
suit	today	waist
summer	together 425	wait
Sunday	tomorrow	wake
supper	tongue	walk
sure	tonight	warm
sweet	touch	warning
take	toward	Washington
teach	travel	watch
tear 400	trouble	water
telegram	trousers	wear
telephone	truly	weather
tenant	twelve	Wednesday
tenth	uncle	week
than	under	weigh
Thanksgiving	understand	welcome
that	United States	well
theater	until	went
them	upon	were
there	used	what
they	usual	whether 475
thing	valley	which
thirteen	value	while
this	variety	white
though	vegetable	whole
thousand	very	whose

continued

Five Hundred Basic Words (*continued*)

wife	work	year
window	world	yesterday
winter	worth	yet
without	would	young
woman	writing	your
wonder	written	you're **500**
won't	wrong	

TIP Two spelling mistakes that students often make are to write *a lot* as one word (*alot*) and to write *all right* as one word (*alright*). Do not write either *a lot* or *all right* as one word.

Vocabulary Development

A good vocabulary is a vital part of effective communication. A command of many words will make you a better writer, speaker, listener, and reader. Studies have shown that students with a strong vocabulary, and students who work to improve a limited vocabulary, are more successful in school. And one research study found that *a good vocabulary, more than any other factor, was common to people enjoying successful careers.* This section describes three ways of developing your word power: (1) regular reading, (2) vocabulary wordsheets, and (3) vocabulary study books. You should keep in mind from the start, however, that none of the approaches will help unless you truly decide that vocabulary development is an important goal. Only when you have this attitude can you begin doing the sustained work needed to improve your word power.

Regular Reading

Through reading a good deal, you will learn words by encountering them a number of times in a variety of sentences. Repeated exposure to a word in context will eventually make it a part of your working language.

You should develop the habit of reading a daily newspaper, one or more weekly magazines, and monthly magazines suited to your interests. In addition, you should try to read some books for pleasure. This may be especially difficult at times when you also have textbook reading to do. Try, however, to redirect a regular half hour to one hour of your recreational time to reading books. Doing so, you may eventually reap the rewards of an improved vocabulary *and* discover that reading can be truly enjoyable. You might want to check with your instructor for recommendations about lists of classics, modern classics, and well-regarded books in different genres. Such lists are also available online.

Vocabulary Wordsheets

Vocabulary wordsheets are another means of vocabulary development. Whenever you read, you should mark off words that you want to learn. After you have accumulated a number of words, sit down with a dictionary and look up basic information about each of them. Put this information on a wordsheet like the one shown in Activity 1. Be sure also to write down a sentence in which each word appears. A word is always best learned not in a vacuum but in the context of surrounding words.

Study each word as follows. To begin with, make sure you can correctly pronounce the word and its derivations. (Pages 493–495 explain the dictionary pronunciation key that will help you pronounce each word properly.) Next, study the main meanings of the word until you can say them without looking at them. Finally, spend a moment looking at the example of the word in context. Follow the same process with the second word. Then, after testing yourself on the first and the second words, go on to the third word. After you learn each new word, remember to continue to test yourself on all the words you have studied. Repeated self-testing is a key to effective learning.

ACTIVITY 1

In your reading, locate four words that you would like to master. Using the completed example as a model, enter your words in the spaces on the vocabulary wordsheet on page 510 and fill in all the needed information. Your instructor may then check your wordsheet and perhaps give you a quick oral quiz on selected words.

You may receive a standing assignment to add several words a week to a wordsheet and to study the words. Note that you can create your own wordsheets using a notebook or a computer file, or your instructor may give you copies of the wordsheet that appears on the next page.

Vocabulary Wordsheet

Word: _____ *formidable* _____ Pronunciation: _____ *(fôr′ mi də bəl)*

Meanings: _____ *1. feared or dreaded*

_____ *2. extremely difficult*

Other forms of the word: _____ *formidably formidability*

Use of the word in context: _____ *Several formidable obstacles stand*

between Matt and his goal.

Vocabulary Wordsheet

1. Word:_____Pronunciation:_____

    Meanings: _____

    _____

    Other forms of the word: _____

    Use of the word in context: _____

2. Word: _____ Pronunciation: _____

    Meanings: _____

    _____

    Other forms of the word: _____

    Use of the word in context: _____

    _____

3. Word: _____ Pronunciation: _____

    Meanings: _____

    _____

    Other forms of the word: _____

    Use of the word in context: _____

    _____

4. Word: _____ Pronunciation: _____

    Meanings: _____

    _____

    Other forms of the word: _____

    Use of the word in context: _____

    _____

Vocabulary Study Books

A third way to increase your word power is to use vocabulary study books. Many vocabulary books and programs are available. The best are those that present words in one or more contexts and then provide several reinforcement activities for each word. These books will help you increase your vocabulary if you work with them on a regular basis.

Commonly Confused Words

> This chapter will list homonyms and other commonly confused words and provide activities to help you learn to distinguish them.

Homonyms

The commonly confused words on the following pages have the same sounds but different meanings and spellings; such words are known as *homonyms*. Complete the activity for each set of homonyms, and check off and study the words that give you trouble. You may want to work in groups of two or three.

all ready completely prepared
already previously; before

> We were *all ready* to start the play, but the audience was still being seated.
> I have *already* bought the tickets.

Fill in the blanks: I am _____ for the economics examination because

I have _____ studied the chapter three times.

brake stop; the stopping device in a vehicle
break come apart

> His car bumper has a sticker reading, "I *brake* for animals."
> "I am going to *break* up with Evan if he keeps seeing other women," said Elise.

Fill in the blanks: When my car's emergency _____ slipped, the car rolled back and demolished my neighbor's rose garden, which caused a

_____ in our good relations with each other.

coarse rough
course part of a meal; a school subject; direction; certainly (as in *of course*).

> By the time the waitress served the customers the second *course* of the meal, she was aware of their *coarse* eating habits.

Fill in the blanks: Ted felt that the health instructor's humor was too _____ for his taste and was glad when he finished the _____.

hear　perceive with the ear
here　in this place

> "The salespeople act as though they don't see or *hear* me, even though I've been standing *here* for fifteen minutes," the woman complained.

Fill in the blanks: "Did you _____ about the distinguished visitor who just came into town and is staying _____ at this very hotel?"

hole　an empty spot
whole　entire

> "I can't believe I ate the *whole* pizza," moaned Ralph. "I think it's going to make a *hole* in my stomach lining."

Fill in the blanks: The _____ time I was at the party I tried to conceal the _____ I had in my pants.

its　belonging to it
it's　shortened form of *it is* or *it has*

> The car blew *its* transmission (the transmission belonging to it, the car).
> *It's* (it has) been raining all week and *it's* (it is) raining now.

Fill in the blanks: _____ hot and unsanitary in the restaurant kitchen I work in, and I don't think the restaurant deserves _____ good reputation.

knew　past form of *know*
new　not old

> "I had *new* wallpaper put up," said Amelia.
> "I *knew* there was some reason the place looked better," said Charlie.

Fill in the blanks: Lola _____ that getting her hair cut would give her face a _____ look.

know　to understand
no　a negative

> "I don't *know* why my dog Fang likes to attack certain people," said Phoebe.
> "There's *no* one thing the people have in common."

Fill in the blanks: I _____ of _____ way to tell whether that politician is honest or not.

pair   set of two
pear   fruit

"What a great *pair* of legs Dustin has," said Olivia to Vonnie. Dustin didn't hear her, for he was feeling very sick after munching on a green *pear.*

Fill in the blanks: In his lunch box was a _____ of _____ s.

passed   went by; succeeded in; handed to
past   time before the present; beyond, as in "We worked past closing time."

Someone *passed* him a wine bottle; it was the way he chose to forget his unhappy *past.*

Fill in the blanks: I walked _____ the instructor's office but was afraid to ask her whether or not I had _____ the test.

peace   calm
piece   part

Nations often risk world *peace* by fighting over a *piece* of land.

Fill in the blanks: Natalie did not have any _____ until she gave her dog a _____ of meat loaf.

plain   simple
plane   aircraft

The movie star dressed in *plain* clothes and wore no makeup so she would not stand out on the *plane.*

Fill in the blanks: The game-show contestant opened the small box wrapped in _____ brown paper and found inside the keys to his own jet _____.

principal main; a person in charge of a school
principle law, standard, or rule

Tim's high school *principal* had one *principal* problem: Tim. This was because there were only two *principles* in Tim's life: rest and relaxation.

Fill in the blanks: The _____ reason she dropped out of school was that she believed in the _____ of complete freedom of choice.

TIP It might help to remember that the *e* in *principle* is also in *rule*—the meaning of *principle*.

right   correct; opposite of *left*
write   put words on paper

If you have the *right* course card, I'll *write* your name on the class roster.

Fill in the blanks: Drew thinks I'm weird because I _____ with both

my _____ and my left hands.

than   used in comparisons
then   at that time

When we were kids, my friend Kathryn had prettier clothes *than* I did. I really envied her *then.*

Fill in the blanks: Rachael thought she was better _____ the rest of us,

but _____ she got the lowest grade on the history test.

TIP It might help to remember that *then* (with an **e**) is also a tim**e** signal.

their   belonging to them
there   at that place; neutral word used with verbs like *is, are, was, were, have,*
         and *had*
they're shortened form of *they are*

Two people own that van over *there* (at that place). *They're* (they are) going to move out of *their* apartment (the apartment belonging to them) and into the van, in order to save money.

Fill in the blanks: _____ not going to invite us to _____ table

because _____ is no room for us to sit down.

threw   past form of *throw*
through from one side to the other; finished

The fans *threw* so much litter onto the field that the teams could not go *through* with the game.

Fill in the blanks: When Mr. Jefferson was _____ screaming about the

violence on television, he _____ the newspaper at his dog.

to   verb part, as in *to smile;* toward, as in "I'm going *to* heaven"

too   overly, as in "The pizza was *too* hot"; also, as in "The coffee was hot, *too.*"

two   the number 2

> Tony drove *to* the park *to* be alone with Cassie. (The first *to* means "toward"; the second *to* is a verb part that goes with *be.*)

> Tony's shirt is *too* tight, *too.* (The first *too* means "overly"; the second *too* means "also.")

> You need *two* hands (2 hands) to handle a Whopper.

Fill in the blanks: _____ times tonight, you have been _____ ready _____ make assumptions without asking questions first.

wear   to have on

where   in what place

> Sean wanted to *wear* his light pants on the hot day, but he didn't know *where* he had put them.

Fill in the blanks: Exactly _____ on my leg should I _____ this elastic bandage?

weather   atmospheric conditions

whether   if it happens that; in case; if

> Some people go on vacations *whether* or not the *weather* is good.

Fill in the blanks: I always ask Ryan _____ or not we're going to have a storm, for his bad knee can feel rainy _____ approaching.

whose   belonging to whom

who's   shortened form of *who is* and *who has*

> *Who's* the instructor *whose* students are complaining?

Fill in the blanks: _____ the guy _____ car I saw you in?

your   belonging to you

you're   shortened form of *you are*

> *You're* (meaning "you are") not going to the fair unless *your* brother (the brother belonging to you) goes with you.

Fill in the blanks: _____ going to have to put aside individual differences and play together for the sake of _____ team.

Other Words Frequently Confused

Following is a list of other words that people frequently confuse. Working in groups of two or three, complete the activities for each set of words, and check off and study the words that give you trouble.

a, an   Both *a* and *an* are used before other words to mean, approximately, "one."

Generally you should use *an* before words starting with a vowel (*a, e, i, o, u*):

    an ache   an experiment   an elephant   an idiot   an ox

Generally you should use *a* before words starting with a consonant (all other letters):

    a Coke   a brain   a cheat   a television   a gambler

Fill in the blanks: The women had _____ argument over _____ former boyfriend.

accept (ăk sĕpt′)   receive; agree to
except (ĕk sĕpt′)   exclude; but

    "I would *accept* your loan," said Liam to the bartender, "*except* that I'm not ready to pay 25 percent interest."

Fill in the blanks: _____ for the fact that she can't _____ any criticism, Lori is a good friend.

advice (ăd vīs′)   noun meaning "an opinion"
advise (ăd vīz′)   verb meaning "to counsel, to give advice"

    I *advise* you to take the *advice* of your friends and stop working so hard.

Fill in the blanks: I _____ you to listen carefully to any _____ you get from your boss.

affect (uh fĕkt′)   verb meaning "to influence"
effect (i fĕkt′)   verb meaning "to bring about something"; noun meaning "result"

    The full *effects* of marijuana and alcohol on the body are only partly known; however, both drugs clearly *affect* the brain in various ways.

Fill in the blanks: The new tax laws go into _____ next month, and they are going to _____ your income tax deductions.

among   implies three or more
between   implies only two

We had to choose from *among* fifty shades of paint but *between* only two fabrics.

Fill in the blanks: The layoff notices distributed _____ the unhappy workers gave them a choice _____ working for another month at full pay and leaving immediately with two weeks' pay.

beside   along the side of
besides   in addition to

I was lucky I wasn't standing *beside* the car when it was hit.

Besides being unattractive, these uniforms are impractical.

Fill in the blanks: _____ the alarm system hooked up to the door, our neighbors keep a gun _____ their beds.

collage (kō läzh′)   an artistic composition of materials and objects pasted over a surface
college (kŏl′ ĭj)   an educational institution providing higher education

The artist made a *collage* of pictures from an old magazine.

The student studied art history in *college.*

Fill in the blanks: After I graduated from _____ and moved to a new city, I created a _____ of photos on my computer desktop to remember all the friends I had made.

defiantly   to boldly challenge or resist
definitely   unquestionably, free of uncertainty

The toddler *defiantly* screamed as his mother took away the toy.

She was *definitely* taller than her brother.

Fill in the blanks: I _____ remember how upset my mother was the first time my brother _____ refused to eat his dinner.

desert (dĕz′ ərt)   stretch of dry land; (di zûrt′) to abandon one's post or duty
dessert (dĭ zûrt′)   last part of a meal

Sweltering in the *desert,* I was tormented by the thought of an icy *dessert.*

Fill in the blanks: After their meal, Gabriel and Candice carried their _____ into the living room so that they would not miss the start of the old _____ movie about Lawrence of Arabia.

fewer   used with things that can be counted
less   refers to amount, value, or degree

There were *fewer* than seven people in all my classes today.

I seem to feel *less* tired when I exercise regularly.

Fill in the blanks: With _____ people able to stay home with children, to-day's families spend _____ time together than in the past.

loose (lōōs)   not fastened; not tight-fitting
lose (lōōz)   misplace; fail to win

Phil's belt is so *loose* that he always looks ready to *lose* his pants.

Fill in the blanks: At least once a week our neighbors _____ their dog; it's because they let him run _____.

quiet (kwī'ĭt)   peaceful
quite (kwīt)   entirely; really; rather

After a busy day, the children are now *quiet,* and their parents are *quite* tired.

Fill in the blanks: The _____ halls of the church become _____ lively during square-dance evenings.

though (thō)   despite the fact that
thought (thôt) past form of *think*

Even *though* she worked, she *thought* she would have time to go to school.

Fill in the blanks: Yoshiko _____ she would like the job, but even _____ the pay was good, she hated the traveling involved.

ACTIVITY 1   These sentences check your understanding of *its, it's; there, their, they're; to, too, two;* and *your, you're.* Underline the two incorrect spellings in each sentence. Then spell the words correctly in the spaces provided.

_____ 1. There still complaining about the weather even though its sunny and warm.

_____ 2. The dog ate it's bone while too other dogs watched.

_____ 3. Although I told them not to park by the tree, there car is parked
_____   their.

_____ 4. "Your going to be late," said his mother. "The carpool is not
_____   going too wait for you."

_____ 5. Since your the fastest runner on the team, you're going two run the anchor leg.

_____ 6. Your clothes are to wild for me, but I think their perfect for you.

_____ 7. Their were to things I needed to buy at the store, but I forgot both.

_____ 8. You're aunt has a very nice house, but she has two many pillows on her furniture, and I couldn't even sit down!

_____ 9. John and Sarah spent to much money on there wedding, but their honeymoon was a free gift.

_____10. It's to late to return their car since I wrecked it this afternoon and _____ its totaled!

REVIEW TEST 1

Underline the correct word in the parentheses. Don't try to guess. If necessary, look back at the explanations of the words.

1. At the beginning of the year, the school's (principal, principle) announced that all students would be required to take a personal finance class before they could graduate—(weather, whether) or not they planned to go to (college, collage).

2. He said (two, too) many students were overspending and getting themselves into a financial (whole, hole) before they were twenty-one.

3. Those who had already taken the class (knew, new) the teacher was going to provide a very helpful method for students to learn how to manage (their, they're) finances.

4. Instead of taking a lecture-based approach, this teacher taught (threw, through) hands-on learning, as she believed this type of direct experience would make (quiet, quite) an impact.

5. By the second month of school, the class had (all ready, already) had an (affect, effect) on many students.

6. Students who used to (wear, where) new clothes every day began purchasing (less, fewer) new items.

7. In fact, one student who used to purchase a new (pair, pear) of shoes every month, decided he (definitely, defiantly) didn't need to buy so many new shoes.

8. Another student realized that (its, it's) easier to save money (than, then) she originally believed, (though, thought) she still likes to buy a new (peace, piece) of jewelry every once in a while.

9. The (advice, advise) offered in the course wound up helping many students (break, brake) their bad spending habits.

10. The principal expressed the hope that everyone who (passed, past) the (coarse, course) would now (no, know) how to manage a budget and avoid getting into debt.

REVIEW TEST 2

On a separate paper, write short sentences using the ten words shown below.

dessert	principal
its	affect
you're	past
too	through
than	knew

Effective Word Choice

Choose your words carefully when you write. Always take the time to think about your word choices rather than simply using the first word that comes to mind. You want to develop the habit of selecting words that are appropriate and exact for your purposes. One way you can show sensitivity to language is by avoiding slang, clichés, and pretentious words.

Slang

We often use slang expressions when we talk because they are so vivid and colorful. However, slang is usually out of place in formal writing. Here are some examples of slang expressions:

- Rick spent all Saturday *messing around* with his car's sound system.
- My boss keeps *gettin' on my case* for coming to work late.
- Ruth needs a *triple* from Starbucks if she plans to *pull an all-nighter*.
- My sister knows how to *dish it out*, but I can *throw* some *'tude*, too.

Slang expressions have a number of drawbacks: They go out of date quickly, they become tiresome if used excessively in writing, and they may communicate clearly to some readers but not to others. Also, the use of slang can be a way of evading the specific details that are often needed to make one's meaning clear in writing. For example, in "The tires on the Corvette make the car look like something else," the writer has not provided the specific details about the tires necessary for us to understand the statement clearly. In general, then, you should avoid slang in your writing. If you are in doubt about whether an expression is slang, it may help to check a recently published hardbound dictionary.

Work with a partner to rewrite the following sentences, replacing the italicized slang words with more formal ones.

ACTIVITY 1

EXAMPLE

If the instructor would stop *hasslin'* me, I could *get my act together* in the course.

If the instructor would stop bothering me, I would perform better in the course.

1. Keira's so busy that she's always *IM-ing* her friends rather than giving them *face time*.

   _____

   _____

2. When I first met Nick, I thought he was *dope*, but he turned out to be *a hater* and didn't want me to have other friends.

   _____

   _____

3. Jason thought it would be *cool* to *flash* his Patrolmen's Benevolent Association card, but it didn't stop the *cop* from *nailing* him for speeding.

   _____

   _____

Clichés

A *cliché* is an expression that has been worn out through constant use. Some typical clichés are listed below.

Clichés

all work and no play	saw the light
at a loss for words	short but sweet
better late than never	sigh of relief
drop in the bucket	singing the blues
easier said than done	taking a big chance
had a hard time of it	time and time again
in the nick of time	too close for comfort
in this day and age	too little, too late
it dawned on me	took a turn for the worse
it goes without saying	under the weather
last but not least	where he (she) is coming from
make ends meet	word to the wise
on top of the world	work like a dog
sad but true	

Clichés are common in speech but make your writing seem tired and stale. Also, clichés—like slang—are often a way of evading the specific details that you must work to provide in your writing. You should, then, avoid clichés and try to express your meaning in fresh, original ways.

Underline the cliché in each of the following sentences. Then substitute specific, fresh words for the trite expression.

ACTIVITY 2

EXAMPLE

I passed the test by the skin of my teeth.

I barely passed the test.

1. Hal decided not to eat anything because he was feeling under the weather.

    _____

2. Sara arrived at the train station in the nick of time.

    _____

3. Clarence was asked to make his speech short but sweet.

    _____

Pretentious Words

Some people feel they can improve their writing by using fancy, elevated words rather than simple, natural words. They use artificial, stilted language that more often obscures their meaning than communicates it clearly. This frequently occurs when students attempt to use a dictionary or thesaurus, but just pick words at random to replace the simpler words. Using college-level vocabulary is a way to improve your writing, but you must be careful in choosing words. Not only can certain choices sound artificial, but another problem may arise when words are chosen without enough thought. Since many words can act as nouns, verbs, adjectives, and adverbs, using the wrong part of speech often leads to obscured meaning.

Here are some unnatural-sounding sentences:

- It was a marvelous gamble to procure some slumber.
- We relished the delectable noon-hour repast.
- The officer apprehended the imbibed vehicular operator.
- The female had an affectionate spot in her heart for domesticated felines.

The same thoughts can be expressed more clearly and effectively by using plain, natural language, as below:

- It was an excellent chance to get some sleep.
- We enjoyed the delicious lunch.

- The officer arrested the drunk driver.
- The woman had a warm spot in her heart for cats.

Here are some other inflated words and simpler words that could replace them:

Inflated Words	Simpler Words
amplitude	fullness or abundance
terminate	finish
subsequent to	after
delineate	describe or explain
facilitate	assist or help
moribund	dying or wasting away
manifested	established or shown
to endeavor	to attempt or to try
habituated	accustomed or familiar

ACTIVITY 3   Cross out the pretentious words in each sentence. Then substitute clear, simple language for the artificial words.

EXAMPLE

The chemistry ~~educator~~ asked each of his ~~budding scholars~~ not to ~~prevaricate~~ when explaining how everyone in the ~~assemblage~~ had gotten an A on the exam.

The chemistry teacher asked each of his students not to lie when explaining how

everyone in the class had gotten an A on the exam.

1. Only Tanner comprehended what transpired at the finalization of the movie.

    _____

    _____

2. John utilized Natalie's conceptualization to create a video on YouTube.

    _____

    _____

3. Leanne aspires to legally change her identification to "Li Ann."

    _____

    _____

REVIEW TEST

Certain words are italicized in the following paragraph. These words are either slang, cliché, or inflated. In the space between the lines, replace the italicized words with more effective diction. One italicized phrase is not needed at all; simply cross that one out.

Performance evaluations can be *the worst of times* for both employee and employer. Employers *check out* how the employee has performed over a certain period of time and *facilitate an interview with* the employee. One of the things employers focus on is improvement. Under areas of improvement, employers write things like: *needs to initiate proper arrival time at work, needs to facilitate excellent group collaboration,* and needs to increase production. Another area that employers focus on is goal setting because this gives an employee something to work toward. Sometimes goal setting might identify skill areas that need improvement, but often it involves something simple like increasing production *by a big percent* or setting up a fifteen-minute break every afternoon. After focusing on the things that employees need to improve, employers will often *chew the fat about* the employee's accomplishments. This is when both the employee and employer have a chance to *revel in* the positive part of the review. Accomplishments that employers like to highlight are things like *working like a dog,* landing large accounts, or overall positive behavior. Although performance evaluations can *generate heart palpitations,* they often help employers and employees *implement changes that attain positive personnel performance.*

HOW MUCH PRACTICE DO YOU NEED?

When you are learning a new skill, how much practice do you put in to improve? Think of a time when practice paid off for you, and write a narrative paragraph about the experience. You may want to review Chapter 15, "Narration."

Editing Tests

This chapter will give you practice in editing, or revising, to correct sentence-skills mistakes.

Twelve Editing Tests

The twelve editing tests in this chapter will give you practice in revising for sentence-skills mistakes. Remember that if you don't edit carefully, you run the risk of sabotaging much of the work you have put into a paper. If readers see too many surface flaws, they may assume you don't place much value on what you have to say, and they may not give your ideas a fair hearing. Revising to eliminate sentence-skills errors is a basic part of clear, effective writing.

In five tests, the spots where errors occur have been underlined; your job is to identify and correct each error. In the rest of the tests, you must locate as well as identify and correct the errors.

Following are hints that can help you edit the next-to-final draft of a paper for sentence-skills mistakes.

Editing Hints

1. Have at hand two essential tools: a good dictionary (see page 490) and a grammar handbook (you can use Chapter 5 and Part 4 of this book).
2. Use a sheet of paper to cover your essay so that you will expose only one sentence at a time. Look for errors in grammar, spelling, and typing. It may help to read each sentence out loud. If a sentence does not read clearly and smoothly, chances are something is wrong.
3. Pay special attention to the kinds of errors you yourself tend to make. For example, if you tend to write run-ons or fragments, be especially on the lookout for those errors.
4. Proofreading symbols that may be of particular help are the following:

✐	**omit**	in the ~~the~~ meantime
∧	**insert missing letter or word**	bel∧eve
cap, lc	**add a capital (or a lowercase) letter**	My persian Cat

EDITING TEST 1

Identify the five mistakes in paper format in the student paper that follows. From the box below, choose the letters that describe the five mistakes and write those letters in the spaces provided.

> a. The title should not be underlined.
> b. The title should not be set off in quotation marks.
> c. There should not be a period at the end of a title.
> d. All the major words in a title should be capitalized.
> e. The title should be a phrase, not a complete sentence.
> f. The first line of a paper should stand independently of the title.
> g. A line should be skipped between the title and the first line of the paper.
> h. The first line of a paragraph should be indented.
> i. The right-hand margin should not be crowded.
> j. Hyphenation should occur only between syllables.

	Writing a Successful Research Paper Requires Planning	
	This task requires three important steps: planning, planning, and planning.	
	First, determine if enough information about the chosen topic can be found	
	in the college library or online. If not, choose another topic. Next, determine	
	if the topic is too broad to write about in a relatively short paper. If so, limit	
	the topic. Next, design a research plan. Begin this part of the process by framing	
	a research question about the topic. For example, such a question for a paper	
	on the topic of bilingual education might be this: "Is the bilingual approach	
	the best way to mainstream second-language speakers?" Next, make	
	a preliminary list of sources—books, articles, and online resources—in	
	which useful information might be found. Now, start taking notes!	

1. _____ 2. _____ 3. _____ 4. _____ 5. _____

NAME: _____

DATE: _____

Identify the sentence-skills mistakes at the underlined spots in the paragraph that follows. From the box below, choose the letter that describes each mistake and write it in the space provided. The same mistake may appear more than once.

a. fragment	d. apostrophe mistake
b. run-on	e. faulty parallelism
c. mistake in subject-verb agreement	

Looking Out for Yourself

Academic

It's sad but true: "If you don't look out for yourself, no one else will." For example, some people have a false idea about the power of a college <u>degree, they</u> think that
1
once they <u>possesses</u> the degree, the world will be waiting on their doorstep. In fact, nobody
2
is likely to be on their doorstep unless, through advance planning, they <u>has</u> prepared them-
3
selves for a career. <u>The kind in which good job opportunities exist.</u> Even after a person
4
has landed a job, however, a healthy amount of self-interest is needed. People who hide in
corners or <u>with hesitation</u> to let others know about their skills <u>doesn't</u> get promotions or
5   **6**
raises. <u>Its</u> important to take credit for a job well done, whether the job involves writing a
7
report, <u>organized the office filing system</u>, or calming down an angry customer. Also, people
8
should feel free to ask the boss for a raise. <u>If they work hard and really deserve it.</u> Those
9
who look out for themselves get the <u>rewards, people</u> who depend on others to help them
10
along get left behind.

1. _____ 2. _____ 3. _____ 4. _____ 5. _____

6. _____ 7. _____ 8. _____ 9. _____ 10. _____

EDITING TEST 3

Identify the sentence-skills mistakes at the underlined spots in the paragraph that follows. From the box below, choose the letter that describes each mistake and write it in the space provided. The same mistake may appear more than once.

a. fragment	e. missing comma after introductory words
b. run-on	f. misplaced modifier
c. mistake in verb tense	
d. mistake in irregular verb	

Personal

Treating People with Dignity

<u>While preparing for a recent chemistry exam</u> I witnessed a true act of humanity. It
1
was a really hot day. <u>One of those days that makes the news.</u> Not only <u>does</u> the thermom-
2 3
eter read 101 degrees, but the humidity was so high that just stepping outside could cause
a person to become dehydrated. I was studying at my local Starbucks. <u>When I noticed two
4
men slowly enter the coffee shop.</u> Both were homeless <u>from their appearance.</u> Their clothes
5
were <u>raggedy, they</u> both had multiple bags of items that they clung to. As they walked in,
6
the barista poured two tall glasses of ice water, and <u>slided</u> them across the counter. The
7
men took the water and sat down at a <u>table no</u> money was exchanged. For more than three
8
hours <u>I</u> observed both men sit and savor their water and the cool air-conditioning. No one
9
bothered them or asked them to leave. It was obvious that the employees <u>recognize</u> the
10
importance of treating people with dignity and kindness.

1. _____ 2. _____ 3. _____ 4. _____ 5. _____

6. _____ 7. _____ 8. _____ 9. _____ 10. _____

NAME: _____

DATE: _____

Identify the sentence-skills mistakes at the underlined spots in the paragraph that follows. From the box below, choose the letter that describes each mistake and write it in the space provided. The same mistake may appear more than once.

a. fragment
b. run-on
c. irregular verb mistake
d. missing comma after introductory words
e. apostrophe mistake
f. misplaced modifier
g. missing quotation marks

Corsica: a Brief History

The island of Corsica <u>lays</u> only a short distance from the southern coast of
          1
France. <u>Just north of the Italian island of Sardinia.</u> <u>Mountainous and rugged,</u> Napoleon
           2   *3*
Bonaparte, the Emperor of the French, was born on this island. Corsica is also the setting
of Alexander <u>Dumas</u> *The Corsican Brothers,* a novel about twins, who were supposed to
       4
feel each other's physical pain. <u>Early in its history</u> Corsica was occupied by the Carthag-
             5
inians, the Phoenicians, the Greeks, the Etruscans, and the <u>Romans, becoming</u> the prop-
                    6
erty of the Italian city-state of Genoa in the fourteenth century, the island stayed in Italian
hands for four hundred years. In fact, <u>existing as an independent nation for a short while</u>
<u>during the eighteenth century,</u> the official language remained Italian. That changed. <u>After</u>
       7
<u>the French took control 1769.</u> Genoa is said to have sold its interests in Corsica to <u>France,</u>
  8   *9*
<u>however,</u> Professor Cavour, my Italian teacher, once claimed that <u>"those sneaky French</u>
                                                              10
<u>stole it.</u>

1. _____ 2. _____ 3. _____ 4. _____ 5. _____

6. _____ 7. _____ 8. _____ 9. _____ 10. _____

EDITING TEST 5

Identify the sentence-skills mistakes at the underlined spots in the paragraph that follows. From the box below, choose the letter that describes each mistake and write it in the space provided. The same mistake may appear more than once.

a. fragment	e. missing quotation mark
b. run-on	f. missing comma between two complete thoughts
c. faulty parallelism	g. missing comma after introductory words
d. missing apostrophe	h. misspelled word

Billy Budd, Sailor

Herman Melville's novel *Moby Dick* is his masterpiece but the Melville book that most
                                          ‾‾‾‾‾‾‾‾‾‾‾‾‾‾‾‾‾‾‾‾‾‾‾‾‾‾‾‾‾‾‾‾
                                                          1
students know best is *Billy Budd*. The story of an innocent, handsome young sailor by that name.
                                     ‾‾‾
                                                               2
While he is serving on the American ship *Rights of Man,* a British warship comes alongside his

and takes several American seamen prisoner, Billy is among them. After serving on the British
                             ‾‾‾‾‾‾‾‾‾‾‾‾‾‾‾‾‾‾‾‾‾‾‾‾‾‾‾‾‾‾   ‾‾‾‾‾‾‾‾‾‾‾‾‾‾‾‾‾‾‾‾‾‾‾‾‾‾‾‾‾‾
                                      3   4
ship for only a little while the noble Billy succeeds in winning the admiration of the British
‾‾‾‾‾‾‾‾‾‾‾‾‾‾‾‾‾‾‾‾‾‾‾‾‾‾

captain, Edward Vere, and that of most of the crew. Except for John Claggart, the evil master-of-
                                                     ‾‾‾‾‾‾‾‾‾‾‾‾‾‾‾‾‾‾‾‾‾‾‾‾‾‾‾‾‾‾‾‾‾‾‾‾‾‾‾
                                                                          5
arms, whose hatred Billy has drawn for no apparent reason. Eventually, Claggart accuses Billy of
‾‾

starting a mutiny, this charge is clearly untrue. However, the master-of-arms accusation enrages
          ‾‾‾‾‾‾‾‾   ‾‾‾‾‾‾‾‾‾‾‾‾‾‾‾‾‾‾‾‾‾‾‾‾‾‾‾‾‾‾
             6   7
the seaman, who loses his composure, strikes Claggart, and killing him. Realizing that Claggart's
                                     ‾‾‾‾‾‾‾‾‾‾‾‾‾‾‾‾‾‾‾‾‾‾‾‾‾‾‾‾‾‾
                                                     8
accusation provoked Billy, the captain sympathizes with the young man, but he knows he has

to try Billy before a jury on board ship. Following navel law to the letter, the jury convicts him.
                                                    ‾‾‾‾‾
                                                      9
Shortly thereafter, Billy is hanged, much to the regret of all those involved, but not before he

utters one of the most memorable lines in American literature: "God bless Captain Vere!
                                                                ‾‾‾‾‾‾‾‾‾‾‾‾‾‾‾‾‾‾‾‾‾‾‾
                                                                         10

1. _____   2. _____   3. _____   4. _____   5. _____

6. _____   7. _____   8. _____   9. _____   10. _____

NAME: _____

DATE: _____

Locate and correct the ten sentence-skills mistakes in the following passage. The mistakes are listed in the box below. As you locate each mistake, write the number of the word group in the space provided. Then in the space between the lines, edit and correct each mistake.

5	fragments	_____	_____	_____	_____	_____
5	run-ons	_____	_____	_____	_____	_____

The Language Evolves

Academic

¹Forty years ago, no one would have batted an eye over inadvertent sexism in the media, in newspapers and magazines, and on the radio and television, people used words such as "fisherman" to refer to everyone who fished. ²"Policeman" to refer to all police officers. ³"Postman" for anyone who carried the mail. ⁴Indeed, print journalists and television broadcasters called themselves "newsmen," advertising executives were known as "ad men." ⁵Even the word "mankind" was used as a blanket term to refer to the human race. ⁶Despite the fact that at least half of its members were female. ⁷Today the situation has changed, women figure prominently in the professions, in government, and in business. ⁸As a result, more respect seems to be given them in the media. ⁹In fact, many women serve as executives in the media industry itself. ¹⁰In 1984 and in 2008, the major political parties nominated women as their vice-presidential candidates, no one doubts that someday soon a woman will be her party's candidate for the land's highest office. ¹¹Perhaps in the next presidential election. ¹²As a result, the media are, more and more, granting women equal status. ¹³A status that they deserve and have earned. ¹⁴The media no longer call all fire-fighters "firemen," when referring to a nonspecific doctor, lawyer, politician, scientist, or other professional, they have replaced the pronoun "he" with the more representative "he or she."

EDITING TEST 7

Locate and correct the ten sentence-skills mistakes in the following letter. The mistakes are listed in the box below. As you locate each mistake, write the number of the word group in the space provided. Then in the space between the lines, edit and correct each mistake.

2 fragments: _____ _____

2 missing commas between items in a series: _____ _____

2 missing commas after introductory word(s): _____ _____

1 irregular verb mistake: _____

1 apostrophe mistake: _____

1 run-on: _____

1 missing comma between two complete thoughts: _____

Personal

Houston 43-B

Wallace Residence Center

University of Idaho

Moscow, Idaho 83843

September 28, 2014

Dear Mom,

¹I know you prefer letters to e-mails so I decided to sit down and write you a letter to get you caught up on my life at school. ²First I wanted to thank you so much for the great care package from Hip Kits. ³What a nice surprise it was to open the GoGo Gluten Free box. ⁴My roommate was very envious as I unloaded the cookies chips and chocolate bars. ⁵Don't worry, you raised me well. ⁶And I shared some of the goodies.

    ⁷Classes are good. ⁸I am so excited about getting into the Ecology and Conservation Biology program. ⁹Even though it means that my class loads are going to be very heavy over the next several semesters. ¹⁰My advisor told me

that as long as my grades continue to stay high, I should be able maintain my current scholarships. [11]He also explained there were some additional scholarships I may qualify for by next semester.

[12]As you know, this weekend was Homecoming. [13]It was a great ending to a week of activities. [14]The parade was well attended over fifty different groups were represented with elaborate floats depicting this years theme—Vandal Pride, Planet Wide. [15]Our game against Temple University was one of the best I have seen. [16]It was a great weekend to be a Vandal!

[17]As much as I would like to write more I really have to get back to studying. [18]I have quite a few tests coming up, and I want my grades to make you proud.

[19]Lots of love,
Sam

EDITING TEST 8

Locate and correct the ten sentence-skills mistakes in the following passage. The mistakes are listed in the box below. As you locate each mistake, write the number of the word group in the space provided. Then in the space between the lines, edit and correct each mistake.

---

1 run-on _____	1 missing comma between items in a series _____
1 mistake in subject-verb agreement _____	2 apostrophe mistakes _____ _____
1 missing comma after introductory words _____	2 missing quotation marks _____ _____
2 missing commas around an interrupter _____ _____	

Walking Billboards

¹Many Americans have turned into driving, walking billboards. ²As much as we all claim to hate commercials on television we dont seem to have any qualms about turning ourselves into commercials. ³Our car bumpers for example advertise lake resorts underground caverns, and amusement parks. ⁴Also, we wear clothes marked with other peoples initials and slogans. ⁵Our fascination with the names of designers show up on the backs of our sneakers, the breast pockets of our shirts, and the right rear pockets of our blue jeans. ⁶Also, we wear T-shirts filled with all kinds of advertising messages. ⁷For instance, people are willing to wear shirts that read, "Dillon Construction," "Nike," or even I Got Crabs at Ed's Seafood Palace. ⁸In conclusion, we say we hate commercials, we actually pay people for the right to advertise their products.

NAME: _____

DATE: _____

Locate and correct the ten sentence-skills mistakes in the following passage. The mistakes are listed in the box below. As you locate each mistake, write the number of the word group in the space provided. Then in the space between the lines, edit and correct each mistake.

2 fragments _____ _____	2 apostrophe mistakes _____ _____
2 missing commas between items in a series _____ _____	1 subject-verb agreement _____
2 missing commas after introductory words _____ _____	1 faulty parallelism _____

My Daughter, the Future Park Ranger

Personal

1When my daughter was five and we were visiting Great Smoky Mountains National Park. 2She decided that she wanted to earn as many Jr. Ranger badges as she could before she turned thirteen. 3The United States National Park Systems Junior Ranger program is designed to enhance the experience of children while they are visiting the nations parks. 4Each time we go to a national park my daughter immediately seeks out a Park Ranger to ask about the activities she will need to complete in order to earn a new badge. 5Once she gets the information, she sits down with her father and me to plan out our visit. 6Most badges requires participating in one Ranger-led activity. 7So far, we have attended numerous historical talks and nature hikes a presentation by a Blackfoot Indian and a guided walk through historical Boston. 8In addition to the Ranger-led activities my daughter usually has to fill out a workbook that is designed for her age group. 9These workbooks help guide her through the park and highlight important information like natural wonders, historically significant buildings, and the features of the park that are important. 10She has earned thirty-seven badges and is looking forward to our trip to Washington D.C. 11Because she is certain she will be able to earn enough badges to bring her total to fifty.

EDITING TEST 10

Locate and correct the ten sentence-skills mistakes in the following cover letter. The mistakes are listed in the box below. As you locate each mistake, write the number of the word group in the space provided. Then in the space between the lines, edit and correct each mistake.

1	missing colon: _____	2	homonym mistakes: _____
1	missing apostrophe: _____		_____
1	mistake in capitalization: _____	1	dangling modifier: _____
1	mistake in verb tense: _____	1	fragment: _____
1	missing comma: _____	1	run-on: _____

Melissa Kueny
Personnel Officer
Longview Recreation Inc.
Longview, WA 98632

¹Dear Ms. Kueny

²I am replying to your post on Craigs List that indicated an opening at Longview Recreation Inc. for an activities coordinator. ³Familiar with the outdoors and outgoing, the position seems ideal for me.

⁴I spend the past three years working at Tall Oaks Conference Center wear I developed and implemented activities for children in grades 4-12. ⁵My job required me to think of creative and safe ways to promote physical fitness. ⁶And encourage a love of the outdoors and cooperation among the children.

⁷Also, I took several recreational counseling classes at the university of Washington. ⁸I learned about recreational leadership and planning, I even took a class on exercise techniques.

⁹Please feel free to call me for an interview. ¹⁰Thank you for you're consideration.

¹¹Sincerely

Tanya Grubechek

NAME: _____

DATE: _____

Each underlined area in the resume excerpt below contains a sentence-skills mistake. Identify the mistake and write its item number in the appropriate space in the box below. Then correct the mistake in the space above each error.

Missing capital letter(s): _____ _____	Inconsistent verb tense: _____
Dangling modifier: _____	Run-on: _____
Faulty parallelism: _____	Apostrophe mistake: _____
Fragment: _____ _____	Missing comma: _____

Alyssa Leong

1597 bagley Street

2Torrance CA 90501

Phone: (310) 555-5555 aleong@xyz.net

Objective

I hope to find a position as a certified nurse assistant at a nursing facility that will offer me rewarding work, 3hours that are full time, and medical benefits.

Summary of Qualifications

4Compassionate, competent, and hardworking, my experience caring for people is extensive. 5Having volunteered at an adult residential care home for two years. I am aware of the responsibilities for providing basic care. 6At the care home. 7I helped staff members and sometimes fed, bathed, and dress clients. 8My supervisors' encouraged me to enroll in a certified nursing assistant program. 9In 2009, I completed a six-month training, I also received my CNA certification.

Education

2011	Certified Nursing Assistant	Los Angeles Adult Community School
2009	Diploma	Roosevelt High School

Work History

9/2009-6/2011	Volunteer 10South central adult residential Care Home

- Assisted clients with personal hygiene and recreational activities
- Provided companionship

539

NAME: _____

DATE: _____

Each numbered box in the sample application form contains a sentence-skills mistake. Identify each of the ten mistakes. As you find each, write the type of mistake you found in the space provided. Then correct it next to your answer. The first one has been done for you.

1. _missing comma: August 15, 2014_

3. _____

_____

_____

(Work)

2. _____

4. _____

_____

_____

DT Food Services Ltd. Employment Application		1. Date of Application *August 15 2014*	
Social Security # *123-45-6789*	Last Name *Lee-Thomas*	First Name *Leona*	Middle Initial *F.*
Address (Street number and name) *550 Tenth Avenue*		2. City, State, and Zip Code *carson city, NV 89706*	
3. Desired Position *"Food Server"*	4. Date Available *Tomorow*	Home Phone *(123) 555-5566*	Cell Phone *(456) 777-8899*

EDUCATION

Schools	Name Location	Dates Attended From: To:	Grad?	Major/Minor Course Work	Type of Degree
High School	5. *Kennedy High school*	*9/07 to 6/11*	YES X NO		
College or University	*Washoe Community College*	*9/11 to 6/12*	YES NO X		
Other Training or Education	6. *Coarse in typing*		YES X NO		

WORK HISTORY (include volunteer experience. Use additional sheets if necessary.)			
7. Current or Last Employer: *Grocery outlet*		8. Address: *120 South Carson Street* *Carson City NV 89706*	
9. Job Title: *Sales' Clerk*		Supervisor's Name and Title *Julie Leroy, Manager*	Telephone Number
Dates Employed (mo/yr-mon/yr) *10/13 to present*	Starting Salary *$8.25/hour*	Ending or Current Salary *$9.00/hour*	Reason for Leaving *N/A*
10. List major duties in order of their importance in the job: *I operate the cash register. Also stock shelves.*			

5. _____   8. _____

_____   _____

6. _____   9. _____

_____   _____

7. _____   10. _____

_____   _____

Correction Symbols

Here is a list of symbols the instructor may use when marking papers. The numbers in parentheses refer to the pages that explain the skill involved.

Agr	Correct the mistake in agreement of subject and verb (410–425) or pronoun and the word the pronoun refers to (416–421).
Apos	Correct the apostrophe mistake (460–467).
Bal	Balance the parts of the sentence so they have the same (parallel) form (112–113).
Cap	Correct the mistake in capital letters (447–455).
Coh	Revise to improve coherence (90–92; 146–148).
Comma	Add a comma (476–484).
CS	Correct the comma splice (381–393).
DM	Correct the dangling modifier (435–440).
Det	Support or develop the topic more fully by adding details (61–66; 76–82).
Frag	Attach the fragment to a sentence or make it a sentence (367–380).
lc	Use a lowercase (small) letter rather than a capital (447–455).
MM	Correct the misplaced modifier (433–435).
¶	Indent for a new paragraph.
No ¶	Do not indent for a new paragraph.
Pro	Correct the pronoun mistake (416–421).
Quot	Correct the mistake in quotation marks (468–475).
R-O	Correct the run-on (381–393).
Sp	Correct the spelling error (499–507).
Trans	Supply or improve a transition (92–98).
Und	Underline or italicize (471–473).
Verb	Correct the verb or verb form (402–415).
Wordy	Omit needless words (119–121).
WW	Replace the word marked with a more accurate one (521–525).
?	Write the illegible word clearly.
/	Eliminate the word, letter, or punctuation mark so slashed.
^	Add the omitted word or words.
;/:/-/—	Add semicolon (486), colon (485); hyphen (487), or dash (486).
✓	You have something fine or good here: an expression, a detail, an idea.

Readings for Writers

What do you notice about the student in this photograph? Although he most likely has use of a smartphone, laptop, or tablet, he is choosing to read a printed text. Will computers and the Internet ever replace the need for printed books? Think about this question and write a response.

Introduction to the Readings

The reading selections in Part 5 will help you find topics for writing. Some of the selections provide helpful practical information. For example, you'll learn how to deal with interpersonal conflict and how to avoid being manipulated by clever ads. Other selections deal with thought-provoking aspects of contemporary life. One article, for instance, examines modern young adult literature and how it addresses controversial topics relevant to teens. Still other selections are devoted to a celebration of human goals and values; one essay, for example, reminds us of the power that praise and appreciation can have in our daily lives. The varied subjects should inspire lively class discussions as well as serious individual thought. The selections should also provide a continuing source of high-interest material for a wide range of writing assignments.

The selections serve another purpose as well. They will help you develop reading skills that will directly benefit you as a writer. First, through close reading, you will learn how to recognize the main idea or point of a selection and how to identify and evaluate the supporting material that develops the main idea. In your writing, you will aim to achieve the same essential structure: an overall point followed by detailed, valid support for that point. Second, close reading will help you explore a selection and its possibilities thoroughly. The more you understand about what is said in a piece, the more ideas and feelings you may have about writing on an assigned topic or a related topic of your own. A third benefit of close reading is becoming more aware of authors' stylistic devices—for example, their introductions and conclusions, their ways of presenting and developing a point, their use of transitions, their choice of language to achieve a particular tone. Recognizing these devices in other people's writing will help you enlarge your own range of writing techniques.

The Format of Each Selection

Each selection begins with a short overview that gives helpful background information. The selection is then followed by three sets of questions.

- First, there are **Vocabulary in Context** questions to help you expand your knowledge of selected words.

- **Reading Comprehension Questions** foster several important reading skills: recognizing a subject or topic, determining the thesis or main idea, identifying key supporting points, and making inferences. Answering the questions will enable you and your instructor to check quickly your basic understanding of a selection. More significantly, as you move from one selection to the next, you will sharpen your reading skills as well as strengthen your thinking skills— two key factors in making you a better writer.

- Following the comprehension questions are several **Discussion Questions.** In addition to dealing with **Content**, these questions focus on **Structure, Style,** and **Tone.**

Finally, several **Writing Assignments** accompany each selection. Many of the assignments provide guidelines on how to proceed, including suggestions for prewriting and appropriate methods of development. Some readings also feature related images and writing prompts intended to help you probe and analyze the images. When writing your responses to the readings, you will have opportunities to apply all the methods of development presented in Part 2 of this book.

How to Read Well: Four General Steps

Skillful reading is an important part of becoming a skillful writer. Following are four steps that will make you a better reader—both of the selections here and in your reading at large.

1 Concentrate as You Read

To improve your concentration, follow these tips. First, read in a place where you can be quiet and alone. Don't choose a spot where a TV or a video game is on or where friends or family are talking nearby. Next, sit in an upright position when you read. If your body is in a completely relaxed position, sprawled across a bed or nestled in an easy chair, your mind is also going to be completely relaxed. The light muscular tension that comes from sitting upright in a chair promotes concentration and keeps your mind ready to work. Finally, consider using your index finger (or a pen) as a pacer while you read. Lightly underline each line of print with your index finger as you read down a page. Hold your hand slightly above the page and move your finger at a speed that is a little too fast for comfort. This pacing with your index finger, like sitting upright in a chair, creates a slight physical tension that will keep your body and mind focused and alert.

2 Skim Material before You Read It

In skimming, you spend about two minutes rapidly surveying a selection, looking for important points and skipping secondary material. Follow this sequence when skimming:

- Begin by reading the overview that precedes the selection.

- Then study the title of the selection for a few moments. A good title is the shortest possible summary of a selection; it often tells you in just a few words what a selection is about.

- Next, form a basic question (or questions) out of the title. Forming questions out of the title is often a key to locating a writer's main idea— your next concern in skimming.

- Read the first two or three paragraphs and the last two or three paragraphs in the selection. Very often a writer's main idea, *if* it is directly stated, will appear in one of these paragraphs and will relate to the title.

- Finally, look quickly at the rest of the selection for other clues to important points. Are there any subheads you can relate in some way to the title? Are there any words the author has decided to emphasize by setting them off in *italic* or **boldface** type? Are there any major lists of items signaled by words such as *first, second, also, another,* and so on?

3 Read the Selection Straight Through with a Pen Nearby

Don't slow down or turn back; just aim to understand as much as you can the first time through. Place a check or star beside answers to basic questions you formed from the title, and beside other ideas that seem important. Number lists of important points 1, 2, 3, ... Circle words you don't understand. Put question marks in the margin next to passages that are unclear and that you will want to reread.

4 Work with the Material

Go back and reread passages that were not clear the first time through. Look up words that block your understanding of ideas, and write their meanings in the margin. Also, reread carefully the areas you identified as most important; doing so will enlarge your understanding of the material. Now that you have a sense of the whole, prepare a short outline of the selection by answering the following questions on a sheet of paper:

- What is the main idea?

- What key points support the main idea?

- What seem to be other important points in the selection?

By working with the material in this way, you will significantly increase your understanding of a selection. Effective reading, just like effective writing, does not happen all at once. Rather, it is a process. Often you begin with a general impression of what something means, and then, by working at it, you move to a deeper level of understanding of the material.

How to Answer the Vocabulary in Context Questions

To decide on the meaning of an unfamiliar word, consider its surrounding context. Ask yourself, "Are there any clues in the sentence that suggest what this word means?"

How to Answer the Comprehension Questions: Specific Hints

Several important reading skills are involved in the reading comprehension questions that follow each selection. The skills are

- Summarizing the selection by providing a title for it
- Determining the main idea
- Recognizing key supporting details
- Making inferences

The following hints will help you apply each of these reading skills:

- *Subject or title.* Remember that the title should accurately describe the *entire* selection. It should be neither too broad nor too narrow for the material in the selection. It should answer the question "What is this about?" as specifically as possible. Note that you may at times find it easier to do the "title" question *after* the "main idea" question.

- *Main idea.* Choose the statement that you think best expresses the main idea or thesis of the entire selection. Remember that the title will often help you focus on the main idea. Then ask yourself, "Does most of the material in the selection support this statement?" If you can answer "yes" to this question, you have found the thesis.

- *Key details.* If you were asked to give a two-minute summary of a selection, the major details are the ones you would include in that summary. To determine the key details, ask yourself, "What are the major supporting points for the thesis?"

- *Inferences.* Answer these questions by drawing on the evidence presented in the selection and on your own common sense. Ask yourself, "What reasonable judgments can I make on the basis of the information in the selection?"

On page 671 is a chart on which you can keep track of your performance as you answer the vocabulary and comprehension questions for each selection. The chart will help you identify reading skills you need to strengthen.

* * *

The readings begin on the next page. Enjoy!

All the Good Things

Sister Helen Mrosla

PREVIEW

Sometimes the smallest things we do have the biggest impact. A teacher's impulsive idea, designed to brighten a dull Friday-afternoon class, affected her students more than she ever dreamed. Sister Helen Mrosla's moment of classroom inspiration took on a life of its own, returning to visit her at a most unexpected time. Her account of the experience reminds us of the human heart's endless hunger for recognition and appreciation.

He was in the first third-grade class I taught at Saint Mary's School in Morris, 1 Minnesota. All thirty-four of my students were dear to me, but Mark Eklund was one in a million. He was very neat in appearance but had that happy-to-be-alive attitude that made even his occasional mischievousness delightful.

Mark talked incessantly.* I had to remind him again and again that talking 2 without permission was not acceptable. What impressed me so much, though, was his sincere response every time I had to correct him for misbehaving—"Thank you for correcting me, Sister!" I didn't know what to make of it at first, but before long I became accustomed to hearing it many times a day.

One morning my patience was growing thin when Mark talked once too often, 3 and then I made a novice teacher's mistake. I looked at him and said, "If you say one more word, I am going to tape your mouth shut!"

It wasn't ten seconds later when Chuck blurted out, "Mark is talking again." I 4 hadn't asked any of the students to help me watch Mark, but since I had stated the punishment in front of the class, I had to act on it.

I remember the scene as if it had occurred this morning. I walked to my desk, 5 very deliberately opened my drawer, and took out a roll of masking tape. Without saying a word, I proceeded to Mark's desk, tore off two pieces of tape and made a big X with them over his mouth. I then returned to the front of the room. As I glanced at Mark to see how he was doing, he winked at me.

That did it! I started laughing. The class cheered as I walked back to Mark's **6** desk, removed the tape, and shrugged my shoulders. His first words were, "Thank you for correcting me, Sister."

At the end of the year I was asked to teach junior-high math. The years flew **7** by, and before I knew it Mark was in my classroom again. He was more handsome than ever and just as polite. Since he had to listen carefully to my instruction in the "new math," he did not talk as much in ninth grade as he had talked in the third.

One Friday, things just didn't feel right. We had worked hard on a new concept **8** all week, and I sensed that the students were frowning, frustrated with themselves— and edgy* with one another. I had to stop this crankiness before it got out of hand. So I asked them to list the names of the other students in the room on two sheets of paper, leaving a space after each name. Then I told them to think of the nicest thing they could say about each of their classmates and write it down.

It took the remainder of the class period to finish the assignment, and as the **9** students left the room, each one handed me the papers. Charlie smiled. Mark said, "Thank you for teaching me, Sister. Have a good weekend."

That Saturday, I wrote down the name of each student on a separate sheet of **10** paper, and I listed what everyone else had said about that individual.

On Monday I gave each student his or her list. Before long, the entire class **11** was smiling. "Really?" I heard whispered. "I never knew that meant anything to anyone!" "I didn't know others liked me so much!"

No one ever mentioned those papers in class again. I never knew if the students **12** discussed them after class or with their parents, but it didn't matter. The exercise had accomplished its purpose. The students were happy with themselves and one another again.

That group of students moved on. Several years later, after I returned from **13** a vacation, my parents met me at the airport. As we were driving home, Mother asked me the usual questions about the trip—the weather, my experiences in general. There was a slight lull in the conversation. Mother gave Dad a sideways glance and simply said, "Dad?" My father cleared his throat as he usually did before something important. "The Eklunds called last night," he began. "Really?" I said. "I haven't heard from them in years. I wonder how Mark is."

Dad responded quietly. "Mark was killed in Vietnam," he said. "The funeral is **14** tomorrow, and his parents would like it if you could attend." To this day I can still point to the exact spot on I-494 where Dad told me about Mark.

I had never seen a serviceman in a military coffin before. Mark looked so hand- **15** some, so mature. All I could think at that moment was, Mark, I would give all the masking tape in the world if only you would talk to me.

The church was packed with Mark's friends. Chuck's sister sang "The Battle **16** Hymn of the Republic." Why did it have to rain on the day of the funeral? It was difficult enough at the graveside. The pastor said the usual prayers, and the bugler played Taps. One by one those who loved Mark took a last walk by the coffin and sprinkled it with holy water.

I was the last one to bless the coffin. As I stood there, one of the soldiers who had 17 acted as pallbearer came up to me. "Were you Mark's math teacher?" he asked. I nodded as I continued to stare at the coffin. "Mark talked about you a lot," he said.

After the funeral, most of Mark's former classmates headed to Chuck's farmhouse 18 for lunch. Mark's mother and father were there, obviously waiting for me. "We want to show you something," his father said, taking a wallet out of his pocket. "They found this on Mark when he was killed. We thought you might recognize it."

Opening the billfold, he carefully 19 removed two worn pieces of notebook paper that had obviously been taped, folded and refolded many times. I knew without looking that the papers were the ones on which I had listed all the good things each of Mark's classmates had said about him. "Thank you so much for doing that," Mark's mother said. "As you can see, Mark treasured it."

Mark's classmates started to gather 20 around us. Charlie smiled rather sheepishly and said, "I still have my list. it's in the top drawer of my desk at home." Chuck's wife said, "Chuck asked me to put his list in our wedding album." "I have mine too," Marilyn said. "It's in my diary." Then Vicki, another classmate, reached into her pocketbook, took out her wallet, and showed her worn and frazzled list to the group. "I carry this with me at all times," Vicki said without batting an eyelash. "I think we all saved our lists."

That's when I finally sat down and 21 cried. I cried for Mark and for all his friends who would never see him again.

FROM LOOKING AT THIS PHOTOGRAPH, WHAT CAN you tell about the relationship between the students and their instructor? What specific visual clues help you draw these conclusions? Write a paragraph that describes the kind of relationship that is being demonstrated and why this is or is not, in your opinion, a good student-teacher relationship.

VOCABULARY IN CONTEXT

1. The word *incessantly* in "Mark talked incessantly. I had to remind him again and again that talking without permission was not acceptable" (paragraph 2) means
    a. slowly.
    b. quietly.
    c. constantly.
    d. pleasantly.

2. The word *edgy* in "We had worked hard on a new concept all week, and I sensed that the students were frowning, frustrated with themselves—and edgy with one another. I had to stop this crankiness before it got out of hand" (paragraph 8) means
   a. funny.
   b. calm.
   c. easily annoyed.
   d. dangerous.

READING COMPREHENSION QUESTIONS

1. Which of the following would be the best alternative title for this selection?
   a. Talkative Mark
   b. My Life as a Teacher
   c. More Important Than I Knew
   d. A Tragic Death

2. Which sentence best expresses the main idea of the selection?
   a. Although Sister Helen sometimes scolded Mark Eklund, he appreciated her devotion to teaching.
   b. When a former student of hers died, Sister Helen discovered how important one of her assignments had been to him and his classmates.
   c. When her students were cranky one day, Sister Helen had them write down something nice about each of their classmates.
   d. A pupil whom Sister Helen was especially fond of was tragically killed while serving in Vietnam.

3. Upon reading their lists for the first time, Sister Helen's students
   a. were silent and embarrassed.
   b. were disappointed.
   c. pretended to think the lists were stupid, although they really liked them.
   d. smiled and seemed pleased.

4. In the days after the assignment to write down something nice about one another,
   a. students didn't mention the assignment again.
   b. students often brought their lists to school.
   c. Sister Helen received calls from several parents complaining about the assignment.
   d. Sister Helen decided to repeat the assignment in every one of her classes.

5. According to Vicki,
   a. Mark was the only student to have saved his list.
   b. Vicki and Mark were the only students to have saved their lists.
   c. Vicki, Mark, Charlie, Chuck, and Marilyn were the only students to have saved their lists.
   d. all the students had saved their lists.

6. The author implies that
   a. she was surprised to learn how much the lists had meant to her students.
   b. Mark's parents were jealous of his affection for Sister Helen.
   c. Mark's death shattered her faith in God.
   d. Mark's classmates had not stayed in touch with one another over the years.

7. *True or False?* _____ The author implies that Mark had gotten married.

8. We can conclude that when Sister Helen was a third-grade teacher, she
   a. was usually short-tempered and irritable.
   b. wasn't always sure how to discipline her students.
   c. didn't expect Mark to do well in school.
   d. had no sense of humor.

DISCUSSION QUESTIONS

About Content

1. What did Sister Helen hope to accomplish by asking her students to list nice things about one another?

2. At least some students were surprised by the good things others wrote about them. What does this tell us about how we see ourselves and how we communicate our views of others?

3. "All the Good Things" has literally traveled around the world. Not only has it been reprinted in numerous publications, but many readers have sent it out over the Internet for others to read. Why do you think so many people love this story? Why do they want to share it with others?

About Structure

4. This selection is organized according to time. What three separate time periods does it cover? What paragraphs are included in the first time period? The second? The third?

5. Paragraph 8 includes a cause-and-effect structure. What part of the paragraph is devoted to the cause? What part is devoted to the effect? What transition word signals the break between the cause and the effect?

6. What does the title "All the Good Things" mean? Is this a good title for the essay? Why or why not?

About Style and Tone

7. Sister Helen is willing to let her readers see her weaknesses as well as her strengths. Find a place in the selection in which the author shows herself as less than perfect.

8. What does Sister Helen accomplish by beginning her essay with the word "he"? What does that unusual beginning tell the reader?

9. How does Sister Helen feel about her students? Find evidence that backs up your opinion.

10. Sister Helen comments on Mark's "happy-to-be-alive" attitude. What support does she provide that makes us understand what Mark was like?

WRITING ASSIGNMENTS

Assignment 1: Writing a Paragraph

Early in her story, Sister Helen refers to a "teacher's mistake" that forced her to punish a student in front of the class. Write a paragraph about a time you gave in to pressure to do something because others around you expected it. Explain what the situation was, what happened, and how you felt afterward. Here are two sample topic sentences:

> Even though I knew it was wrong, I went along with some friends who shoplifted at the mall.

> Just because my friends did, I made fun of a kid in my study hall who was a slow learner.

Assignment 2: Writing a Paragraph

Sister Helen Mrosla was teaching math when she deviated from her lesson plan, seized the "teachable moment," and had the students create the lists that they carried with them through adulthood. Write a paragraph that defines the qualities of a good teacher. You don't have to limit your focus to a classroom teacher; instead, you could expand your definition of a teacher to include parents, religious leaders, or even mentors at work. Start your paragraph with a topic sentence that has a persuasive tone to it, so you can focus on convincing your reader that your definition is a valid one.

Assignment 3: Writing an Essay

It's easy to forget to let others know how much they have helped us. Only after one of the students died did Sister Helen learn how important the list of positive comments had been to her class. Write an essay about someone to whom you are grateful and explain what that person has done for you. In your thesis statement, introduce the person and describe his or her relationship to you. Also include a general statement of what that person has done for you. Your thesis statement can be similar to any of these:

> My brother Roy has been an important part of my life.

> My best friend Ginger helped me through a major crisis.

> Mrs. Morrison, my seventh-grade English teacher, taught me a lesson for which I will always be grateful.

Use freewriting to help you find interesting details to support your thesis statement. You may find two or three separate incidents to write about, each in a paragraph of its own. Or you may find it best to use several paragraphs to give a detailed narrative of one incident or two or three related events. (Note how Sister Helen uses several separate "scenes" to tell her story.) Whatever your approach, use some dialogue to enliven key parts of your essay. (Review the reading to see how Sister Helen uses dialogue throughout her essay.)

Alternatively, write an essay about three people to whom you are grateful. In that case, each paragraph of the body of your essay would deal with one of those people. The thesis statement in such an essay might be similar to this:

> There are three people who have made a big difference in my life.

Rowing the Bus
Paul Logan

PREVIEW

There is a well-known saying that goes something like this: All that is necessary in order for evil to triumph is for good people to do nothing. Even young people are forced to face cruel behavior and to decide how they will respond to it. In this essay, Paul Logan looks back at a period of schoolyard cruelty in which he was both a victim and a participant. With unflinching honesty, he describes his behavior then and how it helped to shape the person he has become.

When I was in elementary school, some older kids made me row the bus. Row- 1 ing meant that on the way to school I had to sit in the dirty bus aisle littered with paper, gum wads, and spitballs. Then I had to simulate* the motion of rowing while the kids around me laughed and chanted, "Row, row, row the bus." I was forced to do this by a group of bullies who spent most of their time picking on me.

I was the perfect target for them. I was small. I had no father. And my mother, 2 though she worked hard to support me, was unable to afford clothes and sneakers that were "cool." Instead she dressed me in outfits that we got from "the bags"— hand-me-downs given as donations to a local church.

Each Wednesday, she'd bring several bags of clothes to the house and pull out 3 musty, wrinkled shirts and worn bell-bottom pants that other families no longer wanted. I knew that people were kind to give things to us, but I hated wearing clothes that might have been donated by my classmates. Each time I wore something from the bags, I feared that the other kids might recognize something that was once theirs.

Besides my outdated clothes, I wore thick glasses, had crossed eyes, and spoke 4 with a persistent lisp. For whatever reason, I had never learned to say the "s" sound properly, and I pronounced words that began with "th" as if they began with a "d." In addition, because of my severely crossed eyes, I lacked the hand and eye coordination necessary to hit or catch flying objects.

As a result, footballs, baseballs, soccer balls and basketballs became my en- 5 emies. I knew, before I stepped onto the field or court, that I would do something clumsy or foolish and that everyone would laugh at me. I feared humiliation so much that I became skillful at feigning illnesses to get out of gym class. Eventually I learned how to give myself low-grade fevers so the nurse would write me an excuse. It worked for a while, until the gym teachers caught on. When I did have to play, I was always the last one chosen to be on any team. In fact, team captains did everything in their power to make their opponents get stuck with me. When the unlucky team captain was forced to call my name, I would trudge over to the team, knowing that no one there liked or wanted me. For four years, from second through fifth grade, I prayed nightly for God to give me school days in which I would not be insulted, embarrassed, or made to feel ashamed.

I thought my prayers were answered when my mother decided to move dur- 6 ing the summer before sixth grade. The move meant that I got to start sixth grade in a different school, a place where I had no reputation. Although the older kids laughed and snorted at me as soon as I got on my new bus—they couldn't miss my thick glasses and strange clothes—I soon discovered that there was another kid who received the brunt of their insults. His name was George, and everyone made fun of him. The kids taunted him because he was skinny; they belittled him because he had acne that pocked and blotched his face; and they teased him because his voice was squeaky. During my first gym class at my new school, I wasn't the last one chosen for kickball; George was.

George tried hard to be friends with me, coming up to me in the cafeteria on 7 the first day of school. "Hi. My name's George. Can I sit with you?" he asked with a peculiar squeakiness that made each word high-pitched and raspy. As I nodded for him to sit down, I noticed an uncomfortable silence in the cafeteria as many of the students who had mocked George's clumsy gait during gym class began watching the two of us and whispering among themselves. By letting him sit with me, I had violated an unspoken law of school, a sinister code of childhood that demands there must always be someone to pick on. I began to realize two things. If I befriended George, I would soon receive the same treatment that I had gotten at my old school. If I stayed away from him, I might actually have a chance to escape being at the bottom.

Within days, the kids started taunting us whenever we were together. "Who's 8 your new little buddy, Georgie?" In the hallways, groups of students began mumbling about me just loud enough for me to hear, "Look, it's George's ugly boyfriend." On the bus rides to and from school, wads of paper and wet chewing gum were tossed at me by the bigger, older kids in the back of the bus.

It became clear that my friendship with George was going to cause me sev- 9 eral more years of misery at my new school. I decided to stop being friends with George. In class and at lunch, I spent less and less time with him. Sometimes I told him I was too busy to talk; other times I acted distracted and gave one-word responses to whatever he said. Our classmates, sensing that they had created a rift* between George and me, intensified their attacks on him. Each day, George grew more desperate as he realized that the one person who could prevent him from being completely isolated was closing him off. I knew that I shouldn't avoid him, that he was feeling the same way I felt for so long, but I was so afraid that my life would become the hell it had been in my old school that I continued to ignore him.

Then, at recess one day, the meanest kid in the school, Chris, decided he had 10 had enough of George. He vowed that he was going to beat up George and anyone else who claimed to be his friend. A mob of kids formed and came after me. Chris led the way and cornered me near our school's swing sets. He grabbed me by my shirt and raised his fist over my head. A huge gathering of kids surrounded us, urging him to beat me up, chanting "Go, Chris, go!"

"You're Georgie's new little boyfriend, aren't you?" he yelled. The hot blast 11 of his breath carried droplets of his spit into my face. In a complete betrayal of the only kid who was nice to me, I denied George's friendship.

"No, I'm not George's friend. I don't like him. He's stupid," I blurted out. Sev- 12 eral kids snickered and mumbled under their breath. Chris stared at me for a few seconds and then threw me to the ground.

"Wimp. Where's George?" he demanded, standing over me. Someone pointed 13 to George sitting alone on top of the monkey bars about thirty yards from where we were. He was watching me. Chris and his followers sprinted over to George and yanked him off the bars to the ground. Although the mob quickly encircled them, I could still see the two of them at the center of the crowd, looking at each other.

George seemed stoic, staring straight through Chris. I heard the familiar chant of "Go, Chris, go!" and watched as his fists began slamming into George's head and body. His face bloodied and his nose broken, George crumpled to the ground and sobbed without even throwing a punch. The mob cheered with pleasure and darted off into the playground to avoid an approaching teacher.

Chris was suspended, and after a few days, George came back to school. I 14 wanted to talk to him, to ask him how he was, to apologize for leaving him alone and for not trying to stop him from getting hurt. But I couldn't go near him. Filled with shame for denying George and angered by my own cowardice, I never spoke to him again.

Several months later, without telling any students, George transferred to an- 15 other school. Once in a while, in those last weeks before he left, I caught him watching me as I sat with the rest of the kids in the cafeteria. He never yelled at me or expressed anger, disappointment, or even sadness. Instead he just looked at me.

In the years that followed, George's silent stare remained with me. It was there 16 in eighth grade when I saw a gang of popular kids beat up a sixth-grader because, they said, he was "ugly and stupid." It was there my first year in high school, when I saw a group of older kids steal another freshman's clothes and throw them into the showers. It was there a year later, when I watched several seniors press a wad of chewing gum into the hair of a new girl on the bus. Each time that I witnessed another awkward, uncomfortable, scared kid being tormented, I thought of George, and gradually his haunting stare began to speak to me. No longer silent, it told me that every child who is picked on and taunted deserves better, that no one—no matter how big, strong, attractive, or popular—has the right to abuse another person.

Finally, in my junior year when a loudmouthed, pink-skinned bully named 17 Donald began picking on two freshmen on the bus, I could no longer deny George. Donald was crumpling a large wad of paper and preparing to bounce it off the back of the head of one of the young students when I interrupted him.

"Leave them alone, Don," I said. By then I was six inches taller and, after two 18 years of high-school wrestling, thirty pounds heavier than I had been in my freshman year. Though Donald was still two years older than me, he wasn't much bigger. He stopped what he was doing, squinted, and stared at me.

"What's your problem, Paul?" 19

I felt the way I had many years earlier on the playground when I watched the 20 mob of kids begin to surround George.

"Just leave them alone. They aren't bothering you," I responded quietly. 21

"What's it to you?" he challenged. A glimpse of my own past, of rowing the 22 bus, of being mocked for my clothes, my lisp, my glasses, and my absent father flashed in my mind.

"Just don't mess with them. That's all I am saying, Don." My fingertips were 23 tingling. The bus was silent. He got up from his seat and leaned over me, and I rose from my seat to face him. For a minute, both of us just stood there, without a word, staring.

"I'm just playing with them, Paul," he said, chuckling. "You don't have to go **24** psycho on me or anything." Then he shook his head, slapped me firmly on the chest with the back of his hand, and sat down. But he never threw that wad of paper. For the rest of the year, whenever I was on the bus, Don and the other troublemakers were noticeably quiet.

Although it has been years since my days on the playground and the school bus, **25** George's look still haunts me. Today, I see it on the faces of a few scared kids at my sister's school—she is in fifth grade. Or once in a while I'll catch a glimpse of someone like George on the evening news, in a story about a child who brought a gun to school to stop the kids from picking on him, or in a feature about a teenager who killed herself because everyone teased her. In each school, in almost every classroom, there is a George with a stricken face, hoping that someone nearby will be strong enough to be kind—despite what the crowd says—and brave enough to stand up against people who attack, tease, or hurt those who are vulnerable.

If asked about their behavior, I'm sure the bullies would say, "What's it to you? **26** It's just a joke. It's nothing." But to George and me, and everyone else who has been humiliated or laughed at or spat on, it is everything. No one should have to row the bus.

VOCABULARY IN CONTEXT

1. The word *simulate* in "Then I had to simulate the motion of rowing while the kids around me laughed and chanted, 'Row, row, row the bus'" (paragraph 1) means

    a. sing.

    b. ignore.

    c. imitate.

    d. release.

2. The word *rift* in "I decided to stop being friends with George. . . . Our classmates, sensing that they had created a rift between George and me, intensified their attacks on him" (paragraph 9) means

    a. friendship.

    b. agreement.

    c. break.

    d. joke.

READING COMPREHENSION QUESTIONS

1. Which of the following would be the best alternative title for this selection?

    a. A Sixth-Grade Adventure

    b. Children's Fears

    c. Dealing with Cruelty

    d. The Trouble with Busing

2. Which sentence best expresses the main idea of the selection?

   a. Although Paul Logan was the target of other students' abuse when he was a young boy, their attacks stopped as he grew taller and stronger.

   b. When Logan moved to a different school, he discovered that another student, George, was the target of more bullying than he was.

   c. Logan's experience of being bullied and his shame at how he treated George eventually made him speak up for someone else who was teased.

   d. Logan is ashamed that he did not stand up for George when George was being attacked by a bully on the playground.

3. When Chris attacked George, George reacted by

   a. fighting back hard.

   b. shouting for Logan to help him.

   c. running away.

   d. accepting the beating.

4. Logan finally found the courage to stand up for abused students when he saw

   a. Donald about to throw paper at a younger student.

   b. older kids throwing a freshman's clothes into the shower.

   c. seniors putting bubble gum in a new student's hair.

   d. a gang beating up a sixth-grader whom they disliked.

5. *True or False?*_____ After Logan confronted Donald on the bus, Donald began picking on Logan as well.

6. *True or False?* _____ The author suggests that his mother did not care very much about him.

7. The author implies that, when he started sixth grade at a new school,

   a. he became fairly popular.

   b. he decided to try out for athletic teams.

   c. he was relieved to find a kid who was more unpopular than he.

   d. he was frequently beaten up.

8. We can conclude that

   a. the kids who picked on George later regretted what they had done.

   b. George and the author eventually talked together about their experience in sixth grade.

   c. the author thinks kids today are kinder than they were when he was in sixth grade.

   d. the author is a more compassionate person now because of his experience with George.

DISCUSSION QUESTIONS

About Content

1. Logan describes a number of incidents involving students' cruelty to other students. Find at least three such events. What do they seem to have in common? Judging from such incidents, what purpose does cruel teasing seem to serve?

2. Throughout the essay, Paul Logan talks about cruel but ordinary school behavior. But in paragraph 25, he briefly mentions two extreme and tragic consequences of such cruelty. What are those consequences, and why do you think he introduces them? What is he implying?

About Structure

3. Below, write three time transitions Logan uses to advance his narration.

   _____   _____   _____

4. Logan describes the gradual change within him that finally results in his standing up for a student who is being abused. Where in the narrative does Logan show how internal changes may be taking place within him? Where in the narrative does he show that his reaction to witnessing bullying has changed?

5. Paul Logan titled his selection "Rowing the Bus." Yet very little of the essay actually deals with the incident the title describes. Why do you think Logan chose that title? In groups of two or three, come up with alternative titles and discuss why they would or would not be effective.

About Style and Tone

6. Give examples of how Logan appeals to our senses in paragraphs 1–4.

   Sight _____

   Smell _____

   Hearing _____

7. What is Logan's attitude toward himself regarding his treatment of George? Find three phrases that reveal his attitude and write them on a separate piece of paper.

WRITING ASSIGNMENTS

Assignment 1: Writing a Paragraph

Logan writes, " In each school, in almost every classroom, there is a George with a stricken face." Think of a person who filled the role of George in one of your classes. Then write a descriptive paragraph about that person, explaining why he or she was a target and what form the teasing took. Be sure to include a description of your own thoughts and actions regarding the student who was teased. Your topic sentence might be something like one of these:

> A girl in my fifth-grade class was a lot like George in "Rowing the Bus."

> Like Paul Logan, I suffered greatly in elementary school from being bullied.

Try to include details that appeal to two or three of the senses.

Assignment 2: Writing a Paragraph

Paul Logan feared that his life at his new school would be made miserable if he continued being friends with George. So he ended the friendship, even though he felt ashamed of doing so. Think of a time when you have wanted to do the right thing but felt that the price would be too high. Maybe you knew a friend was doing something dishonest and wanted him to stop but were afraid of losing his friendship. Or perhaps you pretended to forget a promise you had made because you decided it was too difficult to keep. Write a paragraph describing the choice you made and how you felt about yourself afterward.

LOGAN'S ESSAY FOCUSES ON what happens to kids who are picked on and ostracized. This photo, however, shows what it is like when a child belongs and has a friend. Write a paragraph explaining how schools and parents can work together to create more positive environments that encourage friendship and belonging.

Assignment 3: Writing an Essay

Logan provides many vivid descriptions of incidents in which bullies attack other students. Reread these descriptions, and consider what they teach you about the nature of bullies and bullying. Then write an essay that supports the following main idea:

> Bullies seem to share certain qualities.

Identify two or three qualities; then discuss each in a separate paragraph. You may use two or three of the following as the topic sentences for your supporting paragraphs, or come up with your own supporting points:

> Bullies are cowardly.

> Bullies make themselves feel big by making other people feel small.

> Bullies cannot feel very good about themselves.

> Bullies are feared but not respected.

> Bullies act cruelly in order to get attention.

Develop each supporting point with one or more anecdotes or ideas from any of the following: your own experience, your understanding of human nature, and "Rowing the Bus."

"Extra Large," Please

Diane Urbina

PREVIEW

Why are so many kids today overweight or even obese? According to Diane Urbina, the number-one culprit is junk food, which is available anytime, anywhere—and in ever-increasing portion sizes. Urbina argues that schools, fast-food restaurants, and the media have a responsibility to raise awareness about nutrition and save people of all ages from a public-health disaster.

School lunches have always come in for criticism. When I was a kid, we com- 1 plained about "mystery meat" and "leftover surprise casserole." Half a canned pear in a shaky nest of Jell-O didn't do much to excite our tastebuds. I hid my share of limp green beans under my napkin, the better to escape the eagle eye of lunchroom monitors who encouraged us to eat our soggy, overcooked vegetables.

But the cafeteria lunches were there, and so we ate them. (Most of them. OK, I 2 hid the gooey tapioca pudding, too.) I think we accepted the idea that being delicious was not the point. The meals were reasonably nutritious and they fueled our young bodies for the mental and physical demands of the day. In my case, that demand in- cluded walking a quarter-mile to and from school, enjoying three recesses a day, and taking part in gym class a couple of times a week. After-school hours, at least when the weather was good, were spent outdoors playing kickball or tag with neighbor kids.

I can imagine you wondering, "Who cares?" I don't blame you. My memories 3 of schooldays in northern Indiana thirty-some years ago aren't all that fascinating even to me. And yet I think you should care, because of one fact I haven't men- tioned yet. When I was a kid and looked around at other kids my age, I saw all kinds of differences. There were tall ones and short ones and black and white and brown ones, rude ones and polite ones, popular ones and geeky ones, athletic ones and uncoordinated ones. But you know what? There weren't many heavy ones. The few there were stood out because they were unusual. I think that if you had asked me at the time, I would have told you that kids are just naturally skinny.

Flash forward to the present. Walk down any city street in America. Sit in a mall 4 and watch the people stream by. You don't need to be a rocket scientist to notice something's changed. Whether you call them big-boned, chubby, husky, or plus- sized, kids are heavy, lots of them. If your own eyes don't convince you, here are the statistics: Since 1980, the number of American kids who are dangerously over- weight has tripled. More than 16 percent of our children—that's 1 in 6—qualify as "obese." Hordes* of them are developing diet-related diabetes, a disease that used to be seen almost always in adults. When California's students grades 5 through 12 were given a basic fitness test, almost 8 out of 10 failed.

Part of the problem is that many kids don't have good opportunities to exer- 5 cise. They live in neighborhoods without sidewalks or paths where they can walk, bike, or skate safely. Drug activity and violent crime may make playing outside dangerous. They can reach their schools only by car or bus. Many of those schools are so short of money they've scrapped their physical-fitness classes. Too few communities have athletic programs in place.

Electronic entertainment also plays a role in the current state of affairs. Kids 6 used to go outside to play with other kids because it was more fun than sitting around the house. Today, kids who sit around the house have access to dozens of cable TV channels, the Internet, DVD players, and a dizzying assortment of video games.

Still another cause is the lack of parental supervision. When I was a kid, most 7 of us had a mom or an older sibling at home telling us to get off our butts and go outside. (The alternative was often to stay inside and do chores. We chose to go out and play.) Now, most American families have two working parents. For most of the daylight hours, those parents just aren't around to encourage their kids to get some exercise. A related problem is that parents who can't be home much may feel guilty about it. One way of relieving that guilt is to buy Junior the game system of his dreams and a nice wide-screen TV to play it on.

These are all complicated* problems whose solutions are equally complicated. 8 But there is one cause of the fattening of America's kids that can be dealt with more easily. And that cause is the enormous influence that fast-food restaurants and other sources of calorie-laden junk have gained over America's kids.

I'm no health nut. I like an occasional Quarter Pounder as well as the next 9 mom. There is no quicker way to my kids' hearts than to bring home a newly released DVD, a large pepperoni pie and a bag of Chicken McNuggets. But in our home, an evening featuring extra mozzarella and bottles of 7-Up is a once-in-a-while treat—sort of a guilty pleasure.

To many of today's kids, fast food is not a treat—it's their daily diet. Their nor- 10 mal dinnertime equals McDonald's, Pizza Hut, Domino's, Burger King, Taco Bell, or Kentucky Fried Chicken, all washed down with Pepsi. And increasingly, lunchtime at school means those foods too. About 20 percent of our nation's schools have sold chain restaurants the right to put their food items on the lunch line. Many schools also allow candy and soft-drink vending machines on their campuses. The National Soft Drink Association reports that 60 percent of public and private middle schools and high schools make sodas available for purchase.

Believe me, when I was a kid, if the lunchline had offered me a couple of slices 11 of double-crust stuffed pepperoni-sausage pizza instead of a Turkey Submarine, I would have said yes before you could say the words "clogged arteries." And when I needed a mid-afternoon pick-me-up, I would have gladly traded a handful of change for a Coke and a Snickers bar.

And then I would have gone back into algebra class and spent the hour bounc- 12 ing between a sugar high and a fat-induced coma.

Stopping off at Taco Bell for an occasional Seven-Layer Burrito is one thing. 13 But when fast foods become the staple of young people's diets, it's the kids who become Whoppers. And it has become the staple for many. According to researchers at Children's Hospital Boston, during any given week, three out of four children eat a fast-food meal one or more times a day. The beverages they chug down are a problem, too. The U.S. Department of Agriculture says that every day, the average adolescent drinks enough soda and fruit beverages to equal the sugar content of 50 chocolate-chip cookies.

The problem isn't only that burgers, fries, and sodas aren't nutritious to begin 14 with—although they aren't. What has made the situation much worse is the increasingly huge portions sold by fast-food restaurants. Back when McDonald's began business, its standard meal consisted of a hamburger, two ounces of French fries, and a 12-ounce Coke. That meal provided 590 calories. But today's customers don't have to be satisfied with such modest portions. For very little more money, diners can end up with a quarter-pound burger, extra-large fries, and extra-large cup of Coke that add up to 1,550 calories. A whole generation of kids is growing up believing that this massive shot of fat, sugar, and sodium equals a "normal portion." As a result, they're becoming extra large themselves.

As kids sit down to watch the after-school and Saturday-morning shows designed 15 for them, they aren't just taking in the programs themselves. They're seeing at least an hour of commercials for every five hours of programming. On Saturday mornings, nine out of 10 of those commercials are for sugary cereals, fast foods, and other non-nutritious junk. Many of the commercials are tied in with popular toys or beloved cartoon characters or movies aimed at children. Watching those commercials makes the kids hungry—or at least they think they're hungry. (Thanks to all the factors mentioned here, many children can no longer tell if they're genuinely hungry or not. They've been programmed to eat for many reasons other than hunger.) So they snack as they sit in front of the TV set. Then at mealtime, they beg to go out for more junk food. And they get bigger, and bigger, and bigger.

IN WHAT WAYS DOES THIS PRODUCT REFLECT THE PROBLEMS that Urbina discusses? Write a paragraph that argues the pros and cons of such products. Use the points Urbina makes in her essay as well as your own reasons to support your argument.

There is no overnight 16 solution to the problem of American children's increasing weight and decreasing level of physical fitness. But can anything be done? To begin with, fast-food meals and junk-food vending machines should be banned from schools. Our education system should be helping children acquire good nutritional habits, not assisting them in committing slow nutritional suicide.

In addition, commercials for junk food should be banned from TV during chil- 17 dren's viewing time, specifically Saturday mornings.

And finally, fast-food restaurants should be required to do what tobacco 18 companies—another manufacturer of products known to harm people's health— have to do. They should display in their restaurants, and in their TV and print ads as well, clear nutritional information about their products. For instance, a young woman at Burger King who was considering ordering a Double Whopper with Cheese, a king-size order of fries and a king-size Dr. Pepper could read something like this:

Your meal will provide 2030 calories, 860 of those calories from fat. **19**

Your recommended daily intake is 2000 calories, with no more than 600 of 20 *those calories coming from fat.*

At a glance, then, the customer could see that in one fast-food meal, she was 21 taking in more calories and fat than she should consume in an entire day.

Overweight kids today become overweight adults tomorrow. Overweight 22 adults are at increased risk for heart disease, diabetes, stroke, and cancer. Schools, fast-food restaurants, and the media are contributing to a public-health disaster in the making. Anything that can be done to decrease the role junk food plays in kids' lives needs to be done, and done quickly.

VOCABULARY IN CONTEXT

1. The word *hordes* in "More than 16 percent of our children—that's 1 in 6— qualify as 'obese.' Hordes of them are developing diet-related diabetes, a disease that used to be seen almost always in adults" (paragraph 4) means

   a. few.

   b. many.

   c. hardly any.

   d. a handful.

2. The word *complicated* in "These are all complicated problems whose solutions are equally complicated" (paragraph 8) means

   a. simple.

   b. interesting.

   c. complex.

   d. easy.

READING COMPREHENSION QUESTIONS

1. Which of the following would be the best alternative title for this selection?

   a. Healthy School Lunches

   b. Solving Childhood Obesity

   c. The Dangers of Childhood Obesity

   d. Too Much of a Junk Thing

2. Which sentence best expresses the central idea of the selection?

   a. Electronic entertainment is responsible for childhood obesity.

   b. More physical-fitness classes are needed to solve childhood obesity.

   c. We need to reduce the role that junk food plays in children's lives and help children acquire good nutritional habits.

   d. School lunches are much more nutritious than junk food.

3. According to the author, which of the following does *not* contribute to childhood obesity?

   a. Electronic entertainment

   b. Fewer opportunities to exercise

   c. Occasional fast-food treats

   d. Lack of parental supervision

4. *True or False?* _____ Today, 1 in 6 children in America qualifies as "obese."

5. The author argues that fast-food restaurant chains should be required to

   a. provide nutritional information about their products.

   b. reduce the portion sizes of their products.

   c. use healthier ingredients in their products.

   d. reduce the amount of saturated fats contained in their products.

6. Many public and private middle schools and high schools

   a. provide students with healthy lunch options.

   b. refuse to allow candy vending machines on their campuses.

   c. make soft drinks available for purchase.

   d. refuse to offer items from fast-food restaurant chains.

7. From the article, we can infer that the author

   a. believes her readers are genuinely concerned about her topic.

   b. is trying to convince her readers about the importance of her topic.

   c. is trying to encourage her readers to lobby for school lunch reform.

   d. believes that the solution to childhood obesity is simple.

8. When the author suggests that fast-food restaurants should be required to display nutritional information about their products, she is assuming that

    a. many of the items will exceed the recommended daily intake of calories.

    b. the tobacco companies will also display information about their products.

    c. fast-food restaurants will feel pressured to offer healthier menu items.

    d. people will then choose to eat more wisely.

DISCUSSION QUESTIONS

About Content

1. In paragraph 3, the author says to her readers, "I can imagine you wondering, 'Who cares?'" Does she blame her readers? Why does she think they should care?

2. Do you feel that the author's solutions in paragraphs 16–18 will solve "the problem of American children's increasing weight and decreasing level of physical fitness"? With a partner, discuss what other solutions are needed to counteract this problem.

3. How might the author revise her essay to appeal directly to children and teenagers? What might she say to them? What might convince them to change their eating habits?

About Structure

4. What patterns of development does the author use in her essay? Explain.

5. The author uses *addition words* to signal added ideas. Locate and write three of these words:

    _____   _____   _____

6. The author uses the first-person approach, which relies on her own experiences. Do you feel that she is credible? What details does she include in her essay to convince us of her trustworthiness?

About Style and Tone

7. In paragraph 1, the author recounts her experiences eating school lunches. She could have simply written, "I ate casseroles, canned fruits, and cooked vegetables." Instead she writes, "Half a canned pear in a shaky nest of Jell-O didn't do much to excite our tastebuds. I hid my share of limp green beans under my napkin, the better to escape the eagle eye of lunchroom monitors who encouraged us to eat our soggy, overcooked vegetables." Why do you think she provides such vivid details? What is the effect on her readers?

8. The author uses statistics as well as personal experiences. Find three places in the selection where statistics are cited:

Paragraph _____

Paragraph _____

Paragraph _____

What do statistics accomplish that anecdotes cannot?

9. What are a few words that the author would probably use to describe the people who are responsible for fast-food marketing? Find evidence in the selection to support your opinion.

WRITING ASSIGNMENTS

Assignment 1: Writing a Paragraph

Diane Urbina discusses why 1 in 6 children in our country is considered obese. Choose one of the problems she identifies, such as lack of opportunities for children to exercise, and write a paragraph in which you discuss what could be done to help solve the problem. Following are a few possible topic sentences for this assignment:

> Children would have more opportunities to exercise if the government would allocate funds to build playgrounds, fields, and basketball courts.

> Parents should spend time with their children doing physical activities, such as riding bikes, going for hikes, or swimming at the neighborhood pool.

Assignment 2: Writing a Paragraph

What did you learn from the selection, or what do you already know, about obesity that might influence your own future? Write a paragraph in which you list three or four ways in which you could minimize or avoid some of the problems often faced by those struggling with their weight. For instance, you may decide to do whatever you can to remain as healthy as possible throughout your life. That might involve taking daily walks, eating less junk food, and cooking more nutritious meals. Your topic sentence might simply be "There are three important ways in which I hope to avoid some of the problems often faced by those struggling with obesity."

Assignment 3: Writing an Essay

Diane Urbina offers several suggestions to address the obesity problem in children. Recently, many cities have started writing laws that require restaurants to post the nutrition facts on the menu or menu board. Other cities have tried to pass laws limiting the portion sizes of foods and beverages being sold in restaurants.

City officials have often cited the growing obesity problem as a reason to require making this information more public. One argument against these laws is that it hurts sales, thus cutting into restaurants' profits. Write an essay either supporting or arguing against such laws. You may need to do some research about proposed and current laws before you are able to write a persuasive paper with good support. Remember if you use any information from your research, either direct quotes or general ideas, you need to tell your reader where the information originates.

What Good Families Are Doing Right

Dolores Curran

PREVIEW

It isn't easy to be a successful parent these days. Pressured by the conflicting demands of home and workplace, confused by changing moral standards, and drowned out by the constant barrage of new media, today's parents seem to be facing impossible odds in their struggle to raise healthy families. Yet some parents manage to "do it all"—and even remain on speaking terms with their children. How do they do it? Dolores Curran's survey offers some significant suggestions; her article could serve as a recipe for a successful family.

I have worked with families for fifteen years, conducting hundreds of semi- 1
nars, workshops, and classes on parenting, and I meet good families all the time. They're fairly easy to recognize. Good families have a kind of visible strength. They expect problems and work together to find solutions, applying common sense and trying new methods to meet new needs. And they share a common shortcoming— they can tell me in a minute what's wrong with them, but they aren't sure what's right with them. Many healthy families with whom I work, in fact, protest at being called *healthy*. They don't think they are. The professionals who work with them do.

To prepare the book on which this article is based, I asked respected workers in 2
the fields of education, religion, health, family counseling, and voluntary organizations to identify a list of possible traits of a healthy family. Together we isolated fifty-six such traits, and I sent this list to five hundred professionals who regularly work with families—teachers, doctors, principals, members of the clergy, scout directors, YMCA leaders, family counselors, social workers—asking them to pick the fifteen qualities they most commonly found in healthy families.

While all of these traits are important, the one most often cited as central to 3
close family life is communication: The healthy family knows how to talk—and how to listen.

"Without communication you don't know one another," wrote one family 4 counselor. "If you don't know one another, you don't care about one another, and that's what the family is all about."

"The most familiar complaint I hear from wives I counsel is 'He won't talk to 5 me' and 'He doesn't listen to me,'" said a pastoral marriage counselor. "And when I share this complaint with their husbands, they don't hear *me,* either."

"We have kids in classes whose families are so robotized by television that 6 they don't know one another," said a fifth-grade teacher.

Professional counselors are not the only ones to recognize the need. The phe- 7 nomenal growth of communication groups such as Parent Effectiveness Training, Parent Awareness, Marriage Encounter, Couple Communication, and literally hundreds of others tells us that the need for effective communication—the sharing of deepest feelings—is felt by many.

Healthy families have also recognized this need, and they have, either instinc- 8 tively or consciously, developed methods of meeting it. They know that conflicts are to be expected, that we all become angry and frustrated and discouraged. And they know how to reveal those feelings—good and bad—to each other. Honest communication isn't always easy. But when it's working well, there are certain recognizable signs or symptoms, what I call the hallmarks of the successfully communicating family.

The Family Exhibits a Strong Relationship between the Parents

According to Dr. Jerry M. Lewis—author of a significant work on families, *No* 9 *Single Thread*—healthy spouses complement, rather than dominate, each other. Either husband or wife could be the leader, depending on the circumstances. In the unhealthy families he studied, the dominant spouse had to hide feelings of weakness while the submissive spouse feared being put down if he or she exposed a weakness.

Children in the healthy family have no question about which parent is boss. 10 Both parents are. If children are asked who is boss, they're likely to respond, "Sometimes Mom, sometimes Dad." And, in a wonderful statement, Dr. Lewis adds, "If you ask if they're comfortable with this, they look at you as if you're crazy—as if there's no other way it ought to be."

My survey respondents echo Dr. Lewis. One wrote, "The healthiest families I 11 know are ones in which the mother and father have a strong, loving relationship. This seems to flow over to the children and even beyond the home. It seems to breed security in the children and, in turn, fosters the ability to take risks, to reach out to others, to search for their own answers, become independent and develop a good self-image."

The Family Has Control over Television

Television has been maligned, praised, damned, cherished, and even thrown out. 12 It has more influence on children's values than anything else except their parents. Over and over, when I'm invited to help families mend their communication ruptures, I hear "But we have no time for this." These families have literally turned their "family-together" time over to television. Even those who control the quality of programs watched and set "homework-first" regulations feel reluctant to intrude upon the individual's right to spend his or her spare time in front of the set. Many families avoid clashes over program selection by furnishing a set for each family member. One of the women who was most desperate to establish a better sense of communication in her family confided to me that they owned nine sets. Nine sets for seven people!

Whether the breakdown in family communication leads to excessive viewing 13 or whether too much television breaks into family lives, we don't know. But we do know that we can become out of one another's reach when we're in front of a TV set. The term *television widow* is not humorous to thousands whose spouses are absent even when they're there. One woman remarked, "I can't get worried about whether there's life after death. I'd be satisfied with life after dinner."

In family-communication workshops, I ask families to make a list of phrases 14 they most commonly hear in their home. One parent was aghast* to discover that his family's most familiar comments were "What's on?" and "Move." In families like this one, communication isn't hostile—it's just missing.

But television doesn't have to be a villain. A 1980 Gallup Poll found that the 15 public sees great potential for television as a positive force. It can be a tremendous device for initiating discussion on subjects that may not come up elsewhere, subjects such as sexuality, corporate ethics, sportsmanship, and marital fidelity.

Even very bad programs offer material for values clarification if family mem- 16 bers view them together. My sixteen-year-old son and his father recently watched a program in which hazardous driving was part of the hero's characterization. At one point, my son turned to his dad and asked, "Is that possible to do with that kind of truck?"

"I don't know," replied my husband, "but it sure is dumb. If that load shifted 17 . . ." With that, they launched into a discussion on the responsibility of drivers that didn't have to originate as a parental lecture. Furthermore, as the discussion became more engrossing* to them, they turned the sound down so that they could continue their conversation.

Parents frequently report similar experiences; in fact, this use of television was 18 recommended in the widely publicized 1972 Surgeon General's report as the most effective form of television gatekeeping by parents. Instead of turning off the set, parents should view programs with their children and make moral judgments and initiate discussion. Talking about the problems and attitudes of a TV family can be a lively, nonthreatening way to risk sharing real fears, hopes, and dreams.

The Family Listens and Responds

"My parents say they want me to come to them with problems, but when I do, either 19 they're busy or they only half-listen and keep on doing what they were doing—like shaving or making a grocery list. If a friend of theirs came over to talk, they'd stop, be polite, and listen," said one of the children quoted in a *Christian Science Monitor* interview by Ann McCarroll. This child put his finger on the most difficult problem of communicating in families: the inability to listen.

It is usually easier to react than to respond. When we react, we reflect our own 20 experiences and feelings; when we respond, we get into the other person's feelings. For example:

> *Tom, age seventeen:* "I don't know if I want to go to college. I don't think I'd do very well there."
>
> *Father:* "Nonsense. Of course you'll do well."

That's reacting. This father is cutting off communication. He's refusing either 21 to hear the boy's fears or to consider his feelings, possibly because he can't accept the idea that his son might not attend college. Here's another way of handling the same situation:

> *Tom:* "I don't know if I want to go to college. I don't think I'd do very well there."
>
> *Father:* "Why not?"
>
> *Tom:* "Because I'm not that smart."
>
> *Father:* "Yeah, that's scary. I worried about that, too."
>
> *Tom:* "Did you ever come close to flunking out?"
>
> *Father:* "No, but I worried a lot before I went because I thought college would be full of brains. Once I got there, I found out that most of the kids were just like me."

This father has responded rather than reacted to his son's fears. First, he 22 searched for the reason behind his son's lack of confidence and found it was fear of academic ability (it could have been fear of leaving home, of a new environment, of peer pressure, or of any of a number of things); second, he accepted the fear as legitimate; third, he empathized by admitting to having the same fear when he was Tom's age; and, finally, he explained why his, not Tom's, fears turned out to be groundless. He did all this without denigrating or lecturing.

And that's tough for parents to do. Often we don't want to hear our children's 23 fears, because those fears frighten us; or we don't want to pay attention to their dreams because their dreams aren't what we have in mind for them. Parents who deny such feelings will allow only surface conversation. It's fine as long as a child says, "School was OK today," but when she says, "I'm scared of boys," the parents are uncomfortable. They don't want her to be afraid of boys, but since they don't quite know what to say, they react with a pleasant "Oh, you'll outgrow it." She probably will, but what she needs at the moment is someone to hear and understand her pain.

In Ann McCarroll's interviews, she talked to one fifteen-year-old boy who said 24 he had *"some* mother. Each morning she sits with me while I eat breakfast. We talk about anything and everything. She isn't refined or elegant or educated. She's a terrible housekeeper. But she's interested in everything I do, and she always listens to me—even if she's busy or tired."

That's the kind of listening found in families that experience real communica- 25 tion. Answers to the routine question "How was your day?" are heard with the eyes and heart as well as the ears. Nuances are picked up and questions are asked, although problems are not necessarily solved. Members of a family who really listen to one another instinctively know that if people listen to you, they are interested in you. And that's enough for most of us.

The Family Recognizes Unspoken Messages

Much of our communication—especially our communication of feelings—is non- 26 verbal. Dr. Lewis defines *empathy* as "someone responding to you in such a way that you feel deeply understood." He says, "There is probably no more important dimension in all of human relationships than the capacity for empathy. And healthy families teach empathy." Their members are allowed to be mad, glad, and sad. There's no crime in being in a bad mood, nor is there betrayal in being happy while someone else is feeling moody. The family recognizes that bad days and good days attack everyone at different times.

Nonverbal expressions of love, too, are the best way to show children that par- 27 ents love each other. A spouse reaching for the other's hand, a wink, a squeeze on the shoulder, a "How's-your-back-this-morning?" a meaningful glance across the room—all these tell children how their parents feel about each other.

The most destructive nonverbal communication in marriage is silence. Silence 28 can mean lack of interest, hostility, denigration, boredom, or outright war. On the part of a teen or preteen, silence usually indicates pain, sometimes very deep pain. The sad irony discovered by so many family therapists is that parents who seek professional help when a teenager becomes silent have often denied the child any other way of communicating. And although they won't permit their children to become angry or to reveal doubts or to share depression, they do worry about the withdrawal that results. Rarely do they see any connection between the two.

Healthy families use signs, symbols, body language, smiles, and other gestures 29 to express caring and love. They deal with silence and withdrawal in a positive, open way. Communication doesn't mean just talking or listening; it includes all the clues to a person's feelings—his bearing, her expression, their resignation. Family members don't have to say, "I'm hurting," or, "I'm in need." A quick glance tells that. And they have developed ways of responding that indicate caring and love, whether or not there's an immediate solution to the pain.

The Family Encourages Individual Feelings and Independent Thinking

Close families encourage the emergence of individual personalities through open 30 sharing of thoughts and feelings. Unhealthy families tend to be less open, less accepting of differences among members. The family must be Republican, or Bronco supporters, or gun-control advocates, and woe to the individual who says, "Yes, but . . . ."

Instead of finding differing opinions threatening, the healthy family finds them 31 exhilarating. It is exciting to witness such a family discussing politics, sports, or the world. Members freely say, "I don't agree with you," without risking ridicule or rebuke. They say, "I think it's wrong . . ." immediately after Dad says, "I think it's right . . ."; and Dad listens and responds.

Give-and-take gives children practice in articulating their thoughts at home 32 so that eventually they'll feel confident outside the home. What may seem to be verbal rambling by preteens during a family conversation is a prelude to sorting out their thinking and putting words to their thoughts.

Rigid families don't understand the dynamics of give-and-take. Some label it 33 disrespectful and argumentative; others find it confusing. Dr. John Meeks, medical director of the Psychiatric Institute of Montgomery County, Maryland, claims that argument is a way of life with normally developing adolescents. "In early adolescence they'll argue with parents about anything at all; as they grow older, the quantity of argument decreases but the quality increases." According to Dr. Meeks, arguing is something adolescents need to do. If the argument doesn't become too bitter, they have a good chance to test their own beliefs and feelings. "Incidentally," says Meeks, "parents can expect to 'lose' most of these arguments, because adolescents are not fettered by logic or even reality." Nor are they likely to be polite. Learning how to disagree respectfully is a difficult task, but good families work at it.

Encouraging individual feelings and thoughts, of course, in no way presumes 34 that parents permit their children to do whatever they want. There's a great difference between permitting a son to express an opinion on marijuana and allowing him to use it. That his opinion conflicts with his parents' opinion is OK as long as his parents make sure he knows their thinking on the subject. Whether he admits it or not, he's likely at least to consider their ideas if he respects them.

Permitting teenagers to sort out their feelings and thoughts in open discus- 35 sions at home gives them valuable experience in dealing with a bewildering array of situations they may encounter when they leave home. Cutting off discussion of behavior unacceptable to us, on the other hand, makes our young people feel guilty for even thinking about values contrary to ours and ends up making those values more attractive to them.

The Family Recognizes Turn-Off Words and Put-Down Phrases

Some families deliberately use hurtful language in their daily communication. 36 "What did you do all day around here?" can be a red flag to a woman who has spent her day on household tasks that don't show unless they're not done. "If only we had enough money" can be a rebuke to a husband who is working as hard as he can to provide for the family. "Flunk any tests today, John?" only discourages a child who may be having trouble in school.

Close families seem to recognize that a comment made in jest can be insulting. 37 A father in one of my groups confided that he could tease his wife about everything but her skiing. "I don't know why she's so sensitive about that, but I back off on it. I can say anything I want to about her cooking, her appearance, her mothering— whatever. But not her skiing."

One of my favorite exercises with families is to ask them to reflect upon phrases 38 they most like to hear and those they least like to hear. Recently, I invited seventy-five fourth- and fifth-graders to submit the words they most like to hear from their mothers. Here are the five big winners:

> *"I love you."*
>
> *"Yes."*
>
> *"Time to eat."*
>
> *"You can go."*
>
> *"You can stay up late."*

And on the children's list of what they least like to hear from one another are 39 the following:

> *"I'm telling."*
>
> *"Mom says!"*
>
> *"I know something you don't know."*
>
> *"You think you're so big."*
>
> *"Just see if I ever let you use my bike again."*

It can be worthwhile for a family to list the phrases members like most and 40 least to hear, and post them. Often parents aren't even aware of the reaction of their children to certain routine comments. Or keep a record of the comments heard most often over a period of a week or two. It can provide good clues to the level of family sensitivity. If the list has a lot of "shut ups" and "stop its," that family needs to pay more attention to its relationships, especially the role that communication plays in them.

The Family Interrupts, but Equally

When Dr. Jerry M. Lewis began to study the healthy family, he and his staff video- 41 taped families in the process of problem solving. The family was given a question, such as "What's the main thing wrong with your family?" Answers varied, but what was most significant was what the family actually did: who took control, how individuals responded or reacted, what were the put-downs, and whether some members were entitled to speak more than others.

The researchers found that healthy families expected everyone to speak openly 42 about feelings. Nobody was urged to hold back. In addition, these family members interrupted one another repeatedly, but no one person was interrupted more than anyone else.

Manners, particularly polite conversational techniques, are not hallmarks of 43 the communicating family. This should make many parents feel better about their family's dinner conversation. One father reported to me that at their table people had to take a number to finish a sentence. Finishing sentences, however, doesn't seem all that important in the communicating family. Members aren't sensitive to being interrupted, either. The intensity and spontaneity of the exchange are more important than propriety in conversation.

The Family Develops a Pattern of Reconciliation

"We know how to break up," one man said, "but who ever teaches us to make up?" 44 Survey respondents indicated that there is indeed a pattern of reconciliation in healthy families that is missing in others. "It usually isn't a kiss-and-make-up situation," explained one family therapist, "but there are certain rituals developed over a long period of time that indicate it's time to get well again. Between husband and wife, it might be a concessionary phrase to which the other is expected to respond in kind. Within a family, it might be that the person who stomps off to his or her room voluntarily reenters the family circle, where something is said to make him or her welcome."

When I asked several families how they knew a fight had ended, I got re- 45 markably similar answers from individuals questioned separately. "We all come out of our rooms," responded every member of one family. Three members of another family said, "Mom says, 'Anybody want a Pepsi?'" One five-year-old scratched his head and furrowed his forehead after I asked him how he knew the family fight was over. Finally, he said, "Well, Daddy gives a great big yawn and says, 'Well . . .'" This scene is easy to visualize, as one parent decides that the unpleasantness needs to end and it's time to end the fighting and to pull together again as a family.

Why have we neglected the important art of reconciling? "Because we have 46 pretended that good families don't fight," says one therapist. "They do. It's essential to fight for good health in the family. It gets things out into the open. But we need to learn to put ourselves back together—and many families never learn this."

Close families know how to time divisive and emotional issues that may cause 47 friction. They don't bring up potentially explosive subjects right before they go out, for example, or before bedtime. They tend to schedule discussions rather than allow a matter to explode, and thus they keep a large measure of control over the atmosphere in which they will fight and reconcile. Good families know that they need enough time to discuss issues heatedly, rationally, and completely— and enough time to reconcile. "You've got to solve it right there," said one father. "Don't let it go on and on. It just causes more problems. Then when it's solved, let it be. No nagging, no remembering."

The Family Fosters Table Time and Conversation

Traditionally, the dinner table has been a symbol of socialization. It's probably the 48 one time each day that parents and children are assured of uninterrupted time with one another.

Therapists frequently call upon a patient's memory of the family table during 49 childhood in order to determine the degree of communication and interaction there was in the patient's early life. Some patients recall nothing. Mealtime was either so unpleasant or so unimpressive that they have blocked it out of their memories. Therapists say that there is a relationship between the love in a home and life around the family table. It is to the table that love or discord eventually comes.

But we are spending less table time together. Fast-food dining, even within the 50 home, is becoming a way of life for too many of us. Work schedules, individual organized activities, and television all limit the quantity and quality of mealtime interaction. In an informal study conducted by a church group, 68 percent of the families interviewed in three congregations saw nothing wrong with watching television while eating.

Families who do a good job of communicating tend to make the dinner meal 51 an important part of their day. A number of respondents indicated that adults in the healthiest families refuse dinner business meetings as a matter of principle and discourage their children from sports activities that cut into mealtime hours. "We know which of our swimmers will or won't practice at dinnertime," said a coach, with mixed admiration. "Some parents never allow their children to miss dinners. Some don't care at all." These families pay close attention to the number of times they'll be able to be together in a week, and they rearrange schedules to be sure of spending this time together.

The family that wants to improve communication should look closely at its at- 52 titudes toward the family table. Are family table time and conversation important? Is table time open and friendly or warlike and sullen? Is it conducive to sharing more than food—does it encourage the sharing of ideas, feelings, and family intimacies?

We all need to talk to one another. We need to know we're loved and appreci- 53 ated and respected. We want to share our intimacies, not just physical intimacies but all the intimacies in our lives. Communication is the most important element

BASED ON THE TRAITS THAT CURRAN DESCRIBES IN HER ESSAY, IS EITHER OF THE FAMILIES pictured here a "successful" family? What is it about the family's appearance and interaction with one another that lets you know this? In what ways is the "successful" family different from the other family pictured? Considering these questions and the essay you've just read, write a paragraph in which you contrast the two families pictured here.

of family life because it is basic to loving relationships. It is the energy that fuels the caring, giving, sharing, and affirming. Without genuine sharing of ourselves, we cannot know one another's needs and fears. Good communication is what makes all the rest of it work.

VOCABULARY IN CONTEXT

1. The word *aghast* in "One parent was aghast to discover that his family's most familiar comments were 'What's on?' and 'Move'" (paragraph 14) means

   a. horrified.

   b. satisfied.

   c. curious.

   d. amused.

2. The word *engrossing* in "as the discussion became more engrossing to them, they turned the sound down so that they could continue their conversation" (paragraph 17) means

   a. disgusting.

   b. intellectual.

   c. foolish.

   d. interesting.

READING COMPREHENSION QUESTIONS

1. Which of the following would be the best alternative title for this selection?

    a. Successful Communication

    b. How to Solve Family Conflicts

    c. Characteristics of Families

    d. Hallmarks of the Communicating Family

2. Which sentence best expresses the article's main point?

    a. Television can and often does destroy family life.

    b. More American families are unhappy than ever before.

    c. A number of qualities mark the healthy and communicating family.

    d. Strong families encourage independent thinking.

3. *True or False?* _____ According to the article, healthy families have no use for television.

4. Healthy families

    a. never find it hard to communicate.

    b. have no conflicts with each other.

    c. know how to reveal their feelings.

    d. permit one of the parents to make all final decisions.

5. The author has found that good families frequently make a point of being together

    a. in the mornings.

    b. after school.

    c. during dinner.

    d. before bedtime.

6. *True or False?* _____ The article implies that the most troublesome nonverbal signal is silence.

7. The article implies that

    a. verbal messages are always more accurate than nonverbal ones.

    b. in strong families, parents practice tolerance of thoughts and feelings.

    c. parents must avoid arguing with their adolescent children.

    d. parents should prevent their children from watching television.

8. From the article, we can conclude that

    a. a weak marital relationship often results in a weak family.

    b. children should not witness a disagreement between parents.

    c. children who grow up in healthy families learn not to interrupt other family members.

    d. parents always find it easier to respond to their children than to react to them.

DISCUSSION QUESTIONS

About Content

1. What are the nine hallmarks of a successfully communicating family? Which of the nine do you feel are most important?

2. How do good parents control television? How do they make television a positive force instead of a negative one?

3. In paragraph 20, the author says, "It is usually easier to react than to respond." What is the difference between the two terms *react* and *respond*?

4. Why, according to Curran, is a "pattern of reconciliation" (paragraph 44) crucial to good family life? Besides those patterns mentioned in the essay, can you describe a reconciliation pattern you have developed with friends or family?

About Structure

5. What is the thesis of the selection? Write here the number of the paragraph in which it is stated: _____

6. What purpose is achieved by Curran's introduction (paragraphs 1–2)? Why is a reader likely to feel that her article will be reliable and worthwhile?

7. Curran frequently uses dialogue or quotations from unnamed parents or children as the basis for her examples. The conversation related in paragraphs 16–17 is one instance. Find three other dialogues used to illustrate points in the essay and write the numbers below:

    Paragraph(s) _____

    Paragraph(s) _____

    Paragraph(s) _____

About Style and Tone

8. Curran enlivens the essay by using some interesting and humorous remarks from parents, children, and counselors. One is the witty comment in paragraph 5 from a marriage counselor: "And when I share this complaint with their husbands,

they don't hear *me,* either." Find two other places where the author keeps your interest by using humorous or enjoyable quotations, and write the numbers of the paragraphs here:

_____   _____

WRITING ASSIGNMENTS

Assignment 1: Writing a Paragraph

Write a definition paragraph on the hallmarks of a *bad* family. Your topic sentence might be "A bad family is one that is _____, _____, and _____." To get started, you should first reread the features of a good family explained in the selection. Doing so will help you think about what qualities are found in a bad family. Prepare a list of as many bad qualities as you can think of. Then go through the list and decide on the qualities that seem most characteristic of a bad family.

Assignment 2: Writing a Paragraph

Curran tells us five phrases that some children say they most like to hear from their mothers (paragraph 38). When you were younger, what statement or action of one of your parents (or another adult) would make you especially happy—or sad? Write a paragraph that begins with a topic sentence like one of the following:

A passing comment my grandfather once made really devastated me.

When I was growing up, there were several typical ways my mother treated me that always made me sad.

A critical remark by my fifth-grade teacher was the low point of my life.

My mother has always had several lines that make her children feel very pleased.

You may want to write a narrative that describes in detail the particular time and place of a statement or action. Or you may want to provide three or so examples of statements or actions and their effect on you.

To get started, make up two long lists of childhood memories involving adults—happy memories and sad memories. Then decide which memory or memories you could most vividly describe in a paragraph. Remember that your goal is to help your readers see for themselves why a particular time was sad or happy for you.

Assignment 3: Writing an Essay

In light of Curran's description of what healthy families do right, examine your own family. Which of Curran's traits of communicative families fit your family? Write an essay pointing out three things that your family is doing right in creating a communicative climate for its members. Or, if you feel your family could work harder at communicating, write the essay about three specific ways your family could improve. In either case, choose three of Curran's nine "hallmarks of the successfully communicating family" and show how they do or do not apply to your family.

In your introductory paragraph, include a thesis statement as well as a plan of development that lists the three traits you will talk about. Then present these traits in turn in three supporting paragraphs. Develop each paragraph by giving specific examples of conversations, arguments, behavior patterns, and so on, that illustrate how your family communicates. Finally, conclude your essay with a summarizing sentence or two and a final thought about your subject.

To get ideas flowing, draw a picture of your family, and consider what the word *family* means to you. In groups of two or three, share your pictures and definitions, discussing how your family communicates. Compare and contrast your experiences with "successful" communication.

Different Is Just Different

Suzanne Fisher Staples

PREVIEW

Cultural understanding doesn't always come easily, especially when one's only knowledge of another nation or culture comes primarily from news coverage of wars and disasters. In this essay, Suzanne Fisher Staples describes how her experiences in Afghanistan and in Pakistan influenced her to write her novels. She also challenges her readers to see that one culture is not superior to another, but merely different, and explains how appreciating those differences is so vital to creating a more compassionate world.

In Lake County, Florida, where I live, the school board passed a resolution last 1 winter that allows teaching multicultural studies provided they are taught from the perspective that "American culture" is superior. America's growing preference for challenging First Amendment rights over exercising tolerance* is alarming. The good news in Florida is that the resolution has sparked discussion where people didn't know much about multicultural studies before. The mother of a student said to me recently: "I've never been clear on what multicultural means. I thought my kids would be reading about African-American and Hispanic people. I never realized it could make a difference in how America acts as a member of the world community."

There's more to it than that, but she was on the right track.   2

I'm often asked why I was moved to write my first two books, *Shabanu* and **3** *Haveli,* both set in Pakistan, both with Islamic characters. Many people wonder why they should know or care at all about the Islamic world.

The idea of writing fiction first struck me when I was a news reporter for **4** United Press International in Asia. The most important story I covered during that time was the war in Afghanistan. It was, like all wars, tragic and terrible, perhaps more so than others because so many children were involved. After news reporters were denied visas to Afghanistan, we had to cover events from the border area. Often I visited the field hospitals that treated refugees and the Islamic rebels who fought the Soviet invaders. In one clinic in a remote area south of rebel headquarters, I met six boys who were around the age of thirteen. They were all that was left of a ragtag group of one hundred unarmed boys who had fought and killed twenty-odd Soviet soldiers in hand-to-hand combat.

During the Afghanistan War, I began to be troubled by Americans' lack of **5** understanding of people who are very different from us. Every day at news desks all over the country, editors lobbied for space for national, local, and state news in their newspapers. Most days the Afghanistan story was relegated to a paragraph in "News in Brief" columns. It was not because the editors didn't understand the strategic importance of Afghanistan. They knew the Soviet Union had invaded because they needed a warm-water port, and more important, access to the Persian Gulf and the shipping lanes that carry Middle Eastern oil to the West.

What these editors did not understand about Afghanistan, an Islamic nation, **6** was its culture, the ways of its people. It was as if the war were happening somewhere unimaginable, in outer space perhaps. The editors didn't have the sense that these were people just like you and me, whose mothers, grandfathers, husbands, wives, and children were being killed, people who get cold in winter when there's no heat, and are terrified when they hear gunfire outside their houses—just as you and I would be.

The news, important as it is, is not the best way to promote cultural understand- **7** ing. News is based on facts about politics and economics. But fiction invites us into the lives of people who may seem very different from us, but nevertheless share our emotions and hopes and dreams—the stuff of the hearts of every one of us.

I had the opportunity to return to Pakistan in 1985 to do a study of women and **8** poverty for the U.S. Agency for International Development. While the major thrust of USAID's projects was to build or improve roads, tunnels, bridges, and irrigation canals, the agency sought ways to improve the lives of the poorest people of Pakistan, those who live in rural areas. The idea was to improve health, nutrition, and housing for families by concentrating on women. The first step, we decided, should be to teach the women to read. If you teach people the meaning of words on paper, they more readily understand ideas—for example, that things they can't see in their drinking water will make their babies sick or that certain foods will make them grow strong. Teaching people to read makes hope a reality, for many for the first time in their lives.

It was exciting to study the mysteries of poverty and how to break into its 9 cycles. It was also exquisitely* frustrating because the solutions were so complex. It's very difficult to motivate women to learn unless you provide a concrete reason, like showing how it will help them earn money. Otherwise they see little sense in sparing their valuable time and finding other people to care for their children and animals. And it's virtually impossible to teach them to read or make money if they're always sick because their drinking water is too close to their toilets or because they don't have enough to eat.

USAID ultimately decided that this approach to improving people's lives was 10 too complicated and didn't spend enough money fast enough to be politically acceptable, either in Washington or Islamabad. In the end a small step was taken. USAID contributed to a literacy center where women from the countryside would take instruction and return to their villages to teach other women to read. In the face of the crushing problems in their lives, funding the literacy center seemed a small token step.

Now, eight years later, the literacy rate among women in rural Pakistan re- 11 mains at about five percent. Children still go hungry and many die in infancy. USAID no longer funds the literacy center, nor roads nor tunnels.

I can think of little that does more damage to bodies, minds, and spirits than 12 poverty. Change is particularly difficult in economically backward Islamic countries, and many American development experts regard progress there as almost impossible. On the other hand, my moderate Muslim friends regarded our effort in behalf of literacy as a great victory. They're used to small steps, while Americans are of a mind to have it all.

When I came back from Pakistan, people asked: "How could you stand the 13 poverty and ignorance?" It made me want to say: "Look around you! It's not so different here."

Poverty does not define the lives of poor people. Their lives have as much value 14 as ours do. There is more to Islam than repression. All of us have in common the entire range of emotion and experience: love—passionate love of men and women and tender love of parents and children, girl children included; humor—they love to see a bully brought down, an unkind deed backfire.

During my time in Pakistan, I learned something with my heart that my head 15 already knew: "different" does not mean "better" or "worse"—it just means different.

It's important for people to understand that Islam is more than terrorism and 16 fundamentalism and suppression of women—that it's a religion of compassion and justice and poetry not at all dissimilar from Christianity and Judaism in its prescriptions for how we should behave toward each other.

Like it or not, we're politically and economically linked to the Middle East 17 by way of our dependence on oil. Islam is the world's largest and fastest-growing religion. And now we find ourselves yet again in the forefront of making and keeping peace in the Middle East.

A great struggle is being waged for the very soul of Islam. While we know 18 of attacks such as the one on the World Trade Center, we don't know the significance of terrorist activities that don't actually affect us. In Pakistan, fundamentalists have arrested Akhtar Hameed Khan, a poet and philanthropist who once wrote that he admired Buddha. In Turkey, they gunned down the secular journalist Ugur Mumcu. These events were barely mentioned in the American press, yet our not knowing about them is a big help to fundamentalists.

In a *New York Times* editorial in July, 1993, Salman Rushdie wrote that acts 19 of persecution against moderates in the Islamic world are common: "[These acts are] part of a deliberate, lethal program, whose purpose is to criminalize, denigrate and even to assassinate the Muslim world's best, most honorable voices: its voices of dissent. And remember that those dissidents need your support. More than anything, they need your attention."

I went to the Cholistan Desert to gather information for the USAID study. 20 As an outward show of respect, I wore Pakistani clothes. I had reservations about wearing the *chadr,* or veil, which to me symbolized the repression of women. I was mistaken about the veil, as I was in most of my other preconceived ideas about Islam. The *chadr,* when tied between the branches of a tree, makes a fine cradle. It is a backpack for carrying fodder and kindling, a screen to dress and bathe behind, a sheet, protection from the sun, a bandage, a towel. Life in the desert is inconceivable without it.

I slept on the ground with the women and worked beside them learning to make 21 *chapatis* and hauling water. I studied Urdu, the language of Pakistan, so I could listen to their stories and tell them my own. We laughed and cried together and became friends. Their stories became the framework for *Shabanu* and *Haveli.*

The Pakistani are people of extreme courage. Living as they do on the very 22 edge of survival, they depend on each other too much for triviality* to creep into their relationships. They see joy and humor everywhere it hides, and they train themselves to find the best in every situation.

As difficult as it had been to adjust to living there, it was easier than coming 23 home. By comparison Americans seemed petty in their dealings with each other. I was appalled at how much energy we spend on unimportant concerns, such as whether our shoes are in style, or our teacups are chipped when company is coming. (I've been back five years now, and I must report that I now worry over what to serve guests at dinner, what to wear to parties, the state of my teacups.)

But living among the people of the wind forced me constantly to stretch to 24 understand and to make myself understood. It made me grow in ways I never knew were possible. My hope for *Shabanu* and *Haveli* and all good books about people who are different from us is that they will inspire us to grow beyond our limits to learn understanding. And that this understanding will foster peace in the world by teaching us not to fear differences but to become more compassionate people.

VOCABULARY IN CONTEXT

1. The word *tolerance* in "challenging First Amendment rights over exercising tolerance is alarming" (paragraph 1) means
    a. capacity to endure pain or hardship.
    b. sympathy for beliefs or practices differing from or conflicting with one's own.
    c. allowable deviation from a standard.
    d. the capacity of the body to endure or become less responsive to a substance.

2. The word *exquisitely* in "It was also exquisitely frustrating because the solutions were so complex" (paragraph 9) means
    a. carefully selected.
    b. marked by flawless craftsmanship.
    c. intense or extreme.
    d. ingeniously devised or thought out.

3. The word *triviality* in "they depend on each other too much for triviality to creep into their relationships" (paragraph 22) means
    a. something of little worth or importance.
    b. characterized by having all variables equal to zero.
    c. commonplace; everyday.
    d. a remark that is hurtful.

READING COMPREHENSION QUESTIONS

1. Which of the following would be the best alternative title for this selection?
    a. Reporting the Truth
    b. Understanding Creates Compassion
    c. USAID's Positive Impact
    d. Why I Wrote My Books

2. Which of the following best expresses the main idea of this selection?
    a. Afghanistan and Pakistan are two different countries that have been involved in a multitude of wars.
    b. Poverty is everywhere and affects women and children differently than it does men.
    c. Understanding that different doesn't mean better or worse will help us become more compassionate.
    d. American culture is superior and different cultures need to incorporate American values.

3. According to the author, about how old were the boys she met at the field hospital south of rebel headquarters?

    a. thirteen

    b. seventeen

    c. nineteen

    d. twenty-five

4. Why did the author return to Pakistan in 1985?

    a. to visit the refugees she had met during her reporting career

    b. to help distribute medications to the sick and needy

    c. to interview women for her novels

    d. to conduct a study on women and poverty

5. *True or False?*_____ USAID's literacy project improved the literacy of Pakistani women.

6. The author learned that the *chadr,* or veil, could be used for all of the following except a

    a. cradle.

    b. backpack.

    c. skirt.

    d. screen.

7. We can infer that the author of this selection

    a. grew close to the Pakistani women she observed and studied.

    b. wishes she lived in Pakistan instead of America.

    c. believes that "American culture is superior."

    d. became so discouraged by what she witnessed that she wanted to give up.

DISCUSSION QUESTIONS

About Content

1. Why does Staples believe much of the Afghanistan War (1979–1989) wasn't reported in American newspapers?

2. Pakistan's illiteracy rate in the twenty-first century remains very high, especially among women. Do you think if USAID had continued to fund the education programs started in 1985 the literacy rates would be better? Why or why not?

3. When Staples returned from Pakistan, she was often asked how she could stand the poverty and ignorance. Her silent response was that people should "Look around you! It's not so different here" (paragraph 13). Do you agree/disagree with her? Why/why not?

4. In paragraph 18, Staples references the 1993 attack on the World Trade Center and comments that "not knowing about them [terrorist activities that don't directly affect Americans] is a big help to fundamentalists." What do you think Staples means?

About Structure

5. What in the introduction to this essay captures the attention of readers and motivates them to read on?

6. What patterns of development does the author use in her essay? Explain.

About Style and Tone

7. In the introduction, a mother is quoted as saying, "I never realized it could make a difference in how America acts as a member of the world community." How does the final sentence in the essay relate to the mother's statement?

8. To convey her point, what tone does the author utilize? Give examples from the essay to support your answer.

WRITING ASSIGNMENTS

Assignment 1: Writing a Paragraph

In paragraph 5, Staples states, "I began to be troubled by Americans' lack of understanding of people who are very different from us." Write a paragraph in which you react to this statement. Your topic sentence will need to include a claim that expresses your view. Here are two sentences that might begin different paragraphs. One agrees with her statement and the other disagrees with her statement:

> Americans' lack of understanding of other cultures is going to hinder our ability to be a leader in the global economy.

> New York City is a principal example of Americans' positive acceptance and integration of new and different cultures.

Assignment 2: Writing a Paragraph

Staples claims that Americans worry over inconsequentialities. She even admits that she, too, is guilty of such worry. Write a persuasive paragraph in which you explain why Americans need to stop worrying over things like what to wear to parties, whether or not one has the "right" car or house, or who the Bachelor is going to choose. Your topic sentence might be similar to one of these:

> Americans need to stop being concerned about petty matters and should put their energy into important problems like poverty, illness, and human rights.

> Because of their obsession with trivial concerns, Americans are disconnected from the world community.

Alternatively, you might choose to write a persuasive paragraph that disagrees with Staples's point. Your topic sentence might be similar to one of these:

> Americans' aspirations for the latest and most fashionable items continue to keep the economy strong.

> Deciding what to wear, what food to serve, and what dishes to use at a party represent important decisions because they demonstrate consideration of good etiquette.

Assignment 3: Writing an Essay

Staples mentions two terrorist incidents that were not reported in the American press because they didn't directly affect American citizens. She points out that there can be serious consequences when such events are not covered.

For this assignment, you will need to access Newseum.org and click on the link, "Today's Front Pages." You will be able to compare over nine hundred different newspapers' front pages. Choose a major American newspaper like *The New York Times* or a smaller newspaper like the *Anchorage Daily News* and compare its headlines to a newspaper from another country. Many newspapers like *The Calgary Sun, The Wall Street Journal Asia,* and *The Asian Age* are printed in English. Since the front pages change daily, you may want to print copies or save pdf copies of the pictures, so you can continue to work with them even after the headlines change.

Once you have chosen your front pages, you will want to read them over carefully, taking notes about the similarities and differences of the headlines. You may also want to try to answer the following questions as you read over your newspapers:

- Are there any similar stories/headlines? If yes, what is their significance? Is the coverage of each story the same?
- If there are no similar stories, what is significant about the chosen stories?
- Why do you think the editors chose the stories they did?
- Were the stories effectively covered?
- Why do you think the layout of the front page appears as it does?
- What was conveyed by the photos that were used?

Then write an essay in which you compare and contrast the front pages and analyze why you think the editors of the papers chose the stories they did for the front page. You will want to create a thesis that has a claim. Instead of just saying the two papers are similar (or different), you might write "The coverage of international news in *The Anchorage Daily News* was superior to the coverage in *The Calgary Sun.*"

Share your rough draft with a partner to get and give feedback for revision. Refer to the checklist on the inside back cover.

What Students Need to Know About Today's Job Crisis

Don Bertram

PREVIEW

Finding a job in America may be more difficult than it has ever been before. What are the factors that make the job hunt so much more challenging today—and what must students do to increase their chances for employment? Above all, how can students avoid an all-too-common trap in today's economy: post-high-school study and significant debt, but no job to show for it?

Many Jobs Have Disappeared Forever

To begin with, students must recognize a hard truth: Many jobs in America have disappeared forever. There is a well-known story about a meeting that President Barack Obama had with the late Steve Jobs of Apple Computer, America's most profitable corporation. Apple at one time boasted that its products were made in the United States. But now almost all of its millions of iPods, iPhones, iPads, and other products are manufactured overseas—benefiting hundreds of thousands of workers there. "Why can't all that work making Apple products come home?" Obama was said to have asked. Jobs's reply was unambiguous*: "Those jobs aren't coming back," he said. 1

The globalization of jobs is simply a reality of today. Many American companies, like Apple, have shipped their jobs overseas to places like China, India, and Latin America, where workers are willing to work for a fraction of the pay they would receive in the United States. Companies go overseas because they are increasingly owned by institutional investors who focus on the bottom line, rather than on what might be better, in the long run, for American workers. "American business is about maximizing shareholder value," says Allen Sinai, chief global economist at the research firm Decision Economics. 2

Once companies decided to set up manufacturing sites in other countries, with **3** cheaper costs and higher profits, American manufacturing could not compete, and many blue-collar manufacturing jobs for the middle class disappeared. Thirty or forty years ago, the country had an abundance of low-skill, decent-paying manufacturing jobs in the automobile, steel, textile, furniture, apparel and electronics assembly industries, among others. Instead of going to college, a person could work in a factory and still enjoy a middle-class life with a house, a yearly vacation, and the chance to eat steak in a restaurant on a Saturday night. But those days are gone.

Relatedly, the manufacturing jobs that *do* remain in America have been re- **4** duced by automation, which has helped companies cut over six million jobs since 2000. As one executive said, "You basically don't want workers. You try to find capital equipment to replace them." Today there are all kinds of factory robots that perform tasks that once gave people a living wage.

The rapid growth of computer-based technology has also eliminated many tradi- **5** tional jobs. Picture the 1960s advertising agency in the cable TV show *Mad Men,* and think about the abundance of people there who were hired to do jobs now handled electronically by small machines. Secretaries have been replaced by word processing, voice mail, e-mail and scheduling software; accounting staff by Excel; people in the art department by desktop design programs. And today the need for workers of all kinds has been reduced by, for example, online banking, self-service checkouts at the supermarket, and the use of home computers or smartphones to do one-click ordering of food, clothing, shoes, health and beauty aids, books, music, movies, games, tools, and an endless range of sports, electronics, and automotive products.

Also cutting deeply into American jobs has been "outsourcing"—the transfer **6** of many white-collar jobs to the much cheaper labor market overseas. Enabled by global computer networks, questions and problems that were once dealt with by workers in the U.S. are now answered by someone at a computer and phone station in India. The back-office operations of banks, investment houses, and insurance companies are increasingly handled by bright, talented people, hired at low wages, in countries halfway around the world. And many companies have or plan to set up white-collar operations in other countries. A case in point: Pharmaceutical giant Merck & Co. Inc., which operates a plant near Philadelphia, announced plans to invest $1.5 billion in research development in China—enough to build a facility large enough to house six hundred employees, who will work on discovering new drugs, testing them, and getting regulatory approval. Global competition for jobs with people in other parts of the world is a reality that is likely to increase over time.

The Reduced Value of a College Degree

A second key factor in today's economy is that not only have many jobs dis- 7 appeared, but a college degree no longer means what it once did. In the past, a student with a college diploma could walk out the college door, and companies would almost be waiting on the doorstep, ready to offer him or her an interesting white-collar job. Today, chances are that unless students have prepared themselves for jobs in marketable areas, there will be no one waiting at their doorstep except the lenders who have provided them with the loans needed to earn their degree.

Here are a few all-too-typical stories; there are countless others just like them. 8

1. Kelsey, 23, graduated from a university in Ohio with a degree in marketing and 9 $120,000 in student debt. Unable to get a job in her major, she is now working two restaurant jobs and has given up her apartment to live with her parents. Her mother, who co-signed on the loans, took out a life insurance policy on her daughter. "If anything ever happened, God forbid, that is my debt also," said her mother.

   Kelsey didn't seem like a perfect financial fit for a school that costs nearly 10 $50,000 a year. Her father and mother have modest incomes, and she has four sisters. But when she visited the school, she was won over by faculty and admissions staff members who urge students to pursue their dreams rather than obsess on the sticker price. "I was an 18-year-old and they really sold me," Kelsey says. "But no one told me that when I would graduate, I'd owe like $900 a month."

2. Michael, 22, graduated in 2010 with a creative writing degree. Today he is 11 making just above the minimum wage in his job as a barista, serving customers at a Seattle coffeehouse. In the beginning he sent three or four résumés a day, but employers questioned his lack of experience or the practical worth of his major, and he has lost his job-hunting momentum. He is fortunate in getting financial help from his parents to help pay off student loans.

3. Laura, 29, unemployed and with $100,000 in student debt, graduated with hon-12 ors and two B.A.s, served in the Peace Corps, then graduated with a master's degree in public administration. Despite her accomplishments, she searches fruitlessly for work and lives on food stamps in South Philadelphia. At last count, she had applied for more than 250 jobs, from government service to boutique clerk to waitress. She talked about the blue-collar parents that have supported her along the way: "My parents' hopes are in me, and I feel I'm letting them down. My generation wants to succeed, and given the chance, we could shine. But so many things are holding us back."

4. Wanda makes $8.50 an hour working for an employment training center in 13 Florida. She dropped out of a for-profit college after she ran out of money, even with the loans. She has stopped opening her student loan bills but thinks they now total over $90,000. She's a single mother who knows she cannot pay it. "She's worse off than when she started," an advisor says. "Debt with no degree."

5. "I always used to say that I couldn't wait to get out of here when I gradu-14 ate and have a career instead of just a job," Reid, 24, says as he sweeps the grocery store aisles where he still works as what he calls a "glorified janitor."

Reid graduated eighteen months ago with a degree in corporate finance. He hasn't been able to find a job in investment banking or wealth management as he had hoped, and his student loans are over $50,000 and growing. After a year of fruitless job searching, Reid lowered his expectations. No one was hiring investment specialists, because far fewer people had money to invest. "So I changed my approach and expectations," Reid explains. Although he was overqualified, he began applying for low-paying positions at call centers. "But even with those," he says, "they were looking for older, more experienced, and even better qualified workers. That's how bad the job situation is."

6. Eric got a degree in history from the University of Pennsylvania, and he still 15 owes $20,000 for his degree. He's applied for a least a hundred jobs—"any job that looked like something I can do"—but nothing has developed. Now he's a chess tutor for elementary school kids. He believes he was misled: "The good schools project this image that if you have our degree, it's a ticket to any job you want—which is obviously total B.S.," he says. "I don't think I was properly informed of the negative side to all this." And he adds: "If this is what it's like for people who go to the best colleges, how is it for everyone else?"

Five Important "Don't's"

Given the loss of so many jobs in America, and the fact that a college degree 16 no longer means what it once did, here are five guidelines that students should keep in mind:

1. **Don't choose a college because you've fallen in love with it.** Parents and stu- 17 dents often fall in love with pretty campuses. To compete for the parent dollar, education experts say, college officials have long believed that they must manufacture nothing short of Shangri-La University: heaven on earth, with cable and Internet, health facilities, major athletic complexes, libraries, speedy online service—an entire society replicated. "On the college tour," says one student advisor, "they don't take you to the philosophy department. They show you the gym." The appealing extras cost money, and all too often schools pass along those costs to incoming students in the form of ever-increasing tuition.

    Listen to the advice of Barmak Nassirian, associate executive director of 18 the American Association of Collegiate Registrars and Admissions Officers in Washington. Too many students, he says, don't understand that when they go to college, they're entering places of business, not cathedrals on a hill: "A lot of schools have stopped being anything but self-sustaining bureaucracies." His advice: **"Pick a more Spartan school near home, and commute."**

2. **Don't assume a college will give you important advice about either career 19 prospects or student debt.** Some schools are responsible in educating students about today's job challenges. But as one expert has said, "Many colleges are just trying to fill seats. Warm bodies in classrooms help pay for the

comfortable salaries of tenured faculty and administrative personnel. They present school as an opportunity, but it reaches a point where they're just taking people's money. As a result, students leave school with serious debt and without a marketable degree."

Carl Van Horn, director of the John J. Heldrich Center for Workforce Development at Rutgers University, is one of an increasing number of voices saying that colleges need to do better to prepare their students for today's changed labor market. Van Horn says, "Colleges have a moral responsibility to educate students about job prospects, but few offer anything other than advice to start a job search six weeks before graduation." 20

Today's reality is that a college degree itself is no ticket to success. About 50 percent of college graduates are working in jobs that don't require a bachelor's degree, according to economist Paul Harrington of Drexel University. Students in four-year colleges, he says, don't give sufficient thought to how their majors connect to jobs in the real world. 21

As for student debt, the Obama administration has tried to make college pricing easier to understand. Colleges and universities are now required to post calculators on their websites that explain the net tuition price after grants and loans, but critics say the calculators can be confusing, misleading, or hard to find. And the administration has proposed that colleges be required to offer a "shopping sheet" to make it easier for families to measure the true costs and benefits. "We just have to get them much more information," said Education Secretary Arne Duncan. "If you're going to college, you need to know not what the first year costs. You need to know what it's going to cost for the long haul." One student advisor has said, "When a college suggests that students take out $5,000 in loans, I wish they'd put 5,000 one-dollar bills on a table in front of them and explain that debt will follow them for life. Then maybe they could see just what they're getting into." Nassarian adds that lenders have been only too happy to work with schools. "What's better than owning a piece of a student for life?" 22

In light of the above, an important rule of thumb is to not get into major debt. Regard any student loan for more than $2,500 a year as a danger to your future. Like mortgages lugged around for life, student loans can follow you to the grave and can't be discharged in bankruptcy. Lenders can legally collect on those loans by attaching money from your wages and even from your Social Security. 23

3. **Don't start college unless you're reasonably sure you can finish.** The one thing worse than student debt is student debt without a diploma. Only about 40 percent of all four-year college students who start school ever complete it, and among community college students, just one in five earns an associate's degree within three years. Students drop out due to family demands and the need to find some kind of work. As a result, the United States has the highest 24

college dropout rate in the industrialized world. The danger of dropping out is especially high for children of low-income families.

4. **Don't go to a for-profit school.** (To see a list of such schools, Google "for- 25 profit schools" or go to specific online sites dedicated to these types of schools.) Students at for-profit schools often complain that they were misled about educational costs and that their job prospects were exaggerated. Many for-profit institutions have a track record of very high tuitions—sometimes twice that of nonprofit schools—and low graduation rates. Government reports and lawsuits have accused some for-profit colleges of outright fraud, including doctoring attendance records or peddling near-worthless degrees. Never go to a for-profit school without checking first to see if there is a comparable program offered at a nearby community college.

5. **Don't assume that you will need a college degree. Instead, you may want 26 to get a certification or some other postsecondary training in a growing career field.** Former Labor Secretary Robert Reich says, "Too many families cling to the mythology that their child can be a success only if he or she has a college degree." Such an assumption poorly serves candidates who might be better off taking career-related courses, attending a vocational-training school, or learning about other ways to enter the work force.

A report called *Pathways to Prosperity* recently released by Harvard Uni- 27 versity states, in some of the strongest terms yet, that a "college for all" emphasis may actually harm many American students—keeping them from having a smooth transition from adolescence to adulthood and a viable career. The Harvard report concludes: "The American system for preparing young people to lead productive and prosperous lives as adults is clearly badly broken." It is a system that doesn't do a good job showing students the link between their learning and the jobs to which they aspire. The college-for-all rhetoric should be broadened to become "post-high-school credential for all."

And writing recently in *The Atlantic*, Jordan Weissman adds: "When 28 there were fewer graduates, a generic* college degree used to be a valuable credential. Now that the market is flooded, diplomas count less, and specific skills count more. This means that, in many instances, associate's and technical degrees may be more financially valuable than a liberal-arts degree. After all, some of the fastest growing job categories are expected to be in so-called 'middle-skill' positions such as nursing, which do not require a full, four-year education. It's one more sign that, for people seeking to fix America's employment picture, 'college for all' is the wrong mantra.* We need to be talking about 'skills for all' instead."

Other voices express a similar conclusion: One unemployed college grad- 29 uate observed, "I was raised to think that what you needed was a college degree," he said. "That's not the game anymore. It's what you major in." And an employment advisor comments: "Our current college system doesn't work.

You get a degree but wind up in a high school labor market job you could have had before college. But now you're worse off because you have all the debt you incurred getting that college degree." And an education researcher concludes: "The mainstream American approach to education is obsolete. The solution to today's problems starts with education—specifically, work-linked education, the teaching of particular skills to do a particular job. We should not be emphasizing college but career training."

Two Important "Do's"

1. **Do pursue some kind of post-high-school skills development.** In today's economy, job applicants with only high school degrees are among the worst off; just three out of ten can expect to make $35,000 a year or more in their lifetimes, predicts Georgetown University economist Jeff Strohl. One education reporter has said that in today's world facing the future even with a post-secondary degree "is like being in a lifeboat in a roiling sea," but "facing the future with a high school degree is like being in the water." 30

   And writes Adam Davidson in the *New York Times*: "Though it's no guarantee, a B.A. or some kind of technical training is at least a prerequisite for a decent salary. It's hard to see any great future for high-school dropouts or high-school graduates with no technical skills. They most often get jobs that require little judgment and minimal training, like stocking shelves, cooking burgers, and cleaning offices. Employers generally see these unskilled workers as commodities—one is as good as any other—and thus each worker has very little bargaining power, especially now that unions are weaker. There are about forty million of these low-skilled people in our work force. They're vying for jobs that are likely to earn near the minimum wage with few or no benefits, and they have a high chance of being laid off many times in a career. . . . The rest of us, meanwhile, should go to school, learn some skills and prepare for a rocky road." 31

   It's worth noting that most community colleges remain a bargain—a way to make postsecondary education affordable. Average tuition is often about $3,000 a year, compared to a four-year school costing tens of thousands more. And a student can save thousands more by commuting to a community college close to home. 32

2. **Do sail your own ship in looking for a job.** The Harvard report *Pathways to Prosperity* notes that much so-called career counseling is inadequate and nonexistent, with counselors lacking the expertise needed for quality career guidance in today's world. For that reason, you need to take charge of the fact *that it's up to you* to research career and job possibilities. Some students lack street smarts, and they just drift passively and blindly with the tide, not looking or planning ahead for the challenges and dangers that await. Don't be a patsy; your life is in your hands—no one else's. 33

Here's what you should start to do: Educate yourself about what all the 34 adults in your life do to make a living. Educate yourself about the kinds of jobs that are available in the region of the country where you live. Educate yourself about the strongest jobs possibilities by visiting the *Occupational Outlook Handbook* (www.bis.gov/ooh/)—the government Web site that lists the strongest job possibilities for today. (Right now the fastest growing occupations up to 2020 are projected to be personal care aides, home health aides, masonry, carpenter and plumber helpers, veterinary technicians, physical and occupational therapy assistants, meeting and event planners, interpreters and translators, medical secretaries, and family therapists.) Use the Internet to educate yourself as well about how to prepare a good résumé and a good cover letter when applying for jobs, as well as how to handle a job interview.

And, in general, keep in mind that the U.S. economy is one that has shifted 35 from the production of vital goods to a service-based collection of jobs. Ask yourself, "What kind of service-providing job can I prepare for?" For example, one of the largest growth fields in the country today is health care. If your funds are severely limited, consider earning a certificate as a personal care aide or home health aide; chances are that certificate will quickly get you a job with a regular paycheck you can use to gradually take courses in a promising career direction.

Final Thoughts

Knowledge is power. To secure a meaningful job, you must first understand the 36 challenges in today's economy. The first challenge is that many jobs have disappeared, and the second is that a college degree no longer leads to a job in the way it once did. With these facts in mind, apply the "Don't's" and "Do's" presented here. Then proceed one careful step at a time in exploring directions you feel will have the best chance of opening job doors. Remember it's up to you to make the search for a good job a primary and ongoing goal in your life. I wish you success.

VOCABULARY IN CONTEXT

1. The word *unambiguous* in "Why can't all that work making Apple products come home?" Obama was said to have asked. Jobs's reply was unambiguous: 'Those jobs aren't coming back,' he said" (paragraph 1) means

   a. promising.

   b. clever.

   c. straightforward.

   d. indirect.

2. The word *generic* in "When there were fewer graduates, a generic college degree used to be a valuable credential. Now that the market is flooded, diplomas count less, and specific skills count more" (paragraph 28) means

   a. genuine.

   b. specific.

   c. competitive.

   d. general.

3. The word *mantra* in "It's one more sign that, for people seeking to fix America's employment picture, 'college for all' is the wrong mantra. We need to be talking about 'skills for all' instead" (paragraph 28) means

   a. image.

   b. message.

   c. explanation.

   d. definition.

READING COMPREHENSION QUESTIONS

1. Which of the following would be the best alternative title for this selection?

   a. College: The Gateway to Guaranteed Employment

   b. Avoid College, Avoid Debt

   c. College and Employment: A Losing Combination

   d. Employment Realities in the Twenty-First Century

2. Which sentence best expresses the central point of the entire selection?

   a. Globalization, automation, and outsourcing are the reasons why it is now difficult for many Americans to get good-paying jobs.

   b. Because many American jobs have disappeared, students need to pursue some kind of post-high school education that will provide them with marketable skills.

   c. There are ways that today's students can avoid falling into the trap of becoming unemployed or underemployed.

   d. Because they have failed to prepare themselves for the current job market, about 50 percent of college graduates are working in jobs that don't require a college degree.

3. The implied main idea of paragraphs 8–16 is that

   a. today it's common for young, college graduates to be deeply in debt and unemployed or underemployed.

   b. many young American college graduates are deeply in debt due to the high cost of their college education.

   c. today a college degree is worthless.

   d. many of today's recent college graduates are surprised that they have to work so hard to obtain even low-paying jobs.

4. Which sentence best expresses the main idea of paragraph 35?

   a. There are many reasons why it is important to become well educated.

   b. The *Occupational Outlook Handbook* lists the strongest job possibilities for today.

   c. There are lots of job openings in the field of health care and in certain trades such as masonry, carpentry, and plumbing.

   d. It's important to educate yourself about the strongest job possibilities for today and the near future.

5. According to the selection, students who are shopping for a college should enroll at

   a. the one with the best overall academic reputation.

   b. the one with the newest health facilities, athletic complexes, and libraries.

   c. the Spartan one close to home.

   d. the one that functions more like a business, not a cathedral on a hill.

6. According to Secretary of Education Arne Duncan,

   a. not all students need to acquire a post-high school education.

   b. students need to know what college will cost for the long haul.

   c. it is only important for students to know what the first year of college will cost.

   d. students should avoid taking out any loans to pay for their college education.

7. According to Bertram, students should ***not***

   a. expect that their college will prepare them for today's job market.

   b. automatically think that they need a four-year college degree.

   c. enroll at a for-profit school when a community college offers a comparable program.

   d. all of the above.

DISCUSSION QUESTIONS

About Content

1. According to the author, why have so many American jobs been outsourced to countries like China, India, and Latin America?

2. On the basis of paragraphs 19–21, we can infer that like other businesses, colleges need to make money to survive. Do you agree with this statement? Do you think, as the author implies, that this need to make money sometimes overshadows quality of education?

3. Were you surprised by any of the information presented in this article? Did you expect that your degree would guarantee you a high paying job? Explain.

About Structure

4. In the section "The Reduced Value of a College Degree," Bertram highlights six different students' experiences. What is the purpose in presenting these stories? Why do you believe he presented them numerically?

5. Bertram employs the use of bold text and headlines throughout the essay. Why do you think the author chose this strategy?

About Style and Tone

6. Bertram often uses testimony by authorities to support his points. Where in his essay does he use such support? What do you think it adds to his piece?

7. Is the author's purpose to educate readers about the job crisis or to persuade readers to do something? What specific points in the article lead you to that opinion?

WRITING ASSIGNMENTS

Assignment 1: Writing a Paragraph

Imagine that you have completed your post-secondary education and that you now have skills for which there is a steady demand. Write a cover letter for a job that you would like to have. In your cover letter, describe the personal qualities and educational background that would make you an ideal candidate for the job. The cover letter will accompany your resume, which you are submitting for a particular job. Examine the cover letter presented on page 538 to learn the proper format for this kind of letter; examine, as well, the resume on page 539. You might also locate sample cover letters on the Internet to expand your understanding of what is expected in such correspondence.

Assignment 2: Writing a Paragraph

In the selection, Bertram recommends educating yourself about what the adults in your life do to make a living. Take his advice and speak with three people you know about their careers. Be sure to ask them how and why they got into this field, and whether or not they are satisfied with what they are currently doing. After your interviews, write a paragraph summing up what you've learned by talking with these adults. Your topic sentence might be similar to the following:

"Talking with _____, _____, and _____ about what they do for a living was an eye-opening experience."

or

"I learned several things about the working world after speaking with _____, _____, and _____."

Assignment 3: Writing an Essay

Don Bertram states that because much career counseling is either inadequate or even nonexistent, it's up to you to research career and job possibilities. Take a few minutes and brainstorm a list of careers and/or jobs that you are interested in. Then pick three items from your list and research these three, using such resources as the *Occupational Outlook Handbook* (www.bis.gov/ooh/); United States Jobs, Careers, and Education Resources (http://usa.careers.org); and others. Afterward, write an essay that, in your own words, presents the results of your research. Your thesis statement might be similar to one of the following:

According to my research, three strong job possibilities in my region of the country are _____, _____, and _____.

or

According to my research, there is a strong demand for _____ and _____, but not for _____.

BERTRAM'S ESSAY MENTIONS
that one of the causes of the job crisis is outsourcing. Some jobs, like plumbers, electricians, and police officers cannot be outsourced. As you think about preparing for a future job, can you come up with some possible career choices that might ensure that you are entering an industry that won't be outsourced? Write a paragraph about the career you feel would be a good choice for your future and why you believe it won't be outsourced.

The body of your essay should describe in detail what the occupational outlook is for each career; enumerate the expected salary ranges; and define the steps, including training and education, that a person would need to follow to prepare for each career. You might conclude your essay by identifying which career most appeals to you, and explain why.

Do It Better

Ben Carson, M.D., with Cecil Murphey

PREVIEW

If you suspect that you are now as "smart" as you'll ever be, then read this selection. Taken from the book *Think Big*, it is about Dr. Ben Carson, who was sure he was "the dumbest kid in the class" when he was in fifth grade. Carson tells how he turned his life totally around from what was a path of failure. Today he is a famous neurosurgeon at the Johns Hopkins University Children's Center in Baltimore, Maryland.

"Benjamin, is this your report card?" my mother asked as she picked up the 1 folded white card from the table.

"Uh, yeah," I said, trying to sound casual. Too ashamed to hand it to her, I had 2 dropped it on the table, hoping that she wouldn't notice until after I went to bed.

It was the first report card I had received from Higgins Elementary School 3 since we had moved back from Boston to Detroit, only a few months earlier.

I had been in the fifth grade not even two weeks before everyone considered 4 me the dumbest kid in the class and frequently made jokes about me. Before long I too began to feel as though I really was the most stupid kid in fifth grade. Despite Mother's frequently saying, "You're smart, Bennie. You can do anything you want to do," I did not believe her.

No one else in school thought I was smart, either. 5

Now, as Mother examined my report card, she asked, "What's this grade in 6 reading?" (Her tone of voice told me that I was in trouble.) Although I was embarrassed, I did not think too much about it. Mother knew that I wasn't doing well in math, but she did not know I was doing so poorly in every subject.

While she slowly read my report card, reading everything one word at a time, I 7 hurried into my room and started to get ready for bed. A few minutes later, Mother came into my bedroom.

"Benjamin," she said, "are these your grades?" She held the card in front of me 8 as if I hadn't seen it before.

"Oh, yeah, but you know, it doesn't mean much." 9

"No, that's not true, Bennie. It means a lot."   10

"Just a report card."   11

"But it's more than that."   12

Knowing I was in for it now, I prepared to listen, yet I was not all that inter- 13
ested. I did not like school very much and there was no reason why I should. Inas-
much as I was the dumbest kid in the class, what did I have to look forward to? The
others laughed at me and made jokes about me every day.

"Education is the only way you're ever going to escape poverty," she said. 14
"It's the only way you're ever going to get ahead in life and be successful. Do you
understand that?"

"Yes, Mother," I mumbled.   15

"If you keep on getting these kinds of grades you're going to spend the rest 16
of your life on skid row, or at best sweeping floors in a factory. That's not the
kind of life that I want for you. That's not the kind of life that God wants for
you."

I hung my head, genuinely ashamed. My mother had been raising me and my 17
older brother, Curtis, by herself. Having only a third-grade education herself, she
knew the value of what she did not have. Daily she drummed into Curtis and me
that we had to do our best in school.

"You're just not living up to your potential," she said. "I've got two mighty 18
smart boys and I know they can do better."

I had done my best—at least I had when I first started at Higgins Elementary 19
School. How could I do much when I did not understand anything going on in our
class?

In Boston we had attended a parochial school, but I hadn't learned much because 20
of a teacher who seemed more interested in talking to another female teacher than in
teaching us. Possibly, this teacher was not solely to blame—perhaps I wasn't emotionally able to learn much. My parents had separated just before we went to Boston,
when I was eight years old. I loved both my mother and father and went through
considerable trauma* over their separating. For months afterward, I kept thinking
that my parents would get back together, that my daddy would come home again
the way he used to, and that we could be the same old family again—but he never
came back. Consequently, we moved to Boston and lived with Aunt Jean and Uncle
William Avery in a tenement building for two years until Mother had saved enough
money to bring us back to Detroit.

Mother kept shaking the report card at me as she sat on the side of my bed. 21
"You have to work harder. You have to use that good brain that God gave you,
Bennie. Do you understand that?"

"Yes, Mother." Each time she paused, I would dutifully say those words.   22

"I work among rich people, people who are educated," she said. "I watch how 23
they act, and I know they can do anything they want to do. And so can you." She
put her arm on my shoulder. "Bennie, you can do anything they can do—only you
can do it better!"

Mother had said those words before. Often. At the time, they did not mean 24 much to me. Why should they? I really believed that I was the dumbest kid in fifth grade, but of course, I never told her that.

"I just don't know what to do about you boys," she said. "I'm going to talk to 25 God about you and Curtis." She paused, stared into space, then said (more to herself than to me), "I need the Lord's guidance on what to do. You just can't bring in any more report cards like this."

As far as I was concerned, the report card matter was over.   26

The next day was like the previous ones—just another bad day in school, an- 27 other day of being laughed at because I did not get a single problem right in arithmetic and couldn't get any words right on the spelling test. As soon as I came home from school, I changed into play clothes and ran outside. Most of the boys my age played softball, or the game I liked best, "Tip the Top."

We played Tip the Top by placing a bottle cap on one of the sidewalk cracks. 28 Then taking a ball—any kind that bounced—we'd stand on a line and take turns throwing the ball at the bottle top, trying to flip it over. Whoever succeeded got two points. If anyone actually moved the cap more than a few inches, he won five points. Ten points came if he flipped it into the air and it landed on the other side.

When it grew dark or we got tired, Curtis and I would finally go inside and 29 watch TV. The set stayed on until we went to bed. Because Mother worked long hours, she was never home until just before we went to bed. Sometimes I would awaken when I heard her unlocking the door.

Two evenings after the incident with the report card, Mother came home about 30 an hour before our bedtime. Curtis and I were sprawled out, watching TV. She walked across the room, snapped off the set, and faced both of us. "Boys," she said, "you're wasting too much of your time in front of that television. You don't get an education from staring at television all the time."

Before either of us could make a protest, she told us that she had been praying 31 for wisdom. "The Lord's told me what to do," she said. "So from now on, you will not watch television, except for two preselected programs each week."

"Just *two* programs?" I could hardly believe she would say such a terrible 32 thing. "That's not—"

"And *only* after you've done your homework. Furthermore, you don't play 33 outside after school, either, until you've done all your homework."

"Everybody else plays outside right after school," I said, unable to think of 34 anything except how bad it would be if I couldn't play with my friends. "I won't have any friends if I stay in the house all the time—"

"That may be," Mother said, "but everybody else is not going to be as success- 35 ful as you are—"

"But, Mother—"   36

"This is what we're going to do. I asked God for wisdom, and this is the answer 37 I got."

I tried to offer several other arguments, but Mother was firm. I glanced at 38 Curtis, expecting him to speak up, but he did not say anything. He lay on the floor, staring at his feet.

"Don't worry about everybody else. The whole world is full of 'everybody 39 else,' you know that? But only a few make a significant achievement."

The loss of TV and play time was bad enough. I got up off the floor, feeling as 40 if everything was against me. Mother wasn't going to let me play with my friends, and there would be no more television—almost none, anyway. She was stopping me from having any fun in life.

"And that isn't all," she said. "Come back, Bennie." 41

I turned around, wondering what else there could be. 42

"In addition," she said, "to doing your homework, you have to read two books 43 from the library each week. Every single week."

"Two books? Two?" Even though I was in fifth grade, I had never read a whole 44 book in my life.

"Yes, two. When you finish reading them, you must write me a book report just 45 like you do at school. You're not living up to your potential, so I'm going to see that you do."

Usually Curtis, who was two years older, was the more rebellious. But this time 46 he seemed to grasp the wisdom of what Mother said. He did not say one word.

She stared at Curtis. "You understand?" 47

He nodded. 48

"Bennie, is it clear?" 49

"Yes, Mother." I agreed to do what Mother told me—it wouldn't have occurred 50 to me not to obey—but I did not like it. Mother was being unfair and demanding more of us than other parents did.

The following day was Thursday. After school, Curtis and I walked to the local 51 branch of the library. I did not like it much, but then I had not spent that much time in any library.

We both wandered around a little in the children's section, not having any idea 52 about how to select books or which books we wanted to check out.

The librarian came over to us and asked if she could help. We explained that 53 both of us wanted to check out two books.

"What kind of books would you like to read?" the librarian asked. 54

"Animals," I said after thinking about it. "Something about animals." 55

"I'm sure we have several that you'd like." She led me over to a section of 56 books. She left me and guided Curtis to another section of the room. I flipped through the row of books until I found two that looked easy enough for me to read. One of them, *Chip, the Dam Builder*—about a beaver—was the first one I had ever checked out. As soon as I got home, I started to read it. It was the first book I ever read all the way through even though it took me two nights. Reluctantly I admitted afterward to Mother that I really had liked reading about Chip.

Within a month I could find my way around the children's section like 57
someone who had gone there all his life. By then the library staff knew Curtis and me and the kind of books we chose. They often made suggestions.
"Here's a delightful book about a squirrel," I remember one of them telling me.

As she told me part of the story, I tried to appear indifferent, but as soon as she 58
handed it to me, I opened the book and started to read.

Best of all, we became favorites of the librarians. When new books came in 59
that they thought either of us would enjoy, they held them for us. Soon I became
fascinated as I realized that the library had so many books—and about so many
different subjects.

After the book about the beaver, I chose others about animals—all types of 60
animals. I read every animal story I could get my hands on. I read books about
wolves, wild dogs, several about squirrels, and a variety of animals that lived in
other countries. Once I had gone through the animal books, I started reading about
plants, then minerals, and finally rocks.

My reading books about rocks was the first time the information ever became 61
practical to me. We lived near the railroad tracks, and when Curtis and I took the
route to school that crossed by the tracks, I began paying attention to the crushed
rock that I noticed between the ties.

As I continued to read more about rocks, I would walk along the tracks, search- 62
ing for different kinds of stones, and then see if I could identify them.

Often I would take a book with me to make sure that I had labeled each stone 63
correctly.

"Agate," I said as I threw the stone. Curtis got tired of my picking up stones 64
and identifying them, but I did not care because I kept finding new stones all the
time. Soon it became my favorite game to walk along the tracks and identify the
varieties of stones. Although I did not realize it, within a very short period of time,
I was actually becoming an expert on rocks.

Two things happened in the second half of fifth grade that convinced me of the 65
importance of reading books.

First, our teacher, Mrs. Williamson, had a spelling bee every Friday afternoon. 66
We'd go through all the words we'd had so far that year. Sometimes she also called
out words that we were supposed to have learned in fourth grade. Without fail, I
always went down on the first word.

One Friday, though, Bobby Farmer, whom everyone acknowledged* as the 67
smartest kid in our class, had to spell "agriculture" as his final word. As soon as the
teacher pronounced his word, I thought, *I can spell that word.* Just the day before,
I had learned it from reading one of my library books. I spelled it under my breath,
and it was just the way Bobby spelled it.

If I can spell "agriculture," I'll bet I can learn to spell any other word in the 68
world. I'll bet I can learn to spell better than Bobby Farmer.

Just that single word, "agriculture," was enough to give me hope.   69

The following week, a second thing happened that forever changed my life. 70
When Mr. Jaeck, the science teacher, was teaching us about volcanoes, he held

CARSON'S LIFE BEGAN TO change when his mother required him to read two books a week and write a report on each. Many libraries and schools have programs to encourage children to read during both the school year and the summer. Write a paragraph about whether or not you participated in one of these programs, why you did or did not participate, and whether or not you believe school- or library-sponsored incentive programs work.

up an object that looked like a piece of black, glass-like rock. "Does anybody know what this is? What does it have to do with volcanoes?"

Immediately, because of my reading, I [71] recognized the stone. I waited, but none of my classmates raised their hands. I thought, *This is strange. Not even the smart kids are raising their hands.* I raised my hand.

"Yes, Benjamin," he said.   [72]

I heard snickers around me. The other [73] kids probably thought it was a joke, or that I was going to say something stupid.

"Obsidian," I said.   [74]

"That's right!" He tried not to look star- [75] tled, but it was obvious he hadn't expected me to give the correct answer.

"That's obsidian," I said, "and it's [76] formed by the supercooling of lava when it hits the water." Once I had their attention and realized I knew information no other student had learned, I began to tell them everything I knew about the subject of obsidian, lava, lava flow, supercooling, and compacting of the elements.

When I finally paused, a voice behind [77] me whispered, "Is that Bennie Carson?"

"You're absolutely correct," Mr. Jaeck [78] said and he smiled at me. If he had announced that I'd won a million-dollar lottery, I couldn't have been more pleased and excited.

"Benjamin, that's absolutely, absolutely right," he repeated with enthusiasm [79] in his voice. He turned to the others and said, "That is wonderful! Class, this is a tremendous piece of information Benjamin has just given us. I'm very proud to hear him say this."

For a few moments, I tasted the thrill of achievement. I recall thinking, *Wow, look* [80] *at them. They're all looking at me with admiration. Me, the dummy! The one everybody thinks is stupid. They're looking at me to see if this is really me speaking.*

Maybe, though, it was I who was the most astonished one in the class. Although [81] I had been reading two books a week because Mother told me to, I had not realized how much knowledge I was accumulating. True, I had learned to enjoy reading, but until then I hadn't realized how it connected with my schoolwork. That day—for the first time—I realized that Mother had been right. Reading is the way out of ignorance, and the road to achievement. I did not have to be the class dummy anymore.

For the next few days, I felt like a hero at school. The jokes about me stopped. **82** The kids started to listen to me. *I'm starting to have fun with this stuff.*

As my grades improved in every subject, I asked myself, "Ben, is there any rea- **83** son you can't be the smartest kid in the class? If you can learn about obsidian, you can learn about social studies and geography and math and science and everything."

That single moment of triumph pushed me to want to read more. From then **84** on, it was as though I could not read enough books. Whenever anyone looked for me after school, they could usually find me in my bedroom—curled up, reading a library book—for a long time, the only thing I wanted to do. I had stopped caring about the TV programs I was missing; I no longer cared about playing Tip the Top or baseball anymore. I just wanted to read.

In a year and a half—by the middle of sixth grade—I had moved to the top of **85** the class.

VOCABULARY IN CONTEXT

1. The word *trauma* in "I loved both my mother and father and went through con-siderable trauma over their separating. For months afterward, I kept thinking that my parents would get back together, . . . but he never came back" (para-graph 20) means

    a. love.

    b. knowledge.

    c. distance.

    d. suffering.

2. The word *acknowledged* in "One Friday, though, Bobby Farmer, whom every-one acknowledged as the smartest kid in our class, had to spell 'agriculture' as his final word" (paragraph 67) means

    a. denied.

    b. recognized.

    c. forgot.

    d. interrupted.

READING COMPREHENSION QUESTIONS

1. Which of the following would be the best alternative title for this selection?

    a. The Importance of Fifth Grade

    b. The Role of Parents in Education

    c. The Day I Surprised My Science Teacher

    d. Reading Changed My Life

2. Which sentence best expresses the main idea of this selection?

    a. Children who grow up in single-parent homes may spend large amounts of time home alone.

    b. Because of parental guidance that led to a love of reading, the author was able to go from academic failure to success.

    c. Most children do not take school very seriously, and they suffer as a result.

    d. Today's young people watch too much television.

3. Bennie's mother

    a. was not a religious person.

    b. spoke to Bennie's teacher about Bennie's poor report card.

    c. had only a third-grade education.

    d. had little contact with educated people.

4. To get her sons to do better in school, Mrs. Carson insisted that they

    a. stop watching TV.

    b. finish their homework before playing.

    c. read one library book every month.

    d. all of the above.

5. *True or False?* _____ Bennie's first experience with a library book was discouraging.

6. We can conclude that Bennie Carson believed he was dumb because

    a. in Boston he had not learned much.

    b. other students laughed at him.

    c. he had done his best when he first started at Higgins Elementary School, but still got poor grades.

    d. all of the above.

7. We can conclude that the author's mother believed

    a. education leads to success.

    b. her sons needed to be forced to live up to their potential.

    c. socializing was less important for her sons than a good education.

    d. all of the above.

8. From paragraphs 70–80, we can infer that

    a. Bennie thought his classmates were stupid because they did not know about obsidian.

    b. Mr. Jaeck knew less about rocks than Bennie did.

   c. this was the first time Bennie had answered a difficult question correctly in class.

   d. Mr. Jaeck thought that Bennie had taken too much class time explaining about obsidian.

DISCUSSION QUESTIONS

About Content

1. How do you think considering himself the "dumbest kid in class" affected Bennie's schoolwork?

2. The author recalls his failure in the classroom as an eight-year-old child by writing, "perhaps I wasn't emotionally able to learn much" (paragraph 20). Why does he make this statement? What do you think parents and schools can do to help children through difficult times?

3. How did Mrs. Carson encourage Bennie to make school—particularly reading—a priority in his life? What effect did her efforts have on Bennie's academic performance and self-esteem?

4. As a child, Carson began to feel confident about his own abilities when he followed his mother's guidelines. How might Mrs. Carson's methods help adult students build up their own self-confidence and motivation?

About Structure

5. What is the main order in which the details of this selection are organized—time order or emphatic order? Locate and write below three of the many transitions that are used as part of that time order or emphatic order.

   _____   _____   _____

6. In paragraph 65, Carson states, "Two things happened in the second half of fifth grade that convinced me of the importance of reading books." What two transitions does Carson use in later paragraphs to help readers recognize those two events? Write those two transitions here:

   _____   _____

About Style and Tone

7. Instead of describing his mother, Carson reveals her character through specific details of her actions and words. Find one paragraph in which this technique is used, and write its number here: _____. What does this paragraph tell us about Mrs. Carson?

8. Why do you suppose Carson italicizes sentences in paragraphs 67, 68, 71, 80, and 82? What purpose do the italicized sentences serve?

WRITING ASSIGNMENTS

Assignment 1: Writing a Paragraph

The reading tells about some of Carson's most important school experiences, both positive and negative. Write a paragraph about one of your most important experiences in school. To select an event to write about, consider the following questions and discuss them in groups of two or three:

- Which teachers or events in school influenced how I felt about myself?
- What specific incidents stand out in my mind as I think back to elementary school?

To get started, you might use freewriting to help you remember and record the details. Then begin your draft with a topic sentence similar to one of the following:

A seemingly small experience in elementary school encouraged me greatly.

If not for my sixth-grade teacher, I would not be where I am today.

My tenth-grade English class was a turning point in my life.

Use concrete details—actions, comments, reactions, and so on—to help your readers see what happened.

Assignment 2: Writing a Paragraph

Reading helped Bennie, and it can do a lot for adults, too. Most of us, however, don't have someone around to make us do a certain amount of personal reading every week. In addition, many of us don't have as much free time as Bennie and Curtis had. How can adults find time to read more? Write a paragraph listing several ways adults can add more reading to their lives.

To get started, simply write down as many ways as you can think of—in any order. Here is an example of a prewriting list for this paper:

Situations in which adults can find extra time to read:

- Riding to and from work or school
- In bed at night before turning off the light
- While eating breakfast or lunch
- Instead of watching some TV
- In the library

Feel free to use items from the list above, but see if you can add at least one or two of your own points as well. Use descriptions and examples to emphasize and dramatize your supporting details.

Assignment 3: Writing an Essay

Mrs. Carson discovered an effective way to boost her children's achievement and self-confidence. There are other ways as well. Write an essay whose thesis statement is "There are several ways parents can help children live up to their potential."

Then, in the following paragraphs, explain and illustrate two or three methods parents can use. In choosing material for your supporting paragraphs, you might consider some of these areas, or think of others on your own:

- Assigning regular household "chores" and rewarding a good job

- Encouraging kids to join an organization that fosters achievement: Scouts, Little League, religious group, or neighborhood service club

- Going to parent-teacher conferences at school and then working more closely with children's teachers—knowing when assignments are due, and so on

- Giving a child some responsibility for an enjoyable family activity, such as choosing decorations or food for a birthday party

- Setting up a "Wall of Fame" in the home where children's artwork, successful schoolwork, and so on, can be displayed

- Setting guidelines (as Mrs. Carson did) for use of leisure time, homework time, and the like

Draw on examples from your own experiences or from someone else's—including those of a classmate or Bennie Carson, if you like.

Anxiety: Challenge by Another Name

James Lincoln Collier

PREVIEW

What is your basis for making personal decisions? Do you aim to rock the boat as little as possible, choosing the easy, familiar path? There is comfort in sticking with what is safe and well known, just as there is comfort in eating bland mashed potatoes. But James Lincoln Collier, author of numerous articles and books, decided soon after leaving college not to live a mashed-potato sort of life. In this essay, first published in *Reader's Digest,* he tells how he learned to recognize the marks of a potentially exciting, growth-inducing experience, to set aside his anxiety, and to dive in.

Between my sophomore and junior years at college, a chance came up for me   1
to spend the summer vacation working on a ranch in Argentina. My roommate's father was in the cattle business, and he wanted Ted to see something of it. Ted said he would go if he could take a friend, and he chose me.

The idea of spending two months on the fabled Argentine pampas was excit- **2** ing. Then I began having second thoughts. I had never been very far from New England, and I had been homesick my first weeks at college. What would it be like in a strange country? What about the language? And besides, I had promised to teach my younger brother to sail that summer. The more I thought about it, the more the prospect daunted* me. I began waking up nights in a sweat.

In the end I turned down the proposition. As soon as Ted asked somebody else **3** to go, I began kicking myself. A couple of weeks later I went home to my old summer job, unpacking cartons at the local supermarket, feeling very low. I had turned down something I wanted to do because I was scared, and I had ended up feeling depressed. I stayed that way for a long time. And it didn't help when I went back to college in the fall to discover that Ted and his friend had had a terrific time.

In the long run that unhappy summer taught me a valuable lesson out of which **4** I developed a rule for myself: *do what makes you anxious, don't do what makes you depressed.*

I am not, of course, talking about severe states of anxiety or depression, which **5** require medical attention. What I mean is that kind of anxiety we call stage fright, butterflies in the stomach, a case of nerves—the feelings we have at a job interview, when we're giving a big party, when we have to make an important presentation at the office. And the kind of depression I am referring to is that downhearted feeling of the blues, when we don't seem to be interested in anything, when we can't get going and seem to have no energy.

I was confronted by this sort of situation toward the end of my senior year. As **6** graduation approached, I began to think about taking a crack at making my living as a writer. But one of my professors was urging me to apply to graduate school and aim at a teaching career.

I wavered. The idea of trying to live by writing was scary—a lot more scary **7** than spending a summer on the pampas, I thought. Back and forth I went, making my decision, unmaking it. Suddenly, I realized that every time I gave up the idea of writing, that sinking feeling went through me; it gave me the blues.

The thought of graduate school wasn't what depressed me. It was giving up on **8** what deep in my gut I really wanted to do. Right then I learned another lesson. To avoid that kind of depression meant, inevitably, having to endure a certain amount of worry and concern.

The great Danish philosopher Søren Kierkegaard believed that anxiety always **9** arises when we confront the possibility of our own development. It seems to be a rule of life that you can't advance without getting that old, familiar, jittery feeling.

Even as children we discover this when we try to expand ourselves by, say, learn- **10** ing to ride a bike or going out for the school play. Later in life we get butterflies when we think about having that first child, or uprooting the family from the old hometown to find a better opportunity halfway across the country. Anytime, it seems, that we set out aggressively to get something we want, we meet up with anxiety. And it's going to be our traveling companion, at least part of the way, in any new venture.

When I first began writing magazine articles, I was frequently required to inter- 11 view big names—people like Richard Burton, Joan Rivers, sex authority William Masters, baseball great Dizzy Dean. Before each interview I would get butterflies and my hands would shake.

At the time, I was doing some writing about music. And one person I particu- 12 larly admired was the great composer Duke Ellington. On stage and on television, he seemed the very model of the confident, sophisticated man of the world. Then I learned that Ellington still got stage fright. If the highly honored Duke Ellington, who had appeared on the bandstand some ten thousand times over thirty years, had anxiety attacks, who was I to think I could avoid them?

I went on doing those frightening interviews, and one day, as I was getting onto 13 a plane for Washington to interview columnist Joseph Alsop, I suddenly realized to my astonishment that I was looking forward to the meeting. What had happened to those butterflies?

Well, in truth, they were still there, but there were fewer of them. I had ben- 14 efited, I discovered, from a process psychologists call "extinction." If you put an individual in an anxiety-provoking situation often enough, he will eventually learn that there isn't anything to be worried about.

Which brings us to a corollary* to my basic rule: *you'll never eliminate anxiety* 15 *by avoiding the things that caused it.* I remember how my son Jeff was when I first began to teach him to swim at the lake cottage where we spent our summer vacations. He resisted, and when I got him into the water he sank and sputtered and wanted to quit. But I was insistent. And by summer's end he was splashing around like a puppy. He had "extinguished" his anxiety the only way he could—by confronting it.

The problem, of course, is that it is one thing to urge somebody else to take on 16 those anxiety-producing challenges; it is quite another to get ourselves to do it.

Some years ago I was offered a writing assignment that would require three 17 months of travel through Europe. I had been abroad a couple of times on the usual "If it's Tuesday this must be Belgium"[1] trips, but I hardly could claim to know my way around the continent. Moreover, my knowledge of foreign languages was limited to a little college French.

I hesitated. How would I, unable to speak the language, totally unfamiliar with 18 local geography or transportation systems, set up interviews and do research? It seemed impossible, and with considerable regret I sat down to write a letter begging off. Halfway through, a thought—which I subsequently made into another corollary to my basic rule—ran through my mind: *you can't learn if you don't try.* So I accepted the assignment.

There were some bad moments. But by the time I had finished the trip I was 19 an experienced traveler. And ever since, I have never hesitated to head for even the

---

[1]Reference to a film comedy about a group of American tourists who visited too many European countries in too little time.

most exotic of places, without guides or even advance bookings, confident that somehow I will manage.

The point is that the new, the different, is almost by definition scary. But each time 20 you try something, you learn, and as the learning piles up, the world opens to you.

I've made parachute jumps, learned to ski at forty, flown up the Rhine in a 21 balloon. And I know I'm going to go on doing such things. It's not because I'm braver or more daring than others. I'm not. But I don't let the butterflies stop me from doing what I want. Accept anxiety as another name for challenge, and you can accomplish wonders.

VOCABULARY IN CONTEXT

1. The word *daunted* in "The more I thought about [going to Argentina], the more the prospect daunted me. I began waking up nights in a sweat" (paragraph 2) means

   a. encouraged.

   b. interested.

   c. discouraged.

   d. amused.

2. The word *corollary* in "Which brings us to a corollary to my basic rule: *you'll never eliminate anxiety by avoiding the things that caused it*" (paragraph 15) means

   a. an idea that follows from another idea.

   b. an idea based on a falsehood.

   c. an idea that creates anxiety.

   d. an idea passed on from one generation to another.

READING COMPREHENSION QUESTIONS

1. Which of the following would be the best alternative title for this selection?

   a. A Poor Decision

   b. Don't Let Anxiety Stop You

   c. Becoming a Writer

   d. The Courage to Travel

2. Which sentence best expresses the main idea of the selection?

   a. The butterflies-in-the-stomach type of anxiety differs greatly from severe states of anxiety or depression.

   b. Taking on a job assignment that required traveling helped the author get over his anxiety.

c. People learn and grow by confronting, not backing away from, situations that make them anxious.

d. Anxiety is a predictable part of life that can be dealt with in positive ways.

3. When a college friend invited the writer to go with him to Argentina, the writer

a. turned down the invitation.

b. accepted eagerly.

c. was very anxious about the idea but went anyway.

d. did not believe his friend was serious.

4. *True or False?* _____ As graduation approached, Collier's professor urged him to try to make his living as a writer.

5. *True or False?*_____ The philosopher Søren Kierkegaard believed that anxiety occurs when we face the possibility of our own development.

6. *Extinction* is the term psychologists use for

a. the inborn tendency to avoid situations that make one feel very anxious.

b. a person's gradual loss of confidence.

c. the natural development of a child's abilities.

d. the process of losing one's fear by continuing to face the anxiety-inspiring situation.

7. The author implies that

a. it was lucky he didn't take the summer job in Argentina.

b. his son never got over his fear of the water.

c. Duke Ellington's facing stage fright inspired him.

d. one has to be more daring than most people to overcome anxiety.

8. The author implies that

a. anxiety may be a signal that one has an opportunity to grow.

b. he considers his three-month trip to Europe a failure.

c. facing what makes him anxious has eliminated all depression from his life.

d. he no longer has anxiety about new experiences.

DISCUSSION QUESTIONS

About Content

1. Collier developed the rule "Do what makes you anxious, don't do what makes you depressed" (paragraph 4). How does he distinguish between feeling anxious and feeling depressed?

2. With a partner, discuss the following questions, and then share your ideas with the whole class: In what way does Collier believe that anxiety is positive? How, according to him, can we eventually overcome our fears? Have you ever gone ahead and done something that made you anxious? How did it turn out?

About Structure

3. Collier provides a rule and two corollary rules that describe his attitude toward challenge and anxiety. Below, write the location of that rule and its corollaries.

   Collier's rule: paragraph _____

   First corollary: paragraph _____

   Second corollary: paragraph _____

   How does Collier emphasize the rule and its corollaries?

4. Collier uses several personal examples in his essay. Find three instances of these examples and explain how each helps Collier develop his main point.

About Style and Tone

5. In paragraph 3, Collier describes the aftermath of his decision not to go to Argentina. He could have just written, "I worked that summer." Instead he writes, "I went home to my old summer job, unpacking cartons at the local supermarket." Why do you think he provides that bit of detail about his job? What is the effect on the reader?

6. Authors often use testimony by authorities to support their points. Where in Collier's essay does he use such support? What do you think it adds to his piece?

7. In the last sentence of paragraph 10, Collier refers to anxiety as a "traveling companion." Why do you think he uses that image? What does it convey about his view of anxiety?

8. Is Collier just telling about a lesson he has learned for himself, or is he encouraging his readers to do something? How can you tell?

WRITING ASSIGNMENTS

Assignment 1: Writing a Paragraph

Collier explains how his life experiences made him view the term *anxiety* in a new way. Write a paragraph in which you explain how a personal experience of yours has given new meaning to a particular term. Following are some terms you might consider for this assignment:

Failure	Homesickness
Friendship	Maturity
Goals	Success

Here are two sample topic sentences for this assignment:

I used to think of failure as something terrible, but thanks to a helpful boss, I now think of it as an opportunity to learn.

The word *creativity* has taken on a new meaning for me ever since I became interested in dancing.

Assignment 2: Writing a Paragraph

The second corollary to Collier's rule is "You can't learn if you don't try" (paragraph 18). Write a paragraph using this idea as your main idea. First, you will need to find a topic that could be developed using this idea. For instance, you could write a paragraph about the amount of time and practice a particular professional musician has put in to become the accomplished artist he or she is, including any failures he or she may have had. Alternately, you might write a paragraph about how a student can learn to take useful lecture notes through trial and error. To support your topic, find factual details through research or by interviewing someone who is an expert in this area. For example, if you decide to write a paragraph about how to come across well in a college admissions interview, talking to an admissions representative from your college would provide good, expert advice to support your paragraph.

To get your started, below is a list of things adults often need to go to some trouble to learn.

- Driving with a stick shift
- Efficiently studying for an exam
- Knowing how to do well on a job interview
- Planning a trip abroad
- Making a presentation
- Effectively canvassing for a cause

Assignment 3: Writing an Essay

Collier describes three rules he follows when facing anxiety. In an essay, write about one or more rules, or guidelines, that you have developed for yourself through experience. If you decide to discuss two or three such guidelines, mention or refer to them in your introductory paragraph. Then go on to discuss each in one or more paragraphs of its own. Include at least one experience that led you to develop a given guideline, and tell how it has helped you at other times in your life. You might end with a brief summary and an explanation of how the guidelines as a group have helped. If you decide to focus on one rule, include at least two or three experiences that help to illustrate your point.

To prepare for this assignment, spend some time freewriting about the rules or guidelines you have set up for yourself. Continue writing until you feel you have a central idea for which you have plenty of interesting support. Then organize that support into a scratch outline, such as this one:

Thesis: I have one rule that keeps me from staying in a rut—Don't let the size of a challenge deter you; instead, aim for it by making plans and taking steps.

Topic sentence 1: I began to think about my rule one summer in high school when a friend got the type of summer job that I had only been thinking about.

Topic sentence 2: After high school, I began to live up to my rule when I aimed for a business career and entered college.

Topic sentence 3: My rule is also responsible for my having the wonderful boyfriend (*or* girlfriend *or* spouse *or* job) I now have.

Let's Really Reform Our Schools

Anita Garland

PREVIEW

A few years ago, the National Commission on Excellence in Education published *A Nation at Risk,* in which commission members described what they saw as a "rising tide of mediocrity" in our schools. Other studies have pointed to students' poor achievement in science, math, communication, and critical thinking. What can our schools do to improve students' performance? Anita Garland has several radical ideas, which she explains in this selection. As you read it, think about whether or not you agree with her points.

American high schools are in trouble. No, that's not strong enough. American 1 high schools are disasters. "Good" schools today are only a rite of passage for American kids, where the pressure to look fashionable and act cool outweighs any concern for learning. And "bad" schools—heaven help us—are havens for the vicious and corrupt. There, metal detectors and security guards wage a losing battle against the criminals that prowl the halls.

Desperate illnesses require desperate remedies. And our public schools are 2 desperately ill. What is needed is no meek, fainthearted attempt at "curriculum revision" or "student-centered learning." We need to completely restructure our thinking about what schools are and what we expect of the students who attend them.

The first change needed to save our schools is the most fundamental one. Not only must we stop *forcing* everyone to attend school; we must stop *allowing* the attendance of so-called students who are not interested in studying. Mandatory school attendance is based upon the idea that every American has a right to basic education. But as the old saying goes, your rights stop where the next guy's begin. A student who sincerely wants an education, regardless of his or her mental or physical ability, should be welcome in any school in this country. But "students" who deliberately interfere with other students' ability to learn, teachers' ability to teach, and administrators' ability to maintain order should be denied a place in the classroom. They do not want an education. And they should not be allowed to mark time within school walls, waiting to be handed their meaningless diplomas while they make it harder for everyone around them to either provide or receive a quality education.

By requiring troublemakers to attend school, we have made it impossible to deal with them in any effective way. They have little to fear in terms of punishment. Suspension from school for a few days doesn't improve their behavior. After all, they don't want to be in school anyway. For that matter, mandatory attendance is, in many cases, nothing but a bad joke. Many chronic troublemakers are absent so often that it is virtually impossible for them to learn anything. And when they *are* in school, they are busy shaking down other students for their lunch money or jewelry. If we permanently banned such punks from school, educators could turn their attention away from the troublemakers and toward those students who realize that school is a serious place for serious learning.

You may ask, "What will become of these young people who aren't in school?" But consider this: What is becoming of them now? They are not being educated. They are merely names on the school records. They are passed from grade to grade, learning nothing, making teachers and fellow students miserable. Finally they are bumped off the conveyor belt at the end of twelfth grade, oftentimes barely literate, and passed into society as "high school graduates." Yes, there would be a need for alternative solutions for these young people. Let the best thinkers of our country come up with some ideas. But in the meanwhile, don't allow our schools to serve as a holding tank for people who don't want to be there.

Once our schools have been returned to the control of teachers and genuine students, we could concentrate on smaller but equally meaningful reforms. A good place to start would be requiring students to wear school uniforms. There would be cries of horror from the fashion slaves, but the change would benefit everyone. If students wore uniforms, think of the mental energy that could be redirected into more productive channels. No longer would young girls feel the need to spend their evenings laying out coordinated clothing, anxiously trying to create just the right look. The daily fashion show that currently absorbs so much of students' attention would come to a halt. Kids from modest backgrounds could stand out because of their personalities and intelligence, rather than being tagged as losers because they can't wear the season's hottest sneakers or jeans. Affluent* kids might learn they have something to offer the world other than a fashion statement. Parents would be relieved of the pressure to deal with their offspring's constant demands for wardrobe additions.

Next, let's move to the cafeteria. What's for lunch today? How about a Milky **7** Way bar, a bag of Fritos, a Coke, and just to round out the meal with a vegetable, maybe some french fries. And then back to the classroom for a few hours of intense mental activity, fueled on fat, salt, and sugar. What a joke! School is an institution of education, and that education should be continued as students sit down to eat. Here's a perfect opportunity to teach a whole generation of Americans about nutrition, and we are blowing it. School cafeterias, of all places, should demonstrate how a healthful, low-fat, well-balanced diet produces healthy, energetic, mentally alert people. Instead, we allow school cafeterias to dispense the same junk food that kids could buy in any mall. Overhaul the cafeterias! Out with the candy, soda, chips, and fries! In with the salads, whole grains, fruits, and vegetables!

Turning our attention away from what goes on during school hours, let's **8** consider what happens after the final bell rings. Some school-sponsored activities are all to the good. Bands and choirs, foreign-language field trips, chess or skiing or drama clubs are sensible parts of an extracurricular plan. They bring together kids with similar interests to develop their talents and leadership ability. But other common school activities are not the business of education. The prime example of inappropriate school activity is in competitive sports between schools.

Intramural sports are great. Students need an outlet for their energies, and friendly **9** competition against one's classmates on the basketball court or baseball diamond is fun and physically beneficial. But the wholesome fun of sports is quickly ruined by the competitive team system. School athletes quickly become the campus idols, encouraged to look down on classmates with less physical ability. Schools concentrate enormous amounts of time, money, and attention upon their teams, driving home the point that competitive sports are the *really* important part of school. Students are herded into gymnasiums for "pep rallies" that whip up adoration of the chosen few and encourage hatred of rival schools. Boys' teams are supplied with squads of cheerleading girls . . . let's not even get into what the subliminal message is *there*. If communities feel they must have competitive sports, let local businesses or even professional teams organize and fund the programs. But school budgets and time should be spent on programs that benefit more than an elite few.

Another school-related activity that should get the ax is the fluff-headed, **10** money-eating, misery-inducing event known as the prom. How in the world did the schools of America get involved in this showcase of excess? Proms have to be the epitome of everything that is wrong, tasteless, misdirected, inappropriate, and just plain sad about the way we bring up our young people. Instead of simply letting the kids put on a dance, we've turned the prom into a bloated nightmare that ruins young people's budgets, their self-image, and even their lives. The pressure to show up at the prom with the best-looking date, in the most expensive clothes, wearing the most exotic flowers, riding in the most extravagant form of transportation, dominates the thinking of many students for months before the prom itself. Students cling to doomed, even abusive romantic relationships rather than risk being dateless for this night of nights. They lose any concept of meaningful values as they implore* their parents for more, more, more money to throw into the jaws of the prom god. The adult trappings of the prom—the slinky dresses, emphasis on romance, slow dancing, nightclub atmosphere—all encourage kids to engage in behavior that can have tragic consequences. Who knows how many unplanned pregnancies and alcohol-related accidents can be directly attributed to the pressures of prom night? And yet, not going to the prom seems a fate worse than death to many young people—because of all the hype about the "wonder" and "romance" of it all. Schools are not in the business of providing wonder and romance, and it's high time we remembered that.

We have lost track of the purpose of our schools. They are not intended to 11 be centers for fun, entertainment, and social climbing. They are supposed to be institutions for learning and hard work. Let's institute the changes suggested here—plus dozens more—without apology, and get American schools back to business.

VOCABULARY IN CONTEXT

1. The word *affluent* in "Kids from modest backgrounds could stand out because of their personalities and intelligence. . . . Affluent kids might learn they have something to offer the world other than a fashion statement" (paragraph 6) means

   a. intelligent.

   b. troubled.

   c. wealthy.

   d. poor.

2. The word *implore* in "They lose any concept of meaningful values as they implore their parents for more, more, more money to throw into the jaws of the prom god" (paragraph 10) means

   a. beg.

   b. ignore.

   c. pay.

   d. obey.

READING COMPREHENSION QUESTIONS

1. Which of the following would be the best alternative title for this selection?
   a. America's Youth
   b. Education of the Future
   c. Social Problems of Today's Students
   d. Changes Needed in the American School System

2. Which sentence best expresses the main idea of the selection?
   a. Excesses such as the prom and competitive sports should be eliminated from school budgets.
   b. Major changes are needed to make American schools real centers of learning.
   c. Attendance must be voluntary in our schools.
   d. The best thinkers of our country must come up with ideas on how to improve our schools.

3. Garland believes that mandatory attendance at school
   a. gives all students an equal chance at getting an education.
   b. allows troublemakers to disrupt learning.
   c. is cruel to those who don't really want to be there.
   d. helps teachers maintain control of their classes.

4. Garland is against school-sponsored competitive sports because she believes that
   a. exercise and teamwork should not have a role in school.
   b. they overemphasize the importance of sports and athletes.
   c. school property should not be used in any way after school hours.
   d. they take away from professional sports.

5. We can infer that Garland believes
   a. teens should not have dances.
   b. proms promote unwholesome values.
   c. teens should avoid romantic relationships.
   d. proms are even worse than mandatory education.

6. The author clearly implies that troublemakers
   a. are not intelligent.
   b. really do want to be in school.
   c. should be placed in separate classes.
   d. don't mind being suspended from school.

7. *True or False?* _____ We can conclude that the author feels that teachers and genuine students have lost control of our schools.

8. The essay suggests that the author would also oppose
   a. school plays.
   b. serving milk products in school cafeterias.
   c. the selection of homecoming queens.
   d. stylish school uniforms.

DISCUSSION QUESTIONS

About Content

1. What reforms does Garland suggest in her essay? Think back to your high school days. Which of the reforms that Garland suggests do you think might have been most useful at your high school?

2. Garland's idea of voluntary school attendance directly contradicts the "stay in school" campaigns. Do you agree with her idea? What do you think might become of students who choose not to attend school?

3. At the end of her essay, Garland writes, "Let's institute the changes suggested here—plus dozens more." What other changes do you think Garland may have in mind? What are some reforms you think might improve schools?

About Structure

4. The thesis of this essay can be found in the introduction, which is made up of the first two paragraphs. Find the thesis statement and write it here:

   _____

   _____

5. The first point on Garland's list of reforms is the elimination of mandatory (that is, required) education. Then she goes on to discuss other reforms. Find the transition sentence that signals that she is leaving the discussion about mandatory education and going on to other needed changes. Write that sentence here:

   _____

   _____

6. What are two transitional words that Garland uses to introduce two of the other reforms?

   _____   _____

About Style and Tone

7. Garland uses some colorful images to communicate her ideas. For instance, in paragraph 5 she writes, "Finally [the troublemakers] are bumped off the conveyor belt at the end of twelfth grade, oftentimes barely literate, and passed into society as 'high school graduates.'" What does the image of a conveyor belt imply about schools and about the troublemakers? What do the quotation marks around *high school graduates* imply?

8. What do the italicized words in the following three colorful images from the essay imply about today's schools and students?

    . . . don't allow our schools to serve as a *holding tank* for people who don't want to be there. (paragraph 5)

    A good place to start would be requiring students to wear school uniforms. There would be cries of horror from the *fashion slaves* . . . (paragraph 6)

    Students are *herded* into gymnasiums for "pep rallies" that whip up adoration of the chosen few . . . (paragraph 9)

9. To convey her points, does the author use a formal, straightforward tone or an informal, impassioned tone? Give examples from the essay to support your answer.

WRITING ASSIGNMENTS

Assignment 1: Writing a Paragraph

Write a persuasive paragraph in which you agree or disagree with one of Garland's suggested reforms. Your topic sentence may be something simple and direct, like these:

I strongly agree with Garland's point that attendance should be voluntary in our high schools.

I disagree with Garland's point that high school students should be required to wear uniforms.

Alternatively, you may want to develop your own paragraph calling for reform in some other area of American life. Your topic sentence might be like one of the following:

We need to make radical changes in our treatment of homeless people.

Strong new steps must be taken to control the sale of guns in our country.

Major changes are needed to keep television from dominating the lives of our children.

Assignment 2: Writing a Paragraph

If troublemakers were excluded from schools, what would become of those troublemakers? Write a paragraph in which you suggest two or three types of programs that troublemakers could be assigned to. Explain why each program would be beneficial to the troublemakers themselves and to society in general. You might want to include in your paragraph one or more of the following:

- Apprentice programs
- Special neighborhood schools for troublemakers
- Reform schools
- Work-placement programs
- Community service programs

Assignment 3: Writing an Essay

Garland suggests ways to make schools "institutions for learning and hard work" (paragraph 11). She wants to get rid of anything that greatly distracts students from their education, such as having to deal with troublemakers, overemphasis on fashion, and interschool athletics. When you were in high school, what tended most to divert your attention from learning? Write an essay explaining in full detail the three things that interfered most with your high school education. You may include any of Garland's points, but present details that apply specifically to you. Organize your essay by using emphatic order—in other words, save whatever interfered most with your education for the last supporting paragraph.

It is helpful to write a sentence outline for this kind of essay. Here, for example, is one writer's outline for an essay titled "Obstacles to My High School Education."

Thesis: There were three main things that interfered with my high school education.

Topic sentence 1: Concern about my appearance took up too much of my time and energy.

a. Since I was concerned about my looking good, I spent too much time shopping for clothes.

b. In order to afford the clothes, I worked twenty hours a week, drastically reducing my study time.

c. Spending even more time on clothes, I fussed every evening over what I would wear to school the next day.

Topic sentence 2: Cheerleading was another major obstacle to my academic progress in high school.

a. I spent many hours practicing in order to make the cheerleading squad.

b. Once I made the squad, I had to spend even more time practicing and then attending games.

c. Once when I didn't make the squad, I was so depressed for a while that I couldn't study, and this had serious consequences.

Topic sentence 3: The main thing that interfered with my high school education was my family situation.

a. Even when I had time to study, I often found it impossible to do so at home, since my parents often had fights that were noisy and upsetting.

b. My parents showed little interest in my schoolwork, giving me little reason to work hard for my classes.

c. When I was in eleventh grade, my parents divorced; this was a major distraction for me for a long time.

To round off your essay with a conclusion, you may simply want to restate your thesis and main supporting points. After you finish a first draft, swap essays with a classmate and share revision advice; use the checklist on the inside back cover to guide your critique.

How They Get You to Do That

Janny Scott

PREVIEW

So you think you're sailing along in life, making decisions based on your own preferences? Not likely! Janny Scott brings together the findings of several researchers to show how advertisers, charitable organizations, politicians, employers, and even your friends get you to say "yes" when you should have said "no"—or, at least, "Let me think about that."

The woman in the supermarket in a white coat tenders a free sample of "lite" 1 cheese. A car salesman suggests that prices won't stay low for long. Even a penny will help, pleads the door-to-door solicitor. Sale ends Sunday! Will work for food.

The average American exists amid a perpetual torrent of propaganda. Everyone, 2 it sometimes seems, is trying to make up someone else's mind. If it isn't an athletic shoe company, it's a politician, a panhandler, a pitchman, a boss, a billboard company, a spouse.

The weapons of influence they are wielding* are more sophisticated than ever, 3 researchers say. And they are aimed at a vulnerable target—people with less and less time to consider increasingly complex issues.

As a result, some experts in the field have begun warning the public, tipping 4 people off to precisely how "the art of compliance" works. Some critics have taken to arguing for new government controls on one pervasive form of persuasion—political advertising.

The persuasion problem is "the essential dilemma of modern democracy," 5 argue social psychologists Anthony Pratkanis and Elliot Aronson, the authors of *Age of Propaganda: The Everyday Use and Abuse of Persuasion.*

As the two psychologists see it, American society values free speech and 6 public discussion, but people no longer have the time or inclination to pay attention. Mindless propaganda flourishes, they say; thoughtful persuasion fades away.

The problem stems from what Pratkanis and Aronson call our "message-dense 7 environment." The average television viewer sees nearly 38,000 commercials a year, they say. "The average home receives . . . [numerous] pieces of junk mail annually and . . . [countless calls] from telemarketing firms."

Bumper stickers, billboards and posters litter the public consciousness. Ath- 8 letic events and jazz festivals carry corporate labels. As direct selling proliferates, workers patrol their offices during lunch breaks, peddling chocolate and Tupperware to friends.

Meanwhile, information of other sorts multiplies exponentially. Technology 9 serves up ever-increasing quantities of data on every imaginable subject, from home security to health. With more and more information available, people have less and less time to digest it.

"It's becoming harder and harder to think in a considered way about any- 10 thing," said Robert Cialdini, a persuasion researcher at Arizona State University in Tempe. "More and more, we are going to be deciding on the basis of less and less information."

Persuasion is a democratic society's chosen method for decision making 11 and dispute resolution. But the flood of persuasive messages in recent years has changed the nature of persuasion. Lengthy arguments have been supplanted by slogans and logos. In a world teeming with propaganda, those in the business of influencing others put a premium on effective shortcuts.

Most people, psychologists say, are easily seduced by such shortcuts. Humans are 12 "cognitive misers," always looking to conserve attention and mental energy—leaving themselves at the mercy of anyone who has figured out which shortcuts work.

The task of figuring out shortcuts has been embraced by advertising agencies, 13 market researchers, and millions of salespeople. The public, meanwhile, remains in the dark, ignorant of even the simplest principles of social influence.

As a result, laypeople underestimate their susceptibility to persuasion, psychol- 14 ogists say. They imagine their actions are dictated simply by personal preferences.

Unaware of the techniques being used against them, they are often unwittingly outgunned.

As Cialdini tells it, the most powerful tactics work like jujitsu: They draw their 15 strength from deep-seated, unconscious psychological rules. The clever "compliance professional" deliberately triggers these "hidden stores of influence" to elicit a predictable response.

One such rule, for example, is that people are more likely to comply with a 16 request if a reason—no matter how silly—is given. To prove that point, one researcher tested different ways of asking people in line at a copying machine to let her cut the line.

When the researcher asked simply, "Excuse me, I have five pages. May I use 17 the Xerox machine?" only 60 percent of those asked complied. But when she added nothing more than "because I have to make some copies," nearly every one agreed.

The simple addition of "because" unleashed an automatic response, even 18 though "because" was followed by an irrelevant reason, Cialdini said. By asking the favor in that way, the researcher dramatically increased the likelihood of getting what she wanted.

Cialdini and others say much of human behavior is mechanical. Automatic 19 responses are efficient when time and attention are short. For that reason, many techniques of persuasion are designed and tested for their ability to trigger those automatic responses.

"These appeals persuade not through the give-and-take of argument and de- 20 bate," Pratkanis and Aronson have written. ". . . They often appeal to our deepest fears and most irrational hopes, while they make use of our most simplistic beliefs."

Life insurance agents use fear to sell policies, Pratkanis and Aronson say. Par- 21 ents use fear to convince their children to come home on time. Political leaders use fear to build support for going to war—for example, comparing a foreign leader to Adolf Hitler.

As many researchers see it, people respond to persuasion in one of two ways: If 22 an issue they care about is involved, they may pay close attention to the arguments; if they don't care, they pay less attention and are more likely to be influenced by simple cues.

Their level of attention depends on motivation and the time available. As David 23 Boninger, a UCLA psychologist, puts it, "If you don't have the time or motivation, or both, you will pay attention to more peripheral* cues, like how nice somebody looks."

Cialdini, a dapper man with a flat Midwestern accent, describes himself as an 24 inveterate sucker. From an early age, he said recently, he had wondered what made him say yes in many cases when the answer, had he thought about it, should have been no.

So in the early 1980s, he became "a spy in the wars of influence." He took a sab- 25 batical and, over a three-year period, enrolled in dozens of sales training programs,

learning firsthand the tricks of selling insurance, cars, vacuum cleaners, encyclope-
dias, and more.

He learned how to sell portrait photography over the telephone. He took a job 26
as a busboy in a restaurant, observing the waiters. He worked in fund-raising, advertising, and public relations. And he interviewed cult recruiters and members of
bunco squads.

By the time it was over, Cialdini had witnessed hundreds of tactics. But he 27
found that the most effective ones were rooted in six principles. Most are not new,
but they are being used today with greater sophistication on people whose fast-
paced lifestyle has lowered their defenses.

Reciprocity People have been trained to believe that a favor must be repaid in 28
kind, even if the original favor was not requested. The cultural pressure to return
a favor is so intense that people go along rather than suffer the feeling of being
indebted.

Politicians have learned that favors are repaid with votes. Stores offer free 29
samples—not just to show off a product. Charity organizations ship personalized
address labels to potential contributors. Others accost pedestrians, planting paper
flowers in their lapels.

Commitment and Consistency People tend to feel they should be consistent— 30
even when being consistent no longer makes sense. While consistency is easy,
comfortable, and generally advantageous, Cialdini says, "mindless consistency"
can be exploited.

Take the "foot in the door technique." One person gets another to agree to a small 31
commitment, like a down payment or signing a petition. Studies show that it then
becomes much easier to get the person to comply with a much larger request.

Another example Cialdini cites is the "lowball tactic" in car sales. Offered a 32
low price for a car, the potential customer agrees. Then at the last minute, the sales
manager finds a supposed error. The price is increased. But customers tend to go
along nevertheless.

Social Validation People often decide what is correct on the basis of what other 33
people think. Studies show that is true for behavior. Hence, sitcom laugh tracks, tip
jars "salted" with a bartender's cash, long lines outside nightclubs, testimonials,
and "man on the street" ads.

Tapping the power of social validation is especially effective under certain con- 34
ditions: When people are in doubt, they will look to others as a guide; and when
they view those others as similar to themselves, they are more likely to follow their
lead.

Liking People prefer to comply with requests from people they know and like. 35
Charities recruit people to canvass their friends and neighbors. Colleges get

alumni to raise money from classmates. Sales training programs include groom-
ing tips.

According to Cialdini, liking can be based on any of a number of factors. 36
Good-looking people tend to be credited with traits like talent and intelligence.
People also tend to like people who are similar to themselves in personality, back-
ground, and lifestyle.

Authority People defer to authority. Society trains them to do so, and in many sit- 37
uations deference is beneficial. Unfortunately, obedience is often automatic, leaving people vulnerable to exploitation by compliance professionals, Cialdini says.

As an example, he cites the famous ad campaign that capitalized on actor 38
Robert Young's role as Dr. Marcus Welby, Jr., to tout the alleged health benefits of
Sanka decaffeinated coffee.

An authority, according to Cialdini, need not be a true authority. The trappings 39
of authority may suffice. Con artists have long recognized the persuasive power of
titles like doctor or judge, fancy business suits, and expensive cars.

Scarcity Products and opportunities seem more valuable when the supply is 40
limited.

As a result, professional persuaders emphasize that "supplies are limited." Sales 41
end Sunday and movies have limited engagements—diverting attention from whether
the item is desirable to the threat of losing the chance to experience it at all.

The use of influence, Cialdini says, is ubiquitous.   42

Take the classic appeal by a child of a parent's sense of consistency: "But you 43
said . . ." And the parent's resort to authority: "Because I said so." In addition,
nearly everyone invokes the opinions of like-minded others—for social validation—in vying to win a point.

One area in which persuasive tactics are especially controversial is political ad- 44
vertising—particularly negative advertising. Alarmed that attack ads might be alien-
ating voters, some critics have begun calling for stricter limits on political ads.

In Washington, legislation pending in Congress would, among other things, 45
force candidates to identify themselves at the end of their commercials. In that
way, they might be forced to take responsibility for the ads' contents and be unable
to hide behind campaign committees.

"In general, people accept the notion that for the sale of products at least, there 46
are socially accepted norms of advertising," said Lloyd Morrisett, president of the
Markle Foundation, which supports research in communications and information
technology.

"But when those same techniques are applied to the political process—where 47
we are judging not a product but a person, and where there is ample room for
distortion of the record or falsification in some cases—there begins to be more
concern," he said.

On an individual level, some psychologists offer tips for self-protection.   48

- Pay attention to your emotions, says Pratkanis, an associate professor of   49
  psychology at UC Santa Cruz: "If you start to feel guilty or patriotic, try to
  figure out why." In consumer transactions, beware of feelings of inferiority
  and the sense that you don't measure up unless you have a certain product.

- Be on the lookout for automatic responses, Cialdini says. Beware foolish   50
  consistency. Check other people's responses against objective facts.
  Be skeptical of authority, and look out for unwarranted liking for any
  "compliance professionals."

Since the publication of his most recent book, *Influence: The New Psychology*   51
of Modern Persuasion, Cialdini has begun researching a new book on ethical uses
of influence in business—addressing, among other things, how to instruct salespeople and other "influence agents" to use persuasion in ways that help, rather than
hurt, society.

"If influence agents don't police themselves, society will have to step in to   52
regulate . . . the way information is presented in commercial and political settings,"
Cialdini said. "And that's a can of worms that I don't think anybody wants to get into."

HAVE YOU NOTICED HOW MUCH ADVERTISING SURROUNDS US? DO YOU THINK
overwhelming people with advertisements, as illustrated in this photo, should be
allowed in public venues? Write a paragraph arguing whether or not advertisers
should be permitted to inundate audiences with their messages and defend your
argument with specific details and examples.

VOCABULARY IN CONTEXT

1. The word *wielding* in "The weapons of influence they are wielding are more sophisticated than ever" (paragraph 3) means
   a. handling effectively.
   b. giving up.
   c. looking for.
   d. demanding.

2. The word *peripheral* in "As David Boninger . . . puts it, 'If you don't have the time or motivation, or both, you will pay attention to more peripheral cues, like how nice somebody looks'" (paragraph 23) means
   a. important.
   b. dependable.
   c. minor.
   d. attractive.

READING COMPREHENSION QUESTIONS

1. Which of the following would be the best alternative title for this selection?
   a. Automatic Human Responses
   b. Our Deepest Fears
   c. The Loss of Thoughtful Discussion
   d. Compliance Techniques

2. Which sentence best expresses the selection's main point?
   a. Americans are bombarded by various compliance techniques, the dangers of which can be overcome through understanding and legislation.
   b. Fearful of the effects of political attack ads, critics are calling for strict limits on such ads.
   c. With more and more messages demanding our attention, we find it harder and harder to consider any one subject really thoughtfully.
   d. The persuasion researcher Robert Cialdini spent a three-year sabbatical learning the tricks taught in dozens of sales training programs.

3. *True or False?* _____ According to the article, most laypeople think they are more susceptible to persuasion than they really are.

4. According to the article, parents persuade their children to come home on time by appealing to the children's sense of
   a. fair play.
   b. guilt.

c. humor.

d. fear.

5. When a visitor walks out of a hotel and a young man runs up, helps the visitor with his luggage, hails a cab, and then expects a tip, the young man is depending on which principle of persuasion?

a. reciprocity

b. commitment and consistency

c. social validation

d. liking

6. An inference that can be drawn from paragraph 49 is that

a. Anthony Pratkanis is not a patriotic person.

b. one compliance technique involves appealing to the consumer's patriotism.

c. people using compliance techniques never want consumers to feel inferior.

d. consumers pay too much attention to their own emotions.

7. One can infer from the selection that

a. the actor Robert Young was well known for his love of coffee.

b. Sanka is demonstrably better for one's health than other coffees.

c. the actor Robert Young was also a physician in real life.

d. the TV character Marcus Welby Jr. was trustworthy and authoritative.

8. We can conclude that to resist persuasive tactics, a person must

a. buy fewer products.

b. take time to question and analyze.

c. remain patriotic.

d. avoid propaganda.

DISCUSSION QUESTIONS

About Content

1. What unusual method did Robert Cialdini apply to learn more about compliance techniques? Were you surprised by any of the ways he used his time during that three-year period? Have you ever been employed in a position in which you used one or more compliance techniques?

2. What are the six principles that Cialdini identifies as being behind many persuasion tactics? Describe an incident in which you were subjected to persuasion based on one or more of these principles.

3. In paragraph 16, we learn that "people are more likely to comply with a request if a reason—no matter how silly—is given." Do you find that to be true? Have you complied with requests that, when you thought about them later, were backed up with silly or weak reasons? Describe such an incident. Why do you think such requests work?

4. In paragraphs 44–47, the author discusses persuasive tactics in political advertising. Why might researchers view the use of such tactics in this area as "especially controversial"? Discuss this issue in groups of two or three, taking into consideration the question of "attack ads" (see page 631).

About Structure

5. What is the effect of Janny Scott's introduction to the essay (paragraphs 1–2)? On the basis of that introduction, why is a reader likely to feel that the selection will be worth his or her time?

6. Which of the following best describes the conclusion of the selection?

    a. It just stops.

    b. It restates the main point of the selection.

    c. It focuses on possible future occurrences.

    d. It presents a point of view that is the opposite of views in the body of the selection.

    Is this conclusion effective? Why or why not?

About Style and Tone

7. Why might Robert Cialdini have identified himself to the author as an "inveterate sucker"? How does that self-description affect how you regard Cialdini and what he has to say?

8. The author writes, "People defer to authority. Society trains them to do so; and in many situations deference is beneficial" (paragraph 37). Where does the author himself use the power of authority to support his own points? In what situations would you consider authority to be beneficial?

WRITING ASSIGNMENTS

Assignment 1: Writing a Paragraph

According to the article, "laypeople underestimate their susceptibility to persuasion. . . . They imagine their actions are dictated simply by personal preferences. Unaware of the techniques being used against them, they are often unwittingly outgunned" (paragraph 14). After having read the selection, do you believe that statement is true of you? Write a paragraph in which you either agree with or argue against the statement. Provide clear, specific examples of ways in which you are or are not influenced by persuasion.

Your topic sentence might be like either of these:

> After reading "How They Get You to Do That," I recognize that I am more influenced by forms of persuasion than I previously thought.

> Many people may "underestimate their susceptibility to persuasion," but I am not one of those people.

Assignment 2: Writing a Paragraph

Robert Cialidini identifies "social validation" as a strong persuasion technique. Social validation involves people's need to do what they hope will gain them approval from the crowd; this often means that people stop thinking for themselves. The essay provides several examples of social validation, such as laughing along with a laugh track and getting in a long line to go to a nightclub.

Choose a person you know for whom the need for social validation is very strong. Write a paragraph about that person. Explain how the need for social validation has had an impact on specific areas of his or her life. Develop your paragraph with colorful, persuasive examples of the person's behavior. (You may wish to write about an invented person, in which case, feel free to use humorous exaggeration to make your points.)

Here are some possible topic sentences:

> My cousin Nina's strong need for social validation is especially obvious when she is introduced to people she's never met before.

> My friend Terry wears only the newest and most popular clothing styles in order to "be in."

> Jadon, my neighbor, never asserts any opinions of his own, but adopts the opinions of the people he is with.

Assignment 3: Writing an Essay

Scott describes multiple principles—including reciprocity, social validation, and authority—that are used to influence people to desire and/or purchase items.

Write an essay in which you analyze a print or TV advertisement. Decide which guiding principles the ad uses to persuade its audience. You will want to choose an advertisement that uses at least three principles. In your introduction, you should describe the ad that you are analyzing and identify what principles it utilizes. Then, as you develop each paragraph, include a topic sentence that defines one of the principles and provide details about the elements of the advertisement that employ that particular principle. Your conclusion should restate your thesis and bring your essay to a strong ending.

After you finish a first draft, exchange essays with a classmate and share revision advice; use the checklist on the inside back cover to guide your critique.

from A Tale of Two Cities
Charles Dickens

PREVIEW

Have you ever been so upset about something that you decided you could no longer tolerate it? Would you be willing to give up your life to fight to change it? This selection, which comprises Chapter 1 and the first five paragraphs of Chapter 5 from *A Tale of Two Cities*, introduces you to the period of oppression that incited the French to revolt against the aristocracy. Through Dickens's descriptions, you will experience the poverty and cruelty the citizens of France suffered at that time. As you read this excerpt, think about what you would do in these situations.

Chapter 1: The Period

It was the best of times, it was the worst of times, it was the age of wisdom, it was the 1 age of foolishness, it was the epoch* of belief, it was the epoch of incredulity, it was the season of Light, it was the season of Darkness, it was the spring of hope, it was the winter of despair, we had everything before us, we had nothing before us, we were all going direct to Heaven, we were all going direct the other way—in short, the period was so far like the present period, that some of its noisiest authorities insisted on its being received, for good or for evil, in the superlative* degree of comparison only.

There were a king with a large jaw and a queen with a plain face, on the throne 2 of England; there were a king with a large jaw and a queen with a fair face, on the throne of France. In both countries it was clearer than crystal to the lords of the State preserves of loaves and fishes, that things in general were settled for ever.

It was the year of Our Lord one thousand seven hundred and seventy-five. 3 Spiritual revelations were conceded to England at that favoured period, as at this. Mrs. Southcott had recently attained her five-and-twentieth blessed birthday, of whom a prophetic private in the Life Guards had heralded the sublime appearance by announcing that arrangements were made for the swallowing up of London and Westminster. Even the Cock-lane ghost had been laid only a round dozen of years, after rapping out its messages, as the spirits of this very year last past (supernaturally deficient in originality) rapped out theirs. Mere messages in the earthly order of events had lately come to the English Crown and People, from a congress of British subjects in America: which, strange to relate, have proved more important to the human race than any communications yet received through any of the chickens of the Cock-lane brood.

France, less favoured on the whole as to matters spiritual than her sister of 4 the shield and trident, rolled with exceeding smoothness down hill, making paper money and spending it. Under the guidance of her Christian pastors, she entertained herself, besides, with such humane achievements as sentencing a youth to have his hands cut off, his tongue torn out with pincers, and his body burned alive, because he had not kneeled down in the rain to do honour to a dirty procession of monks which passed within his view, at a distance of some fifty or sixty yards. It is likely enough that, rooted in the woods of France and Norway, there were growing trees, when that sufferer was put to death, already marked by the Woodman, Fate, to come down and be sawn into boards, to make a certain movable framework with a sack and a knife in it, terrible in history. It is likely enough that in the rough outhouses of some tillers of the heavy lands adjacent to Paris, there were sheltered from the weather that very day, rude carts, bespattered with rustic mire, snuffed about by pigs, and roosted in by poultry, which the Farmer, Death, had already set apart to be his tumbrils of the Revolution. But, that Woodman and that Farmer, though they work unceasingly, work silently, and no one heard them as they went about with muffled tread: the rather, forasmuch as to entertain any suspicion that they were awake, was to be atheistical and traitorous.

In England, there was scarcely an amount of order and protection to justify 5 much national boasting. Daring burglaries by armed men, and highway robberies, took place in the capital itself every night; families were publicly cautioned not to go out of town without removing their furniture to upholsterers' warehouses for security; the highwayman in the dark was a City tradesman in the light, and, being recognized and challenged by his fellow-tradesman whom he stopped in his character of 'the Captain', gallantly shot him through the head and rode away; the mail was waylaid by seven robbers, and the guard shot three dead, and then got shot dead himself by the other four, 'in consequence of the failure of his ammunition': after which the mail was robbed in peace; that magnificent potentate, the Lord Mayor of London, was made to stand and deliver on Turnham Green, by one highwayman, who despoiled the illustrious creature in sight of all his retinue; prisoners in London gaols* fought battles with their turnkeys, and the majesty of the law fired blunderbusses in among them, loaded with rounds of shot and ball; thieves snipped off diamond crosses from the necks of noble lords at Court drawing rooms; musketeers went into St Giles's, to search for contraband goods, and the mob fired on the musketeers, and the musketeers fired on the mob; and nobody thought any of these occurrences much out of the common way. In the midst of them, the hangman, ever busy and ever worse than useless, was in constant requisition; now, stringing up long rows of miscellaneous criminals; now, hanging a housebreaker on Saturday who had been taken on Tuesday; now, burning people in the hand at Newgate by the dozen, and now burning pamphlets at the door of

Westminster Hall; to-day, taking the life of an atrocious murderer, and tomorrow of a wretched pilferer who had robbed a farmer's boy of sixpence.

All these things, and a thousand like them, came to pass in and close upon the **6** dear old year one thousand seven hundred and seventy-five. Environed by them, while the Woodman and the Farmer worked unheeded, those two of the large jaws, and those other two of the plain and the fair faces, trod with stir enough, and carried their divine rights with a high hand. Thus did the year one thousand seven hundred and seventy-five conduct their Greatnesses, and myriads of small creatures—the creatures of this chronicle among the rest—along the roads that lay before them.

Opening paragraphs of Chapter 5: The Wine-Shop

A large cask of wine had been dropped and broken, in the street. The accident had **7** happened in getting it out of a cart; the cask had tumbled out with a run, the hoops had burst, and it lay on the stones just outside the door of the wine-shop, shattered like a walnut-shell.

All the people within reach had suspended their business, or their idleness, **8** to run to the spot and drink the wine. The rough, irregular stones of the street, pointing every way, and designed, one might have thought, expressly to lame all living creatures that approached them, had dammed it into little pools; these were surrounded, each by its own jostling group or crowd, according to its size. Some men kneeled down, made scoops of their two hands joined, and sipped, or tried to help women, who bent over their shoulders, to sip, before the wine had all run out between their fingers. Others, men and women, dipped in the puddles with little mugs of mutilated earthen ware, or even with handkerchiefs from women's heads, which were squeezed dry into infants' mouths; others made small mud-embankments, to stem the wine as it ran; others, directed by lookers-on up at high windows, darted here and there, to cut off little streams of wine that started away in new

DICKENS USED WORDS TO DESCRIBE EVENTS IN FRANCE during the eighteenth century, ultimately asserting his opinion of the monarchy. The artist who created this picture was also emphasizing a point. What do you think he is saying in this image? What types of symbols does he use to convey his opinion? Do you think this picture is effective? Why or why not?

directions; others, devoted, themselves to the sodden and lee-dyed pieces of the cask, licking, and even champing the moister wine-rotted fragments with eager relish. There was no drainage to carry off the wine, and not only did it all get taken up, but so much mud got taken up along with it, that there might have been a scavenger in the street, if anybody acquainted with it could have believed in such a miraculous presence.

A shrill sound of laughter and of amused voices—voices of men, women, and children—resounded in the street while this wine game lasted. There was little roughness in the sport, and much playfulness. There was a special companionship in it, an observable inclination on the part of every one to join some other one, which led, especially among the luckier or lighter-hearted, to frolicsome embraces, drinking of healths, shaking of hands, and even joining of hands and dancing, a dozen together. When the wine was gone, and the places where it had been most abundant were raked into a gridiron-pattern by fingers, these demonstrations ceased, as suddenly as they had broken out. The man who had left his saw sticking in the firewood he was cutting, set it in motion again; the woman who had left on a door-step the little pot of hot ashes, at which she had been trying to soften the pain in her own starved fingers and toes, or in those of her child, returned to it; men with bare arms, matted locks, and cadaverous faces, who had emerged into the winter light from cellars, moved away to descend again; and a gloom gathered on the scene that appeared more natural to it than sunshine.

The wine was red wine, and had stained the ground of the narrow street in the suburb of Saint Antoine, in Paris, where it was spilled. It had stained many hands, too, and many faces, and many naked feet, and many wooden shoes. The hands of the man who sawed the wood, left red marks on the billets; and the forehead of the woman who nursed her baby, was stained with the stain of the old rag she wound about her head again. Those who had been greedy with the staves of the cask, had acquired a tigerish smear about the mouth; and one tall joker so besmirched, his head more out of a long squalid bag of a nightcap than in it, scrawled upon a wall with his finger dipped in muddy wine lees—blood.

The time was to come, when that wine too would be spilled on the street-stones, and when the stain of it would be red upon many there.

VOCABULARY IN CONTEXT

1. The word *epoch* in "it was the age of foolishness, it was the epoch of belief, it was the epoch of incredulity" (paragraph 1) means
   a. beginning.
   b. highpoint.
   c. a distinct period of time.
   d. the mean longitude of a planet.

2. The word *superlative* in "authorities insisted on its being received, for good or for evil, in the superlative degree of comparison only" (paragraph 1) means

   a. the highest degree of comparison.

   b. the lowest degree of comparison.

   c. superior or outstanding.

   d. the lowest point or second-class.

3. The word *gaols* in "prisoners in London gaols" (paragraph 5) means

   a. suburbs.

   b. slums.

   c. castles.

   d. prisons.

READING COMPREHENSION QUESTIONS

1. The novel opens in the year _____.

   a. 1753

   b. 1764

   c. 1775

   d. 1786

2. Which two countries are being described in Chapter 1?

   a. London and Paris

   b. England and France

   c. England and the United States

   d. France and the United States

3. Which of the following would be the best alternative title for this selection?

   a. Two Countries at War

   b. Four Terrible Monarchs

   c. The Final Straw

   d. A Brewing Revolution

4. Which sentence best expresses the central idea of the selection?

   a. Life was terrible in both England and France for the working class and poor.

   b. The kings and queens of England and France thought things were perfectly fine.

   c. Wine was a luxury that the people of France rarely enjoyed.

   d. People had terrible manners and treated one another poorly in the 1700s.

5. Who are the Woodman and the Farmer?

    a. Fate and Death

    b. Death and Wealth

    c. servants to the king of France

    d. workers at the wine store

6. We can infer from paragraph 2 that Queen Marie Antoinette of France was

    a. ugly.

    b. kind.

    c. pretty.

    d. honest.

7. We can infer from paragraph 11 that

    a. more wine casket accidents are going to happen.

    b. wine is going to become a scarce commodity.

    c. people are going to continue to starve in France.

    d. many people are going to die in the streets.

DISCUSSION QUESTIONS

About Content

1. List two of the instances of violence and cruelty mentioned in Chapter 1.

2. In paragraph 3, which war is alluded to?

About Structure

3. In the beginning of the selection, Dickens describes "The Period" with four characteristics. What are these characteristics?

    _____   _____

    _____   _____

4. In paragraph 5, Dickens uses personification, attributing human characters to inanimate objects or abstract notions. Find the examples of personification.

    _____

    _____

5. In the first two paragraphs of Chapter 5, what details does Dickens use to introduce the reader to the setting?

_____

_____

About Style and Tone

6. Why do you think Dickens focuses solely on the setting, rather than the main characters, in his opening chapter?

7. In the section from Chapter 5, what type of atmosphere does Dickens create with his images?

WRITING ASSIGNMENTS

Assignment 1: Writing a Paragraph

Write a paragraph that mimics the opening paragraph of Chapter 1. Instead of trying to describe something historical, describe your life. For instance, you might write a paragraph about an extremely stressful year that brought about major changes in your life. You could start your paragraph with "It was the hottest of summers; it was the coolest of winters; it was a year of extremes in my life." Make sure your details support your opening line and create a picture in your reader's mind.

Assignment 2: Writing a Paragraph

Historically, the working class has been oppressed by the nobility, the poor have been exploited by the rich, and those without power have suffered at the hands of those with power. Write a paragraph that examines an instance you believe demonstrates inequality between socio-economic classes, and offer suggestions about how such inequalities can be addressed and ultimately eliminated.

Assignment 3: Writing an Essay

Many revolutions have been ignited when those who are oppressed revolt against those in power. Some revolutions, like the American Revolution, help establish new countries. Other revolutions, like the French Revolution, help establish better or new governments.

For this assignment, you are to research a revolution, exploring its causes and its outcomes. You may want to look at a revolution that occurred hundreds of years ago like the Haitian Revolution, or you may want to research a more recent revolution, such as those in Egypt, Iran, or Turkey. Write an essay about either the three major causes of the revolution or the three major effects of the revolution. Remember that any information you use from another source, whether it is word for word or rewritten in your own words, needs to be properly credited.

Share your rough draft with a partner to get and give feedback for revision. Refer to the checklist on the inside back cover.

Duel at High Noon: A Replay of Cormier's Works

Kathy Neal Headley

PREVIEW

Robert Cormier's young adult novels have been popular since *The Chocolate War* was first published in 1974. In this essay, Kathy Neal Headley explores his writings and examines why these books have been perceived as controversial. At the same time, she offers an analysis of why they have been so well liked and why they will likely continue to be read, admired, and discussed well into the twenty-first century.

Today's baby boomers were reared in times of romanticism. Wars were won, the 1 American Dream was a real possibility, and even the turbulent 60s were colored with strokes of idealism. According to formula, literature for adolescents through the 50s and into the 60s was didactic* and predictable, with the teenaged protagonist eventually adopting behavior that was acceptable to adults. Given such a vision of the world, one can comprehend why Robert Cormier has faced criticism for his portrayals of good versus evil in many of his works. His books are avidly read by teenagers, but many parents have difficulty with his dark view of life and negative portrayal of humanity (Ellis, 1985). All too often, parents are protective and controlling of their children's lives, but kids want books to reflect reality. They know that the "good guys don't always win" (West, 1987). Cormier defends his harsh look at reality since "Kids know the language they hear and what's going on in the locker rooms and the school buses. They know my books are mild in comparison" (Silvey, 1985b, p. 295).

Influenced at a young age by movies of the 1930s, Cormier is intrigued by 2 the development of characters and story plots with slight twists (Silvery, 1985b). During these Depression times, movies such as gangster films and budget westerns provided escape mechanisms, entertaining the young and old alike. Traditionally, the heroes were easily spotted as rebels, outcasts, or loners. The good guy might be disguised as an outlaw, but by movie's end, the outcome was one of triumph for "doing the right thing." Cormier's character and plot developments mirror the 30s images, but the happy endings seem to be left on the cutting room's floor.

In his novels, Cormier strives for shocks of recognition and hopes that people 3 react, "Yes, this is the way it is or could be" (Silvey, 1985b, p. 293). He writes realistically, not didactically, since "it's impossible to write about kids of that age without going into certain things that are on their minds" (Silvey, 1985b, p. 294). To allow young people to be viewed as individuals, mothers and fathers are often absent in Cormier's works (Bugniazet, 1985). As for role models, Cormier states that "I can't be concerned with that. I'm not worrying about corrupting youth. I'm worrying about writing realistically and truthfully to affect the reader. What I worry about is good taste and getting my message across by whatever means I can" (Silvey, 1985b, p. 294).

Of concern to Cormier are the morality issues and individual development cri- 4 ses that dominate the genre of adolescent literature. Cormier, however, deals with a different morality than the personal concerns of most adolescent novels.

Not one of Cormier's characters is concerned with "alcoholism, drug use (except 5 when imposed by institutions), premarital sex, childbirth, physical handicaps, social and racial problems, divorce, mental illness (except where imposed by institutions), and homosexuality (Duncan, p. 1)." His focus has not been on menstruation, rape or prostitution. Cormier's characters stepped boldly and independently into the world of adolescent literature where most characters finally got their first bra, reached a decision about having intercourse, chose to have an abortion or a baby, kicked a drug habit or adjusted to a single-parent home. . . . it took the good sense … to have a larger view and see the much greater problems that young people face (Ellis, 1985, p. 11).

Interested in the operation of society, Cormier writes political novels. In 6 doing so, the situation is primary in importance and characterization is secondary (MacLeod, 1981). Hence, the central theme in his novels has been the struggle between individuals and institutions. Cormier "focuses our attention on individuals. In doing so, he causes us to see, through these individuals, that the boundaries and the controls need not be accepted passively. They can be challenged; indeed, they must be challenged" (Ellis, 1985, p. 11). Cormier is "frightened by today's world, terrified by it . . . that comes out in the books" (Silvey, 1985a, p. 155).

More than just a story of peer pressure and schools, *The Chocolate War* par- 7 allels Nazi Germany throughout the text (MacLeod, 1981). The world of power and manipulation creates shock waves of possibilities. In Cormier's own words, "Never does the book fail to get a response" (Cormier, 1985b, p. 4).

His casual references to topics such as masturbation offer reassurances to to- 8 day's youth (Bugniazet, 1985). The opening scenes, short reminders of cinematographic inter-cuts (March-Penny, 1978), set the troubled tone for the episodes to follow. The twisted teacher image sends conflicting messages of good and evil while the repetition of games pushes against individuality. In the end, survival through conformity* comes too late for Jerry, but the message is clear: "Don't disturb the universe" (Cormier, 1974, p. 187).

In an unusual attempt to respond to unanswered questions in *The Chocolate* 9 *War*, Cormier penned *Beyond the Chocolate War*. Without a doubt, Archie must get the black marble in this sequel to prove that he is human. With the sharp illusion of the guillotine, Cormier ignites the action and reminds us that life is made of choices and that we choose whether to follow or lead (Silvey, 1985a).

The realities of government, bureaucracy, secrecy, betrayal, and other aspects 10 of politics describe the survival of the organization in *I Am the Cheese*. The pitch and frenzy of the drama increase as Cormier refuses to answer the why's for the adolescent reader. *I Am the Cheese* is like a mystery novel, forcing the reader to focus on what has already happened while blinding him to the present. The reader believes the wrong things and ignores the right ones. The biggest lie of all, that Adam is not on his way to Rutterburg, is hidden beneath the question of insanity. Cormier disguises truth as delusion and fantasy as the truth. Like *The Chocolate War*, the failure of individuals to protect themselves from corruption of the powerful emerges in *I Am the Cheese* (Nodelman, 1983).

Harsh realities are not covered up by parents in *After the First Death*. Instead, [11] "violence initiated by the terrorists is matched by the equally violent response of the government, and the children are the victims of both" (MacLeod, 1981, p. 79). The extremes of patriotism turned into terrorism define innocence as a potentially evil quality, particularly political innocence.

References to the 1933 film, *The Invisible Man*, a favorite of Cormier's, are in- [12] terspersed in scenes throughout *Fade*. Using an autobiographical approach, Cormier weaves such an intricate tale of power and its misuse that the reader is almost persuaded to believe that the fade is a reality. Cormier shatters our childhood fantasies of becoming invisible when scenes of incest and brutality force the reader to turn away with Paul, sharing the destruction of innocence and the burden of secrets (Campbell, 1985).

MacLeod (1981) charges that Cormier has departed from the standard models of [13] writing and has gone beyond the limits of contemporary realism. His novels violate the unwritten rule that, no matter how realistic, there should be some glimmer of hope with a positive message. "Cormier has abandoned an enduring American myth to confront his teenaged readers with life as it more often is—with the dangers of dissent, the ferocity of systems as they protect themselves, the power of the pressure to conform" (p. 76). Life, after all, isn't a B-Western flickering inside a darkened theater. "The lone dissent has not only failed, it is repudiated.... Gary Cooper lies in his own blood in the street at high noon" (MacLeod, 1981, p. 76). With intentional foresight, "evil is not conquered in Cormier's novels. His heroes are more tragic than not. It maybe suggested that their flaw is an unwillingness to 'play by the established rules'" (Ellis, 1985, p. 52). Perhaps, however, contrary to MacLeod's view, "the struggle is not hopeless, . . . but formidable. . . .[A]dolescents have an innate sense of immortality, and they perennially carry the seeds of the idealism which is the lifeblood of humanity. No one is better suited for recognizing and taking up the challenge" (Ellis, 1985, p. 53).

Even in a hospital permeated by experimentation and death, Cormier manages [14] to interject a fragment of hope in his book, *The Bumblebee Flies Anyway*. The challenge of doing the impossible spurs Barney on as he works to see the makeshift car, the Bumblebee, soar through the night sky. The Complex, as the hospital is called, compels us to feel the boundaries of confinement and reminds us of our own mortality: we will all, eventually, face death. Just like Barney, the voyage of the Bumblebee impacts within us the hope of victory over death, the only key to survival (Campbell, 1989).

Cormier is "always trying to affect the reader because . . . ultimately the book, [15] as a whole, becomes a catharsis and causes some kind of emotional responses" (Bugniazet, 1985, p. 15). There is some hope in his books; "maybe it's what the individual reader brings to the books," says Cormier, "but I thought I had this element in my books all the time. Adam's out there pumping on his bike. I said it all in *The Bumblebee Flies Anyway* when I had Barney say, 'The bad thing is to do nothing'" (Bugniazet, 1985, p. 15).

Robert Cormier appeals to adolescents to reach beyond self-centered concerns 16 to address more global issues such as political manipulations that can create or prevent nuclear war, environmental devastation, and economic fluctuations. Perhaps, the final act of justice and the difference between right and wrong may reside in the destruction of apathy* and the disillusion of innocence. The adolescent reader, drawing the camera back slowly from the blood shed by Jerry on the field beneath the lights, is reminded of the duel at high noon. Sometimes, justice is lost, but it is never forgotten. Neither will be the powerful writings of Robert Cormier. "His are among the few books written for young adults which, in all probability, will still be discussed in the twenty-first century" (Campbell, 1989).

References

Bugniazet, J. A telephone interview with Robert Cormier. *The ALAN Review*, Winter, 1985, pp. 14–18.

Campbell, P. J. *Presenting Robert Cormier*. Dell, 1989.

Cormier, R. *The Chocolate War*. Dell, 1975.

_____. *After the First Death*. Avon Books, 1980.

_____. *The Bumblebee Flies Anyway*. Pantheon Books, 1983.

_____. *I Am the Cheese*. Dell, 1983.

_____. *Beyond the Chocolate War*. Pantheon Books, 1985a.

_____. "The Pleasures and Pains of Writing a Sequel," *The ALAN Review*, Winter, 1985b, pp. 1–4.

_____. *Fade*. Delacorte Press, 1988.

Ellis, W.G. "Cormier and the Pessimistic View," *The ALAN Review*, Winter, 1985, pp. 10–12, 52–53.

MacLeod, A. S. "Robert Cormier and the Adolescent Novel," *Children's Literature in Education*, Summer, 1981, pp. 74–81.

March-Penny, R. "From Hardback to Paperback: The Chocolate War, by Robert Cormier," *Children's Literature in Education*, Summer, 1978, pp. 78–84.

Nodelman, P. "Robert Cormier Does a Number," *Children's Literature in Education*, Summer, 1983, pp. 94–103.

Silvey, A. "An Interview with Robert Cormier," *The Horn Book*, March-April, 1985a, pp. 145–155.

_____. "An Interview with Robert Cormier," *The Horn Book*, May-June, 1985b, pp. 289–296.

West, M. I. "Censorship on Children's Books: Authors and Editors Provide New Perspectives on the Issue," *Publishers Weekly*, July, 1987, pp. 108–111.

VOCABULARY IN CONTEXT

1. The word *didactic* in "literature for adolescents through the 50s and into the 60s was didactic and predictable" (paragraph 1) means
   a. intended to be entertaining and pleasing.
   b. intended to lecture and offer textbook instruction.
   c. intended to convey moral instruction.
   d. intended to be as one would expect.

2. The word *conformity* in "In the end, survival through conformity comes too late" (paragraph 8) means
   a. mental struggle resulting from incompatible needs.
   b. correspondence to a higher ideal.
   c. having the same shape, outline, or contour.
   d. action in accordance with prevailing standard or authority.

3. The word *apathy* in "the final act of justice and the difference between right and wrong may reside in the destruction of apathy and the disillusion of innocence" (paragraph 16) means
   a. being freed from a belief or idealism.
   b. absence of feeling or emotion.
   c. mediocre quality; commonplace.
   d. earnestness of feeling; intensity.

READING COMPREHENSION QUESTIONS

1. Which of the following would be the best alternative title for this selection?
   a. Books that Should Be Banned
   b. Cormier's Many Books for Teens
   c. Powerful Messages in Adolescent Fiction
   d. Books Should Always Be Positive

2. Which of the following best expresses the main idea of this selection?
   a. Robert Cormier has written a multitude of books, and young adults should read them.
   b. *The Chocolate War* and *Beyond the Chocolate War* are Cormier's best books.
   c. Robert Cormier's books are very controversial and rarely contain happy endings.
   d. Cormier's books allow adolescents to explore important themes not often found in teen fiction.

3. According to the author, Cormier writes novels that are considered to be
   a. science fiction.
   b. political.
   c. folk literature.
   d. Westerns.

4. *The Chocolate War* parallels
   a. Nazi Germany.
   b. the Revolutionary War.
   c. *Beyond the Chocolate War.*
   d. the Civil War.

5. *True or False?* _____ The central theme in Cormier's novels is the struggle between individuals and institutions.

6. As the essay implies, which of the following is NOT a book by Cormier?
   a. *The Bumblebee Flies Anyway*
   b. *Fade*
   c. *After the First Death*
   d. *The Invisible Man*

7. We can infer that the author of this selection
   a. wishes she could write like Cormier.
   b. admires Cormier's powerful themes and realistic endings.
   c. hopes that schools and libraries will ban Cormier's books.
   d. is looking forward to Cormier's newest book.

DISCUSSION QUESTIONS

About Content

1. In the beginning of the essay, the author explains that Cormier has often faced criticism, especially by parents, because his books have dark views of life. At the same time his books have been popular because adolescents want to read books that reflect reality. Do you agree with this statement? Why or why not?

2. According to the essay, why does Cormier write books that don't end happily?

3. In paragraph 13, Ellis states that "their flaw is an unwillingness to 'play by established rules . . . taking up the challenge'." What does he mean by this?

About Structure

4. To what does the title "Duel at High Noon: A Replay of Cormier's Works" refer? Is this a good title? Why or why not?

5. The author uses numerous quotes throughout the essay. What is the purpose of these quotes?

About Style and Tone

6. Is the author's purpose primarily to inform readers about Cormier's books, or is she hoping that readers will explore the books on their own? Explain.

7. How would you characterize the author's attitude toward ultimate, unquestioned authority? How do you know this?

WRITING ASSIGNMENTS

Assignment 1: Writing a Paragraph

Have you ever read a book or watched a movie with an unrealistic ending? Did you like it? Why or why not? Write a paragraph that describes that book or movie. Be sure to provide specific details about why you did or did not like the ending. Your topic sentence will need to include the title and author of the book (or title and director of the movie) and a claim that expresses your view. Here are two topic sentences that might begin different paragraphs:

> The ending of *A Little Princess* by Frances Hodgson Burnett was disappointing because Sara ended up becoming extremely wealthy again, which is very improbable.

> *The Breakfast Club* by John Hughes created the unrealistic expectation at the end that the popular kids and outsiders would really become friends.

Assignment 2: Writing a Paragraph

Conflict between teens and/or young adults and their parents is common. Sometimes the arguments concern what is considered an appropriate movie, book, or album. Sometimes the disagreements concern larger issues like politics or values. Write a paragraph about a specific issue that you and your parents disagree about. Explain the nature of the difference in opinion. Have you come to a compromise? If not, how do you and they handle the situation? If so, how did you arrive at the compromise?

Assignment 3: Writing an Essay

Cormier's books have tragic heroes who often suffer terrible fates because they have stood up to and challenged authority. In *I Am the Cheese* and *The Chocolate War*, individuals fail to protect themselves from corruption. In *The Bumblebee*

Flies Anyway, Barney has to navigate life in the experimental hospital with little hope of escape. In *After the First Death,* children are victims of violence and extreme patriotism. Taking a stand for your beliefs, especially when those beliefs run counter to societal norms, is never easy, but "the bad thing is to do nothing."

Write an essay about a memorable character in a book you have read—a character who felt compelled to stand up for or against something. This could be a character from a work of fiction or nonfiction. In your essay, you should describe the basic conflict faced by the character and explain why he or she decided to speak up, what the consequences were, and why. You will want to include specific details to support your ideas.

On the other hand, you may want to write about a character who should have stood up to authority, but who was too fearful to do so. Again, this character could be from a work of fiction or nonfiction. For this essay, you will need to explain what the character experienced and why he or she decided not to speak up. You should also evaluate the effects this decision had on the individual's life. Like the other option, you will want to call on specific details to help build a strong argument.

Before you begin writing, describe your topic and your approach to a partner. Ask which supporting details seem most informative, interesting, and relevant to the topic.

Managing Conflicts in Relationships
Rudolph F. Verderber

PREVIEW

How do you handle the conflicts in your life? Do you get angry? Do you give in? Whatever your methods, you will probably recognize them in this excerpt from the widely used textbook *Communicate!* (8th ed.), by Rudolph F. Verderber.

Conflicts include clashes over facts and definitions ("Charley was the first one 1 to talk." "No, it was Mark." or "Your mother is a battle-ax." "What do you mean, a 'battle-ax'?"); over values ("Bringing home pencils and pens from work is not stealing." "Of course it is." or "The idea that you have to be married to have sex is completely outdated." "No, it isn't."); and, perhaps the most difficult to deal with, over ego involvement ("Listen, I've been a football fan for thirty years; I ought to know what good defense is." "Well, you may be a fan, but that doesn't make you an expert.").

Although many people view conflict as bad (and, to be sure, conflict situations 2 are likely to make us anxious and uneasy), it is inevitable in any significant relationship. Moreover, conflict is sometimes useful in that it forces us to make choices; to resolve honest differences; and to test the relative merits of our attitudes, behaviors, needs, and goals. Now let's consider methods of dealing with conflict.

Methods of Dealing with Conflict

Left to their own devices, people engage in many behaviors, both negative and   3
positive, to cope with or manage their conflicts. The various methods of dealing with conflict can be grouped into five major patterns: withdrawal, surrender,
aggression, persuasion, and problem-solving discussion. Let's consider each of
these methods in turn.

Withdrawal   One of the most common, and certainly one of the easiest, ways to 4
deal with conflict is to withdraw. When people *withdraw*, they physically or psychologically remove themselves from the situation.

Physical withdrawal is, of course, easiest to identify. Suppose Eduardo and 5
Justina get into a conversation about Eduardo's smoking. Justina says, "Eduardo,
I thought you told me that whether you stopped smoking completely or not, you
weren't going to smoke around the house. Now here you are lighting up!" Eduardo
may withdraw physically by saying "I don't want to talk about it" and going to the
basement to finish a project he was working on.

Psychological withdrawal may be less noticeable but is every bit as common. 6
Using the same example, when Justina begins to talk about Eduardo's smoking in
the house, Eduardo may sit quietly in his chair looking at Justina, but all the time
she speaks he is thinking about the poker game he will be going to the next evening.

Besides being quite common, both kinds of withdrawal are basically nega- 7
tive. Why? Because they neither eliminate nor attempt to manage the conflict. As
researchers Roloff and Cloven note, "Relational partners who avoid conflicts have
more difficulty resolving disputes." In the case of the physical withdrawal, Justina
may follow Eduardo to the basement, where the conflict will be resumed; if not, the
conflict will undoubtedly resurface later—and will probably be intensified—when
Justina and Eduardo try to resolve another, unrelated issue. In the case of the psychological withdrawal, Justina may force Eduardo to address the smoking issue,
or she may go along with Eduardo's ignoring it but harbor* a resentment that may
negatively affect their relationship.

Another reason why withdrawal is negative is that it results in what Cloven and 8
Roloff call "mulling behavior." By *mulling* they mean thinking about or stewing over
an actual or perceived problem until the participants perceive the conflict as more severe and begin engaging in blaming behavior. Thus, in many cases, not confronting
the problem when it occurs only makes it more difficult to deal with in the long run.

Nevertheless, conflicts do occasionally go away if left alone. There appear to 9
be two sets of circumstances in which withdrawal may work. First, when the withdrawal represents temporary disengagement for the purpose of letting the heat of the
conflict subside, it can be an effective technique for managing conflict. Consider this
example: Bill and Margaret begin to argue over inviting Bill's mother for Thanksgiving dinner. During the conversation, Margaret begins to get angry about what
her mother-in-law said to her recently about the way she and Bill are raising their

daughter. Margaret says, "Hold it a minute; let me make a pot of coffee. We can both relax a bit, and then we'll talk about this some more." A few minutes later, having calmed down, she returns, ready to approach the conflict more objectively. Margaret's action is not true withdrawal; it's not meant as a means of avoiding confrontation. Rather, it provides a cooling-off period that will probably benefit them both.

The second set of circumstances in which withdrawal may work is when a 10 conflict occurs between people who communicate infrequently. Consider Josh and Mario, who work in the same office. At two office gatherings, they have gotten into arguments about whether the company really cares about its employees. At the next office gathering, Mario avoids sitting near Josh. Again, this form of withdrawal serves as a means of avoiding conflict rather than contributing to it. In this case, Mario judges that it simply isn't that important to resolve the disagreement. It is fair to say that not every conflict needs to be resolved. Withdrawal is a negative pattern only when it is a person's major way of managing conflict.

Surrender   A second method of managing conflict is to surrender. As you might 11 suspect, *surrender* means giving in immediately to avoid conflict. Although altering a personal position in order to accommodate* another can be positive when it's done in the spirit of cooperation, using surrender as a primary coping strategy is unhealthy.

Some people are so upset by the prospect of conflict that they will do anything 12 to avoid it. For instance, Juan and Mariana are discussing their vacation plans. Juan would like just the two of them to go, but Mariana has talked with two of their friends who will be vacationing the same week about going together. After Juan mentions that he'd like the two of them to go alone, Mariana says, "But I think it would be fun to go with another couple, don't you?" Juan replies, "OK, whatever you want." Even though Juan really wants the two of them to go alone, rather than describe his feelings or give reasons for his position, he gives in to avoid conflict.

Habitual surrender is a negative way of dealing with conflict for at least two rea- 13 sons. First, decisions should be made on their merits, not to avoid conflict. If one person gives in, there is no testing of the decision—no one knows what would really be best. Second, surrender can be infuriating to the other person. When Mariana tells Juan what she thinks, she probably wants Juan to see her way as the best. But if Juan simply surrenders, Mariana might believe that Juan still dislikes her plan but is playing the martyr. And his unwillingness to present his reasons could lead to even more conflict.

The contention that surrender is a negative way of dealing with conflict should 14 be qualified to the extent that it reflects a Western cultural perspective. In some cultures, surrendering is a perfectly legitimate way of dealing with conflict. In Japanese culture, for instance, it is thought to be more humble and face-saving to surrender than to risk losing respect through conflict.

Aggression   A third method of dealing with conflict is through aggression. *Ag-* 15 *gression* entails the use of physical or psychological coercion to get one's way. Through aggression, people attempt to force others to accept their ideas or wishes, thereby emerging as "victors" in conflicts.

Aggression seldom improves a relationship, however. Rather, aggression is an 16 emotional reaction to conflict. Thought is short-circuited, and the person lashes out physically or verbally. People who use aggression are concerned not with the merits of an issue but only with who is bigger, who can talk louder, who can act nastier, or who can force the other to give in. With either physical or verbal aggression, conflict is escalated or obscured but not managed.

Persuasion   A fourth method of managing conflict is by persuasion. *Persuasion* 17 is the attempt to change either the attitude or the behavior of another person in order to seek accommodation. At times during the discussion of an issue, one party may try to persuade the other that a particular action is the right one. Suppose that at one point in their discussion about buying a car, Sheila says, "Don't we need a lot of room?" Kevin might reply, "Enough to get us into the car together, but I don't see why we need more than that." Sheila and Kevin are now approaching a conflict situation. At this point, Sheila might say, "Kevin, we are constantly complaining about the lack of room in our present car. Remember last month when you were upset because we couldn't even get our two suitcases into the trunk and we had to put one of them in the backseat? And how many times have we been embarrassed when we couldn't drive our car with friends because the backseat is too small for even two normal-sized people?" Statements like these represent an attempt at resolving the conflict through persuasion.

When persuasion is open and reasonable, it can be a positive means of resolv- 18 ing conflict. However, persuasion can also degenerate into manipulation, as when a person says, "You know, if you back me on this, I could see to it that you get a few more of the good accounts, and if you don't, well . . ." Although persuasive efforts may fuel a conflict, if that persuasion has a solid logical base, it is at least possible that the persuasion will resolve the conflict.

Discussion   A fifth method of dealing with conflict is *problem-solving* 19 *discussion*—the verbal weighing and considering of the pros and cons of the issues in conflict. Discussion is the most desirable means of dealing with conflict in a relationship because it provides for open consideration of issues and because it preserves equality. Resolving conflict through discussion is often difficult to accomplish, however, because it requires all parties involved to cooperate: The participants must be objective in their presentation of issues, honest in stating their feelings and beliefs, and open to the solution that proves to be most satisfactory and in the best interests of those involved.

Problem-solving discussion includes defining and analyzing the problem, 20 suggesting possible solutions, selecting the solution that best fits the analysis, and working to implement the decision. In everyday situations, all five steps are not always considered completely, nor are they necessarily considered in the order given. But when two people perceive a conflict emerging, they need to be willing to step back from the conflict and proceed systematically toward a solution.

Does this process sound too idealized? Or impracticable? Discussion is diffi- 21
cult, but when two people commit themselves to trying, chances are that they will
discover that through discussion they arrive at solutions that meet both their needs
and do so in a way that maintains their relationship.

From Rudolph F. Verderber, *Communicate!* 8th ed. © 1996 Wadsworth, a part of Cengage Learning, Inc.
Reproduced by permission. www.cengage.com/permissions

VOCABULARY IN CONTEXT

1. The word *harbor* in "Justina may force Eduardo to address the smoking issue,
   or she may go along with Eduardo's ignoring it but harbor a resentment that
   may negatively affect their relationship" (paragraph 7) means

   a. hold on to.

   b. avoid.

   c. give up.

   d. pretend.

2. The word *accommodate* in "Although altering a personal position in order to
   accommodate another can be positive when it's done in the spirit of cooperation . . ." (paragraph 11) means

   a. to disagree with.

   b. to adjust to.

   c. to agree with.

   d. to insult.

READING COMPREHENSION QUESTIONS

1. Which sentence best expresses the main point of the selection?

   a. Many people have a negative view of conflict.

   b. There are five main ways, both positive and negative, with which people
      deal with conflict.

   c. Conflicts can force people to make choices and to test their attitudes, ac-
      tions, needs, and aims.

   d. It is better not to intensify or hide conflict.

2. The main idea of paragraphs 9–10 can be found in the

   a. second sentence of paragraph 9.

   b. third sentence of paragraph 9.

   c. first sentence of paragraph 10.

   d. second sentence of paragraph 10.

3. From the reading, we can infer that the author believes that
   a. withdrawal never works.
   b. whether or not surrender is generally a good way to manage conflict is related to one's cultural perspective.
   c. aggression is an attempt to change either the attitude or the behavior of another person in order to seek accommodation.
   d. discussion is the easiest way of dealing with conflict in a relationship.

4. What is the relationship between the following two sentences:
   "When persuasion is open and reasonable, it can be a positive means of resolving conflict. However, persuasion can also degenerate into manipulation . . ." (paragraph 18)?
   a. comparison
   b. contrast
   c. cause and effect
   d. illustration

5. Three of the following sentences are supporting details for an argument. Which of the sentences expresses the point of those supporting details?
   a. People who use aggression are concerned not with the merits of an issue but only with who can force the other person to give in.
   b. Aggression usually harms a relationship.
   c. In aggression, thought is short-circuited and the person lashes out physically or verbally.
   d. With either physical or verbal aggression, conflict is escalated or obscured but not managed.

6. We can infer that the author of this selection
   a. believes that conflict should be avoided at all costs.
   b. feels that conflict is the best way to strengthen a relationship.
   c. feels that conflict can be positive if handled appropriately.
   d. believes that withdrawal is never an appropriate method of dealing with conflict.

7. *True or False?* _____ In healthy relationships, conflict can always be avoided.

8. *True or False?* _____ One reason that discussion is effective in resolving conflicts is that it preserves equality.

DISCUSSION QUESTIONS

About Content

1. Which of Verderber's five methods of dealing with conflict do you—or do people you know—typically use? Give examples.

2. Why do you think Verderber regards discussion as "the most desirable means of dealing with conflict in a relationship" (paragraph 19)? And why might he feel that discussion "is often difficult to accomplish" (paragraph 19)?

3. Verderber writes that conflict is sometimes useful because it forces us to make choices and test attitudes. When in your life has conflict been a good thing? What did you learn from it?

4. Suggest ways that someone you know could be encouraged to deal effectively with his or her specific conflict.

5. Why does Verdeber believe that withdrawing from a conflict rarely results in a long-term resolution?

About Structure

6. What technique explained in Chapter 17 of this textbook does Verderber use to introduce this material?

7. Why does Verderber use subheadings?

About Style and Tone

8. What method does the author use most often to define concepts such as "psychological withdrawal" and "surrender"?

9. How would your describe the author's tone (his attitude toward his subject)?
   a. emotional
   b. objective and fair
   c. cold and withdrawn
   d. excited

WRITING ASSIGNMENTS

Assignment 1: Writing a Paragraph

Think of a person you know whom you would define as one of the following: a withdrawer, a surrenderer, an aggressor, or a persuader. Write a paragraph in which you describe this person and his or her approach to dealing with conflict. Include at least one specific example of his or her behavior. Here are two sample topic sentences like the one you might use.

> Henry's approach to problem-solving is sometimes too aggressive.

> Alicia is afraid of personal conflict and usually lets her husband and children get their way.

Assignment 2: Writing a Paragraph

Verderber uses personal examples to discuss five major patterns of dealing with conflict. However, conflict doesn't occur solely in personal relationships; it is often experienced in the workplace as well. For instance, in order to avoid doing a particular task, a coworker may pass projects or assignments on to other workers. Or certain coworkers may aggressively strong arm people to agree with their opinions and decisions. Interview a coworker about a conflict he or she has had at work and describe how that conflict was resolved. Or write a paragraph about a coworker with whom you have experienced conflict and describe how you resolved that conflict. In either case, refer specifically to Verderber's five methods and explain which were utilized.

Assignment 3: Writing an Essay

When have you and another person had an important conflict that you needed to deal with? (To be "important," the conflict need not be earth-shattering, just a conflict you were unwilling to ignore.) Write an essay that describes the nature of the conflict, and then take the reader through the process that occurred as you and the other person dealt with it. Use transitional words such as *first, next,* and *finally* to help the reader follow the action. In the final paragraph, provide a conclusion that states how satisfied or dissatisfied you felt about the process or that explains what you learned from this experience. Here are two sample thesis statements like the one you might use.

> I know now that Melissa had manipulated me when she convinced me to let her submit one of my English papers as her own.

> Being aggressive is not the best way to fight a traffic ticket.

Group Pressure

Rodney Stark

PREVIEW

We've all experienced group pressure at one time or another, but how much do we really know about how that phenomenon affects us? The following selection from the college textbook *Sociology* (3rd ed.) by Rodney Stark, will give you a fascinating view of this common behavioral situation.

It is self-evident that people tend to conform to the expectations and reactions 1 of others around them. But what are the limits of group pressure? Can group pressure cause us to deny the obvious, even physical evidence?

Over thirty-five years ago, Solomon Asch performed the most famous experi- 2 mental test of the power of group pressure to produce conformity. Since then his study has been repeated many times, with many variations confirming his original results. Perhaps the best way to understand what Asch discovered is to pretend that you are a subject in his experiment.

You have agreed to take part in an experiment on visual perception. Upon arriv- 3 ing at the laboratory, you are given the seventh in a line of eight chairs. Other students taking part in the experiment sit in each of the other chairs. At the front of the room the experimenter stands by a covered easel. He explains that he wants you to judge the length of lines in a series of comparisons. He will place two decks of large cards upon the easel. One card will display a single vertical line. The other card will display three vertical lines, each of a different length. He wants each of you to decide which of the three lines on one card is the same length as the single line on the other card. To prepare you for the task, he displays a practice card. You see the correct line easily, for the other lines are noticeably different from the comparison line.

The experiment begins. The first comparison is just as easy as the practice com- 4 parison. One of the three lines is obviously the same length as the comparison line, while the other two are very different. Each of the eight persons answers in turn, with you answering seventh. Everyone answers correctly. On the second pair of cards, the right answer is just as easy to spot, and again all eight subjects are correct. You begin to suspect that the experiment is going to be a big bore.

Then comes the third pair. The judgment is just as easy as before. But the first 5 person somehow picks a line that is obviously wrong. You smile. Then the second person also picks the same obviously wrong line. What's going on? Then the third, fourth, fifth, and sixth subjects answer the same way. It's your turn. You know without doubt that you are right, yet six people have confidently given the wrong answer. You are no longer bored. Instead, you are a bit confused, but you go ahead and choose the line you are sure is right. Then the last person picks the same wrong line everyone else has chosen.

A new pair is unveiled, and the 6 same thing happens again. All the others pick an obviously wrong line. The experimenter remains matter-of-fact, not commenting on right or wrong answers but just marking down what people pick. Should you

CAN YOU TELL WHICH LINES ARE EXACTLY THE same? Do you believe you would be able to stick to your opinion if everyone else in the room disagreed? Why or why not?

stick it out? Should you go along? Maybe something's wrong with the light or with your angle of vision. Your difficulty lasts for eighteen pairs of cards. On twelve of them, all the others picked a line you knew was incorrect.

When the experiment is over, the experimenter turns to you with a smile and 7 begins to explain. You were the only subject in the experiment. The other seven people were stooges* paid by Professor Asch to answer exactly the way they did. The aim of the experiment was to see if social pressure could cause you to reject the evidence of your own eyes and conform.

In his first experiment, Asch tested fifty people in this situation. Almost a third of them 8 went along with the group and gave the wrong answer at least half of the time. Another 40 percent yielded to the group some of the time, but less than half of the time. Only 25 percent refused to yield at all. Those who yielded to group pressure were more likely to do so as the experiment progressed. Nearly everyone withstood the group the first several times, but as they continued to find themselves at odds with the group, most subjects began to weaken. Many shifted in their chairs, trying to get a different line of vision. Some blushed. Finally, 75 percent of them began to go along at least a few times.

The effects of group pressure were also revealed in the behavior of those who 9 steadfastly refused to accept the group's misjudgments. Some of these people be-came increasingly uneasy and apologetic. One subject began to whisper to his neighbor, "Can't help it, that's the one," and later, "I always disagree—darn it!" Other subjects who refused to yield dealt with the stress of the situation by giving each nonconforming response in a progressively louder voice and by casting chal-lenging looks at the others. In a recent replication* of the Asch study, one subject loudly insulted the other seven students whenever they made a wrong choice. One retort was "What funny farm did you turkeys grow up on, huh?"

The Asch experiment shows that a high number of people will conform even 10 in a weak group situation. They were required merely to disagree with strang-ers, not with their friends, and the costs of deviance were limited to about half an hour of disapproval from people they hardly knew. Furthermore, subjects were not faced with a difficult judgment—they could easily see the correct response. Little wonder, then, that we are inclined to go along with our friends when the stakes are much higher and we cannot even be certain that we are right.

VOCABULARY IN CONTEXT

1. The word stooges in "The other seven people were stooges paid by Professor Asch to answer exactly the way they did" (paragraph 7) means

    a. comedians.

    b. people who played a role.

    c. true subjects in an experiment.

    d. educators.

2. The word *replication* in "In a recent replication of the Asch study, one subject loudly insulted the other seven students . . . " (paragraph 9) means

   a. memory.

   b. repeat.

   c. image.

   d. prediction.

READING COMPREHENSION QUESTIONS

1. Which of the following is the topic of the selection?

   a. visual perception

   b. Solomon Asch

   c. Asch's experiment on group pressure

   d. stooges in an experiment

2. Which sentence from the reading comes closest to expressing the main idea of the selection?

   a. "Upon arriving at the laboratory, you are given the seventh in a line of eight chairs."

   b. "The experimenter remains matter-of-fact, not commenting on right or wrong answers but just marking down what people pick."

   c. "In his first experiment, Asch tested fifty people in this situation."

   d. "The Asch experiment shows that a high number of people will conform even in a weak group situation."

3. In Solomon Asch's experiment, when does the subject realize that he or she is the subject?

   a. soon after the experiment begins.

   b. during the experiment.

   c. after the experiment ends.

   d. never.

4. Most of the people Professor Asch tested

   a. refused to yield to group pressure.

   b. yielded to group pressure immediately.

   c. yielded to group pressure eventually.

   d. got angry because other members of the group gave incorrect answers.

5. What percentage of the subjects in the experiment refused to conform?

    a. 33

    b. 50

    c. 25

    d. 75

6. The author implies that

    a. the power of group pressure is limited.

    b. Asch's findings are not supported by other research.

    c. group pressure makes people deny what they know to be true.

    d. group pressure can be easily withstood.

7. We can conclude from this essay that people react to group pressure

    a. in ways that are similar.

    b. in many different ways.

    c. by conforming almost immediately.

    d. by conforming only when threatened.

8. We can infer that, during the experiment, many of Asch's subjects became

    a. bored.

    b. violent.

    c. excited.

    d. insecure.

DISCUSSION QUESTIONS

About Content

1. Were you at all surprised by the results of Solomon Asch's experiment? If you had been one of the subjects, do you think you would have stuck to your answers, or would you have gone along with the group? Why?

2. What reasons might the subjects in the Asch experiment have had for eventually giving in and accepting the group's wrong answers?

3. Stark refers to the Asch experiment as a "weak group situation," one in which the group is made up of strangers and the stakes are not very high. What might a "strong group situation" be? Give examples.

4. Have you ever been in a situation when you wanted to resist group pressure? What was the situation, and why did you want to resist? What could you have done to resist?

About Structure

5. This essay uses several different patterns of development (as presented in Part 2 and Chapter 17). Identify two of these patterns and provide support from the essay to explain your answer.

6. Why does Stark address the reader directly by using "you"?

About Style and Tone

7. What effect does including direct quotations in paragraph 9 have in helping Stark achieve his purpose?

8. Should what Stark says in the last paragraph be placed earlier in the essay? Explain why or why not.

WRITING ASSIGNMENTS

Assignment 1: Writing a Paragraph

Have you had the following experience? From conversation with a friend, you believe you know his or her opinion on some matter. But when the two of you are with a larger group, you hear the friend agree with the general group opinion, even though it is different from the opinion he or she held before. The opinion might be about something unimportant, such as the quality of a new movie or TV show. Or it may be about something more important, such as whether or not someone is likable. Write a description of that experience. An opening statement for this paper might be something like this one:

> Group pressure caused _____ to change his (her) opinion about someone new at school.

Assignment 2: Writing a Paragraph

The "lines on the card" experiment gives just a hint of the kind of pressure that group opinion can bring to bear on an individual. Advertising companies play into group pressure to influence people to purchase products. For instance, restaurants often show groups of happy, attractive people enjoying their food. Clothing companies often depict their models as successful, forward-moving people. These images influence people when they decide which restaurant to patronize or when they purchase a new pair of pants. Write a paragraph in which you describe one or more examples from your own life in which group pressure through advertising has influenced you to purchase a certain item, visit a certain restaurant, or participate in a certain activity.

Assignment 3: Writing an Essay

The Stark essay explains an experiment done to determine how peer pressure exerted by strangers can affect someone. However, the author believes that pressure from friends is often much stronger and, therefore, might make someone give in more quickly than the subjects in the experiment did. Do you agree? Write an essay in which you discuss three examples of peer pressure on someone to do things he or she really didn't want to do. Take these examples from historical figures like President Truman or Rosa Parks; people you know well, such as your parents or teachers; or your own personal experiences. Try answering questions such as the following when you draft your essay:

- Who was the source of the pressure?

- How did he, she, or they exert this pressure?

- How did the person being pressured feel (angry, anxious, fearful, uncomfortable, etc.)?

- What were the effects of the subject's giving in to—or resisting—the pressure?

From Father to Son, Last Words to Live By

Dana Canedy

PREVIEW

On October 14, 2006, Dana Canedy's fiancé, First Sgt. Charles Monroe King, died in combat in Baghdad; their son Jordan was only seven months old. Before Charles was deployed to Iraq, he began recording a journal—a blend of stories from his life and pieces of advice—for Jordan. In this essay, Canedy, a *New York Times* editor, describes the acute pain of losing her son's father and seeks comfort in the words he left behind.

He drew pictures of himself with angel wings. He left a set of his dog tags on 1 a nightstand in my Manhattan apartment. He bought a tiny blue sweat suit for our baby to wear home from the hospital.

Then he began to write what would become a 200-page journal for our son, in 2 case he did not make it back from the desert in Iraq.

For months before my fiancé, First Sgt. Charles Monroe King, kissed my swol- 3 len stomach and said goodbye, he had been preparing for the beginning of the life we had created and for the end of his own.

He boarded a plane in December 2005 with two missions, really—to lead his 4 young soldiers in combat and to prepare our boy for a life without him.

Dear son, Charles wrote on the last page of the journal, "I hope this book is 5 somewhat helpful to you. Please forgive me for the poor handwriting and grammar. I tried to finish this book before I was deployed to Iraq. It has to be something special to you. I've been writing it in the states, Kuwait and Iraq."

The journal will have to speak for Charles now. He was killed Oct. 14 when **6** an improvised explosive device detonated near his armored vehicle in Baghdad. Charles, 48, had been assigned to the Army's First Battalion, 67th Armored Regiment, Fourth Infantry Division, based in Fort Hood, Tex. He was a month from completing his tour of duty.

For our son's first Christmas, Charles had hoped to take him on a carriage ride **7** through Central Park. Instead, Jordan, now 9 months old, and I snuggled under a blanket in a horse-drawn buggy. The driver seemed puzzled about why I was riding alone with a baby and crying on Christmas Day. I told him.

"No charge," he said at the end of the ride, an act of kindness in a city that can **8** magnify loneliness.

On paper, Charles revealed himself in a way he rarely did in person. He thought **9** hard about what to say to a son who would have no memory of him. Even if Jordan will never hear the cadence of his father's voice, he will know the wisdom of his words.

Never be ashamed to cry. No man is too good to get on his knee and humble **10** himself to God. Follow your heart and look for the strength of a woman.

Charles tried to anticipate questions in the years to come. Favorite team? I am **11** a diehard Cleveland Browns fan. Favorite meal? Chicken, fried or baked, candied yams, collard greens and cornbread. Childhood chores? Shoveling snow and cutting grass. First kiss? Eighth grade.

In neat block letters, he wrote about faith and failure, heartache and hope. He **12** offered tips on how to behave on a date and where to hide money on vacation. Rainy days have their pleasures, he noted: Every now and then you get lucky and catch a rainbow.

Charles mailed the book to me in July, after one of his soldiers was killed and **13** he had recovered the body from a tank. The journal was incomplete, but the horror of the young man's death shook Charles so deeply that he wanted to send it even though he had more to say. He finished it when he came home on a two-week leave in August to meet Jordan, then 5 months old. He was so intoxicated by love for his son that he barely slept, instead keeping vigil over the baby.

I can fill in some of the blanks left for Jordan about his father. When we met in **14** my hometown of Radcliff, Ky., near Fort Knox, I did not consider Charles my type at first. He was bashful, a homebody and got his news from television rather than newspapers (heresy, since I'm a *New York Times* editor).

But he won me over. One day a couple of years ago, I pulled out a list of the **15** traits I wanted in a husband and realized that Charles had almost all of them. He rose early to begin each day with prayers and a list of goals that he ticked off as he accomplished them. He was meticulous,* even insisting on doing my ironing because he deemed my wrinkle-removing skills deficient. His rock-hard warrior's body made him appear tough, but he had a tender heart.

He doted on Christina, now 16, his daughter from a marriage that ended in **16** divorce. He made her blush when he showed her a tattoo with her name on his arm.

Toward women, he displayed an old-fashioned chivalry,* something he expected
of our son. Remember who taught you to speak, to walk and to be a gentleman,
he wrote to Jordan in his journal. These are your first teachers, my little prince.
Protect them, embrace them and always treat them like a queen.

Though as a black man he sometimes felt the sting of discrimination, Charles 17
betrayed no bitterness. It's not fair to judge someone by the color of their skin,
where they're raised or their religious beliefs, he wrote. Appreciate people for who
they are and learn from their differences.

He had his faults, of course. Charles could be moody, easily wounded and 18
infuriatingly quiet, especially during an argument. And at times, I felt, he put the
military ahead of family.

He had enlisted in 1987, drawn by the discipline and challenges. Charles 19
had other options—he was a gifted artist who had trained at the *Art Institute of
Chicago*—but felt fulfilled as a soldier, something I respected but never really understood. He had a chest full of medals and a fierce devotion to his men.

He taught the youngest, barely out of high school, to balance their checkbooks, 20
counseled them about girlfriends and sometimes bailed them out of jail. When he
was home in August, I had a baby shower for him. One guest recently reminded
me that he had spent much of the evening worrying about his troops back in Iraq.

Charles knew the perils of war. During the months before he went away and 21
the days he returned on leave, we talked often about what might happen. In his
journal, he wrote about the loss of fellow soldiers. Still, I could not bear to answer
when Charles turned to me one day and asked, "You don't think I'm coming back,
do you?" We never said aloud that the fear that he might not return was why we
decided to have a child before we planned a wedding, rather than risk never having
the chance.

But Charles missed Jordan's birth because he refused to take a leave from Iraq 22
until all of his soldiers had gone home first, a decision that hurt me at first. And he
volunteered for the mission on which he died, a military official told his sister, Gail
T. King. Although he was not required to join the resupply convoy in Baghdad, he
believed that his soldiers needed someone experienced with them. "He would say,
'My boys are out there, I've got to go check on my boys'," said First Sgt. Arentea-
nis A. Jenkins, Charles's roommate in Iraq.

In my grief, that decision haunts me. Charles's father faults himself for not 23
begging his son to avoid taking unnecessary risks. But he acknowledges that it
would not have made a difference. "He was a born leader," said his father, Charlie
J. King. "And he believed what he was doing was right."

Back in April, after a roadside bombing remarkably similar to that which 24
would claim him, Charles wrote about death and duty.

The 18th was a long, solemn night, he wrote in Jordan's journal. We had a 25
memorial for two soldiers who were killed by an improvised explosive device.
None of my soldiers went to the memorial. Their excuse was that they didn't want
to go because it was depressing. I told them it was selfish of them not to pay their
respects to two men who were selfless in giving their lives for their country.

Things may not always be easy or pleasant for you, that's life, but always pay **26** your respects for the way people lived and what they stood for. It's the honorable thing to do.

When Jordan is old enough to ask how his father died, I will tell him of **27** Charles's courage and assure him of Charles's love. And I will try to comfort him with his father's words.

God blessed me above all I could imagine, Charles wrote in the journal. I have **28** no regrets, serving your country is great.

He had tucked a message to me in the front of Jordan's journal. This is the let- **29** ter every soldier should write, he said. For us, life will move on through Jordan. He will be an extension of us and hopefully everything that we stand for. . . . I would like to see him grow up to be a man, but only God knows what the future holds.

VOCABULARY IN CONTEXT

1. The word *meticulous* in "He was meticulous, even insisting on doing my ironing because he deemed my wrinkle-removing skills deficient" (paragraph 15) means

    a. sloppy.

    b. careful and precise.

    c. generous and warm.

    d. careless.

2. The word *chivalry* in "Toward women, he displayed an old-fashioned chivalry, something he expected of our son. Remember who taught you to speak, to walk and to be a gentleman, he wrote to Jordan in his journal" (paragraph 16) means

    a. politeness.

    b. outlook.

    c. rudeness.

    d. attitude.

READING COMPREHENSION QUESTIONS

1. Which of the following would be the best alternative title for this selection?

    a. A Soldier's Letter

    b. Jordan's Early Years

    c. A Father's Gift to His Son

    d. Charles's Military Experience

2. Which sentence best expresses the main idea of the selection?

   a. Charles Monroe King writes about his experiences as a soldier in Iraq.

   b. Charles Monroe King provides his son Jordan with personal proverbs.

   c. Both Jordan's father, Charles Monroe King, and Jordan's mother, Dana Canedy, provide their son with words to live by.

   d. Dana Canedy writes an article for the *New York Times* about her fiancé's love for their son, Jordan.

3. Charles Monroe King was killed

   a. a month after starting his tour of duty in Iraq.

   b. a month before taking leave to visit Jordan for the first time.

   c. a month before completing his tour of duty in Iraq.

   d. a month after witnessing a roadside bombing that killed two of his soldiers.

4. *True or False?* _____ Charles's father begged his son to avoid taking unnecessary risks by joining a resupply convoy in Baghdad.

5. Charles and his fiancé first met in

   a. Radcliff, Kentucky.

   b. New York, New York.

   c. Cleveland, Ohio

   d. Chicago, Illinois.

6. Which of the following did Charles *not* write in his journal?

   a. Always be ashamed to cry.

   b. It's not fair to judge someone by the color of their skin.

   c. Every now and then you get lucky and catch a rainbow.

   d. Always pay your respects for the way people lived and what they stood for.

7. Charles wrote in his journal, "Follow your heart and look for the strength of a woman" (paragraph 10). From this passage, we can infer that he

   a. did not trust his mind.

   b. felt that women were stronger than men.

   c. felt that men were stronger than women.

   d. was sincere and respected women.

8. The author writes, "And at times, I felt, he put the military ahead of family" (paragraph 18). After reading the entire selection, we can infer that she

   a. never forgave Charles for putting the military ahead of his family.

   b. should have begged Charles not to sign up for the dangerous convoy mission.

   c. understood Charles's duty to his country.

   d. did not understand why Charles could not put his family ahead of the military.

DISCUSSION QUESTIONS

About Content

1. What did Charles hope to accomplish by writing the journal? Do you feel that he was successful? What does the author, Charles's fiancée, hope to accomplish by writing her article and publishing it in the *New York Times*?

2. The author writes that "on paper, Charles revealed himself in a way he rarely did in person" (paragraph 9). Why do you think this occurred?

3. What are some words of wisdom that you received from your parents or family members? What words do you have to inspire others?

About Structure

4. What patterns of development does the author use in her essay? Explain.

5. The author uses several time transition words to signal time relationships. Find three of these time words, and write them here:

   _____   _____

6. In paragraphs 22 and 23, the author includes information told to her by people other than Charles, such as his sister and his roommate in Iraq. Why do you think she chose this narrative strategy?

About Style and Tone

7. In paragraphs 1 and 2, the author does not indicate whom the pronoun "he" refers to: "He drew pictures of himself with angel wings. He left a set of his dog tags on a nightstand in my Manhattan apartment. He bought a tiny blue sweat suit for our baby to wear home from the hospital. Then he began to write what would become a 200-page journal for our son, in case he did not make it back from the desert in Iraq." Why do you think she waited until the third paragraph to provide a pronoun reference?

8. How do you think the author feels about America's military involvement in Iraq? Find evidence in the selection to support your opinion.

WRITING ASSIGNMENTS

Assignment 1: Writing a Paragraph

Author Dana Canedy weaves excerpts from her fiancé Charles's journal into her own essay about him. Write a paragraph about a person in your life whom you care about—such as a relative, a spouse, or a close friend—but whom you recognize has "faults, of course" (paragraph 18). Perhaps you enjoy this person's company but are annoyed by her grumbling. Or you admire the person's work ethic but find his flirting uncomfortable. In your topic sentence, state both sides of your feelings, as in the following sample topic statement:

> While Jim is a terrific supervisor, he sometimes flirts too much with the office staff.

Then fully describe one side of your subject's personality before you begin describing the other. Throughout the paragraph, illustrate your point with specific revealing comments and incidents.

Before you begin writing, describe your subject to a partner. Ask which supporting details seem most interesting and most relevant to the topic.

Assignment 2: Writing a Paragraph

Describe a person who has managed to positively touch the lives of nearly everyone around him or her. Divide your paragraph into three sections. These sections could be about *individuals* the person has impacted, such as any of these:

- A grandchild
- A former student
- A coworker

Assignment 3: Writing an Essay

Charles Monroe King was a person who did not judge others by the color of their skin, where they were raised, or their religious beliefs, perhaps because, as his fiancé pointed out, he "sometimes felt the sting of discrimination" (paragraph 17). Write an essay about how it feels to be discriminated against. Select several specific instances in your life when you felt that someone was judging you unfairly. In your essay, devote each supporting paragraph to one such anecdote, describing what happened and how you responded.

Reading Comprehension Chart

Write an X through the numbers of any questions you missed while answering the questions for each selection in Part 5, "Readings for Writers." Then write in your comprehension score. If you repeatedly miss questions in any particular skill, the chart will make that clear. Then you can pay special attention to that skill in the future. Note that, just as in the book, there are two separate sets of Questions 1 and 2—the first set references the Vocabulary in Context questions and the second set applies to the Reading Comprehension questions. This should not affect your recording or your scoring.

Selection	Vocabulary in Context	Title and Main Idea	Key Details	Inferences	Comprehension Score
Mrosla	1 2	1 2	3 4 5	6 7 8	%
Logan	1 2	1 2	3 4 5	6 7 8	%
Urbina	1 2	1 2	3 4 5 6	7 8	%
Curran	1 2	1 2	3 4 5	6 7 8	%
Fisher	1 2 3	1 2	3 4 5 6	7	%
Bertram	1 2 3	1 2 3 4	5 6 7		%
Carson	1 2	1 2	3 4 5	6 7 8	%
Collier	1 2	1 2	3 4 5 6	7 8	%
Garland	1 2	1 2	3 4 5	6 7 8	%
Scott	1 2	1 2	3 4 5	6 7 8	%
Dickens	1 2 3	3 4	1 2 5	6 7	%
Headley	1 2 3	1 2	3 4 5	6 7	%
Verderber	1 2	1 2	5	3 4 6 7 8	%
Stark	1 2	1 2	3 4 5	6 7 8	%
Canedy	1 2	1 2	3 4 5 6	7 8	%

APPENDIX A: ESL Pointers

This section covers rules that most native speakers of English take for granted but that are useful for speakers of English as a second language (ESL).

Articles

An *article* is a noun marker—it signals that a noun will follow. There are two kinds of articles: indefinite and definite. The *indefinite* articles are *a* and *an*. Use *a* before a word that begins with a consonant sound:

a carrot, **a p**ig, **a u**niform

(*A* is used before *uniform* because the u in that word sounds like the consonant y plus u, not a vowel sound.)

Use *an* before a word beginning with a vowel sound:

an excuse, **an o**nion, **an h**onor

(*Honor* begins with a vowel because the *h* is silent.)

The *definite* article is *the*:

the lemon, **the** fan

An article may come right before a noun:

a circle, **the** summer

Or an article may be separated from the noun by words that describe the noun:

a large circle, **the** long hot summer

> **TIP**
>
> There are various other noun markers, including quantity words (*a few, many, a lot of*), numerals (*one, ten, 120*), demonstrative adjectives (*this, these*), adjectives (*my, your, our*), and possessive nouns (*Vinh's, the school's*).

Articles with Count and Noncount Nouns

To know whether to use an article with a noun and which article to use, you must recognize count and noncount nouns. (A *noun* is a word used to name something—a person, place, thing, or idea.)

Count nouns name people, places, things, or ideas that can be counted and made into plurals, such as *window, table,* and *principal* (*one window, two tables, three principals*).

Noncount nouns refer to things or ideas that cannot be counted and therefore cannot be made into plurals, such as *weather, anger,* and *happiness*. The box below lists and illustrates common types of noncount nouns.

> ## COMMON NONCOUNT NOUNS
>
> *Abstractions and emotions:* joy, humor, patience, mercy, curiosity
>
> *Activities:* soccer, gardening, reading, writing, searching
>
> *Foods:* sugar, spaghetti, fudge, chicken, lettuce
>
> *Gases and vapors:* air, nitrogen, oxygen, smoke, steam
>
> *Languages and areas of study:* Laotian, German, social studies, calculus, biology
>
> *Liquids:* coffee, gasoline, soda, milk, water
>
> *Materials that come in bulk or mass form:* lumber, soil, dust, detergent, hay
>
> *Natural occurrences:* gravity, hail, snow, thunder, rust
>
> *Other things that cannot be counted:* clothing, furniture, homework, machinery, money, news, transportation, work

The quantity of a noncount noun can be expressed with a word or words called a *qualifier,* such as *some, more, a unit of,* and so on. In the following two examples, the qualifiers are shown in *italic* type, and the noncount nouns are shown in **boldface** type.

I hear *a little* **anger** in your voice.

The pea soup had gotten thick overnight, so Kala added *more* **water** to it.

Some words can be either count or noncount nouns, depending on whether they refer to one or more individual items or to something in general:

The yearly **rains** in India are called monsoons.

(This sentence refers to individual rains; *rains* in this case is a count noun.)

Rain is something that farmers cannot live without.

(This sentence refers to rain in general; in this case, *rain* is a noncount noun.)

Using *a* or *an* with Nonspecific Singular Count Nouns

Use *a* or *an* with singular nouns that are nonspecific. A noun is nonspecific when the reader doesn't know its specific identity.

A penguin cannot fly; it uses its "wings" to "fly" through the water.

(The sentence refers to any penguin, not a specific one.)

There was **a** fire today in our neighborhood.

(The reader isn't familiar with the fire. This is the first time it is mentioned.)

Using *the* with Specific Nouns

In general, use *the* with all specific nouns—specific singular, plural, and noncount nouns. A noun is specific—and therefore requires the article *the*—in the following cases:

- When the noun has already been mentioned once

    There was a fire today in our neighborhood. **The** fire destroyed the Smiths' garage.

    (*The* is used with the second mention of *fire*.)

- When the noun is identified by a word or phrase in the sentence

    The lights in the bathroom do not work.

    (*Lights* is identified by the words *in the bathroom*.)

- When the noun's identity is suggested by the general context

    The coffee at Billy's Diner always tastes a week old.

    (*Coffee* is identified by the words *at Billy's Diner*.)

- When the noun names something that is unique

    Scientists warn that there is a growing hole in **the** ozone layer.

    (Earth has only one ozone layer.)

- When the noun comes after a superlative adjective (*best, biggest, wisest*)

    Many of *the* best distance runners come from East Africa.

Omitting Articles

Omit articles with nonspecific plurals and nonspecific noncount nouns. Plurals and noncount nouns are nonspecific when they refer to something in general.

Lights were on all over the empty house.

Coffee should be stored in the refrigerator or freezer if possible.

Runners from Kenya, Ethiopia, and Tanzania often win world-class races.

Using *the* with Proper Nouns

Proper nouns name particular people, places, things, or ideas and are always capitalized. Most proper nouns do not require articles; those that do, however, require *the*. Following are general guidelines about when and when not to use *the*.

Do not use *the* for most singular proper nouns, including names of the following:

- *People and aeapnimals* (Rosa Parks, Skipper)
- *Continents, states, cities, streets, and parks* (Asia, North Dakota, San Diego, Rodeo Boulevard, Fairmount Park)
- *Most countries* (Thailand, Argentina, England)
- *Individual bodies of water, islands, and mountains* (Lake Tahoe, Prince Edward Island, Mount Saint Helens)

Use *the* for the following types of proper nouns:

- *Plural proper nouns* (the Jacksons, the United Arab Emirates, the Great Lakes, the Appalachian Mountains)
- *Names of large geographic areas, deserts, oceans, seas, and rivers* (the Northeast, the Gobi Desert, the Indian Ocean, the Mediterranean Sea, the Hudson River)
- *Names with the format* "the _____ of _____" (the king of Sweden, the Gulf of Aden, the University of New Hampshire)

ACTIVITY 1

Underline the correct form of the noun in parentheses. Compare your answers with a partner's.

1. (A telephone, Telephone) is found in almost every American home.
2. Franz has registered for (the, a) course in Asian history.
3. (The car, A car) Kim bought is four years old but in very good condition.
4. Dark (cloud, clouds) filled the skies over (the, a) valley.
5. My grandparents and cousins all live in (New Jersey, the New Jersey).
6. Adults should have (patience, the patience) when dealing with children.

7. My dog is afraid of (thunder, thunders).

8. Cats are known for having a great deal of (curiosity, the curiosity).

9. Through the ages, (wine, the wine) has been made out of many fruits other than grapes, such as apples and blueberries.

10. People often get lost when hiking through (Pine Barrens, the Pine Barrens), a forest in New Jersey.

Subjects and Verbs

Avoiding Repeated Subjects

In English, a particular subject can be used only once in a word group with a subject and a verb. Don't repeat a subject in the same word group by following a noun with a pronoun.

>   Incorrect: My *friend she* is a wonderful cook.
>
>   Correct: My **friend** is a wonderful cook.
>
>   Correct: **She** is a wonderful cook.

Even when the subject and verb are separated by several words, the subject cannot be repeated in the same word group.

>   Incorrect: The *flowers* that are blooming in the yard they are called snapdragons.
>
>   Correct: The **flowers** that are blooming in the yard **are called** snapdragons.

Including Pronoun Subjects and Linking Verbs

Some languages may omit a pronoun as a subject, but in English, every sentence other than a command must have a subject. (In a command, the subject *you* is understood: [**You**] Hand in your papers now.)

>   Incorrect: The party was a success. *Was* lots of fun.
>
>   Correct: The party was a success. **It was** lots of fun.

Every English sentence must also have a verb, even when the meaning of the sentence is clear without the verb.

>   Incorrect: Rosa's handwriting very neat.
>
>   Correct: Rosa's handwriting **is** very neat.

Including *There* and *Here* at the Beginning of Sentences

Some English sentences begin with *there* or *here* plus a linking verb (usually a form of *to be: is, are,* and so on). In such sentences, the verb comes before the subject.

>   **There are** oranges in the refrigerator.
>
>   (The subject is the plural noun *oranges,* so the plural verb *are* is used.)
>
>   **Here is** the book you wanted.
>
>   (The subject is the singular noun *book,* so the singular verb *is* is used.)

In sentences like those above, remember not to omit *there* or *here.*

>   Incorrect: *Are* many good reasons to quit smoking.
>
>   Correct: **There are** many good reasons to quit smoking.

> **TIP** The topic of subjects and verbs is covered more comprehensively in Chapter 18, "Subjects and Verbs," and Chapter 24, "Subject-Verb Agreement."

Not Using the Progressive Tense of Certain Verbs

The progressive tenses are made up of forms of *be* plus the *-ing* form of the main verb. They express actions or conditions still in progress at a particular time.

Iris **will be running** for student-body president this year.

However, verbs for mental states, the senses, possession, and inclusion are normally not used in the progressive tense.

Incorrect: **I am loving** chocolate.

Correct: **I love** chocolate.

Incorrect: Sonia **is having** a lovely singing voice.

Correct: Sonia **has** a lovely singing voice.

Common verbs not generally used in the progressive tense are listed in the box below.

COMMON VERBS NOT GENERALLY USED IN THE PROGRESSIVE

Thoughts, attitudes, and desires: agree, believe, imagine, know, like, love, prefer, think, understand, want, wish

Sense perceptions: hear, see, smell, taste

Appearances: appear, seem, look

Possession: belong, have, own, possess

Inclusion: contain, include

Using Gerunds and Infinitives after Verbs

A *gerund* is the *-ing* form of a verb that is used as a noun:

Complaining is my cousin's favorite activity.

(*Complaining* is the subject of the sentence.)

An *infinitive* is *to* plus the basic form of the verb (the form in which the verb is listed in the dictionary), as in **to eat.** The infinitive can function as an adverb, an adjective, or a noun.

We were delighted **to eat** dinner on the porch.

(*To eat dinner on the porch* functions as an adverb that describes the verb adjective *delighted.*)

Simon built a shelf **to hold** his DVD collection.

(*To hold his DVD collection* functions as an adjective describing the noun *shelf.*)

To have good friends is a blessing.

(*To have good friends* functions as a noun—the subject of the verb *is.*)

Some verbs can be followed by only a gerund or only an infinitive; other verbs can be followed by either. Examples are given in the following lists. There are many others; watch for them in your reading.

Verb + gerund (dislike + studying)
Verb + preposition + gerund (insist + on + paying)

Some verbs can be followed by a gerund but not by an infinitive. In many cases, there is a preposition (such as *for, in,* or *of*) between the verb and the gerund. Following are some verbs and verb-preposition combinations that can be followed by gerunds but not by infinitives.

admit	deny	look forward to
apologize for	discuss	postpone
appreciate	dislike	practice
approve of	enjoy	suspect of
avoid	feel like	talk about
be used to	finish	thank for
believe in	insist on	think about

Incorrect: Sometimes I *enjoy to eat* by myself in a restaurant.

Correct: Sometimes I **enjoy eating** by myself in a restaurant.

Incorrect: Do you *feel like to dance*?

Correct: Do you **feel like dancing**?

Verb + infinitive (agree + to leave)

Following are common verbs that can be followed by an infinitive but not by a gerund.

agree	decide	manage
arrange	expect	refuse
claim	have	wait

Incorrect: I *agreed taking* Grandma shopping this afternoon.

Correct: I **agreed to take** Grandma shopping this afternoon.

Verb + noun or pronoun + infinitive (cause + them + to flee)

Below are common verbs that are first followed by a noun or pronoun and then by an infinitive, not a gerund.

cause	force	remind
command	persuade	warn

Incorrect: The queen *commanded the prince obeying.*

Correct: The queen **commanded the prince to obey.**

Below are common verbs that can be followed either by an infinitive alone or by a noun or pronoun and an infinitive.

ask	need	want
expect	promise	would like

Jerry **would like to join** the army.

Jerry's parents **would like him to go** to college.

Verb + gerund or infinitive
(begin + packing, or begin + to pack)

Below are verbs that can be followed by either a gerund or an infinitive.

begin	hate	prefer
continue	love	start

The meaning of each of the verbs above remains the same or almost the same whether a gerund or an infinitive is used.

I prefer **eating** dinner early.

I prefer **to eat** dinner early.

With the verbs below, the gerunds and the infinitives have very different meanings.

forget	remember	stop

Nadia **stopped to put on** makeup.

(She interrupted something to put on makeup.)

Nadia **stopped putting on** makeup.

(She discontinued putting on makeup.)

 TIP The topic of verbs is covered more comprehensively in Chapter 22, "Regular and Irregular Verbs," Chapter 23, "Standard English Verbs," and Chapter 24, "Subject-Verb Agreement."

ACTIVITY 2

Underline the correct form in parentheses.

1. The waiter (he recited, recited) a list of dinner specials so long that I got a headache.

2. The rain seems to have stopped. (It's, Is) going to be a beautiful day.

3. (Are paints and crayons, There are paints and crayons) in that cupboard.

4. That book (contains, is containing) photos of our wedding.

5. My midterm math grade persuaded me (getting, to get) a tutor.

6. After walking in the hot sun, we (very thirsty, were very thirsty).

7. Professor Wilhelm agreed (to repeat, repeat) the lecture for students who had not been able to attend it.

8. Lucia (expects earning, expects to earn) a B in the class.

9. The pigeons on the sidewalk (pick up, they pick up) crumbs of food that people drop.

10. For lunch today I (want, am wanting) a big salad.

Adjectives

Following the Order of Adjectives in English

Adjectives describe nouns and pronouns. In English, an adjective usually comes directly before the word it describes or after a linking verb (a form of *be* or a "sense" verb such as *look, seem,* and *taste*), in which case it modifies the subject. In each of the following two sentences, the adjective is **boldfaced** and the noun it describes is *italicized.*

That is a **bright** *light.*

That *light* is **bright.**

When more than one adjective modifies the same noun, the adjectives are usually stated in a certain order, though there are often exceptions. Following is the typical order of English adjectives.

> ## TYPICAL ORDER OF ADJECTIVES IN A SERIES
>
> 1. *An article or another noun marker:* a, an, the, Joseph's, this, three, your
> 2. *Opinion adjective:* exciting, plain, annoying, difficult
> 3. *Size:* enormous, huge, petite, tiny
> 4. *Shape:* circular, short, round, square
> 5. *Age:* newborn, recent, old, new, young
> 6. *Color:* pink, yellow, orange, white
> 7. *Nationality:* Italian, Chinese, Guatemalan, Russian
> 8. *Religion:* Buddhist, Catholic, Jewish, Muslim
> 9. *Material:* plastic, silver, cement, cotton
> 10. *Noun used as an adjective:* school (as in school bus), closet (as in closet shelf), birthday (as in birthday *party*)

Here are some examples of the order of adjectives:

an interesting old story

the long orange cotton dress

your elderly Hungarian cousin

Rafael's friendly little black dog

In general, use no more than two or three adjectives after the article or other noun marker. Numerous adjectives in a series can be awkward: **the lovely little old Methodist stone** church.

Using the Present and Past Participles as Adjectives

The present participle ends in *-ing.* Past participles of regular verbs end in *-ed* or *-d;* a list of the past participles of many common irregular verbs appears on pages 394–397. Both types of participles may be used as adjectives. A participle used as an adjective may come before the word it describes:

It was a **boring** *lecture.*

A participle used as an adjective may also follow a linking verb and describe the subject of the sentence:

The *lecture* was **boring.**

While both present and past participles of a particular verb may be used as adjectives, their meanings differ. Use the present participle to describe whoever or whatever causes a feeling:

a **surprising** *conversation*

(The conversation *caused* the surprise.)

Use the past participle to describe whoever or whatever experiences the feeling:

the **surprised** *waitress*

(The waitress *is surprised.*)

Here are two more sentences that illustrate the differing meanings of present and past participles.

The horror movie was **frightening.**
The audience was **frightened.**

(The movie caused the fear; the audience experienced the fear.)

Following are pairs of present and past participles with similar distinctions:

annoying / annoyed	exhausting / exhausted
boring / bored	fascinating / fascinated
confusing / confused	tiring / tired
depressing / depressed	surprising / surprised
exciting / excited	

 TIP The topic of adjectives is covered more comprehensively in Chapter 27, "Adjectives and Adverbs."

ACTIVITY 3

Underline the correct form in parentheses.

1. The (green large snake, large green snake) slithered on the lawn.
2. At the party, Julie sang a(n) (Vietnamese old, old Vietnamese) song.
3. Joanna wore a (silk blue scarf, blue silk scarf) over her beautiful red hair.
4. The long walk home from the supermarket left Mira feeling (exhausting, exhausted).
5. The constant barking of our neighbor's dog is very (annoying, annoyed).

Prepositions Used for Time and Place

In English, the use of prepositions is often not based on their common meanings, and there are many exceptions to general rules. As a result, correct use of prepositions must be learned gradually through experience. Following is a chart showing how three of the most common prepositions are used in some customary references to time and place.

> ## USE OF *ON, IN,* AND *AT* TO REFER TO TIME AND PLACE
>
> ### Time
> *On a specific day:* on Saturday, on June 12, on your birthday
> *In a part of a day:* in the morning, in the daytime (*but* at night)
> *In a month or a year:* in November, in 1492
> *In a period of time:* in a minute, in a couple of days, in a while
> *At a specific time:* at 10:00 A.M., at dawn, at sunset, at dinnertime
>
> ### Place
> *On a surface:* on the dresser, on the porch, on the roof
> *In a place that is enclosed:* in my bedroom, in the hallway, in the drawer
> *At a specific location:* at the pool, at the bar, at the racetrack

Underline the correct preposition in parentheses.

1. We'll resume the meeting (on, in) fifteen minutes.
2. The sailboat drifted (on, at) the quiet bay as the crew waited for the wind to return.
3. I plan to watch the game (on, in) a large TV.
4. Sonia is moving to Florida (in, at) a month.
5. The children's birthday party was held (on, at) the bowling alley.

ACTIVITY 4

REVIEW TEST

Underline the correct form in parentheses.

1. When I looked out the window, I was surprised to see large puddles of (rain, rains).
2. (Is there, Is) enough room for our luggage in the trunk?
3. There are plenty of fish (in, at) the sea, Elisa told Serena, who had just broken up with her boyfriend.
4. Owls hunt (at, in) night and sleep most of the day.
5. Larry (postponed to go, postponed going) on vacation because he broke his foot.
6. My English teacher wears a (silver small, small silver) ring in his ear.
7. Marta (has, is having) a very bad cold.
8. (On, In) Valentine's Day, friends and lovers send each other affectionate cards.
9. Skinless (chicken, chickens) breasts are a food most doctors recommend because of the low fat content.
10. The customers (annoying, annoyed) by the rude waiter complained to the restaurant manager.

APPENDIX B: Sentence-Skills Diagnostic Test

Part 1

This test will help you check your knowledge of important sentence skills. Certain parts of the following word groups are underlined. Write *X* in the answer space if you think a mistake appears at the underlined part. Write *C* in the answer space if you think the underlined part is correct.

A series of headings ("Fragments," "Run-Ons," and so on) will give you clues to the mistakes to look for. However, you do not have to understand the label to find a mistake. What you are checking is your own sense of effective written English.

Fragments

_____ 1. Because I could not sleep. I turned on my light and read. I finished my book by 6:00 a.m.

_____ 2. Calling his dog's name, Todd walked up and down the street. He finally found his dog at the local park.

_____ 3. My little sister will eat anything. Except meat, vegetables, and fruit.

_____ 4. A country in Central American bordered by Mexico to the north. Guatemala is famous for its coffee.

_____ 5. The reporter turned on her laptop. Then she began to type quickly as the defendant gave his testimony.

_____ 6. One of my greatest joys in life is eating desserts. Such as blueberry cheesecake and vanilla cream puffs. Almond fudge cake makes me want to dance.

Run-Ons

_____ 7. We couldn't view the Picasso exhibit because the museum is closed on Mondays.

_____ 8. The window shade snapped up like a gunshot her cat leaped four feet off the floor.

_____ 9. The chain on my bike likes to chew up my pants, it leaves grease marks on my ankle as well.

_____ 10. The Allies landed in Normandy in June 1944, the war in Europe was over in less than a year.

_____ 11. My first boyfriend was five years old. We met every day in the playground sandbox.

_____ 12. The store owner watched the shopper carefully, she suspected him of stealing from her before.

Regular and Irregular Verbs

13. Henry Folger <u>gived</u> the money to establish the Folger Shakespeare Library in Washington, D.C.   _____

14. She had <u>written</u> four poems and a short story before she was twelve.   _____

15. When the mud slide <u>started</u>, the whole neighborhood began going downhill.   _____

16. Juan has <u>rode</u> the bus to school for two years while saving for a car.   _____

Standard English Verbs

17. Jed <u>sells</u> cars for a living and enjoys his job.   _____

18. You <u>snored</u> like a chain saw last night.   _____

19. After Massachusetts exiled Roger Williams in 1635, he <u>settle</u> in what is now Providence, Rhode Island.   _____

20. Charlotte <u>react</u> badly whenever she gets caught in a traffic jam.   _____

Consistent Verb Tense

21. The South had a rural economy before the Civil War <u>begins</u> in 1861.   _____

22. The first thing Jerry does every day is weigh himself. The scale <u>informs</u> him what kind of meals he can eat that day.   _____

23. Sandy eats a nutritional breakfast, <u>skips</u> lunch, and then enjoys a big dinner.   _____

24. His parents stayed together for his sake; only after he <u>graduates</u> from college were they divorced.   _____

Subject-Verb Agreement

25. There <u>is</u> long lines at the checkout counter.   _____

26. Two cookies <u>were</u> left on the plate.   _____

27. One of the crooked politicians <u>was</u> jailed for a month.   _____

28. The Allegheny and Monongahela Rivers <u>joins</u> in Pittsburgh to form the Ohio River.   _____

Pronoun Agreement, Reference, and Point of View

29. Someone in my neighborhood lets <u>their</u> dog run loose.   _____

30. I enjoy movies, like *Saw*, that frighten <u>me</u>.   _____

31. Every guest at the party dressed like <u>their</u> favorite cartoon character.   _____

32. People who visit foreign countries must carry <u>their</u> passports.   _____

33. After Tony reviewed his notes with Bob, <u>he</u> passed the exam with ease.   _____

34. I love hot peppers, but <u>they</u> do not always agree with me.   _____

Pronoun Types

_____ 35. <u>Him</u> and Antoine joined the soccer team.

_____ 36. No one is a better cook than <u>she</u>.

Adjectives and Adverbs

_____ 37. Bonnie ran <u>quick</u> up the steps, taking them two at a time.

_____ 38. Parts of Holland are <u>more lower</u> than sea level.

Misplaced Modifiers

_____ 39. Clyde and Charlotte decided to have two children <u>on their wedding day</u>.

_____ 40. Charlotte returned the hamburger <u>that was spoiled</u> to the supermarket.

_____ 41. Jamal test-drove a car at the dealership <u>with power windows and a sunroof</u>.

_____ 42. The students no longer like the math instructor <u>who failed the test</u>.

Dangling Modifiers

_____ 43. <u>Tapping a pencil on the table</u>, Ms. Garcia asked for the students' attention.

_____ 44. <u>Walking across the field</u>, a river came into view.

_____ 45. <u>Busy talking on a cell phone</u>, his car went through a red light.

_____ 46. <u>Falling to the ground</u>, the rising sun was greeted by the tan beachcombers.

Faulty Parallelism

_____ 47. The sky got dark, lightning flashed, the wind howled, and a massive storm <u>approaching</u> the city.

_____ 48. The recipe instructed me to chop onions, to peel carrots, and <u>to boil a pot of water</u>.

_____ 49. In London, we ate fish and chips, visited the British Museum, and <u>traveling</u> around the city in a double-decker bus.

_____ 50. Jackie enjoys shopping for new clothes, <u>surfing the Internet</u>, and walking her dog.

Capital Letters

_____ 51. After being out in a cold drizzling rain, I looked forward to a bowl of <u>campbell's</u> soup for lunch.

_____ 52. Julio is taking a vacation in <u>august</u> this year.

_____ 53. I asked my friend, "<u>Were</u> you born in <u>Idaho</u>?"

_____ 54. During the <u>Winter</u> months, my grandfather burns wood in his Franklin stove.

Numbers and Abbreviations

55. After we completed the class activity, the <u>prof.</u> told us we could go home.   _____

56. At the age of <u>18</u>, a person is considered an adult.   _____

Apostrophe

57. It was a twist to see a long line outside the <u>men's</u> room.   _____

58. <u>Clydes</u> quick hands reached out to break his son's fall.   _____

59. We <u>can't</u> go to Paris without visiting the Eiffel Tower.   _____

60. They <u>didn't</u> study as hard as they should have for the test.   _____

Quotation Marks

61. Mark Twain once said, <u>"The</u> more I know about human beings, the more I like my dog."   _____

62. Say something tender to me, <u>"whispered Tony to Lola."</u>   _____

63. "Ask not what your country can do for <u>you, said President Kennedy."</u>   _____

64. "To err is human," Alexander Pope wrote, <u>"to forgive divine."</u>   _____

Comma

65. Some major European capitals include <u>London Paris Rome Madrid and Berlin.</u>   _____

66. Although he had little formal <u>education Thomas</u> Alva Edison became a great inventor.   _____

67. Sandra didn't have to study much for her algebra <u>final, for</u> she was a mathematical genius.   _____

68. The large clock <u>which was in the library's foyer</u> told us that the place was closing.   _____

69. <u>Dogs, according to most cat lovers,</u> are inferior pets.   _____

70. His father <u>shouted</u> "Why don't you go out and get a job?"   _____

Spelling

71. We studied very hard for our <u>grammer</u> test.   _____

72. My thirteen-year-old brother <u>recieved</u> an award at the end of eighth grade.   _____

73. <u>Neither</u> her husband nor her son wanted to go to the home decorating store.   _____

Commonly Confused Words

_____ 74. We were grateful to hear that the storm would not <u>effect</u> us.

_____ 75. <u>Your</u> never too old to learn a foreign language.

_____ 76. <u>It's</u> important to get this job done properly.

_____ 77. Will you <u>except</u> this job if it's offered to you, or keep looking for something <u>better?</u>

Effective Word Choice

_____ 78. The movie was a <u>real bomb</u>, so we left early.

_____ 79. Arthur never goes to fast-food restaurants; he <u>avoids them like the plague</u>.

_____ 80. Jason's face turned red <u>in color</u> after he swallowed the hot peppers.

Part 2 (Optional)

Do Part 2 at your instructor's request. This second part of the test will provide more detailed information about skills you need to know. On a separate piece of paper, number and correct all the items in Part 1 that you marked with an X. For example, suppose you had marked the following word groups with an X. (Note that these examples are not taken from the test.)

4. <u>If football games disappeared entirely from television.</u> I would not even miss them. Other people in my family would perish.

7. The kitten suddenly saw her reflection in the <u>mirror, she</u> jumped back in surprise.

15. <u>Nashville Tennessee</u> is the capital of country music.

29. The first woman to obtain a medical license <u>in Italy Maria</u> Montessori was a pioneer in education for children.

Here is how you should write your corrections on a separate sheet of paper.

4. television, I

7. mirror, and

15. Nashville, Tennessee

29. in Italy, Maria

There are more than forty corrections to make in all.

Part 1

This test will help you measure your improvement in important sentence skills. Certain parts of the following word groups are underlined. Write *X* in the answer space if you think a mistake appears at the underlined part. Write *C* in the answer space if you think the underlined part is correct.

The headings ("Fragments," "Run-Ons," and so on) will give you clues to the mistakes to look for.

Fragments

1. After a careless driver hit my motorcycle, I decided to buy a car. At least I would have more protection against other careless drivers. _____

2. Because of her work with autistic children. Dr. Marie Sorrentino was awarded a National Science Foundation grant. As a result, she was able to continue her research. _____

3. In 1918, Francis March wrote *A History of the World War. Which is what World War I was then called.* That name changed when World War II broke out. _____

4. Waiting for the box office to open for six hours was exhausting, but we were the third people to get tickets to the concert. It was sold out within an hour. _____

5. My brother and I seldom have fights about what to watch on television. Except with baseball games. I get bored watching baseball. _____

6. My new roommate and I have split the chores. She is responsible for vacuuming and cleaning the kitchen. I am responsible for cleaning the bathroom and dusting. In addition, we both clean our own rooms. _____

Run-Ons

7. The snow on most roads had been cleared off quite well, traffic was moving normally. _____

8. The bald eagle is also known as the American eagle, for it is the national bird of the United States. _____

9. I got through the interview without breaking out in a sweat I also managed to keep my voice under control. _____

10. My local bookshop struggles to make a profit in this age of online shopping. I go there as often as possible to purchase my books. _____

_____ 11. My most valued possession is my slow cooker, I can make entire meals in it at a low cost.

_____ 12. The shopping carts outside the supermarket seemed welded together, Rita could not separate one from another.

Regular and Irregular Verbs

_____ 13. The large pile of snow had shrank significantly after the weather got warm.

_____ 14. That woman has never ran for political office before.

_____ 15. They remembered to shut the car windows; in any case, it didn't rain.

_____ 16. They had ate the gallon of natural vanilla ice cream in just one night.

Standard English Verbs

_____ 17. Danielle work at a local ice cream shop called Poppi's.

_____ 18. For recreation he sets up hundreds of dominoes, and then he knocks them over.

_____ 19. He stopped taking a nap after lunch because he then had trouble sleeping at night.

_____ 20. There was no bread for sandwiches, so he decided to drive to the store.

Consistent Verb Tense

_____ 21. On the night of his surprise party, Alex wanted to stay home, but his sister convinced him to accompany her to the restaurant where the guests are waiting.

_____ 22. Jan plays a tennis match every Tuesday night, and she has lessons every Thursday and Saturday.

_____ 23. Juan ran down the hall without looking and trips over the toy truck lying on the floor.

_____ 24. Debbie enjoys riding her bike in the newly built park, which features a special path for bikers and runners.

Subject-Verb Agreement

_____ 25. The children watch as the six geese, which have just landed on the meadow, waddles into the pond.

_____ 26. There are two minutes left in the football game.

_____ 27. He believes films that feature violence is a disgrace to our society.

_____ 28. The closet bursting with shoes and clothes were the largest I had ever seen.

Pronoun Agreement, Reference, and Point of View

29. The museum guides assigned to the students' tour were willing to discuss any of the exhibits that you asked them about.   _____

30. We did not return to the amusement park, for we had to pay too much for the rides and meals.   _____

31. Drivers should check the oil level in their cars every three months.   _____

32. Someone who wastes money as much as Anton puts their family's financial security in jeopardy.   _____

33. Sharon's mother was overjoyed when Sharon became pregnant.   _____

34. His cell phone is so old you have to flip it open to make or answer a call.   _____

Pronoun Types

35. Tawnya and us are going out to eat at a new restaurant tonight.   _____

36. No one in the class is better at computer programming than he.   _____

Adjectives and Adverbs

37. The old gentleman had really bad arthritis, so he walked very awkward.   _____

38. Let's hope the weather doesn't get any more worse.   _____

Misplaced Modifiers

39 To be cooked well, people should steam their vegetables.   _____

40. With a mile-wide grin, Betty turned in her winning raffle ticket.   _____

41. I bought a beautiful shirt in a local store with long sleeves and French cuffs.   _____

42. I first spotted the turtle playing tag on the back lawn.   _____

Dangling Modifiers

43. While still a little girl, her father was appointed company president.   _____

44. Running across the field, I caught the baseball.   _____

45. Going down the elevator from the rooftop restaurant, a crowd awaited us on the ground floor.   _____

46. Looking into the window, the living room was cozy and homey.   _____

Faulty Parallelism

47. The book was well written, interesting, and many instructors assigned it.   _____

48. I put my books in a locker, changed into my gym clothes, and hurried to the yoga class.   _____

_____ 49. Jogging, playing tennis, and a daily swim kept John from gaining back the weight he had lost.

_____ 50. In the evening I plan to write a paper, to watch a movie, and to read two chapters in my biology text.

Capital Letters

_____ 51. I asked Cindy, "what time will you be leaving?"

_____ 52. On the breakfast table sat a carton of orange juice, a banana, and a bowl of cheerios cereal.

_____ 53. Mother ordered a raincoat from the catalog on Monday, and it arrived four days later.

Numbers and Abbreviations

_____ 54. Every Tues. afternoon, I have to prepare a report for my boss.

_____ 55. Ray has more than 100 copies of *Highlights for Children.*

Apostrophe

_____ 56. Marians attention was focused on the bride's gown, a Paris original.

_____ 57. He's failing the course because he doesn't have any confidence in his ability to do the work.

_____ 58. Clyde was incensed at the dentist who charged him ninety dollars to fix his son's tooth.

_____ 59. Sophia spoiled her dogs' so much that their food dishes were made from real crystal.

Quotation Marks

_____ 60. In Greek mythology, Daedalus warned his son Icarus, "Don't fly too near the sun.

_____ 61. Martha said to Fred at bedtime, "Why is it that men's pajamas always have such baggy bottoms?" "You look like a circus clown in that flannel outfit."

_____ 62. The red sign on the door read, "Warning—open only in case of an emergency."

_____ 63. "I adore eating gourmet food," said Rick. "Could we try this new restaurant I was reading about?"

Comma

_____ 64. Artie attended his morning classes, ate lunch, studied for his math test, went to work, got home, and fell right to sleep.

_____ 65. Although we wanted to visit France we spent all of our vacation in Spain.

66. He wanted a new car, so he took on a second job to earn extra money.   ————

67. "Thank goodness I'm almost done" I said aloud with every stroke of the broom.   ————

68. Last night I ran into my old friend Sasha who was studying for a physics exam in the library.   ————

Spelling

69. Rosemary was glad she had taken the course on American goverment.   ————

70. My brothers have alot of toys in their room.   ————

71. I had hoped to study for my foreign language exam yesterday, but I had a migraine, so I slept instead.   ————

Commonly Confused Words

72. The principal upon which the economist based his predictions seemed a bit strange.   ————

73. Fortunately, I was not driving very fast when my car lost it's brakes.   ————

74. There are too many steps in the math formula for me to understand it.   ————

75. The counseling center can advise you on how to prepare for an interview.   ————

76. To many students seem to give up after getting a poor grade on one exam.   ————

Effective Word Use

77. The instructor used the telephone to make a phone call to discuss Ron's social maladjustment difficulties.   ————

78. I thought the course would be a piece of cake, but a ten-page paper was required.   ————

79. The economy has taken a turn for the worse, but it goes without saying that it will improve soon.   ————

80. Spike gave away his television owing to the fact that it distracted him from studying.   ————

Part 2 (Optional)

Do Part 2 at your instructor's request. This second part of the test will provide more detailed information about your improvement in sentence skills. On a separate piece of paper, number and correct all the items you have marked with an *X*. For examples, see page 686. There are more than forty corrections to make in all.

Preview

This Appendix provides answers for the Sentence-Skills Diagnostic Test, Appendix B.

SENTENCE-SKILLS DIAGNOSTIC TEST *(Appendix B)*

Fragments
1. X
2. C
3. X
4. X
5. C
6. X

Run-Ons
7. C
8. X
9. X
10. X
11. C
12. X

Regular and Irregular Verbs
13. X
14. C
15. C
16. X

Standard English Verbs
17. C
18. C
19. X
20. X

Consistent Verb Tense
21. X
22. C

23. C
24. X

Subject-Verb Agreement
25. X
26. C
27. C
28. X

Pronoun Agreement, Reference, and Point of View
29. X
30. C
31. X
32. C
33. X
34. C

Pronoun Types
35. X
36. C

Adjectives and Adverbs
37. X
38. X

Misplaced Modifiers
39. X
40. C
41. X
42. X

Dangling Modifiers
43. C
44. X
45. X
46. X

Faulty Parallelism
47. X
48. C
49. X
50. C

Capital Letters
51. X
52. X
53. C
54. X

Numbers and Abbreviations
55. X
56. X

Apostrophe
57. C
58. X
59. C
60. C

Quotation Marks
61. C
62. X
63. X
64. C

Comma
65. X
66. X
67. C
68. X
69. C
70. X

Spelling
71. X
72. X
73. C

Commonly Confused Words
74. X
75. X
76. C
77. X

Effective Word Choice
78. X
79. X
80. X

APPENDIX E: Writing a Research Paper

HOW DO YOU SELECT A FOCUSED TOPIC? If you

were to write a research paper on college, what would you focus on? "College" itself is too broad a topic to cover in one paper. You would need to select a more limited topic. For example, you could focus on the first-class treatment received by many college star athletes or the benefits of attending smaller colleges over larger universities. Based on one or all of these photos, come up with a focused college-themed topic and write a thesis statement for your paper.

This chapter will explain and illustrate

- the six steps in writing a research paper:

  Step 1: Select a topic that you can readily research

  Step 2: Limit your topic, make the purpose of your paper clear, and assess your audience

  Step 3: Gather information on your limited topic

  Step 4: Plan your paper and take notes on your limited topic

  Step 5: Write the paper

  Step 6: Use an acceptable format and method of documentation

This chapter also provides

- a model research paper

Step 1: Select a Topic That You Can Readily Research

Researching at a Local or College Library

Start with a *subject* search of your library's catalog, and see whether there are several books on your general topic. For example, if you choose the broad topic "divorce," try to find at least three books on that topic. Make sure the books are available on the library shelves.

Next, go to a *periodicals index* in your library to see if there are a fair number of magazine, newspaper, or journal articles on your topic. You can use the *Readers' Guide to Periodical Literature* (found in just about every library) to find articles in back issues of periodicals that your library may keep. Also, your library may subscribe to electronic databases such as Academic Search Premier, JSTOR, and Wilson Humanities Index, which will allow you to find articles published in a far greater range of publications. For instance, when Sarah Hughes, author of the model research paper "Divorce Mediation," visited her local library, she typed the search term "divorce" into a computer that connected her to Academic Search Premier. In searching this database, she found hundreds of titles, with publication information and the complete text of articles about divorce.

Note that further information about the topics and processes discussed above and below can be found in the chapter, "Using the Library," and/or in Chapter 7, "Writing in the Digital Age."

Researching on the Internet

The first step is to go to the *subjects* section of the Web site of a large bookseller—such as Barnes and Noble or Amazon.com—or library catalog to find books. (You don't have to buy the books; you're just browsing for information.)

Sarah Hughes checked out both Barnes and Noble and Amazon. "At Barnes and Noble, the category I clicked on first was 'Parenting and Families.' Under that were many subcategories, including 'Divorce.' I clicked on it, and got back 733 books! Scrolling through these titles, I noticed that there were several different themes: mostly 'how to survive a divorce' books, but also books on other topics, like 'how to stay involved in your children's lives when you're not living with them.' Others were about all kinds of emotional, legal, and financial aspects of divorce." There were so many books that Sarah felt frustrated and decided to return to Barnes and Noble later, after searching online for newspaper and magazine articles.

She started with the Internet search engine Google. "First I typed the word 'divorce' in the keyword box," says Sarah. "But I got more than a hundred million hits! Then I narrowed my topic to 'the process of divorce,' but that was still too general, so I kept narrowing to things like 'divorce costs' and 'divorce alternatives.'

I was still getting too many hits, but I saw that some of the first ones seemed really promising.

"In order to look just for newspaper or magazine articles, I went directly to the sites of some popular publications such as *Time* (time.com), *Newsweek* (newsweek.com), and *USA Today* (usatoday.com). I was able to search each one for recent articles on divorce; however, I would have had to pay about two dollars to read each article online. So I wrote down the title, date, and page number of the articles I was interested in and looked up the ones that were available in the back-issue section of the library and on the electronic databases my library subscribes to. I found plenty of recent material on my subject. In *USA Today*, I found an article entitled 'A Kindler, Gentler Divorce?', which really grabbed my attention. In it was a term I had never heard before: 'divorce mediation.' I learned that divorce mediation helps people divorce without becoming bitter enemies in the process. It definitely sounded like a topic worth exploring. So I went back to Google and typed in 'divorce mediation'. I began to read these articles and realized that this was a far more limited topic than the one I had before. Now I was beginning to have a focus."

Encouraged, Sarah returned to the Barnes and Noble site and typed in "divorce mediation." That brought up a far more manageable list of forty-one books. As she clicked on their titles, she noticed that for some of them she could access reviews, a summary and a table of contents. That helped her narrow her focus even more; she decided to write about the advantages of divorce mediation over traditional divorce. With that in mind, she picked out ten books that looked promising. When she went to her college library, she found that it had six of the ten; she then bought one more book in paperback at a local bookstore. (Remember that if you can't find a book in your local or college library, you can always ask the librarians to obtain it from another library through interlibrary loan. However, be aware that interlibrary loans often take several days.)

Sarah's search was successful. However, for your own research, if not enough books and articles are available to you, try changing your topic. After all, you can't write a research paper for which research materials are not readily available.

Step 2: Limit Your Topic, Make the Purpose of Your Paper Clear, and Assess Your Audience

A research paper should *thoroughly* develop a *limited* topic. It should be narrow and deep, rather than broad and shallow. Therefore, as you read through books and articles on your general topic, look for ways to limit the topic.

For instance, as Sarah read through materials on the general topic "divorce," she chose to limit her paper to divorce mediation. Furthermore, she decided to limit it even more by focusing on the advantages of mediated divorce over more traditional adversarial divorce. The general topic "violence in the media" might be narrowed to instances of copycat crimes inspired by movies or TV. After doing some reading on protests against the death penalty, you might decide to limit your paper to cases in which executed people were later proved innocent. The broad subject "learning disabilities" could be reduced to the widespread use of the drug Ritalin or possible causes of dyslexia. "AIDS" might be limited to federal funding to fight the disease; "personal debt" could be narrowed to the process an individual goes through in declaring bankruptcy.

The subject headings in your library's catalog and periodicals index will give you helpful ideas about how to limit your subject. For example, under the subject heading "Divorce" in the book file at Sarah's library were titles suggesting many limited directions for research: helping children cope with divorce, cooperative parenting after a divorce, the financial toll of divorce, fathers and custody rights. Under the subject heading "Divorce" in the library's periodicals index were subheadings and titles of many articles that suggested additional limited topics that a research paper might explore: how women can learn more about family finances in the event of a divorce, how parents can move past their own pain to focus on children's welfare, becoming a divorce mediator, divorce rates in second marriages. The point is that *subject headings and related headings, as well as book and article titles, may be of great help to you in narrowing your topic.* Take advantage of them.

Do not expect to limit your topic and make your purpose clear all at once. You may have to do quite a bit of reading as you work out the limited focus of your paper. Note that many research papers have one of two general purposes. Your purpose might be to make and defend a point of some kind. (For example, your purpose in a paper might be to provide evidence that gambling should be legalized.) Or, depending on the course and the instructor, your purpose might simply be to present information about a particular subject. (For instance, you might be asked to write a paper describing the most recent scientific findings about what happens when we dream.)

In Chapters 2 and 17, you learned that assessing the needs of an audience is an important step in the writing process. Chances are that your research paper will probably be read only by your instructor, although he or she might want to share it with the rest of the class. Even if your instructor is your only reader, you will need to keep his or her needs in mind as you research your paper. For example, pretend you are writing a paper on the medical breakthroughs resulting from adult-stem-cell research. Your composition instructor's training is probably in English, not biology or medicine, so he or she might not be familiar with certain technical terms like *undifferentiated cells* (cells that have not yet developed into specific cell types) or *somatic stem cells* (another term for the stem cells of an adult body). Of course, you will have become familiar with such terms through your research; nonetheless, you will have to define them for your reader to make sure that he or she can follow your paper easily.

To introduce a reader to a process with which he or she is unfamiliar, you might want to determine the most frequently asked questions (called "FAQs" online) about the subject. As such, you might be able to anticipate the reader's needs even better. For example, Sarah Hughes, the student writing a paper on "divorce mediation," came upon a Web site that listed several frequently asked questions about her topic. Some of these seemed so important to her (*What is the cost? How long does mediation take?* for example) that she made a point of discussing them in her paper because there was a good chance her reader might ask such questions.

Step 3: Gather Information on Your Limited Topic

After you have a good sense of your limited topic, you can begin gathering information. A helpful way to proceed is to sign out the books that you need from your library. In addition, make copies of all relevant articles from magazines, newspapers, or journals. If your library has an online periodicals database, you may be able to print copies of those articles.

In other words, take the steps needed to get all your important source materials together in one place. You can then sit and work on these materials in a quiet, unhurried way in your home or some other place of study.

Step 4: Plan Your Paper and Take Notes on Your Limited Topic

Preparing a Scratch Outline

As you carefully read through the material you have gathered, think constantly about the specific content and organization of your paper. Begin making decisions about exactly what information you will present and how you will arrange it. Prepare a scratch outline for your paper that shows both its thesis and the areas of support for the thesis. It may help to try to plan at least three areas of support.

Thesis: _____

Support: 1. _____

2. _____

3. _____

Here, for example, is the brief outline that Sarah Hughes prepared for her paper on divorce mediation:

Thesis: Divorce mediation is an alternative to the painful, expensive process of a traditional divorce.

Support: 1. Saves time and money
2. Produces less hostility
3. Produces more acceptable agreement between ex-spouses

Taking Notes

With a tentative outline in mind, you can begin taking notes on the information that you expect to include in your paper. Write your notes on four- by six-inch or five- by eight-inch cards or on computer files. The notes you take can be in the form of *direct quotations*, *paraphrases*, *summaries*, or all three.

A *direct quotation* must be written *exactly* as it appears in the original work. But as long as you don't change the meaning, you may omit words from a quotation if they are not relevant to your point. Show such an omission with three spaced periods (known as an *ellipsis*) in place of the deleted words.

Original Passage

If you choose to follow the traditional path through this adversarial system, you will each hire lawyers who will fight on your behalf like ancient knights, charging each other with lances. Each knight, highly skilled in the intricacies of jousting but untrained in other ways to resolve conflict, will try to win by seizing for his client as much booty (children and property) as possible.

Direct Quotation with Ellipsis

"[Y]ou will each hire lawyers who will fight on your behalf like ancient knights, charging each other with lances. Each knight . . . will try to win by seizing for his client as much booty (children and property) as possible."

(Note that the capital letter in brackets shows that the word was capitalized by the student and did not begin the sentence in the original source.)

A *paraphrase* uses about the same number of words as the original. However, you express the information in your own words, structuring the ideas in your own way. A paraphrase accurately reports the original information, but it does so in a completely new way.

Reread the original statement on Sarah's direct-quotation note card. Then compare it to a paraphrase of that statement.

Paraphrase

People who decide to hire highly skilled and experienced divorce attorneys usually end up in a bitter fight (the only strategies the attorneys know how to use) in which one side tries to deprive the other of as much as it can, including the house, the cars, the furniture, and even the kids.

In a *summary,* you condense the original material by expressing it in your own words. Summaries may be written as lists, as brief paragraphs, or both. Following is one of Sarah Hughes's summary note cards.

Summary Note Card

Abusive spouse

If there has been a recent history of physical abuse, mediation should not be attempted. If the abuse has been mental/verbal, mediation may not be successful if abused partner is very intimidated.

Butler/Walker, 46–47

Keep in mind the following points about your research notes:

- Write on only one side of each card or sheet of paper.

- Write only one kind of information, from one source, on any one card or sheet. For example, the sample card above has information on only one idea (abusive spouse) from one source (Butler/Walker).

- At the top of each card or sheet, write a heading that summarizes its content. This will help you organize the different kinds of information that you gather.

- Identify the source and page number at the bottom.

Whether you quote, paraphrase, or summarize, be sure to record the exact source and page from which you take each piece of information. In a research paper, you must document all information that is not common knowledge or a matter of historical record. For example, the birth and death dates of Dr. Martin Luther King Jr. are established facts and do not need documenting. On the other hand, the number of adoptions granted to single people in 2008 is a specialized fact that should be documented. As you read several sources on a subject, you will develop a sense of what authors regard as generally shared or common information and what is more specialized information that must be documented.

A Caution about Plagiarism

If you do not document information that is not your own, you will be stealing. The formal term is *plagiarizing*—using someone else's work as if it were your own, whether you borrow a single idea, a sentence, or an entire essay. Plagiarism is a direct violation of academic ethics; if you pass someone else's work off as your own, you risk being failed or even expelled. Equally, plagiarism deprives you of what can be a most helpful and organizational experience—researching and writing about a selected topic in detail.

There are two types of plagiarism: intended and unintended. The first is worse than the second, but both must be avoided.

One example of *intended plagiarism* is submitting someone else's paper as if it were your own. Another is copying an article from a magazine, newspaper, the Internet, or any other source and turning it in as your own. Keep in mind that teachers can easily discover whether a student has taken material from an Internet source by typing a sentence or two from the student's paper into a search engine such as Google; the source is often quickly identified.

Intended plagiarism, described above, is rather obvious and easy to avoid. Unintended plagiarism, the other type, is trickier. *Unintended plagiarism* occurs when the note taker writes a paraphrase or summary that too closely resembles the original because it uses some of the same structure or some of the same words as the original.

An acceptable paraphrase based on an original passage about "divorce mediation" was presented earlier. Here is an example of an unacceptable paraphrase of that original passage. Compare it to the acceptable paraphrase.

Unacceptable Paraphrase

People who decide to use the <u>traditional path</u> and pursue an <u>adversarial</u> divorce will each hire attorneys <u>who will fight</u> each other for their clients. Each lawyer will probably be very good at what he or she does but will probably be <u>untrained in other ways to resolve</u> the problem. And each side will try to <u>seize as much</u> from the other (houses, <u>children</u>, etc.) <u>as possible</u>.

As you can see, similar or identical phrases are underlined. In addition, the structure of the unacceptable paraphrase is identical to that of the original source.

With the possibility of plagiarism in mind, then, be sure to take careful, documented notes during your research. Remember that if you use another person's material—whether you quote directly, paraphrase, or summarize—*you must acknowledge your source.* Moreover, when you cite a source properly, you give credit where it is due, you provide your readers with a way to locate the original material on their own, and you demonstrate that your work has been carefully researched.

Step 5: Write the Paper

After you have finished reading and note taking, you should have a fairly clear idea of the plan of your paper. Make a *final outline* and use it as a guide to write your first full draft. If your instructor requires an outline as part of your paper, you should prepare either a *topic outline,* which contains your thesis plus supporting words and phrases, or a *sentence outline,* which contains all complete sentences. In the model paper shown later in this chapter, a topic outline is provided. You will note that Roman numerals are used for first-level headings, capital letters for second-level headings, and Arabic numerals for third-level headings.

In your *introduction,* include a thesis statement expressing the purpose of your paper and indicate the plan of development that you will follow. The section on writing an introductory paragraph for an essay is also appropriate for the introductory section of a research paper.

As you move from *introduction* to *main body* to *conclusion,* strive for unity, support, and coherence so that your paper will be clear and effective. Repeatedly ask yourself, "Does each of my supporting paragraphs develop the thesis of my paper?" Use the checklist on the inside back cover of this book to make sure that your paper touches all four bases of effective writing.

Step 6: Use an Acceptable Format and Method of Documentation

Format

The model paper presented in this chapter shows acceptable formats for a research paper, including the style recommended by the Modern Language Association (MLA). Be sure to note carefully the comments and directions set in small print in the margins of each page.

Documentation of Sources

You must tell the reader the sources (books, articles, and so on) of the borrowed material in your paper. Whether you quote directly, paraphrase, or summarize ideas in your own words, you must acknowledge your sources. In the past, you may have used footnotes and a bibliography to cite your sources. Here you will learn a simplfed and widely accepted documentation style used by the Modern Language Association.

Citations within a Paper

When citing a source, you must mention the author's name and the relevant page number. The author's name may be given either in the sentence you are writing or in parentheses following the sentence. Here are two examples:

> Paula James, the author of *The Divorce Mediation Handbook*, has witnessed the divorce process from both sides—actually, *three* sides. First, she went through a traditional divorce herself. In her words, "we simply turned our destinies over to our two attorneys. . . . Many thousands of dollars later we were divorced, but with resentment and distrust and no idea of how we would jointly raise our child" (xvi).
>
> By contrast, mediation costs are far more reasonable. Most mediators charge between $100 and $350 an hour (Friedman 19).

There are several points to note about citations within the paper:

- When an author's name is provided within the parentheses, only the last name is given.
- There is no punctuation between the author's name and the page number.
- The parenthetical citation is placed after the borrowed material but before the period at the end of the sentence.
- If you are using more than one work by the same author, include a shortened version of the title within the parenthetical citation. For example, suppose you were using two books by Paula James and you included a second quotation from her book *The Divorce Mediation Handbook*. Your citation within the text would be (James, *Handbook* 39).

    Note that a comma separates the author's last name from the abbreviated title and page number.
- Use the abbreviation *qtd. in* when citing a quotation from another source. For example, a quotation from Lynn Jacob on the third page of Sarah Hughes's paper is from a work written not by Jacob but by Ann Field. The citation is therefore handled as follows:

> As pointed out by Lynn Jacob, president of the Academy of Family Mediators, "the legal system is designed so that the more the couples fight, the more money the lawyers earn" (qtd. in Field 136).

Citations at the End of a Paper

End your paper with a list of works cited that includes all the sources actually used in the paper. (Don't list other sources, no matter how many you have read.) Look at the "Works Cited" list in the research paper, and note the following:

- Begin the "Works Cited" list on a new page, not on the last page of the paper's text.

- Organize entries alphabetically according to the authors' last names. Do not number the entries.

- Double-space the entries, and insert no extra space between entries.

- After the first line of an entry, indent each additional line in that entry half an inch.

- Italicize (do not underline) titles of books, periodicals, and other independently published works.

- Include URLs or DOIs in Web entries.

Model Entries for a "Works Cited" List

Model entries for a "Works Cited" list are given below. Use these entries as a guide when you prepare your own list.

Book by One Author

> Maggio, Theresa. *The Stone Boudoir: Travels through the Hidden Villages of Sicily.* Perseus, 2003.

Note that the author's last name is written first. In addition, when citing a book, always provide the full title, which you should copy from the inside title page. Include a subtitle by placing a colon after the main title and then copying the subtitle word for word.

Two or More Entries by the Same Author

> Nuland, Sherman B. *How We Die: Reflections on Life's Final Chapter.* Vintage, 1995.

> —. *The Mysteries Within: A Surgeon Reflects on Medical Myths.* Simon & Schuster, 2000.

If you cite two or more entries by the same author (in the example above, the second book is also by Nuland), do not repeat the author's name. Instead, substitute for it three hyphens followed by a period. Then give the remaining information as usual. Arrange works by the same author alphabetically by title. Ignore the words *A*, *An*, and *The* when alphabetizing by title.

Book by Two Authors

Baxandall, Rosalyn, and Elizabeth Ewen. *Picture Windows: How the Suburbs Happened.* Basic Books, 2000.

For a book with three or more authors, give the first author's name (last name, first name), followed by a comma and the words "et al." (meaning "and others").

Magazine Article

Bowden, Charles. "Unseen Sahara." *National Geographic,* Oct. 2009, pp. 100–11.

Newspaper Article

Zoroya, Gregg. "A Hunger for Heroes." *USA Today,* 28 Feb. 2000, pp. D1–2.

The final letter and numbers refer to pages 1 and 2 of section D. If the article is not printed on consecutive pages, list the first page, followed by a plus sign "+" (in that case, the example above would read "D1+"). Also, when citing newspaper and periodical titles, include the introductory *The* (for example, *The Boston Globe* or *The New Yorker*).

Article in Professional Journal

Andrews, Elmer. "The Gift and the Craft: An Approach to the Poetry of Seamus Heaney." *Twentieth Century Literature,* vol. 31, no. 4, 1985, pp. 368–69.

Editorial or Letter

"Drugs and Preschoolers." Editorial. *The Philadelphia Inquirer,* 28 Feb. 2000, p. A10.

Selection in an Edited Collection

Feist, Raymond E. "The Wood Boy." *Legends: Short Novels by the Masters of Modern Fantasy,* edited by Robert Silverberg, Tor Books, 1998, pp. 176–211.

Revised or Later Edition

Davis, Mark H. *Social Psychology.* 4th ed., McGraw-Hill, 2000.

Note that the abbreviations *Rev. ed., 2nd ed., 3rd ed.,* and so on, are placed right after the title.

Chapter or Section in a Book by One Author

Secunda, Victoria. "A New Sense of Family." *Losing Your Parents, Finding Yourself: The Defining Turning Point of Adult Life.* Hyperion, 2000, pp. 242–59.

Pamphlet

Health Scams: Don't Take the Risk. United States Food and Drug Administration, 2009.

Television Program

"Not As Private As You Think." *60 Minutes.* Narrated by Lesley Stahl, produced by Rome Hartman, CBS, 13 Aug. 2000.

Film

Scorsese, Martin, director. *The Departed.* Warner Brothers, 2006.

Sound Recording

Mayer, John. "Gravity." *Continuum,* Aware Records, 2006.

DVD or Videocassette

"To the Moon." *Nova.* Narrated by Liev Schrieber, PBS Video, 1999.

Personal Interview

Cornell, Matthew R. Personal interview. 17 Sept. 2009.

Article in a Reference Database

De Sousa, Avinash. "The Role of Music Therapy in Psychiatry." *Alternative Therapies in Health & Medicine,* vol. 11, no. 6, 2005, pp. 52–53. *Academic Search Premier,* http://ezproxy.mcckc.edu:2337/ehost/pdfviewer.

Citations for articles found in online databases should include the URL or DOI for the article.

Article in an Online Magazine

Begley, Sharon. "Why the Power of DNA Is Overrated." *Newsweek,* 25 Nov. 2009, www.newsweek.com/begley-why-power-dna-overrated-76827.

Article on a Web Site

"Galileo's Telescope." *The Galileo Project.* Rice U, 1995, galileo.rice.edu/.

No author is given, so the article is cited first, followed by the title of the Web site (*The Galileo Project*), followed by the sponsor of the Web site (Rice University, which has been abbreviated as "Rice U" per MLA). Finally, the URL for the Web site is included (do not include "http://" before the URL) and the citation ends with a period.

Electronic Mail (E-mail) Posting

Capuana, Louis. "Re: Once upon a Time." Message to John Verga, 10 Apr. 2008.

ACTIVITY 1

On a separate sheet of paper, convert the information in each of the following references into the correct form for a "Works Cited" list. Use the appropriate model above as a guide.

1. An article by Alex Yannis titled "In New League, Women Get Payoff and Payday" on page D5 of the April 13, 2001, issue of *The New York Times*.

2. An article by Nancy Franklin titled "Nonsense and Sensibility" on pages 96–97 of the March 6, 2000, issue of *The New Yorker*.

3. A book by Francis McInerney and Sean White called *Futurewealth: Investing in the Second Great Wave of Technology* and published by St. Martin's in 2000.

4. A book by Ellen N. Junn and Chris Boyatzis titled *Child Growth and Development* and published in a seventh edition by McGraw-Hill in 2000.

5. An article by Melinda Liu and Leila Abboud titled "Generation Superpower" dated April 11, 2001, and found on April 12, 2007, in the online version of *Newsweek*.

Model Paper

While the *MLA Handbook* does not require a title page or an outline for a paper, your instructor may ask you to include one or both. Here is a model title page.

Option 1: Model Title Page

The title should begin about one-third of the way down the page. Center the title. Double-space between lines of the title and your name. Also center and double-space the instructor's name and the date.

Divorce Mediation: A Better Alternative

by

Sarah Hughes

English 101

Professor Martinez

8 March 2016

Papers written in MLA style use the simple format shown below. There is no title page or outline.

½ inch

1 inch

Hughes 1

Option 2: Model First Page with Top Heading

Double-space between lines. Leave a one-inch margin on all sides.

Sarah Hughes

Professor Martinez

English 101

8 March 2016

Divorce Mediation: A Better Alternative

Divorce is never easy. Even if two people both want to part, ending a marriage is a painful experience. In order to become divorced, most people go through a process that increases this pain. Starting with the lawsuit that one partner has to file against the other, the two take on the roles of enemies. . . .

Use this format if your instructor asks you to submit an outline of your paper.

Hughes i

Outline

Thesis: Divorce mediation offers several advantages over the traditional process of divorce.

I.   Introduction
   A. Traditional divorce
      1. Casts divorcing couple in the role of enemies
      2. Expensive and painful
   B. Mediation
      1. Description of mediation process
      2. Growing popularity of mediation
II. Advantages of mediation in terms of money and time
   A. Traditional divorce
      1. Lawyers' fees charged for every step
      2. Lawyers' and courts' involvement slows process down
   B. Mediation
      1. Mediators' fees lower than lawyers'
      2. Couple controls costs of case
      3. Mediated divorces completed more quickly
III. Emotional benefits of mediation
   A. Traditional divorce
      1. Pits clients against one another
      2. Produces hostility and distrust
   B. Mediation encourages clients to work cooperatively
IV. Advantages of mediation in terms of divorce agreement
   A. Traditional divorce leaves clients with attorney-negotiated agreement that may not work well for them
   B. Mediation creates agreement that both clients can live with
V.   Who shouldn't use mediation
VI. Conclusion

Here is a full model paper. It assumes that the writer has included a title page.

Hughes 1

Divorce Mediation: A Better Alternative

Divorce is never easy. Even if two people both want to break up, ending a marriage is a painful experience. In order to become divorced, most people go through a process that increases this pain. Starting with the lawsuit that one partner files against the other, the two take on the roles of enemies. As author Paula James describes it,

> You will each hire lawyers who will fight on your behalf like ancient knights, charging each other with lances. Each knight . . . will try to win by seizing for his client as much booty (children and property) as possible. You will stand on the sidelines wringing your hands while you watch the battle—and, of course, pay your knight a high hourly fee. One peculiarity of this battle is that the wounds inflicted don't appear on the other warrior; they appear on you, your spouse, and your children. (3)

But there is an alternative to this traditional, ugly divorce process. It is called divorce mediation. Couples who use divorce mediation find that it saves them time and money, it produces less hostility, and it leaves them with an agreement they can respect.

What is divorce mediation? According to a 2009 article entitled "Divorce Litigation Alternatives," it is a process in which "the parties engage the services of a specially trained impartial third party to facilitate a mutually satisfactory resolution of the divorce" (Schonfeld and Kessler). The mediator, who is usually a lawyer or a therapist, helps the couple hammer out a divorce agreement they both find acceptable. This is done in as few or as many meetings as necessary. Each spouse will probably hire a personal lawyer to review the agreement before it is made final. But the spouses, not "hired gun" lawyers, are responsible

---

Academic

Double-space between lines of the text. Leave a one-inch margin all the way around the page. Your name and the page number should be typed one-half inch from the top of the page.

Source is identified by name.

Direct quotations of five typed lines or more are indented five spaces from the left margin. Quotation marks are not used.

The spaced periods (ellipsis) show that material from the original source has been omitted.

Only the page number is needed, as the author has already been named in the text.

Thesis, followed by plan of development.

Both authors' names are given in a work by two authors.

for creating it. In fact, as Cathy Gale, an Australian divorce law specialist, indicates, if lawyers are involved at all, their job is "to coach and support their clients to do the negotiating themselves" (qtd. in Towers 29).

Source is identified by name and area of expertise.

During the process, the mediator doesn't favor one partner over the other. Instead, the mediator maintains, in the words of the lawyer and mediator Gary Friedman, an attitude of "positive neutrality." Friedman explains the term by saying, "While I am largely neutral as to the outcome, . . . I am not neutral as to process. On the contrary, I am actively engaged in trying to ensure that each party takes responsibility for him- or herself, and making sure that all decisions are sound for both of them" (26).

Once the couple is satisfied with the agreement, it is filed in court and approved by a judge in a brief hearing. In many states, the couple does not even need to attend that hearing. Couples can thus complete a divorce without ever seeing the inside of a courtroom.

This typical citation is made up of the author's last name and the relevant page number. "Works Cited" then provides full information about the source.

There are no official statistics to tell how many divorcing couples use mediation, but it is definitely becoming a popular option. According to the Academy of Family Mediators in Boston, the number of mediators has increased exponentially (Valente B7). And courts in twenty-five states now *require* couples involved in child-custody disputes to work with a mediator (Field 136).

One practical advantage of mediation is that it is less expensive and less time-consuming. In a traditional divorce, after each partner retains a lawyer and sets the divorce machine in motion, costs mount up quickly. A lawyer's fee "may exceed $500 per hour . . . for each spouse" ("Avoiding the War"). The lawyers bill their clients for every phone call made, every letter written, every hearing attended, every

Citation for an online source. No page number is given because the online document does not provide one.

Hughes 3

meeting held to iron out another wrinkle in the process. In addition, when people divorce, they must make decisions about countless details. Even if the spouses are not far apart in their thinking, those decisions take time. If the husband and wife are deeply divided, the bills can become staggering. According to Field, "An uncontested, amiable divorce may cost $5,000 per partner and drag on for more than a year. . . . A warring duo . . . could wind up spending $30,000 apiece, and the case might span an entire Presidential administration" (136). The couple's financial welfare is not the top concern of courts and attorneys. As pointed out by Lynn Jacob, president of the Academy of Family Mediators, "the legal system is designed so that the more the couples fight, the more money the lawyers earn" (qtd. in Field 136).

By contrast, mediation costs are far more reasonable. Most mediators charge between $100 and $350 an hour (Friedman 19). Because both spouses are present for all mediating sessions, they are in control of how high the costs mount. Although there is no "typical" divorce, it is clear that mediated divorces tend to be much less expensive than others. In Friedman's experience, a mediated divorce in which there is "substantial disagreement" costs between $2,000 and $5,000 (19). Ken Waldron, a mediator with the Madison (Wisconsin) Center for Divorce Mediation, estimates that most mediated divorces end up costing one-half to one-third less than an attorney-negotiated divorce (Schuetz 10). Mediator Paula James describes mediated divorces as costing "a fraction" of attorney-negotiated ones (60).

Second, mediated divorces are finalized much more quickly than divorces fought out in the courts. Couples divorcing in the traditional way spend a long time going through the following cycle: meet with attorney, wait for attorney to talk with spouse's attorney, wait for

The abbreviation "qtd." means quoted. The quoted material is not capitalized because the student has blended it into a sentence with an introductory phrase.

Quotation marks acknowledge that the phrase is copied from the previous citation.

spouse's attorney to talk with spouse, wait for spouse's attorney to return with response. Mediating couples don't have to do any of that. They also don't have the ordeal of endless hearings, court delays, and their attorneys' own schedule problems. Mediating couples can do a large part of the work of their divorce agreement outside their meetings with the mediator. Most mediating couples really want to get their agreement finished, for both financial and emotional reasons. Because they have the guidance of a professional to help them work through difficult points, they tend to work efficiently. According to an article by Meg Lundstrom in *BusinessWeek*, most mediated divorces are completed in four to eight sessions, or six to twenty-four hours (228). Gary Friedman's estimate is about the same: four to six meetings spaced over a period of two to three months (18). A typical mediation center advertising online, Divorce Solutions of New York, N.Y., says, "The entire divorce process takes approximately 2–3 months, as opposed to 2–3 years in the adversarial process" ("Mediation: How It Works").

Citation for an online source with no author.

A third important point is that mediated divorces leave less hostility behind them. It's true that a divorce produces feelings of grief, anger, and frustration for almost everyone. But mediation can help people deal with these feelings. By contrast, an attorney-fought divorce seems designed to make the splitting partners hate each other as much as possible. Before she wrote *The Divorce Mediation Handbook*, Paula James had witnessed the divorce process from both sides—actually, *three* sides. First, she went through a traditional divorce herself. In her words, "we simply turned our destinies over to our two attorneys. . . . Many thousands of dollars later we were divorced, but with resentment and distrust and no idea of how we would jointly raise our child" (xvi).

Hughes 5

Later, James became an attorney herself and represented clients in traditional divorces. She describes how she and her colleagues routinely dug for dirt about possible affairs, alcohol abuse, shady business dealings, child neglect, and any other personal weaknesses they could use as ammunition in court. By the end of such an ordeal, she writes, couples were "deeply in debt, very angry, and distrustful of one another" (10).

Finally, James began working as a divorce mediator. As a mediator she works with many clients who may no longer be the best of friends but who want to remain on decent terms with their ex-spouses, for their own sake as well as for the sake of any children. One such client, Terri, expressed the feelings of many people who want a mediated divorce. She called James after having talked with an attorney. Terri was horrified by the attorney's fee ($5,000 to start) and what he told her. " 'He said that Eli and I are now adversaries, that I must do everything I can to protect myself from him and to get as much money as possible. . . . ,' Terri said. 'That's not what I want. I'm sorry that our marriage hasn't worked out, but I'm not trying to take Eli to the cleaners' " (10). Terri and Eli then started working with James. By listening carefully to them both, and stepping in occasionally to help them explain their fears and priorities rather than attack one another, James helped Terri and Eli work out an agreement in a short time and for a reasonable fee. "They left my office looking more relaxed than when they had entered," she reported (15). According to the Divorce Law Information Service Center's home page, "In family law disputes, mediation is often preferred over litigation because it facilitates future communication between the parties which is necessary when the future of the children is at stake."

In the long run, the biggest advantage of mediated divorce is that it helps couples develop an agreement they will be willing to live with.

Single quotation marks are used for a quotation within a quotation.

The authors of "Divorce Litigation Alternatives" assert, "[A]s mediated agreements represent a genuine compromise between the interests of the parties, the likelihood of future disputes is reduced. Most importantly, where the welfare of the children is a concern, mediation promotes their best interest, by discouraging the escalation of parental conflict" (Schonfeld and Kessler). Attorney-negotiated agreements tend to fall into rigid, traditional patterns: She gets the house; he gets the car; the kids spend every other weekend and six weeks in the summer with him. But mediated agreements are generally more creative and in tune with the divorcing couple's lives. One couple described by Field, in a *Cosmopolitan* article, Vivian and Bill, had been fighting bitterly over the mail-order business they had built together. Each insisted that he or she should take over the business entirely.

> Without lawyers, judges, or formal courtroom rules to get in the way, the mediator got Vivian and Bill to agree on a general plan whereby one spouse would keep the business, buy out the other, and lend him or her enough money to start a new venture. Then he instructed them to calculate their company's net worth. Finally, the material helped them realize on their own that Vivian, who'd had more contact with overseas suppliers, should keep the business; Bill, who was more aggressive, would do better taking the loan and launching a new product line. (Field 137)

Once they are used to the idea, most couples like the idea of creating an agreement that really works for them. In the words of Paula James, "[The divorcing couple] aren't ignorant children who must be silenced while their lawyers do the talking" (xvii).

Although mediation has clear advantages, it is not right for everyone. Most mediation experts agree with Butler and Walker, who

Brackets indicate that the words inside them were supplied by the student and did not appear in the original source.

Hughes 7

say that mediation "would not be an appropriate way to negotiate a fair settlement" if one of the divorcing partners feels unable or too frightened to stand up to the other. Examples are situations characterized by "intimidation or fear of violence," "a recent history of domestic violence or child abuse," or "severe intellectual or emotional limitations" (6). In such cases, it is probably best for the weaker partner if an attorney does his or her negotiating.

In conclusion, while divorce is never a pleasant experience, divorce mediation can save a couple time and money, help them keep a civil relationship, and produce an agreement that they both feel is reasonable. According to the Academy of Family Mediators, 70 to 90 percent of couples are satisfied with the terms of their mediated divorces (Lundstrom 228). This high figure shows that mediation is a more civilized and respectful way to achieve a divorce than the traditional courtroom method.

A mediating couple, Sam and Jane, said it best:

> [Sam said,] "I really do appreciate your help. This was a lot easier than I thought it would be."
>
> Jane smiled. "We both thought we were going to end up in a huge fight. Doing it this way was so much better." (Qtd. in James xi)

The conclusion provides a summary and restates the thesis.

Works Cited

"Avoiding the War." *Divorce without War*. Divorce Without War, 2016,
www.divorcewithoutwar.com/why-choose-us/control-the-outcome/.

Butler, Carol A., and Dolores D. Walker. *The Divorce Mediation
Answer Book*. Kodansha America, 1999.

Divorce Law Information Service Center. "Mediation." *DivorceLawInfo.
com*, 2006–2015, www.divorcelawinfo.com/aboutus.htm#4.

Field, Ann. "Divorce Mediation and Other (Cheap) Ways to Split."
Cosmopolitan, Aug. 1995, pp. 136–37.

Friedman, Gary J. *A Guide to Divorce Mediation*. Workman, 1993.

James, Paula. *The Divorce Mediation Handbook*. Jossey-Bass, 1997.

Lundstrom, Meg. "A Way to 'Take the War Out' of Divorce."
BusinessWeek, 16 Nov. 1998, p. 228.

"Mediation: How It Works." *Divorce Solutions*, 2001, www.
divorcesolutions.com/askus.asp.

Schonfeld, Esther, and Deena Kessler. "Divorce Litigation Alternatives."
5 Towns Jewish Times, 27 Nov. 2009, 5tjt.com/divorce-
mediation-2/.

Schuetz, Lisa. "Mediation Offers an Alternative When Dealing with
Divorce." *Wisconsin State Journal,* 31 May 1998, p. 10.

Towers, Katherine. "Parting with Dignity." *Herald Sun* [Melbourne], 27
Apr. 2009, pp. 29–30.

Valente, Judith. "A Kinder, Gentler Divorce?" *USA Today,* 25 Aug.
1997, p. B7.

"Works Cited" should be centered at the top of a new page.

The list should be double-spaced.

Titles of books, magazines, newspapers, Web sites, and database services should be italicized.

The URL for the online source is noted at the end of the citation.

CREDITS

Line Art/Text Credits

Chapter 5
Page 119: Kate Taylor/www.CartoonStock.com

Chapter 8
Page 197: Dan Rosandich/www.CartoonStock.com

Chapter 13
Page 276: Leo Cullum/The New Yorker Collection/www.cartoonbank.com

Chapter 14
Page 291: Dan Reynolds/www.CartoonStock.com

Chapter 16
Page 307: Real Life Adventures © 2003 GarLanCo. Dist. By Universal Uclick. Reprinted with permission. All rights reserved.

Chapter 33
Page 475: Baby Blues © 2007 Baby Blues Partnership. Dist. by King Features Syndicate.

Chapter 43
Page 548: "All the Good Things" by Sister Helen P. Mrosla, O.S.F. Originally published in *Proteus,* Spring 1991. Reprinted by permission of Franciscan Sisters of Little Falls, c/o Briggs and Morgan, Minneapolis, as edited and published by *Reader's Digest* in October 1991; **p. 562:** "'Extra Large,' Please" by Diane Urbina. Reprinted by permission of the author; **p. 569:** "What Good Families Are Doing Right" by Dolores Curran. Reprinted from *McCall's,* March 1983. Reprinted by permission of Dolores Curran, author and parent-educator; **p. 582:** Suzanne Fisher Staples, "Different Is Just Different," *The ALAN Review,* vol. 22, no. 2 (Winter 1995). Reprinted by permission of The ALAN Review.

Chapter 44
Page 602: "Do It Better!" Taken from *Think Big* by Ben Carson. M.D., with Cecil Murphey. Copyright © 1992 by Benjamin Carson, M.D. Used by permission of Zondervan; **p. 612:** James Lincoln Collier, "Anxiety: Challenge by Another Name." Originally published by *Reader's Digest,* December 1986. Reprinted by permission of the author; **p. 619:** "Let's Really Reform Our Schools" by Anita Garland. Copyright © 1994. Reprinted by permission of the author; **p. 627:** Janny Scott, "How They Get You to Do That," *Los Angeles Times,* July 23, 1992. Copyright © 1992, Los Angeles Times. Reprinted with permission.

Chapter 45
Page 644: Kathy Neal Headley, "Duel at High Noon: A Replay of Cormier's Works," *The ALAN Review,* vol. 21, no. 2 (Winter 1994). Reprinted by permission of The ALAN Review; **p. 651:** From Rudolph F. Verderber, *Communicate!* 8th ed. © 1996 Wadsworth, a part of Cengage Learning, Inc. Reproduced by permission. www.cengage.com/permissions; **p. 658:** From Rodney Stark, *Sociology,* 3rd ed. © 1989 Wadsworth, a part of Cengage Learning, Inc. Reproduced by permission. www.cengage.com/permissions; **p. 664:** Dana Canedy, "From Father to Son, Last Words to Live By." From *The New York Times,* January 1, 2007. © 2007 The New York Times. All rights reserved. Used by permission and protected by the Copyright Laws of the United States. The printing, copying, redistribution, or retransmission of this Content without express written permission is prohibited. www.nytimes.com

Photo Credits

About the Authors
Page v (top): Courtesy of John Langan; **p. v (bottom):** Courtesy of Zoé L. Albright.

Part 1
Opener: © Getty Images/Digital Vision RF.

Chapter 1
Opener: © Hero Images/Getty Images; **p. 15:** © Jeff Greenberg/PhotoEdit.

Chapter 2
Opener: © Asia Images Group/Getty Images RF; **p. 34:** © PhotoAlto/Alamy RF.

Chapter 3
Opener: © Aping Vision/Photodisc/Getty Images.

Chapter 4
Opener: © PhotoAlto/Sigrid Olsson/Getty Images RF.

Chapter 5
Opener: © Bill Pugliano/Getty Images.

Chapter 6
Opener: © S. Olsson/PhotoAlto RF.

Chapter 7
Opener: © Tim Robberts/The Image Bank/Getty Images; **p. 171:** © Wavebreakmedia Ltd/Getty Images RF; **p. 173:** © IanDagnall Computing/Alamy; **p. 176:** Google and the Google logo are registered trademarks of Google Inc., used with permission. Photo illustration by David A. Tietz/Editorial Image, LLC.

Part 2
Opener: © Royalty-Free/Corbis RF.

Chapter 8
Opener: © Zia Soleil/Getty Images.

Chapter 9
Opener (top): © Iain Masterton/Media Bakery; **Opener (bottom):** © Ian Dagnall/Alamy.

Chapter 10
Opener: © David L. Ryan/The Boston Globe via Getty Images; **p. 220:** © PhotoSpin, Inc/Alamy RF; **p. 226:** © Exactostock/SuperStock RF.

Chapter 11
Opener: © Jason Miller/Getty Images; **p. 231:** © Hill Street Studios/Getty Images RF; **p. 241 (left):** © UpperCut Images/Getty Images RF; **p. 241 (right):** © Digital Vision/PunchStock RF.

Chapter 12
Opener: © Shaun Botterill/Getty Images; **p. 257:** © Jose Luis Pelaez, Inc./Corbis; **p. 262:** © Scott Rovak/epa/Corbis.

Chapter 13
Opener (all): National Gallery of Art, Washington; **p. 272:** © Steve Prezant/Corbis.

Chapter 14
Opener (both): National Gallery of Art, Washington; **p. 285:** © Rodger Tamblyn/Alamy.

Chapter 15

Opener: © Ariel Skelley/Blend Images/Getty Images RF.

Chapter 16

Opener: © Sam Toren/Alamy; **p. 312 (top):** Courtesy of Adbusters Media Foundation; **p. 312 (bottom):** © Bill Aron/PhotoEdit.

Part 3

Opener: © Ryan McVay/Getty Images RF.

Chapter 17

Opener: © ML Harris/Getty Images; **p. 334:** The Advertising Archives; **p. 353:** © HBO/Photofest; **p. 355 (left):** NASA; **p. 355 (middle):** © Douglas Kirkland/Corbis; **p. 355 (right):** © Reuters/Corbis.

Part 4

Opener (top): © Stuart Forster/Alamy; **Opener (bottom):** © Jeff Greenberg/Alamy.

Section I

Opener: © Kim Karpeles/Alamy.

Section II

Opener (both): Photo illustration by David A. Tietz/Editorial Image, LLC.

Section III

Opener (top): © Douglas Graham/Roll Call/Getty Images.

Section III

Opener (bottom): © Peter Tsai Photography/Alamy.

Section IV

Opener: © Lisa Beebe.

Chapter 36

Opener (left): Courtesy of Houghton Mifflin Harcourt Publishing Company; **Opener (right):** Book Cover, copyright © Random House LLC; from RANDOM HOUSE WEBSTER'S COLLEGE DICTIONARY by Random House LLC. Used by permission of Random House Reference and Information Publishing, a division of Random House LLC. All rights reserved. Photo by David A. Tietz/Editorial Image, LLC; **p. 491:** By permission from Merriam-Webster's Collegiate® Dictionary, 11th Edition © 2013 by Merriam-Webster, Inc. (www.Merriam-Webster.com). Digital image created by David A. Tietz/Editorial Image, LLC.

Section V

Opener: © AP Photo/Richard Vogel.

Part 5

Opener: © Tara Moore/Taxi/Getty Images; **p. 548:** Courtesy of the Franciscan Sisters of Little Falls, Minnesota; **p. 550:** © Davis Barber/PhotoEdit; **p. 554:** © Kevin Winter/Getty Images; **p. 561:** © Photodisc RF; **p. 564:** © Spencer Platt/Getty Images; **p. 578 (left):** © Ariel Skelley/Blend Images/Getty Images RF; **p. 578 (right):** © Maartje van Caspel/E+/Getty Images; **p. 601:** © Fuse/Getty Images RF; **p. 602:** © Joe Giza/Reuters/Corbis; **p. 607:** © BananaStock/JupiterImages RF; **p. 612:** Courtesy of James Lincoln Collier; **p. 627:** © Mark Peterson/Corbis; **p. 632:** © Len Holsborg/Alamy; **p. 637:** © Ingram Publishing; **p. 639:** Tate, London/Art Resource.

INDEX

Google, 176–177
Google Docs, 168, 169, 172
Google Scholar, 176, 177
Grammar
  adjectives and adverbs, 428–432
  fragments, 367–380
  misplaced and dangling
    modifiers, 433–440
  pronoun agreement, 416–421
  pronoun types, 422–427
  regular and irregular verbs,
    394–401
  run-ons, 381–393
  sentence sense, 364–366
  subject-verb agreement,
    410–415
  subjects and verbs, 359–363
"Group Pressure" (Stark)
  content, 659–660
  discussion questions, 662–663
  preview, 658
  reading comprehension
    questions, 661–662
  vocabulary in context, 660–661
  writing assignments, 663–664

Headley, Kathy Neal, "Duel at
  High Noon: A Replay of
  Cormier's Works," 644–651
Historical periods and events,
  capitalization of, 452
Holidays, capitalization of, 448
Homonyms, 511–515, 538
"How They Get You to Do That"
  (Scott)
  content, 627–632
  discussion questions, 634–635
  preview, 627
  reading comprehension
    questions, 633–634
  vocabulary in context, 633
  writing assignments, 635–636
Hyphen, 487, 528

iCloud, 169
Illustration signals, 96
Images, using in a paper, 173
Incident, as essay introduction,
  329, 342–344
Indefinite article, 672–675

Indefinite pronouns, 413, 417
Indirect quotations, 471
Inferences, reading comprehension
  and, 547
Infinitives, ELS pointers for,
  676–678
Inform, as writing purpose, 7
-ing and to fragments, 371–374
-ing word, 125
Internet
  evaluating sources, 178–181
  find articles on your topic,
    175–177
  find books on your topic,
    174–175
  using when writing, 173
Internet Explorer, 177
Introductory material, comma
  after, 477–478
Introductory paragraph, 327,
  328–330, 342–344
Irregular nouns, in dictionary
  entries, 496
Irregular verbs
  achievement test, 688
  common irregular verbs, 406–408
  defined, 394
  diagnostic test, 682–683
  in dictionary entries, 495–496
  list of, 395–397
  practice identifying, 398–401,
    530, 531, 534–535
Items in a series
  comma between, 476–477
  semicolon between, 486

JDarkRoom, 171
Joining word, correcting run-ons
  with, 384–386
Journal keeping, 15–16
JSTOR (Journal Storage), 176

Keeping a journal, 15–16
Key details, reading
  comprehension and, 547

Languages, capitalization of, 451
"Let's Really Reform Our
  Schools" (Garland)
  content, 619–622

discussion questions, 624–625
preview, 619
reading comprehension
  questions, 623–624
vocabulary in context, 622
writing assignments, 625–627
Letters
  capitalizing opening and
    closing, 452
  commas in opening and
    closing, 482
Library of Congress, 174
Library subscription services,
  175–176
Linking verbs, 675
Links, using in a paper, 173
Lists
  colon in, 485
  making as prewriting
    technique, 23–24
Logan, Paul, "Rowing the Bus,"
  554–561
Logical support, 306–307
Long quotation, colon in, 485
-ly word, 125

Macintosh, 492
Main idea, reading comprehension
  and, 547
Making a list, as prewriting
  technique, 23–24
"Managing Conflicts in
  Relationships" (Verderber)
  content, 651–655
  discussion questions, 657
  preview, 651
  reading comprehension
    questions, 655–656
  vocabulary in context, 655
  writing assignments,
    657–658
Mapping, as prewriting technique,
  24–25
Meanings, in dictionary entries,
  496–497
Mechanics
  capital letters, 447–455
  numbers and abbreviations,
    456–458
  paper format, 442–446